T0180398

Lecture Notes in Computer Science 13328

More information about this series at https://link.springer.com/bookseries/558

Panayiotis Zaphiris · Andri Ioannou (Eds.)

Learning and Collaboration Technologies

Designing the Learner and Teacher Experience

9th International Conference, LCT 2022
Held as Part of the 24th HCI International Conference, HCII 2022
Virtual Event, June 26 – July 1, 2022
Proceedings, Part I

 Springer

Editors
Panayiotis Zaphiris 🆔
Department of Multimedia and Graphic Art
Cyprus University of Technology
Limassol, Cyprus

Andri Ioannou 🆔
Research Center on Interactive Media, Smart
Systems and Emerging Technologies
(CYENS)
Cyprus University of Technology
Limassol, Cyprus

ISSN 0302-9743   ISSN 1611-3349 (electronic)
Lecture Notes in Computer Science
ISBN 978-3-031-05656-7   ISBN 978-3-031-05657-4 (eBook)
https://doi.org/10.1007/978-3-031-05657-4

This Springer imprint is published by the registered company Springer Nature Switzerland AG
The registered company address is: Gewerbestrasse 11, 6330 Cham, Switzerland

Foreword

Human-computer interaction (HCI) is acquiring an ever-increasing scientific and industrial importance, as well as having more impact on people's everyday life, as an ever-growing number of human activities are progressively moving from the physical to the digital world. This process, which has been ongoing for some time now, has been dramatically accelerated by the COVID-19 pandemic. The HCI International (HCII) conference series, held yearly, aims to respond to the compelling need to advance the exchange of knowledge and research and development efforts on the human aspects of design and use of computing systems.

The 24th International Conference on Human-Computer Interaction, HCI International 2022 (HCII 2022), was planned to be held at the Gothia Towers Hotel and Swedish Exhibition & Congress Centre, Göteborg, Sweden, during June 26 to July 1, 2022. Due to the COVID-19 pandemic and with everyone's health and safety in mind, HCII 2022 was organized and run as a virtual conference. It incorporated the 21 thematic areas and affiliated conferences listed on the following page.

A total of 5583 individuals from academia, research institutes, industry, and governmental agencies from 88 countries submitted contributions, and 1276 papers and 275 posters were included in the proceedings to appear just before the start of the conference. The contributions thoroughly cover the entire field of human-computer interaction, addressing major advances in knowledge and effective use of computers in a variety of application areas. These papers provide academics, researchers, engineers, scientists, practitioners, and students with state-of-the-art information on the most recent advances in HCI. The volumes constituting the set of proceedings to appear before the start of the conference are listed in the following pages.

The HCI International (HCII) conference also offers the option of 'Late Breaking Work' which applies both for papers and posters, and the corresponding volume(s) of the proceedings will appear after the conference. Full papers will be included in the 'HCII 2022 - Late Breaking Papers' volumes of the proceedings to be published in the Springer LNCS series, while 'Poster Extended Abstracts' will be included as short research papers in the 'HCII 2022 - Late Breaking Posters' volumes to be published in the Springer CCIS series.

I would like to thank the Program Board Chairs and the members of the Program Boards of all thematic areas and affiliated conferences for their contribution and support towards the highest scientific quality and overall success of the HCI International 2022 conference; they have helped in so many ways, including session organization, paper reviewing (single-blind review process, with a minimum of two reviews per submission) and, more generally, acting as goodwill ambassadors for the HCII conference.

This conference would not have been possible without the continuous and unwavering support and advice of Gavriel Salvendy, founder, General Chair Emeritus, and Scientific Advisor. For his outstanding efforts, I would like to express my appreciation to Abbas Moallem, Communications Chair and Editor of HCI International News.

June 2022   Constantine Stephanidis

HCI International 2022 Thematic Areas
and Affiliated Conferences

Thematic Areas

- HCI: Human-Computer Interaction
- HIMI: Human Interface and the Management of Information

Affiliated Conferences

- EPCE: 19th International Conference on Engineering Psychology and Cognitive Ergonomics
- AC: 16th International Conference on Augmented Cognition
- UAHCI: 16th International Conference on Universal Access in Human-Computer Interaction
- CCD: 14th International Conference on Cross-Cultural Design
- SCSM: 14th International Conference on Social Computing and Social Media
- VAMR: 14th International Conference on Virtual, Augmented and Mixed Reality
- DHM: 13th International Conference on Digital Human Modeling and Applications in Health, Safety, Ergonomics and Risk Management
- DUXU: 11th International Conference on Design, User Experience and Usability
- C&C: 10th International Conference on Culture and Computing
- DAPI: 10th International Conference on Distributed, Ambient and Pervasive Interactions
- HCIBGO: 9th International Conference on HCI in Business, Government and Organizations
- LCT: 9th International Conference on Learning and Collaboration Technologies
- ITAP: 8th International Conference on Human Aspects of IT for the Aged Population
- AIS: 4th International Conference on Adaptive Instructional Systems
- HCI-CPT: 4th International Conference on HCI for Cybersecurity, Privacy and Trust
- HCI-Games: 4th International Conference on HCI in Games
- MobiTAS: 4th International Conference on HCI in Mobility, Transport and Automotive Systems
- AI-HCI: 3rd International Conference on Artificial Intelligence in HCI
- MOBILE: 3rd International Conference on Design, Operation and Evaluation of Mobile Communications

List of Conference Proceedings Volumes Appearing Before the Conference

39. CCIS 1582, HCI International 2022 Posters - Part III, edited by Constantine Stephanidis, Margherita Antona and Stavroula Ntoa
40. CCIS 1583, HCI International 2022 Posters - Part IV, edited by Constantine Stephanidis, Margherita Antona and Stavroula Ntoa

http://2022.hci.international/proceedings

Preface

In today's knowledge society, learning and collaboration are two fundamental and strictly interrelated aspects of knowledge acquisition and creation. Learning technology is the broad range of communication, information, and related technologies that can be used to support learning, teaching, and assessment, often in a collaborative way. Collaboration technology, on the other hand, is targeted to support individuals working in teams towards a common goal, which may be an educational one, by providing tools that aid communication and the management of activities as well as the process of problem solving. In this context, interactive technologies do not only affect and improve the existing educational system but become a transformative force that can generate radically new ways of knowing, learning, and collaborating.

The 9th Learning and Collaboration Technologies Conference (LCT 2022), affiliated to HCI International 2022, addressed theoretical foundations, design and implementation, and effectiveness and impact issues related to interactive technologies for learning and collaboration, including design methodologies, developments and tools, theoretical models, and learning design or learning experience (LX) design, as well as technology adoption and use in formal, non-formal, and informal educational contexts.

Learning and collaboration technologies are increasingly adopted in K-20 (kindergarten to higher education) classrooms and lifelong learning. Technology can support expansive forms of collaboration; deepened empathy; complex coordination of people, materials, and purposes; and development of skill sets that are increasingly important across workspaces of the 21st century. The general themes of the LCT conference aim to address challenges related to understanding how to design for better learning and collaboration with technology, support learners to develop relevant approaches and skills, and assess or evaluate gains and outcomes. To this end, topics such as extended reality (XR) learning, embodied and immersive learning, mobile learning and ubiquitous technologies, serious games and gamification, learning through design and making, educational robotics, educational chatbots, human-computer interfaces, and computer supported collaborative learning, among others, are elaborated in LCT conference proceedings. Learning (experience) design and user experience design remain a challenge in the arena of learning environments and collaboration technology. LCT aims to serve a continuous dialog while synthesizing current knowledge.

Two volumes of the HCII 2022 proceedings are dedicated to this year's edition of the LCT 2022 conference, entitled Learning and Collaboration Technologies: Designing the Learner and Teacher Experience (Part I) and Learning and Collaboration Technologies: Novel Technological Environments (Part II). The first focuses on topics related to designing and developing learning technologies, learning and teaching online, and diversity in learning as well as practices and experiences of technology in education, while the second focuses on topics related to XR in learning and education, chatbots, robots and virtual teachers, and collaboration technology.

Papers of these volumes are included for publication after a minimum of two single-blind reviews from the members of the LCT Program Board or, in some cases, from members of the Program Boards of other affiliated conferences. We would like to thank all of them for their invaluable contribution, support, and efforts.

June 2022

Panayiotis Zaphiris
Andri Ioannou

9th International Conference on Learning and Collaboration Technologies (LCT 2022)

Program Board Chairs: **Panayiotis Zaphiris**, Cyprus University of Technology, Cyprus, and **Andri Ioannou** Cyprus University of Technology and Research Center on Interactive Media, Smart Systems and Emerging Technologies (CYENS), Cyprus

- Fisnik Dalipi, Linnaeus University, Sweden
- Camille Dickson-Deane, University of Technology Sydney, Australia
- David Fonseca, La Salle, Ramon Llull University, Spain
- Francisco Jose García-Peñalvo, University of Salamanca, Spain
- Aleksandar Jevremovic, Singidunum University, Serbia
- Elis Kakoulli Constantinou, Cyprus University of Technology, Cyprus
- Tomaž Klobučar, Jozef Stefan Institute, Slovenia
- Birgy Lorenz, Tallinn University of Technology, Estonia
- Nicholas H. Müller, University of Applied Sciences Würzburg-Schweinfurt, Germany
- Anna Nicolaou, Cyprus University of Technology, Cyprus
- Antigoni Parmaxi, Cyprus University of Technology, Cyprus
- Dijana Plantak Vukovac, University of Zagreb, Croatia
- Maria-Victoria Soulé, Cyprus University of Technology, Cyprus
- Sonia Sousa, Tallinn University, Estonia
- Alicia Takaoka, University of Hawaii at Hilo, USA
- Sara Villagrá-Sobrino, Valladolid University, Spain

The full list with the Program Board Chairs and the members of the Program Boards of all thematic areas and affiliated conferences is available online at

http://www.hci.international/board-members-2022.php

HCI International 2023

The 25th International Conference on Human-Computer Interaction, HCI International 2023, will be held jointly with the affiliated conferences at the AC Bella Sky Hotel and Bella Center, Copenhagen, Denmark, 23–28 July 2023. It will cover a broad spectrum of themes related to human-computer interaction, including theoretical issues, methods, tools, processes, and case studies in HCI design, as well as novel interaction techniques, interfaces, and applications. The proceedings will be published by Springer. More information will be available on the conference website: http://2023.hci.international/.

General Chair
Constantine Stephanidis
University of Crete and ICS-FORTH
Heraklion, Crete, Greece
Email: general_chair@hcii2023.org

http://2023.hci.international/

Contents – Part I

Learning and Teaching Online

Diversity in Learning

Technology in Education: Practices and Experiences

Contents – Part II

Chatbots, Robots and Virtual Teachers

Collaboration Technology

Designing and Developing Learning Technologies

Serious Video Game Interaction for Collaborative Problem Solving in Elementary School

Rebeca Almonacid[✉] and Jaime Sánchez

University of Chile, Santiago, Chile
rebeca.almonacid@ug.uchile.cl, jsanchez@dcc.uhile.cl

Abstract. Teamy is a serious video game in a mobile application format, which was tested and evaluated in terms of interface usability, as well as its impact on collaborative work for problem solving at elementary level. To achieve this, research and development methodology was used in this project, pursuing the construction, evaluation, and implementation of educational products. The first tests and evaluations made by experts regarding usability and functionality allowed improvements to be made during the development of the serious video game, which allowed a correct implementation with end users. These users, after using Teamy, were able to carry out a usability test to also provide their feedback. Subsequently, evaluations pertinent to collaborative work in relation to the use of Teamy were made, such as questionnaires to end users, class observation and a focus group. The results of the various evaluations were favorable since end users validated the video game both in its interface usability and its use as a tool that facilitates collaborative work.

Keywords: Serious video game · Collaborative work · Problem solving

1 Introduction

To create conducive learning environments, teachers must use different didactic resources that consider the context students are living. Because of COVID-19 global pandemic, during the years 2020 and 2021, many educational institutions were forced to close their doors to students; nevertheless, all instructional processes had to be continued online. This has made, among other things, peer interaction and collaborative work activities difficult or null for students.

The main purpose of this work is the construction and evaluation of a serious video game interaction as a tool to develop collaborative problem-solving skills in elementary school students, in the context of online synchronous classes. To achieve this objective, three steps have been followed: (1) To develop a serious video game from a prototype; (2) To test the serious video game in terms of usability, interface, and interaction; and (3) To evaluate its use to develop collaborative problem-solving skills in end-users.

P. Zaphiris and A. Ioannou (Eds.): HCII 2022, LNCS 13328, pp. 3–12, 2022.
https://doi.org/10.1007/978-3-031-05657-4_1

2 Literature Review

In today's world, technology has had an impact in many aspects of our lives, including education. Information and communication technologies (ICT) applied to teaching and learning have created a discipline that studies the converge of computing and education for the development of strategies and practices (Nuñez 2006).

To have a better understanding of the research's topics underlying this study, it was necessary to make a review of the concepts of collaborative work, problem solving, and serious video games.

2.1 Collaborative Work

One of the fundamental skills to develop in education is collaborative work, which is defined as the process of group work in an integrated way to meet a common goal. Also, collaborative learning arises as the teacher's intention to strengthen pre-existing relationships between students and use them as tools so that the performance of each one is reflected in the result (Ruffnelli et al. 2017). Collaboration allows participation in a conscious and voluntary way, and collaborative objects foster skills and competencies in students that favor interaction, in which consensus is made on routes for the construction group knowledge (Lizcano et al. 2019). Respecting the use of ICT as collaborative working tools, teachers point the great motivation digital tools generate in students, as well as their perception on how practical is to use them for these purposes (García-Valcárcel 2014).

2.2 Collaborative Problem Solving

Collaborative problem solving is the activity made by a group of students with a common goal where a relational dimension is present, which requires interaction and group analysis (Negrón 2021). Adding to that, collaborative problem solving requires social skills, such as participation, perspective, and social regulation, as well as cognitive skills, such as task regulation and the building of knowledge (Csapó and Funke 2017). Considering technology for these purposes, information and communication technologies constitute a great mean of representation that can produce favorable outcomes in learning, because they foster students to develop new skills through novel ways of transmission, processing, and use of information (Jaramillo and Chávez 2015).

2.3 Serious Video Games

The impact of video games in our lives has extended not only in their use in spare time but also in areas related to work and education, and they can be defined as games which main objective is education beyond entertainment (Shobel et al. 2021).

Serious video games can be a great tool for students to apply the skills above mentioned, because they have the potential to allow the interaction with other people and the device itself, fostering the participation and motivation in learning activities (Sánchez and Olivares 2011). Serious video games focus on problem solving through significant tasks with the objective of involving players in real situations that include learning elements according to planned learning objectives (Casañ-Pitarch 2021).

3 Methodology

The methodology used in this research has been R + D (Research and Development), which consists in the development and evaluation of a product by testing it in educational environments.

3.1 Research and Development R&D

R&D is a process used to develop and validate educational products, which consists in a cycle of 10 steps that go from the study of findings related to the product to be developed, the making of the product based on those findings, testing the product, and the improvement of any possible deficiencies found in the testing phase (Borg and Gall 1987). Though this model is effective, the extensive use of this model has led researchers to modify or adapt it in their own research, generally shortening the process from 10 to 4 or 5 steps (Gustiani 2019).

3.2 Plomp's Model

Considering the above, Plomp's model offers a model with 5 steps (Plomp 1997). This model is more flexible, for it can be adapted to the context of the research and the researchers' characteristics. The first step is *Research*, where information is collected and analyzed, and the problem is defined. The second step, *Design*, consists in designing a model/prototype/solution. Third step is *Construction*, which is to produce and the making of the previous step product. The fourth step is *Testing, Evaluation and Revision*, in which information is collected, processed, and analyzed systematically to have feedback for the product improvement. Finally, the fifth step, *Implementation*, is where the product is implemented on end users. This model was chosen to conduct this research.

Below are shown Borg & Gall model compared to Plomp's adapted model (Figs. 1 and 2):

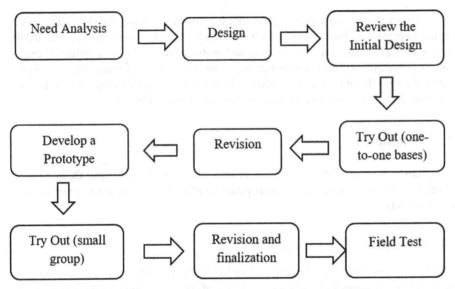

Fig. 1. Research & development, Borg and Gall model (1987)

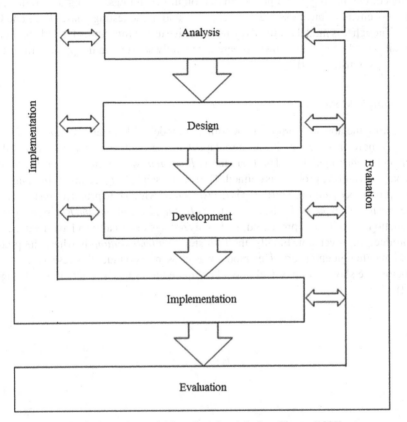

Fig. 2. Generic model for educational design, Plomp (1997)

In the first phase of this study, Teamy was developed from a prototype created in the Human-Computer Interaction course as part of the Master of Education (educational technology) Program at the University of Chile. In the second phase, experts tested the video game in terms of usability and interface. Finally, Teamy was evaluated in terms of usability and collaborative work skills by end users, which were 6th grade students.

3.3 Serious Video Game, Teamy

Teamy is a serious video game prototype in a mobile application format with characteristics that foster collaborative work. For that, the objective of the video game is to work in teams to complete different missions (previously programmed by teachers' activities) that give points, so that the team with higher score is the winner.

The missions can be of three kinds, and were chosen because of the following educational purposes:

i. *Multiple choice*: Multiple choice items are widely used in education because they allow the measurement of varied knowledge, skills, and competencies in a large range of disciplines and areas of content, including the ability to comprehend concepts and principles, make judgements, to infer, reason, complete sentences, interpret data and apply information (Griel et al. 2017).

ii. *Collaborative writing*: Collaborative writing is defined as the activity to produce a text by two or more people. It is a social process, in which the participants focus in a common objective, they negotiate and discuss while producing a text using a common language, which can result in better final outcomes (Ho 2021).

iii. *Collaborative drawing:* Drawing consists in producing graphic objects, usually sketches id 2D, to express ideas. Its collaborative functions can include to preserve group information to later use, as well as to express ideas, which involve the creation of tangible group ideas representations (Greenberg et al. 1992).

To carry out the missions collaboratively, Teamy includes a chat and a voting system for decision making with the members of the same team, and functions to interact with other teams, though these functions discount score from the team's score. In this way, students can complete group activities related to any subject, created, and programmed by the teacher, without distance being an impediment.

The aforementioned features of Teamy are illustrated below:

Figure 1. Start screen

Figure 2. Access and avatar selection

Figure 3.Group designation

Figure 4. Multiple choice mission. Once every member of the group had answered correctly, the next exercise will display.

Figure 5. Collaborative writing mission. The text from every member will show in different colors.

Figure 6. Collaborative drawing mission. All the members of the group can draw on the screen at the same time.

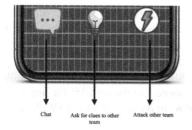

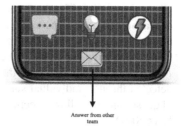

Chat	Ask for clues to other team	Attack other team

Answer from other team

Figure 7 & 8. Interaction. These features allow interaction between the member of the group and interaction with other groups.

Figure 9. Chat. Feature that allows interaction and communication within the members of the group.

Figure 10. Voting system. Feature for decision making.

Figure 11.Final results. Screen that shows all the groups' final scores.

3.4 Instruments

The instruments used in this research were chosen to, on the one hand, evaluate Teamy's usability and, on the other hand, its performance as a tool to facilitate collaborative work in end users, and are detailed as it follows:

I. *Unity test*: Used to test in an efficient way particular components, such as functions y graphs, in the code of the serious video game.

II. *Heuristic evaluation*: Inspection in which one or more experts evaluate a specification, prototype or product using a list of usability principles or user experience (Wilson 2014).

III. *Usability test for end users*: Questionnaire that asks the same questions to a group of people to obtain data related to their experiences, opinions, interests, etc. (Borg et al. 2003). It also provides objectivity, replicability, quantification, economy, communication, and scientific generalization (Lewis 2006). This questionnaire was applied to two kind of end users, students, and a teacher.

IV. *Class observation*: This instrument provides valid and evidence to measure quality of teaching, which helps to streamline the supervision and evaluation of teachers (White 2018). This observation provided an outlook on the end users behavior when using the video game in the context of hybrid classes.

V. *Focus group*: Technique with the potential to provide data that may have not be detected through individual surveys, furthermore, combined with the application of questionnaires, allows a better understanding of the research topic (Williams and Katz 2001).

4 Results

This study used the Research & Development methodology to develop and evaluate a serious video game in a school context with 6th grade students. For that purpose, different techniques were used to, on the one hand, help the correct development of the video game, and on the other hand, evaluate its incidence in the collaborative work skills of the end users. The results were the following:

I. Usability

a) Unity test. While the video game was developed, unity tests were applied to the code, which indicated that the functions and graphics work correctly.

b) Heuristic evaluation. Two experts evaluated the video game and the results showed that it was efficient in aspects such as the of the game state visibility, game and real-world relation, player control and freedom, flexibility and use efficiency, aesthetic and minimalistic design, content treatment, help and documentation, and interactivity. Aspects related to error prevention had to be improved due to the experts' feedback.

c) Usability test. Both usability tests applied to end users, students, and a teacher, gave favorable results. The test applied to students indicated that most of them would use Teamy again, highlighted the aesthetic of the game and the functions that allow to work with their classmates. The test applied to the teacher, indicated that she thinks the dynamic of the game is conducive to the students, she liked the transversality of the game to be used in different subjects, and highlighted its aesthetic.

II. Collaborative work

The results indicate that the students perceived Teamy as a tool that facilitates collaborative working, because of its goal oriented dynamic, as well as the functions that allow a fluid interaction and ideas and information exchange.

a) Observation. The comments made by the students during the observations indicated that they wanted to use Teamy again. Most of the comments were related to the group formations, whether they would like to be on the same team or a different one next time.

b) Focus group. With the implementation of the focus group many aspects revealed before were reinforced, such as the aesthetic of the game and its functions related to the interaction between classmates.

5 Conclusion

The idea to create a teaching tool that facilitates collaborative working raised from the need to cover the lack of peer interaction during the COVID-19 pandemic that affects the world since 2019. Teamy is a serious video game for mobile phones, which was developed and tested though different evaluation methods in aspects related to its usability and its incidence in educational aspects such as collaborative work and problem solving.

The usability tests were implemented using different methods to students and a teacher, which results indicated that Teamy is efficient in terms of its components. Firstly, experts indicated that Teamy meets with the following aspects: the of the game state visibility, game and real-world relation, player control and freedom, flexibility and use efficiency, aesthetic and minimalistic design, content treatment, help and documentation, and interactivity. Secondly, students and the teacher highlighted the aesthetics of the video game.

The tests that evaluated Teamy's performance to promote collaborative work, indicated that students perceived Teamy as a tool that facilitates collaborative working, due to its functions that allow a fluid interaction and ideas and information exchange, as well as the transversality of the software for its use in different subjects.

The previously mentioned evaluations revealed positive and promising results, indicating that Teamy's functions are usable, understandable, pertinent, efficient, and they facilitate and promote collaborative work and problem-solving skills.

Acknowledgements. This work was funded by CONICYT's Basal Funds for Centers of Excellence, Project FB0003.

References

Nuñez, G.: Informática Educativa: Conceptualización y Aplicaciones. Conference: Informática Educativa: Conceptualización y Aplicaciones, Veraguas, Panamá (2006). https://www.researchgate.net/publication/348513552

Ruffinelli, R., Domínguez, L., Hermosilla, M.: Aprendizaje colaborativo con apoyo tecnológico. Revista Científica Estudios e Investigaciones, 91–92 (2017). https://doi.org/ https://doi.org/10.26885/rcei.foro.2017.91

Lizcano-Dallos, A.R., Barbosa-Chacón, J.W., Villamizar-Escobar, J.D.: Aprendizaje colaborativo con apoyo en TIC: concepto, metodología y recursos. magis, Revista Internacional de Investigación en Educación, 12 (24), 5–24 (2019)

García-Varcárcel, A., Basilotta, V., López, C.: Las TIC en el aprendizaje colaborativo en el aula de Primaria y Secundaria. Revista Científica de Educomunicación **42**(21), 65–74 (2014). https://doi.org/10.3916/C42-2014-06

Negrón, J.: Habilidad de resolución colaborativa de problemas en actividades de indagación en clases de ciencias: un análisis de interacciones educativas en primer ciclo básico. Universidad de Chile, Tesis de Magister en Educación con Mención en Informática Educativa (2021)

Csapó, B., y Funke, J.: The Nature of Problem Solving: Using Research to Inspire 21st Century Learning. OECD Publishing, Paris (2017)

Jaramillo, C., Chávez, J.: TIC y educación en Chile: Una revisión sistemática de la literatura (J. Sánchez, Ed.; pp. 221–231). TISE, International Conference on Computers and Education, Santiago de Chile (2015)

Schobel, S., Saqr, M., Jaonson, A.: Two decades of game concepts in digital learning environments – a bibliometric study and research agenda. two decades of game concepts in digital learning environments – a bibliometric study and research agenda. Comput. Edu. **173**, 1–23 (2021). https://doi.org/10.1016/j.compedu.2021.104296

Sánchez, J., Olivares, R.: Problem solving and collaboration using mobile serious games. Comput. Educ. **57**, 1943–1942 (2011)

Casañ-Pitarch, R.: Videojuegos Serios en educación [Poster presentation]. Cátedra estratégica Videojuegos Gamificación Juegos Serios, Málaga, España (2021)

Borg, W.R., Gall, M.D.: Educational Research: An Introduction. Longman, New York (1983)

Gustiani, S.: Reseach and development (R&D) method as a model design in educational research and its alternatives. Holist. J. **11**(2), 12–22 (2019). https://jurnal.polsri.ac.id/index.php/holistic/article/view/1849

Plomp, T.: Development Research on/in Educational Development. Twente University, Netherlands (1997)

Gierl, M., Bulut, O., Guo, Q., Zhang, X.: Developing, analyzing, and using distractors for multiple-choice tests in education: a comprehensive review. Am. Educ. Res. Assoc. **87**(6), 1082–1116 (2017). https://www.jstor.org/stable/ 44667687

Ho, P.: The Effects of Collaborative Writing on Students' Writing Fluency: An Efficient Framework for Collaborative Writing. SAGE Open, 1–11 (2021). https://doi.org/ https://doi.org/10.1177/2158244021998363

Greenberg, S., Roseman, M., Webster, D., Bohnet, R.: Issues and experiences designing and implementing two group drawing tools. In: Proceedings of Hawaii International Conference on System Sciences, **4**, pp. 138–150, Kuwaii, Hawaii, January, IEEE Press. Reprinted in Baecker, R. (ed) (1993) Readings in Computer Supported Cooperative Work, Morgan-Kaufmann (1992)

Wilson, C.: Heuristic Evaluation. User Interface Inspection Methods, 1–32 (2014). https://doi.org/10.1016/b978-0-12-410391-7.00001-4

Gall, M., Borg, W., Gall, J.: Educational research: an introduction. Br. J. Educ. Stud. **32** (2003). https://doi.org/10.2307/3121583

Lewis, J.R.: Handbook of Human Factors and Ergonomics (3rd ed.). John Wiley (2006). https://doi.org/10.1002/0470048204.ch49

White, M.: Rater performance standards for classroom observation instruments. Am. Educ. Res. Assoc. **47**(8), 492–501 (2018). https:// www.jstor.org/stable/44971832

Williams, A., Katz, L.: The use of focus group methodology in education: some theoretical and practical considerations. Int. Electr. J. Leader. Learn. **5**(3) (2001). https://www.researchgate.net/publication/228941039

Semantic and Interactive Search in an Advanced Note-Taking App for Learning Material

Aryobarzan Atashpendar[✉], Christian Grévisse, Jean Botev,
and Steffen Rothkugel

University of Luxembourg, Av. de la Fonte 6, 4364 Esch-sur-Alzette, Luxembourg
{aryobarzan.atashpendar,christian.grevisse,
jean.botev,steffen.rothkugel}@uni.lu

Abstract. Note-taking apps on tablets are increasingly becoming the go-to space for managing learning material as a student. In particular, digital note-taking presents certain advantages over traditional pen-and-paper approaches when it comes to organizing and retrieving a library of notes thanks to various search functionalities. This paper presents improvements to the classic textual-input-based search field, by introducing a semantic search that considers the meaning of a user's search terms and an automatic question-answering process that extracts the answer to the user's question from their notes for more efficient information retrieval. Additionally, visual methods for finding specific notes are proposed, which do not require the input of text by the user: through the integration of a semantic similarity metric, notes similar to a selected document can be displayed based on common topics. Furthermore, a fully interactive process allows one to search for notes by selecting different types of dynamically generated filters, thus eliminating the need for textual input. Finally, a graph-based visualization is explored for the search results, which clusters semantically similar notes closer together to relay additional information to the user besides the raw search results.

Keywords: Learning material · Semantic search ·
Question-answering · Note similarity · Interactive search

1 Introduction

Regular tasks of students comprise taking notes during their lectures, reviewing a course's learning material for an exam, or skimming articles for further research.

A common factor among these various chores is organization: firstly, students might not be able to follow along with the lecture while simultaneously writing down what the teacher is saying. While note-taking has been shown to improve how much a student recalls from an oral lecture [10], it is still dependent on whether they also review their notes [7,12], preferably shortly after writing them. As such, if the student is trying to retrieve an older note they have not

© The Author(s), under exclusive license to Springer Nature Switzerland AG 2022
P. Zaphiris and A. Ioannou (Eds.): HCII 2022, LNCS 13328, pp. 13–29, 2022.
https://doi.org/10.1007/978-3-031-05657-4_2

yet reviewed, they may use misleading keywords as their search terms, e.g., synonyms or paraphrasing, because they do not remember the exact technical terms mentioned in the lecture.

Secondly, note-taking is a mentally taxing activity [31], as it requires the student to think of how to format their notes while listening to the lecturer, e.g., by coming up with abbreviations and formatting their sentences to link them together. Generally, writing is much slower than speaking, meaning the student tends to lag behind the lecturer's speech. This can result in the student rushing to keep up, thus ending up with scattered notes across their library.

An active student can overcome these issues by organizing their notes at the end of the day and doing weekly revisions, though this is naturally not a given for every individual. To that end, digital note-taking can come to the forefront to simplify some of these tasks, e.g., the student can more easily organize their various courses' material in different folders and use a dedicated search field to retrieve specific notes, both of which tend to be common features offered by most document-based apps on tablets.

However, both folder organization and text-based search queries can falter: categorizing various notes in appropriate folders can become easier digitally when the person does not have to shuffle tens of paper sheets, though this task still requires patience and traditional file systems do not permit a "heterarchy" [2].

On the other hand, while a text-based search field has proven to be an effective method for information retrieval, it comes with its inherent weaknesses: its accuracy highly depends on the student's choice of search terms. Individuals well-versed in their domains of study tend to use the correct technical words [41] and manage to retrieve very specific documents using longer queries. On the other hand, non-experts of a domain might input misleading words, e.g., incorrect designations for technical terms, and their queries tend to be shorter. Additionally, experts and non-experts of a domain can end up writing too long queries, pointing towards a lack of understanding in adequately formatting their requests to the search engine [19].

In this paper, we present a note-taking app for the iPad which improves the classic search field by leveraging semantics, allowing the app to analyze the user's search terms at the level of meaning, thus supporting the usage of synonyms and paraphrasing in queries. Additionally, an automatic question-answering process helps retrieve the information the user is seeking more quickly from their library of notes. Furthermore, alternatives to the text-based search field are integrated which solely rely on visual interaction: users can retrieve similar notes for the document they are viewing based on common topics and find specific notes by selecting various auto-generated filters. Finally, a graph-based visualization is explored for displaying the search results, which offers additional information to the user as to which notes in the results are most similar to each other.

Thus, the app focuses on the organization and retrieval of notes for the user, specifically for students taking notes on a new subject. The goal is to provide alternative methods for searching through their library such that the student manages to find what they are looking for and that they do so more efficiently.

Ultimately, refining the note-taking process helps the user focus more on their learning and less on the technicalities of formulating the correct search query.

The remainder of this paper is organized as follows. In Sect. 2, we discuss related work covering information retrieval methods relevant to our work. The contributions of our app are described in Sect. 3. Finally, we conclude in Sect. 4 along with future work possibilities.

2 Related Work

Various approaches have been explored for integrating semantics into search.

"TAP" [16] provides facilities for setting up a Semantic Web, i.e., a graph capturing relations between words such as "Paris" and "France", as well as methods to retrieve data from said graph based on an input word. "Semantic Search" [17] makes use of TAP to set up such a web of information and augments the search results for the user's query with additional documents, e.g., the keyword "Hamlet" will not only display documents that contain the word but also details on its publishing data, who the author is, et cetera. These relations are fetched from the previously set up web of semantic information, typically a directed graph.

Similarly, "SemSearch" [23] makes use of ontologies stemming from different sources, e.g., web resources, and retrieves documents based on the relations in the former which satisfy the user's keywords: SemSearch adopts a simple query format for the user, who specifies the subject of their search, e.g., "movie", and a variable number of additional search terms to narrow down the possible results, e.g., "noir" and "short". The search will thus fetch all entities from the underlying graph structure of a given ontology which match the user's query, e.g., all entities of type "movie" which are associated with the concepts "noir" and "short". The contribution is mainly a user-friendly query format for indicating the semantic subject of the user's search.

Another method [6] uses semantics to refine the user's original query to find highly matching documents. To that end, the lexical database WordNet [27] provides additional options to the user, e.g., when entering a search term X, the search engine will retrieve the different senses for X from WordNet and ask the user which meaning of the word they meant. WordNet is also used to augment the query with hypernyms, i.e., documents that do not explicitly mention the user's keyword but their category, e.g., "Shakespeare" and "author", respectively, can also be deemed results.

Semantics also help interpret the terms in a given search query while considering their context: a single word may have multiple meanings that can be retrieved from a knowledge base, though the difficulty lies in selecting the correct meaning for each search term that leads to the same intended context. One method to determine both the meaning of the query words while respecting their context is to determine all the possible combinations of the meanings associated with each term and determining which combination leads to the most common context, e.g., where the majority of the chosen term meanings relate to the same category such as "biology".

Recent methods deploy word embeddings [3,26], which essentially represent words of a given vocabulary in a 2D vector space where the cosine distance between two words' vectors indicates their semantic similarity. One such approach [15] trained a word embedding based on a mathematical dataset of expressions and definitions: by retrieving other words in the word embedding which are positioned closest to the user's search terms, the engine can find documents that semantically match the user's query, i.e., the original search terms do not need to occur as such, but similar concepts suffice.

Regarding interactive search, several distinct methods exist which help cut down the need for manual textual input. An early approach [34] consists in performing the document search based on an initial textual query, then asking the user to indicate which retrieved documents are relevant. Using this feedback, the query is modified with common terms stemming from relevant documents and the search is performed again.

A different technique lies in auto-completion, or so-called query expansion [28], where the search engine can suggest additional search terms as the user is typing their query. Such suggested query expansions originate from the user's library of existing documents, thus allowing the final search to retrieve some results, i.e., it avoids the user inputting misleading terms.

Document similarity can also be integrated into search, where users can retrieve other documents which are similar in terms of topics to their current one. An earlier approach [18] uses WordNet [27] to compute the semantic similarity between documents, enabling this search experience in the context of medical data to fetch conceptually similar documents. At the same time, newer methods [5] rely on word embeddings to represent two documents numerically as matrices, allowing the usage of metrics such as the matrix norm for similarity measurements.

Other tools deviate from textual input altogether, instead providing the user with search options that can visually be selected through the program interface. Faceted search [21] does this by integrating filters, which can either be pre-determined, e.g., product types on e-commerce websites, or dynamically generated based on the user's experience, e.g., items they may have previously inspected in a shopping app. "Mimir" [37] adopts a similar technique by offering different categories of filters to the user whose selections gradually shrink the possible search results set: for example, in a medical database, when the user selects the category "disease", they can further narrow their search by choosing "bacterial disease" or "viral disease". The idea is to slowly present the user with the possible filter choices, allowing them to explore documents as they search.

In the context of knowledge bases, search results can also be presented graphically [22,32] for known entities, allowing the user to explore other concepts related to their query. Such visualizations can use graphs laying out similar concepts as linked vertices or hierarchical views that let the user explore concepts step by step.

"Thalia" [35] presents a hybrid engine which combines semantics and faceted search: by integrating named-entity recognition, which includes both acronyms and textual variations of the same term, it can recognize concepts in both the articles and the user's entered query. These concepts are associated with corresponding entities from biomedical ontologies. After outputting matching documents based on concepts similar to the user's input, e.g., "Alzheimer" is related to "disease", the faceted search provides additional filters to narrow the results, such as year of publication and journal for the articles deemed as search results. Furthermore, related concepts are suggested as new queries, e.g., for the search term "diabetes", the concept "obesity" is also suggested as they are closely related in the underlying knowledge bases.

Finally, steps can also be taken to reduce the need for the user to open a given search result for the exact answer they seek. Automatic question-answering [9, 29,36] is deployed in this area to extract the passage of text in a document corresponding with the answer to the user's queried question, which will directly be presented to them.

3   Enhanced Search

To facilitate information retrieval, improvements to the textual input-based search and interactive alternatives are integrated into an existing note-taking app, from now on referred to as "Sketchnoting" [1]. For context, this app supports two distinct features that will be re-utilized for this work: firstly, certain shapes drawn by the user are automatically recognized, e.g., the app can label a "light bulb" drawing, which can be used as a search query.

Secondly, Sketchnoting integrates semantic annotators [24,30,40] for different domains, which essentially annotate the content of a given note with related documents originating from web resources, e.g., a note about Shakespeare will automatically display the corresponding Wikipedia article within the app, and it will be associated with the concept of "author". These web resources can also be used when searching for specific notes in the user's library.

This work expands the previously described app's search to render it less strict and thus easier to use for a student. Notably, by leveraging semantics to analyze search terms at the level of their meaning rather than just their syntactical structure, the user can retrieve notes even when entering synonyms or paraphrasing concepts. Furthermore, an automated process is introduced to answer the user's query if forms a question, extracting the relevant passage from a note resulting from the standard search. This improves the efficiency as the user no longer needs to open and read a given search result to obtain the information they were looking for. On the other hand, alternatives to the textual input approach are offered to help less tech-adept users who do not know how to form their textual queries without resorting to natural language. These alternatives forego the input of text and instead rely on visual interaction with the app's interface: firstly, users can fetch notes deemed semantically similar to a given selected note, which not only reduces the need for manually grouping notes based on a common topic but also allows the student to continue their learning through related material. Secondly, a filter-selection-based process is also introduced, narrowing the possible set of search results in a step-wise fashion as the user selects various filters to describe the notes being searched for.

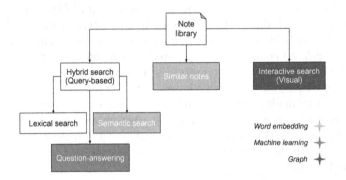

Fig. 1. Components of the proposed app

Each proposed functionality is presented in this section, following the overview in Fig. 1. A hybrid search (Sect. 3.1) combining lexical and semantic approaches supports the textual input-based search. A question-answering module (Sect. 3.2) is layered on top of the standard search to extract the answer to the user's question directly from the search results. A semantic similarity metric enables one to view related notes (Sect. 3.3) for a selected note. Finally, a filter-based process (Sect. 3.4) allows users to find the notes they are looking for interactively.

3.1   Semantic Search

Hybrid Search. A standard option for information retrieval in document-based apps is a dedicated text field where search terms are entered.

Typically, to find matching notes across the user's library, either exact occurrences of the user's keywords are searched for, or at least partial occurrences, e.g., substrings of the original search term. An established measure is the Damerau-Levenshtein [8] metric, which compares two words' lexical similarity by computing how many edits are needed to transform a given word into another. This method exclusively relies on the structural make-up of the user's search terms, i.e., comparisons at the character level.

This leads to the hybrid approach proposed by our app: in addition to the lexical search, search terms are also analyzed at the level of meaning. The latter denotes the so-called semantic search, which computes the similarity between two words by considering whether they refer to related concepts, e.g., "car" and "wheel" are semantically similar but not lexically as they share no common characters.

The goal of this hybrid search is to support more search terms, especially when the user's entered keywords do not occur as such in their notes: misspellings are always possible, which the lexical search can already handle to a certain degree, e.g., through the usage of partial matching rather than only accepting exact occurrences.

However, the lexical search can fail when the user enters entirely different words that do not appear in the notes they are looking for. For example, if users look for a note on one of Shakespeare's works but do not remember the title or the characters' names, they may resort to a more generic search query such as "theatre production". As these words do not appear in the note, the lexical search can not retrieve it, yet the semantic search can capture the meaning of the search terms, e.g., that "theatre" and "Hamlet" are semantically related, as shown in Fig. 2.

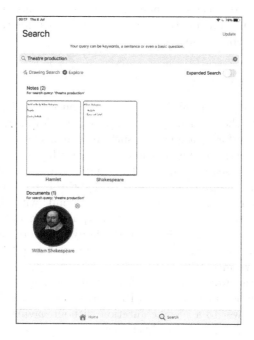

Fig. 2. Example of a user query where two notes are found through the semantic search

The semantic search thus acts as a backup measure for the traditional lexical search, which can find results even when the user does not accurately remember the specific terms used in their notes.

Concretely, the app integrates a word embedding [4], which positions words of a given language's vocabulary in a 2D vector space such that semantically similar terms are closer together when applying metrics such as the cosine distance. This embedding allows the app to compare two given words' similarities based on meaning by computing their distance in the vector space, e.g., using cosine distance [14].

Pre-processing. In addition to the proposed hybrid search, pre-processing steps are introduced to shorten the user's entered query down to its most relevant terms.

Firstly, part-of-speech tagging [20] is applied to reduce the user's query down to its main keywords, such as nouns and adjectives. In contrast, other words such as prepositions and particles are omitted as they generally only help form grammatically correct sentences, i.e., they do not contribute additional information about what the user is searching for.

Secondly, a query splitting procedure is introduced to increase the likelihood that the app finds at least one match for the user's entered query, separating the individual search terms into semantically similar groups. To that end, the same word embedding used by the semantic search is applied here to compute the semantic similarities between each pair of search terms. This means the original query can be split up into multiple smaller sub-queries, for each of which the app will perform a separate search.

3.2   Question-Answering

Answer Extraction. The app integrates an automatic question-answering module to improve the efficiency of information retrieval. Specifically, whenever the user's query forms a question such as "when was work X published", the app directly answers to the question on the search page. The user does not have to open a given search result to find the answer manually. To that end, notes resulting from the previously described hybrid search (Sect. 3.1) are used to extract the specific passage of text that corresponds with the answer to the user's question. In the previous example, the publishing date of the work X would be displayed as it is mentioned in the body of a note on said work. The answer can also vary by type, e.g., rather than a date being expected, it may be a definition as shown in Fig. 3.

This automatic answer extraction can especially be helpful when a document, e.g., a scientific article in the form of a PDF, was imported and the user merely wants to find an answer to a specific question without having to read the entire article. The hybrid search retrieves likely paragraphs of text which may contain the answer based on both search term occurrence and semantically similar words, i.e., the user does not need to know the exact terms used in the document, and the automatic question-answering will finally display a direct answer to the user's question using these extracted paragraphs.

Technically, the app uses a machine learning (ML) model based on a variant of the BERT [9,39] architecture and trained on the question-answering dataset SQuAD [33] to extract the answer given a question and a paragraph of text which may contain said answer.

As for the actual question-answering process, the hybrid search first identifies up to five paragraphs of text that might contain the answer (3.1). These paragraphs can stem from both the textual content or the abstract of related documents retrieved for a note through semantic annotators.

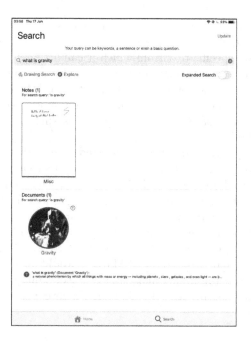

Fig. 3. Example of the automatic question-answering, where the user's question is answered with the corresponding definition from the Wikipedia article on 'Gravity', which itself stems from the semantic annotator recognizing the concept of gravity mentioned in the user's note 'Misc'.

The main requirement is to only use continuous text that forms at least one sentence, i.e., not the title of a note typically composed of a few words. The reason for this is that the used ML model was similarly trained on longer text, meaning shorter input may negatively impact the accuracy of the answer extraction.

Finally, while the model provides a confidence score in its answer extraction, it may not always be reliable as it still constitutes a somewhat black-box process owing to its machine learning-based nature. As such, the chosen approach is to display up to five possible answers to the user's question, which have each been extracted from different texts.

The idea is to inform the user about the source of the answer and the confidence of the ML model and to provide them with multiple answers in case the one with the highest confidence does not correspond with the expected answer, while another answer with a slightly lower confidence does.

Meta-information. An additional use case of the question-answering model is to extract answers from meta-information, i.e., not the actual content of the user's notes, but details such as the document creation date.

The idea is to exploit the generic nature of the model whose only requirements for the input are a question and a paragraph of text, i.e., it is not necessarily restricted to domain-specific text from which it can attempt to extract answers.

Consequently, the app also supports other types of queries from the user, which do not pertain to the content of notes, but rather their meta information. The goal is to enable queries such as "what are my most recent notes", "which note contains a PDF", or more specific questions such as "which note did I modify in September".

Typically, such questions might be supported by introducing visual elements in the app, e.g., a date selector to restrict search results to a specific time period. In this sense, the need for additional tools for the user is reduced, and "meta" queries are instead supported through the existing search field.

Technically, the same ML model used for the answer extraction is applied to this task, but sentences based on the user's library are additionally generated, which are then input into the model. For example, the sentence "Note X was created on 20 March and updated on 24 March." would be generated for a given note X and input into the model alongside the user's question. This step thus allows the app to make other aspects of the user's notes searchable besides their content.

3.3 Similar Notes

In some instances, the user may already be viewing a certain note and wish to retrieve other related notes from their library. The user may want to retrieve other material related to the note they are currently viewing, e.g., to either study a given subject further or to find the rest of their writing in case they had previously written about a topic across several notes located in different folders of their library. To that end, a process is introduced which only requires visual interaction from the user, i.e., no textual input: we propose a "similar notes" feature, where the user selects a given note in their library and asks for other notes which are similar to it, as showcased in Fig. 4.

To enable this feature, a metric [5] is integrated to assess the semantic similarity of two given notes, which bases itself on using the same word embedding that enables the app's semantic search (Sect. 3.1). Specifically, each note is represented as a matrix whose rows denote the vector representation (provided by the word embedding) of each word contained in the note's body.

Consequently, a matrix representation is available for each of the two notes we want to compare at the level of semantics, and we can compute the matrix norm, e.g., the Frobenius norm, between two of these given matrices to obtain the semantic similarity.

However, the chosen algorithm is intended for shorter pieces of text, while our app is geared towards general note-taking, meaning notes can range from a few keywords to multiple pages of text. To optimize the user's library for this similarity computation, we integrate a keyword extraction [25] pre-processing step for each note and instead use these keywords to compute the matrix for each note. This means that the length of the notes will not have a significant

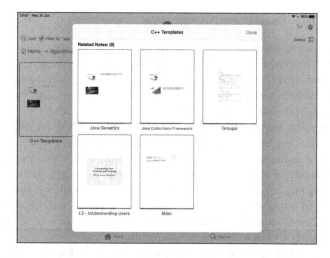

Fig. 4. Example of the 'similar notes' feature, where other notes similar to the user's selected note "C++ templates" are shown, with a colored bar indicating the level of similarity.

impact on the similarities, as we want to rely on semantics for this comparison rather than word frequency (statistics).

For example, by combining this keyword extraction with the semantic similarity, a note X composed of only ten words on climate change and another note Y composed of ten sentences on climate change would share a relatively high semantic similarity. In contrast, a statistical approach, e.g., based on word frequency, would not recognize the common topics shared by the two notes and instead conclude that they are entirely different due to their stark difference in length.

Overall, the goal of a semantic similarity measure rather than a statistical alternative is to better grasp the topics mentioned in each note, which helps the app recognize other notes that may interest the user.

More generally, this similarity metric can also help organize the user's notes: when importing a new PDF document, the app can compute the PDF's semantic similarity to each existing note in the user's library and determine the folder which would be most relevant to store this new document in.

The app can further automate the app usage by cutting down on the time needed for the user to select in which folder to import each new document manually. To conclude, the note similarity feature facilitates the retrieval of multiple notes covering the same topics without requiring the formulation of a complex textual query, e.g., when the student wants to study particular learning material for an exam. It also reduces the manual organization task as new notes can be stored in existing folders based on their similarity.

3.4 Interactive Search

Query-based search reliant on textual input by the user has an inherent weakness, namely that it is dependent on the chosen search terms: the app will only have access to these terms to locate the relevant documents, meaning its performance can falter if the user's entered query is misleading, too long and complex, or it simply contains too many typos.

More generally, textual input can be a difficult method for amateur users, e.g., people who are less familiar with how search engines work, manifesting due to a lack of understanding on how to phrase their queries in search of very specific documents. For example, inexperienced users might write a complete sentence describing what they are looking for, thus requiring the underlying search engine to support natural language processing to handle such a query. On the other hand, experienced users would likely know to restrict their query to select keywords to improve the search results.

As such, an alternative search process is proposed, based solely on visual interaction by the user. Specifically, different filters can be selected to narrow down the possible search results: the idea is to eliminate the weak link that was the unrestricted entry of keywords by the user and instead let the app generate the filters which the user can choose.

Concretely, Sketchnoting proposes four types of filters: the user can indicate whether the notes they are looking for are recent (modified in the past week) or older, and whether they are short (fewer than 200 characters).

The other two types of filters are more dynamic. Firstly, the "drawings" category presents the labels of drawings present in different notes by the user and recognized by the app. The user can thus restrict the search results to notes containing certain drawings, e.g., a "lightning" and a "light bulb".

The other dynamic category is "related documents", which presents all the documents that have been associated with the user's notes through the usage of semantic annotators. For example, by selecting the document "Gravity" stemming from Wikipedia, the app retrieves only the notes annotated with the same document.

The goal of the interactive search is also to speed up the overall information retrieval process. In contrast to the text-based approach, where the user has to think of the keywords and consequently enter them in a search field via keyboard or pencil input, the interactive search attempts to present the available options quickly. To that end, the order in which the different types of filters are shown is important: the time frame and length filters both offer only two possible filters, e.g., "short" or "long" in the case of length, meaning the user can rather quickly choose in these cases. This initial selection can help reduce the possible number of filters that the user is presented with in the two final categories, namely "drawings" and "related documents": as these are dynamic categories, the possible filters shown to the user depend on the previous filters selected. For example, if the user has chosen the "recent" filter in the time frame category, the drawings category will not present the user with the option "light bulb" if all the notes containing said drawing are not recent.

This leads to the second aspect of the interactive search: the filters across all the categories are dynamically generated such that any combination of filters will always lead to at least one result. The app thus ensures that the user never chooses a combination of filters yielding no results.

In addition to the general process of the interactive search, a special visualization is integrated for the search results: as the app has information about what links different notes together, i.e., commonly related documents stemming from the semantic annotators, it can present this same information to the user.

The chosen approach is to display a graph structure containing both the notes and their related documents, with the documents (circular vertices) being linked (edges) to the notes (rectangular vertices) they are related to. Furthermore, to better relay the similarity of two notes to the user, a force-directed graph [11, 13, 38] is used: this graph makes use of attractive and repulsive forces to place vertices (notes, related documents) closer together when they are linked, while vertices that have no links to other vertices are pushed away from the rest. An example results page is highlighted in Fig. 5.

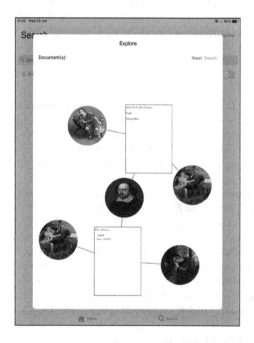

Fig. 5. Example of the interactive search: the graph highlights the common link that is the "William Shakespeare" document stemming from Wikipedia, which connects both notes on "Hamlet" and "Shakespeare". Notes have a square shape, while related documents have a circular visualization.

As such, the user is presented with a graph-based visualization of their search results which clusters similar notes together, thus allowing to identify similarities at a glance.

4 Conclusions and Future Work

Several techniques were explored for improving the search experience in a learning material-focused app. The integration of a word embedding facilitates understanding the user's queries at the level of meaning and enables the comparison of notes to group them based on common topics. On the other hand, question-answering reduces the time for retrieving specific information by directly surfacing possible answers in the search page, while the interactive search allows the retrieval of notes without requiring textual input. Finally, the alternative visualization for search results based on a force-directed graph relays additional information to the user about relations between different notes.

Two ventures exist for future research: firstly, sentence embeddings could be explored as an alternative to word embeddings, which represent entire sentences as vectors to capture their semantics numerically. These sentence embeddings could be integrated into both the semantic search and the note similarity metric. Secondly, the graph-based visualization for search results could be expanded to allow further interaction, e.g., by tapping a vertex (note or related document). The graph would display other notes and documents linked to the user's selection, thus introducing further exploration of certain topics.

References

1. Atashpendar, A., Grévisse, C., Rothkugel, S.: Enhanced sketchnoting through semantic integration of learning material. In: Florez, H., Leon, M., Diaz-Nafria, J.M., Belli, S. (eds.) ICAI 2019. CCIS, vol. 1051, pp. 340–353. Springer, Cham (2019). https://doi.org/10.1007/978-3-030-32475-9_25
2. Beaudoin, L.: Cognitive Productivity: Using Knowledge to Become Profoundly Effective. CogZest (2013)
3. Bengio, Y., Ducharme, R., Vincent, P., Janvin, C.: A neural probabilistic language model. J. Mach. Learn. Res. **3**, 1137–1155 (2003)
4. Bojanowski, P., Grave, E., Joulin, A., Mikolov, T.: Enriching word vectors with subword information. Trans. Assoc. Comput. Linguist. **5**, 135–146 (2017)
5. vor der Brück, T., Pouly, M.: Text similarity estimation based on word embeddings and matrix norms for targeted marketing. In: Proceedings of the 2019 Conference of the North American Chapter of the Association for Computational Linguistics: Human Language Technologies, Volume 1 (Long and Short Papers), pp. 1827–1836 (2019). https://doi.org/10.18653/v1/N19-1181
6. Burton-Jones, A., Storey, V.C., Sugumaran, V., Purao, S.: A heuristic-based methodology for semantic augmentation of user queries on the web. In: Song, I.-Y., Liddle, S.W., Ling, T.-W., Scheuermann, P. (eds.) ER 2003. LNCS, vol. 2813, pp. 476–489. Springer, Heidelberg (2003). https://doi.org/10.1007/978-3-540-39648-2_37
7. Carter, J.F., Van Matre, N.H.: Note taking versus note having. J. Educ. Psychol. **67**(6), 900 (1975). https://doi.org/10.1037/0022-0663.67.6.900
8. Damerau, F.J.: A technique for computer detection and correction of spelling errors. Commun. ACM **7**(3), 171–176 (1964). https://doi.org/10.1145/363958.363994

9. Devlin, J., Chang, M.W., Lee, K., Toutanova, K.: BERT: pre-training of deep bidirectional transformers for language understanding. In: Proceedings of the 2019 Conference of the North American Chapter of the Association for Computational Linguistics: Human Language Technologies, vol. 1 (Long and Short Papers), pp. 4171–4186. Association for Computational Linguistics, Minneapolis, Minnesota, June 2019. https://doi.org/10.18653/v1/N19-1423,https://aclanthology.org/N19-1423

10. Di Vesta, F.J., Gray, G.S.: Listening and note taking. J. Educ. Psychol. **63**(1), 8 (1972). https://doi.org/10.1037/H0032243

11. Eades, P.: A heuristic for graph drawing. Congressus Numerantium **42**, 149–160 (1984)

12. Fisher, J.L., Harris, M.B.: Effect of note taking and review on recall. J. Educ. Psychol. **65**(3), 321 (1973). https://doi.org/10.1037/h0035640

13. Fruchterman, T.M., Reingold, E.M.: Graph drawing by force-directed placement. software. Pract. Exper. **21**(11), 1129–1164 (1991). https://doi.org/10.1002/spe.4380211102

14. Gomaa, W.H., Fahmy, A.A., et al.: A survey of text similarity approaches. Int. J. Comput. Appl. **68**(13), 13–18 (2013). https://doi.org/10.5120/11638-7118

15. Greiner-Petter, A., et al.: Math-word embedding in math search and semantic extraction. Scientometrics **125**(3), 3017–3046 (2020). https://doi.org/10.1007/s11192-020-03502-9

16. Guha, R., McCool, R.: Tap: a semantic web platform. Comput. Netw. **42**(5), 557–577 (2003). https://doi.org/10.1016/S1389-1286(03)00225-1

17. Guha, R., McCool, R., Miller, E.: Semantic search. In: Proceedings of the 12th International Conference on World Wide Web, pp. 700–709 (2003). https://doi.org/10.1145/775152.775250

18. Hliaoutakis, A., Varelas, G., Voutsakis, E., Petrakis, E.G., Milios, E.: Information retrieval by semantic similarity. Int. J. Seman. Web Inf. Syst. (IJSWIS) **2**(3), 55–73 (2006). https://doi.org/10.4018/jswis.2006070104

19. Hölscher, C., Strube, G.: Web search behavior of internet experts and newbies. Comput. Netw. **33**(1–6), 337–346 (2000). https://doi.org/10.1016/S1389-1286(00)00031-1

20. Huston, S., Croft, W.B.: Evaluating verbose query processing techniques. In: Proceedings of the 33rd International ACM SIGIR Conference on Research and Development in Information Retrieval, pp. 291–298 (2010). https://doi.org/10.1145/1835449.1835499

21. Koren, J., Zhang, Y., Liu, X.: Personalized interactive faceted search. In: Proceedings of the 17th International Conference on World Wide Web, pp. 477–486 (2008). https://doi.org/10.1145/1367497.1367562

22. Kurteva, A., De Ribaupierre, H.: Interface to query and visualise definitions from a knowledge base. In: Brambilla, M., Chbeir, R., Frasincar, F., Manolescu, I. (eds.) ICWE 2021. LNCS, vol. 12706, pp. 3–10. Springer, Cham (2021). https://doi.org/10.1007/978-3-030-74296-6_1

23. Lei, Y., Uren, V., Motta, E.: SemSearch: a search engine for the semantic web. In: Staab, S., Svátek, V. (eds.) EKAW 2006. LNCS (LNAI), vol. 4248, pp. 238–245. Springer, Heidelberg (2006). https://doi.org/10.1007/11891451_22

24. Mendes, P.N., Jakob, M., García-Silva, A., Bizer, C.: Dbpedia spotlight: shedding light on the web of documents. In: Proceedings of the 7th International Conference on Semantic Systems, pp. 1–8 (2011). https://doi.org/10.1145/2063518.2063519

25. Mihalcea, R., Tarau, P.: Textrank: bringing order into texts. In: Proceedings of the 2004 Conference on Empirical Methods in Natural Language Processing, pp. 404–411 (2004)
26. Mikolov, T., Sutskever, I., Chen, K., Corrado, G., Dean, J.: Distributed representations of words and phrases and their compositionality. In: Proceedings of the 26th International Conference on Neural Information Processing Systems - vol. 2, pp. 3111–3119. NIPS 2013, Curran Associates Inc., Red Hook, NY (2013)
27. Miller, G.A.: WordNet: An Electronic Lexical Database. MIT press (1998)
28. Mitra, M., Singhal, A., Buckley, C.: Improving automatic query expansion. In: Proceedings of the 21st Annual International ACM SIGIR Conference on Research and Development in Information Retrieval, pp. 206–214 (1998). https://doi.org/10.1145/290941.290995
29. Pasca, M.A., Harabagiu, S.M.: High performance question/answering. In: Proceedings of the 24th Annual International ACM SIGIR Conference on Research and Development in Information Retrieval, pp. 366–374 (2001). https://doi.org/10.1145/383952.384025
30. Piccinno, F., Ferragina, P.: From tagme to wat: a new entity annotator. In: Proceedings of the First International Workshop on Entity Recognition and Disambiguation, pp. 55–62. ERD 2014. ACM, New York, NY (2014). https://doi.org/10.1145/2633211.2634350
31. Piolat, A., Olive, T., Kellogg, R.T.: Cognitive effort during note taking. Appl. Cogn. Psychol. **19**(3), 291–312 (2005). https://doi.org/10.1002/acp.1086
32. Plake, C., Schiemann, T., Pankalla, M., Hakenberg, J., Leser, U.: AliBaba: PubMed as a graph. Bioinformatics **22**(19), 2444–2445 (2006). https://doi.org/10.1093/bioinformatics/btl408
33. Rajpurkar, P., Zhang, J., Lopyrev, K., Liang, P.: SQuAD: 100,000+ questions for machine comprehension of text. In: Proceedings of the 2016 Conference on Empirical Methods in Natural Language Processing, pp. 2383–2392. Association for Computational Linguistics, Austin, Texas, November 2016. https://doi.org/10.18653/v1/D16-1264, https://aclanthology.org/D16-1264
34. Rocchio, J.: Relevance feedback in information retrieval. Smart Retrieval Syst. Exper. Autom. Doc. Process. 313–323 (1971)
35. Soto, A.J., Przybyła, P., Ananiadou, S.: Thalia: semantic search engine for biomedical abstracts. Bioinformatics **35**(10), 1799–1801 (2019). https://doi.org/10.1093/bioinformatics/bty871
36. Srihari, R., Li, W.: Information extraction supported question answering. Tech. rep, CYMFONY NET INC WILLIAMSVILLE NY (1999)
37. Tablan, V., Bontcheva, K., Roberts, I., Cunningham, H.: Mímir: an open-source semantic search framework for interactive information seeking and discovery. J. Web Semant. **30**, 52–68 (2015). https://doi.org/10.1016/j.websem.2014.10.002
38. Tutte, W.T.: How to draw a graph. Proc. London Math. Soc. **3**(1), 743–767 (1963). https://doi.org/10.1112/plms/s3-13.1.743
39. Wang, W., Wei, F., Dong, L., Bao, H., Yang, N., Zhou, M.: Minilm: deep self-attention distillation for task-agnostic compression of pre-trained transformers. In: NeurIPS 2020. ACM, February 2020. https://www.microsoft.com/en-us/research/publication/minilm-deep-self-attention-distillation-for-task-agnostic-compression-of-pre-trained-transformers/

40. Whetzel, P.L., et al.: Bioportal: enhanced functionality via new web services from the national center for biomedical ontology to access and use ontologies in software applications. Nucleic acids Res. **39**(suppl_2), W541–W545 (2011). https://doi.org/10.1093/nar/gkr469
41. White, R.W., Dumais, S.T., Teevan, J.: Characterizing the influence of domain expertise on web search behavior. In: Proceedings of the Second ACM International Conference on Web Search and Data Mining, pp. 132–141 (2009). https://doi.org/10.1145/1498759.1498819

An Argument for Visualization Technologies in Spatial Skills Assessment

Kristin A. Bartlett[ID] and Jorge D. Camba[✉][ID]

Purdue University, West Lafayette, IN 47906, USA
jdorribo@purdue.edu

Abstract. Spatial skills assessment is popular in educational research, with correlations found with success in STEM disciplines. One type of spatial assessment involves recognition and manipulation of drawings of 3D shapes. However, the use of 2D media to evaluate 3D abilities has inherent limitations that are a threat to the validity of the instruments. We propose that emerging visualization technologies can and should be used to create updated, more accurate instruments for the assessment of 3D spatial thinking. We examine the application of advanced computer rendering, virtual and augmented reality, eye-tracking, adaptive testing, and randomized question banks, and discuss how advanced visualization technologies can dramatically improve our ability to accurately evaluate spatial abilities in STEM educational contexts.

Keywords: Spatial skills · Visualization technology · Augmented reality

1 Introduction

Spatial skills assessment is popular in research and STEM education, with correlations found with success in STEM [1, 2]. Spatial ability is comprised of multiple separate abilities [3] and different authors have categorized these abilities in different ways, for example: visualization, spatial orientation, and speeded rotation [4]. One common type of spatial assessment requires the recognition and manipulation of 3D drawings, or small-scale, across-plane manipulation tasks [5]. This particular category of assessment is popular in STEM education research. Some of the most popular instruments in this area include the Mental Rotation Test (MRT; [6]), Purdue Spatial Visualization Test of Rotations (PSVT:R [7]), and Mental Cutting Test (MCT; [8]), [9–11]. The MRT, PSVT:R, and MCT all use black and white line drawings of three dimensional shapes as stimuli, and are presented in a multiple-choice format. Example problems from the tests are shown in Figs. 1, 2 and 3.

The spatial ability assessments shown above were originally designed to be administered on paper, or on a projector for group administration. Some of these tests were later scanned or digitized so they could be taken on computers. Researchers also created revised versions of the instruments because the original copies had degraded [12], or to correct errors in the original projection drawings [13]. However, these revised versions still contain questionable issues that are a threat to the instruments' validity to accurately assess spatial skills.

P. Zaphiris and A. Ioannou (Eds.): HCII 2022, LNCS 13328, pp. 30–39, 2022.
https://doi.org/10.1007/978-3-031-05657-4_3

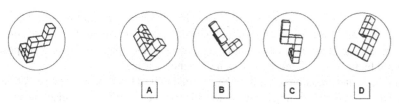

Fig. 1. Problem from the Redrawn MRT [12]

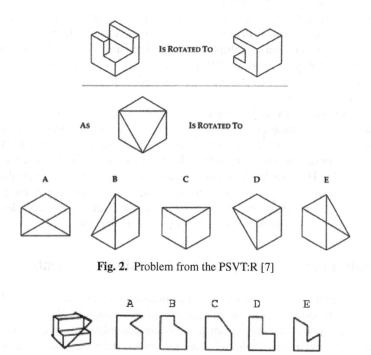

Fig. 2. Problem from the PSVT:R [7]

Fig. 3. Problem from the MCT [8]

2 2D Graphics in the Assessment of 3D Spatial Skills

The use of 2D media to assess 3D abilities has many limitations that are a threat to the validity of the instruments. Any 2D image is inherently ambiguous when it comes to interpreting a 3D shape from the image [14]; the viewer has no way of knowing the shape's depth, or how the shape looks on the obscured side. The tests also use black and white line drawings, which can be ambiguous due to problems like perceptual multi-stability or challenging viewpoints in axonometric projections, which do not naturally replicate human vision and can be confusing to interpret.

Due to the aforementioned factors, test takers must use additional mental processes to interpret the visual stimuli, processes which are not necessarily encompassed under the construct of "spatial ability." The requirement of an additional graphical interpretation step in the assessments represents "construct-irrelevant variance" [15] and is a threat to instrument validity for spatial skills tests [16]. Educators cannot be sure whether a student's low performance on a test of spatial skills was due to a lack of ability to correctly interpret the visual stimuli, or an actual weakness in the spatial construct supposedly measured by the test (i.e. mental rotation or mental cutting).

Graphics interpretation has indeed been found to be a hindrance to test performance. In the MCT, low-scoring subjects were not able to successfully distinguish the test solid from the cutting plane [17, 18]. Tsutsumi et al. (1999) suggested that it is important to learn to "read drawings" to perform well on the MCT [17].

It is reasonable to think that the difficulties with graphics interpretation can result in biases in favor of individuals with more background experience with engineering graphics. In fact, it has been shown in multiple occasions that such individuals tend to perform better on spatial ability assessments [10, 19, 20]. This fact introduces a possibility that spatial skills examinations are not unbiased measures of someone's abilities to visualize 3D manipulations of shapes.

Numerous studies have shown improved performance on tests of mental rotation by manipulating the test stimuli to make the drawings of the shapes clearer and improve the 3D appearance [21–24]. Researchers who have modified spatial ability tests to use physical blocks or various animations of the shapes also observed performance improvements [18, 25, 26]. However, it seems most modifications and improvements to the visual stimuli in spatial tests have not migrated from the research arena into popular use in education. In the next section, we discuss how visualization technologies can be leveraged to develop improved spatial instruments for educational contexts.

3   Visualization Technologies in Spatial Skill Assessments

In this paper, we propose that emerging visualization technologies can and should be used to create updated, more accurate instruments for the assessment of 3D spatial thinking. We discuss the opportunities and advantages of using technologies such as photorealistic computer rendering, animation, virtual and augmented reality, eye-tracking, adaptive testing, and randomized test banks.

3.1   Three-Dimensional Computer Rendering

Three-dimensional computer rendering offers many advantages over traditional black-and-white line drawings in the presentation of images for spatial tests. Advanced photorealistic rendering enables the production of shapes with realistic perspective, textures, color, lighting, shading, and ground shadows. An example of a shape from the PSVT:R is shown in two ways in Fig. 4. Figure 4A shows the original shape from the PSVT:R as a black-and-white line drawing in isometric projection. Figure 4B shows the same shape in a perspective view with shading.

Many viewers will likely find the manner in which Fig. 4A is presented difficult to naturally interpret as a 3D shape at all. The coincidence of lines in the image that do not actually coincide in 3D make the representation challenging. Figure 4B resolves some of these visual problems through the use of perspective and shading. The darker shadow on the lower left section of the shape gives viewers a clue that this particular portion of

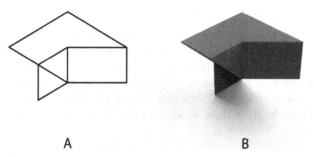

Fig. 4. A shape from the PSVT:R shown in the original style (A) and as a 3D computer rendering from a slightly different viewpoint (B)

the shape is further back in space and underneath the top portion. The use of perspective also makes the shape more natural to interpret.

A few researchers have explored using computer rendering to present images on spatial tests more realistically [24, 27]. Yue (2008) added perspective, shading, and a wood grain texture to shapes in the PSVT:R, and saw an improvement in student performance [24]. Cohen & Hegarty (2012) developed a new test of mental cutting which used computer-rendered shapes presented with color and shading, the Santa Barbara Solids Test [27]. To our knowledge, however, no test has leveraged computer rendering to present shapes with anything close to photorealism.

While 3D computer rendering offers many advantages in making shapes clearer and more intuitive for the viewer to interpret, an important limitation of presenting 3D shapes in 2D static images is still unresolved. The limitation has to do with the fact that a portion of the shape presented to the viewer is always hidden from view, as the front faces which are closer to the observer's point of view partially or completely obscure the back faces that are further away. Therefore, any 2D image of a 3D shape is inherently ambiguous, because we cannot know what the obscured side of the shape looks like. Viewers who look at Fig. 4B may be relatively confident of what the front and top of the shape look like, but may continue to be unsure of how the shape looks from the back. In this regard, test takers are inevitably forced to make assumptions and simplifications when interpreting the 3D shape. In many cases, these assumptions are reasonable, but computer animation technology can facilitate strategies to resolve this limitation more naturally and enable more accurate and creative presentation methods.

3.2 Animation

The use of animations to present the shapes in spatial tests has been found to influence performance. In one case, a video animation of the shape rotating 360° was shown in a study with the Santa Barbara Solids Test [26]. Subjects who viewed animations performed better than subjects who had viewed static images [26] (however, there may have been other differences between the two subject groups that also contributed to this outcome). In another case, test-takers were allowed to control the degree of rotation of the 3D shapes on the MCT with a slider, 180° in either direction around the Y-axis, and performance improved compared to the original test [18].

We suspect that allowing test-takers to interactively control the degree of rotation would be preferred to a video animation that runs automatically, because controlled rotation would allow the subject to investigate any difficult areas of the shape at their own pace. We also speculate that allowing more degrees of freedom of rotation, beyond a 360-degree rotation around the Y-axis, would also be preferable. In some cases, it might be beneficial to be able to see shapes from the top or bottom. Virtual or augmented reality would be a helpful interface for allowing a more intuitive viewing of shapes from multiple angles.

3.3 Virtual Reality

Virtual Reality (VR) aims to provide a convincing immersive experience for the user, typically enabled through a headset which completely blocks out the view of the real world and replaces it with computer-generated imagery. An advantage of VR interfaces in the assessment of spatial skills is that viewers can observe the shapes in a natural manner from any viewpoint.

The researchers who modified the MRT to include physical blocks found that performance improved compared to the paper-and-pencil version of the test [25]. The improvement was likely due to the fact that subjects were able to take in realistic, comprehensive visual information about the shapes by manipulating real blocks. However, using physical blocks is a serious limitation to the widespread availability of a test for educational purposes. Additionally, administering a test this way would be extremely time-consuming as students could only be assessed one-at-a-time. Physical blocks also require significant setup time by a test administrator. Alternatively, a more accessible test could be provided as a downloadable application in VR.

Although some research groups have proposed designing VR-based spatial tests (ex. [28, 29]), we were unable to find any follow-up publications detailing the completion or validation of such tests. Multiple authors have, however, explored the use of virtual reality to *train* spatial skills [30–32]. Because there is apparently no VR-based spatial test that has been completed and validated, we believe that this is an important area of opportunity for spatial researchers and educators to explore.

3.4 Augmented Reality

Augmented reality involves superimposing computer-generated imagery on the user's view of the real-world. While AR headsets and heads-up displays do exist, applications on regular smartphones and computers are more prevalent. Likewise, many people come into contact with AR every day through filters and virtual backgrounds in video communication applications. Because AR is widespread already, users may have a greater level of comfort using the technology in comparison to VR, which may be an advantage in creating a level playing field for spatial testing.

Like VR, AR can also allow subjects to more naturally explore the shapes from multiple angles. Some researchers have examined the use of AR in the training or assessment of spatial abilities. For example, a gamified version of the MCT was developed using augmented reality (AR) in an Android platform [33]. In an exploration of media for teaching spatial skills, it was found that students preferred working with AR models over VR or Portable Document Format 3D [34]. AR-based books have also been created to help develop spatial abilities [35, 36]. Nevertheless, we have not found any widely-distributed AR-based tests of spatial abilities in the scientific literature.

3.5 Tangible Interfaces

Tangible interfaces are defined as physical objects that are used to control a digital display. In the case of spatial ability assessment and training, a tangible interface may consist of a physical block with a marker on it that allows the block to be recognized by a computer. As the user rotates the physical block, an animated version of the same shape may be seen rotating in the same way on the computer screen.

One study that used tangible interfaces for the training of spatial skills found that students preferred the tangible interfaces over just physical or just digital [37]. A similar study used a tangible interface and a projector called Tinkerlamp to teach students about orthographic projections. The tangible interface appeared to aid in student learning [38].

Tangible interfaces have also been explored for the assessment of spatial ability [39–41], though the examples are few. In one case, researchers designed a tangible and embodied interaction system combined with VR to study perspective-taking ability. In this approach, the user wears a VR headset with a tracker that tracks the user's hand movements. The user then interacts with physical blocks to manipulate objects in the VR environment [40, 41].

Since a single tangible interface can be used to control a variety of different digital objects or shapes, this type of interfaces may provide an opportunity for wider distribution of a "physical" spatial test, without requiring as many items to be purchased and distributed.

3.6 Eye Tracking

Eye tracking has been used in spatial research since the 1970s, when it was applied to study the nature of mental rotation, and whether mental rotation was accomplished as a holistic or piecemeal task [42]. Since then, applications of eye tracking to spatial ability assessment have consistently focused on assessing underlying mental processes and problem-solving strategies used in traditional assessments of spatial ability, rather than using eye tracking to improve spatial ability instruments themselves. Recent studies have used eye tracking to investigate the underlying mental processes used in solving mental rotation problems [43], problem solving strategies [44], to predict the difficulty level of spatial problems [45], and to investigate the nature of gender differences in performance on a task [46].

To the best of our knowledge, eye tracking has not yet been applied to any spatial ability assessment tools that are using newer media to present stimuli, such as VR or AR. Some modern VR headsets provide integrated eye tracking capabilities, so the technology could be combined with VR assessments rather seamlessly. Eye tracking data can be helpful to understand how test-takers are solving spatial problems, and can reveal more objective information about strategy choices than self-reports.

3.7 Adaptive Testing or Randomized Question Banks

Adaptive testing and randomized question banks can be leveraged in spatial tests, regardless of what media is used to present the test material. Common standardized tests, such as the Graduate Readiness Exam (GRE) now use adaptive testing, in which the questions that are shown vary depending on the test-taker's performance so far. While spatial tests are increasingly being administered in a digital format, no spatial tests have made use of adaptive testing. Adaptive testing can be used to avoid floor and ceiling effects by automatically adjusting the difficulty of the test to the level of the test-taker. Adaptive testing may also help with student motivation. If a test is too difficult, a student may give up trying. However, an adaptive test would show that student an easier question next, which may help build confidence and engagement.

Many researchers who want to test the effectiveness of a spatial skills training intervention use a pre- and post-test study design. However, many of these studies use the same spatial assessment instrument in the pre- and post-test, which introduces the possibility that improvements were due to practice effects in the spatial assessment rather than due to the effectiveness of the intervention. A randomized question bank can also be leveraged in computerized spatial tests to create multiple versions of a spatial test that are similar, but not identical, and could be more suitable for studies that need a pre- and post-test.

4　Conclusions

Spatial ability tests that attempt to assess 3D abilities through the use of 2D media are likely not accurate assessments of the spatial constructs that they claim to be assessing. In this paper, we identified and discussed how various technologies such as computer rendering, animation, eye-tracking, VR, and AR can be used to present stimuli more realistically and resolve the limitations present in 2D media. Besides using new media to present stimuli more realistically, adaptive testing can enable more precise measurement, and a randomized test bank can facilitate more accurate pre- and post-test studies.

Creating improved and reliable spatial assessment instruments is important, because the current "gold standard" instruments have been used to make various claims, such as the existence of gender differences in spatial ability. Lower performance is also often observed in these tests among other groups that are minoritized in engineering. Relying on inaccurate instruments to assess people's potential for STEM success is problematic. When a particular group is thought to be less capable of spatial problem-solving, this may influence the way teachers interact with their students, the types of careers that parents encourage their children to pursue, as well as the students' self-confidence in STEM. In this regard, improved instruments of spatial ability assessment can help educators train students more fairly and effectively.

References

1. Sorby, S., Veurink, N., Streiner, S.: Does spatial skills instruction improve STEM outcomes? the answer is yes. Learn. Individ. Differ. **67**, 209–222 (2018)
2. Wai, J., Lubinski, D., Benbow, C.P.: Spatial ability for STEM domains: aligning over 50 years of cumulative psychological knowledge solidifies its importance. J. Educ. Psychol. **101**(4), 817–835 (2009)
3. Hegarty, M., Waller, D.A.: Individual differences in spatial abilities. In: the Cam-bridge Handbook of Visuospatial Thinking, pp. 121–169 (2005)
4. Lohman, D.F.: Spatial abilities as traits, processes, and knowledge. In: Advances in the Psychology of Human Intelligence, pp. 181–248. Erlbaum (1988)
5. Eliot, J., Smith, I.M.: An International Directory of Spatial Tasks. NFER-NELSON Publishing Company (1983)
6. Vandenberg, S.G., Kuse, A.R.: Mental rotations, a group test of three-dimensional spatial visualization. Percept. Mot. Skills **47**(2), 599–604 (1978)
7. Guay, R.B.: Purdue spatial visualisation test: rotations. West Lafayette: Purdue Research Foundation (1977)
8. CEEB. College Entrance Examination Board (CEEB) special aptitude test in spatial relations. College Entrance Examination Board (1939)
9. Gorska, R., Sorby, S.: Testing instruments for the assessment of 3D spatial skills. In: 2008 ASEE Annual Conference & Exposition Proceedings, 13.1196.1–13.1196.10, (2008)
10. Kelly, W., Branoff, T.J., Clark, A.: Spatial ability measurement in an introductory graphic communications course. In: Proceedings of 2014 ASEE Annual Conference & Exposition (2014)
11. Khine, M.S.: Visual-spatial Ability in STEM Education. Springer International Publishing (2017)
12. Peters, M., Laeng, B., Latham, K., Jackson, M., Zaiyouna, R., Richardson, C.: A re-drawn Vandenberg and Kuse mental rotations test-different versions and factors that affect performance. Brain Cogn. **28**(1), 39–58 (1995)
13. Yoon, S.Y.: Revised Purdue Spatial Visualization Test: Visualization of Rotations (Revised PSVT:R) [Psychometric Instrument] (2011)
14. Pizlo, Z.: 3D Shape: Its Unique Place in Visual Perception. MIT Press (2008)
15. Messick, S.: Validity of psychological assessment. Am. Psychol. **50**(9), 741–749 (1995)
16. Bartlett, K.A., Camba, J.D.: The role of a graphical interpretation factor in the assessment of spatial visualization: a critical analysis. Spatial Cogn. Comput. 1–30 (2021)
17. Tsutsumi, E., Shiina, K., Suzaki, A., Yamanouchi, K., Saito, T., Suzuki, K.: A mental cutting test on female students using a stereographic system. J. Geo. Graph. **3**(1), 111–119 (1999)
18. Tsutsumi, E., Ishikawa, W., Sakuta, H., Suzuki, K.: Analysis of causes of errors in the mental cutting test – effects of view rotation. J. Geo. Graph. **12**(1), 109–120 (2008)
19. Field, B., Burvill, C., Weir, J.: The impact of spatial abilities on the comprehension of design drawings. In: Presented at the International Conference on Engineering Design ICED 05, Melbourne (2005)
20. Field, B.W.: A course in spatial visualisation. J. Geo. Graph. **3**(2), 201–209 (1999)
21. Aitsiselmi, Y., Holliman, N.S.: Using mental rotation to evaluate the benefits of stereoscopic displays. In: Stereoscopic Displays and Applications XX, vol. 7237, p. 72370Q. IS&T/SPIE Electronic Imaging, San Jose, CA (2009)
22. Branoff, T.J.: Spatial visualization measurement: a modification of the purdue spatial visualization test—visualization of rotations. Eng. Des. Graph. J. **64**(2), 14–22 (2000)
23. Takahashi, G., Connolly, P.: Impact of binocular vision on the perception of geometric shapes in spatial ability testing. In: Proceedings of 67th EDGD Midyear Meeting, pp. 26–31 (2012)

24. Yue, J.: Spatial visualization by realistic 3D views. Eng. Des. Graph. J. **72**(1), 28–38 (2008)
25. Fisher, M.L., Meredith, T., Gray, M.: Sex differences in mental rotation ability are a consequence of procedure and artificiality of stimuli. Evol. Psychol. Sci. **4**(2), 124–133 (2018)
26. Sanandaji, A., Grimm, C., West, R.: Inferring cross-sections of 3D objects: a 3D spatial ability test instrument for 3D volume segmentation. In: Proceedings of the ACM Symposium on Applied Perception, pp. 1–4 (2017)
27. Cohen, C.A., Hegarty, M.: Inferring cross sections of 3D objects: a new spatial thinking test. Learn. Individ. Differ. **22**(6), 868–874 (2012)
28. Hartman, N.W., Connolly, P.E., Gilger, J.W., Bertoline, G.R., Heisler, J.: Virtual reality-based spatial skills assessment and its role in computer graphics education. In: ACM SIGGRAPH 2006 Educators Program on - SIGGRAPH 2006, p. 46 (2006)
29. Kaufmann, H., Csisinko, M., Strasser, I., Strauss, S., Koller, I., Glück, J.: Design of a virtual reality supported test for spatial abilities. In: Proceedings of the International Conference on Geometry and Graphics, Dresden, Germany (2008)
30. Rizzo, A.A., Buckwalter, J.G., Neumann, U., Kesselman, C., Thiebaux, M., Larson, P., Rooyen, A.V.: The virtual reality mental rotation spatial skills project. Cyberpsychol. Behav. **1**(2), 8 (1998)
31. Rahimian, F.P., Ibrahim, R.: Impacts of VR 3D sketching on novice designers' spatial cognition in collaborative conceptual architectural design. Des. Stud. **32**(3), 255–291 (2011)
32. Torner, J., Alpiste, F., Brigos, M.: Virtual reality application to improve spatial ability of engineering students, **9** (2016)
33. Tóth, R., Zichar, M., Hoffmann, M.: Gamified mental cutting test for enhancing spatial skills. In: 2020 11th IEEE International Conference on Cognitive Infocommunications (CogInfoCom), pp. 000229–000304 (2020)
34. Dominguez, M.G., Martin-Gutierrez, J., Gonzalez, C.R., Corredeaguas, C.M.M.: Methodologies and tools to improve spatial ability. Procedia. Soc. Behav. Sci. **51**, 736–744 (2012)
35. Martin-Gutierrez, J., Navarro, R.E., Gonzalez, M.A.: Mixed reality for development of spatial skills of first-year engineering students. In: 2011 Frontiers in Education Conference (FIE), T2D-1-T2D-6 (2011)
36. Camba, J.D., Otey, J., Contero, M., Alcañiz, M.: Visualization and Engineering Design Graphics with Augmented Reality. SDC Publications (2013)
37. Ha, O., Fang, N.: Interactive virtual and physical manipulatives for improving students' spatial skills. J. Educ. Comput. Res. **55**(8), 1088–1110 (2018)
38. Cuendet, S., Bumbacher, E., Dillenbourg, P.: Tangible vs. virtual representations: When tangibles benefit the training of spatial skills. In: Proceedings of the 7th Nordic Conference on Human-Computer Interaction: Making Sense Through Design, pp. 99–108 (2012)
39. Cerrato, A., Siano, G., De Marco, A., Ricci, C.: The importance of spatial abilities in creativity and their assessment through tangible interfaces. In: Popescu, E., Belén Gil, A., Lancia, L., Simona Sica, L., Mavroudi, A. (eds.) MIS4TEL 2019. AISC, vol. 1008, pp. 89–95. Springer, Cham (2020). https://doi.org/10.1007/978-3-030-23884-1_12
40. Chang, J.S.-K.: The design and evaluation of embodied interfaces for supporting spatial ability. In: Proceedings of the Eleventh International Conference on Tangible, Embedded, and Embodied Interaction, pp. 681–684 (2017)
41. Chang, J.S.-K.,et al.: Evaluating the effect of tangible virtual reality on spatial perspective taking ability. In: Proceedings of the 5th Symposium on Spatial User Interaction, pp. 68–77 (2017)
42. Just, M.A., Carpenter, P.A.: Eye fixations and cognitive processes. Cogn. Psychol. **8**(4), 441–480 (1976)
43. Xue, J.: Uncovering the cognitive processes underlying mental rotation: An eye-movement study. Sci. Rep. **7**(1), 1–12 (2017)

44. Khooshabeh, P., Hegarty, M.: Representations of shape during mental rotation. In: Proceedings of AAAI Spring Symposium Cognition Shape Process, pp. 15–20 (2010)
45. Li, X., Younes, R., Bairaktarova, D., Guo, Q.: Predicting spatial visualization problems' difficulty level from eye-tracking data. Sensors **20**(7), 1949 (2020)
46. Toth, A.J., Campbell, M.J.: Investigating sex differences, cognitive effort, strategy, and performance on a computerised version of the mental rotations test via eye tracking. Sci. Rep. 9(1), 1–11 (2019)

An Ontology-based Approach to Annotating Enactive Educational Media: Studies in Math Learning

Raquel da Silva Vieira Coelho[1,2], Fernando Selleri[2],
Julio Cesar dos Reis[3], Francisco Edeneziano Dantas Pereira[4],
and Rodrigo Bonacin[1,4(✉)]

[1] UNIFACCAMP, Campo Limpo Paulista, SP, Brazil
[2] Universidade do Estado de Mato Grosso, Barra do Bugres, MT, Brazil
{raquelcoelho,selleri}@unemat.br
[3] University of Campinas, Campinas, SP, Brazil
jreis@ic.unicamp.br
[4] CTI Renato Archer, Campinas, SP, Brazil
{edeneziano.dantas,rodrigo.bonacin}@cti.gov.br

Abstract. Enactive media bring new possibilities for intelligent interactive educational systems, as they are capable of adapting to the user's emotional expressions and promote an advanced learning experience. This can motivate students and minimize learning problems, attracting and keeping students' attention by showing personalized content according to their emotional states. Annotations are necessary to recovery, adapt, compose and present educational content according to emotional expressions. Aiming at identifying and classifying enactive media, this article presents a novel ontology for semantic annotation. Our solution supports to annotate content (normal media) to be used by enactive (or linked to) educational media. The proposed ontology reuses and extends international standards for media annotation and promotes interoperability with existing models. Our investigation presents an evaluation in the context of teaching mathematics for Computer Science students. We illustrate the instantiation of the proposed ontology and its application in practice. In this study, professors execute scenarios of composition and use of media segments annotated according to the proposed ontology. Obtained results point to the potential contribution of the ontology in a classroom environment and research challenges to be addressed in further studies.

Keywords: Enactive media · Educational media · Web ontology · Semantic annotation · Math learning

This work was financed by the São Paulo Research Foundation (FAPESP) (Grant #2015/16528-0). The opinions expressed here are not necessarily shared by the financial support agency.

1   Introduction

Advanced interactive technologies, such as enactive media, can motivate students and minimize learning problems, attracting and keeping students' attention by showing personalized content according to their emotional states. By doing so, such technologies make abstract thinking and understanding of mathematical concepts easier.

According to Tikka [24], the term enactive media emerged as a new genre of emotion-driven cinema and evolved to a systemic approach applicable to other forms of media. In her view, the concept of enactive media goes beyond the borders of technology, the brain and the body, contributing to the understanding of an embodied dynamics of the human mind.

Human being can be understood as an organism directed by emotions, as they constantly influence human behavior, ability to learn, and understanding of states of things. We understand enactive systems, in a technological view, as computer systems that dynamically link human processes and technology. Enactive systems have feedback cycles, which are based on sensors and data analysis. They may allow a fluid interaction between humans and computers. Hence, these systems should be able to detect human aspects, such as emotions, and properly be coupled to them [11].

The contribution of enactive media technology to learning has been increasing as it can self-adjust to emotional expressions [9]. We argue that proper annotation of media (*e.g.*, videos, games, images and sounds) is a key aspect for developing enactive media as well as its use in learning context. Annotations are necessary to recovery, adapt, compose and present educational content according to emotional expressions, among other students' physiological aspects.

This investigation deals with semantic annotation of enactive educational media. It proposes the *Enactive Educational Media Ontology* (EEMO), an OWL ontology[1] capable of semantically identify enactive media. On this basis, our solution is suited for recovering content (normal media) to be used by enactive media. EEMO models the emotional expressions, a key parameter for selecting suitable medias. To this end, during the design time, we executed an ontology engineering process based on the communication of engineers and educators. Reuse of international standards and interoperability with existing models were considered.

EEMO was instantiated in an educational context study. Such study encompassed EEMO functioning in practice and how it brings benefits to the students' and teachers' experience in learning mathematics. We evaluated what are benefits that having media recovered and composed with the use of semantic annotations (regarding the media features, body and face expressions, and level of understanding) bring during the learning activities. Three teachers, a psychologist and fourteen (14) undergraduate students evaluated the use of the EEMO in distance learning activities during the first semester of 2021.

---

[1] https://www.w3.org/TR/owl-overview/.

Our study contributes in the following topics: (1) definition of a semantic annotation conceptual model for enactive educational media; (2) proposal of a computationally interpretable and expandable OWL ontology, which can be reused by other studies that explore enactive media; and (3) construction and evaluation of scenarios with teachers and students to demonstrate the applicability of EEMO in practice.

The remainder of this article is structured as follows: Sect. 2 describes background concepts and related work; Sect. 3 details the ontology engineering process as well as the conceptual modeling of the problem and the developed OWL ontology; Sect. 4 presents an evaluative study with educators and students; finally, Sect. 5 concludes the article and presents future work.

2 Background and Related Work

This section presents key concepts of our investigation such as enactive systems (Subsect. 2.1) and emotions in interactive systems (Subsect. 2.2). We also present results from literature review on enactive media in math learning (Subsect. 2.3) and technologies for semantic media annotation (Subsect. 2.4).

2.1 Concepts on Enactive Systems

Cognitivism is applied to different perspectives in distinct contexts, such as, Linguistics, Education, and Informatics. Enactive approach uses the concept of embodied cognition, in which cognitive processes belong to the relational domain of the living body coupled to its environment [27].

In a transdisciplinary view, the enactive approach to cognition brings together a set of central ideas regarding the study of the emergence of autonomous systems, production of shared meanings and embodied experience [8]. In this context, learning is understood in a broader sense because we cannot completely dissociate mind, body and environment. Since we are constantly dominated by different emotions [27], in this approach, emotions play a key role in understanding cognitive and learning processes.

We understand enactive systems, in a technological view, as computer systems that dynamically link human processes and technology. Enactive systems have feedback cycles which are based on sensors and data analysis and allow a fluid interaction between humans and computers. Hence these systems should be able to detect human aspects, such as emotions, and properly be coupled to them [11].

According to Tikka [24], enactive media can contain shared spaces where several people mutually execute activities. She emphasizes that the new generations of videogames and the internet are prepared for accepting different types of intelligent interactivity. There are several areas of innovative applications of enactive systems, such as, generative music videos and medical health applications adaptable to physiological states [24]. It is also possible to explore this technology on educational scenarios (*e.g.*, [3,18,26]).

2.2   Emotions in Interactive Systems

Nowadays, several technologies allow automatic recognition of emotional expressions. Such technologies have boosted researches on emotions in Human-Computer Interaction (HCI) area, including solutions to interpret emotional expressions and treat to them in an intelligent way.

In this context, we highlight the Scherer's work [22], which was used in the conception of our model for semantic notation of emotions in media. Scherer [22] presented a model to classify emotions based on octants, which are linked to emotional experience. These octants are the result of the evaluation of four dimensions (Arousal, Sense of control, Valence, and Ease in achieving a goal). From the HCI viewpoint, the impact of these dimensions can be summarized as follows [10]:

- Arousal: impact on user excitement and motivation;
- Sense of control: impact on how users control the interaction/device;
- Valence: users' degree of satisfaction, pleasure and displeasure;
- Ease in achieving a goal: the ease and/or difficulty in reaching a goal.

The Scherer's semantic space makes possible to identify the impact of a given emotion in the dimensions. The "tense" emotion, for example, is directly linked to: 1) a high degree of excitement; 2) difficulties in achieving a goal; and 3) an intermediate satisfaction and feeling of control by the user [4]. The design of our proposed ontology in this investigation used these concepts and octants.

2.3   Enactive Media in Math Learning

We present a subset of studies about social and enactive systems/media for educational contexts, which was selected from a comprehensive literature review that covered 104 studies [9]. On these pre-selected studies combined to an exploratory research on scientific bases, we searched for investigations addressing annotations of educational enactive media or educational enactive media for math learning (scenario of application of our EEMO ontology). As we did not find investigations on semantic annotation of educational enactive media, we present eight studies on applications of enactive media in the math learning context, as follows.

Khoo *et al.* [12] focused on analyzing how children enact, when are viewing and representing addition and subtraction operations. The authors conducted recreational activities with students of five years old. Results showed that digital technology supported the participants to autonomous enact in tasks where they construct their own meanings.

Casano *et al.* [5] studied the application of embodied cognition concept in math learning systems. Wearing wrist devices, students received clues to find hidden geometric objects. Arroyo *et al.* [1] presented educational mathematical games based on embodiment concept. They proposed the use of mobile technology in math learning activities, which require body involvement with the environment.

Trninic and Abrahamson [25] studied how notions of mathematics can be constituted from embodied interaction on instructional activities. King and Smith [13] argued that advances in technologies controlled by body movements have opened up new possibilities for learning mathematics, such as, embodying a mathematical concept while visual feedback is provided. Price and Duffy [20] addressed sensor-based technology for sensorimotor involvement in mathematical learning.

Flood, Harrer and Abrahamson [7] presented an analysis of a productive sequence of interaction between a child and a teacher while they use an embodied learning environment for math learning. Both the child and teacher use a mathematical object shared in a reciprocal interactive process where one draws the other's attention through movements. When analyzing the same system, Abrahamson [6] emphasized that the theory of ecological dynamics is relevant to the study and practice of mathematics education. According to the author, with the embodiment, students build new "anchors" and then identify concepts introduced by teachers.

Literature presents both the benefits of using enactive media in education and potential of embodied learning for math. However, studies on how to annotate enactive media to support their recovery and composition on the fly were not found. This is an essential requirement for providing means for enactive systems to (re)configure them according to parameters related to users' physiological and emotional aspects.

2.4   Technologies for Semantic Media Annotation

This section presents our review on semantic annotation of media on the Web. Several works propose alternatives for automatic semantic annotation of multimedia resources on the web. However, few studies propose new models (e.g., ontology) for media annotation. Selected works are described below.

Lee and Cho [15] proposed an annotation approach that consists of generating new identification tags based on visual similarity using two layered Bayesian networks. According to the authors, tags generation is a key step for managing a large volume of multimedia content. The procedure assigns textual annotations to the content to describe the content to other interested users.

Singhal and Srivastava [23] presented a semantic annotation algorithmic approach based on knowledge bases such as Dbpedia, Yago, Freebase and Wordnet. According to this research, a structured and semantic version of annotations is highly useful for search engines. In this context, documents annotated with these datasets become indexable and semantically searchable.

Rolim, Osório and Avila [21] explored international standards for the description of multimedia content, including semantic Web concepts and OWL ontologies. They proposed a collaborative annotation mechanism for the structuring of a database to store the description of multimedia content on the Web. Their focus was on the construction of search systems that provide results closer to the users' interest. According to the authors, this collaborative model proposal enables a gradual improvement of this repository based on the participants' engagement in the annotation process.

Meiyu *et al.* [17] argued that the need to retrieve images from vast databases led some researchers to propose new technologies, such as those based on the visual characteristics of the image. To this end, the authors proposed the use of the image resource called *SIFT*, which remains invariant to rotation, scale, brightness variations and a certain degree of stability in angle changes, affine transformation and noise. *SIFT* was applied to express the visual features of parts of the image, improving the construction of semantic annotations.

Küçük and Yazıcı [14] proposed a system that uses video texts as the information source and exploits several information extraction techniques (entity recognition, person entity extraction, coreference resolution, and semantic event extraction). The proposed system is used for automatic semantic annotation and video retrieval in Turkish language. Similarly, Borges *et al.* [2,16] proposed a method for recommending educational content by exploring the use of semantic annotations over textual transcriptions from video lectures.

Xu, Luo and Liang [28] proposed a new framework for personalization and ways to summarize sport videos. To this end, the videos were automatically annotated. On the basis of the annotations, their proposal generates tailored clips with highlight events of a match using an indexed video database. According to Nguyen *et al.* [19] users of sport media streams have difficulties to determine whether the information returned is accurate and adequate. They proposed a system with components for ontology-based semantic annotation, ontology learning and domain exploration. The solution was based on adding semantics to the multimedia content of sports websites to achieve the goal of more efficient management and access.

Our literature analysis indicate that most studies emphasize the automatic extraction of annotations (out of the focus of our present study), without delving into the semantic model for annotation. Other investigations focuses on the use of semantic models to provide personalized media in specific domains. Therefore, the construction of a model for information retrieval and composition of enactive media is the main novelty of our investigation. We use as a starting point, the Ontology for Media Resources 1.0^2, as described in the next section.

3   Ontology for Semantic Annotation of Enactive Educational Media

This section presents the ontology engineering process (Subsect. 3.1). We describe our key contribution as the EEMO ontology (Subsect. 3.2) and illustrate its use (Subsect. 3.3).

3.1   The Ontology Engineering Process

EEMO was developed using a five-step engineering process:

---

[2] https://www.w3.org/TR/mediaont-10/.

- *Step 1: Definition of Concepts.* Through a review of the related topics, we selected and described key concepts to be considered within the context of enactive media annotation.
- *Step 2. Codesign of the Conceptual Model.* This model aims to clarify and anticipate the understanding of the involved concepts and elicit concepts, which are necessary to annotate medias' to be recovered during educational practices. This model was developed involving educators and students (stakeholders), who carried out codesign activities to understand the conceptual aspects of the enactive media. Specific concepts related to both the enactive media (*e.g.*, emotions and embodiment) and math education were included. *CmapTools*[3] supported an iterative process of understanding, modeling and analysis of the model with the participation of researchers (coauthors), a lecturer of mathematics at UNEMAT-Brazil, a psychologist and two Computer Science undergraduate students. In this step, concept maps were used because they are less restrictive and lighter than computer interpretable models. This supported the freely expression of ideas and facilitated communication.
- *Step 3. Evaluation of the Conceptual Model.* First, the concept maps were translated to UML (Unified Modeling Language) class diagrams, and then they were instantiated in object diagrams, which contain concepts in scenario of math education used in Computer Science courses. Simplified UML diagrams were used to provide an intermediate level of abstraction between concept maps and OWL models. Details such as data types, attributes and some types of relationships (*e.g.*, inheritances and aggregations) were excluded to prioritize both the visualization and simplicity of the model.
- *Step 4. Development of the OWL ontology.* We used the conceptual model as a basis for our OWL ontology. Reuse and integration with existing media annotation models and descriptors took place during the steps 4 and 5 through an iterative process. Supported by *Protégé*[4] software, this process involved parallel modeling of concept maps, UML diagrams, OWL model and model validation. Interoperability and integration with existing Knowledge Organization Systems (KOS) were also considered.
- *Step 5. Validation of the model.* We created in this step scenarios simulating the use of the model. This emphasized the use of enactive media during the execution of an enactive system in the process.

3.2   The Ontology of Enactive Educational Media

EEMO is an enactive educational media OWL ontology conceived to offer solution about semantic annotation of enactive educational media. First, we present the concept model (cf. Fig. 1) used in the modeling of EEMO. Second, we describe the class hierarchy (Fig. 2) and relationships (Fig. 3).

The concept model summarizes the participants common understanding after a 12-month modeling process. In this model, the upper left corner of Fig. 1 represents *Media* as the most generic concept. Media comprises different types of

---

[3] https://cmap.ihmc.us/cmaptools/.
[4] https://protege.stanford.edu/.

medium, such as *Videos, MediaVR and Games*. *Media* support *PassiveInteraction, ImmersiveInteraction* and *ActiveInteraction*. The media also has a storage *Format*.

EnactiveMedia is a specific type of *Media*. Among other aspects, this type is able to consider *Emotions* and *AutoModify*, and *ProvideEmbodiment*. *Emotions* is a concept that comprises *EmotionName* and *Dimensions*, such as *Valencia, Excitement, SenseofControl* and *EaseofAchieving*. This concept is described by *ExternalModels*, such as ontologies and other types of KOS. The *EnactiveMedia* is able to *AutoModify*. To this end, it uses a *SelectionMechanism*, a *GenerationMechanism* or a *ChangeMechanism*. The media must contain *MechanismsofEmbodiment* to *ProvideEmbodiment*.

The *EducacionalEnativeMedia* is a type of *EnativeMedia*; *Media* is made up of *MediaFragment*. The *EducacionalEnativeMedia* is composed of *EducacionalEnativeMediaFragment*, which includes *EducationalContent*. These fragments aim to improve the *Motivation* and they are able to work on *EmbodiedCognition*.

The *EducacionalEnativeMediaFragment* aims to provide an *Understanding* of an *EducationalContent*, which occurs in *DifferentDifficutLevels*. *Geometry* is an example of *EducationalContent*. *ConcurrentLine* and *Trigonometry* are examples and types of content about *Geometry*. *EducationalConcepts* can be described by *ExternalModels*, including other KOS.

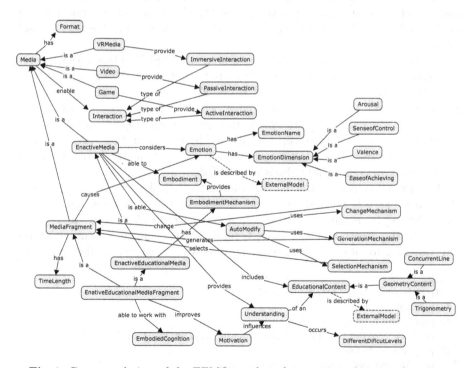

Fig. 1. Conceptual view of the EEMO ontology for enactive educational media.

EEMO is based on the concept model presented in Fig. 1. To prioritize reuse, it expands the Ontology for Media Resources 1.0[5]. Such an ontology is a W3C recommendation that defines a set of properties to describe media resources. This recommendation extends the Dublin Core[6] and provides restrictions on the properties to be used in the Metadata API for Media Resources[7]. It provides mapping for metadata formats used to describe media resources published on the Web, including DIG35[8], ID3[9], YouTube Data API Protocol[10], to cite some.

In our proposal, the W3C recommendation was expanded with concepts, properties and logical axioms related to the characteristics of enactive media for educational content. Such expansion kept compatibility with existing formats and integration with concepts of education ontologies and description of emotions.

Figure 2 presents the EEMO class hierarchy. The classes reused from *Ontology for Media Resources* are identified with the prefix "ma:". This study modeled the key enactive media concepts (*EnactiveConcept* class) used in the annotation process. This includes *AutoReconfiguration*, *Embodiment* and *Emotion* classes. *AutoReconfiguration* is organized into *AutoGeneration*, *AutoSelection* and *AutoUpdate* subclasses. *EmbodiedCognition* is a *Embodiment* and is a *LearningConcept* (multiple inheritance).

Other learning concepts are modeled as classes in EEMO, including *LearningContent* and *LearningMotivation*. As an example, *GeometryContent* was modeled as subclass of *LearningContent*[11]. In addition, subclasses of *ma:MediaResource* included *EducationalMedia*, *EnactiveMedia*, *GameMedia* and *VRMedia*.

Figure 3 presents the relationships among the EEMO classes that represent W3C standard expansion. As illustrated, an *EnactiveMedia* is defined as a *ma:MediaResource*, which is linked to an *EnactiveConcept*; an *EducationalMedia* is defined as a *ma:MediaResource*, which is linked to a *LearningContent*. An *EnactiveEducationalMedia* is defined as both *EducationalMedia* and *EnactiveMedia*. *LearningMotivation* is affected by *Emotion*; *AutoUpdate* updates *ma:MediaResource*; *AutoSelection* selects individuals of *ma:MediaResource*; and *AutoGeneration* creates individuals of *ma:MediaResource*.

To express values of the individuals of the EEMO, a set of additional *DataProperties* was created. It includes: *EmbodimentMechanism*; *InteractionType* (Active, Immersive and Passive); *ReconfigurationMechanism*; and values to specify the *EmotionDimension* (Arousal, EaseinAchieving, SenseofControl and Valence), to cite some examples. Axioms were created to define and infer

---

[5] https://www.w3.org/TR/mediaont-10/.
[6] http://dublincore.org/.
[7] https://www.w3.org/TR/mediaont-api-1.0/.
[8] https://www.bgbm.org/TDWG/acc/Documents/DIG35-v1.1WD-010416.pdf.
[9] https://www.id3.org/.
[10] https://developers.google.com/youtube/v3/docs.
[11] we decided to model the learning content domains as subclasses because they may contain unshared properties and specific features.

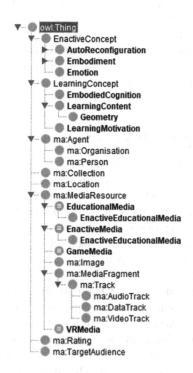

Fig. 2. EEMO class hierarchy.

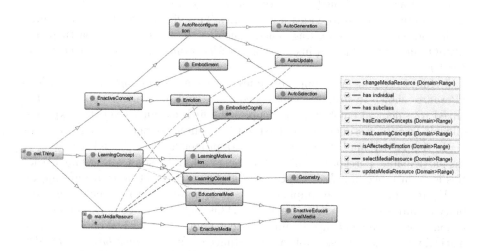

Fig. 3. Overview of EEMO core classes relationship.

individuals, such as: *VRMedia* is a *ma:MediaResource* that provides an immersive *InteractionType*. The full set of axioms and properties are omitted in the interest of readability and space constraints.

EEMO ontology includes links to external definitions of concepts related to leaning and emotions. To enable more accurate classification and recovering based on concepts related to learning and emotions, efforts were made to integrate EEMO with external knowledge sources.

3.3   EEMO Ontology in a Illustrative Scenario

To illustrate the use of EEMO, an educational scenario in the context of math learning is presented. In this sense, we chose an educational video that addresses the teaching of geometry. It contains visual elements and presents a theme easily understood by students. Furthermore, it is long enough to evaluate changes in the annotations between its fragments. The video addresses the subject of "lines" with illustration resources and practical examples. Six fragments of the video were analyzed. The entire video is available on the YouTube platform: https://youtu.be/8Gd1gihKgK0

A lecturer, a psychologist and other two participants who played the students roles formed the development team. They provided feedback about each video fragment and answered a form, which were used to manually generate instances of EEMO. This form includes multiple-choice questions regarding the expected emotional states of the students after watching each video fragment, as well as their level of understanding of each video fragment. The researchers simulated the automatic annotation by updating directly in the ontology the emotions associated with the fragment as well as their level of understanding.

The scenario illustrates the annotation of enactive media as well as the annotation of fragments of media. Figure 4 presents an instance of a *MediaResource* that represents the entire video under study. This video is related to a learning topic and encompasses six fragments, which are identified by the participants. EEMO infers that this is a instance of an *EducationalMedia* and is a *Learning-Content*.

Figure 4 presents an example of an instance of a *MediaFragment* of the *MediaResource* shown in Figure *MediaResource*. At runtime, this *MediaFragment* is linked to a neutral emotion and occupies the fifth learning level (the expected difficult level of a student to understand the content of the fragment), according to the participants. These values of data properties are updated according to the participants' perception while interacting with the system. EEMO infers that this is an instance of a *LearningContent* and is a fragment of a *MediaResource*.

Figure 6 presents an example of a media annotated with the enactive capability of auto selecting medias fragments. This includes the composition of (*i.e.*, to join *MediaFragment* on) learning content about "lines". The ontology automatically classifies this example as an instance of an *EnactiveEducationalMedia*. The fragments were used by enactive media of Fig. 6 via SPARQL[12] queries.

---

[12] https://www.w3.org/TR/rdf-sparql-query/.

Fig. 4. Example of annotation of a geometry class video.

Fig. 5. Example of annotation of a fragment of a video about geometry.

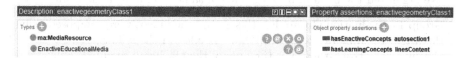

Fig. 6. Example of annotation of media with enactive concepts.

Both the EEMO instantiation and feedback from the participants show the capability of annotating educational media with enactive characteristics in a practical scenario. Although this scenario is limited in terms of scope and number of instances, it was able to provide an initial feedback about the main desired characteristics and functionality, which includes: (1) media annotation with aspects related to emotions and content understanding, which provides information for recovery and use by enactive media in self-selection mechanisms; (2) representation of media with enactive capabilities; (3) representation of educational content media, with possible connection with other KOS; (4) execution of axioms that allow inferring properties and automatic classification of educational enactive media; and (5) media recovery according to the characteristics presented in annotations.

4   Evaluation with Educators and Students

This section presents the evaluations carried out with teachers, psychologists and students. Subsection 4.1 describes the objectives, context, participants and methods. Subsection 4.2 describes, analyzes and discusses the results.

4.1   Objectives, Context, Participants and Evaluation Methods

This study aimed to understand how the EEMO ontology works in practice as well as how it could benefit the experience of students and teachers in teaching mathematics. More specifically in the discipline of analytical geometry. In other words, we investigated what are the benefits of having a media with semantic annotations provided by the proposed ontology. To this end, we opted for a qualitative research approach, based on researchers' observations and questionnaires responses.

Due to the Covid-19 pandemic, the activities were all conducted online using Google Meet. Different groups of collaborators were composed as follows: (a) three lecturers (university lecturers), two of them with background in Mathematics and one with background in Computer Science; (b) twelve students, eight of them take Computer Science undergraduate course (main focus) and other four take a specialization specialisation course in Science and Mathematics Teaching. All are enrolled in the State University of Mato Grosso - Brazil.

We organized the class into two groups of same size, in a random way:

- Group 1 - Evaluation Group. For this group, the videos were composed using the fragments annotated by EEMO, as detailed in the following.
- Group 2 - Control Group. For this group, the teachers presented the content using "fixed" videos, i.e., without using the EEMO.

This study was carried out in four stages as follows:

1. *Theme and scope definition.* With the support of a lecturer of the analytical geometry discipline of the Computer Science course, we defined the theme "parables" for our study. The content was developed jointly with the researcher (first author of this article) and two lecturers with prior experience in teaching this theme.
2. *Video preparation and ontology annotation.* The lecturers followed the following steps in the video preparation: (1) selection of a content; (2) dimensioning of the time to be used; (3) choice of tools that would be used; and (4) construction and/or use of learning objects. The videos were created in addition to other materials such as slides, books and YouTube videos. The following criteria were used in the initial section of videos: videos lengths must be kept under the limit for the subject; each video must be focused on a specific content; and, different learning methodologies must be used for each video. After all the material was selected, the videos were fragmented and annotated according to the EEMO ontology' concepts. A researcher with the support of a lecturer included all the fragments as instances of EEMO, including the

expected emotions, difficulty level, use of embodied cognition, among others (cf. Section 3).

3. *Use of annotated media in classes.* Each lecturer received a "descriptive" (table) version of the annotations. This was because the ontology reading requires specialized knowledge. The lecturers themselves selected the videos during their classes, according to what had been previously annotated by EEMO and the students' reactions (including emotions) at run-time. That is, at the current stage, we did not develop a full system to select or propose the use of media fragments in a automatic way. Four videos, composed of several fragments, were dynamically created and presented to the students.

4. *Evaluation after classes.* After reading and accepting a free and informed consent term, the groups performed the activities and answered a questionnaire on Google Forms. Participants analyzed the solution individually, without interference or previous discussion with the researchers. The students had access to the annotations after executing the activities. One lecturer applied a assessment test to the two groups with questions about the covered topics, as complementary evaluation.

4.2   Synthesis and Discussion of the Results

This section describes the results according to each assessment category/audience.

Results on the Lecturers' Responses. Table 1 presents a summary of the teachers responses for the following questions:

– Q1. How do you analyze the use of enactive media in the classroom?
– Q2. What were the benefits of relying on an annotated media including aspects such as subject, emotional elements, level of understanding, use of the body, and level of difficulty?
– Q3. Did the annotated media provide support to choose the most appropriate teaching material for students?
– Q4. What would be the benefits of having this information available on a database?
– Q5. Were test group students more interested than control group?
– Q6. What benefits did the annotated media bring to you?

The lecturers reported that benefits of annotated media may include: 1) enriched classes, by presenting the same content in different ways (approaches); 2) greater interaction among lectures and students, and student-student. One of the lecturers reported that a lot of work is necessary to implement annotated media in the classroom. However, he pondered that this is normal/expected when a new approach is introduced in classroom. Furthermore, he emphasized that teachers were supported by annotation in choosing different methods to quickly respond to the student's learning difficulties and emotional expressions. The teachers agreed that the annotations provided by the proposed enactive media positively improve the content presented to the class and acknowledged that annotations make personalized classes to students feasible.

Table 1. Summary of teachers responses

#	Responses
Q1.	It's the future, but it requires a lot of work to develop it.
	Enactive media brings new possibilities to classroom teaching, such as
	different approaches to the same content and greater interaction.
	It requires a greater effort as in other cases that differ from the usual ...
Q2.	It is an attempt to understand why a student is not understanding the subject.
	The annotation allowed to select a more suitable media for the class or student ...
	The benefits are in the possibility of personalization of teaching, with
	indicators that go beyond those externalized by the students ...
Q3.	Of course, yes.
	Yes, it helps, mainly to choose content suitable to the class and students ...
	I believe so, because an understanding of individual doubts ...
Q4.	Reconciling the various forms of presentation of a subject ...
	It allows the teacher to choose a set of media according to students ...
	Having a better diagnosis of what should be presented or is misunderstood.
Q5.	I saw few changes in the faces of the students.
	Yes. It is observed that as the media is switched, the students' attention is resumed.
	I wouldn't be able to answer.
Q6.	Classes are enriched.
	Possibility of exploring the contents on different approaches ...
	The benefit is a better understanding of learning processes

Results on the Psychologist Responses. Table 2 presents a summary of the psychologist's, who watched class videos, responses to the following questions:

– Q1. What was the influence of enactive media on students' motivation?
– Q2. Was the type of emotion produced different when the teacher uses different resources like: books, blackboards, videos, games, etc.?
– Q3. Did annotated media help the teacher in the learning process?

The psychologist declared that each person has a different way of learning, and emphasized that enactive media can positively influence this process. This can make the learning process more pleasurable and meaningful. According to the psychologist, from the moment that such differences are taken into account, enactive media make students feel more motivated and open to participation.

The psychologist indicated that annotated media make students feel a sense of care (for them), and special. Consequently, this generates motivation and increases the possibilities for better learning. She reported that enactive media can generate a perception of a higher teaching quality because it provides individualized and adaptive content. At the same time, it can serve as a motivational tool for teachers because it provides feedback from students.

Table 2. Summary of psychologist responses

#	Responses
Q1.	... taking into account that people learn in a different way, enactive media has a lot to positively influence students' learning process, because it provides carefully choice of the media to which they will be used for teaching ...
Q2.	Yes. The type of emotion generated in each individual is different, ...
Q3.	Yes. However, the teachers need to carry out an investigative process to better understand what alternatives to facilitate learning ...

Results on the Students Responses. Table 3 presents a summary of the students' responses for the following questions:

- Q1. Did the media (in fact) rise the emotion described in the annotation?
- Q2. Did the media changes (based on the annotations) adequate ?
- Q3. Based on what you experienced in the study, do you find it interesting to have media annotated with the level of understanding, the level of difficulty and expected emotion?

In Group 1 (evaluation group), only one student negatively answered the questions Q1 and Q2. The other ones acknowledged the potential positive contribution of annotated media to the learning process. Next paragraphs, detail both the main positive and negative aspects.

Main Positive Aspects: Media annotations, including the level of understanding, difficulty and emotional aspects, can bring improvements in the result of the learning process. This occurs because teachers can have the media annotated according to the parameters they need to adapt and select the content. In this sense, each teacher can increase or decrease the level of difficulty and students' emotional (or corporal) experience according to the annotations linked to the media.

Main Negative Aspects: Among the students responses, one reported that "the videos were repetitive and only had an explanation of definitions ...". This may be related to the fact that we focused on only one theme. The same student mentioned a situation in which the teacher used the blackboard to demonstrate a definition and he (the teacher) had to erase the board to continue. It is expected that in real situations theses issues can be avoided by tackling a wider range of topics and by editing the media.

Table 3. Summary of students responses (Group 1)

#	Student	Responses
Q1.	St. 1	Yes.
	St. 2	Yes.
	St. 3	Yes.
	St. 4	I believe so! I was very motivated...
	St. 5	I did not understand this question... the videos were very repetitive ...
	St. 6	Yes.
Q2.	St. 1	Yes.
	St. 2	Yes, because it was possible to have different points of view ...
	St. 3	Yes.
	St. 4	Yes, it helped us to see the same content from different perspectives.
	St. 5	... the videos used the digitizing table and the blackboard, both of which had limited space for visualization ...
	St. 6	Yes.
Q3.	St. 1	Yes.
	St. 2	Yes.
	St. 3	Yes.
	St. 4	I found it quite interesting, it helps to filter and find content...
	St. 5	Yes, but with varied examples ...
	St. 6	Yes, it is very valid in facilitating learning

Observations, Test Results and Discussion. According to our observations, we notice that, after the study with Group 1, there was an intense discussion among the students and the lectures. The teachers asked opinions about the classes. The students replied that they considered this "type" (adaptive) of class very interesting. They expressed that it would be interesting for all lectures to adopt such a method. Another addressed issue referred to the fact that only one topic was selected (due to time limitation). On doing so, students and lectures imagined and discussed what should be a complete course using these technologies. The students were open to use these technologies in a complete course.

By observing group 2 (control), we concluded that there were need to adapt videos according to students' perceptions from the contents. We observed that some students were dispersed, and expressed changes in their faces. As such adaptation was not presented, we concluded that there is insufficient interaction between "teacher-student-didactic content". In the group 2, we perceived that the lecturer was less interactive in the virtual classroom than in the group 1. A possible impact of the technology on the attitude of the lecturer can explain this finding (to be further studied).

In the complementary assessment of the students' performance, group 1 reached 93% of correct answers on average; group 2 reached 83% in a test with the same questions. Although group 1 had a better result, this was not the main focus of this study, and additional researches are needed.

Additional studies are also necessary to evaluate the use of EEMO on a large scale use; as well as to evolve it in terms of representativeness and annotation capabilities. We consider that a construction of an API that extends Metadata API for Media Resources 1.0[13] can be an alternative to enable the use of EEMO in practice in future studies.

5   Conclusion

This article presented EEMO, an OWL ontology for annotating enactive educational content. It was codesigned with a lecturer of mathematics, a psychologist and two students, focusing on mathematics teaching domain. The development was based on a five-step engineering process including: a) definition of concepts; b) codesign of conceptual models; c) evaluation of the conceptual model; d) development of the ontology; and e) a final validation. EEMO extended well-known standards and provided interoperability with existing KOSs. Our study aimed to evaluate the use of the EEMO in practice and its instantiation in an illustrative scenario. Three lecturers, twelve students and a psychologist participated in the evaluation study. It was conducted in the context of teaching mathematics (concepts for undergraduate Computer Science students). The obtained results showed that EEMO provides capabilities for bringing new perspectives for exploring enactive media in educational settings. Next steps include development of EEMO extensions, which aim at covering themes from other areas and evaluating it in other educational scenarios. We plan to develop an API to enable the use of EEMO as a component of other computer systems.

Acknowledgements. This work was financed by the São Paulo Research Foundation (FAPESP) (Grant #2015/16528-0)([18]The opinions expressed here are not necessarily shared by the financial support agency.)

References

1. Arroyo, I., Micciollo, M., Casano, J., Ottmar, E., Hulse, T., Rodrigo, M.M.: Wearable learning: multiplayer embodied games for math. In: Proceedings of the Annual Symposium on Computer-Human Interaction in Play CHI PLAY 2017, pp. 205–216. ACM, New York, NY (2017). https://doi.org/10.1145/3116595.3116637
2. Borges, M.V.M., dos Reis, J.C., Gribeler, G.P.: Empirical analysis of semantic metadata extraction from video lecture subtitles. In: 2019 IEEE 28th International Conference on Enabling Technologies: Infrastructure for Collaborative Enterprises (WETICE), pp. 301–306. IEEE (2019)
3. Caceffo, R., et al.: Collaborative meaning construction in socioenactive systems: study with the *mBot*. In: Zaphiris, P., Ioannou, A. (eds.) HCII 2019. LNCS, vol. 11590, pp. 237–255. Springer, Cham (2019). https://doi.org/10.1007/978-3-030-21814-0_18

---

[13] https://www.w3.org/TR/mediaont-api-1.0/.

4. Campanari Xavier., R.A., de Almeida Neris., V.P.: A hybrid evaluation approach for the emotional state of information systems users. In: 14th International Conference on Enterprise Information Systems, vol. 3, pp. 45–53. INSTICC, SciTePress (2012). https://doi.org/10.5220/0004003600450053

5. Casano, J., Tee, H., Agapito, J., Arroyo, I., Rodrigo, M.M.T.: Migration and evaluation of a framework for developing embodied cognition learning games. In: Proceedings of the 3rd Asia-Europe Symposium on Simulation & Serious Gaming, pp. 199–203 (2016)

6. Abrahamson, D.: The ecological dynamics of mathematics education: the emergence of proportional reasoning in fields of promoted action. In: Kaiser, G. (ed.) Proceedings of the 13th International Congress on Mathematical Education, pp. 1–8. Hamburg (2016)

7. Flood, V.J., Harrer, B.W., Abrahamson, D.: The interactional work of configuring a mathematical object in a technology-enabled embodied learning environment. In: International Conference of the Learning Sciences, pp. 122–129 (2016)

8. Froese, T., Di Paolo, E.A.: The enactive approach: theoretical sketches from cell to society. Pragmatics amp; Cogn. **19**(1), 1–36 (2011). https://doi.org/10.1075/pc.19.1.01fro

9. Gonçalves, D.A., et al.: Revisão de Literatura e Análise de Metadados e Descritores sobre Tecnologias Ubíquas em Sistemas Sociais e Enativos de Contextos Educacionais. Tech. Rep. IC-21-02, Institute of Computing, University of Campinas

10. Gonçalves, V.P.: An approach to indicate the users' emotional state at interaction time. Ph.D. thesis, ICMC - University of São Paulo, Brazil (2016)

11. Kaipainen, M., et al.: Enactive systems and enactive media: Embodied human-machine coupling beyond interfaces. Leonardo **44**, 433–438 (2011). https://doi.org/10.1162/LEON_a_00244

12. Khoo, K.Y.: Enacting App-Based Learning Activities with Viewing and Representing Skills in Preschool Mathematics Lessons. In: Churchill, D., Lu, J., Chiu, T.K.F., Fox, B. (eds.) Mobile learning design. LNET, pp. 351–372. Springer, Singapore (2016). https://doi.org/10.1007/978-981-10-0027-0_21

13. King, B., Smith, C.P.: Mixed-reality learning environments: what happens when you move from a laboratory to a classroom? J. Res. Educ. Sci. **4**(2), 577–594 (2018)

14. Küçük, D., Yazıcı, A.: Exploiting information extraction techniques for automatic semantic video indexing with an application to Turkish news videos. Knowl.-Based Syst. **24**(6), 844–857 (2011). https://doi.org/10.1016/j.knosys.2011.03.006

15. Lee, Y.S., Cho, S.B.: Automatic image tagging using two-layered Bayesian networks and mobile data from smart phones. In: Proceedings of the 10th International Conference on Advances in Mobile Computing amp; Multimedia, pp. 39–46. MoMM 2012, Association for Computing Machinery, New York (2012). https://doi.org/10.1145/2428955.2428971

16. Macêdo Borges, M.V., dos Reis, J.C.: Semantic-enhanced recommendation of video lectures. In: IEEE 19th International Conference on Advanced Learning Technologies (ICALT), vol. 2161–377X, pp. 42–46 (2019). https://doi.org/10.1109/ICALT.2019.00013

17. Meiyu, L., Junping, D., Yingmin, J., Zengqi, S.: Image semantic description and automatic semantic annotation. In: ICCAS 2010, pp. 1192–1195 (2010). https://doi.org/10.1109/ICCAS.2010.5669742

18. Mendoza, Y.L.M., Baranauskas, M.C.C.: Tangitime: designing a (socio) enactive experience for deep time in an educational exhibit. In: Proceedings of the 18th Brazilian Symposium on Human Factors in Computing Systems, pp.1–11 (2019)

19. Nguyen, Q.M., Cao, T.D., Nguyen, H.C., Hagino, T.: Towards efficient sport data integration through semantic annotation. In: 2012 Fourth International Conference on Knowledge and Systems Engineering, pp. 99–106 (2012). https://doi.org/10.1109/KSE.2012.21
20. Price, S., Duffy, S.: Opportunities and challenges of bodily interaction for geometry learning to inform technology design. Multi. Technol. Interact. **2**(3), 41 (2018)
21. Rolim, L., Osorio, A., Avila, I.: Collaborative system for semantic annotation of audiovisual contents - applications in the context of brazilian independent culture. In: 2010 Brazilian Symposium on Collaborative Systems II - Simposio Brasileiro de Sistemas Colaborativos II, pp. 1–4 (2010). https://doi.org/10.1109/SBSC-II.2010.10
22. Scherer, K.R.: What are emotions? and how can they be measured? Soc. Sci. Inf. **44**(4), 695–729 (2005). https://doi.org/10.1177/0539018405058216
23. Singhal, A., Srivastava, J.: Generating semantic annotations for research datasets. In: Proceedings of the 4th International Conference on Web Intelligence, Mining and Semantics (WIMS14). WIMS 2014. Association for Computing Machinery, New York, NY (2014). https://doi.org/10.1145/2611040.2611056
24. Tikka, P.: Enactive media - generalising from enactive cinema. Digital Creativity **21**(4), 205–214 (2010). https://doi.org/10.1080/14626268.2011.550028
25. Trninic, D., Abrahamson, D.: Embodied Interaction as Designed Mediation of Conceptual Performance. Springer (2013)
26. Valente, J.A., et al.: A robot-based activity for kindergarten children: an embodied exercise. In: Constructionism Conference, pp. 137–146. The University of Dublin (2020)
27. Varela, F.J., Thompson, E., Rosch, E.: The Embodied Mind, revised edition: Cognitive Science and Human Experience. MIT press (2017)
28. Xu, H., Luo, X., Liang, C.: Personalized sports video customization based on multimodal analysis for mobile devices. In: 2010 International Conference on Electrical and Control Engineering, pp. 4725–4730 (2010). https://doi.org/10.1109/iCECE.2010.1143

Analyzing Information-Gathering Behavioral Sequences During Game-Based Learning Using Auto-recurrence Quantification Analysis

Daryn A. Dever[1]([✉]), Mary Jean Amon[1], Megan D. Wiedbusch[1],
Elizabeth B. Cloude[2], and Roger Azevedo[1]

[1] University of Central Florida, Orlando, FL 32816, USA
`daryn.dever@ucf.edu`
[2] SoarTechnology, Inc., Orlando, FL 32816, USA

Abstract. Analyzing behavioral sequences is essential for identifying how inter-action with scientific texts built into a game-based learning environment (GBLE) relates to learning. Undergraduate students ($n = 82$) were recruited to learn with Crystal Island, a GBLE that teaches learners about microbiology. Learners were randomly assigned to either the full agency (i.e., complete control over one's own actions) or partial agency condition (i.e., restricted control). As participants learned with Crystal Island, log-file data captured their information-gathering behaviors, defined as their interactions with scientific information—i.e., posters, books, research articles, or talking to non-player characters.. To examine how learners deployed information-gathering behaviors, this paper used auto-Recurrence Quantification Analysis (aRQA). This analysis extracts the entropy (i.e., the number of unique sequential patterns denoting behavioral novelty) of learners' information-gathering behaviors. Results found that learners with restricted agency demonstrated greater entropy, or more novel information-gathering behaviors than learners with full agency. Further, results suggested an interaction between agency and entropy on learning gains, where learners with greater entropy in the partial agency condition demonstrated greater learning gains. We conclude GBLEs should scaffold learners' actions while promoting increased diversity in information-gathering behaviors to improve learning outcomes.

Keywords: Game-based learning · Self-regulated learning · Auto-recurrence quantification analysis

1 Game-Based Learning

Compared to traditional classroom learning environments, game-based learning oscillates between play and education, ultimately increasing learning through heightened engagement [1]. Game-based learning environments (GBLEs) are defined by the implementation of rules and responsive to player input, provide some level of difficulty or challenge, evoke learning outcomes, and motivate learners to engage in content [1, 2].

Human-computer interaction GBLE research has focused on the development and utilization of learner-interaction spanning several domains including science [3–6], math [7–9], second-language learning [10, 11], and history [12]. GBLEs have unique interactive features unavailable in other advanced learning technologies that incorporate learning mechanics. GBLEs harness these features and interactive elements, such as visuals, sounds, and incentives, supporting learners' ability to achieve their instructional objectives [1]. One such learning mechanic, game-integrated narrative, serves several functions including providing storyline and instructional content via digital text, dialogue with non-player characters (NPCs), etc. However, as the narrative design contributes to how learners obtain instructional content, it is essential to explore how narrative-based GBLEs present instructional materials and how learners' interaction with these materials influences their learning. The goal of this study is to investigate how learning is related to the sequence of interaction with instructional materials.

1.1 Narrative-Based GBLEs

Narrative is central to the learning design of most GBLEs as it creates the framework for instructional information to be integrated while maintaining an engaging atmosphere [13]. Several GBLEs have implemented narrative within their structure to increase learning across several domains. River City [14], for example, is a narrative-based GBLE that attempts to aid learners in forming scientific skills including proposing research questions, collecting data, forming hypotheses, and testing those hypotheses. Throughout this environment, learners are asked to identify illnesses that are being spread throughout a city by talking to virtual characters and interacting with artifacts (e.g., medical records). Similar to River City, Operation ARA [15] aims to increase learners' scientific inquiry skills. Learners are given the role of junior Federal Bureau of Science (FBS) agents to identify which aliens dressed as humans are publishing bad research in terms of the scientific method and research design. Learners progress through three modules containing virtual texts to read about different research designs, talk with peer, teacher, and researcher virtual characters to ask questions about the lessons and administer assessments, and read research descriptions of studies.

Compared to these narrative-based GBLEs, Crystal Island [3] not only supports learners in acquiring scientific method skills but it also aims to increase learners' knowledge about microbiology concepts. Because of this, Crystal Island is used as a research tool within the current study to examine how learners interact with instructional materials while learning with a narrative-based GBLE. Learners playing Crystal Island have the role as a Center for Disease Control (CDC) agent to diagnose an illness that is infecting researchers on a virtual island. To identify the illness, learners are required to engage in the scientific reasoning process of gathering information, forming a hypothesis, and then testing that hypothesis. The information required to learn about microbiology is integrated into the storyline of Crystal Island where instructional materials support the information-gathering phase. Specifically, learners gathered information by (1) reading books and research articles which held long blocks of text, (2) viewing posters which had both text and diagrams to support the text, and (3) engaged in dialogue with virtual NPCs such as patients who explained their symptoms or researchers who provided microbiology knowledge (see Fig. 1). While within a narrative-based GBLE, specifically Crystal

Island, learners are forced to encounter large amounts of information across different types of representations (e.g., text versus dialogue). It is essential to explore the way learners interact with these instructional materials, and the various factors (e.g., prior knowledge, environmental constraints) that may influence their learning and informational gathering approaches. That is, when highly dense material is embedded in GBLEs, how does informational processing occur?

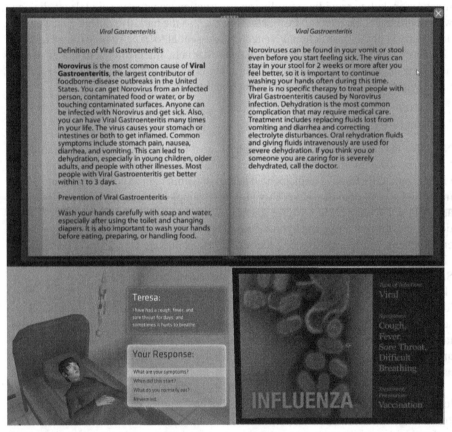

Fig. 1. Example of Crystal Island book and research article (top), NPC dialogue (bottom left), and poster (bottom right).

1.2 Information-Processing in GBLEs

To engage in information processing, learners must select information from their environment, organize selected information into mental models, and then integrate prior knowledge into these mental models to create new representations of information [16]. However, while learning with narrative-based GBLEs, learners are required to engage with an abundance of incoming information that can be both irrelevant to learning goals (e.g., aesthetic visual design) and relevant (e.g., instructional materials) to learning goals. As learners can only process a limited amount of information at once, learning within GBLEs can be extremely challenging [17–21]. Because of this, learning within narrative-based GBLEs requires the use of self-regulated learning (SRL) strategies to maximize essential and generative processing while minimizing extraneous processing to selectively identify which materials should be attended to while learning within the environment [18]. SRL involves the monitoring and modulation of learners' cognitive, affective, metacognitive, and motivational processes to effectively and efficiently interact with and comprehend information presented within GBLEs as instructional materials [22]. SRL processes can include both cognitive and metacognitive strategies. For this study, we examine how learners engage in the cognitive strategy of information-gathering and processing during learning with a GBLE.

2   Theoretical Framework

This paper is theoretically grounded in Winne's (2018) information-processing theory (IPT) of self-regulated learning (SRL) which states that learning occurs over several phases including: (1) defining the task; (2) setting goals and plans to achieve those goals; (3) deploying learning strategies to achieve those goals; and (4) adapting strategies, plans, and goals. Winne (2018) further extends this model to include how learners' conditions, operations, products, evaluations, and standards (COPES) are incorporated within these learning phases to give rise to their change in learning outcomes. We use both models to examine how learners' sequences of information-gathering behaviors during game-based learning changes over time and is related to the several factors presented in COPES. This model acknowledges how the external and internal conditions set during a task can influence how learners deploy operations such as cognitive strategies during learning. The deployed operations can then be controlled and monitored through learners' SRL processes, resulting in products such as greater learning outcomes where are then evaluated against internal and external standards.

Specific to this paper, we examine learners' conditions, operations, and products. Conditions can be either internal (i.e., prior knowledge) or external (i.e., task constraints) and relate to how learners deploy operations during learning. For example, greater prior knowledge about a domain may indicate a greater knowledge about how to engage in different SRL processes while simultaneously gaining greater conceptual understanding about a complex topic [23–25]. External conditions, such as decreased agency from system restraints, can provide structure in how learners deploy cognitive strategies throughout learning, thereby increasing learning gains [3, 22, 26, 27]. Operations are engagement in information-gathering behaviors with content (i.e., GBLEs' virtual texts and pedagogical agents) with the goal of increasing learners' products, or learning gains. Succinctly, this paper examines how learners' information-gathering behaviors demonstrated while learning with a GBLE were related to the agency afforded to learners throughout the environment, prior knowledge about the topic, and overall learning gains.

3   Measuring Learning Behaviors

This study uses a novel approach for analyzing learners' behaviors within the literature of game-based learning to examine behavioral sequences as they relate to learning outcomes within GBLEs. Recurrence Quantification Analyses (RQA; [28]) provides tools to uncover learners' recurrent patterns of interactions—in our case, continuous time series of learners' interactions with text representations. Within this paper, we utilize one type of RQA called auto-RQA (aRQA) to examine whether there were coordinated sequences of information-gathering behavior over time within each participant's single time series [29] (Fig. 2). From this analysis, multiple measures are output, including entropy, a measure of novelty between sequences of behavior [30, 31]. The novelty between sequences of behaviors is a new approach to studying agency with GBLEs and provides information as to how the learner's overall level of repetitious behavior is influenced by the external constraints (e.g., restricted agency) of the environment. In turn, findings will identify how adaptive agency may be implemented within GBLEs to promote learning behaviors.

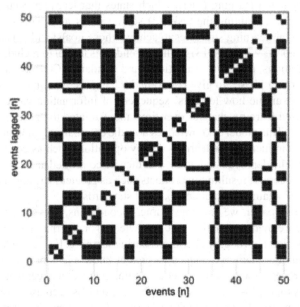

Fig. 2. Recurrence plot of a learner's time series data (n = 50) across all instructional materials as they learned with Crystal Island.

In the context of aRQA, entropy measures the degree of repetitive versus unique sequential patterns that are identified within a time series, describing the novelty of sequential behaviors in a system (see [30] for review; [32]). By identifying entropy, researchers can describe the level of novelty a system demonstrates where lower entropy denotes less novel sequential patterns. In turn, higher entropy reflects a system with a greater amount of less similar sequential patterns, or more novel behavior. Entropy has been measured throughout multiple domains and systems such as gas-liquid flow patterns in chemical engineering [33]. However, limited studies have examined entropy during game-based learning. A study by Likens et al. [34] examined how linguistic patterns of self-explanations were predictive of the quality of the explanations using dynamical systems theory. This study found that entropy, identified using RQA, was not related to comprehension and therefore not included in the overall model. Another study by Allen et al. [35] examined how cognitive processes during reading comprehension are related to how learners verbalized self-explanations. Similar to the study by Likens et al. [34], entropy was not significantly correlated with comprehension scores. However, both studies examined learners' interactions with instructional materials wholistically without examining how learners' sequences of interacting across different types of text representations (e.g., dialogue versus text) was related to overall learning outcomes. This current study extends previous research by examining whether the novelty of information-gathering actions is associated with prior knowledge, agency, and greater learning outcomes during learning with GBLEs.

4 Current Study

As limited studies have examined how learners engage in sequences of information-seeking behaviors while learning with GBLEs, the goal of this study is to understand how learners' prior knowledge and restricted agency within a GBLE relate to how learners engage in information gathering to increase their knowledge about a complex topic. To examine these interactions, we propose three research questions: (1) Does prior knowledge relate to information-gathering behavior novelty? (2) Does information-gathering behavior novelty differ between agency conditions? And (3) How do learning gains relate to information-gathering behavior novelty and level of agency? Based on prior research, we hypothesize that learners with restricted agency and lower prior knowledge will show less novel information-gathering behavioral sequences, and therefore will have greater learning outcomes [22, 24, 31].

5 Method

5.1 Participants

Data from undergraduate students ($n = 82$; 31.7% female) enrolled in a public North American university were collected as they learned with Crystal Island, a GBLE used to teach about microbiology ($M_{age} = 20.1$, $SD_{age} = 1.69$, $Range_{age}$: 18–26). Participants were randomly assigned into either the *full agency* condition ($n = 47$) or the *partial agency* condition ($n = 35$; see below for information on agency conditions). From the original dataset of 120 participants, 38 participants were removed due to missing or incomplete data, resulting in our current dataset of 82 participants. Participants were compensated $10 an hour (up to $30) for participating in the study.

5.2 Embedded Conditions

Participants were randomly assigned to one of two conditions, an experimental and control condition, which were embedded within Crystal Island. The control condition allowed participants *full agency*, or control over their actions, while interacting with Crystal Island. This version of Crystal Island did not include scaffolds or restrictions on agency where participants were able to fully interact with all features of Crystal Island whenever they wanted. The experimental condition, or *partial agency*, embedded within Crystal Island restricted participants in the order in which they interacted with the environment. This condition required participants to enter buildings on the virtual island sequentially. Once they entered the first building, participants had to interact with all materials before they were allowed to exit that building to explore the next.

5.3 Apparati and Experimental Procedure

Participants completed pre-task measures including a demographics survey and microbiology assessment consisting of 21 questions on microbiology which measured learners' prior knowledge of microbiology prior to learning with Crystal Island. Participants were then randomly assigned to either the full or partial agency conditions. Before interacting with Crystal Island, participants were calibrated to an eye tracker, electrodermal activity bracelet, and a facial expression classifier (note these measures were not used in these analyses). In game, participants were required to interact with NPCs, books and research articles, posters, and other features within the environment (e.g., worksheet for note-taking). While learning, participants' log-file data were collected, recording which features the participant interacted with and at what time the action was initiated. Once the participants completed the game ($M = 86.0$ min, $SD = 19.5$ min), they were given post-task measures, including a post-test for microbiology content knowledge similar to the pre-test. Participants were then thanked for their time and compensated.

5.4 Coding and Scoring

Prior Knowledge. This construct was calculated using participants' pre-test scores on the microbiology content knowledge quiz prior to learning with Crystal Island.

Information-gathering Behavior. Information-gathering behaviors were defined as participants' interactions (i.e., opening a single instructional material) with books and research articles, NPCs, and posters spread throughout Crystal Island. Instances of information-gathering were identified using log-file data which recorded which type of instructional material was engaged with and the order in which participants engaged in these materials.

Novelty. This construct is identified using the entropy metric from aRQA output. Entropy measures the novelty of participants' behaviors where novel behaviors refer to a greater number of different behavioral sequences whereas less novel behaviors refer to a lower number of behavioral sequences. In other words, greater entropy is equal to greater information-gathering novelty, where lower entropy is equal to a greater repetition of information-gathering behaviors.

Learning Gains. Participants' pre- and post-test scores on the microbiology content knowledge quizzes were used to calculate their learning gains. Marx and Cummings' [36] normalized change score equations calculated learning gains while controlling for prior knowledge. This used a series of equations which were applied based off if participants' quiz scores increased, decreased, or remained stagnant after learning with Crystal Island.

5.5 Data Processing

Data pre-processing was completed in RStudio [37]. Default parameters for categorical data were set for aRQA analyses in R using the 'crqa' package [30] where delay $= 0$, radius $= 0$, embedding $= 1$, and norm $=$ 'euc' for Euclidean distance.

6 Results

6.1 Research Question 1: Does Prior Knowledge Relate to Information-Gathering Behavior Novelty?

A Pearson's correlation was run to identify the relationship between learners' prior knowledge and entropy. A significant relationship was not found ($p > .05$), indicating that learners' prior knowledge was not related to the novelty of their information-gathering behaviors while learning with a GBLE.

6.2 Research Question 2: Does Information-Gathering Behavior Novelty Differ Between Agency Conditions?

A t-test was conducted to examine if learners' varying in levels of afforded agency differed in the overall entropy displayed in their information-gathering behaviors. The test revealed a significant difference between the two conditions where learners with full agency ($M = 1.61, SD = 0.32$) had a significantly lower entropy score than learners with partial agency ($M = 1.76, SD = 0.27; t(78.4) = -2.22, p < .05$). As lower entropy scores indicate less novel behavior due to the lower number of different behavioral sequences and higher entropy scores indicate more novel behavior due to a greater number of behavioral sequences [31, 32], these analyses indicate that learners with full agency demonstrate less novel and diverse information-gathering behavior than learners with less control over their actions.

6.3 Research Question 3: How Do Learning Gains Relate to Information-Gathering Behavior Novelty and Level of Agency?

To examine if learning outcomes are related to the entropy of learners' information-gathering behaviors, a multiple linear regression was run with entropy and condition as predictors of normalized change scores. While entropy and condition both did not have significant main effects on normalized change scores ($ps < .05$), there is a significant effect of the interaction between condition and entropy on learning gains ($F(3,78) =$

4.11, $p = .01$). For every point increase in entropy, full agency participants' normalized change score increased by approximately 0.31 points whereas participants in the partial agency condition had an increase of 0.74 points on their normalized change score (see Fig. 1). From these results, we conclude that a system whose information-gathering behaviors are more novel and diverse is (1) present when learners' control is restricted; and (2) indicative of greater learning outcomes. In other words, the order in which cognitive operations are deployed and the level of novelty displayed in the sequences of these operations is dependent on learners' external conditions and significantly relate to learners' products during game-based learning.

7 Discussion

The objective of this paper was to examine how learners' sequences of information-gathering behaviors during game-based learning were related to the level of agency afforded by the environment, prior knowledge of individual learners, and overall learning outcomes. We examined an aRQA metric, entropy, which measures the degree of novelty demonstrated by learners' in-game behaviors across three research questions related to learners' conditions, operations, and products. The *first research question* examined how learners' prior knowledge related to the degree of novelty observed through their information-gathering behaviors. Results did not support our hypotheses where we found that learners' prior knowledge did not relate to how learners interacted with instructional materials while learning with Crystal Island. This contrasts with current literature as previous studies have found that learners with higher prior knowledge tend to deploy SRL strategies, including cognitive strategies such as reading instructional materials, differently than learners with lower domain prior knowledge [23–25].

The *second research question* examined how learners varying in the agency afforded to them within Crystal Island differed in the degree of novelty in their information-gathering behaviors. Results found that learners with full agency over their actions demonstrated lower entropy, or less novel behaviors, than learners with restricted agency. In other words, learners engaging in a GBLE without embedded scaffolding techniques tended to have more repetition in their information-gathering behaviors whereas learners with a scaffold displayed a greater degree of novel behaviors. This result does not support our hypothesis as we hypothesized that restricted agency would enforce the use of repetitive behaviors. However, from these results, we infer that learners who have complete agency attempt to reduce cognitive load from information processing by engaging in more repetitive behavior whereas learners receiving external support were comfortable in engaging in novel, less repetitive, behaviors while processing information. However, as we did not directly measure cognitive load, more research is needed to substantiate this claim.

The *third research question* attempts to examine the interaction between learners' conditions and operations on products. Specifically, this question examined how agency within Crystal Island and the entropy displayed in learners' information-gather behaviors contributed to overall learning gains. Results found that, when inputted as predictors in a model, agency and entropy did not have main effects on learning gains. However, the interaction between these two predictors found that learners in the partial agency condition who demonstrated greater entropy had a greater increase in learning gains than learners in the full agency condition who demonstrated greater entropy. These results support Winne's [21] COPES paper in that learners' interaction between conditions and operations were related to their products while learning with a GBLE.

8   Conclusion and Future Directions

This paper aimed to understand how learners' internal and external conditions interacted with their sequences of information-gathering behaviors to increase products during learning with a narrative-based GBLE. Specifically, we examined how prior knowledge and agency were related to learners' novel and repetitive sequences of information-gathering behaviors across different types of instructional materials and how this is related to learning gains. From the results, we found that while prior knowledge did not relate to the degree in behavior novelty, restricted agency and more novel behavioral sequences were related to greater learning gains. As such, future narrative-based GBLE design should focus on promoting novel behaviors while still scaffolding learners, striking a balance between restricting agency and encouraging the use of a broader range of instructional materials. Theoretically, and in relation to Winne's COPES model, future studies should further examine the novelty of learners' deployment of operations including the intersection of both cognitive and metacognitive SRL strategies. Overall, these results encourage the integration of dynamical systems analytical approaches, such as aRQA, to extend contemporary theoretical, methodological and analytical methods to studying information-gathering behaviors and self-regulation with real-time trace data [38, 39].

Acknowledgments. This research was supported by funding from the Social Sciences and Humanities Research Council of Canada (SSHRC 895–2011-1006). Any opinions, findings, conclusions, or recommendations expressed in this material are those of the author(s) and do not necessarily reflect the views of the Social Sciences and Humanities Research Council of Canada. The authors would also like to thank members of the SMART Lab and the intelliMEDIA group at NCSU for their assistance and contributions.

References

1. Plass, J.L., Homer, B.D., Mayer, R.E., Kinze, C.K.: Theoretical foundations of game-based and playful learning. In: Plass, J.L., Mayer, R.E., Homer, B.D. (eds.) The Handbook of Game-based Learning, pp. 3–24. MIT Press, Cambridge (2020)
2. Mayer, R.E.: Incorporating motivation into multimedia learning. Learn. Instr. **29**, 171–173 (2014)
3. Dever, D.A., Azevedo, R., Cloude, E.B., Wiedbusch, M.: The impact of autonomy and types of informational text presentations in game-based environments on learning: converging multi-channel processes data and learning outcomes. Int. J. Artif. Intell. Educ. **30**, 581–615 (2020)
4. Nelson, B., Kim, B.: Multimedia design principles in game-based learning. In: Plass, J.L., Mayer, R.E., Homer, B.D.,(eds.) The Handbook of Game-based Learning, pp. 307–327. MIT Press, Cambridge (2020)

5. Wang, M., Zheng, X.: Using game-based learning to support learning science: a study with middle school students. Asia Pac. Educ. Res. **30**, 167–176 (2021)
6. Zeng, H., Zhou, S.N., Hong, G.R., Li, Q.Y., Su, X.Q.: Evaluation of interactive game-based learning in physics domain. J. Balt. Sci. Educ. **19**, 484–496 (2020)
7. Hwa, S.P.: Pedagogical change in mathematics learning: harnessing the power of digital game-based learning. J. Educ. Technol. Soc. **21**, 259–276 (2018)
8. Moon, J., Ke, F.: Exploring the relationships among middle school students' peer interactions, task efficiency, and learning engagement in game-based learning. Simul. Gaming **51**, 310–335 (2020)
9. Tokac, U., Novak, E., Thompson, C.J.: Effects of game-based learning on students' mathematics achievement: a meta-analysis. J. Comput. Assist. Learn. **35**, 407–420 (2019)
10. Eltahir, M.E., Alsalhi, N.R., Al-Qatawneh, S., AlQudah, H.A., Jaradat, M.: The impact of game-based learning (GBL) on students' motivation, engagement and academic performance on an Arabic language grammar course in higher education. Educ. Inf. Technol. **26**(3), 3251–3278 (2021). https://doi.org/10.1007/s10639-020-10396-w
11. Yukselturk, E., Altiok, S., Başer, Z.: Using game-based learning with kinect technology in foreign language education course. J. Educ. Technol. Soc. **21**, 157–173 (2018)
12. Trista, S., Rusli, A.: HistoriAR: experience Indonesian history through interactive game and augmented reality. Bullet. Electr. Eng. Inform. **9**, 1518–1524 (2020)
13. Dickey, M.D.: Narrative in game-based learning. In: Plass, J.L., Mayer, R.E., Homer, B.D. (eds.) The Handbook of Game-based Learning, pp. 283–306. MIT Press, Cambridge (2020)
14. Ketelhut, D.J., Schifter, C.C.: Teachers and game-based learning: Improving understanding of how to increase efficacy of adoption. Comput. Educ. **56**, 539–546 (2011)
15. Millis, K.A., Graesser, C., Halpern, D.F.: Operation ARA: A serious game that combines intelligent tutoring and learning principles to teach science. In: Benassi, V.A., Overson, C.E., Hakala, C.M. (eds.) Applying science of learning in education: Infusing psychological science into the curriculum, pp. 169–183 (2014)
16. Mayer, R.E.: How multimedia can improve learning and instruction. In: Dunlosky, J., Rawson, K. (eds.) Handbook of Cognition and Education, pp. 460–479. Cambridge University Press, Cambridge (2019)
17. Kintsch, W.: Revisiting the construction-integration model of text comprehension and its implications for instruction. In: Alvermann, D.E., Unrau, N.J., Sailors, M., Ruddell, R.B. (eds.) Theoretical Models and Processes of Literacy, pp. 178–203. Routledge (2018)
18. Mayer, R.E.: Cognitive foundations of game-based learning. In: Plass, J.L., Mayer, R.E., Homer, B.D. (eds.) The Handbook of Game-based Learning, pp. 83–110. MIT Press, Cambridge (2020)
19. Sweller, J: Cognitive load theory. In: Mestre, J.P., Ross, B.H. (eds.) The Psychology of Learning and Motivation: Cognition in Education, pp. 37–76. Elsevier Academic Press (2011)
20. Taub, M., Mudrick, N., Bradbury, A.E., Azevedo, R.: Self-regulation, self-explanation, and reflection in game-based learning. In: Plass, J.L., Mayer, R.E., Homer, B.D. (eds.) The Handbook of Game-based Learning, pp. 239–262. MIT Press, Cambridge (2019)
21. Winne, P.H.: Cognition and metacognition within self-regulated learning. In: Schunk, D. H., Greene, J. A. (eds.) Educational Psychology Handbook Series, Handbook Of Self-Regulation of Learning and Performance, pp. 36–48. Routledge/Taylor & Francis Group (2018)
22. Dever, D.A., Wiedbusch, M.D., Cloude, E.B., Lester, J., Azevedo, R.: Emotions and the comprehension of single versus multiple texts during game-based learning. Discourse Process. **58** (2021)
23. Bernacki, M.L., Byrnes, J.P., Cromley, J.G.: The effects of achievement goals and self-regulated learning behaviors on reading comprehension in technology-enhanced learning environments. Contemp. Educ. Psychol. **37**, 148–161 (2012)

24. Taub, M., Azevedo, R.: How does prior knowledge influence eye fixations and sequences of cognitive and metacognitive SRL processes during learning with an intelligent tutoring system? Int. J. Artif. Intell. Educ. **29**(1), 1–28 (2019)
25. Yang, T.C., Chen, M.C., Chen, S.Y.: The influences of self-regulated learning support and prior knowledge on improving learning performance. Comput. Educ. **126**, 37–52 (2018)
26. Dever, D.A., Azevedo, R.: Autonomy and types of informational text presentations in game-based learning environments. In: Isotani, S., Millán, E., Ogan, A., Hastings, P., McLaren, B., Luckin, R. (eds.) AIED 2019. LNCS (LNAI), vol. 11625, pp. 110–120. Springer, Cham (2019). https://doi.org/10.1007/978-3-030-23204-7_10
27. Sawyer, R. Smith, A., Rowe, J., Azevedo, R., Lester, J.: Enhancing student models in game-based learning with facial expression recognition. In: Proceedings of the 25th Conference on User Modeling, Adaptation, and Personalization, pp. 192–201 (2017)
28. Marwan, N., Romano, M.C., Thiel, M., Kurths, J.: Recurrence plots for the analysis of complex systems. Phys. Rep. **438**, 237–329 (2007)
29. Wallot, S., Roepstorff, A., Mønster, D.: Multidimensional recurrence quantification analysis (MdRQA) for the analysis of multidimensional time-series: a software implementation in MATLAB and its application to group-level data in joint action. Front. Psychol. **7**, 1835 (2016)
30. Coco, M.I., Dale, R.: Cross-recurrence quantification analysis of categorical and continuous time series: an R package. Front. Psychol. **5**, 510 (2014)
31. Vrzakova, H., D'Mello, S., Amon, M.J., Stewart, A.: Dynamics of visual attention on multi-party collaborative problem solving using multidimensional recurrence quantification analysis. In: Proceedings of the 2019 CHI Conference on Human Factors in Computing, Systems, pp. 1–14. ACM, New York (2019)
32. Kuznetsov, N., Bonnette, S., Riley, M.A.: Nonlinear time series methods for analyzing behavioral sequences. In: Complex Systems in Sport, 83–102 (2013)
33. Wei, T., Li, X., Wang, D.: Identification of gas-liquid two-phase flow patterns in dust scrubber based on wavelet energy entropy and recurrence analysis characteristics. Chem. Eng. Sci. **217**, 115504 (2020)
34. Likens, A.D., McCarthy, K.S., Allen, L.K., McNamara, D.S.: Recurrence quantification analysis as a method for studying text comprehension dynamics. In: Proceedings of the International Conference on Learning Analytics and Knowledge, pp. 111–120. ACM, Sydney, Australia (2018)
35. Allen, L.K., Perret, C., Likens, A., McNamara, D.S.: What'd you say again? recurrence quantification analysis as a method for analyzing the dynamics of discourse in a reading strategy tutor. In: Proceedings of the International Conference on Learning Analytics and Knowledge. ACM, Vancouver, Canada (2017)
36. Marx, J., Cummings, K.: Normalized change. Am. J. Phys. **75**, 87–91 (2007)
37. R Core Team: R: A language and environment for statistical computing. R Found. Statist. Comput. (2020)
38. Azevedo, R., Gašević, D.: Analyzing multimodal multichannel data about self-regulated learning with advanced learning technologies: Issues and challenges. Comput. Hum. Behav. **96**, 207–210 (2019)
39. Winne, P.: Paradigmatic dimensions of instrumentation and analytic methods in research on self-regulated learning. Comput. Hum. Behav. **96**, 285–289 (2019)

Towards a Metaphor-Based Tangible Toolkit for Learning Programming Concepts

Ann-Charlott B. Karlsen[✉] ⓘ, Tore Marius Akerbæk ⓘ,
and Susanne Koch Stigberg ⓘ

IT Department, Østfold University College, Halden, Norway
{ann.c.karlsen,tore.m.akerbak,susanne.k.stigberg}@hiof.no

Abstract. This paper reports from design research developing a prototype for a metaphor-based tangible toolkit reifying basic programming concepts. We elicit a list of metaphors using expert interviews with computer science lectures and co-design workshops with programming students and professional software developers. We continue to select metaphors most viable for a tangible toolkit and develop an interactive application for the metaphors mapping 3d models to associated programming code. We assess the application with computer science students to understand how they use the application and how they relate manipulations to the 3d models to changes in the programming code. Our application serves as an example how programming concepts can be represented both as metaphors and tangibles. Our findings build a foundation to guide and inform further research in metaphors and tangibles used in computer science education.

Keywords: Programming concepts · Computer science education · Metaphors · Tangibles

1 Introduction

Programming and computational thinking have emerged as compulsory skills in elementary school education. In recent years, programming has been introduced in primary school curricula across Europe [1]. However, previous research emphasizes that teachers have little or no knowledge of programming or how to introduce programming in schools [5, 26]. There is a substantial need to support teachers in acquiring basic programming knowledge and pedagogical knowledge on how programming can be utilized in the classroom. Moreover, previous research [11, 20, 27] highlights the difficulties in learning programming, especially abstract programming concepts. Here, we explore two promising techniques to teach programming concepts to novices: (1) using metaphors, and (2) tangible material to reify abstract concepts. The theory of metaphors describes that our conceptual system is mainly built from metaphors, which are mappings from our experiences, defined as source domain, to new abstract concepts, defined as target domain [12]. Sanford et al. [23] report on how metaphors are used by university-level Computer Science instructors, providing a foundation for our work on metaphors. Manipulatives as

P. Zaphiris and A. Ioannou (Eds.): HCII 2022, LNCS 13328, pp. 72–88, 2022.
https://doi.org/10.1007/978-3-031-05657-4_6

tangible materials reifying abstract concepts are well established in mathematics education. Previous research has reported that students benefit from long-term use of tangible material in mathematics education. Both their achievements in and motivations for the subject increases when such materials are used [19, 25]. The aim of the project is to develop a tangible toolkit to support teachers to introduce programming concepts to novices in secondary and higher education. In our research project, we explore: (1) what metaphors are common to teach programming concepts and (2) how these metaphors can be reified in a tangible toolkit. We frame our research as design-based research, "the systematic study of designing, developing and evaluating educational interventions as solutions for complex problems in educational practice, which also aims at advancing our knowledge about the characteristics of these interventions and the processes of designing and developing them" [21]. We situate our research in the field of computer science education, focusing on computational metaphors and tangible programming tools. In the following, we present an overview of related work, before describing our research method and results. We conclude with a discussion, presenting two opportunities for future work.

2 Programming Metaphors and Tangible Toolkits

Metaphors are not just linguistic decoration but have a deep impact on our conceptual system and understanding of the world, meaning that the reasons why we think and act as we do might lie in metaphors. Lakoff and Johnson [12] claim that most concepts are partially understood because of our understanding of other concepts, one example being the concept of UP, UP is not understood on its own, but by the rules of gravity, what goes up must come down. But imagine floating through space, where there is no gravity, what would be up and what would down? Then there would not be any up and down because there is no gravity. If something so basic as up and down is understood because of another concept, is there any concept out there that could be understood without a metaphor? Lakoff and Johnson categorize metaphors based on their qualities, organizing them as structural (systematic), orientational metaphors (spatial, system of concepts with respect to each other), or ontological (based on the experiences with physical objects and surfaces). In the digital world, Smith [3] introduced icons and metaphors to make interface applications more intuitive, creating the well know desktop metaphor. However, these metaphors have also been criticized since people tend to overthink them and interpret them too literally. Smith, however, does not agree with the criticism and feels that people's misconceptions are simply a lack of imagination [3]. As a counterpoint, Hurtienne and Israel [10] argue that a graphical user interface (GUI) is not efficient enough to embrace all human senses and our lifetime of acquired skills by interaction with the real world, based on their definition of intuitive: "A technical system is intuitively usable if the user's unconscious application of pre-existing knowledge leads to effective interaction". They present image schemas and their metaphorical extension as a new approach to classify tangible interaction. Ullmer and Ishii interpreted tangible interfaces as being of spatial, relational, constructive, and mixed type and outlined several classes of couplings, including static and dynamic couplings between physical and digital objects [28]. This is relatable to Lakoff and Johnsons categorization of metaphors, and aligns with the framework for tangible interaction presented by Hornecker and Buur [8]:

- Tangible manipulation – how we interact with tangibles is often based on their material representation.
- Spatial interaction – tangible interaction is spatial, we can move tangibles around, up-down, left-right, back-forward, and so on.
- Embodied facilitation – refers to constraints and access points which guide and stimulate interaction.
- Expressive representation – emphasizes the importance to provide tangible access to the salient parts of the digital model to perceive the coupling by the user.

Rossmy og Wiethoff [22] explores new metaphors by designing and building new tangible interfaces to provide users with ways to explore and express themselves in a flexible way through musical interaction. He investigates how the use of metaphors and technologies can create new and meaningful tangible user interfaces. Based on the idea of an instrument's physical qualities and a user's knowledge of how it works, a tangible interface called StringTouch was built using strings as a metaphor to build the conceptual framework. Urbanek and Güldenpfennig proposes a prototyping kit meant for developing tangible audio games. The kit would allow for fast iterative and collaborative prototyping by combining real world objects. Developers can prototype by placing and combining haptic objects. The experimental prototype they used as a tangible kit where composited with LEGO bricks, as they could be combined and disassembled. They were also appropriate for the mapping between tangible objects and the game's actors and objects [29]. Macaranas et al. metaphorically pairs physical representations of image schemas to adjectives. They use the objects attributes and spatial properties as source domains for conceptual metaphors. They provide us with 20 conceptual metaphors identified by participating users, examples being spatial metaphors such as NEAR-FAR being mapped to PRESENT-PAST [14, 15]. Löffler et al. investigated if it's possible to substitute tested haptic attributes (such as IMPORTANT is HEAVY) with color (IMPORTANT is DARK) for the same conceptual model. They identified 15 metaphors, such as FRIENDLY is WARM [13]. These haptic attributes were substituted with colors based on existing literature. Participators then identified which color could be mapped to what metaphorical concept. The results indicate that color could indeed work as substitutes for haptic attributes for tangible artifacts. The use of tangibles to teach programming is not a new idea. In 1997, Ishii and Ulmer [9] published a paper elaborating on their vision of "Tangible Bits", allowing users to manipulate the digital space by interacting with physical objects, aiming to bridge the gap between the physical and digital realm. In 1999, MIT suggested a kit of Tangible Programming Bricks [17]. The purpose with Tangible Programming Bricks was to teach children to understand the principles of their surrounding electronic devices, achieved by constructing tangible programming bricks containing PIC microprocessors. The bricks are put into card slots to control different electronically driven artifacts. In 2011, Wang et. al. launched T-Maze, a kit where children can build a maze and use blocks to sequence moves that lead through the maze [31]. They build upon the previous work on tangible programming kits such as the already mentioned Tangible Programming Bricks, Electronic Blocks [33], roBlock [24], and Tern [6, 7]. Among such kits and materials in the commercial domain are the LEGO MindStorms[1] that combine the popular LEGO building bricks with engines, sensors and block-programming via apps, Gigo smart bricks[2], which is similar to the LEGO MindStorms kit, and mBot[3]), a buildable robot on wheels with sensors and block-programming for building controls. For less pre-conditioned development environments we also find smart boards like Arduino and micro:Bit[4] which kan be extended with physical sensors and materials to create interaction between the physical and digital realm.

In traditional HCI, metaphors play an important role in the design of user interfaces. Metaphors of noun and metaphors of verb refers to the attributes and properties of an object, like shape or motion. Metaphors have also been discussed in the context of tangible interfaces, with spatial, ontological metaphors especially suited, and tangible interaction, e.g., metaphors of optics, light, and shadow. Research indicates positive results in terms of these metaphors linking our understanding of it to a digital meaning, including programming. The challenge with existing tangible kits and tools in regard of teaching and enhance understanding of the concepts in programming are that most of them either 1) have primary school or children as target group, 2) use tangible artefacts that in no or just small regard represent the programming concept the artefact are supposed to perform and/or 3) focus on teaching computational thinking [32] rather than an understanding of the actual programming concepts, meaning they operate on a different abstraction level regarding the metaphorical representation.

3 A Design-Based Research Approach

We chose a design-based research approach to explore: (1) what metaphors are common to teach programming concepts and (2) how can these metaphors be reified in a tangible toolkit. Through prototyping such a tangible toolkit, we aim to support lecturers teaching programming and to advance our knowledge about the characteristics of tangible metaphors for programming and the process to design and develop them. Plomp et al. [21] describe that design research comprises of three phases:

- preliminary research: needs and context analysis, review of literature, development of a conceptual or theoretical framework for the study
- prototyping phase: iterative design phase consisting of iterations with formative evaluation as the most important research activity aimed at improving and refining the intervention
- assessment phase: (semi-) summative evaluation to conclude whether the solution or intervention meets the pre-determined specifications. This phase often results in recommendations for improvement of the intervention.

Design-based research is iterative with repeating cycles of the three phases to find and refine a solution for the initial real-world problem. In this paper, we report from the

---

[1] https://www.lego.com/en-gb/themes/mindstorms/about.

[2] https://www.gigotoys.com/en/about-gigo/.

[3] https://www.makeblock.com/steam-kits/mbot.

[4] https://www.arduino.cc/ and https://microbit.org/.

first cycle of our research project including all three phases and resulting in a prototype and a set of design implications for further research. Our research should be understood as a development study aiming towards design principles for developing innovative interventions and that are relevant for educational practice [21].

McKenney et al. [16] define three tenets to shape design research: rigor, relevance, and collaboration. For design research to be able to result in valid and reliable design principles, the research has to meet rigorous standards. In our research we strive for objectivity and reliability by using literature review, expert interview, and co-design workshop as research methods to understand and design programming metaphors, affording triangulation of the collected metaphors. Furthermore, we apply the theoretical framework by Lakoff and Johnson [12] to analyze and choose metaphors for the tangible toolkit. Finally, we carefully document and report on our design process to secure internal validity of the results. For design research to be relevant for educational practice, the design and development activities must be conducted in collaboration with and not just for professionals from educational practice [21]. We afford participation in our research by including lecturers, students, and programmers during both the preliminary research and assessment phase.

3.1 Preliminary Research Methods

To find metaphors used for teaching programming concepts and answer the first research question, we performed expert interviews [18] with computer science lecturers and two co-design workshops [2] with both computer science bachelor students and software developers. We started with expert interviews with seven computer science lecturers. Following a semi-structured interview guide we explored:

- why lecturers integrate metaphors in their teaching
- how lecturers integrate metaphors in their teaching
- what metaphors they used for which programming concepts
- if they found especially effective metaphors.

Based on their answers, we asked lecturers to elaborate and provide examples of metaphor usage. Finally, lecturers were asked to suggest metaphors specifically for programming concepts: loop, conditional logic (if/else) and return statement, if not mentioned earlier. To see how lecturers' understanding and usage of metaphors correspond with computer science students and software developers, we performed two co-design workshops. The first workshop was conducted with 21 students from a computer science bachelor program and 10 software developers participated in a second workshop. The workshop had two objectives:

- evaluate lecturers' metaphors with participants
- find additional programming metaphors
- agree on a set of metaphors for programming concepts

The workshops resulted in a set of unanimously metaphors for programming concepts. We analyzed these metaphors using Lakoff and Johnson's metaphor framework [12] to select metaphors feasible to be part of a tangible toolkit. The analysis and the resulting metaphors are presented in Sect. 4.

3.2 Methods for Prototyping

We used mood boards and sketches as thinking tools to create more detailed design concepts. Mood boards allow the designer to experience a flow of thoughts, inspirations, and creativity of the design concept, by the provided "space" to arrange a comprehension of the gathered visuals [4]. Sketching as a method supports externalizing our ideas and concepts, reflecting-in-action, and self-communication [10]. Both methods helped to form detailed design concepts for the selected metaphors. The concepts were realized as 3d models using Maya[5] and integrated in an interactive application developed in Unity[6]. The prototype is presented in Sect. 5.

3.3 Assessment Method

To understand (1) how students interact with the created application and (2) how the modeled metaphors convey programming concepts, we performed a user test with 8 bachelor students. All students had basic experience with programming but did not participate in the co-design workshop. The students were given an open task to explore each model and use the think aloud technique [30] to report what happened and how they understood the metaphor. The students were asked explicitly how they understood the mapping between interactive 3d model and the displayed programming code to explore how effective the metaphor is to reify the programming concept. The user test lasted an average of 30 min, the research took notes on how they interacted with the simulation. The user test concluded with a short interview regarding their thoughts about and experiences with the application. Our findings are described in Sect. 6.

4 Finding Tangible Programming Metaphors

All lecturers reported to use metaphors when introducing programming concepts. Especially, in the beginning of programming courses the use of metaphors was seen as useful. They highlight the importance to find commonplace metaphors that many students would recognize based on their previous experiences. One lecturer mentioned that he stopped using metaphors involving VHS or cassette players, since he noticed that students no longer had experience with those technologies. Lecturers highlight the need to find metaphors with appropriate mappings of source and target domain. Metaphors should not underexplain a programming concept, missing important characteristics. On the other hand, metaphors should not overexplain concepts and provide features that are not covered by the programming concept. Furthermore, lectures pointed out the danger of using more than one metaphor to represent a programming concept. They experienced, competing metaphors could confuse students more, since they offer different

---

[5] https://www.autodesk.com/products/maya.
[6] https://unity.com/.

representations. The most used and most recognizable metaphors among the lectures were the box metaphor representing variables, followed by the shopping list metaphor used to illustrate arrays. Another popular group of metaphors were recipes for cooking or baking. Recipe metaphors were used to explain several concepts, and often integrated other concepts, including arrays, functions, loops, or conditional logic. Table 1 presents reported metaphors from the expert interviews. The findings from the expert interview are in line with previous research [23].

Table 1. Source and target domains for metaphors reported by lecturers

Source domain	Target domain
Cooking recipes	Variables, functions, loops, if/else
Box, bucket	Variables
Shopping list, dresser draws, excel sheets	Array, database
Brushing teeth´s/hair, putting on clothes and other everyday activities	Algorithmic thinking
Animal kingdom	Inherit, abstraction, classes
Learning how to ride a bicycle, football training, or any other training one does to become good at something	Learning programming
Black box (radio)	Functions, return statements
Going door to door until certain conditions are met. (example: door-salesman)	Loops
Pointing towards certain objects or people, passing a tread from person to person until the "right" person receives the tread, the tread will then have started at one person and ended up at another one, but it will have been passed between several others to be able to reach its target person	Object referencing, pointers
If you have coffee in the cup, you can drink it, if its empty you must go and refill it	If and else statements
Making food, toaster	Function and return statement
Car engine	Iteration, loop, conditions

During the workshops we collected further metaphors, in total we found 89 unique metaphors. We grouped similar metaphors and removed incomplete metaphors missing a clear programming concept or having a to general source domain. The remaining 42 metaphors are displayed in Table 2. Students and software developers agreed on several of the metaphors reported at the expert interviews including cooking recipe, shopping list, boxes. In general, it was easier to find metaphors for programming concepts such as variable, array and object. Participants had problems finding metaphors for loops, functions and return statements. Roundabout or ring were mentioned to represent the cyclic characteristic of loops.

Table 2. Complete list of metaphors including the number of mentioned

Source domains	Target domains
Cooking recipe	Several concepts (function, array, etc.)
Shopping list	Array
Round about	Loop, for loop
A dressing drawer	Function, variable
Driving to Stockholm / following signs pointing to Stockholm	If/else, while loop, operators
Car	Object
Bucket	Object, variable
Brushing teeth	For loop, algorithmic thinking
A salesman going door to door and trying to sell vacuum cleaners. He must sell 5. If he is invited, he sells 1, otherwise he must go to the next door	Several concepts (if/else, boolean, function)
Asking someone to go to the store to buy milk and they return with milk	Function
A thing, a wallet, a human, a cabinet, shopping mall, world map	Object
A box	Variable
When you have a car and drive until you run out of gas	For loop, while loop
Animals	Inheritance
Ring	Loop
A piece of something	Function
Human brain with memories	Variables
Speech bubble	String
Decisions	If/else
For each Lego block, check if it is red	Foreach
Driving a car	Function
Toasting a slice of bread	Function
Inventory	Array
A block	Function
A cake or instrument you can give a taste or sound	Variable
Backup solution	Else if
A drain	Else if

(*continued*)

Table 2. (*continued*)

Source domains	Target domains
Candy shopping if you have been told to buy chocolate	If/else
Count all the sneakers in the shoe shelf	Foreach
When you make coffee with a coffee machine, you have several different functions. Mocca, espresso etc	Function
Circuit	Loop
Heater that heats a room	Function
Obstacle course	Loop
A school class	Class
Up to eleven	Int
A word or name	String
A lever	Boolean
Road signs telling the driver were to go	Operators
Beading balls	While loop
How many meatballs can we share for dinner today	Int
A cup	Variable
To get a hot slice of bread out of a toaster	Return statement

We analyzed the reported metaphors using the model proposed by Lakoff and Johnson [12], mapping metaphors to ontological, oriental and structural categories. Metaphors with ontological qualities were selected as candidates for the tangible toolkit. Figure 1 illustrates the analysis for the lever-boolean metaphor.

The lever can have one of two states: on or off, or "true" or "false". The two states are defined as ontological elements: the state as a container and the value of the state as an object. The lever itself could also be categorized as ontological, given it is an interactable object in the real world. The action of flipping the lever back and forth is categorized as orientational. The analysis supported our choices for 6 metaphors appropriate for the tangible toolkit as presented in Table 3.

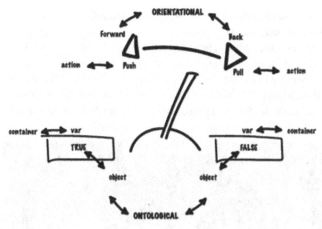

Fig. 1. Analysis of the lever- boolean metaphor based on Lakoff and Johnson [12]

Table 3. Selected concept and metaphors for the tangible toolkit

Concept	Metaphor	Alternative metaphors
Variable	Box	Present, Drawer
Array	Lists in general (shopping list, to-do list etc..)	Excel sheet
For each	Checking LEGOs for red colored bricks	Checking a shoe racket for sneakers, chest of drawers
Object	Car with details	A person, a wallet
For loop	Obstacle course/Game course	A salesperson going door to door
Function	Toaster	Radio, Fancy coffee machine, Black box

5   Prototyping a Tangible Programming Toolkit

In the following, we present our prototype consisting of an interactive application including 3D models for the six selected metaphors. Due to the present pandemic all teaching activities were performed online. To be able to continue with the project, we chose to build an online application using 3d models of the designed tangible programming toolkit instead of physical objects. The 3D simulation can be found at https://simmer. io/@ackarlse/newmetasim. In a second design cycle, we will prototype the presented metaphors as tangibles.

5.1   3D Application of Tangible Toolkit

The developed application included a 3D model of the metaphor. The application allows for direct manipulation. 3D objects can be selected and moved around the screen to simulate tangible interactions. Furthermore, the application included a window with programming code, buttons, and textual information. Figure 2 displays an application screenshot for the box metaphor. The interactive characteristics of the 3D models simulate real-world behavior of the objects, meaning they can be lifted, pressed, and manipulated close to tangible items. In all models, users are given the freedom to explore and interact at their own pace. Simulations can be paused, and the users can switch between models at any time. In the following, we will present each metaphor in more detail.

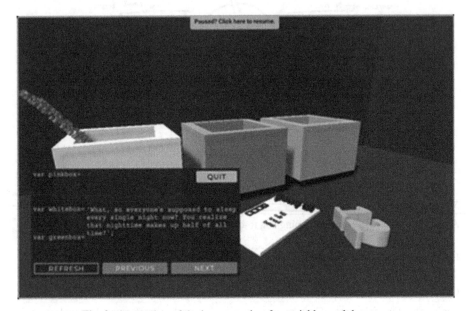

Fig. 2. Screenshot of the box metaphor for variables and data type

5.2 Variables and Data Types

Three different colored boxes represent three empty variables. A shopping list, a text block, and a number represent data types: array, text string and number. The user can move a data type into a box. The code window translates boxes as.

```
var whitebox;
var pinkbox;
var greenbox;
```

If a data type item is moved into a box, the code is updated with a new value, as seen in Fig. 2.

5.3 Array

A box divided in four areas is used to reify an array (see Fig. 3). The box itself represents the array and the separate areas inside the box represent a position in the array. The user can place different items in each area. As the items are placed or removed from the box, the code window is updated accordingly. The box takes the order of indexes into consideration, to emphasize the importance of order in an indexed array.

5.4 Function

A toaster with two loafs of bread is used to reify functions. The user can place the bread in the toaster and turn the toaster on. The bread is lowered into the toaster, and a timer started, representing a function with two parameters given: bread and time, as seen in Fig. 3. The function returns a message: "nicely toasted bread" or "burned".

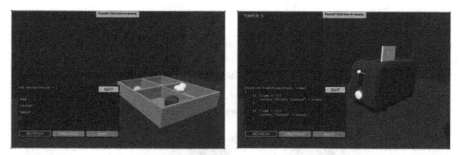

Fig. 3. Screenshots of the array-box metaphor (left) and the toaster-function metaphor (right)

5.5 Object

A car is chosen to represent an object. The application provides information about the car: model, production year and color. Users can "paint" the car by clicking one of the color buttons. The code window is updated accordingly, as seen in Fig. 4.

5.6 Foreach

Two empty boxes, one red and one black are visible. A third box contains several different colored LEGO bricks. The task is to sort read bricks into the red box and all other bricks into the black box. If a brick is sorted into the correct box, a counter is updated. The code window is updated to represent the sorting process, see Fig. 4.

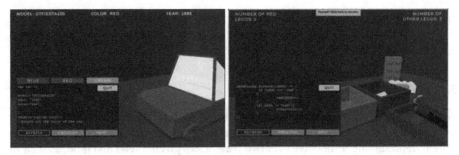

Fig. 4. Screenshots of the car-object metaphor (left) and the lego-foreach metaphor (right)

5.7 Loop

A user can move a box through an obstacle course and collect gold coins. Each completed lab is counted. A lap counter is displayed on the screen. After three laps, the environment changes from day to night. The code window displays the matching code (Fig. 5).

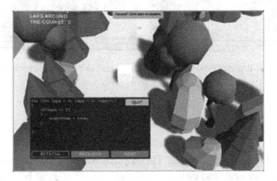

Fig. 5. Screenshot of the obstacle course-loop metaphor

6 Experiencing the Prototype

The user test provided insights how students interact with the application and how they understood the mapping between the interactive 3d models and the programming code. Students started exploring the 3d model, manipulating the objects and exploring what actions were possible in the application. Students noticed that the code in the window changed based on their actions. For example, when students moved objects into boxes in the box example, they noticed that the code in the window changed accordingly. Similar in the other examples, students explored the action possibilities in the 3d model first before looking at the code window and studying how their actions effected the code. The application supported students to explore how manipulating the 3d models changed the code. In the box/array metaphor, several students placed food items in the compartments in the box. When an item was placed in a compartment the item would show up in an array in the code. When all the food items were placed in compartments the students removed one or more items to see how this changed the code. The item removed from a compartment was also removed from the array in code. Other students moved items between the different compartments to see how the item's position in the array changed. They described how the compartments in the box have different positions (indexes) in the array.

However, the user test uncovered mismatches between students' expectations and the behavior of the prototype as well. In the toaster metaphor, students can place bread in the toaster and activate it by pushing a lever. This starts a countdown timer. When the timer reaches 0 the bread will pop up from the toaster, and the message "nicely toasted sourdough bread" is displayed. All students identified this as a metaphor for the concept function, but they were annoyed that they were unable to burn the toast or add more time to the toaster. Some participants pointed out that they expected that functionality since, 1) this was possible with a real toaster and 2) the code in the window indicated the possibility to burn the toast containing an if/else statement in the function.

In summary, students reported that the prototype represented metaphors well and that they were able to manipulate the 3d objects. All students focused on the 3d model first before mapping their actions to changes in the code. Some students restarted the simulation to explore the mapping between their actions and changes in the code starting from the initial state. Students experienced problems when actions from source domain were not possible, or code was not mapped correctly to the model (both described in the toaster-function metaphor).

7   Conclusion

In this paper, we described our research efforts towards a metaphor-based tangible toolkit for learning programming concepts. Using a design-based research approach, we explored: (1) what metaphors are common to teach programming concepts and (2) how can these metaphors be reified in a tangible toolkit. We found common metaphors used for teaching programming proposed by lecturers, students, and software developers alike. This is in line with previous work by Sanford et.al. [23]. The most recognized metaphors are (a) boxes used to represent variables and (b) lists illustrating arrays. Many participants mapped several metaphors to if/else statements such as lever, or decisions and making choices. Many of the metaphors used for complex concepts such as functions or loops contained if/else statements e.g., driving directions, toaster or sorting Lego blocks. Participants reported difficulties finding and agreeing on common metaphors for loops or functions. Here, we present several alternative metaphors that could be explored further. We created an online application integrating interactive 3d models of the metaphors and corresponding programming code to demonstrate how six selected metaphors can be reified into a tangible toolkit. The user test demonstrated that students focused on exploring action possibilities of the 3d model first, before comparing their actions to the changes in the program code. We found that students struggled with the modeled metaphor when expected actions from source domain were not possible, or when there was a mismatch between the code and the interactive 3d model. We argue that the tangible toolkit helps students to explore and understand programming concepts and we aim to implement the 3d models as tangibles in the second design cycle. Furthermore, we are interested probing alternative metaphors reported at the expert interviews and workshops, especially for complex programming concepts such as loops and functions.

References

1. Balanskat, A., et al.: The integration of Computational Thinking (CT) across school curricula in Europe, vol. 2 (2017)
2. Bennett, C.L., et al.: Using a design workshop to explore accessible ideation. In: Proceedings of the 18th International ACM SIGACCESS Conference on Computers and Accessibility, pp. 303–304. Association for Computing Machinery, New York (2016). https://doi.org/10.1145/2982142.2982209
3. Canfield Smith, D.: SIGCHI lifetime research award talk: icons, metaphor, and end-user programming. In: Extended Abstracts of the 2020 CHI Conference on Human Factors in Computing Systems, pp. 1–9. ACM, Honolulu (2020). https://doi.org/10.1145/3334480.3386148
4. Cassidy, T.: The mood board process modeled and understood as a qualitative design research tool. Fash. Pract. **3**(2), 225–251 (2011). https://doi.org/10.2752/175693811X13080607764854
5. Forsström, S.E., Kaufmann, O.T.: A literature review exploring the use of programming in mathematics education. Int. J. Learn. Teach. Educ. Res. **17**, 12 (2019)
6. Horn, M.S., Jacob, R.J.K.: Designing tangible programming languages for classroom use. In: Proceedings of the 1st International Conference on Tangible and Embedded Interaction, pp. 159–162. Association for Computing Machinery, New York (2007). https://doi.org/10.1145/1226969.1227003
7. Horn, M.S., Jacob, R.J.K.: Tangible programming in the classroom with tern. In: CHI 2007 Extended Abstracts on Human Factors in Computing Systems - CHI 2007, p. 1965. ACM Press, San Jose (2007). https://doi.org/10.1145/1240866.1240933
8. Hornecker, E., Buur, J.: Getting a grip on tangible interaction: a framework on physical space and social interaction. In: Proceedings of the SIGCHI Conference on Human Factors in Computing Systems, pp. 437–446. Association for Computing Machinery, New York (2006). https://doi.org/10.1145/1124772.1124838
9. Ishii, H., Ullmer, B.: Tangible bits: towards seamless interfaces between people, bits and atoms. In: Proceedings of the ACM SIGCHI Conference on Human Factors in Computing Systems, pp. 234–241. ACM, Atlanta (1997). https://doi.org/10.1145/258549.258715
10. Israel, J., et al.: Investigating three-dimensional sketching for early conceptual design—results from expert discussions and user studies. Comput. Graph. **33**, 462–473 (2009)
11. Lahtinen, E., et al.: A study of the difficulties of novice programmers. In: Proceedings of the 10th Annual SIGCSE Conference on Innovation and Technology in Computer Science Education, pp. 14–18. Association for Computing Machinery, New York (2005). https://doi.org/10.1145/1067445.1067453
12. Lakoff, G., Johnson, M.: Metaphors We Live By. University of Chicago press, Chicago (2008)
13. Löffler, D., et al.: Substituting color for haptic attributes in conceptual metaphors for tangible interaction design. In: Proceedings of the TEI 2016: Tenth International Conference on Tangible, Embedded, and Embodied Interaction, pp. 118–125. Association for Computing Machinery, New York (2016). https://doi.org/10.1145/2839462.2839485
14. Macaranas, A., et al.: Bridging the gap: attribute and spatial metaphors for tangible interface design. In: Proceedings of the Sixth International Conference on Tangible, Embedded and Embodied Interaction, pp. 161–168 Association for Computing Machinery, New York (2012). https://doi.org/10.1145/2148131.2148166

15. Macaranas, A., et al.: What is intuitive interaction? balancing users' performance and satisfaction with natural user interfaces. Interact. Comput. **27**(3), 357–370 (2015). https://doi.org/10.1093/iwc/iwv003
16. McKenney, S., et al.: Design research from a curriculum perspective. In: Educational design research, pp. 62–90. Routledge, London (2006)
17. McNerney, T.S.: Tangible programming bricks : an approach to making programming accessible to everyone. Massachusetts Institute of Technology (1999)
18. Meuser, M., Nagel, U.: The expert interview and changes in knowledge production. In: Bogner, A. et al. (eds.) Interviewing Experts, pp. 17–42. Palgrave Macmillan, London (2009). https://doi.org/10.1057/9780230244276_2
19. Pires, A.C., et al.: Building blocks of mathematical learning: virtual and tangible manipulatives lead to different strategies in number composition. In: Frontiers in Education, p. 81 Frontiers (2019)
20. Piteira, M., Costa, C.: Learning computer programming: study of difficulties in learning programming. In: Proceedings of the 2013 International Conference on Information Systems and Design of Communication, pp. 75–80. Association for Computing Machinery, New York (2013). https://doi.org/10.1145/2503859.2503871
21. Plomp, T., et al.: Educational design research: an introduction. Netherlands Institute for Curriculum Development (2013)
22. Rossmy, B., Wiethoff, A.: StringTouch: a scalable low-cost concept for deformable interfaces. In: Extended Abstracts of the 2019 CHI Conference on Human Factors in Computing Systems, pp. 1–4. Association for Computing Machinery, New York (2019). https://doi.org/10.1145/3290607.3313245
23. Sanford, J.P. et al.: Metaphors we teach by. In: Proceedings of the 45th ACM Technical Symposium on Computer Science Education, pp. 585–590. Association for Computing Machinery, New York (2014). https://doi.org/10.1145/2538862.2538945
24. Schweikardt, E., Gross, M.D.: roBlocks: a robotic construction kit for mathematics and science education. In: Proceedings of the 8th International Conference on Multimodal Interfaces, pp. 72–75. Association for Computing Machinery, New York (2006). https://doi.org/10.1145/1180995.1181010
25. Sowell, E.J.: Effects of manipulative materials in mathematics instruction. J. Res. Math. Educ. **20**(5), 498–505 (1989)
26. Stigberg, H., Stigberg, S.: Teaching programming and mathematics in practice: a case study from a swedish primary school. Policy Fut. Educ. **18**, 483–496 (2019). https://doi.org/10.1177/1478210319894785
27. Tan, P.-H., et al.: Learning difficulties in programming courses: undergraduates' perspective and perception. In: Proceedings of the 2009 International Conference on Computer Technology and Development, vol. 01, pp. 42–46. IEEE Computer Society (2009). https://doi.org/10.1109/ICCTD.2009.188
28. Ullmer, B., Ishii, H.: Emerging frameworks for tangible user interfaces. IBM Syst. J. **39**(3–4), 915–931 (2000). https://doi.org/10.1147/sj.393.0915
29. Urbanek, M., Güldenpfennig, F.: Tangible audio game development kit: prototyping audio games with a tangible editor. In: Proceedings of the Eleventh International Conference on Tangible, Embedded, and Embodied Interaction, pp. 473–479. Association for Computing Machinery, New York (2017). https://doi.org/10.1145/3024969.3025077
30. Van Someren, M., et al.: The Think Aloud Method: A Practical Approach to Modelling Cognitive, p. 11. Academic Press, London (1994)

31. Wang, D., et al.: T-Maze: a tangible programming tool for children. In: Proceedings of the 10th International Conference on Interaction Design and Children, pp. 127–135. Association for Computing Machinery, New York (2011). https://doi.org/10.1145/1999030.1999045
32. Wing, J.: Computational thinking. Commun. ACM **49**(3), 33–35 (2006)
33. Wyeth, P., Wyeth, G.: Electronic blocks: tangible programming elements for preschoolers. In: Proceedings of the Eighth IFIP TC13 Conference on Human-Computer Interaction (INTERACT) (2001)

Generating Context-Aware Fill-in-Blank Problems for Prompting Reflection on Web-based Investigative Learning

Shinyu Kato[⊠] and Akihiro Kashihara

The University of Electro-Communications, 1-5-1 Chofugaoka, Chofu, Tokyo, Japan
shinyu.kato@uec.ac.jp

Abstract. In recent years, there are a lot of opportunities to investigate any question (initial question) with Web resources and construct knowledge about it. Learners are also expected to elaborate the question for constructing wider and deeper knowledge, which requires them to expand the initial question into related ones as sub-questions to be further investigated. However, it tends to be insufficient since they need to concurrently conduct knowledge construction and question expansion on the Web. In our previous work, we have proposed a model of Web-based investigative learning, and developed a cognitive tool called interactive Learning Scenario Builder (iLSB for short). The results of case studies with iLSB suggest that it promotes self-directed investigative learning involving question expansion, and allows leaners to construct wider and deeper knowledge. The main issue addressed in this paper is how to help learners reflect on the contents learned to further their question expansion. Our approach to this is to provide learners with context-aware fill-in-bank problems for inducing them to reflect on their contents learned, which are automatically generated from the contents learned and the Web resources used for investigation. In this paper, we demonstrate how to generate context-aware fill-in-blank problems for promoting Web-based investigative learning with iLSB. This paper also reports case studies whose purpose were to evaluate fill-in-blank problems generated by the proposed method. The results suggest that these problems are effective to reflection and promotion of question expansion in Web-based investigative learning.

Keywords: Web-based investigative learning · Question expansion · Fill-in-blank problem · Context-awareness

1 Introduction

In recent years, there are a lot of opportunities not only for learning using textbook but also for Web-based investigative learning in the field of education. Web-based investigative learning is expected to be highly effective because it allows learners to construct knowledge from their own perspective about any question to be investigated (initial question) while navigating Web resources/pages [1, 2].

However, learners tend to search a limited number of Web resources/pages for investigating an initial question, which often results in an insufficient investigation and limited

© The Author(s), under exclusive license to Springer Nature Switzerland AG 2022
P. Zaphiris and A. Ioannou (Eds.): HCII 2022, LNCS 13328, pp. 89–100, 2022.
https://doi.org/10.1007/978-3-031-05657-4_7

knowledge construction. In order to construct wider and deeper knowledge of the initial question, it is necessary to facilitate an elaborate investigation. In elaborately investigating an initial question, learners need to identify related questions to be further investigated during navigation and knowledge construction [3]. This corresponds to expanding the initial question into related ones as sub-questions, which would give rise to wider and deeper knowledge construction.

On the other hand, the Web does not provide learners with learning scenarios which indicate questions to be investigated and their sequence such as a table of contents in an instructional textbook [4]. It is necessary for learners to expand a question into the sub-questions while navigating Web resources/pages to construct their knowledge for an elaborate investigation [3]. The question expansion induces learners to construct learning scenarios. Such learner-created scenarios could play a crucial role in self-regulating their navigation and knowledge construction process [5]. On the other hand, the question expansion is concurrently performed with knowledge construction related to the question. Learners' cognitive load could be accordingly high. They also tend to concentrate on knowledge construction about the question, and the question expansion would get stuck.

In our previous work, we have proposed a model of Web-based investigative learning, and developed a cognitive tool called interactive Learning Scenario Builder (iLSB for short), which scaffolds their knowledge construction and question expansion as modeled. The results of case studies with iLSB suggest that it promotes self directed investigative learning involving question expansion, and allows learners to construct wider and deeper knowledge [6]. On the other hand, we also found that some learners often complete their investigation with insufficient question expansion, which is caused by insufficient reflection on the contents they have learned with iLSB. In order to resolve this, it is necessary to help learners reflect on the contents learned to promote question expansion.

Our approach to this is to provide learners with context-aware fill-in-blank problems for inducing them to reflect on their contents learned, which are automatically generated from the contents learned and the Web resources used for investigation. This paper also demonstrates how to generate context-aware fill-in-blank problems for promoting Web-based investigative learning with iLSB. Learners are prompted to fill the blanks in the problems to reflect on the contents learned, which intends them to become aware of sub-questions to be expanded. For example, when learners could not solve a fill-in-blank problem, they are expected to take up a question indicated by the blank to expand.

This paper also reports a case study whose purpose was to ascertain whether solving fill-in-blank problems could promote reflection on the contents learned and question expansion. The results suggest that it is particularly effective in prompting reflection of Web resources/pages. In addition, the problems generated were appropriate to the contents learned, suggesting that they were context-aware problems.

2   Web-Based Investigative Learning

In this section, we describe the model of Web-based investigative learning proposed in our previous work [6], and iLSB for scaffolding the learning process as modeled.

2.1 Model of Web-Based Investigative Learning

In response to the problem of high cognitive load of Web-based investigative learning, we modeled Web-based investigative learning process as shown in Fig. 1. This model includes three cyclic phases: (a) search for Web resources, (b) navigational learning, and (c) question expansion. In phase (a), learners use a search engine such as Google with a keyword representing an initial question and select Web resources suitable for investigating the question. In phase (b), they are expected to navigate the pages in the resources selected in phase (a) to construct knowledge by extracting keywords for representing the contents learned in the pages and by making the relationship among them. In phase (c), they are also expected to find out sub-question related to the initial question to be further investigated from the keywords extracted in phase (b). This corresponds to expanding the initial question into sub-questions. Each sub-question is investigated cyclically in the next phases (a) and (b).

As a result of the question expansion, the learners could create a question tree whose nodes are the question/sub-questions. This tree includes part-of relationships between the question and the sub-questions. The root represents the initial question. Creating the question tree corresponds to building a learning scenario. The learning scenario building is continued until the question extraction does not occur.

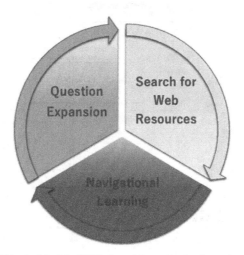

Fig. 1. Model of Web-based Investigative Learning

2.2 Interactive Learning Scenario Builder (iLSB)

We have developed iLSB, which is a cognitive tool for learning as modeled, and which functions as an add-on Firefox [7]. Figure 2 shows the UI (User Interface) of iLSB. iLSB provides learners with three scaffolding functions to promote the investigative learning process:

- Search engine,
- Keyword repository, and
- Question tree viewer.

iLSB focuses on promoting the learning scenario creation involving the question expansion with the question tree viewer. In other phases, iLSB currently provides learners with relatively simple functions such as a search engine and keyword repository. The search engine allows learners to gather and select Web resources/pages for learning. The keyword repository allows learners to extract and store keywords from the searched Web resources/pages, which represents the contents learned. It also allows them to make relationship among the keywords to represent their knowledge constructed. Learners are then expected to find some questions as sub-questions to be further investigated from these keywords. The question tree viewer allows learners to put the sub-questions to create the question tree.

The initial question and sub-questions placed in the question tree are represented as keywords called q-keywords. By clicking on each q-keyword, learners can see the corresponding keywords in the keyword repository that are extracted from Web resources/pages for investigating the question.

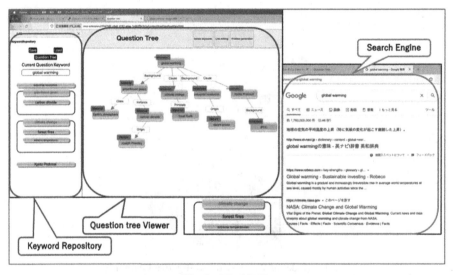

Fig. 2. UI of iLSB

3 Context-Aware Fill-in-Blank Problems Generation

3.1 Context-Aware Systems

Context-aware systems can provide new opportunities for users by collecting contextual data to make adaptive changes to the system's behavior [8]. Dey and Abowd (1999) defined "Context is any information that can be used to characterize the situation of an entity" [9]. The entity referred to here is people, places, and object that are considered relevant to the interaction between the user and the application. In order to generate context-aware problems, we use as a context data of learning contents accumulated by learners using iLSB. Since different learners learn differently, it is expected that the problems will be adapted to them.

3.2 Framework

In this work, we have implemented the generation of fill-in-blank problems as a function of iLSB. Figure 3 shows an overview of generating fill-in-blank problems. First, learners are expected to use iLSB to create a question tree through Web-based investigate learning with an initial question. After learning (the end of the question expansion), they are also expected to reflect on their learning contents. During reflection, they are allowed to select one of the nodes (q-keywords) in the question tree to click on the problem generation button on the UI of iLSB. Fill-in-blank problems are then generated using the information in the keyword repository of the clicked node (stored keywords and URLs of the Web resources/pages from which each keyword was extracted) and the information in the question tree. iLSB performs the following steps to generate fill-in-blank problems to promote question expansion from the clicked node:

1. Split text data in the Web resources/pages from which the stored keywords have been extracted into individual sentences.
2. Extract the sentences containing the stored keyword that are not the q-keyword from the split ones.
3. Select the most problematic sentence from the extracted ones (the selection method describes in Sect. 3.3).
4. Make blanks at the keywords not included in the question tree but stored in the selected sentence.

Fill-in-blank problems generated are then displayed on the top of the UI of iLSB as shown in Fig. 4. Figure 4 shows two problems, which are generated as for 'greenhouse gas' in the question tree. The parts surrounded by brackets correspond to blanks. The upper problem has a statement: 'The best known greenhouse gases, carbon dioxide (CO_2) [] and nitrous oxide, can be found naturally in low concentrations in the atmosphere'. The lower problem has a statement: 'Without greenhouse gases, the average temperature of [] would be about -18 °C(0 °F), rather than the present average of 15 °C (59 °F)'. The answers to be filled in these blanks are 'methane' and 'Earth's surface'. These two answers are stored in the keyword repository of 'greenhouse gases', but they do not exist in the question tree.

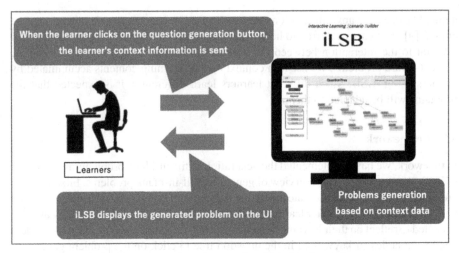

Fig. 3. An overview of generating fill-in-blank problems

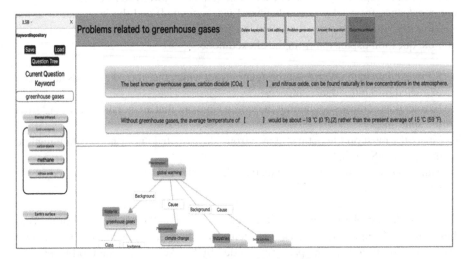

Fig. 4. Generated fill-in-blank problems

iLSB also has an answer function for the generated fill-in-blank problems. Learners can solve the problems by dragging keywords from the keyword repository and dropping them onto the problem text. As shown in Fig. 5, if the answer is correct, the problem text turns green, and if it is wrong, it turns red, so that the learner can visually judge the correctness of the answer.

3.3 Meaningful Fill-in-Blank Problems

In the problem generation, it is not enough to randomly select sentences containing stored keywords from the text data in Web resources/pages and give as a fill-in-blank

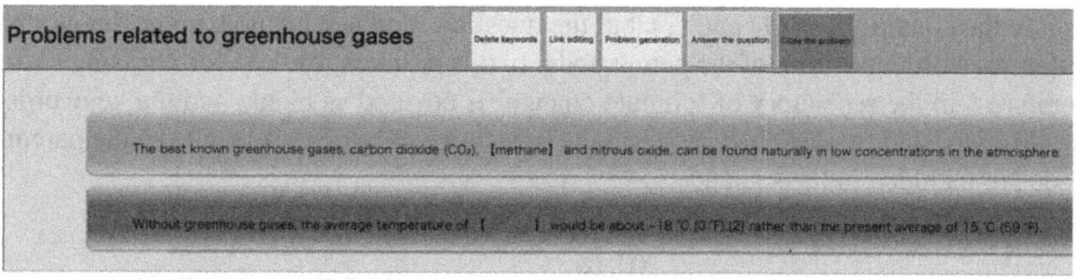

Fig. 5. Visual judgment of correctness when answering problems

problem. In order to generate meaningful problems, iLSB selects sentences under three conditions that are put in a priority order: (1) containing stored keywords that have inclusive relation each other, (2) containing stored keywords in the same keyword repository, and (3) containing stored keywords in the parent node's keyword repository. iLSB then makes fill-in-blank problems. The priority order depends on the relevance between the keywords. This means the inclusive relation between keywords is stronger than the others. In particular, sentences containing more keywords under each condition will be given priority.

Table 1 shows some examples of sentences used for generating fill-in-blank problems by following the conditions (1) to (3). The problems under the conditions (1) and (2) are related to the q-keyword 'global warming', and the problem under (3) is related to 'climate change'. Figure 6 shows the keyword repositories and the question tree used for generating the problems. The numbers above the keyword repositories correspond to the conditions considered in the problems shown in Table 1.

Table 1. Examples of sentences/problems under each condition

Condition	Sentences/Fill-in-blank problems	q-keyword
(1)	They are caused by the emission of [greenhouse gases], mostly carbon dioxide (CO2) and [methane]	Global warming
(2)	Climate change threatens people with food and water scarcity, increased flooding, extreme heat, more disease, and [economic loss]	Global warming
(3)	Burning fossil fuels generates greenhouse gases emissions that act like a blanket wrapped around the Earth, trapping the sun's heat and [raising temperatures]	Climate change

In the keyword repository for 'global warming', the keywords 'carbon dioxide', 'methane', and 'fossil fuels' have inclusive relations with 'greenhouse gases'. The problem under (1) contains some keywords ('greenhouse gases', 'carbon dioxide', 'methane') with inclusive relations. Since carbon dioxide is in the question tree, 'methane' and 'greenhouse gases' become the candidates for blanks. The problem under (2) does not have any keywords inclusive relation, but it contains keywords such as 'climate change' and 'economics loss' in the same keyword repository. The question under (3) does not satisfy the conditions in (1) and (2), but the question sentence includes some keywords in the keyword repository of the parent node. In this problem, the keyword 'raising temperatures' in the repository of 'climate change' is covered as blank, and the keywords 'fossil fuels' and 'greenhouse gases' in the repository of 'global warming' in the parent node are included in the sentence.

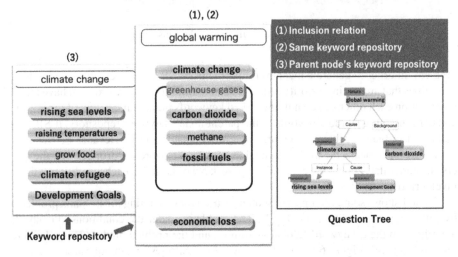

Fig. 6. Keyword repositories and question tree used for problem generation

4   Case Study

4.1   Purpose and Procedure

We have conducted a case study whose purpose was to confirm whether solving context-aware problems could promote reflection on learning contents with iLSB and the question expansion.

The participants were nine graduate and undergraduate students in science and engineering. Five of them were divided into the experimental group and four into the control group. The flow of the experiment is shown in Fig. 7. All participants were given 'separation of powers' as the initial question. First, the participants investigated the initial question for 30 to 60 min using the traditional iLSB. After that, the control group was given from 20 to 30 min to reflect using only what they had learned (question trees, keyword repository, and Web resources/pages). The experimental group was asked to reflect using fill-in-blank problems in addition to what they had learned. Participants in the experimental group generated and solved the problems at their own time. The number of problems to be solved was limited, and two problems each were generated using information from the keyword repository of root node (initial question), one intermediate node (node that have both parents and children), and one leaf node (node that have no children). Since there are multiple leaf nodes and intermediate nodes, they were allowed to arbitrarily choose one leaf node and one intermediate node. During reflection, both groups can add new keywords to the keyword repository and question expansion. After the reflection, the participants were asked to answer a post-questionnaire to evaluate the effectiveness of the fill-in-blank problems. Questionnaire common to both groups are shown in Table 2, and questionnaire only for the experimental group are shown in Table 3. Both questionnaires were conducted using a five-point scale. In order to ascertain whether the fill-in-blank problems could promote reflection and question expansion in web-based investigate learning, we set the following two hypotheses of H1 and H2:

H1: Solving fill-in-blank problems promotes reflection on the contents learned (Web resources/pages, keyword repository and question tree).
H2: Solving fill-in-blank problems makes learners aware of questions that need to be expanded, and promotes question expansion.

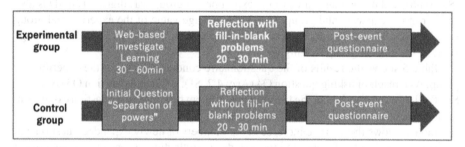

Fig. 7. The flow of the experiment

Table 2. Questionnaire common to both groups

Number	Question
Q1	How much reflection did you do on the Web resources/pages?
Q2	How much reflection did you do on the keyword repository?
Q3	How much reflection did you do on the question tree?

Table 3. Questionnaire for the experimental group

Number	Question
Q4	Did you notice any new questions after solving the fill-in-blank problems?
Q5	How effective was reflection using the fill-in-blank problems in new question expansion?
Q6	How difficult were the fill-in-blank problems?

(continued)

Table 3. (*continued*)

Number	Question
Q7	Were the fill-in-blank questions appropriate to the content you were investigating?
Q8	Did you feel you were prevented from self-directed learning when the fill-in-blank problems induced you to expand a new question?

4.2 Results

Table 4 shows the results of the questionnaire common to both groups. The results of this questionnaire were used to test H1. In Q1, a two-sided t-test was performed with an average of 4.0 (SD: 0.63) in the experimental group and an average of 2.0 (SD: 1.00) in the control group, and a significant difference was found ($p < .05$). In Q2, the average value of the experimental group was 4.4 (SD: 0.49) and that of the control group was 3.5 (SD: 0.86), and the average value of the experimental group was higher. The SD is also smaller in the experimental group. In Q3, the average value of the experimental group was 3.8 (SD: 0.75) and that of the control group was 4.25 (SD: 0.43), and the average value of the control group was higher.

Table 5 shows the results of the questionnaire conducted only for the experimental group. As a result of asking question Q4 (Ave: 4.2, SD: 0.75) and question Q5 (Ave: 4.5, SD: 0.49) to confirm whether the fill-in-blank problem promoted the question expansion, the average score exceeded 4.0 in both cases.

Table 6 shows the average increase in the numbers of newly expanded question and keywords stored in the keyword repository during reflection. There was no significant difference in the increased number of expanded questions, nor was there a significant difference in the number of keywords.

Table 4. Result of Questionnaire (the experimental and control group)

Number	Experimental group Average	Control group Average
Q1	4.00 (SD: 0.63)	2.00 (SD: 1.00)
Q2	4.40 (SD: 0.49)	3.50 (SD: 0.86)
Q3	3.80 (SD: 0.75)	4.25 (SD: 0.43)

[*]five-point scale: 5: I did it very well ……. 1: Not at all

Table 5. Result of Questionnaire (the experimental group)

Number	Five-point scale	Average
Q4	5: I noticed quite a bit ……. 1: I didn't notice at all	4.20 (SD: 0.75)
Q5	5: Very effectively ……. 1: Not at all	4.60 (SD: 0.49)

(*continued*)

Table 5. (*continued*)

Number	Five-point scale	Average
Q6	5: Not easy to solve at all .... 1: Very easy to solve	2.20 (SD: 0.98)
Q7	5: Very appropriate .... 1: Not at all	4.20 (SD: 0.40)
Q8	5: I felt very much .... 1: I didn't feel it at all	1.00 (SD: 0.00)

Table 6. Increased number of expanded question and keywords during reflection

Item name	Experimental group average	Control group average
Expanded question	3.80 (SD: 3.66)	3.25 (SD: 1.30)
Keywords	14.00 (SD: 5.40)	19.5 (SD: 8.20)

4.3 Discussion

In Q1, there was a significant difference between the experimental group and the control group. It is suggested that reflection on the Web resources/pages was promoted in the experimental group rather in the control group. We think this is because the experimental group will have an opportunity to use the web resources/pages to reflect on why they put the keywords into the keyword repository in answering the problem.

In addition, the results of Q2 suggest that the average is higher by 1 or more in the experimental group and the SD is lower in the experimental group, which promotes the reflection of the keyword repository.

From the results of the Q3 questionnaire, no significant difference was found between the two groups. However, the high average in both groups confirmed the effectiveness of the question tree reflection using the iLSB.

There was no significant difference between the two groups in terms of the number of newly expanded question and keywords added during reflection. The results of Q6 in Table 5 (Ave: 2.2) suggest that the participants did not need to expand because the problems were easy.

The results of Q7 also suggest that the generated problem is a context-aware problem. This is probably because iLSB generated problems using what the learner had learned. In addition, the results of Q8 suggest that the generated problems did not interfere with self-directedness. We think this is because the generated problem was a context-aware problem.

5   Conclusion

In this paper we proposed a method for generating context-aware fill-in-blank problems to promote reflection in Web research learning and question expansion. In this work, learning data accumulated by iLSB was used as a context to generate the fill-in-blank problem. We also implemented a function to generate fill-in-blank problems in iLSB and display it on the UI, and a function to answer such problems.

As a result of the case study using iLSB with the added new functions, it became clear that generated problems promote the reflection of the Web resources/pages. In addition, the results of questionnaire suggest that generated problem was in line with learning contents, which means context-aware.

In future, it would be necessary to generate fill-in-blank problems with other Web resources/pages in addition to the Web resources/pages from which keywords to be filled in the blanks were extracted, and to raise the difficulty level of problems and further promote the question expansion.

Acknowledgment. The work presented here is partially supported by JSPS KAKENHI Grant Numbers 18H01053 and 20H04294.

References

1. Fischer, G., Scharff, E.: Learning technologies in support of self-directed learning. J. Interact. Media Educ. **1998**(2) (1998)
2. Hübscher, R., Puntambekar, S.: Adaptive navigation for learners in hypermedia is scaffolded navigation. In: Bra, P., Brusilovsky, P., Conejo, R. (eds.) AH 2002. LNCS, vol. 2347, pp. 184–192. Springer, Heidelberg (2002). https://doi.org/10.1007/3-540-47952-X_20
3. Hill, J.R., Hannafin, M.J.: Cognitive strategies and learning from the World Wide Web. Educ. Tech. Res Dev. **45**(4), 37–64 (1997)
4. Land, S.M.: Cognitive requirements for learning open- ended learning environments. Educ. Technol. Res. Dev. **48**(3), 61–78 (2000)
5. Azevedo, R., Cromley, J.G.: Does training on self-regulated learning facilitate students' learning with hypermedia? J. Educ. Psychol. **96**(3), 523 (2004)
6. Kashihara, A., Akiyama, N.: Learning scenario creation for promoting investigative learning on the web. J. Inf. Syst. Educ. **15**(1), 62–72 (2016)
7. Firefox. https://www.mozilla.org/en-US/firefox/new, Accessed 07 Feb 2022
8. Schahram, D., Florian, R.: A survey on context-aware systems. Int. J. Ad Hoc Ubiquitous Comput. **2**(4), 263–277 (2007)
9. Anind, K., Gregory, D.A.: Towards a better understanding of context and context-awareness. In: Proceedings of the Workshop on the What, Who, Where, and How of Context-Awareness. ACM Press, New York (2000)

Hikari-Tsumiki: Modular Toy that Visualizes Information Flow by Light Emission

Ikkaku Kawaguchi[✉] and Toshimasa Yamanaka

University of Tsukuba, 1-1-1 Tennodai, Tsukuba, Ibaraki, Japan
kawaguchi@cs.tsukuba.ac.jp

Abstract. In existing modular toys, information is transmitted by invisible electrical signals, making it difficult to understand the information flow between modules. This study developed a modular toy, "Hikari-Tsumiki," that visualizes the information flow between modules by light emission. For the development of the system, we set design guidelines based on the design principles of Scratch Jr and developed the actual system. The developed system has the following features: Visualize information flow using light, modules that can work even on their own, various module types, and a wooden appearance. We conducted an experiment to quantitatively evaluate the effect of visualization by light using the developed system. In the experiment, we conducted a function exploration task and a free trial task and compared the conditions with and without visualization by light. The experiment results showed that although understanding the function of each module was not promoted, the positive impression of the system was enhanced in some aspects in light condition.

Keywords: Modular toy · STEAM education · Visual feedback

1 Introduction

In recent years, STEM or STEAM education has been gaining attention [1, 2]. Among them, hardware education has also become a topic of interest [3]. Modular toys, such as littleBits [4,5], have been developed as tools for hardware education. Modular toys can realize various functions via the assembly of various modular parts. However, in current modular toys, information is transmitted by an invisible electric signal, making it difficult to understand the information flow among modules. In this study, we developed a modular toy, "Hikari-Tsumiki," as shown in Fig. 1, that visualizes the information flow between modules by light emission. In Japanese, "Hikari" means light, and "Tsumiki" means wooden building blocks. For the development of the system, we set design guidelines based on the design principles of Scratch Jr [6] and developed the actual system. The developed system has the following features: Visualize information flow using light, modules that can work even on their own, various module types, and a wooden appearance.

P. Zaphiris and A. Ioannou (Eds.): HCII 2022, LNCS 13328, pp. 101–112, 2022.
https://doi.org/10.1007/978-3-031-05657-4_8

In this paper, we describe the developed system and the experiment conducted to investigate the effectiveness of visualization by light.

Fig. 1. Modular toy Hikari-Tsumiki

2   Related Work

2.1   Modular Toy

littleBits [4,5] is a modular toy for hardware education. littleBits consists of several modules containing unique electronic components, which can be assembled to realize various functions. More than 60 different modules are available, each of them divided into four categories: power, input, output, and wire. By combining them, users can build robots, musical toys, IoT devices, etc. However, because the system uses an invisible electric signal to transmit information, it is difficult to understand the information flow between modules intuitively. Information can be visualized by using a bar light module that changes in response to the electric signal. However, to visualize the information of the entire assembly, it is necessary to include a lot of bar graph modules in the assembly, which complicates the configuration. littleBits can only be connected in two dimensions, making it difficult to construct a three-dimensional object without other components like Lego.

Cubelets [7,8] is a modular toy that consists of multiple cubic modules. Cubelets have 18 different modules, consisting of four categories: SENSE, THINK, ACT, and battery. Each module is a cube, and by connecting the surfaces together with magnets placed on each surface, the system itself can create three-dimensional objects. However, Cubelets also use non-visualized electric signals to transmit information, making it difficult to understand the information between the modules intuitively. By connecting the Cubelets to the web application running on the PC via Bluetooth, it is possible to visualize the information transmitted between the modules by a graph, but the information cannot be visualized by the modules itself.

LightUp [9] is a modular toy that helps children learn about circuits. Basic electronic components such as resistors and capacitors and advanced components such as microcontrollers are modularized and can be assembled to build various circuits. LightUp visualizes the invisible electric current using an augmented reality application on a smartphone. However, because the modular toy itself does not visualize the information, it is difficult to check the information in real-time while assembling the modules.

As shown above, existing modular toys [4,5,7–9] have problems in visualizing the information exchanged between modules. In this study, we aim to solve this problem and realize a more intuitive and understandable system. Such a system is expected to be playable even by preschool children.

2.2 Design Guidelines

In designing the new modular toy, we referred to the design principles of Scratch Jr. Scratch Jr[6] is a visual programming language with an intuitive interface that even preschool children can understand. In order to make the existing Scratch[10] accessible to younger children, Scratch Jr adopted the following principles, Low Floor and (Appropriately) High Ceiling, Wide Walls, Tinkerability, Conviviality, Classroom Support. These approaches should also be helpful in designing new modular toys that are intuitive and easy to understand. We set the following design guidelines based on Scratch Jr's design principles.

P1 **Visualize information flow using light:** Visualize information flow between modules by the light emission to help understand the status of each module and the relationship between modules. By changing the brightness of the light corresponding to the information being transmitted, the status of the modules can be intuitively understood.

P2 **Modules that can work even on their own:** Implement a battery for each module to work without connecting to a battery module. In the existing modular toys, connecting the battery module and other modules is necessary to get some action.

P3 **various module types:** Like the existing modular toys, implement various modules to configure various functions.

P4 **Wooden appearance:** Make the module look like a wooden building blocks, often used as a toy for young children.

With the combination of P1 and P2, input modules such as sensors and switches can visualize the information they detect and present visible feedback even when the system is not assembled. It can be the first hint to understand the function of each module and contributes to the realization of Low Floor and Tinkerability. With the combination of P1 and P3, users can create more complex configurations with multiple modules by using the visualized information as a hint. This will contribute to the realization of High Ceilings and Wide Walls. P4 makes preschool children feel that the system is friendly, joyful, inviting, and playful. This will contribute to the realization of Conviviality.

3   System

In this study, we followed the design guidelines we set and developed a new modular toy named "Hikari-Tsumiki" that visualizes the information flow between modules by light emission.

3.1   Hardware

A module consists of an inner chassis and a wooden enclosure(Fig. 2). The inner chassis was printed with a 3D printer, and it holds a Li–fe battery, an FPC, and electronic components specific to each module(e.g., switch, distance sensor, speaker). On the FPC, LEDs and phototransistors for data transmission, a power switch, and a microcontroller(Arduino pro mini) are implemented. The control program is written on the Arduino and runs at a clock frequency of 32 MHz. The wooden enclosure covers the inner chassis. It consists of 4mm thick wooden boards, cut by a laser cutter. The wooden enclosure is cube-shaped, and each face has holes for holding the magnetic balls. The magnetic balls are inserted into the holes in a rotatable state and sealed with a transparent plate so that each surface of each module can be connected without considering the polarity. The size of the modules is standardized to 45 mm cube. The modules have electrodes for charging on the bottom and are charged using an external charger (Fig. 3).

Fig. 2. Wooden enclosure (left) and Inner chassis (right)

Fig. 3. External charger and electrode for charging

3.2   Optical Data Transmission

For data transmission, infrared (IR) light and visible red light are used simultaneously. Data is transmitted by the serial signal of the IR light while the visible red light changes its brightness depending on the data. At first used

PWM modulated visible light signals for both data transmission and visualization. However, there were problems such as errors due to the influence of outside light, so we separated data transmission and visualization and added an IR light for data transmission. The information flow visualization is shown in Fig. 4.

As a protocol for data transmission, we adopted a customized protocol based on the protocol for the IR remote controller. The data to be transmitted is 5 bits, and the strength of the visible light changes linearly according to the data value to be transmitted. For example, when the distance sensor module is moved closer to an object, the light becomes blighter, and when it is moved far away, the light becomes weaker. The data transmission speed is 10 Hz, and up to five ports per module can be used simultaneously.

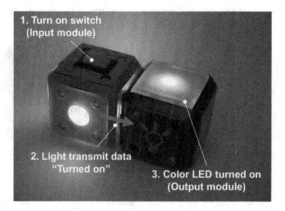

Fig. 4. Information flow visualization by light emission

3.3 Varieties of Modules

Modules can be categorized into three groups: input, output, and joint. An input module detects actions (e.g., flipping a switch) and transmits data. As described in Sect. 3.2, data is transmitted by the IR light, and the visible light changes its brightness depending on the data. The output module receives data from the input module and outputs an action (e.g., turning a motor). The joint module receives data from the input module and transfers it to the output module (e.g., wireless connection).

The varieties of modules are shown in Fig. 5. Thirteen different modules were implemented: six types of inputs, three types of joints, and four types of outputs. We used three kinds of woods to identify three groups.

3.4 Examples of Assembly

Three examples of the assembly are shown in Fig. 6. Figure 6(a) shows a robot made by combining two sets of distance sensors, joints, and DC motors. The distance sensors work as the robot's "eye", and when something approaches, the robot moves away from (or approaches to) the object. Figure 6(b) shows an electronic musical toy made by combining an acceleration sensor, a color LED, and a Speaker. By shaking the device by hand, the acceleration sensor outputs the intensity of the movement as data. The color LED changes the color of the light, and the speaker changes the tone scale according to the received data. Figure 6(c) shows an RC excavator made by combining paired wireless modules, two DC motors, one servo motor, two switches, and one volume. The paired wireless module wirelessly transmits data from the input to the output. In this example, data from the switches and volume connected to the input side is transmitted to the DC motors (wheels) and the servo motor (bucket) and realize remote control.

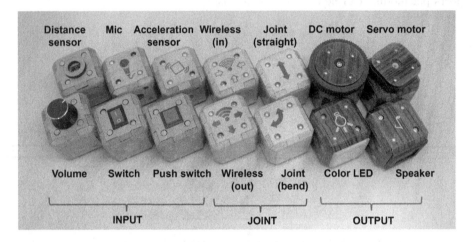

Fig. 5. Varieties of modules

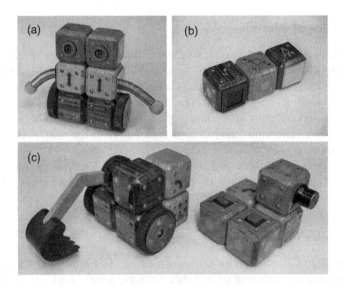

Fig. 6. Examples of assembly

4   User Study

This chapter describes a laboratory experiment using the developed Hikari-Tsumiki to investigate the effect of information visualization by light. The purpose of this experiment was to quantitatively evaluate the effect of the visualization by comparing the system with and without light. Considering the purpose of the proposed system, it is ideal to recruit preschool children as the participants who are assumed to be the target users. However, it is difficult to conduct a quantitative analysis on preschool children. Therefore, in this experiment, we recruited adult participants to analyze the effect of information visualization by light quantitatively.

4.1   Conditions

In this experiment, we compared two conditions to evaluate the effect of visualization of information by light.

– **C1: Light condition:** data was visualized by brightness of light.
– **C2: Without-light condition:** data was not visualized.

Developed Hikari-Tsumiki was used for both conditions, and in the without-light condition, all visible LEDs for data visualization were turned off. Since data transmission between modules is done by IR light, the system's behavior is the same except for the visible light.

We adopted a between-subjects design, with a total of 26 participants(8 females), 13 in each condition(4 females for each). The participants were undergraduate or graduate students at the University of Tsukuba, and their ages ranged from 21 to 33 years old(SD $= 3.62$).

4.2   Hypothesis

In this study, we set the following hypotheses as the effect of information visualization by light.

– **H1:** Promote understanding of the function of each module
– **H2:** Enhance a positive impression of the system

For H1, we thought that the data visualization would promote understanding the functions of input, output, and joint modules. It is possible to immediately feedback the input information (e.g., the value detected by the distance sensor) in the input modules without combining it with other modules. In the output modules, when combined with the input module, the changes in input and output modules can be observed simultaneously. In the joint modules, it is possible to check where the information is being transmitted visually. We thought that understanding would be promoted for input, output, and joint modules from these features.

For H2, the visualization of information will allow the user to get more responses from the system. We thought this would enhance the positive impression of the system.

4.3   Tasks

In this experiment, we set two tasks to verify our hypothesis. Task 1 is a "function exploration" task to understand the functions of each module, and Task 2 is a "free trial" task to play freely after understanding the functions of each module. Hypothesis H1 is verified in Task 1, and H2 is verified in Task 1 and Task 2. In the case of an actual system usage situation, it is considered that the user will go through the phase of function exploration and shift to the free trial.

4.4   Evaluation Items

In this experiment, we set "Questionnaire on the understanding of the functions of each module" as the evaluation item for the verification of H1, and "Questionnaire on the impression of the system" as the evaluation item for the verification of H2. We also measured the time required for each task, because related to H1, if the understanding of the system is promoted, the time required to explore the functions is expected to be shorter(Task 1). Related to H2, if positive impressions are enhanced, the free trial time is expected to be longer(Task 2). A description of each evaluation item is as follows.

Questionnaire on the Understanding of the Functions of Each Module. After the Task 1 was completed, participants answered a questionnaire about their understanding of the functions of each module. The questionnaire included the descriptions of the function of each module, and participants read them before answering the question. After that, for each module, the participants were asked to answer the questions "How well did you understand the function in the task? (degree of understanding)" and "How difficult was it to understand? (difficulty in understanding)" on a 5-point Likert scale.

Questionnaire on the Impression of the System. A questionnaire on the overall impression of the system was conducted after Task 1 and Task 2 were completed. The questions were adapted from studies that evaluated task impressions [11] and consisted of 10 pairs of adjectives. Questions are as follow; Q1. could understand – could not understand, Q2. easy – difficult, Q3. fun – not fun, Q4. task felt short – task felt long, Q5. calm – frustrated, Q6. relaxed – tense, Q7. interesting – boring, Q8. pleasant – unpleasant, Q9. concentrate – distracting, Q10. liked – dislike. Participants answered on a 7-point Likert scale for each question.

Time Required for Each Task. We measured the time required to complete the task in both Task 1 and Task 2. In the Task 1, the task was finished when the participants judged that they understood the functions of all the modules. In the Task 2, the participants were able to freely decide the timing to finish the task by their own will.

4.5 Results

Questionnaire on the Understanding of the Functions of Each Module. The results of degree of understanding and difficulty in understanding on each module are shown in Fig. 7. For questions about degree of understanding and difficulty in understanding, the average of the answers for all modules was calculated for each participant and used as the score. The results of the Shapiro–Wilk test showed that the data were not normally distributed, so we conducted the Mann–Whitney U test for each item. The Mann–Whitney U test result showed no significant difference between conditions.

Questionnaire on the Impression of the System. The results of the questionnaire on the impression of the system are shown in Fig. 8. The results of the Shapiro–Wilk test showed that the data were not normally distributed, so we conducted the Mann–Whitney U test for each item. The result of the Mann–Whitney U test showed a marginally significant difference for the "interesting" of Task 1 (p = 0.096) and "easy" of Task 2 (p = 0.056).

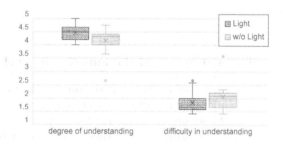

Fig. 7. Result of the degree of understanding and difficulty in understanding.

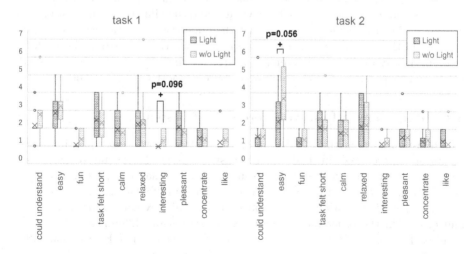

Fig. 8. Result of each item of the questionnaire on the impression of the system.(Smaller values indicate a positive impression.)

Time Required for Each Task. The results of the time required for each task are shown in Fig. 9. The results of the Shapiro-Wilk test showed that the data were not normally distributed, so we conducted the Mann–Whitney U test for each item. The Mann–Whitney U test result showed no significant difference between conditions.

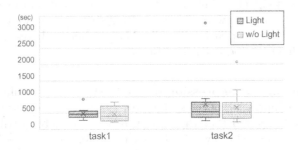

Fig. 9. Results of time required for each task.

5   Discussion

5.1   H1:Promote Understanding of the Function of Each Module

No significant difference was found in the questionnaire on the understanding of the functions of each module. Besides, there was no significant difference in the time required for Task 1. Therefore, we conclude that H1 was not supported.

The reason why the understanding was not significantly promoted is probably that the participants in this study were adults, so they were able to understand without any difficulty, even without visualization. Figure 7 shows that the degree of understanding was more than 4 on average, and the difficulty in understanding was about 2 or less, which indicates that the understanding was easy for participants. On the other hand, in Fig. 7 the Light condition appears to be slightly more positively evaluated. Therefore, future experiments need to be conducted with younger participants who may need more support for understanding.

5.2   H2:Enhance a Positive Impression of System

The questionnaire on the impression of the system showed marginal improvements of "interesting" in Task 1 and "easy" in Task 2. The improvement of "easy" in Task 2 is an interesting result. The fact that the participants felt "easy" in the free trial (task2) despite no significant difference in understanding suggests that visualization may support to think of new configuration by trial and error. On the other hand, there was no significant difference in the time required for Task 2. Based on these results, we consider that H2 was partially supported.

Although some marginally significant differences were observed, the overall enhancement of the impression was slight. The reason for this may be that the system was evaluated positively by the participants, either with or without visualization. In other words, even if there was an effect of the visualization, it is possible that the influence of other aspects such as experience and appearance may be dominant in making the impression of the system. Therefore, we consider conducting a free trial experiment in a within-subjects design to evaluate the slight differences.

5.3   Limitation

One of the main limitations of this study is that the participants were adults, so the effect of visualization of information for the expected users was not evaluated. Therefore, it is necessary to conduct experiments with children in future work. In addition, since the purpose of this study was to make a quantitative comparison within controlled samples, we did not compare the system with existing off-the-shelf products with different form factors, like littleBitss [4,5] and Cubelets [7,8]. In the future, it will be important to compare the proposed system with existing systems with qualitative evaluation.

6   Conclusion

This study developed a modular toy, "Hikari-Tsumiki," which visualizes the information flow between modules by light emission. For the development of the system, we set design guidelines based on the design principles of Scratch Jr [6] and developed the actual system. We also conducted an experiment to quantitatively evaluate the effect of visualization by light using the developed system. We conducted a function exploration task and a free trial task in the experiment and compared the conditions with and without visualization by light. The experiment results showed that although understanding the function of each module was not promoted, the positive impression of the system was enhanced in some aspects. The results also suggest that visualization by light may support the users to think of new configurations by trial and error.

Acknowledgements. This work was supported by INNOvation program from The Ministry of Internal Affairs and Communications.

References

1. Tsupros, N., Kohler, R., Hallinen, J.: STEM education: a project to identify the missing components. Intermed. Unit **1**, 11–17 (2009)
2. Khine, M.S., Areepattamannil, S. (eds.): Steam Education-Theory and Practice. Springer, Cham (2019). https://doi.org/10.1007/978-3-030-04003-1
3. Heradio, R., et al.: Open-source hardware in education: a systematic mapping study. IEEE Access **6**, 72094–72103 (2018)

4. Bdeir, A.: Electronics as material: littleBits. In: Proceedings of the 3rd International Conference on Tangible and Embedded Interaction (TEI 2009), pp. 397–400 (2009)
5. Sphero, Inc. littleBits: Electronic Building Kits for Kids. https://sphero.com/pages/littlebits, Accessed 11 Feb 2022
6. Flannery, L.P., Silverman, B., Kazakoff, E.R., Bers, M.U., Bontá, P., Resnick, M.: Designing ScratchJr: support for early childhood learning through computer programming. In: Proceedings of the 12th International Conference on Interaction Design and Children (IDC 2013), pp. 1–10 (2013)
7. Schweikardt, E.: Modular robotics studio. In: Proceedings of the 5th International Conference on Tangible and Embedded Interaction (TEI 2011), pp. 353–356 (2011)
8. Modular Robotics, Cubelets robot blocks - Modular Robotics. https://modrobotics.com/, Accessed 11 Feb 2022
9. Chan, J., Pondicherry, T., Blikstein, P.: LightUp: an augmented learning platform for electronics. In: Proceedings of the 12th International Conference on Interaction Design and Children (IDC 2013), pp. 491–494 (2013)
10. Resnick, M., et al.: Scratch: programming for all. Commun. ACM **52**(11), 60–67 (2009)
11. Ida, S., Yokoi, T., Yoshioka, K., Hasumi, T., Yamanaka, T.: Analysis of a subjective evaluation and brain activity during handwork and its virtual experience. Trans. Jpn. Soc. Kansei Eng. **13**(3), 449–457 (2014). (in Japanese)

Proposal of a Piano Learning Support System Considering Gamification Based on Reconsolidation

Ryota Matsui[1,2(✉)], Marimo Kumaki[1], Yoshinari Takegawa[1], Keiji Hirata[1], and Yutaka Yanagisawa[2]

[1] Future University Hakodate, Hakodate, Japan
{g3119005,yoshi,hirata}@fun.ac.jp
[2] M plus plus Co., Ltd, Shinagawa, Japan
{r.matsui,kani}@mplpl.com

Abstract. In this paper, we propose a learning support system considering gamification and reconsolidation for piano beginners. The proposed system is a game-based that supports the improvement of motor skills such as piano keying. Practice of motor skills using reconsolidation is more efficient than practice that focuses on specific parts or repetition. On the other hand, what is important in reconsolidation is that the subjects themselves are unaware that they are performing reconsolidation. In this research, gamification is incorporated into a piano learning support system that enables users to practice while using reconsolidation unconsciously. In this way, learners can practice piano motor skills like a game without recognizing the reconsolidation, and can acquire motor skills more efficiently than in previous practice methods that focus on specific parts or repetition. As a result of the comparative experiment, the learning support system in the proposed method was significantly useful for acquiring the set piece of music through the improvement of motor skills.

Keywords: Piano learning support · Reconsolidation · Gamification

1 Introduction

In piano performance, various techniques are required, such as score reading, accurately pressing indicated keys, proper fingering, sense of rhythm, dynamics of keystrokes and tempo. Learning these techniques requires basic practice over a long period of time. Because piano performance requires a lot of time and effort, there are learners who are frustrated due to low learning efficiency. Especially for beginners, it is difficult to perform the series of basic processes involved in practice, i.e. observing notes and fingering on the score, imagining the keying position on the keyboard from the notations, and playing with the designated fingering. Although this basic practice is particularly important, it is

P. Zaphiris and A. Ioannou (Eds.): HCII 2022, LNCS 13328, pp. 113–125, 2022.
https://doi.org/10.1007/978-3-031-05657-4_9

a very simplistic exercise, which makes it a cause of frustration. Therefore, it is important to maintain motivation in piano learning.

Previously, Takegawa et al. has constructed a piano learning support system for beginners [2,3,5]. The proposed system, which utilizes projection mapping to indicate the key(s) to be played with lighting, is designed so that the learner can understand the key pressing positions. These systems can be learned like a game.

Incorporating games into learning is known to increase learning motivation and learning effectiveness. In the past, research has been conducted to incorporate gamification into piano learning systems [6]. In these studies, notes flow, as on a piano roll, to the places that the learner should press. The color of each note corresponds to the fingering finger, so the learner can press the keys like in a rhythm game. In addition, Raymaekers et al. [7]. proposed GAME OF TONES, which applies Weing et al.'s P.I.A.N.O to allow the keyboard to be played on like a Space Invaders game machine. It can be said that, by having learners press keys at the right times as though playing a game, it helps them to handle the instrument casually, reducing the compulsive feeling that they must learn the piano. There are many systems that support piano learning in this way. Beginners can use such systems to lower the learning threshold, making it easier to continue learning. In addition, learners can maintain their motivation by enjoying learning. However, in order to support piano learning more efficiently, it is necessary to focus on the mechanism of the human memory. In these systems, the moment the presentation of keystroke position is eliminated it becomes difficult to know where to play, thus it is difficult to grasp the correspondence between the score and the key to be played on the keyboard, and learners do not progress. Therefore, both a lowering of the threshold for learning by incorporating gamification and a system to establish the memory of keystrokes are required.

Human memories are encoded and temporarily saved as short term memories (STM), then fixed and consolidated as long term memories (LTM). It has been said that consolidated memories are preserved unless they are forgotten. However, Nader et al. proposed that the LTM could be re-modulated by recall and that new information could be incorporated into the memory at the time of recall [16]. This is called reconsolidation. In other words, reconsolidation means that the memory consolidated as an LTM is recalled to an unstable state, and then returns to a stable state again. Wymbs et al. have shown that reconsolidation can help strengthen motor skills [18]. Therefore, we hypothesized that the relationship between reconsolidation and strengthening of motor skills is also effective in piano learning. In piano performance, the movement of pressing an appropriate key is an input, and sound is output as a result. From this, it is thought that the learner can learn the performance of an assigned piece of music (task music) as movement, and, as a result, can learn it efficiently. Therefore, we consider that focusing on keystroke movement and providing learning support incorporating reconsolidation can enable efficient acquisition of task music. In this study, we propose a piano learning support system using reconsolidation.

The proposed system uses reconsolidation to efficiently support keying movements in piano performance.

In this research, gamification is used in a piano learning support system that enables users to practice while using reconsolidation unconsciously, since it is important that the learners do not recognize that they are performing the reconsolidation operation. It is thought that in such a learning method the user can learn more efficiently than in the piano practice methods generally used until now.

2 Related Research

2.1 Presentation and Withdrawal of Support Information

In the case of support for singing, calligraphy and musical instrument performance, it has been confirmed that presenting exemplary motions and indicating errors to learners as support information has been effective in shortening the skill acquisition period. Accordingly, learning systems have been proposed which present both models and current conditions, and indicate errors. For example, in the early stage of playing in piano learning (the stage in which, seeing a piece of music for the first time, a piano beginner practices to remember fingering or keying position), all note names and key striking numbers may be marked on the keyboard in advance using stickers. There are also several instruments sold by instrument manufacturers, such as Lighted Keyboard [1], and software that presents performance support information including which keys to press next. These support methods are useful for learning the keypress movement on the piano.

There are many studies that have incorporated gamification into piano learning [6–9]. By incorporating gamification, it is possible to visualize sounds and keystrokes, to lower the threshold for learning. Therefore, gamification makes the learning process more efficient and enjoyable for beginners than conventional methods do. In research combining gamification and the piano, augmented reality learning using HMDs is often used [10,11]. The HMD method is easy to understand visually and has a sufficient element of gameplay, but it is not used in this study because of the possibility that wearing an HMD may prove an obstacle to performance for beginners.

In addition, Takegawa et al. have proposed a learning system that presents keying position, fingering, rhythm, musical score, etc. on the keyboard and its surroundings, from a projector installed above the keyboard [2,3]. Furthermore, Fukuya et al. have proposed a system to support learning while considering motivation [4]. These systems, in addition to lowering the threshold of learning by presenting a model performance before practice, visually emphasize correct keying position and the learner's current keying position to notify the learner when mis-keying has been performed. The systems have a function to enable the learner to understand the correct keying, by imposing a penalty whereby when a mistake has been made, the next example is not shown and the learner is made to redo the part that was played wrongly. In the early stages of playing, the learner practices while using support information.

In addition, Fukuya et al. [4]. proved that learners can learn efficiently by using a system that produces the correct sound even when the learner presses the wrong key. This result will be useful in our research as well. Takegawa et al. also proposed a system that has a function which visually feeds back to the learner whether or not the support information was used, in order to promote departure from assistance [5]. In this way, there are also proposals for systems that allow learners to gradually reduce support information according to their degree of skill acquisition [12]. In the case of learning support by a system, it is important to aim to gradually withdraw from the support, as in the research described above.

A violin learning support system has also been proposed that includes information such as false and vague information [14]. In this system, the learner can select, with arbitrary timing, the authenticity of the information presented. From the experiment results, it is stated that the group that conducted learning including not only true information, but also information different from traditional information, such as false and vague information, could learn more efficiently than the group that used only conventional true information. Additionally, the experiment results indicate that learning containing false information is more effective than learning containing vague information. This suggests that if the information presented is incorrect, the learner must make active judgements, which may have a positive effect on learning. It is possible that an efficient learning method using reconsolidation is a similar mechanism.

2.2   Human Memory Mechanism

In general, memory is encoded and temporarily stored as short term memory (STM), then fixed and consolidated as long term memory (LTM). Consolidated memories are preserved indefinitely, unless forgotten. Nader et al. proposed that the memory converted to LTM could be re-modulated by being recalled, and at the time of recall new information could be incorporated into the old memory. Recalling a memory once stabilized as an LTM, temporarily resolving it, and then returning to a stable state is called reconsolidation of memory [15–17].

Wymbs et al. proved that reconsolidation is useful for strengthening motor skills. Before that, it was useful for consolidating memories, but whether it was helpful for improving motor skills was unclear [18]. In an experiment on the learning of motor skills, conducted by Wymbs et al. it was revealed that repetitive practice was not an efficient method of strengthening skills, especially in the early stages of learning. In other words, in order for beginners to improve their skills efficiently, methods other than repetitive training are necessary. This is considered to be the same in piano learning. Thus, we design our learning system considering reconsolidation in this study.

In the previous studies, it was important for subjects to perform operations unconsciously when learning skills by reconsolidation [18–20]. In our research,

Fig. 1. Proposed system

we use gamification to make reconsolidation unconscious when learning skills by reconsolidation.

Depending on the scenario of the game, the subject may be required to hit a key that is clearly different from the original. When doing so, the subject can recognize the mistake in the sound but also execute the operation of reconsolidation unconsciously.

3   Design

Figure 1 presents the structure of the proposed system. The piano used in the proposed system is a MIDI-support enabled keyboard. This keyboard is disassembled, and only the keyboard part is fixed directly under the display. In addition, the performance data generated by the MIDI-support enabled keyboard is sent to the PC in MIDI data format via the MIDI device source. The content to be presented is implemented in Unity, and the language used is C#. MIDI data input from the MIDI piano is read with the plug-in of unity-midi-input.

3.1   Design Policy

In the proposed system, the learner practices the task music in accordance with the game, and intentionally performs incorrect keystrokes according to the game

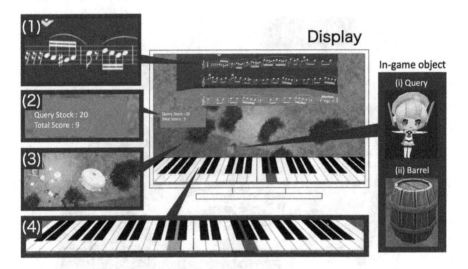

Fig. 2. Contents

scenario, aiming at reconsolidation by gamification. Since learners can learn the task score while playing the game, they do not notice that they themselves are carrying out reconsolidation. Perceiving and remembering keystrokes as movement is useful for practicing task music.

3.2 Information Presented to Learners

The contents presented in Fig. 2 are shown to the learner. The numbers in the figure correspond to the following numbered items.

(1) Presentation of Musical Score. Musical score is presented in the upper part of the content. A light blue arrow pointing downward (1) is presented above the note from which to start playing. A semitransparent red rectangle is superimposed on the next note to be played. In this system, if a learner mis-keys, true (correct) note sound is output and playing moves on to the next note. This method imitates Coloring-in Piano by Oshima et al. [21] and Two Finger Piano by Takeuchi et al. [22], in that correct output is always played regardless of which key is pressed.

This method is the exact opposite of the Suzuki Method, which is widely known as a music learning curriculum. The Suzuki Method is mainly aimed at children learning music following regular stages. When a child in the learning stage performs an operation that outputs a different sound from the keystroke position, the ability to judge correct pitch is not acquired. However, the main target of our study is adult beginners. Adults recognize keystrokes as movement and play through a single piece of music. Since adults tend to learn based on past experiences of success, it is important to provide a reward for being able to play through a single piece. Therefore, in this study, to maintain learner motivation, it is correct to incorporate the operation to output the correct pitch regardless of the keying position.

The set piece of music used in our research was W. A. Mozart's Turkish March (K.331), from the beginning to the 17th measure.

The definition of piano novices who use this system is as follows.

- They can read the score of W. A. Mozart's Turkish March (K.331), which comprises single notes only.
- They do not understand the key positions to press on the piano, from looking at the score.

(2)–(3) Game Mode Capture. The proposed system has a game mode that allows users to perform reconsolidation naturally. In the game mode, receiving a score (2) is a reward for users, as described below. The game score is determined by the number of objects (3) of the character generated by the key, and keying time. A cue tone sounds once every two seconds during keying, and if keying time exceeds this duration points are subtracted from the score at a rate of one point per second. In addition, the current number of generated character objects is also recorded.

(4) Virtual Keyboard. A virtual keyboard is presented on the screen. Also, the real MIDI keyboard is set at the position corresponding to the on-screen keyboard. On the virtual keyboard, the next keying position is shown in red, and the position of the learner's keystroke is shown in blue. The learner learns by memorizing this keying position.

3.3 Manual of Game Mode

The game is an evasion game in which the user must avoid Barrel objects ((ii) in Fig. 2) that decrease the game score, and increase the amount of Query objects ((i) in Fig. 2), by keying, to increase game score. In (4) in Fig. 2, it is necessary to avoid the Barrel objects (ii) with good timing. The user needs to deliberately avoid the Barrel objects because crashing into them will reduce the game score. In-game reconsolidation operations are as follows. The barrel approaches the key that should be struck. The learner knows the position of the correct key, but dares to strike the wrong key to avoid the barrel. Intentional wrong keystrokes by the learner can extend the efficiency of learning [4]. Learners intentionally play the wrong keystrokes in order to progress in the game, and the fact that they themselves are aware of this leads them to reconfirm the keystroke positions.

4 Experiment

To verify the usefulness of the proposed system using reconsolidation, we conducted a user experiment.

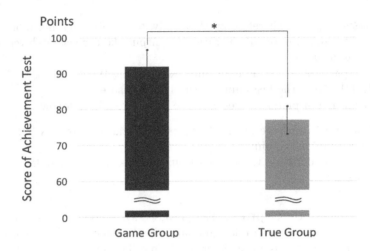

Fig. 3. Average score of each group

Table 1. Questionnaire

Group name	Motivation	Enjoyment
Game group	4.6	4.1
True group	4.1	3.4

4.1   Preparation for the Experiment

The subjects were 17 men and six women, aged between 21 and 26 years. We inserted an additional test for screenings into the first learning session of the first day only, then subjects who scored more than 90% at that time were judged not to be struggling in the first stage of performance and therefore excluded. Therefore, the performance ability among the subjects is uniform to some extent. Accordingly, only 12 subjects out of the total 17 were targeted. The 12 subjects were classified into 2 groups, each consisting of 6 subjects. True Group can use only True Mode, while Game Group can use both True Mode and Game Mode, switching between modes when instructed. We conducted the experiment after confirming that all subjects could read the score and were piano beginners. In this research, we define a piano beginner as someone who, when looking at a note on a score, is unable to imagine the corresponding key position to be pressed on the keyboard. We asked subjects to experiment with the system for approximately 10 min and work out how to use it. In the experiment, we logged the note number of the note to be played, the MIDI value entered by the subject, the current learning mode, the time, the score of the piece of music learned and the game score.

4.2 Experimental Procedure

Subjects played the music of Turkish March as practice, interspersed with breaks of approximately five minutes. In practice, Turkish March is played through to the 17th measure three times, making a total of 252 sounds played only right hand. In practice, the purpose is to look at notes on the score and memorize the keying position on the keyboard from the notes. In the first learning session in the three times, both group subjects practiced using the assigned correct answer mode. In the second learning session, True Group practiced using correct answer mode, while Game Group practiced using Game Mode. In the third learning session, the exercises were exactly the same as in the first learning session, for both groups. After that, as an achievement test, we had subjects play Turkish March up to the 17th measure without instructions on keying position. More than 24 h had passed between each session for both groups. This is the time necessary to perform proper reconsolidation [18]. In one session of the Game Group, the number of times the game makes the subject perform a reconsolidation operation by avoiding the Barrel objects is random.

Also, after completing the experiment, we conducted a motivation survey and questionnaire asking, among other questions, whether subjects were able to enjoy practice.

4.3 Experiment Results

The average achievement test scores, converted from a maximum score of 84 points to a maximum score of 100 points, are shown in Fig. 3. The vertical axis shows the achievement test score and the horizontal axis shows the result of each group.

Comparing the average achievement test scores of each group, Game Group is 92%, and True Group is 77%. When the t-test was applied at the significance level of 5%, a significant difference was observed between the proposed Game Group and the True Group ($t(5) = 2.55, p = 0.03$).

The average in-game score of Game Group is 353.4, but, in contrast, the average achievement test score is 77.3. We found that there was a very high correlation between the in-game scores and the achievement test scores ($r = 0.80, p = 0.03$). Also, comparing the average required completion time of Game Group and True Group, we found that the average required time of Game Group is 12.5 min, and True Group is 14.1 min. Accordingly, there was no correlation between the required times of Game Group and True Group ($r = 0.35, p = 0.44$).

Therefore, the game mode of the proposed system was found to be useful for learning good performance. From this, it can be inferred that the proposed method of piano learning considering reconsolidation is more efficient than the conventional method. We believe that the significance of this method can be proven by increasing the number of subjects and experimenting with task pieces of various difficulty levels.

The questionnaire results are shown in Table 1. MOTIVATION in the table is a question about whether motivation could be maintained. Subjects could answer on a scale of 1–5, in which the nearer the score was to 1 the less they were able to maintain motivation, while the nearer the score was to 5 the more they were able to maintain motivation. As for ENJOYMENT in the table, it is a question about whether subjects were able to feel enjoyment. Subjects could answer on a scale of 1–5: the nearer the score was to 1 the less they were able to feel enjoyment, while the nearer the score was to 5 the more they were able to feel enjoyment.

For both MOTIVATION and ENJOYMENT questions, Game Group had a higher score. Thus, we can infer that the game mode of the proposed system is fun to use and keeps students motivated to learn. This result shows that the avoidance game in Game Mode had sufficient game qualities as a game. Also, comments made in the free description questionnaire suggest that this was due to many negative opinions among True Group that learning was too tedious. However, when a U-test was applied to the questionnaire results for MOTIVATION ($U = 14.0, p > 0.05$) and ENJOYMENT ($U = 17.0, p > 0.05$), there was no significant difference between the two groups.

4.4 Consideration

From the results of the experiment, it can be said that the group that used the proposed method improved efficiently. However, there are some issues in the proposed system that need to be discussed.

The Effects of Pressing the Wrong Keys. Normally, it is not a good idea to press the wrong key. Traditional music education methods emphasize the importance of the correspondence between keys and sounds. These ideas are justified and correct. It is especially important for young children to accurately associate the names of notes with the keys on the keyboard. On the other hand, our experiment included adults as subjects. For adult subjects, the goal was to complete the task quickly rather than to learn the correspondence between the keys and sounds. This is because adults can recognize that incorrect notes and keying are a deliberate operation for the progress of the game. However, in order for the system to be widely used in the future, we need to develop a method to learn the correspondence between the keyboard and sounds.

Whether the Subjects Were Aware of the Aims of the Proposed System. In this experiment, the participants were so absorbed in the operation of the game that they were not aware of the purpose of the system. We did not tell the subjects that our system is a learning system using reconsolidation, because we believed that communicating the aims of the system would have a significant impact on the results.

The Relationship Between Motivation and Progress. Finally, we discuss the relationship between motivation and improvement. In this experiment, the motivation to practice was also investigated. The proposed system allowed users to improve and stay motivated every day. However, the present experiment did not reveal a relationship between progress and motivation. This is because it is impossible to discern whether the subjects remained motivated by the action of the proposed system or whether the subjects' improvement itself was what helped to keep subjects motivated. Therefore, in the future, we need to conduct an experiment to determine whether the system itself or the learner's progress is what maintains motivation.

4.5 Discussion

The details of the experiment need to be discussed. In particular, whether the number and timing of explosions, i.e. reconsolidation operations, were appropriate. In this experiment, the number and timing of appearances of the Barrel objects were randomly controlled by a function. Experimental results showed that the group that performed the reconsolidation operation was more efficient in practice. The purpose of the random control of appearances was to prevent bias in the values between subjects. However, it remains unclear what number of performances of the reconsolidation operation will be useful to learners in piano practice. For example, the practice efficiency rate may differ between a group that incorporated the reconsolidation operation 10 times and a group that incorporated it 3 times. It is also possible that the effect may vary depending on the timing of the operation. It is quite possible that the effect bias may differ between the group that incorporates the reconsolidation operation in the first three minutes of practice and the case of incorporating reconsolidation operation in the last minute. Therefore, the timing and number of appearances must be considered for optimal reconsolidation operations. In order to find the optimal number of reconsolidation operations, we have to experiment with a large number of subjects divided into groups that each perform a specified number of reconsolidation operations.

Reconsolidation destroys information about the keystroke that is fixed in the learners' minds. This corresponds to learners reconsidering the information that should originally be played and organizing their memories. Thus, the learners can reconfirm the keys to be struck. It can be inferred that recognizing the ambiguous parts of the learning process will help to consolidate the memory of keystrokes more powerfully. Furthermore, the insertion of a reconsolidation operation can occur at any point in the piece. On the other hand, when performing live, a performer may make mistakes in unexpected situations. When an unexpected performance mistake occurs at a point that the performer expects to be able to play well, the performer will be greatly upset. However, if learners continue to learn by incorporating reconsolidation, as in the proposed system, they are forced to make mistakes at unexpected points and they learn to recover and play the rest of the song without difficulty. Therefore, it is expected that this system can be used to cope with unexpected mistakes in live performance, which relates to the research of Yokoyama et al. [13].

Normally, a long period of time, such as a week or a month, is required to practice a piece of music. After this long period of practice, learners may become demotivated. However, in this experiment, the subjects only practiced for 3 day. It is conceivable that, in such a short duration of practice, it is difficult to for a difference in motivation and progress to arise depending on the method of practice. In addition, because of the short duration of practice, in the proposed method the effect of practicing for a long period of time, which is what we need to know, is unclear. Therefore, it is necessary to prove that the proposed method of reconsolidation is useful in longer experiments, such as one week or one month. In the future, we will conduct an experiment with subjects classified into several groups of longer duration, and continue the experiment in a more long-term manner.

5   Conclusion

In this research, we proposed a learning support system considering reconsolidation for piano beginners. In the proposed system, gamification is incorporated into a piano learning support system that enables users to practice while using reconsolidation unconsciously. In this way, the learners can practice piano motor skills like a game without recognizing the reconsolidation. The results of the experiment showed that a group of learners using the proposed system were able to learn more efficiently than those using the conventional method.

Future tasks include increasing the number of subjects, using the system for long-term learning, and practicing with other task musics. Increasing the number of subjects and the number of practice days, that will establish the usefulness of gamification and reconsolidation with this method. In addition, by dealing with multiple types of task music, learners can acquire a variety of performance techniques.

Acknowledgments. This work was supported by JST CREST Grant Number JPMJCR18A3, Japan.

References

1. CASIO, Glowing navigation keyboard. https://casio.jp/emi/products/lk511/
2. Takegawa, Y., Terada, T., Tsukamoto, M.: A piano learning support system considering rhythm. In: Proceedings of International Computer Music Conference, pp. 326–332 (2012)
3. Takegawa, Y., Tsukamoto, M., Terada, T.: Design and implementation of a piano practice support system using a real-time fingering recognition technique. In: Proceedings of International Computer Music Conference, pp. 1–8 (2011)
4. Takegawa, Y., Fukuya, Y., Yanagi, H.: Design and implementation of a piano learning support system considering maintenance of motivation. In: Proceedings of EdMedia 2016 World Conference on Educational Media and Technology, pp. 449–463 (2016)

5. Takegawa, Y., Terada, T., Tsukamoto, M.: Design and implementation of piano performance learning system considering withdrawal from system support. Comput. Softw. (J. Jpn. Soc. Softw. Sci. Technol.) **30**(4), 51–60 (2013). (in Japanese)
6. Weing, M., Rhlig, A., Rogers, K., Weber, M.: PIANO: enhancing instrument learning via interactive projected augmentation. In: Proceedings of ACM Conference on Pervasive and Ubiquitous Computing Adjunct Publication, UbiComp 2013, pp. 75–78 (2013)
7. Raymaekers, L., Vermeulen, J., Luyten, K., Coninx, K.: Game of tones: learning to play songs on a piano using projected instructions and games. In: Proceedings of Special Interest Group on Computer-Human Interaction 2014, pp. 411–414 (2014) Special Interest Group on Computer-Human Interaction 2014 , 411–414 (2014)
8. Karola, M., Andreas, W., Thomas, K.: Supporting musical practice sessions through HMD-based augmented reality. In: Proceedings of the Mensch and Computer 2019 - Workshopband (2019)
9. Klepsch, M., Könings, B., Weber, M., Seufert, T.: Fostering piano learning by dynamic mapping of notes. In: Proceedings of EARLI SIG Text and Comprehension (2013)
10. Molero, D., Schez-Sobrino, S., Vallejo, D., Glez-Morcillo, C., Albusac, J.: A novel approach to learning music and piano based on mixed reality and gamification. J. Multimedia Tools Appl. **80**, 165–186 (2020)
11. Gerry, L., Dahl, S., Serafin, S.: ADEPT: exploring the design, pedagogy, and analysis of a mixed reality application for piano training. In: Proceedings of the 16th Sound and Music Computing Conference SMC 2019, pp. 241–239 (2019)
12. Nonami, J., Takegawa, Y.: Construction of a support system for learning character balance in transcription for beginners. In: Proceedings of IEEE Global Conference on Consumer Electronics, pp. 26–30 (2014)
13. Yokoyama, Y., Nishimoto, K.: A piano practice support system for preventing performance cessation caused by performance errors. J. Inf. Process. Soc. Jpn. **2010**(4), 205–208 (2010). (in Japanese)
14. Kumaki, M., Takegawa, Y., Hirata, K.: Design and implementation of a positioning learning support system for violin beginners, using true, vague and false information. J. Inf. Process. Soc. Jpn. **2018**(26), 285–293 (2018)
15. Nader, K., Schafe, G.E., Le Doux, J.E.: Fear memories require protein synthesis in the amygdala for reconsolidation after retrieval. Nature **406**, 722–726 (2000)
16. Nader, K., Hardt, O.: A single standard for memory: the case for reconsolidation. J. Nat. Rev. Neurosci. **10**, 224–234 (2009)
17. Tronson, N.C., Taylor, J.R.: Molecular mechanisms of memory reconsolidation. J. Nat. Rev. Neurosci. **8**, 262–275 (2007)
18. Wymbs, N.F., Bastian, A.J., Celnik, P.A.: Motor skills are strengthened through reconsolidation. J. Curr. Biol. **26**, 338–343 (2009)
19. Walker, M.P., Brakefield, T., Hobson, J.A., Stickgold, R.: Dissociable stages of human memory consolidation and reconsolidation. Nature **425**, 616–620 (2003)
20. Censor, N., Dimyan, M.A., Cohen, L.G.: Modification of existing human motor memories is enabled by primary cortical processing during memory reactivation. J. Curr. Biol. **20**, 1545–1549 (2010)
21. Oshima, C., Miyagawa, Y., Nishimoto, K.: Coloring in piano: a piano that allows a performer to concentrate on musical expression. In: Proceedings of the 7th International Conference on Music Perception and Cognition, pp. 707–710 (2002)
22. Takeuchi, Y., Katayose, H.: Representation of music expression with two finger piano. J. Inf. Process. Soc. Jpn. **1995**, 37–44 (1995)

Development of an Amazon Alexa App for a University Online Search

Jakob Rupitz, Markus Ebner(✉) ⓘ, and Martin Ebner ⓘ

Graz University of Technology, Graz, Austria
{markus.ebner,martin.ebner}@tugraz.at

Abstract. Today, our homes become smarter and smarter. We started to interact with our home with Intelligent Personal Assistants, like Amazon Alexa. In this paper we want to present and give a review on the Alexa skill developed for an online search for resources like rooms, courses, and persons. The goal is to provide the users an easy-to-use way to ask for information like phone numbers, e-mail addresses, room details, … and the Alexa Skill should provide this information also in an easy understandable way. We will describe how we solved to formulate suitable search queries from spoken Alexa commands and how we presented them to the user accordingly. Other obstacles like the presentation of the search results, due to the limited context and prioritization for individual search results, to the user will be discussed.

Keywords: Amazon alexa · Smart home · Voice-based search · Voice user interface · Amazon echo

1 Introduction

Today, more and more technical devices are available in our homes and become smarter and smarter. A smart home helps its residents to increase the standard of living and safety by the aid of additional technical "smart" equipment. These include, for example, remote-controlled lights and shutters, a door lock that can be locked and unlocked with a smartphone, a heating control system connected and controlled over the Internet, a voice-controlled music system and so on.

A possible way to interact with a smart home over voice is the Amazon Alexa platform and its Echo devices. With them, a central point of interaction with the system is offered to the users. For example, Echo devices allow users to use voice commands to turn electronic devices in the home on and off (e.g. lights), change the temperature, or play the next song. Further, learning is supported by Alexa [1], e.g. learning geographic facts [2] and it can be used in mass education [3] as well.

The skill developed and presented in this paper line up in these Skills and is intended to simplify students' daily lives by using a voice query to find out where the lecture hall is located, or which professor is giving the next lecture. This allows the student to save time to get the information on the side while doing other work.

P. Zaphiris and A. Ioannou (Eds.): HCII 2022, LNCS 13328, pp. 126–139, 2022.
https://doi.org/10.1007/978-3-031-05657-4_10

To develop the skill, we started with categorical queries that a student might make. Rooms and courses should support the search initially, as these are also in our everyday language from the language model and therefore easily understood by Amazon Alexa. Later we added the possibility to search for people, which caused us to encounter some problems. Among them, a large error rate when recognizing the name of the person to be searched and the prioritization of the search results.

Beginning with a short introduction of personal Assistants, the paper further focuses in the Background chapter on Amazon Alexa Skills and Voice User Interfaces. The following chapter State of the Art will examine existing Alexa Skills, focus on the communication with the uses and lessons learned for the development of the university search skill. Before discussing the implementation, an overview about the technology used to develop the skill is given. The chapter implementation deals with the implementation of the Amazon Alexa Skills for the search at Graz University of Technology. Finally, the authors will discuss the development and give an outlook on future features to be developed for the skill.

2 Background

This chapter will introduce the history and background of Assistants and focus on existing Amazon Alexa Skills in terms of functions, procedures, and analyzation of their conversation models as well as Voice User Interfaces.

2.1 Personal Digital Assistants

Personal digital assistants (PDAs) are not a new invention. Already in 1984, the first digital assistant came onto the market [4] to simplify daily tasks for users. PDAs were used as calendars, address books or as e-mail devices with steady increasing popularity. Cell phones and smartphones made PDAs useless, as more modern cell phones came with more functions. With the ability to surf the Web and use various apps, the new smartphones became more and more popular; PDAs were hardly used anymore.

Intelligent Personal Assistants. Today's Intelligent Personal Assistants (IPAs) can be compared to earlier PDAs. As Hauswald et al. describe it, *"An IPA is an application that uses inputs such as the user's voice, vision (images), and contextual information to provide assistance by answering questions in natural language, making recommendations, and performing actions"* [5]. An IPA is a more modern PDA, with additional features such as voice recognition, touch screen, camera and so on. In any case, an IPA is normally connected to the Internet and attempts to answer the user's questions with information acquired from the web. Modern IPA devices can further expand their range of functions through machine learning and Artificial Intelligence (AI).

Artificial Intelligence. Artificial Intelligence (AI) refers to a large field of computer science that is characterized by "intelligent behavior". The German Research Center for Artificial Intelligence defines the term as follows: *"Artificial Intelligence is the property of an IT system to exhibit 'human-like' intelligent behavior"* [6].

According to Russel and Norvig, research on AI divides into two categories: Human vs. Rational and Thought vs. Behavior [7]. The combination of the two categories results in four different combinations, each with their own research areas. Further, sub-areas of AI in computer science include Natural Language Processing, Knowledge Representation, Automated Reasoning and Machine Learning.

2.2 Amazon Alexa Platform

Amazon was founded in 1994 by Jeff Bezos in a garage on the US coast [8]. Originally, only books were sold, but due to the simplicity of the purchasing process, the company was a success. Meanwhile, the company operates one of the largest online stores world-wide. To attract even more customers, Amazon is constantly researching new concepts. In addition to Amazon Web Services (AWS) which provides infrastructure in the form of IT resources and servers, the Amazon Prime offering with music and movie streaming services, the company also has other products in stock. One of them, which was created by the employees/staff of the Amazon Development Center, is called Alexa. Alexa is a voice assistant that runs on a wide variety of devices and is designed to simplify the lives of its users. The voice assistant first appeared on the market in 2015, in the form of Amazon Echo devices, and is completely cloud-based [8]. This means everything a user says is processed through AWS to give them the best possible result to their question. Through cloud connectivity, Alexa is constantly learning new features and has become continuously more useful. Alexa now speaks nine languages and can be found on many electronic devices around the world [9].

Functionality. Alexa falls into the category of IPAs [10]. This refers to a speech-enabled device that can understand a user's voice and other important information from context for providing answers to questions in a spoken form. Many new IPAs emerged in the last years. Examples of the most known include Google Now from Alphabet, Siri from Apple, Cortana from Microsoft, and Bixby from Samsung [10]. They are able to understand spoken words, process them and interact with the user. At today's level, these assistants are largely used to perform small tasks that are intended to make the user's life easier. For example, users can utilize voice commands to select the music they want to listen to, adjust the volume, control smart home components such as lights, or set a timer. Alexa is built in such a way that developers can program apps for it - Amazon calls them skills [11]. In this way, Amazon wants to constantly expand the functionality of its voice assistant and give other companies the possibility to develop their own skills.

Structure of the Alexa Platform. When a user asks the voice assistant something, a special procedure runs in the background. The device running Alexa records what is said using speech recognition as well as machine learning. Depending on what was said, Alexa builds a conversation to learn even more information from the user. Once it has learned the necessary facts, Alexa sends a query to a service that can provide the appropriate results. The results are then processed by the skill and presented to the user in the form of a voice output.

Structure of a Request. Amazon's Alexa consists of two modules. On the one hand, there is the user interface, which is in contact with the user. This is a so-called Voice

User Interface (VUI). The VUI differs from a Graphical User Interface (GUI): There is only acoustic communication between the user and the device. Thus, it can be thought of as the front end of Amazon Alexa.

On the other hand, the processing on the server with the help of lambda functions, the communication between the API and the frontend, and the preparation of the data for the voice user interface are all part of the same process. In other words, the backend of Amazon Alexa.

The frontend, the VUI, is there to interpret the requests from the user and to pass them on to the backend. To do so, it must know which function the user wants to call and which data the user provides for this function. For this purpose, there are the so-called intents and utterances.

An intent specifies the function in the backend, and the utterances specify the real words that the user could say to activate this intent. This means an Amazon Alexa skill consists of multiple intents, which in turn consist of multiple utterances. A slot can also be configured for the utterances. The slot works similar to a variable and is used to detect parameters in the utterance and then forward them to the lambda function in the backend [12].

If several slots are needed for a complete intent, and the user does not provide them in the sentence, slot filling can be used. Depending on which slots are missing, Alexa asks the respective ones. The user can then fill in these slots with further utterances. Furthermore, it is possible to have Alexa ask for a confirmation at the end of the intent to check whether the conversation was processed correctly or not.

2.3 Voice-User-Interface

The GUI and the VUI have the same goal: get information from the user and then to do something with this information. There are some differences that are important to think about. The main ones are providing a user-friendly and practical usage of the system.

With a GUI, users usually use physical input devices such as a mouse, keyboard, touch screens to click or enter something in a text field. The user decides what to click, what to type into, and what data to be sent. This type of human-machine interaction has been very successful over the last few decades. In addition, the GUI helps to correct user errors by directly correcting words through spelling programs or displaying suggestions to the user. The interaction between human and machine is quite fast, as the graphical feedback is usually seen immediately after the input.

The VUI on the other side is still relatively new. It has been around only for several years, but since more powerful smartphones reached the mainstream market, this technology has become popular among smartphone users [13]. With Apple's Siri (introduced in 2006) and Google's Google Now (introduced in 2007), the general population is benefitting from VUIs.

These VUIs, which mostly find their way to the customer in the form of digital assistants, are very easy and convenient to use. You no longer have to type, you can simply say out loud what you want and don't even have to look at the screen, because the digital assistant usually also answers by voice.

This means that it is now possible to interact with computers without taking your hands away from the current activity. One problem, however, is still the accuracy of speech recognition, so-called Natural Language Processing (NLP). Many linguistic expressions depend strongly on the surrounding context of the statement for their content. Words that are homonyms denote several concepts.

For example, there are different meanings for the word "the ball". On the one hand the dance event, and on the other hand soccer. So-called phonetic words are very difficult to interpret correctly because there is usually no context [14]. Written out, for example, there are still the capitalization and lower case, which can draw attention to the meaning of a word. Spoken however, these capitalizations do not exist.

For a VUI, the recognition and correct interpretation of the language of the user is therefore very difficult, since there is no other input besides the spoken one, and thus there is no context that could be helpful in interpreting the phrase [14]. Another problem is the privacy of the user. For Amazon Alexa to be activated when someone says the keyword "Alexa", her microphones must be continuously active and picking up ambient sounds. Once the cue is said, the conversation is recorded and stored in Amazon Web Services.

3 State of the Art: Examples for Amazon Alexa Skills with Search Function

This chapter will examine existing Alexa Skills in terms of their structure and functionality. The focus will be on how the communication with its users is structured and how user-friendly the chosen strategy is.

3.1 Deutsche Bahn

The Amazon Alexa Skill from Deutsche Bahn is developed for train connection search. It is designed to make people's everyday lives easier by announcing information about the next departure times and picking out special connections for users. For example, Amazon Alexa answers the question: "Alexa, ask Deutsche Bahn for the next connection to sports." [15] with "Your direct connection from Frankfurt (Main) Hauptbahnhof to Frankfurt (Main) Süd: departure on time at 15:42 with S6 from platform 101. Arrival expected at 15:53." [15] thus giving the user an exact answer without ever having to touch his/her smartphone or computer.

If one starts the skill with "Alexa, start Deutsche Bahn!", one is first greeted with

"Welcome to Deutsche Bahn! What do you want to search for: Connections or Departures?". Here you can already see the first design decision of the developers.

Connections and Departures are two different categories, and the Deutsche Bahn Skill asks for this category first. This is the case because different intents are used for the two categories and thus a large part of the utterances that the user could say are omitted.

If one decides on a category, Amazon Alexa asks for the slots that still must be filled in so that the intent is complete and can make the API call. In this case, they are the origin and destination stations as well as the date and time of departure. The origin and destination stations are of slot type AMAZON.DE_City, the date and time are of slot type AMAZON.DATE and AMAZON.TIME and thus all slots have a build-in slot type.

This means that an NLP model has been trained on the cities, date and time and thus the chance of correct speech recognition is relatively high.

The lambda function in the backend now sends a request to the Deutsche Bahn server. The result is then played back audibly on the Echo device and if the Echo device also has a display, the result is also shown graphically on the screen.

3.2 Spotify

Spotify is a music streaming service that has made over 70 million songs, audio books and podcasts available to 400 million active users since its founding in 2006 [16]. Spotify is available as a program on computers, as an app on Android and iPhone, and also on various voice assistants, including Amazon Alexa. To activate Spotify on Amazon Alexa, the Spotify account must first be linked to the Amazon account. After that, Spotify is saved as a music service on Amazon Alexa and the standard commands, such as play, pause, stop, louder, quieter are all forwarded to the Spotify skill. To play a song, you can activate the Spotify Skill by saying "Alexa, start Spotify!". A song title can also be added directly.

The recognition of song titles by the Spotify Skill works well. However, since there are a lot of songs on Spotify, the artist of the song usually must be named as well, otherwise Amazon Alexa plays the first song with the requested song title. We also noticed that certain artists with non-standard names, such as BLOKHE4D, are not recognized. Even with song title and artist name together it doesn't work very well in this case. However, with 70 million different songs available on Spotify, this is a relatively good performance. Most songs that are relatively high in the charts are still recognized very well.

3.3 Wikinator

Wikinator is an Amazon Alexa Skill, which was developed to find knowledge on the website wikipedia.org and to render it to the user [17]. For the Wikipedia encyclopedia, there are already a lot of skills, but all of them only find generic terms or do not return the correct article. Wikinator takes a different approach. The skill searches for terms and reads the title of the first article. If this is the article the user was looking for, the user can simply repeat the title and the skill reads the article to the user. If the article is not the user's desired search result, the user can simply say, "Next article!" or "Previous article!" [17] and the skill will read the title of the next search result. This allows the user to navigate through the various search results.

In addition to this search function, the user can also subsequently search a Wikipedia article that has been found. This works with the help of keywords. The skill searches the article for the user's keyword and returns relevant information.

3.4 Outcome

The analysis of the three Amazon Alexa Skills reveals a clear picture. Predefined terms or pre-trained speech models are very important for speech recognition to achieve a good usability of the skill. It is also of benefit to leave as little as possible to speech recognition. That means, it should be tried to generate as much information as possible from the context. A categorical search supports this system by minimizing the risk of incorrect input from a single function query. In addition, queries with very similar meanings can lead to conflicts between the individual utterances of the intents, and the user may get a wrong result.

4   Amazon Alexa - Technology Overview

This chapter presents Amazon software used for developing the Alexa skill for the university online search.

4.1   Amazon Alexa Developer Console

The Amazon Alexa Developer Console is the main entry point for all Amazon Alexa developers. Since Amazon Alexa is an online service, it must be stored somewhere and be accessible to all. To make it as easy as possible for developers, Amazon offers this hosting service. An Amazon Alexa Skill is therefore always stored on Amazon's servers from its first initialization, during its development and right up to its publication. The development process also takes place online. For this purpose, Amazon offers software developers an Integrated Development Environment (IDE). This can also be found in the Amazon Developer Console. It is also possible to write the entire code offline in an editor, but this complicates testing because it must be uploaded to the Amazon servers for each test.

Amazon offers three different methods for the backend to host an Alexa Skill. In the first case, Amazon will provide its servers and give the developer a Node.js template as a start file. The skill is then hosted entirely on Amazon's servers, both frontend and backend. Secondly, there is a similar method, but instead of Node.js, Python is used. So only the programming language is different. The third option is to host the skill itself on specifically designed hardware provided from the developer's company. This makes sense if the skill generates or requires very large amounts of data. For example, for music or video streaming applications.

The Developer Console consists of several modules (see Fig. 1). The Dashboard is the entry point for that. Here all current projects are shown where it is possible to edit monetization, view current invoices or payments, set the data rates of the hosting, and set general options for the developer account. Clicking on an ongoing project takes you to the skill-specific page, now you are in the Build module. Here, the basic settings of the Amazon Alexa skill are defined, such as the call name, the intents and utterances, the slots and slot types, multimodal responses, interfaces, and if a separate endpoint is used, this can also be defined here.

Code Module. This page functions as an online IDE. It works like a code editor such as Visual Studio or Notepad++. Here, you can edit the individual files of the lambda function and define what the backend should do. A request from the frontend arrives here, is processed, and a suitable response is created. This is also where the access to

Fig. 1. A Screenshot of the test environment in the Developer Console. The various modules are displayed at the top.

the S3 storage (Amazon's cloud storage for files) and the CloudWatch logs (the log files of the test environment) are located.

Text Module. In this module, the developer can test the programmed skill. Here, you can enter phrases via microphone or keyboard to test the frontend or the backend. This module acts like an Alexa simulator, and you get exactly the same output that a user would get later.

Distribution Module. The distribution module contains the settings for publishing the skill. This means that you can enter the name, a description, examples and other information about the skill.

Certification and Analysis are there to fix bugs and validate the skill, or to track the number of users after publication and get general statistics.

4.2 Alexa Presentation Language

Amazon Alexa is a digital voice assistant. Over time, however, the developers at Amazon have built small screens into the Echo devices. This has the advantage of not only being able to give the user auditory feedback, but also to display the search results graphically. Graphical feedback is much better for user experience than purely auditory feedback, because the user sees all the results at once and does not have to listen to them one after the other from Alexa.

The Alexa Presentation Language is for displaying content on the screens. The way this works is that in the backend, while formulating the result, a JSON file with the answer is passed to the frontend. In this file, the screen layout is defined by "document" and the basic framework for data formulation is provided. In the backend, the developer can now save the search results in a list and add them to the JSON file as "datasources". This basic framework is then populated with content. The JSON code is then passed with the response to the frontend, which then renders the content on the screen.

5 Implementation of the Alexa Skill

This chapter deals with the implementation of the Amazon Alexa Skills for the search at Graz University of Technology. In particular, the frontend, backend, the individual functions, and the queries.

5.1 Skill Invocation

Skill Invocations are used to activate an Amazon Alexa skill. For example:

"Alexa, start TU Graz!". Here you define the name of the skill, it should be short and concise and easy to understand.

In our case, we use t. u. graz. The dots after the letters ("t" and "u") show Amazon Alexa that the letters are pronounced and not spelled out in one word ("T. U. Graz" and not "tu Graz"). The upper and lower case of words makes no difference here, as Amazon Alexa automatically converts all sentences, words and letters to lower case. This simplifies the later parsing of the information.

Furthermore, there is the possibility to create Skill Launch Phrases, which are used to activate the skill without using the Invocation-name. For example, "Alexa, what is the weather for tomorrow?". This Launch Phrase directly activates the Intent of a weather skill and queries the weather for the next day. However, these Launch Phrases can only be created once the Amazon Alexa Skill has been released, so we'll leave it out here.

5.2 Interaction Model

The interaction model defines the conversation between the user and Amazon Alexa. In this chapter the intents are specified, the utterances are defined, and the slots as well as slot types are determined.

Intents. Intents define the various functions of the skill. Depending on which intent the user activates, the specified intent is executed, and the function is called in the backend. There are five intents, which are already included in most interaction models by default. These are AMAZON.CancelIntent, AMAZON.HelpIntent, AMAZON.StopIntent, AMAZON.NavigateHomeIntent and AMAZON.FallbackIntent. These describe the functionalities that every Amazon Alexa Skill should have. The user should be able to "cancel" the skill, ask for "help", "stop" it, and "navigate home" to the welcome message. These four intents call the functions in the backend ("IntentHandler"). These functions are also included by default and should be customized by the developer to fit the design of the rest of the skill [11]. If the user says something that cannot be assigned to an intent, the fallback intent is triggered. It returns an error message that describes the further procedure to the user. This could be something like: "I'm sorry, I didn't understand that. Can you repeat that?".

In addition to these required intents, there are the custom intents that determine the functionality of the skill.

Here we have introduced the intents "room", "person" and "course". These are the three categories for which the TU-Graz-Search should work.

Room-Intent. To search for rooms at Graz University of Technology, there is the room intent. This requires different utterances to trigger this Intent. The elementary utterance is simply "room". This allows the user to select one of the categories after being asked if he/she wants to search for a room, person or course and thus trigger the intent. A few more utterances would be something like "where is the {request}", "I am looking for the lecture hall {request}", "where is the {request}".

Where {request} is always the slot to be filled with the search query. One advantage is that utterances like "room" or "auditorium" can also be said on their own, since the slot fulfillment setting causes the {request} slot to be filled in any case before the intent sends the query to the backend. So even if an utterance like "room" is said and the slot is not yet filled, or if the word is not understood, Amazon Alexa will prompt with a voice prompt to fill the slot. After the utterance says "room", Amazon Alexa prompts the utterance with the question "What room are you looking for?" to name a room.

In addition to Slot Fulfillment, there is also the setting Slot Confirmation or Intent Confirmation. This setting is used to ask the user once again whether what Amazon Alexa has understood is correct and reflects the user's intention. Amazon Alexa asks ("Are you sure you want to search for {request}?") and the user must answer "Yes" or "No".

Person Intent. The principle of the intents and utterances works here very similar to the other intents, only the utterances are different, and the settings vary a bit. In this intent we also have a categorical utterance ("Person") which triggers the intent. Another utterance with slot would be: "give me information about {request}". The filling of the slots happens here again with Slot-Fulfillment and Slot-Confirmation.

Course Intent. The last intent of our skill is responsible for searching for courses. As a categorical utterance there is again the word "course", and as an utterance with slot the sentence "Search for course {request}". The filling of the slots happens here again with Slot-Fulfillment and Slot-Confirmation. Slot-Confirmation.

Problems with Intents. One problem that mainly affects the Person intent is recognizing the language of the user. Amazon Alexa is good at recognizing colloquial words and phrases, but very poor at recognizing proper names or last names. The language model, which is adjusted by the settings in the interaction model, is not trained for the different last names, and thus does not know how or what it should recognize when the user searches for a person. This affects searching for people as well as searching in general. It is very difficult with a voice user interface to develop a language model that can know all the words in a language and all the technical terms and interpret them correctly in context. Amazon Alexa Skills are relatively good at having simple conversations where the manner of the conversation is predictable.

However, Amazon offers a partial solution here with what it calls slot validation. Here, Amazon allows developers to adjust certain slots so that they only recognize values that have been programmed in in advance. For example, in a slot that is supposed to recognize food for a shopping list, the food could be programmed in as a word beforehand. This way, Amazon Alexa subsequently knows what words to expect from the user and can match the user's spoken phrase with this internal list and find the right word. Basically, it works like a dictionary.

One limitation, however, is that this list of pre-programmed words can only be 1000 words long. This is probably sufficient for a grocery shopping list, but a problem for a people search with several thousand different names. Here one would have to filter out and enter the most probable thousand persons to solve this problem.

5.3 Multimodal Responses

Certain Echo devices, such as the Amazon Echo Show 8 or the Amazon Echo Show 15, not only have a microphone and speaker, but they also have a build-in display. This allows developers to create visual feedback in addition to auditory feedback to the user.

Fig. 2. Screenshot of the development environment for visual multimodal responses.

To accomplish this, we use the Alexa Presentation Language (APL). With the help of APL, we can create a graphical user interface that can provide the user with even more information, in addition to the VUI. For this purpose, Amazon provides a tool in the Developer Console that we can use to create such a multimodal response. This tool is shown in Fig. 2.

Using drag-and-drop, individual modular elements can be dragged onto the screen and customized. This mainly uses placeholders, which are later replaced by the actual values in the backend.

Fig. 3. Screenshot of a multimodal response: search results displayed as a list.

We use the display to show a welcome message and a first tip on how to use our Amazon Alexa Skill. In addition, the search results of rooms and courses are displayed in a list. Extra information such as the room number, or the address are additionally displayed in the respective entry in the list. An example of this list can be seen in Fig. 3.

5.4 Lambda-Function

The lambda function processes the requests of the frontend. Each intent in the frontend has a corresponding intent handler in the backend. Thus, if e.g. the room intent is called, it passes the information to the room handler, which then processes this information. The structure of the lambda endpoint is explained in Fig. 4. In the file lambda_funtion.py the intent handlers are registered. The handlers.py file contains all handlers.

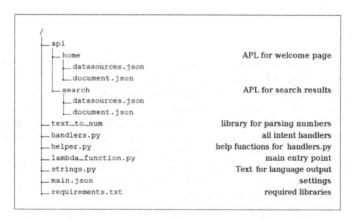

Fig. 4. Representation of the directory of the lambda endpoint.

6 Discussion

Since its release in 2015, Amazon Alexa has become a very large platform with thousands of skills. Most of the skills are small games, puzzles, news, tools, music services or applications that represent companies. Most of them have a very limited repertoire of intents, which makes them quite simple and very easy to use.

One problem with a voice user interface is the small amount of information exchanged compared to the time the user must spend on it. If you give the user the same amount of time to look through an entire list of results on the screen, as it takes Amazon Alexa to read just two of those results aloud, the user has probably already read through the entire list of results. This major disadvantage of VUIs makes them inferior to GUIs and therefore will never have such a presence in the modern world as GUIs.

The developed Amazon Alexa Skill described in this paper is able to recognize three different search categories and give the user an answer to a simple search query. This answer consists of a spoken phrase and a list of search results displayed on a screen.

Combining a voice user interface with a graphical user interface, as is already the case with certain Amazon Echo devices or Google Nest Hub, improves the user experience many times over, as the advantages of both systems add up and the disadvantages are compensated for by the respective other system.

Extensions for our skill in this case would mean even better prioritization of search results. The functionality of the search can be extended by navigating to the lecture hall, writing an email to the person you are looking for, registering for a course, or integrating online services of the TU Graz.

Going further, this skill could be extended to other platforms like Google's "Now" or Microsoft's "Cortana", and even more functionalities could be added. These could include directions to the exact address of the lecture hall, or an appointment calendar that checks the students' online system to find out when their next lecture is scheduled to begin and informs the students accordingly.

References

1. Weiss, M., Ebner, M., Ebner, M.: Speech-based learning with amazon alexa. In: Bastiaens, T. (ed.) Proceedings of EdMedia + Innovate Learning, pp. 156–163. Association for the Advancement of Computing in Education (AACE), United States (2021). Accessed 27 July 2021, https://www.learntechlib.org/primary/p/219651/
2. Bilic, L., Ebner, M., Ebner, M.: A voice-enabled game based learning application using amazon's echo with alexa voice service: a game regarding geographic facts about Austria and Europe. Int. J. Interact. Mob. Technol. (iJIM) 14(3), 226–232 (2020)
3. Schoegler, P., Ebner, M., Ebner, M.: The use of alexa for mass education. In: Proceedings of EdMedia + Innovate Learning, pp. 721–730. Association for the Advancement of Computing in Education (AACE), The Netherlands (2020)
4. Viken, A.: The history of personal digital assistants 1980–2000. Agile Mob. 10 (2009)
5. Hauswald, J., et al.: Sirius: an open end-to-end voice and vision personal assistant and its implications for future warehouse scale computers. ACM SIGPLAN Notices 50, 223–238 (2015). https://doi.org/10.1145/2775054.2694347

6. Bitkom e.V und Deutsches Forschungszentrum für Künstliche Intelligenz. Künstliche Intelligenz. https://www.dfki.de/fileadmin/user/5Fupload/import/9744/5F171012-KI-Gipfel papier-online.pdf, Accessed 30 Oct 2021
7. Russell, S.J., Norvig, P.: Artificial Intelligence: A Modern Approach, 4 edn. Pearson (2020)
8. Amazon. Unsere Geschichte: Was aus einer Garagen-Idee werden kann? (2020). https://www.aboutamazon.de/%C3%BCber-amazon/unsere-geschichte-was-aus-einer-garagen-idee-werden-kann, Accessed 20 Oct 2021
9. Strohbach, T.: Amazon Alexa: 28 unterschiedliche Stimmen in 9 Sprachen verfügbar (2018). https://www.amazon-watchblog.de/technik/1475-amazon-alexa-9-sprachen-28-stimmen.html, Accessed 15 Nov 2021
10. Canbek, N.G., Mutlu, M.: On the track of artificial intelligence: learning with intelligent personal assistants. Int. J. Hum. Sci. **13**, 592 (2016). https://doi.org/10.14687/ijhs.v13i1.3549
11. Amazon. Amazon Alexa Voice AI|Alexa Developer Official Site (2021). https://developer.amazon.com/en-US/docs/alexa/ask-overviews/what-is-the-alexa-skills-kit.html, Accessed 15 Nov 2021
12. Haase, P., et al.: Alexa, Ask Wikidata! voice interaction with knowledge graphs using amazon alexa. In: SEMWEB (2017)
13. Oberoi, A.: The rise of voice user interface (VUI) (2020). https://insights.daffodilsw.com/blog/the-rise-of-voice-user-interface-vui, Accessed 28 Oct 2021
14. Hunt, N.: Voice input: the interface problem - UX Collective (2018). https://uxdesign.cc/voice-input-the-interface-problem-1700be45ec18, Accessed 15 Nov 2021
15. Redaktion, D.B.: Deutsche Bahn Skill auf Amazon Alexa: Reiseauskunft per Sprachsteuerung jetzt noch flexibler (2021). https://inside.bahn.de/amazon-alexa/, Accessed 02 Nov 2021
16. Martin, M., Kühne, F.: Spotify: Test|Kosten|Unterstützte Geräte im Überblick|NETZWELT (2021). https://www.netzwelt.de/spotify/testbericht.html, Accessed 02 Nov 2021
17. Martin, A.: Wikinator: Amazon.de. https://www.amazon.de/Alexander-Martin-Wikinator/dp/B07LFFHYLM, Accessed 03 Nov 2021

Tackling the Challenges of Acquiring Web Videos for STEM Hands-On Learning: Example of a Fake Hologram and a Proposed Learning Model

Yu-Liang Ting[1], Shin-Ping Tsai[2], Yaming Tai[3](✉), and Teng-Hui Tseng[4]

[1] Department of Technology Application and Human Resource Development,
National Taiwan Normal University, Taipei, Taiwan
[2] Department of Special Education, National Taipei University of Education, Taipei, Taiwan
[3] Department of Children English Education, National Taipei University of Education, Taipei,
Taiwan
yaming@tea.ntue.edu.tw
[4] Department of Communication Engineering, Asia Eastern University of Science and
Technology, New Taipei, Taiwan

Abstract. The web offers rich learning resources, including technology education. With the advocate of hands-on learning and STEM education, many web videos teach users how to use technological tools to create an STEM artifacts and acquire related science knowledge. These videos were adopted by teachers in their classroom and followed closely as pro-claimed technology education. As web credibility is a challenge and how students approach the topics to develop systematic knowledge are crucial, this study proposed a learning model to address these challenges. The model was embedded into a teacher training to have teachers self-experience these challenges. Participating teachers were expected to construct their pedagogical knowledge inductively, and their responses to the proposed learning were collected. With the participation of 27 in-service teachers, the results demonstrated teachers' recognition and support of the proposed model. However, their belief and concerns regarding its implementation generated uncertainty. Study results broaden the spectrum of hands-on teacher training.

Keywords: Hands-on learning · Teacher training · Web credibility · STEM

1 Introduction

Hands-on learning motivates students and enhances their learning. It refers to acquiring knowledge and skills from learners' own experiences and placing learners' participation in practice at the center of the learning process. Students engaging in hands-on activities were able to analyze their own learning experience through reflection, evaluation, and reconstruction to draw ideas from the current experience in light of their prior experience [1]. Students participating in hands-on learning considered the course to be interesting, valuable, meaningful, and motivating [2]. However, ideas that develop without any prior knowledge of the subject may be wrong. For example, when determining the causes of science events, people reason linearly rather than systemically and use obvious variables rather than considering nonobvious variables [3]. People make assumptions concerning the causes and effects of phenomena and have expectations for the behavior of nonobvious, implicit causes and effects in scientific phenomena [4]. People also tend to intuitively identify causal relationships, which often results in wrong ideas [3, 5, 6]. For example, when considering pressure and why a balloon partially deflates when driving from the mountains to the coast, students reason using obvious agents, such as a hole in the balloon, rather than considering differences in air pressure between the two regions [3].

Regarding technology-supported scientific phenomena that students have never experienced, their reasoning and learning of technology and related science may be a challenge because it is much easier to focus on the most obvious single concrete variable as an explanation rather than consider the interaction between multiple abstract variables. Moreover, science has problems with the specific terminology and scientific language. In particular, involved substances, mathematics, and symbols are not clearly differentiated [7]. Moreover, inappropriate teaching methods and materials may bring students wrong ideas about the subject content. The problem of the use of inappropriate teaching methods can be solved by equipping teachers with appropriate pedagogical resources, such as by recommending alternative strategies to the traditional approaches and using more structured teaching models [7]. Inappropriate materials, especially those found online, can mislead students and should be avoided by equipping students with digital literacy, such as the ability to critically evaluate the credibility of data.

This study uses the example of holograms. Many websites, such as YouTube, provide inaccurate information on holograms. There are many YouTube videos on how to use smartphones for creating three-dimensional (3D) images, which many web users claim to be holograms. These videos are misused by some teachers as teaching material for hands-on learning. This study addressed this challenge by proposing a model and emphasizing the importance of a developmental learning process to guide students in using technology and exploring related science concepts. Instead of evaluating the proposed model in a students' learning the proposed model was evaluated by in-service teachers to justify its educational value and identify challenges teachers may encounter while implementing it. These results and discussions were expected to broaden the spectrum of teacher training about the adoption of web materials in hands-on education.

2   Literature Review

Misuse of Hologram

The technology displayed in Fig. 1 has widely been referred to as a smartphone-supported hologram.

Most YouTube video aimed to teach learners how to use a smartphone for creating a so-called "hologram." Holography is a technology that involves 3D recording and projection. Developed by Gabor [8], a hologram is an optics technique based on wave physics that is dedicated to wavefront reconstruction. It is a photographic recording of

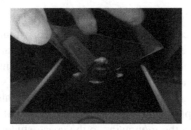

Fig. 1. Still from a video obtained from the work done by author's students

a light field rather than of an image captured using a lens; it displays a fully three-dimensional image of the subject of the holograph, which is seen without the aid of special glasses or other intermediate optics (Wikipedia). Hence, holography should not be confused with lenticular or other 3D display technologies that can produce superficially similar results but are based on conventional lens imaging, such as smartphone-supported 3D image projection.

Web Credibility

As the advance of web technology, various tools and networks provide convenient mechanisms helping students access versatile science knowledge. One of these tools is videos in social networks such as YouTube, where it is easy for teachers to generate interesting content to teach and disseminate science subject content. Some physics instructors even have their students create educational short videos as their homework Tai or laboratory results to present what they learn in the classes [9]. Furthermore, some studies had students create their own mobile applications to learn not only the subject content of physics but also how to collaborate with people from different disciplines [10, 11]. Hence, the web can be referred to as the largest library and laboratory in supporting versatile learning activities; it offers many attractive methods for acquiring instructional information and learning resources [12, 13]. There is an increased focus on web literacy skills, where people search digital information sources and read, assess, and synthesize that information [14]. When people use web resources for learning, three aspects of interconnected web literacy skills have been identified: searching, reading, and evaluating [15]. With the successful acquisition of these three skills, people may coherently integrate different pieces of information to develop knowledge [14]. Among these skills, given the easy accessibility of masses of unregulated information, evaluating skills are crucial because they facilitate the critical differentiation and organization of online information. It is imperative that people adopt a critical approach to information and develop the ability to evaluate the information they encounter.

Challenges in Hands-On Learning

Direct contact with objects and consequence manipulation encourage learners to think as well as formulate and test hypotheses [16]. Some educators assert that such learning contexts, in which students encounter authentic problems in information-rich settings and must construct their own solutions, provide an effective constructivist learning experience. This implies a shift in emphasis from teaching a discipline as a body of knowledge toward an exclusive emphasis on acquiring knowledge of a discipline by experiencing its processes and procedures [17, 18]. Moreover, this suggestion also implies that knowledge can be learned through experience that is based primarily on the procedures of the discipline. This perspective led to the proposal of extensive practical or project work, namely experience-based hands-on activities, which are treated by many educators as constructivist learning that rejects instruction based on the facts, principles, and theories that comprise the content of a discipline [19].

A basic premise of constructivism is that meaningful learning occurs when the learner strives to make sense of the presented material by selecting relevant incoming information, organizing it into a coherent structure, and integrating it with other organized knowledge [20]. Learning involving only hands-on activity may fail to promote the cognitive process of selecting relevant incoming information or fail to support students in accessing the material. Learning should promote appropriate cognitive processing in learners rather than promote hands-on activity as end in itself.

Regarding the structural understanding of science subject content in hands-on learning, Bruner (1966) described knowledge in terms of three levels of representation: enactive, iconic, and symbolic. These modes of representation implicitly indicate the stages of knowledge development, a sequential graduation progressing from working with hands-on physical materials to reasoning with iconic and ultimately symbolic representations [21]. Johnstone [22] gave explicit examples from chemistry to elucidate the connection between another three levels of representation: macroscopic, microscopic, and symbolic. It is difficult for students to develop an intuitive understanding of the connections among these three levels [23].

Effective learning is related to the simultaneous use of the microscopic and symbolic components of knowledge [24]. The use of multiple representations with explicit connections fosters students' visuospatial reasoning [25]. Students should be supported in forging links among these three levels of representation to help them understand the invisible particulate world and connect it to its tangible emergent properties in real-world phenomena. Integrating the three levels of representation provides a greater conceptual understanding of the subject content.

Some concrete experience may be attributed to the ideas used to describe the bulk properties of matter, such as temperature, pressure, and density, and the macro level seems to encompass both actual phenomena and the concepts used to describe them [26, 27]. Hence, teachers like to transition from the macro level directly to the symbolic representation. Students might be unable to understand this transition. Incorporating hands-on practical work is one way to help students strengthen their understanding of the connections between macroscopic and microscopic ideas [28]. Even with hands-on work and experiences, the learning task should provide various types of representations and train students to integrate them. However, making this transition of learning from the macroscopic to the representational level appears to be challenging. Although students do not see any connection between these levels, they are given responsibility for selecting a mental model for the submicroscopic level; in this case, they are develop ideas on their own, and most of these ideas are wrong [7]. For example, the phenomenon of a 3D virtual image is interesting to students, and they may incorrectly use the newly acquired terminology of "hologram" without acquiring knowledge of its scientific properties.

3 Proposed Learning Model

This study asserts that after conducting hands-on experiments, students are asked to describe and interpret the observations not only at the macro level but also micro and symbolic levels as well as describe the interconnections among the three levels. Only when the structural description integrating these levels of representations has been made clearly will a thorough knowledge of the content be successfully attained. For example, touch could provide information that relates to the microstructure of an object, whereas vision could provide information that relates to the macrostructure of it; thus, the combination of these components facilitates a better understanding of a multidimensional object or system [29]. Sensory input originating from corresponding manipulation or motor skills may not be especially crucial for learning. What appears to be important is whether the various aspects of knowledge content are coherently presented to students and retained by them.

An instruction process that employs Kolb's experiential learning model is proposed for enabling students to form interconnections among various representations of a subject's content and develop structural understanding (Fig. 2). The instruction process aims to help novice learners assimilate and accommodate the three aforementioned levels of representations through a developmental process. In this process, the experiential learning cycle is proposed to guide the design of instructional representation and development of students' cognitive activities that integrate these phases (cycles) and allow for a fluent transition among different types of representations. Kolb et al. [30] suggested that learning from experience is an appropriate method for acquiring knowledge. A related supporting argument is embodied cognition research, which demonstrates that people form metaphorical associations between physical activities and conceptual abstractions [31].

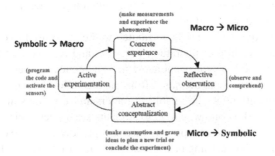

Fig. 2. Proposed learning model, adopted from a modified Kolb's [32] model

The proposed learning model associates representational levels with Kolb's model. Kolb's learning cycle comprises four steps: concrete experience, reflection, abstract conceptualization, and active experimentation. In addition to the four steps, the model also focuses on three levels of knowledge representations: macro (physical experiences), micro (invisible elements), and symbolic (conceptual understanding) representations. With the activities across these four steps, the level of knowledge representation will transform. When students engage in a hands-on activity, they first establish observational experience in the physical world, which refers to the macroscopic representation of knowledge. As the students move to the phase of reflection, they consider their understanding of a learning experience and integrate their knowledge. Through reflective thinking, students conceptualize their phenomenological experience and form a microscopic representation of knowledge. In the fourth phase, "active experimentation," students actively construct their conceptual schemes and revise them with more experiences to establish a symbolic representation of knowledge with fidelity. Finally, students can apply their symbolic representation of knowledge in the physical world.

The proposed learning model aims to address two general concerns regarding hands-on activities, namely that students do not learn the underlying scientific concepts through these activities and that the knowledge to be learned may not be deliverable through direct instruction [19, 33]. In particular, owing to the lack of associations between the qualitative description of a science phenomenon at the macroscopic level and the underlying scientific processes at the microscopic level, students must be guided through the associations between successive levels of scientific representations necessary for proper abstract conceptualization [34]. The proposed learning model aims to increase learners' awareness of the challenge of conceptualizing phenomenological experiences (e.g., observation and description) and acquire understanding of the scientific theories and principles behind it.

Within this broadly "constructivist" perspective, it is believed that learners construct mental representations of the world around them and use these to interpret new situations and guide their actions [35]. These mental representations or conceptual schemes are then revised according to how they fit the experience. Learning is thus seen as an adaptive process in which the learners' conceptual schemes are progressively reconstructed to adhere to a broadening range of experiences and ideas [35]. It is also seen as an active process of "sense-making" over which the learner has some control. Active experimentation is thus the fourth phase of Kolb's learning cycle. It allows learners to test the theory or model they have developed in the previous stage and put it into practice or plan for a subsequent experience [36]. Hence, the focus of active experimentation is not the activity itself but how the activity supports students in testing concepts.

Instead of behavioral activity (e.g., hands-on activity), the type of activity that most effectively promotes meaningful learning is cognitive activity (e.g., selecting, organizing, and integrating knowledge). Instead of depending solely on learning through action or discussion, the most genuine approach to constructivist learning is learning by thinking [37]. Methods that rely on action or discussing should be judged not with respect to the amount of action or discussion involved but rather the degree to which these activities promote appropriate cognitive processing. For example, regarding the topic of the hologram, the proposed activity asks students to answer the following questions on the basis of the newly formed conceptual model: 1) How do you create a smartphone-supported 3D image? 2) How can you use the model to explain the formation of a hologram? and 3) is the smartphone-supported 3D image a hologram?

The proposed model does not equate concrete experience in Kolb's model to macro-level representation. In each phase of Kolb's learning cycle, it is suggested that the three levels of representations be fully utilized to help students achieve the learning goal in each cycle. For example, in the cycle of concrete experience, the technology of augmented reality overlaying symbolic representation on a physical artifact in a hands-on activity helps students focus on and acquire the targeted skills and information. In addition, in discussions related to STEM learning, students explore and integrate their skills and knowledge in science and mathematics and use technological tools to create engineering work [38, 39]. STEM domain content may exist in the four phases of Kolb's learning cycle and present in each phase with these three types of representations. For example, regarding the smartphone-supported fake hologram, students use an app-authoring tool to support the illustration of mirrored images on a screen (concrete phase). Creating the image reflected through a plastic pyramid requires mathematics: namely sketching an appropriate trapezoid shape on the graph paper. Optics is also involved in forming the 3D vision. In the abstract phase, notes can be delivered to students and help them reflect on the math and optics in symbolic format and integrate their understanding with what they have learned in traditional science and mathematics classes. The phases of Kolb's learning cycle and types of knowledge representations interweave to form a systematic approach for helping students construct a structural understanding of a topic.

4 Evaluation

The proposed preliminary teaching model needed to obtain teachers' responses before its implementation in classroom. The evaluation was conducted in a teachers' training program, in which 27 in-service high school teachers of the technology education were invited. The training was held in computer lab with Internet access. The evaluation was to determine whether they misunderstood the term "hologram" and obtain their responses to the proposed learning model. Participants were guided through the following three steps to understand the proposed model and express their opinions.

Step 1)
This step aimed to engage participants in self-exploration of the subject content on the basis of the perceptually oriented image. Participants were presented with Fig. 3 without mentioning any terminology, and their mission was to design a lesson plan for teaching students how to create such works in class. There are many popular web videos for teaching people how to use a smartphone to create such works that are mistakenly referred to as holograms. Most of the videos focus on hands-on activity.

Participants were reminded of STEM education. Because not all of the participants were familiar with STEM or its implementation in class, the teaching goal of STEM was defined as training students to integrate subject content acquired in their prior classes, especially in mathematics, physics, and technology, to solve an engineering problem. For example, in Fig. 1, the cutting angle of the plastic pyramid and the symmetry of the four images on the screen of a smartphone are related to mathematics. In addition, how the 3D images are created is related to light reflection and follows the law of reflection in optics. However, this STEM knowledge is seldom mentioned in most web videos, which focus solely on the hands-on work.

Participants were given 40 min to collect information, design a lesson plan, and prepare a related curriculum supporting a 2-h class for high school students. After that, each participant answered the following survey questions.

Q1: How did you find the material? Which website did you refer to? Please specify.

Q2: What is a hologram? If you were to teach this topic in a class, how would you explain it?

This step aimed to examine how the participants designed their lesson plan and whether they mistakenly identified the image in Fig. 3 as a hologram.

Step 2)

Participants were given a fifteen-minute lecture by the instructor on the topic of holograms. The lecture aimed to present a basic idea of how hologram technology is achieved by using laser light to illuminate the object and then recording the laser light scattered from the object directly onto the recording medium. The recorded information was then used with the laser again to reconstruct and display a fully 3D image of the hologram subject. The reflection of light in optics was then presented to illustrate how the propagation of light is reflected by a mirror. In addition, the structure of human vision was illustrated by referring to the structure of the source, propagation, and reception of light. The final slide presented Fig. 1, which compelled participants to think again about how the image was formed. There are four symmetrically arranged images on the screen of a smartphone, and through reflection, the four images can create what appears to be a 3D virtual image in the air.

After the presentation, participants were asked the following questions.

Q1: What is your opinion about the web information?

Q2: After learning exactly what a hologram is, will you modify the lesson plan you just designed? If so, how?

This step serves to make participants aware of the importance of web literacy, especially skills for evaluating the credibility of information. This design should compel participants to think about what was incorrect in their exploration. By comparing the scientific idea delivered by the instructor and their own ones, the participants could intensify the recently gained idea [7] and recognize the importance of digital literacy. The instruction also aims to make participants think about the kind of optics knowledge they should pursue along with the physical artifacts they learn to make.

Step 3)

This step aimed to present the proposed learning model and collect participants' responses to the model. After participants were equipped with knowledge on the misuse of the term "hologram," they were guided to reflect on how to build optics knowledge in a structural manner such that they can cope with similar challenges in further exploration of optics, especially regarding 3D images. This step also aimed to remind participants of the types of representation other than macro-representation (perceptual experience) for knowledge of physical artifacts. It motivated and helped participants conceptualize the basic model of vision formation, on the basis of which they could differentiate the subtle variations in optics techniques.

In addition to including the Kolb's experiential learning model, the three levels of representations, namely macro, micro, and symbolic (representational), were presented

(Fig. 3) to educate participants regarding the levels of representation for a chemical reaction. The presentation also elaborated on the cognitive roles that these three types of representation may play in delivering subject content and, most importantly, how they can complement and supplement each other to help students construct a correct and comprehensive understanding of a topic.

Fig. 3. Three types of representations in chemistry (Note: This figure may not be correct in a chemistry reaction process)

Participants were also given Fig. 4 as a sample presentation for adopting the proposed teaching model for delivering the topic of the law of the lever in physics.

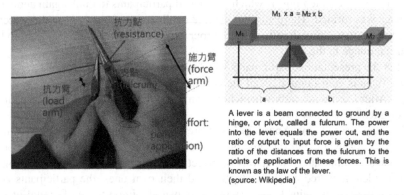

Fig. 4. Three levels of representation for illustrating the law of the lever in physics (The right-hand side is about the law of the lever and accessed from https://en.wikipedia.org/wiki/Lever)

Figure 4 shows the three levels of representation in illustrating the law of the lever in physics. This may refer to Mayer's multimedia learning theory. However, Mayer focused only on multimedia, without mentioning the senses used during hands-on learning, such as the haptic. In Fig. 4, a student uses his bare hands to operate the pliers and acquires a sense of force; he can change the holding position of the plier handles to consolidate his haptic experience with the theory of the law of the lever. This is not to be confused with the provision of concrete experience (macro-representation) in the phase of reflection. Various types of representations are suggested to be adopted in each Kolb's phase of learning for helping students reach the required cognitive status of each phase.

Right after the presentation, participants were asked the following questions.

Q1: What is your opinion of the proposed teaching model? Does it have any educational value? If so, what?

Q2: What kind of topic or subject content can the proposed teaching model be applied to? And why?

Q3: If you apply the proposed teaching model in the classroom, what are the challenges you may face?

5   Results

Step 1) Only given a perceptually oriented image (Fig. 3), participants conducted online self-exploration and design using hands-on learning. Under such circumstances, the participants' responses were as follows.

Q1: How did you find the material? Which website did you refer to? Please specify.

A total of 55 websites were mentioned by the 27 participants: 43 in Chinese and 12 in English. Participants mainly used Google and YouTube as search tools to find the material. Two participants replied that they had done this work before, and by examining their responses to Q2, they still thought the work was a hologram (T2 and T12; the identities of participating teachers were coded as T1–T27).

Q2: What is a hologram? If you were to teach this topic in a class, how would you explain it?

Of the 27 participants, one did not answer the question and 20 participants incorrectly referred to the technology displayed in Fig. 3 as a hologram. T11 drew a diagram (Fig. 5) to demonstrate his answer. However, his diagram and associated writing were about the reflection of light and not related to holograms.

Fig. 5. One participant's wrong answer about how the hologram was created (Translation of the notes: Human eyes can catch the virtual image by reflection and transparency.)

T24 seemed to correctly describe that a hologram is the technique of recording the frequency and phase of the scattered laser. However, T24 mentioned that he will ask students to do the same work in Fig. 3, which is not possible in current high school classrooms. This indicated that T24 was not aware of the contradiction between the definition of the hologram he gave and the hands-on work that he was thinking of.

Step 2) After being instructed regarding what the hologram was, participants responded to the questions as follows.

Q1: What is your opinion about the web information?

Of the 27 participants, credibility was mentioned by 25 participants. In addition to the matter of web credibility, T9 and T11 added that teachers should rely on their expertise to verify the web materials before delivering them to students.

Q2: After understanding exactly what a hologram is, will you modify the lesson plan you just designed? If so, how?

Of the 27 participants, 23 replied that they will modify the title as "light reflection" instead of "hologram." Among the 23 participants, T26 replied that he will attempt to understand more about the topic and only present the content that he is confident about. Of the other four, T4 said he would attempt to integrate the content of both "light reflection" and "hologram"; T2 said that his approach would depend on the classroom circumstance, such as students' needs and course requirements; T12 said he would focus on hands-on work; and T17 said he would not teach this topic.

Step 3) After being presented with the proposed learning model, participants responded to the questions as follows.

Q1: What is your opinion on the proposed teaching model? Does it have any educational value? If so, what?

	Themes and sample response(s)	Number
1	It changed the way I thought that hands-on learning is delivered T25: It increases students' level of cognition	2
2	Science should be explored from multiple perspectives (micro and symbolic levels)	3
3	It clarified the cycle of the learning process (Kolb's) T5: It connected experience with knowledge; T6: It clarified the reciprocal relationship among each stage of learning	15
4	Systematic presentation of the subject content	1
5	This model helps teachers develop pedagogical content knowledge, and teachers need such a model to reflect on their teaching and understand its educational value	1

Q2: What kind of topic or subject content can the proposed teaching model be applied to? Why?

	Topic or subject content	Why?	Num
1	Hands-on learning	To help students reflect on the content and build correct concepts T5: Flying a small airplane to learn about air dynamics; T6: Wall painting (the pigment, binder, and solvent)	15
2	All kinds of topics	T7: Any topic related to living T8: Even if students have prior knowledge of a certain topic, they must engage in design work and deepen their existing knowledge	4

Q3: If you apply the proposed teaching model in the classroom, what are the challenges you may face?

	Statement	Num
1	Class time limitation. It takes students a great deal of time to transition from hands-on work to the reflection on theories	2
2	Teachers need time and experience to understand the topic and apply the teaching model T5: Teachers must understand students' thought and cognitive status T11: Teachers must determine how to make these steps coherent and in sync with each other and how to conduct the evaluation T12: Teachers must understand the extent to which the subject content can be delivered to students T9: Constructing abstract concepts is important in learning; however, it is difficult to find concrete artifacts to support such learning	12
3	Students' lack of prior knowledge, reluctance, incapability of critical thinking, unwillingness to connect theories with experience, and hesitation in performing the experiment	12

6 Discussions and Conclusions

This study aimed to draw attention to concerns that are generally ignored by most teachers, such as web literacy and structural understanding of a scientific topic. In this study, the in-service teachers learned about holograms by watching hands-on-activity videos online, on the basis of which they described how they would teach on the topic of holograms. Participating teachers' responses about such proposal were collected under the theme of linking contemporary important educational issues of web credibility and hands-on learning. The results showed that almost all participants misunderstood the concept of holograms and were unaware of the problem of web credibility. Only two out of the 27 participants emphasized that teachers should rely on their expertise to verify the web materials. The results indicated that participants encountered difficulties in the connection of macro and micro levels of representation. This finding is consistent with the results of Johnson [40]: the directionality of commonsense reasoning from the observable (macro) to the inferential (micro) levels might be related to learners' propensity for applying their macroscopic reasoning in making sense of abstract and inaccessible microscopic phenomena. People tend to use their prior knowledge, which may be everyday knowledge instead of scientific knowledge, to link the observable (macro) to the abstract (micro) phenomena.

Regarding the proposed learning model, participants commented that this model could develop teachers' pedagogical content knowledge, which in turn help students connect their experience with knowledge and increase level of cognition. Participants also suggested other topics to which teachers could further apply this proposed model, such as painting a wall in addressing the pigment, binder, and solvent and flying a small airplane to learn about aerodynamics. Finally, participants also identified challenges that teachers may face in applying the model, including class time limitation, teachers' lack of pedagogical knowledge, and students' lack of prior knowledge, inability to think critically, and inability to conceptualize knowledge. The contribution of this study to science and technology education is the proposal of integrating the macro–micro–symbolic representation framework with Kolb's learning cycle. Integrating Kolb's and Johnstone's models better explains and supports students' hands-on learning and broadens the spectrum of teacher training in hands-on education.

References

1. Andresen, L., Boud, D., Cohen, R.: Experience-based learning. In: Foley, G. (ed.) Understanding Adult Education and Training. Allen & Unwin (1995)
2. Bruguier, L.R., Greathouse Amador, L.M.: New educational environments aimed at developing intercultural understanding while reinforcing the use of English in experience-based learning. Profile: Issues Teach. Prof. Dev. **14**(2), 195–211 (2012)
3. Hung, W.: Enhancing systems-thinking skills with modelling. Br. J. Edu. Technol. **39**(6), 1099–1120 (2008)
4. Grotzer, T.A., Bell, B.: Negotiating the funnel: guiding students toward understanding elusive generative concepts. In: Hetland, L., Veenema, S. (eds.) The Project Zero Classroom. Project Zero, Harvard Graduate School of Education, Cambridge (1999)
5. Barbas, A., Psillos, D.: Causal reasoning as a base for advancing a systemic approach to simple electrical circuits. Res. Sci. Educ. **27**(3), 445–459 (1997)
6. Nisbett, R.: Human Inference: Strategies and Shortcomings of Social Judgment. Prentice-Hall, Englewood Cliffs (1980)
7. Barke, H., et al.: Students' misconceptions and how to overcome them. In: Misconceptions in Chemistry, pp. 21–36. Springer, Heidelberg (2009)
8. Gabor, D.: A new microscopic principle. Nature **161**(4098), 777–778 (1948)
9. Aragoneses, A., Messer, R.: Developing educational YouTube videos as a tool to learn and teach physics. Phys. Teach. **58**(7), 488–490 (2020)
10. Tai, Y., Ting, Y.: English -learning mobile app designing for engineering students' cross-disciplinary learning and collaboration. Australas. J. Educ. Technol. **36**, 120–136 (2019). https://doi.org/10.14742/ajet.4999
11. Tseng, T., et al.: Students' self-authoring mobile App for integrative learning of STEM. Int. J. Electr. Eng. Educ. 0020720918800438 (2018). https://doi.org/10.1177/0020720918800438
12. Tai, Y., et al.: A proposed cohesive use of online discussion board from the aspects of instructional and social interactions in engineering education. Int. J. Online Pedagog. Course Des. **8**(3), 33–44 (2018)
13. Neo, M.: Developing a collaborative learning environment using a web-based design. J. Comput. Assist. Learn. **19**(4), 462–473 (2003)
14. Quintana, C., et al.: A framework for supporting metacognitive aspects of online inquiry through software-based scaffolding. Educ. Psychol. **40**(4), 235–244 (2005)
15. Kuiper, E., et al.: Integrating critical web skills and content knowledge: development and evaluation of a 5th grade educational program. Comput. Hum. Behav. **24**(3), 666–692 (2008)
16. Bertacchini, F., Bilotta, E., Pantano, P., Tavernise, A.: Motivating the learning of science topics in secondary school: a constructivist edutainment setting for studying Chaos. Comput. Educ. **59**(4), 1377–1386 (2012)
17. Handelsman, J., Egert-May, D., Beichner, R., Bruns, P., Change, A., DeHaan, R., et al.: Scientific teaching. Science **304**(5670), 521–522 (2004)
18. Hodson, D.: Experiments in science and science teaching. Educ. Philos. Theory **20**(2), 53–66 (1988)
19. Kirschner, P., et al.: Why minimal guidance during instruction does not work: an analysis of the failure of constructivist, discovery, problem-based, experiential, and inquiry-based teaching. Educ. Psychol. **41**(2), 75–86 (2006)

20. Mayer, R.E.: Learning and Instruction. Prentice Hall, Upper Saddle River (2003)
21. Manches, A., O'Malley, C., Benford, S.: The role of physical representations in solving number problems: a comparison of young children's use of physical and virtual materials. Comput. Educ. **54**(3), 622–640 (2010)
22. Johnstone, A.: Teaching of chemistry-logical or psychological? Chem. Educ. Res. Pract. **1**(1), 9–15 (2000)
23. Harrison, A.G., Treagust, D.F.: The particulate nature of matter: challenges in understanding the submicroscopic world. In: Chemical Education: Towards Research-Based Practice, pp. 189–212. Springer, Netherlands (2002)
24. Treagust, D., et al.: The role of submicroscopic and symbolic representations in chemical explanations. Int. J. Sci. Educ. **25**(11), 1353–1368 (2003)
25. Wu, H., Shah, P.: Exploring visuospatial thinking in chemistry learning. Sci. Educ. **88**(3), 465–492 (2004)
26. Dori, Y., Hameiri, M.: Multidimensional analysis system for quantitative chemistry problems: symbol, macro, micro, and process aspects. J. Res. Sci. Teach. **40**(3), 278–302 (2003)
27. Talanquer, V.: Macro, submicro, and symbolic: the many faces of the chemistry "triplet." Int. J. Sci. Educ. **33**(2), 179–195 (2010)
28. Gabel, D.: Improving teaching and learning through chemistry education research: a look to the future. J. Chem. Educ. **76**(4), 548 (1999)
29. Zacharia, Z.C., Olympiou, G.: Physical versus virtual manipulative experimentation in physics learning. Learn. Instr. **21**(3), 317–331 (2011)
30. Kolb., D., Boyatzis, R.E., Mainemelis, C.: Experiential learning theory: previous research and new directions. Perspectives on cognitive, learning, and thinking styles. Lawrence Erlbaum, pp. 227–247 (2000)
31. Lakoff, G., Johnson, M.: The metaphorical structure of the human conceptual system. Cogn. Sci. **4**(2), 195–208 (1980)
32. Kolb, D.: Experiential Learning: Experience as the Source of Learning and Development. Prentice-Hall, USA (1984)
33. Apedoe, X., et al.: Bringing engineering design into high school science classrooms: the heating/cooling unit. J. Sci. Educ. Technol. **17**(5), 454–465 (2008)
34. Eylon, B.-S., Ganiel, U.: Macro-micro relationships: the missing link between electrostatics and electrodynamics in students' reasoning. Int. J. Sci. Educ. **12**(1), 79–94 (1990)
35. Driver, R.: Students' conceptions and the learning of science. Int. J. Sci. Educ. **11**(5), 481–490 (1989)
36. Akella, D.: Learning together: Kolb's experiential theory and its application. J. Manag. Organ. **16**(1), 100–112 (2010)
37. Mayer, R.: Should there be a three-strikes rule against pure discovery learning? Am. Psychol. **59**(1), 14–19 (2004)
38. Chu, L., Ting, Y.-L., Tai, Y.: Building STEM capability in a robotic arm educational competition. In: Hofmann, Z. (ed.) Learning and Collaboration Technologies. Human and Technology Ecosystems. Springer, Heidelberg [S.l.] (2020). https://doi.org/10.1007/978-3-030-50506-6_28
39. Ting, Y.-L., Lin, Y.-C., Tsai, S.-P., Tai, Y.: Using Arduino in service learning to engage pre-service STEM teachers into collaborative learning. In: Hofmann, Z (ed.) Learning and Collaboration Technologies. Human and Technology Ecosystems. Springer, Heidelberg [S.l.] (2020)
40. Johnson, P.: Children's understanding of substances, part 2: explaining chemical change. Int. J. Sci. Educ. **24**(10), 1037–1054 (2002)

Learning and Teaching Online

Developing a Professional Profile of a Digital Ethics Officer in an Educational Technology Unit in Higher Education

David Andrews[1]([envelope]) [ID], Philipp Leitner[1] [ID], Sandra Schön[2] [ID],
and Martin Ebner[1] [ID]

[1] Graz University of Technology, Graz, Austria
{david.andrews,philipp.leitner,martin.ebner}@tugraz.at
[2] Universitas Negeri Malang, Malang, East Java, Indonesia
sandra.schon.fs@um.ac.id

Abstract. The digitalisation of learning, teaching, and study processes has a major impact on possible evaluations and uses of data, for example with regard to individual learning recommendations, prognosis, or assessments. This also gives rise to ethical issues centered around digital teaching and possible challenges of data use. One possible approach to this challenge might be to install a Digital Ethics Officer (DEO), whose future profile this paper outlines for a Educational Technology unit of a Higher Education Institution (HEI). Therefore, an introductory overview of the tasks and roles of Ethics Officers (EO) is given based on the literature. The authors then describe the current ethics program of a university of technology and collect current and potential ethical issues from the field of educational technologies. Based on this, a first professional profile for a DEO at an educational technology unit of a university is described. From the authors' point of view, the article thus prepares important considerations and steps for the future of this position.

Keywords: Digital ethics officer · Educational technology · Higher education

1 Introduction

The digital transformation has a comprehensive impact on organizations and their daily work. Ever-improving data processing and algorithms present them with considerable ethical challenges, for example with regard to data protection or possible discrimination through automated decision-making. Data breaches in education [52], ethical issues with artificial intelligence [8], and scandals like the mistakenly labeling of black people "gorillas" of Google [9] or the recent incident, where a 10 years old girl was asked by Alexa (Amazon) to insert a coin into the socket [3] illustrates this.

P. Zaphiris and A. Ioannou (Eds.): HCII 2022, LNCS 13328, pp. 157–175, 2022.
https://doi.org/10.1007/978-3-031-05657-4_12

Some organizations are addressing these issues with, among other measures, the establishment of Ethics Officers (EO) [1,29,33,45,53], which have been occurring in the literature since the 1970s [44]. These may also occur in slight variations or specializations as, for example, Chief Ethics and Compliance Officer (CECO) [7,16,28,53], Compliance Officer (CO) [35,37] or Chief AI Ethics Officer (CAIEO) [34]. In a general sense, the EO is responsible for the ethical development of an organization [33,43,44]. The tasks range from the creation of ethical guidelines and the enforcement and control of these, to employee training and the establishment of an ethical work culture [1,33,37,45,53]. This makes us wonder whether an EO is also needed in higher education.

Higher Education Institutions (HEI) and their Educational Technology units, such as ours at Graz University of Technology (TU Graz), are not immune to the challenges posed by digitalization. Teaching and learning processes are increasingly taking place online. This results in new, digital ethical challenges, which we did not face before. These can range from non-discriminatory access to content, to a more diverse presentation in learning materials, all the way to the analysis of contextual data from learning platforms for the creation of learning prognoses. For this reason, the Educational Technology unit at Graz University of Technology thinks about whether and with which profile an EO could make sense for us. It should be noted that our Educational Technology unit is primarily concerned with technology-enhanced teaching issues and services to other units, rather than research issues. Research ethics require other considerations and are usually already widely discussed at universities, which comes with a plethora of frameworks, standards, and guidelines. Therefore, this paper focuses on ethical issues in the aforementioned areas rather than those related to research.

The variants of an EO known so far are, for our purposes, either too generally responsible for the entire ethical development of an organization (e.g. Ethics and Compliance Officer) or too specifically limited to one aspect or technology (e.g. AI Ethics Officer). Since our main focus is on the ethical challenges associated with the digital transformation of our work, in this paper we aim to explore and develop the professional profile of a Digital Ethics Officer (DEO) in a higher education organizational unit responsible for Educational Technology.

2   Research Questions, Related Research and Research Design

In the course of our exploration of the possible profile of an EO for the Educational Technology unit at TU Graz, we found that this topic is currently not comprehensively addressed in the literature. For this reason, our research questions follow a top-down approach: from the general role of an EO and the measures used for the ethical development of an HEI, to the ethical challenges of Educational Technology units, from which we want to develop a possible profile of a DEO.

2.1   Research Questions

The following four research questions are addressed in this paper:

1. *What are the characteristics of an EO and what are their responsibilities for organizations?*
2. *What components of an ethics program are currently in place at a university of technology using TU Graz as an example?*
3. *What ethical issues and needs for action arise in an Educational Technology unit at a HEI?*
4. *What is the professional profile of a (future) DEO in an Educational Technology unit in higher education?*

Research questions 1 to 3 take a descriptive approach, which are then used to prescriptively derive answers to question 4.

2.2   Related Research

Research on professional profiles is executed in different ways. We did not find an overview of their development, but numerous studies that pursued similar goals in different contexts. Lima *et al.* [42] did for example a longitudinal study of nearly 1400 job advertisements for industrial and engineering management (IEM) profiles from 2007 to 2013. With this approach the authors want to contribute to the definition of IEM professional profile by analyzing professional practice areas and counting the mentions of transversal competences. An analysis of international (research) literature was the selected approach of Brookes *et al.* [6] to describe the professional profile of community health nurses. A different approach was chosen by Saldaña *et al.* [49]: An online survey amongst 1427 ICU nursing professionals is the base for the development of a professional profile of their profession.

Similarly, Ingram *et al.* [32] used a survey amongst community health workers to identify a common set of professional characteristics, training preparation, and job activities. Beneath different data sources - literature, job advertisements, survey results - researchers in the field of professional profile development use different methods to analyze the data. Lima *et al.* [42] for example did qualitative analysis and counted the term/category frequency for a simple descriptive statistical analysis. Others apply complex multivariate analysis methods such as factor analysis [54].

The starting point for the present work is different: It is not about developing a professional profile for a de facto existing profession, but about developing a profession that will (presumably) be needed in the future. For example, Zsolnai and Tencati [57] aimed to develop a vision of a "future international manager" with a collection of articles of colleagues about potential important characteristics and competencies. Nevertheless, there is no standard procedure for the development of future professional profiles. Therefore, we have developed a procedure that we would like to present in the following.

2.3 Design and Methodology

This study was developed in three phases. At the beginning, the structure and design were determined. Then, research questions 1 to 3 were addressed using desktop research and literature review. Relevant literature was searched using scientific research portals, such as Google Scholar, SpringerLink and Research-Gate. Keywords such as "ethics officer", "digital ethics officer" or "ethics officer higher education" were of particular interest. Also, the Journal of Business Ethics has been a valuable source for literature.

Within research question 1, frequently occurring concepts were clustered by content in order to collectively present characteristics and job responsibilities of an EO. For this purpose, relevant papers were identified and searched for characteristics and responsibilities. Then the terms were grouped according to similarity. After a manual semantic analysis, this resulted in overarching categories. Answering question 2 involved mapping (non-)existing components of the ethics program at TU Graz to those found in the literature. Furthermore, relevant persons and departments in our own organization as well as the intranet of TU Graz were consulted to answer research questions 2 and 3. For the answer to question 3, the knowledge of the unit head and his deputy was used in particular. The final phase involved consolidation in addressing question 4 on the professional profile of a future DEO. For this purpose, the structure of a job description of TU Graz was adapted for a possible new position of a DEO. The job description was developed from the results of the research questions 1 to 3 and from discussions with the unit management. In the following, the four research questions are addressed in order.

3 Characteristics and Responsibilities of an Ethics Officer

In order to develop the future profile of a DEO, we strived to better understand what qualities an EO should possess and what his or her job responsibilities in general might be.

As a first step, we took a closer look at the role and traits that an EO should have. To do this, we searched the literature for contributions describing characteristics of an EO. This allowed us to select the following four papers with designated descriptions of an EO: Izraeli and BarNir [33], Adobor [1], Llopis et al. [43], as well as Hogenbirk and van Dun [30].

After clustering by meaning, we were able to summarize the characteristics of an EO mentioned by the authors in Table 1. The specified properties were taken directly from the respective papers. We then could identify four overarching categories: *professional management, independent actions, working knowledge* and *ethical expertise*.

Professional management describes an EO's ability to respond appropriately and professionally in any situation and refers to both work attitude and soft skills. *Independent actions* refers to the status of the EO within an organization, in which he or she should be as independent as possible and capable of acting. In

Table 1. Overview of characteristics of EOs in selected sources. Own analysis based on the referred literature. Note: Capitalisation has been slightly adjusted.

Source	Professional management	Independent actions	Working knowledge	Ethical expertise
Izraeli and BarNir [33]	Professionalism	Insider status; Independence	Knowledge of organizational issues	Knowledge of ethics theory
Adobor [1]	Tolerance of ambiguity; Individual orientation and leadership behaviour	Locus of control	Business knowledge; Technical knowledge	Moral character
Llopis et al. [43]	Personal and professional maturity; Rationality in tense interpersonal situations; Solid, broad management skills; Common sense; Discreet and able to protect confidential information	Strong communicators; Ability to establish and maintain credibility and trust throughout the organisation; Ability to quickly assimilate information relating to complex issues; Ability to network on all levels of an organisation; Able and willing to take a difficult or unpopular position if necessary	Deep organisational knowledge; Working knowledge of applicable laws and regulations	Objective and thoughtful; Experience with training and development including best practices in ethics and compliance education; Always show the highest integrity
Hogenbirk and van Dun [30]	Conscientiousness; Openness to experience			

order to fulfill his or her role, the EO should, on the one hand, know the professional concerns of his or her organization and therefore have *working knowledge*. On the other hand, the EO also should have experienced the necessary ethical training and serve as a moral role model, thus having concise *ethical expertise*.

In a second step, we did the same to find out what responsibilities EOs usually (should) have according to the literature. From the literature review, we filtered out papers with dedicated descriptions to the task areas of an EO. This results in the selection of the following five contributions: Izraeli and BarNir [33], Morf *et al.* [45], Adobor [1], Trevino *et al.* [53] and Kaptein [37].

Table 2 shows the responsibilities found in the relevant literature, whereby the mentioned properties were taken directly from the respective papers. Clustering allowed us to identify five broad areas of responsibility for an EO: *ethical guidelines*, *control activities*, *ethics training*, *ethical culture* and *advising management*.

Table 2. Overview of responsibilities of EOs in selected sources. Own analysis based on the referred literature. Note: Capitalisation has been slightly adjusted.

Source	Ethical guidelines	Control activities	Ethics training	Ethical culture	Advising management
Izraeli and BarNir [33]		Monitoring compliance with the codes; Taking remedial action in case of inappropriate behavior by members of the organization	Preparing ethics training programs		Advising management on the development of codes
Morf et al. [45]	Creating and maintaining a company's guiding values, principles, and business practices	Evaluating the company's adherence to its formal ethics code; Investigating alleged violations of the law			Advising top management as to various moral and ethical issues
Adobor [1]	Manage compliance	Investigative oversight; Manage compliance	Ethics education	Corporate social responsibility	Advise top management
Trevino et al. [53]	Developing and distributing codes of conduct	Developing and managing reporting lines and investigation systems	Designing and delivering training programs	Working to create ethical cultures and climates; Legitimacy work	Contributing to the design of performance management systems
Kaptein [37]	Accountability policies; Code of ethics	Investigation and correction policies; Monitoring and auditing; Ethics report line	Ethics training and communication	Incentive policies	

An EO should play a significant role in determining the ethical direction of an organization, which includes developing *ethical guidelines* often in the form of a code or policy. *Control activities* refers to the need to monitor, investigate, and respond appropriately to potentially unethical behaviors within an organization, all to ensure that ethical principles do not only exist on paper. To promote ethical behavior and prevent unethical behavior, another task of the EO is *ethics training* within the workforce. By establishing an *ethical culture* within the organization, ethical behavior can be further normalized and made visible to the outside world. The EO is the central point of contact for ethical issues, which top management in particular should have recourse to, which is why *advising management* is one of the five areas of responsibility.

Based on our analysis, we can see that the requirements for EOs are complex and individually demanding. This is also due to the fact that the tasks of an EO extend deep into the structures of an organization, even to the point of completely changing established ways of working. Accordingly, the installation of this position requires great commitment and trust from the management so that the EO is not hindered by potential conflicts of interest [1,29,55]. Otherwise, the EO could find him or herself in a constant struggle for legitimacy and ultimately represent nothing more than ethics washing [53]. Some research indicates that installing ethics programs and establishing an EO reduces unethical behavior in organizations [37,48], especially when relying on innovative methods [30], though more research is certainly needed here. Based on the preceding analysis, the increased visibility of ethical efforts, the benefits of a one-stop shop for ethical concerns, and the need to address these challenges, we believe that EOs have a high chance to increase ethical behavior in organizations.

4   Components of a Current Ethics Program at a Technical University

In order to better understand the potential uses of an EO in issues of technology-enhanced teaching in higher education, we first want to investigate what measures to promote ethical behavior already are in place. For this purpose, we analyzed our own organization at TU Graz, for such components. In an empirical study, Kaptein [36,37] identifies eight components of ethics programs that directly or indirectly lead to less unethical behavior within organizations, while suggesting the following order of implementation: (1) code of ethics, (2) ethics training and communication, (3) accountability policies, (4) monitoring and auditing, (5) investigation and correction policies, (6) an ethics office(r), (7) ethics report line, and (8) incentive policies. To determine which components already are installed, the intranet of the university was searched on the one hand and relevant employees were contacted on the other. Whereupon these insights were matched with Kaptein's components (Table 3).

In the year 2008, TU Graz implemented an "ethics code" [24] to commit its students and staff to scientific conduct. However, this code is limited to scientific work and does not contain any general ethical values or principles, for which it was also criticized by the student representation [2]. Therefore, we do not consider the component (1) code of ethics in the sense of Kaptein to be fulfilled. We also could not find a corresponding implementation for components (2) ethics training and communication, (4) monitoring and auditing and (8) incentive policies.

TU Graz operates a Commission for Scientific Integrity and Ethics [19], which is mainly composed of faculty members. Its main task is to advise about and investigate scientific misconduct. However, it is only active upon request and does not actively shape the ethical orientation of the university, which is why we consider it too passive to be considered a full equivalent of (5) investigation and correction policies and (6) ethics office.

Furthermore, TU Graz has published a code of conduct [27] corresponding to component (3) accountability policies and a whistleblowing website [20] corresponding to the (7) ethics report line. Apart from the components just mentioned, there is a Science, Technology and Society Unit (STS) [21] at TU Graz. However, this unit is primarily dedicated to research and teaching in the area of

Table 3. Components of the ethics program of TU Graz. Meaning of the characters: ✗ not fulfilled, ∼ partly fulfilled, ✓ fulfilled.

Component	Fulfillment level	Equivalent at TU Graz
(1) Code of ethics	✗	
(2) Ethics training and communication	✗	
(3) Accountability policies	✓	Code of conduct
(4) Monitoring and auditing	✗	
(5) Investigation and correction policies	∼	Commission for Scientific Integrity and Ethics
(6) Ethics office(r)	∼	Commission for Scientific Integrity and Ethics
(7) Ethics report line	✓	Whistleblowing website
(8) Incentive policies	✗	

the social impact of technology and not so much to the internal development of the university. This is why it does not appear in the matching of Kaptein's components, but it could be an important building block in the future development of TU Graz's ethical efforts. In addition, TU Graz has set up a sustainability advisory board, which, for example, strives to establish a sustainability strategy and advises the rectorate in these matters [22].

Our analysis shows that there is room for improvement with regard to the ethics program at TU Graz. In our experience, however, we assume that this is not much different at many other European universities and especially technical universities, as priorities have been set differently so far. Although there are also critics to the introduction of EOs at universities [4] and Kaptein [37] proposes them later in the sequence (for economic reasons), we think that EOs could directly make an impact as they would bundle the implementation of these components [55]. However, care must be taken that this commitment would be deeply embedded in the culture of the university for it to be effective, as Weber [55] recommends after implementing an ethics program in his academic unit.

5   Ethical Issues and Needs for Action Arising in an Educational Technology Unit at a Higher Education Institution

TU Graz is constantly pursuing new, modern and innovative paths in teaching and learning and tries to support these in particular through digital technologies. The organizational unit Educational Technology was established in 2005 as a working group for this purpose, becoming a separate organizational unit in 2015. Since the Covid-19 pandemic in 2020 [12], it has been classified as system critical and currently employs twelve full-time equivalent staff and a few more dozen project staff (January 2022). In addition to the technical challenges, a wide range of media-didactic and media-pedagogical measures are additionally taken into account. The successive expansion of online teaching is strategically anchored in order to enable flexible and target group-oriented studying at the university of tomorrow. Therefore, digital education at TU Graz is now taken for granted and increasingly corresponds to the natural use of teaching and learning technologies for any purpose. The scope of the organizational unit Educational Technology of TU Graz includes among others the enhancement of face-to-face teaching and learning activities with the help of digital technologies, the development of new applications and technologies and of course to foster also the pure online teaching and learning. Strategically, the unit is the main driver of digital transformation of learning and teaching at TU Graz [11].

A large field of activity is the operation of online platforms. The unit operates the learning management system TeachCenter, which is based on Moodle, the first and so far only MOOC platform in Austria, iMooX [10,31], as well as the university's own video portal TUbe [23] with the possibility of streaming lectures live or making videos available for viewing. What these online platforms have in common is that they enable the collection of a wide variety of data about their users. Potential ethical fields of action range from how students are tracked to barrier-free access and the universal design of these. TU Graz has committed itself to climate neutrality by 2030 [18], whereby video portals especially consume a lot of energy and therefore have an environmentally critical component. The fundamental question for all platforms is how they can best be used to promote education.

The establishment of the above-mentioned platforms further enables the use of the collected data for learning and academic analytics. Learning analytics involves the analysis, presentation, and interpretation of data from teaching and learning settings for the purpose of enabling learners to directly transform their learning [40]. Among other things, the unit is developing dashboards for various target groups, from students to deans of studies. In the case of students, this should provide insights into their own performance, and for deans, into the functioning of study programs. Special attention must be paid to how sensitive data is handled so that the privacy and autonomy needs of students are taken seriously and they do not degenerate into vitreous students [41], but rather perceive these services as empowered demanders [17]. Slade and Tait [51] mention other ethical challenges in learning analytics, such as transparency, data ownership and control, consent, accessibility of data, communication, institutional responsibility and obligation to act, or inclusion, among others. In general, careful consideration is needed between the goal of providing the best possible education and the influence that can be exerted on students through analysis and its presentation. Last but not least, learning analytics also places great organizational demands on universities [50].

Another relatively new task is to provide e-assessment tools. Here, the organizational unit Educational Technology operates Knowledge CheckR [38] for digital exams with the possibility to automatically monitor students and, if necessary, report them to the supervisor. In addition, exams can be administered via the TeachCenter platform using TeachCenter Exam. Particularly controversial is the automated observation of students via their webcams, which raises some ethical questions of privacy and trust issues, and possibly even human dignity. In addition, the safety and robustness of the system must be granted to ensure flawless and tamper-proof examination [13].

A further area of responsibility is the production of video material. The organizational unit Educational Technology helps teachers with the recording and streaming of lectures, as well as with the creation of didactic explanatory videos. In video production, issues of diversity and non-discrimination have become increasingly important, especially in recent times. This involves a diverse and gender-neutral representation of people in the videos and didactic methods with a focus on all target groups, as well as barrier-free access, for example through subtitles or the consideration of color blindness.

The organizational unit Educational Technology is the first point of contact within the university when it comes to support in didactic matters, continuing education and Technology-Enhanced Learning (TEL) counseling. An important project within these tasks is TELucation [5], which can be seen as an overall concept for the empowerment of teachers for creative, technology-supported teaching. In 2020, the TU Graz [25] has published its Open Educational Resources (OER) policy, where the unit is responsible for. Nearly all resources of the unit are published under open licenses. OER consulting, OER further education and an OER repository [39] are some of the related activities. Within OER, copyright issues and the question of how to ensure free access in a fair way often arise. TELucation is based on OER and asks the question how learning designs can be created in a learner-centered, diverse and gender-sensitive way and how education can be promoted in the best possible way.

Although the organizational unit Educational Technology is operated primarily as a service facility, it also conducts research projects in the field of teaching and learning technologies. Frequent ethical issues arise from the handling of potentially sensitive learner data, such as if underagers are involved [46] or usage of external students' marks for MOOC evaluation [14].

In 2019, the High-Level Expert Group on Artificial Intelligence (AI HLEG), established by the EU Commission, published a highly regarded document on "Ethics Guidelines for Trustworthy AI" [15]. Their goal is to set up a framework for the development of trustworthy AI. To this end, the group was able to establish four overarching ethical principles: respect for human autonomy, prevention of harm, fairness and explicability. Starting from these, they develop their framework more and more concretely to seven key requirements and finally an assessment list. The seven key requirements are: 1. *human agency and oversight*, 2. *technical robustness and safety*, 3. *privacy and data governance*, 4. *transparency*, 5. *diversity, non-discrimination and fairness*, 6. *environmental and societal well-being* and 7. *accountability*. For a detailed description of the key requirements, the previously mentioned AI HLEG document [15] can be consulted. Although the AI HLEG developed this framework specifically for AI applications, we believe that these basic principles are also applicable to other digital technologies, which is why we want to use the key requirements to guide our listing of ethical challenges. Figure 1 shows a non-exhaustive selection of our unit's activities with a mapping to ethical issues and to the aforementioned key requirements. It should be noted that when assigning the key requirements, only those that are particularly clearly affected were selected, since many requirements can often be reflected to a small degree. The ethical issues listed are a selection of particularly prominent issues that we have derived from the analysis of our activities and our daily work.

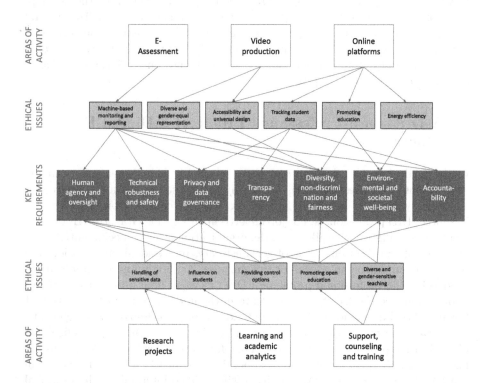

Fig. 1. Mapping of the areas of activity of the Educational Technology unit to ethical issues and key requirements of the AI HLEG.

The present result illustrates the diverse questions and areas of activity of the organizational unit Educational Technology. These are only an excerpt, and the individual challenges require more in-depth analyses. Dealing with these sometimes very critical ethical issues is often left directly to the employees involved, who in many cases have not received any ethical training. One example is the handling of tracking data from learning management systems. What data should be collected? How and for how long should it be stored? Which data analyses are permissible? How can this data be used for the best possible benefit? Leaving employees alone to deal with these issues can result in overwhelm and indifference. This is precisely where the installation of an EO could come into play and serve as a central point of contact and for steering ethical concerns. In summary, we see that the unit "Educational Technology" faces a variety of recurring and pressing ethical challenges on the one hand, and a desire to advance ideas such as ethics by design and responsible innovation [8] on the other. Therefore, we believe that addressing them could be better guided by an explicit EO.

Among all the aspects and developments mentioned, two topics have been discussed particularly intensively or time-consumingly with an ethical focus in the last two years: One is proctoring in e-assessment during pure distance learning phases. In particular, the (planned) use of a tool that uses artificial intelligence-based proctoring (Knowledge CheckR) was a topic [47]. Secondly, the development of a learning analytics application for better personal visualization and monitoring of one's own study progress led to some discussions about access to and inclusion of data. Finally, the decision was made to make it available only to students and not to teachers or others, and to use only information that is already accessible to them [41].

6   A Draft of a Professional Profile of a Digital Ethics Officer

In the field of technical employees there is already long experience with job descriptions at universities [56]. Typically, job descriptions are prepared or adapted by the job holder or supervisor, also in consultation with Human Resource (HR) professionals. For job advertisements at TU Graz, the HR department collects information like job title, organizational unit, specific authorities, objective of the position, areas of responsibility, professional qualification and personal requirements in a form for this purpose [26]. For a practical application, we develop the professional profile of a DEO as a job description based on this information (see Fig. 2). It was derived from the findings of research questions 1 through 3 and discussions with the unit Educational Technology management.

It was determined that with the current size of the unit, it is unlikely to fill a full-time position with this role. Therefore, the following two scenarios are likely: either the position will be co-supervised by an EO who is also active in other units, for example, or the position will be filled internally with additional duties. The description of the areas of responsibility provides a rough orientation and is additionally fed by the ethical requirements of the organizational unit

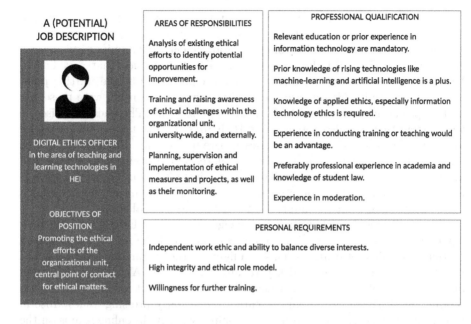

A (POTENTIAL) JOB DESCRIPTION	AREAS OF RESPONSIBILITIES	PROFESSIONAL QUALIFICATION

A (POTENTIAL) JOB DESCRIPTION

DIGITAL ETHICS OFFICER in the area of teaching and learning technologies in HEI

OBJECTIVES OF POSITION
Promoting the ethical efforts of the organizational unit, central point of contact for ethical matters.

AREAS OF RESPONSIBILITIES

Analysis of existing ethical efforts to identify potential opportunities for improvement.

Training and raising awareness of ethical challenges within the organizational unit, university-wide, and externally.

Planning, supervision and implementation of ethical measures and projects, as well as their monitoring.

PROFESSIONAL QUALIFICATION

Relevant education or prior experience in information technology are mandatory.

Prior knowledge of rising technologies like machine-learning and artificial intelligence is a plus.

Knowledge of applied ethics, especially information technology ethics is required.

Experience in conducting training or teaching would be an advantage.

Preferably professional experience in academia and knowledge of student law.

Experience in moderation.

PERSONAL REQUIREMENTS

Independent work ethic and ability to balance diverse interests.

High integrity and ethical role model.

Willingness for further training.

Fig. 2. Job description of a DEO in an Educational Technology unit in a HEI.

Educational Technology. In the face of multifaceted technologies, we believe it is important for a future DEO to have experienced technical education as well. This makes communication and practical work with the technicians involved easier. The required ethical training can be provided, for example, as part of additional training or a university degree.

7   (Summary and) Discussion

This paper developed a possible professional profile of a DEO at an Educational Technology unit of an HEI. First, the responsibilities and characteristics of EOs in general were examined. Four characteristics were extracted from the literary analysis: professional management, independent actions, working knowledge and ethical expertise. In addition, five broad areas of responsibility were identified: ethical guidelines, control activities, ethics training, ethical culture and advising management. This analysis shows us that EOs can influence the ethical orientation of an organization in various different aspects. The literature was selected by desktop research using keywords. This selection may be incomplete and reflect only part of the available literature. The clustering of related concepts from the literature contributions was a manual and subjective process, which naturally would have allowed for alternative results. Nevertheless, we think that the concepts found cover a wide range and are useful for better understanding the concept of an EO as a whole and is a valuable first step.

The second step was to examine our university for the presence of components of an ethics program. Using Kaptein's suggested ethics components, it was determined that there is room for improvement in the university's overall ethical efforts. From this finding, we were able to conclude that a dedicated DEO position at our subunit might make sense and could be the starting point of further efforts in this direction. Kaptein's ethics components were presented by him primarily with regard to business organizations. The question arises to what extent they are also applicable to HEIs. In our view, they provide a useful overview of possible parts of an ethics program, although they should not be understood as absolute and final. Furthermore, organizations can operate well and ethically without having these components installed, and they can have them implemented and still fail on ethical issues. Thus, these are neither necessary, nor sufficient, but certainly improve the visibility of ethical efforts.

Third, we looked at what ethical challenges arise at our Educational Technology unit as a result of the digitization of teaching. In doing so, we have assigned particularly salient ethical problems in a figure to the overarching areas of activity of the unit and the ethical key requirements of the AI HLEG. The areas include: online platforms, e-assessment, learning and academic analytics, video production, TEL counseling and research. Particularly pressing issues arose in proctoring in e-assessment and how to monitor students in online exams on the one hand, and data collection and processing on online platforms in the context of learning analytics on the other. These examples in particular show some very sensitive issues, which up to now have mainly been left to the employees involved. Here, the position of the DEO could have a decisive influence. The ethical challenges presented in this chapter are only a sample of all the activities of the Educational Technology unit. Moreover, they are formulated in relatively general terms for the sake of simplicity and must be considered in a much more complex and multi-layered manner in individual cases. In addition, the areas of responsibility and the associated problem areas change rapidly, as was impressively demonstrated not least by the covid-19 pandemic [47] and the sudden need for online examinations.

Finally, we thought about what the position of a DEO for our Educational Technology unit might look like. To do this, we packaged the previous findings and our requirements for this person into a job description. It turned out that for our case a full-time position is unlikely and the position could be, for example, filled internally with the tasks of the DEO being done in addition. Therefore, it seems particularly important that this person brings technical knowledge as a priority and additionally an ethical qualification. Clearly, one weakness of this job description is its hypothetical nature. Individual needs and thus job requirements can and certainly will change through practical experience. However, the development of this professional profile is intended to provide some initial guidance on what to look for in this position. Although we tried to include general considerations, the present description is tailored to the requirements and needs of our Educational Technology unit and can therefore only be adopted to a limited extent for other units of HEIs.

The most critical question we faced was whether there is actually a need for a separate EO and then a DEO in particular? The fact that our ethical needs relate to the digital use of teaching and learning technologies and not to research work, as is usually the case in large parts of universities, makes a differentiated consideration necessary. Precisely because we must face specific ethical problems of digital teaching, we believe that our Educational Technology unit would benefit from filling the position of a DEO at the university. A university-wide EO might also lead to an improvement, but it would be expected that this EO would not be able to deal with these specific problems in detail, since this position would have to be very broadly positioned and cover many different areas, including the important area of research ethics or the general ethical development of the university. Since this topic only became relevant to us through the widespread use of digital technology and the opportunities it offers, we believe that a focus on the digital aspects makes sense. This would allow the DEO to be selected and deployed in a targeted manner. Ideally, this DEO would then be part of a university-wide ethics board with the overarching position of a Chief Ethics Officer. For this position to succeed, beyond a qualified individual, it also requires management commitment to it [1], otherwise EOs are just as likely to face legitimacy challenges within their organization [53]. As a result, this position could not prove its worth and would be doomed to failure. Furthermore, the impact of a DEO is difficult to measure and its potential benefits are therefore subject to doubt [30,53]. It is also in the realm of possibility that a DEO is too cumbersome in practice and that invested resources would have been better spent directly on employee training or other approaches to improve ethical efforts.

8   Outlook

Based on this paper, the potential need of a dedicated DEO in our Educational Technology unit will be further evaluated. A possible introduction will depend on many factors, such as the will of the management, the urgency of the ethical challenges and, last but not least, financial and organizational resources. The work presented here represents a starting point, and further research projects may subsequently arise, for example on the concrete implementation, evaluation of the benefits or possible unfulfilled expectations of a DEO.

Acknowledgements. Contributions and development were partly delivered within the project "Learning Analytics: Effects of data analysis on learning success" (01/2020-12/2021) with TU Graz and University of Graz as partners and the Province of Styria as funding body (12. Zukunftsfonds Steiermark). We would also like to thank Armin Spök and Günter Getzinger from the Science, Technology and Society Unit at TU Graz for their helpful comments and feedback on our work.

References

1. Adobor, H.: Exploring the role performance of corporate ethics officers. J. Bus. Ethics **69**, 57–75 (2006). https://doi.org/10.1007/s10551-006-9068-7

2. Bayer, M., Hauser, I., Zöggeler, A.: Zitieren nach ethischen Grundsätzen? (nd). https://diglib.tugraz.at/download.php?id=4d2daecd474b4&location=browse
3. BBC: Alexa tells 10-year-old girl to touch live plug with penny (December 2021). https://www.bbc.co.uk/news/technology-59810383
4. Bennett, J.B.: Do colleges and universities need ethics officers? Acad. Leadersh.: Online J. 1(2), 4 (2003). https://scholars.fhsu.edu/alj/vol1/iss2/4
5. Braun, C.: Technologiegestützte Lehre vermitteln - TELucation an der TU Graz (2021). https://hochschulforumdigitalisierung.de/de/blog/telucation-tu-graz. Accessed 10 Feb 2022
6. Brookes, K., Davidson, P., Daly, J., Hancock, K.: Community health nursing in Australia: a critical literature review and implications for professional development. Contemp. Nurse 16, 195–207 (2004). https://doi.org/10.5172/conu.16.3.195
7. Chief Ethics and Compliance Officer (CECO) Definition Working Group: Leading Corporate Integrity: Defining the Role of the Chief Ethics and Compliance Officer. Ethics Resource Center (June 2010). https://www.ethics.org/wp-content/uploads/2010-ECI-WP-Leading-Corporate-Integrity.pdf
8. Coeckelbergh, M.: Artificial intelligence: some ethical issues and regulatory challenges. Technol. Regul. 2019, 31–34 (2019). https://doi.org/10.26116/techreg.2019.003
9. Dougherty, C.: Google photos mistakenly labels black people 'gorillas' (July 2015). https://bits.blogs.nytimes.com/2015/07/01/google-photos-mistakenly-labels-black-people-gorillas/
10. Ebner, M.: iMooX - a MOOC platform for all (universities). In: 2021 7th International Conference on Electrical, Electronics and Information Engineering (ICEEIE), pp. 537–540 (December 2021). https://doi.org/10.1109/ICEEIE52663.2021.9616685
11. Ebner, M., Schön, S., Dennerlein, S., Edelsbrunner, S., Haas, M., Nagler, W.: Digitale Transformation der Lehre an Hochschulen - ein Werkstattbericht (December 2021)
12. Ebner, M., Schön, S., Braun, C., Ebner, M., Grigoriadis, Y., Haas, M., et al.: Covid-19 epidemic as e-learning boost? Chronological development and effects at an Austrian university against the background of the concept of "e-learning readiness". Future Internet 12(6), 94 (2020). https://doi.org/10.3390/fi12060094
13. Edelsbrunner, S.: Entwicklungspapier E-Assessment an der TU Graz. Workingpaper, Graz University of Technology (February 2022). https://doi.org/10.3217/s2rpc-x5g66
14. Edelsbrunner, S., Steiner, K., Schön, S., Ebner, M., Leitner, P.: Promoting digital skills for Austrian employees through a MOOC: results and lessons learned from design and implementation. Educ. Sci. 12(2), 89 (2022). https://doi.org/10.3390/educsci12020089
15. European Commission and Directorate-General for Communications Networks, Content and Technology: Ethics guidelines for trustworthy AI. Publications Office (2019). https://doi.org/10.2759/177365
16. Gnazzo, P.J.: The chief ethics and compliance officer: a test of endurance. Bus. Soc. Rev. 116(4), 533–553 (2011). https://doi.org/10.1111/j.1467-8594.2011.00396.x
17. Gosch, N., Andrews, D., Barreiros, C., Leitner, P., Staudegger, E., Ebner, M., et al.: Learning analytics as a service for empowered learners: from data subjects to controllers. In: LAK21: 11th International Learning Analytics and Knowledge Conference, pp. 475–481. Association for Computing Machinery (2021). https://doi.org/10.1145/3448139.3448186

18. Graz University of Technology: Climate-neutral TU Graz. Roadmap. https://www.tugraz.at/en/tu-graz/university/climate-neutral-tu-graz/roadmap/#c367923. Accessed 17 Jan 2022
19. Graz University of Technology: Commission for scientific integrity and ethics. https://www.tugraz.at/en/tu-graz/organisational-structure/representative-bodies-for-members-of-tu-graz/commission-for-scientific-integrity-and-ethics/. Accessed 15 Jan 2022
20. Graz University of Technology: Electronic mailbox for anonymous tips (whistleblowing). https://www.tugraz.at/en/about-this-page/electronic-mailbox-for-anonymous-tips-whistleblowing/. Accessed 15 Jan 2022
21. Graz University of Technology: STS - science, technology and society unit. https://www.tugraz.at/arbeitsgruppen/sts/home/. Accessed 15 Jan 2022
22. Graz University of Technology: Sustainability Advisory Board. https://www.tugraz.at/en/tu-graz/organisational-structure/committees/sustainability-advisory-board/. Accessed 10 Feb 2022
23. Graz University of Technology: TUbe. https://tube.tugraz.at/. Accessed 10 Feb 2022
24. Graz University of Technology: Ethischer Kodex der TU Graz (October 2008). https://mibla-archiv.tugraz.at/08_09/Stk_1/EthikKodex1_0_1008.pdf
25. Graz University of Technology: Richtlinie zu offenen Bildungsressourcen an der Technischen Universität Graz (OER-Policy) (November 2020). https://www.tugraz.at/fileadmin/user_upload/tugrazExternal/02bfe6da-df31-4c20-9e9f-819251ecfd4b/2020_2021/Stk_5/RL_OER_Policy_24112020.pdf
26. Graz University of Technology: Stellen- und Funktionsbeschreibung (2020). internal document
27. Graz Universtity of Technology: Verhaltenskodex (Compliance Richtlinie) (June 2021). https://www.tugraz.at/fileadmin/public/Studierende_und_Bedienstete/Richtlinien_und_Verordnungen_der_TU_Graz/Verhaltenskodex_Compliance_Richtlinie_Deutsch.pdf
28. Greenberg, M.D.: Perspectives of Chief Ethics and Compliance Officers on the Detection and Prevention of Corporate Misdeeds: What the Policy Community Should Know. RAND Corporation, Santa Monica (2009)
29. Hoffman, W.M., Neill, J.D., Stovall, O.S.: An investigation of ethics officer independence. J. Bus. Ethics **78**(1/2), 87–95 (2008). https://doi.org/10.1007/s10551-006-9312-1
30. Hogenbirk, S., van Dun, D.: Innovative ethics officers as drivers of effective ethics programs: an empirical study in the Netherlands. Bus. Ethics Eur. Rev. **30**, 76–89 (2021). https://doi.org/10.1111/beer.12310
31. iMoox Homepage. https://imoox.at/. Accessed 10 Feb 2022
32. Ingram, M., Reinschmidt, K., Schachter, K., Davidson, C., Sabo, S., Zapien, J., et al.: Establishing a professional profile of community health workers: results from a national study of roles, activities and training. J. Community Health **37**, 529–37 (2011). https://doi.org/10.1007/s10900-011-9475-2
33. Izraeli, D., BarNir, A.: Promoting ethics through ethics officers: a proposed profile and an application. J. Bus. Ethics **17**(11), 1189–1196 (1998). https://doi.org/10.1023/A:1005770732000
34. Janssen, M., Brous, P., Estevez, E., Barbosa, L.S., Janowski, T.: Data governance: organizing data for trustworthy artificial intelligence. Gov. Inf. Q. **37**(3), 101493 (2020). https://doi.org/10.1016/j.giq.2020.101493
35. Kaptein, M.: Guidelines for the development of an ethics safety net. J. Bus. Ethics **41**(3), 217–234 (2002). https://doi.org/10.1023/A:1021221211283

36. Kaptein, M.: Ethics programs and ethical culture: a next step in unraveling their multi-faceted relationship. J. Bus. Ethics **89**, 261–281 (2008). https://doi.org/10.1007/s10551-008-9998-3
37. Kaptein, M.: The effectiveness of ethics programs: the role of scope, composition, and sequence. J. Bus. Ethics **132**, 415–431 (2014). https://doi.org/10.1007/s10551-014-2296-3
38. Knowledge CheckR Homepage. https://www.knowledgecheckr.com/. Accessed 10 Feb 2022
39. Ladurner, C., Ortner, C., Lach, K., Ebner, M., Haas, M., Ebner, M., et al.: The development and implementation of missing tools and procedures at the interface of a university's learning management system, its OER repository and the Austrian OER referatory. Int. J. Open Educ. Resour. **3**(2), 25065 (2020)
40. Leitner, P., Ebner, M., Ammenwerth, E., Andergassen, M., Csanyi, G., Gröblinger, O., et al.: Learning Analytics: Einsatz an österreichischen Hochschulen. Workingpaper, Verein Forum neue Medien in der Lehre Austria, Austria (November 2019)
41. Leitner, P., Ebner, M., Geisswinkler, H., Schön, S.: Visualization of learning for students: a dashboard for study progress – development, design details, implementation, and user feedback. In: Sahin, M., Ifenthaler, D. (eds.) Visualizations and Dashboards for Learning Analytics. Advances in Analytics for Learning and Teaching. Springer, Cham (2021). https://doi.org/10.1007/978-3-030-81222-5_19
42. Lima, R., Mesquita, D., Rocha, C., Rabelo, M.: Defining the industrial and engineering management professional profile: a longitudinal study based on job advertisements. Production **27**, e20162299 (2017). https://doi.org/10.1590/0103 6513.229916
43. Llopis, J., Gonzalez, R., Gasco, J.: Corporate governance and organisational culture: the role of ethics officers. Int. J. Discl. Gov. **4**, 96–105 (2007). https://doi.org/10.1057/palgrave.jdg.2050051
44. Mazur, T.C.: Ethics Officers, pp. 2028–2034. Springer, Heidelberg (2018). https://doi.org/10.1007/978-3-319-20928-9_2378
45. Morf, D.A., Schumacher, M.G., Vitell, S.J.: A survey of ethics officers in large organizations. J. Bus. Ethics **20**(3), 265–271 (1999). https://doi.org/10.1023/A:1006000131803
46. Murr, T., Schön, S., Ebner, M.: By pupils for students: experience with the MOOC "Tenses Explained" (April 2021). https://doi.org/10.13140/RG.2.2.28346.11209
47. Pausits, A., Oppl, S., Schön, S., Fellner, M., Campell, D.: Distance Learning an österreichischen Universitäten und Hochschulen im Sommersemester 2020 und Wintersemester 2020/21. Bundesministerium für Bildung, Wissenschaft und Forschung (July 2021)
48. Remišová, A., Lašáková, A., Kirchmayer, Z.: Influence of formal ethics program components on managerial ethical behavior. J. Bus. Ethics **160**(1), 151–166 (2019). https://doi.org/10.1007/s10551-018-3832-3
49. Saldaña, D., Achury, L., Colmenares, S., Romero, H., Cavallo, E., Ulloa, A., et al.: Professional profile and work conditions of nurses working in intensive care units: a multicentre study. J. Clin. Nurs. (2021). https://doi.org/10.1111/jocn.16026
50. Scheidig, F., Holmeier, M.: Learning Analytics aus institutioneller Perspektive: Ein Orientierungsrahmen für die hochschulische Datennutzung, pp. 215–231 (October 2021). https://doi.org/10.1007/978-3-658-32849-8_13
51. Slade, S., Tait, A.: Global guidelines: ethics in learning analytics. Tech. rep. (March 2019). https://www.learntechlib.org/p/208251

52. Thomas, B.J., Hajiyev, J.: The direct and indirect effects of personality on data breach in education through the task-related compulsive technology use: M-learning perspective. IJCDS J. **9**, 457–467 (2020). https://doi.org/10.12785/ijcds/090310

53. Treviño, L., den Nieuwenboer, N., Kreiner, G., Bishop, D.: Legitimating the legitimate: a grounded theory study of legitimacy work among ethics and compliance officers. Organ. Behav. Hum. Decis. Process. **123**, 186–205 (2014). https://doi.org/10.1016/j.obhdp.2013.10.009

54. Vangarov, I.A., Belichev, M.G., Ilieva, N.I.: Application of statistical software SPSS to study the professional profile of engineers (nd)

55. Weber, J.: Implementing an organizational ethics program in an academic environment: the challenges and opportunities for the Duquesne university schools of business. J. Bus. Ethics **65**(1), 23–42 (2006). https://doi.org/10.1007/s10551-005-3970-2

56. Wohinz, J.W.: Die Arbeitsplatzbeschreibung im Angestelltenbereich, pp. 1–8 (1976)

57. Zsolnai, L., Tencati, A.: The Future International Manager: A Vision of the Roles and Duties of Management. Palgrave Macmillan, London (2009)

Whose Interests and Knowledge are Recognized? An Empirical Study of Teachers' Reflections on Integrating Digital Technologies in Teaching Activities

Eva Brooks[1]([📧]) [iD] and Marie Bengtsson[2] [iD]

[1] Aalborg University, Kroghstræde 3, 9220 Aalborg, Denmark
eb@hum.aau.dk
[2] Halmstad University, Kristian IV:s väg 3, 301 18 Halmstad, Sweden
marie.bengtsson@hh.se

Abstract. The integration of digital technology in teaching activities has shown to be challenging for teachers. To approach this, the article investigated the foundation of teachers' stance about developing their use of digital technology in teaching. The study draws on an action research approach, involving 35 teachers (K-2) in workshops and interaction-based facilitation. Based on content analysis, we identified how the teachers reasoned about their agency or lack of it, and children's knowledge and experiences, as well as guardians' viewpoints. The result is presented in four themes: *Exchanging experiences across different school settings*, *Acknowledging accessibility to digital tools*, *Teachers' considerations about children's influence*, and *Teachers' considerations about guardians' influence*. The study supports the theoretical framework of funds of knowledge; however, the teachers need to move from 'talking the talk' to 'walking the walk'. They wish to give space for children's experiences, but do not reveal any tools to do so. Hence, the children's home domain is lacking in teachers' discussions and their stance in including children's interests is shadowed by their own needs. The analysis shows that the local context is a foundational support and constitutes a framework for the teachers to step by step becoming digitally competent and, hence, being able to a greater extent give space for children's funds of knowledge – i.e. moving from talk to implementation. The study contributes to a local perspective to the debate on how to integrate digital technology in classrooms and how teachers can be empowered to gradually build digital agency.

Keywords: Digital technology · Education · Children's interest · Funds of knowledge · Teachers' needs and agency · Local context

1 Introduction

This paper contributes to knowledge about the ways teachers recognize their own as well as children's knowledge and experiences when integrating digital technology in classroom settings. In line with Gray et al. [1] and Ertmer and Ottenbreit-Lerfwich [2],

P. Zaphiris and A. Ioannou (Eds.): HCII 2022, LNCS 13328, pp. 176–196, 2022.
https://doi.org/10.1007/978-3-031-05657-4_13

Blackwell et al. [3] underline that the increased access but underuse of technology in teaching and learning activities require sufficient support to teachers as well as a strong technology vision to alleviate this problem. The ways in which technology is integrated are still very much dependent upon teachers' beliefs, values, and skills [3, 4]. We agree with Mertala [5] who argues that if digital technology should be genuinely meaningful in teaching activities, it should give space for children's views, values, and experiences of using this kind of technology in their homes. Thus, we underline that to understand the complexity of what this means for teachers, it is crucial to investigate teachers' stance about children's use of digital technology in their homes. In particular concerning how they consider that such experiences can be used in classroom settings.

Children bring different experiences into the classroom, and this also goes for their experiences of digital technology. According to Brito et al. [6] these differences can be understood from children's home settings, for example related to the variation of their access to technology that exist in different families, or the way guardians mediate technology use [7]. To further exemplify, guardians often become more restrictive in letting their child spend time on digital technology if he or she starts to use digital tools more extensively [6]. In this way, guardians tend to take on a role as gatekeepers rather than scaffolding or encouraging the child's technology use [7]. For the youngest children, up to 3 years of age, guardians have concerns about touchscreens and how such devices would replace traditional play and learning [8, 9]. However, research shows that when teachers embed digital technologies in their teaching activities, guardians are more likely to accept the use of these for educational purposes. They are also more disposed to support children's technology usage at home and, thereby, less focused on, for example, the duration of the child's use but rather on the content of use and a purposeful usage [7, 10, 11].

Mertala [12] emphasizes that there is an uncertainty among teachers to see themselves teaching when digital technology is included. Therefore, they are likely to view children as self-driven learners resulting in teachers taking on a passive role in supporting children's digital learning processes. The author highlights this as a pedagogical pitfall. With this in mind, we underline that when teachers are occupied by their own beliefs, values, and skills there is a risk that children's perspectives and experiences are put behind. Thus, the issue for teachers to move from beliefs and values to give space for children's participation requires a greater consideration of how they as teachers experience children's as well as their own usage of digital technology across the 'home-and-school' domains to, in a meaningful way, connect these two worlds [13, 14]. Based on the above including the fact that children and adults often have different views on the use of digital technology [15], this study investigates the foundation of teachers' stance about developing their use of digital technology in teaching activities. In doing so, we focus on the following research questions:

1. In what ways do teachers consider their own knowledge of and experience with integrating digital technology in teaching activities?
2. In what ways do teachers recognize children's knowledge of and experiences with digital technology?
3. In what ways do teachers acknowledge guardians' approaches to children's technology use?

The present study includes 35 preschool teachers, after-school teachers, and primary school teachers in a school district in southwest Sweden and is part of an ongoing project, Digi-DIA. The project focuses on developing children's and teachers' digital competence through participation, influence, and responsibility, conceptualized as the DIA-model[1].

1.1 Context of the Study

In Sweden, the curriculum for preschools [16] is designed for children aged from one to five/six years of age. It values children as competent learners and highlights play as the foundation for children's development, learning, and well-being, where a lively social community contributes to children's safety as well as their desire to learn. Furthermore, it identifies children's interest and experiences as sources for their curiosity and creativity as well as valuing a participative teaching approach influenced by the children to encourage them to become responsible citizens.

The Swedish curriculum for compulsory schools [17] includes children between six and fifteen/sixteen years of age. It follows the values from the preschool's curriculum when it comes to a democratic and humanistic approach advocating for each individual child to find his or her unique individuality, and through this be able to participate as active and responsible citizens. It highlights creativity, exploration, and play (in relation to the younger children) as crucial parts of active learning. Furthermore, it identifies children's opportunities to take initiative, and responsibility.

Both curricula acknowledge that schools should offer children opportunities to develop their abilities to work on their own as well as together with others. Furthermore, the curricula identify that schools should contribute to children's understanding of digitalization and to develop their abilities to use digital technology. In other words, it is stressed that education should foster children's development of digital competence. Also, both curricula highlight the importance of collaborating with the homes to support each child's opportunity to develop as an individual based on his or her own specific circumstances [16, 17].

The previously mentioned pedagogical model of Participation, Influence and Responsibility (PIR) applied by the preschool and school district involved in this study, should give both children and teachers a real influence on methods and content of teaching. It takes a holistic approach to the mission of preschools, leisure-time centers, and schools to follow the intentions of the curricula and at the same time secure quality of the education. As such it is a leadership model encouraging teachers to act as leaders in their classrooms. To manage this, the teachers regularly develop so-called PIR-plans to support their pedagogical work. This PIR-planning tool consists of three levels (T. Roth, personal communication, August 2020):

---

[1] DIA is the Swedish abbreviation, which stands for *Participation, Influence, Responsibility* and is a model developed by Tony Roth, Principal at Harplinge-Steninge Schools in Halmstad, Sweden. In the following text we will use the English abbreviation PIR when referring to this model.

- Level 1: Goal setting.
- Level 2: Planning of the work process.
- Level 3: Evaluation of the leadership.

The main aim of the goal-setting activity (Level 1) is for the teachers to involve the children as much as possible in the process. Children's participation process is considered as key as they through this, together with the teacher, can influence their learning, which should strengthen their engagement and sense of responsibility as well as their understanding of the subject. The latter is multidimensional as it can be related to several learning aspects, for example to the topic that should be learned, how different methods and tools can support the targeted goals, as well as to the children's learning about democratic and collaborative processes. When planning the work process (Level 2), teachers should involve the children by asking them questions about their skills and knowledge related to the specific topic that they are going to deal with. in doing so, a so-called 'current situation' is established, which forms a foundation for how the teacher will plan the learning activities. This is followed by the teacher asking the children about what they would like to know more about the topic and, based on this, the teacher and the children jointly form an action plan. This requires the teacher to test different methods to, for example, establish fruitful dialogues where the children can sense that they are part of the process as well as influencing it. The evaluation of the leadership (Level 3) is based on an assessment of how the children experienced the lecture and what they learned from the learning activities that was carried out. By evaluating specifically chosen outcomes, for example, learning achievements, motivation, as well as making sure that children's previously mentioned experiences on the specific subject were taken care of, a so-called 'new-situation' is established. Through this, the teacher (i.e. the leader) gets indications of how their leadership has been received by the children.

While applying this PIR-planning tool, teachers systematically evaluate their own actions and leadership related to their interaction with the children. Through this, professional learning is considered as a synthesis of teachers' leadership, their experiences, knowledge, and co-creation (with the children as well as with colleagues).

2 Related Studies

In context of the present study, the organization of preschools and schools apply a participation-oriented pedagogy, where children's involvement is pivotal. Aligned with the curricula [16, 17], teaching and learning activities should be informed by children's interest, experience, and choices and, thereby, supposed to strengthen teachers' pedagogical decisions. However, research shows that when technology is practiced, it is seldom used in child-centered ways, but rather integrated in more traditional pedagogical practices [2, 18]. Moreover, children's interests and experiences in digital play and learning lack acknowledgement from teachers [19].

Hedges [20] argues that learning activities built on children's interests might strengthen their motivation and attention. Within the theoretical field of funds of knowledge, it is argued that educational instruction would gain from being closely connected to children's lives as well as to their local histories and community contexts [21]. Involving children's interests in this way is increasingly being recognized as a useful source for learning within a school context [20]. Chesworth [22] underlines that a pedagogical practice informed by dialogue with children and their families can enhance teachers' professional understandings of how such interests emerge from children's everyday practices. Expressed differently, if teachers critically understand how children's different experiences inform their interest, they will gain an increased sensitivity to the meanings that children ascribe to their play and learning situations. Hedges, Cullen, and Jordan [23] describe funds of knowledge as a framework that provides teachers with a way to recognize and respond to children's interests and experiences. In the context of the present study, this relates to the questions about what the teachers count as valid knowledge and, in this regard, whose interests and whose knowledge that will be recognized; children's and/or teachers'?

Iivari [24] stresses the importance of children's active engagement with digital tools in their education, not only for learning about a topic but also to become critical masters of the technology as such. By using digital tools from critical standpoints, Iivari [24] argues that children are empowered, both individually and collectively, for example in the form of motivational and relational constructs. According to Iivari [24] this creates opportunities for children's active participation as makers and shapers of a digital culture rather than being merely users.

In their study, Biesta et al. [25] explored the dynamics of teacher agency and identified that teachers' beliefs influenced the ways they were able to achieve agency. To address this matter, the authors underline the importance of creating conditions for teachers to engage in collective activities where they can reflect, develop, and consider teaching ideas and solutions. This collective engagement enables teachers to deal with the mismatch between their individual beliefs and values, and the wider institutional discourses, which opens for opportunities to develop educational arguments and visions [25]. Similarly, Vidal-Hall et al. [26] address a need for professional learning to provide teachers with try-out experiences of how to use and implications of using digital tools in teaching activities. Extending teachers' experiences in this way, teachers attain agency, which implies resources for supporting child-oriented digital learning approach [26].

3   Methodology

The present research is based on a collaborative action research methodology [27] carried out in different action cycles focusing on developing an inter-professional practice, where the participants' involvement and influence were core features. The data were gathered from a workshop, which involved 35 teachers divided into six mixed groups with five to six participants in each group. The teachers represented different school forms, from kindergarten, 1st and 2nd grades, and leisure-time centers (including children aged 1–12), situated at five different workplaces. The design of the workshop was based on outcomes from a previous (action-cycle) workshop, which took place in May 2019, where the teachers were divided into the same groups as in the present study. This May workshop was anchored around the question of how the teachers could develop their work with digital tools by means of the PIR-model (see Sect. 1.1). The outcomes showed that the teachers wished for increased communication between schools and preschools. This to inspire each other and to become more digitally competent, for example through sharing of tools and exchanging experiences. The teachers also noted that they liked to be better at including the use of digital tools in their PIR-plans (see Sect. 1.1). These outcomes framed this second workshop, which next will be described in more detail.

3.1 Study Design

The workshop on which this study is based on was carried out in September 2019, four months after the first one. Targeting a continuation of the two workshop activities, the teachers worked in the same mixed groups as the previous workshop. Further, the workshop was guided by statements that the teachers formulated then. Each group received a compilation of these statements, for example:

- We need to get better at making use of the children's wishes and knowledge and to further develop their experiences.
- It is difficult to identify children's and teachers' progression in using and pedagogically applying digital tools in learning activities (from preschool to K1-2).
- We need to be better at observing and be involved in children's learning when it comes to digital tools.
- We need to show parents what we are doing when using the iPad, and what this usage means. That we do more than just playing games.
- We need to learn from each other – cross-over school forms (from preschool to primary school). We need to meet each other. We use different kinds of digital tools and can exchange experiences.
- Joint workshops including hands-on with digital tools.

In addition to this framework, the second workshop included an action point where the teachers were asked to bring digital technologies from their classrooms to be shared among the group members for them to play around with and exchange experiences. The intention was that the teachers should inspire each other to further develop their previous perspectives regarding how they could develop their work on implementing digital tools in their teaching. Through this, we had an interest in identifying what aspects and arguments they put forward when they elaborated different points while playing around with the technology. Our interest was related to how the core features of the PIR-model were acknowledged, i.e. in what ways the teachers' own as well as the children's participation, influence, and responsibility were dealt with when considering teaching and learning with digital technology.

The group discussions were sound recorded by means of iPads placed on each of the groups' workstation. In total, we gathered 180 min of recorded data. In addition, the empirical data included the participants' answers and comments to the different statements, which they after the workshop emailed to the study secretary. The participants were informed about the study on beforehand and agreed to having the workshop session sound recorded. In line with ethical guidelines, all names of the participants as well as their workplaces are anonymized and thus no identifying information is provided.

3.2 Analytical Approach

Our analytical procedure was based on content analysis starting with transcribing the workshop recordings and reading the emailed documents several times. Broadly content analysis can be understood as a complied analytical method where written/transcribed data is systematically analyzed, and then categorized according to specific criteria to present data in an accessible way and, lastly, to provide a ground for future research [28–30]. In this way, the method allows discovering and describing a focus on individual, group, organization, or social attention [29]. In line with this definition, we have analyzed the data by systematically compressing several words of text into fewer content categories based on coding [29–31].

4 Findings

Aligned with the analytical framework, the empirical data were transcribed verbatim and reviewed by both authors to find patterns and through coding divide the material in more detailed units. The next step included a condensation of several data units into fewer components. These components were again coded and categorized, including choosing quotations from the empirical material to exemplify the categories. This process resulted in the identification of four categories namely: (1) Exchanging experiences across different school settings; (2) Acknowledging accessibility to digital tools; (3) Teachers' considerations about children's influence; and (4) Teachers' considerations about guardians' influence. These categories are elaborated in the following subsections.

All names are anonymized and due to the gender distribution among the teachers being dominated by female participants (the males were only a few), we have chosen to use only female names. As this paper does not have a specific gender framework or approach, this kind of name-anonymizing is considered not to affect the outcomes, but rather ensure the male participants' anonymity.

4.1 Exchanging Experiences Across Different School Settings

Our first category illustrates how all the participants acknowledged the importance of exchanging experiences and visiting each other across the different school practices. While discussing this topic they realized that this most probably would lead to a need of bringing in external substitute teachers. In one of the groups, they came up with a solution to this problem. They recognized the relevance of also bringing the children when they as teachers visited each other. If doing so, they would not need any external substitutes, but could internally solve potential manning problems. They agreed upon that sharing experiences and learning from each other, even teaching each other crossover age groups would inspire both teachers and children. Excerpt 1 demonstrates a conversation where the teachers discuss this topic.

Excerpt 1.

Madison: This about substitute teachers – as a substitute for us so that we can visit each other.
[...]
Lilian: Also, this about visiting each other and bringing the children. Different ages [will be mixed]… hmm … [But] we do work with the same things anyway, like books and <u>this</u> [pointing at the digital technologies on the table]. Then, one can do [such things] on different [difficulty] levels and so on.
Madison: Mm, crossover groups.
Mia: Children /…/ should join in and [also]visit each other.
Lilian: They should come with us when we visit each other. And, then one does not need [to bring in] a substitute teacher. Let's start visiting each other!
Madison: But one could visit the other schools and preschools [within the district and not only within the school where you work].
Lilian: And then the school children could see that this is how you do it in preschool. Or [school children] present things [for the preschool children].
Mia: We need to share more with each other, what we do, what we have done.

The joy and inspiration of exchanging knowledge and experiences with each other were visible in the workshop when the teachers tried out the different technologies that they had brought to the session. They demonstrated to each other how the technologies could be used, laughed together, and enjoyed both managing the different tools and sometimes failing to do what they intended. The following excerpt exemplifies how they tried out an Easi-Scope Microscope[2], the Osmo game kit[3], and when they instead of adding a user by mistake erased one from the system:

---

[2] Easi-Scope Microscope is a handheld microscope, which a child can hold over an object, which can take videos or still images using a single control button at up to 43x magnification.
[3] Osmo game kit consists of tangible pieces encouraging children to tactile explorations with digital technology, see link: https://www.playosmo.com/en/.

Excerpt 2.

Madison: And this is an egg.
Lilian: What is it?
Madison: A magnification egg.
Lilian: How should it be used? Well, I can take a photo and then /.../ [mumbling and testing the egg].
Mia: So, one takes a photo here then [pointing]?
Lilian: One can take a photo of a flower or insect or alike and then it is possible to enlarge, or?
Madison: Yes, it must be like that. Is this yours, or? [asking Lilian while pointing at another tool]
Lilian: No, it is not ours. [Changing attention to the Osmo game kit] It is a simple mirror [camera and reflector], which mirrors [scans] what the children are doing on the table [which the come alive on the screen]. /.../ And the children can work in pairs. And I must be logged in [while playing the game]. Oups, now I am logged in as someone else [laughing].
Madison: We need to change that [laughs]. We need to take away [this user and add you]. But how do I do it? [laughing]. What a panic!
Bella: No, you must be able to change this [from one user to another]. Wonderful!
Lilian: They [the children] are really good at it. And when they try it out, they like to work together.
[Several people talking and laughing]
Bella: We have so much fun. Erasing accounts... How do I start [the Osmo game] again, from the beginning? No! But if I do it this way? We share our digital knowledge - right now we do it.

Besides trying out how the different digital tools functioned, they also advised each other about how the tools pedagogically can be used in daily preschool/school activities. This is exemplified when Madison shows the others how Quviver[4] coloring app works. She explains that the app can support children with coloring and animating. They discuss that coloring a butterfly can be challenging for some children and how this often results in their failing to finish coloring activities. They agree that this app could be helpful in such situations:

---

[4] https://quivervision.com/.

Excerpt 3.

> Catherin: It somehow becomes animated. Wow, that's cool!
> Mia: Most help to those who never finish anything.
> Madison: Yes, then something happens for them as well.

To summarize this category, the workshop talks offered opportunities for the teachers to experiment with different digital tools and jointly explore learning opportunities as well as exchange knowledge between their different practices in a relaxed and pleasant way. They did so by demonstrating the various digital tools to each other, giving educational advice, and shared learning incidents as well as pitfalls when experimenting with the digital tools. Moreover, the teachers exchanged novel ideas about how they could visit each other's practices by bringing the children as well and thus avoiding substitutes. They discussed how this would imply not only their own knowledge exchange but also the children's.

4.2   Acknowledging Accessibility to Digital Tools

While the teachers experienced that they became more knowledgeable through sharing conversations and hands-on activities within a workshop activity, some of them also emphasized the importance of having access to various digital tools. They emphasized that having access determined their own as well as the children's possibility to become digitally literate. Hence, acknowledging issues that provide or hinder accessibility to digital tools are unfolded within this theme.

Accessibility issues were on the agenda in all group discussions. The preschool teachers acknowledged this by explaining that they stored robotic equipment like Ozobot[5], Beebot,[6] and Bluebot[7] so that the children could pick them up by themselves. They argued this kind of availability was important as it enables the children to, naturally and by themselves, include such tools in their play, which they, according to the teachers, frequently do: "If it [digital play] is to work, it must be part of their everyday life, the same as we have scissors and pencils". One of the groups concluded that "access and logistics influence how we use technology". Another group discussed how sharing procedures of digital tools can be arranged through a booking system. This would allow them to invest in a variety of tools that can circulate between the different units instead of having the same kind of equipment. This would as well increase contacts between the different school settings.

---

[5] Ozobot is a coding robot https://ozobot.com/.

[6] Bee-Bot is a programmable floor robot https://www.tts-group.co.uk/bee-bot-programmable-floor-robot/1015268.html.

[7] Bluebot is a programmable floor robot https://www.tts-group.co.uk/blue-bot-bluetooth-programmable-floor-robot/1015269.html.

All groups addressed problems related to the technical infrastructure, for example, lagging caused by unstable or a not-working internet, which created pedagogical obstacles. Another issue related to accessibility concerned practicalities like charging and storing of tablets. These two kinds of problematic aspects of the teachers' work are illustrated in the below excerpt.

Excerpt 4.

> Sophia: The technology just needs to work.
> Amelia: Today's biggest [time]thief. And sometimes it [the technology] is just lagging and lagging.
> Sophia: Yes, lagging.
> Amelia: Technology should just work!
> Evelyn: /…/ These metal cabinets are great, security cabinets. Yes, we just put the iPads there and plug them in.
> /…/
> Amelia: What are they called?
> Sophia: Charging cabinets? They [the iPads] are charged there overnight. And they are fully charged when we arrive in the morning. Locked in and charged.

In another group, they talked about the issue of charging tablets as sometimes problematic.

Excerpt 5.

> Layla: Our iPads are not only used in the class but also by the leisure time center, which often is problematic as no one really takes the responsibility of charging them. So, when I come in the morning all iPads can be without power.

To summarize this category, the accessibility to digital tools was identified as crucial for the possibility to integrate them in the teachers' practical work and for the children's use in their play activities. In the preschool practice, the teachers put forward that the children had access to digital tools such as educational robots, which they easily could pick up by themselves and spontaneously include in their play. Furthermore, the teachers had ideas about how they could establish a joint booking system so that different tools could be available for all. Additionally, this system would create meeting opportunities across the different school and classroom settings. All groups described that they had experienced infrastructural problems that restricted the use and caused practical, pedagogical, and time-oriented obstacles.

4.3   Teachers' Considerations About Children's Influence

The issue of how to involve the children in decision-making regarding what kind of activities and tools to be used in learning activities was one of the group discussion points. This was aligned with the previously mentioned PIR-model that frames the pedagogical approach applied in this preschool and school district. When the teachers talk about this, they all underline that they need to ask questions to the children to be able to involve their experiences of using digital technology. Some of the teachers acknowledged that it is not only about talking and asking questions, but also about implementing the children's ideas: "we need to listen to the children and show that their suggestions and wishes are important". In one of the groups, they emphasized that a genuine interest in children's experiences from the teachers' side is important (Excerpt 6):

Excerpt 6.

> Layla: We need to ask questions more specifically to the children and show interest in their experiences, what they know from preschool and school and from classroom to their leisure time. Children can tell each other. What do they already know? And what do they want to learn more about? What is important for them?

At school level the teachers have included a question in the PIR-planning tool when preparing for a new topic. This question should address children's involvement in the planning, "we always ask the children how they want to work with digital tools". However, in one of the groups, Nora states that this is not enough, they as teachers also need to observe the children and actively participate in their activities to better understand their interests and what they are occupied with. While discussing this, two of the teachers recognized the challenge of identifying what the children actually learn from interacting with digital tools. This is illustrated in the below excerpt.

Excerpt 7.

> Nora: It's about documenting what is going on in the present, like a logbook, I mean while they [the children] are active. Then, one can in a way observe how their learning looks like when they are doing stuff. It's about doing a 'new-situation' observation to watch how they interact with each other.
> /.../
> Nora: But you observe a lot in the preschool.
> Amelia: Yes, but it is this about learning, the learning.
> Nora: Mm.
> Amelia: I don't know, but there one could do more [regarding what the children actually learn when using digital tools].
> Nora: Yes, one doesn't really get to that.

This discussion continued by acknowledging limitations that exist when involving, in particular the youngest preschool children in the planning of teaching activities. They compared how children's participation differ between the youngest in preschool and the children in school. This is illustrated in Excerpt 8.

Excerpt 8.

> Amelia: For us who are working with the youngest children, it is a bit more difficult. Where I work, we need to observe to find out the children's interests.
> Evelyn: We [in school context] have more determined ways of working…
> Nora: Yes, but the school children tell us what they think about what we are doing. So, we pick the tools we consider relevant, and we see if the children find it good.
> Sophia: But most of it is based on what we as teachers think. For example, we take out a Beebot because we think it fits.
> Amelia: For the youngest children, it is mostly we as teachers adding tools.
> Sophia: I, myself, constitute a limitation. I am limited by my own lack of knowledge and thereby not competent enough. What fits to what topic, to which age group, I don't know. And then, well, no, I am so uncertain.
> Nora: But you have the things [the digital tools].
> Sophia: Yes, I have, I have access to them, it is not about that part of it.

The groups also discussed the importance of giving the children opportunity to become involved with each other, "It is important that the children interact with each other." In one of the groups, a teacher acknowledged that they as teachers not only can learn from the children's use of digital technology, but through this they also can learn about the children. This is illustrated in Excerpt 9.

Excerpt 9.

> Evelyn: The children most often manage much more than we think. It is about making use of this. On Tuesday's I work with some girls who do a lot with iMovie. They do amazing films. And now they want to teach me about making iMovies.
> Ella: That's cool.
> Evelyn: Yeah, in that way I can learn about them.
> Nora: And perhaps it is more fun and better compared to trying to deal with it yourself.

To summarize this category, when the issue of children's involvement were on the agenda, the teachers talked about how to include them in decision-making. They underlined the importance of asking children questions about their experiences of and ideas about using digital technology. This to have grounding for including the children's perspectives in learning activities. It was emphasized that it was not only important to ask questions to the children but also to show them that their contributions were put into play. It differed between how the preschools and the schools involved children in the pedagogical planning; the schools ask the children, for example which digital tools they want to use, and the teachers include this in the PIR-planning tool, and in the preschools, they observe the children to identify their interests and based on this they decide which kind of tools that could be relevant to include. However, even though the schoolteachers asked the children about digital tools, they put forward that they as teachers often decided what to use. All teachers agreed that it was important to observe children and to participate in their activities. One of the teachers underlined that it was crucial not only to focus on learning from the children (e.g. through observations) but also on learning about them. Another teacher stressed the need of considering the learning aspect when it comes to 'learning with digital tools' as this was rarely the case.

4.4 Teachers' Considerations About Guardians' Influence

The discussions about children's involvement also evoked talks about the guardians' involvement and responsibility. What was most recognizable in the conversations is the teachers' experience of parents' most often resistant viewpoints to their child's use of digital technology, particularly in the preschools. One of the groups exemplified this by acknowledging that the guardians do not want their children to 'sit' with an iPad, "The parents also need to be involved. It is difficult though when parents question the use of digital tools, especially in the preschool". In another group, the teachers agreed that it was up to them (the teachers) to motivate the use of digital tools to encourage the guardians to understand the importance of pedagogically focusing on digitalization from an early age. However, in yet another group they were of another position, which is illustrated in the below excerpt.

Excerpt 10.

> Evelyn: This about parents and iPads /.../ In our
> activities, we work in a certain way … well, in-
> stead of having viewpoints on their child's screen
> time…
> Ella: Do they say so?
> Evelyn: Yes, it happens, instead of asking what we
> actually do with the iPads. I don't think that it
> is always our responsibility to inform. Our idea
> was to inform at the meeting with the guardians,
> but too few parents signed up for the event.
> Nora: It is the responsibility of parents to come
> to such meetings to be informed. To inform them-
> selves through different channels, like our blog
> and the curriculum.

Nora, however, expressed that she can understand the guardians' concern and compared it with her own situation (Excerpt 11).

Excerpt 11.

> Nora: Yes, but I know myself. I don't want to see
> my child sitting alone in a corner with an iPad
> when I come in the afternoon. I want my son to be
> creative and play with other children. /…/ then I
> would rather see him sitting with a regular book.
> Or just like being outdoors playing. The issue
> about screen time will come later anyway. You want
> them to do things together [with other children].

In another group, the teachers concluded that guardians are not a heterogeneous group, but simply think differently and that it is the ones who primarily are against the technology that make their voice heard. The teachers experienced this as a challenge as the curricula for both preschools and schools have clear goals about digitalization. While discussing this issue, they concluded that the implementation of digital technology is a relatively new topic in preschools and as such more established in school contexts. This is illustrated in the below Excerpt 12.

Excerpt 12.

> Lilian: In schools it [digital technology] has been
> around for a while. /.../ there is scientific evi-
> dence saying that one trains one's reading and
> writing by using computers. This is a motivational
> aspect towards parents. /.../ In a way, it [the use
> of digital tools] gets de-dramatized.
> Mia: Parents think that we should offer other
> things, at least they do in preschool. They think
> their children are <u>just</u> sitting and playing.

To summarize this category, the teachers considered guardians as merely being interested in their children's screen time rather than the how the digital tools were pedagogically used for learning. In this regard, the preschool teachers referred to the guardians considered screen time as a passive activity. One of the teachers agreed with this view referring to that she as a parent would not like to find her child occupied with an iPad, but rather with a book or outdoor playing. As digital tools have been used in schools for a longer time compared to in preschools, the schoolteachers found a greater acceptance of using digital tools in schools compared to in preschools.

5   Discussion

We have identified several ways used by teachers in this study to recognize their own and children's knowledge and experiences, and in what ways they consider guardians' viewpoints when integrating digital technologies in teaching activities, presented in four themes: *Exchanging experiences across different school settings, Acknowledging accessibility to digital tools, Teachers' considerations about children's influence*, and *Teachers' considerations about guardians' influence*. In line with previously published research [3, 4], this study showed that the teachers' integration of digital technology in teaching activities were related to their limited agency in handling the ways to do so. However, the findings revealed that when the teachers had the opportunity to share their knowledge and experiences, or lack of it, with each other in a workshop context, they could explore technology and exchange ideas, beliefs, pitfalls, and pedagogical thoughts about how to integrate it in teaching activities. By having the opportunity to express themselves freely, the teachers were able to develop visions about how they collaboratively could improve their own and the children's digital agency. In this way, the research extends related literature by demonstrating how a collaborative workshop format allowed the teachers to reflect and take a step towards not only collective learning but also their own [3, 12, 26]. Despite that the teachers expressed uncertainty, this created the first steps towards a digital technology vision closely connected to anticipate themselves as digital agents acknowledging pedagogical opportunities and limitations as well as the importance of having access to appropriate technologies. In line with Biesta et al. [25], the present study points to the pivotal role of creating conditions for teachers to explore and express their agency dynamically and collectively. Thus, our research revealed that teachers' exchanging of experiences was a way to recognize their own needs and skills.

In line with the PIR-model, the teachers acknowledged the fact that children's knowledge of and experiences with digital technology should be taken into consideration when deciding about what technology to use in the classroom. However, while underlining the importance of actively involving the children in the decision-making about using digital technology in learning activities, one of the teachers questioned whether they properly show the children that their contributions really matter. One of the teachers mentioned that it is vital to know more about the children's digital culture and based on this involve them more actively in decision-making, but how this could be done in practice was not further discussed. The study further showed that even though acknowledging children's knowledge about and experience with digital technology, they are however themselves decided what to use. The research also showed that while the teachers discussed how children's digital culture could be involved in decision-making [15, 24], they did not consider how this could contribute to children's learning in a school context. When this is related to the levels included in the PIR-planning, the research reveals that the teachers involve children in the goal-setting of their teaching (level 1) and the planning of the work processes (level 2), but since they do not reach level 3 (evaluation of leadership) as the goals and processes they formulate do most often not lead to implementation in practice. This means that the teachers have limited opportunities to assess the children's learning outcomes related to the inclusion of digital technology.

In this study, the teachers acknowledge collaboration with guardians. However, one of the groups did so in a negative way by considering them as being gatekeepers rather than scaffolders [7], for example by being more interested in the children's screen time rather than in pedagogical matters. While one of the teachers aligned with the parents by expressing her understanding of why the guardians were critical and restrictive, most of the teachers wanted to find ways of collaborating with the guardians on this aspect. The results from this study show that the teachers merely critically acknowledge the guardians' viewpoints about children's general use of technology rather than expressing any recognition of how digital technologies are used in the children's home environment [13, 14].

While the teachers involved in this study discuss children's and guardians' contributions to the classroom practice, i.e. their funds of knowledge [23] when it comes to integrating digital technology in teaching and learning, this study has found that the teachers primarily recognize their interests and knowledge. They wish to give space for the children's experiences, but do not really have any tools to do so. This means that the home domain is lacking in the teachers' discussions and their stance on including children's interests is shadowed by their own needs.

6 Conclusion

The findings of this study point to the need for teachers to collectively develop their digital agency to sufficiently integrate digital technology in teaching activities. We argue that if digital technology shall be truly meaningful in teaching activities, it needs to consider children's interests and experiences. The results showed that the teachers recognized the children as active agents, but this was merely related to the educational context and not the children's spare time use of digital technology. The teachers also involved the children in choosing digital technologies in educational activities, but only to a certain extent. In their discussions, they primarily acknowledged their skills and needs, rather than giving voice to the children's interests and knowledge related to the digital culture that they are involved in. This may lead to a fragmentation of children's everyday domains.

Through the workshop activities and the accompanying facilitation, the local context was shown to be a foundational support and constitute a framework for the teachers to step by step becoming digitally competent and, hence, being able to a greater extent give space for children's funds of knowledge – i.e. take the talking to implementation. Thus, we argue that the local context is essential when working with digitization, in particular when employees are occupied by their own beliefs, values, and skills. An example of the benefits of acknowledging the local context (which was done through the workshop setting) was the teachers' recognition of similarities and differences between the different school forms. Thus, the issue of moving from own needs and values to give space for children's participation in developing digital skills, requires greater consideration of how teachers experience children's as well as their own agency and usage of digital technology across different domains of their lives to, in a meaningful way, connect these two worlds. This study contributes to a local perspective to the ongoing debate on how to integrate digital technology in classroom settings. In this regard, the findings contribute to how teachers can be empowered through establishing collective communities that truly can involve children's voices and through this being able to step by step build their digital agency.

References

1. Gray, L., Thomas, N., Lewis, L.: Teachers' Use of Educational Technology in U.S. Public Schools: 2009 (NCES 2010–040) (No. NCES 2010–040). Washington, D.C. (2010)
2. Ertmer, P.A., Ottenbreit-Lerfwich, A.: Removing obstacles to the pedagogical changes required by Jonassen's vision of authentic technology-enabled learning. Comput. Educ. **64**, 175–182 (2013). https://doi.org/10.1016/j.compedu.2012.10.008
3. Blackwell, C.K., Lauricella, A.R., Wartella, E.: Factors influencing digital technology use in early childhood education. Comput. Educ. **77**, 82–90 (2014)
4. Tondeur, J., Aesaert, K., van Braak, J., Pynoo, B., Freyman, N., Erstadt, O.: Developing a validated instrument to measure pre-service teachers' ICT competencies: meeting the demands of the 21st-century. Br. J. Edu. Technol. **48**(2), 462–472 (2017). https://doi.org/10.1111/bjet.12380
5. Mertala, P.: Two worlds collide? Mapping the third space of ICT integration in early childhood education (2018)
6. Brito, R., Francisco, R., Dias, P., Chaudron, S.: Family dynamics in digital homes: the role played by parental mediation in young children's digital practices around 14 European countries. Contemp. Fam. Ther. **39**, 271–280 (2017). https://doi.org/10.1007/s10591-017-9431-0
7. Dias, P., et al.: The role of parents in the engagement of young children with digital technologies: exploring tensions between rights of access and protection, from 'Gatekeepers' to 'Scaffolders.' Glob. Stud. Child. **6**(4), 414–427 (2016). https://doi.org/10.1177/2043610616676024

8. O'Connor, J., Fotakopoulou, O.: A threat to childhood innocence or the future of learning? Parents' perspectives on the use of touch-screen technology by 0–3. Contemp. Issues Early Child. **17**(2), 235–247 (2016). https://doi.org/10.1177/1463949116647290

9. Hatcigianni, M., Kalaitzidits, I.: Early childhood educators' attitudes and beliefs around the use of touchscreen technology by children under three years of age. Br. J. Educ. Technol. **49**(5), 883–895 (2018). https://doi.org/10.1111/bjet.12649

10. Johston, K., Highfield, K., Hadley, F.: Supporting young children as digital citizens: the importance of shared understandings of technology to support integration in play-based learning. Br. J. Educ. Technol. **49**(5), 896–910 (2018)

11. van Kruistum, C., van Steensel, R.: The tacit dimension of parental mediation. Cyberpsychol.: J. Psychosoc. Res. Cyberspace **11**(3) (2017)

12. Mertala, P.: Misunderstanding child-centeredness: the case of "child 2.0" and media education. J. Media Lit. Educ. **12**(1), 26–41 (2020). https://doi.org/10.23860/JMLE-2020-12-1-3

13. Burnett, C.: Pre-service teachers' digital literacy practices: exploring contingency in identity and digital literacy in and out of educational contexts. Lang. Educ. **25**(5), 433–449 (2011). https://doi.org/10.1080/09500782.2011.584347

14. Edwards, S., Henderson, M., Gronn, D., Scott, A., Mirkhil, M.: Digital disconnect or digital difference? A socio-ecological perspective on young children's technology use in the home and the early childhood centre. Technol. Pedagog. Educ. **26**(1), 1–17 (2017). https://doi.org/10.1080/1475939X.2016.1152291

15. Nilsen, M., Lundin, M., Wallerstedt, C., Pramling, N.: Evolving and re-mediated activities when preschool children play analogue and digital memory games. Early Years **41**, 232–247 (2018). https://doi.org/10.1080/09575146.2018.1460803

16. Läroplan för förskolan. Skolverket (2018). https://www.skolverket.se/download/18.6bfaca41169863e6a65d5aa/1553968116077/pdf4001.pdf. Accessed 07 Aug 2019

17. Läroplan för Grundskolan samt för Förskoleklassen och Fritidshemmen (Lgr 11). Stockholm: Skolverket (2011). https://www.skolverket.se/undervisning/grundskolan/laroplan-och-kursplaner-for-grundskolan/laroplan-lgr11-for-grundskolan-samt-for-forskoleklassen-och-fritidshemmet. Accessed 14 Aug 2019

18. Cuban, L.: Oversold & Underused: Computers in the classroom. Harvard University Press Cambridge, Massachusetts (2001)

19. Nuttall, J., Edwards, S., Grieshaber, S., et al.: The role of cultural tools and motive objects in early childhood teachers' curriculum decision-making about digital and popular culture play. Prof. Dev. Educ. **45**(5), 790–800 (2019)

20. Hedges, H.: What counts and matters in early childhood: narratives of interests and outcomes. J. Early Child. Res. **19**, 179–194 (2020). https://doi.org/10.1177/1476718X20942939

21. González, N., Moll, L.C., Amanti, C. (eds.): Funds of Knowledge: Theorizing Practices in Households, Communities, and Classrooms. Lawrence Erlbaum Associates Publishers (2005)

22. Chesworth, L.: A funds of knowledge approach to examining play interests: listening to children's and parents' perspectives. Int. J. Early Years Educ. **24**(3), 294–308 (2016). https://doi.org/10.1080/09669760.2016.1188370

23. Hedges, H., Cullen, J., Jordan, B.: Early years curriculum: funds of knowledge as a conceptual framework for children's interests. J. Curric. Stud. **43**(2), 185–205 (2011). https://doi.org/10.1080/00220272.2010.511275

24. Iivari, N.: Empowering children to make and shape our digital futures – from adults creating technologies to children transforming cultures. Int. J. Learn. Technol. **37**(5), 279–283 (2020)

25. Biesta, G., Priestley, M., Robinson, S.: The role of beliefs in teacher agency. Teach. Teach. **21**(6), 624–640 (2015). https://doi.org/10.1080/13540602.2015.1044325

26. Vidal-Hall, C., Flewitt, R., Wyse, D.: Early childhood practitioner beliefs about digital media: integrating technology into a child-centred classroom environment. Eur. Early Child. Educ. Res. J. **28**(2), 167–181 (2020)

27. Lofthouse, R., Flanagan, J., Wigley, B.: A new model of collaborative action research; theorising from inter-professional practice development. Educ. Action Res. Connect. Res. Pract. Prof. Commun. **24**(4), 519–534 (2016). https://doi.org/10.1080/09650792.2015.1110038
28. Berelson, B.: Content Analysis in Communication Research. Free Press, New York (1952)
29. Weber, R.P.: Basic Content Analysis, 2nd edn. Newbury Park, CA (1990)
30. Fraenkel, J.R., Wallen, N.E., Hyun, H.H.: How to design and evaluate research in education, 7th edn. McGraw – Hill, New York (2012)
31. Cohen, L., Manion, L., Morrison, K.: Research methods in education, 8th edn. Routledge Falmer, London and New York (2018)

The Effect of Multitasking During an E-learning Video Conference on Learning Performance: A Psychophysiological Experiment

Rosetta Chang, Constantinos K. Coursaris[✉], Pierre-Majorique Léger[✉], and Sylvain Sénécal[✉]

HEC Montreal, Montreal, QC 3T27, Canada
{rosetta.chang,constantinos.coursaris,pierre-majorique.leger,
sylvain.senecal}@hec.ca

Abstract. Due to the pandemic-induced mobility restrictions, time spent in front of a device, videoconferencing, and, in particular, e-learning increased significantly. Zoom and other video conferencing applications will continue to be part of our everyday life as organizations decide to continue to work remotely in the years to come. Multitasking has been long researched, however, due to the pandemic, it has prompted the need to investigate multitasking in contexts where the primary task is to attend an e-learning video conference session. In general, there has been limited research on the effects of multitasking in remote settings. Moreover, most studies on multitasking have involved the use of diaries or self-reported testimonies for data collection. To fill the abovementioned theoretical void and methodological limitation, we collect physiological data to better understand how task volume and visual attention in a multitasking setting affect learning performance during an e-learning video conference session. Results suggest that multitasking does not affect information retention but it does affect users' perceived information retention. The practical implications discussed are important for the education sector, as well as, and more broadly, for organizations using video conferencing to communicate and collaborate, as they help explain how multitasking behaviors may affect work productivity and performance.

Keywords: Multitasking · Visual attention · Performance · e-learning · Video conferencing · Eye-tracking

1 Introduction

As employees continue to work remotely during the pandemic, to collaborate and work productively, remote meetings are crucial in the functioning of an organization. Time spent in front of devices, videoconferencing, and e-learning, in particular, increased significantly. At the same time, modern technology and remote work have enabled and amplified the level of an individual's multitasking behaviors [2]. For example, splitting your screen using keyboard shortcuts or using multiple monitors allows a user to view

© The Author(s), under exclusive license to Springer Nature Switzerland AG 2022
P. Zaphiris and A. Ioannou (Eds.): HCII 2022, LNCS 13328, pp. 197–208, 2022.
https://doi.org/10.1007/978-3-031-05657-4_14

and work on multiple things at the same time. Although multitasking has been well documented and researched, limited research has been done on multitasking in a remote learning setting and on its impact on work productivity [1] and performance. Moreover, most studies on multitasking have been limited primarily to the use of diaries or self-reported testimonies as data collection methods [1, 3, 4]. In this study, we use physiological data to better understand how task volume and visual attention in a multitasking setting affect learning performance during an e-learning video conference session. Specifically, this study is guided by the following research questions (RQ):

RQ1: What is the effect of an incremental number of peripheral task-based distractions on learning performance during a video conference session?
RQ2: How does a learner's attention get divided between the primary learning task and secondary peripheral tasks during a video conference session?

The remainder of this article is structured as follows: we begin with a literature review and establishing the theoretical foundation for this study. The research methodology is presented next, followed by a presentation of the results. We conclude with the theoretical and practical implications and by proposing opportunities for future research.

2 Literature Review and Theoretical Foundation

2.1 Multitasking

Originally stemming from the Computer Science field, multitasking is defined as doing multiple tasks at the same time [5]. Multitasking can be categorized into three different ways or strategies of multitasking, namely sequential, parallel, and interleaved [2]. It is argued that sequential strategy does not constitute multitasking since tasks are performed one after the other. Parallel and interleaved strategies are more representative to how multitasking is defined in the context of this study. The parallel strategy is described as performing all concurrent tasks simultaneously. However, humans possess a finite level of cognitive resources available to engage in true parallel multitasking, and it has been shown that when attention is divided, performance can be impacted severely [6, 7]. Interleaved multitasking is described as voluntarily or involuntarily stopping a task to perform another and then resuming the initial task [2]. This last definition of multitasking is the one used in the context of this study.

Other researchers have examined the motivations of multitasking. It can be separated into two conditions, self and external interruptions. External interruptions are defined as interruptions from an external source that needs immediate attention [8]. Self-interruption is also described as voluntary interruption often used as a break from the current task or way to entertain oneself since the primary task is monotonous [8]. In the context of a video conference setting, people multitask by interleaving between another task and the videoconference session and then only to engage again with the latter when the topic of discussion is deemed to be relevant to them [9].

2.2 Dual Task Interference and Cognitive Load Theory

Prior research has suggested that, due to the limits of human cognition, each task performed during multitasking mobilizes resources involved in information processing and memory [10]. This basic principle defines the capacity-sharing model which aims to describe how similar cognitive processes triggered by different activities affect task performance [11–13]. More precisely, it has been suggested under this model that tasks carried simultaneously and that involve the same area of the brain tend to have similar needs such that the allocation of resources to the cognitive processes involved is shared [13]. Many studies have shown how performance suffers when multitasking such as using a laptop during an in-person class lecture [14]. Capacity-sharing is one of the two perspectives through which researchers have theorized dual task interference—i.e., the interference arising when someone attempts to complete two tasks at the same time [11]. A second perspective, cross-talk, aims to describe the interference of dissimilar cognitive processes [11]. Cross-talk theory suggests that when a person initiates tasks simultaneously, communication between areas of the brain responsible for their processing might conflict, thus affecting performance [11]. In the case of this study, we are particularly interested in both objective and subjective or perceived learning performance.

Given the above conceptualizations and prior evidence, and in relation to RQ1 presented earlier on, we propose the following hypotheses:

H1a: As the number of peripheral tasks during an e-learning video conference session increases, subjective learning performance will decrease.
H1b: As the number of peripheral tasks during an e-learning video conference session increases, objective learning performance will decrease.

2.3 Visual Attention

Visual attention is better described as a collection of cognitive mechanisms that control signals to the visual system [15]. Visual attention serves four different purposes: data reduction/stimulus selection, stimulus enhancement, feature binding, and recognition [15].

Since the human brain has limited capacity in terms of cognition, visual attention serves as a filter suppressing irrelevant stimuli thus enabling an individual to focus on what is relevant. This is called data reduction or stimulus selection [16]. This is similar to the filter theory proposed by Broadbent [17], i.e., given our limited capability in processing information, we limit the quantity of information we pay attention to. This selective attention can also be described as the spotlight metaphor. It represents a mental beam where a specific object or space in the visual field is illuminated, and the rest is ignored [21]. Also described as the attentional beam, attention can also be voluntarily redirected to another object or space, however relevant it might be to the task at hand. Stimulus enhancement, on the other hand, is described as either focusing on a specific stimulus (e.g., space and object-based attention) or focusing on an attribute of a stimulus (e.g., feature-based attention) [15]. Feature binding or the binding problem [18] refers to how humans decompose signals to process in different areas of our brain and then resolve it through visual attention; humans do so either by generating a representation that is not "hard-wired" in the visual system [19] or dynamically altering the selectivity or spatial extent of the receptive field of a neuron to resolve ambiguities [20]. Lastly, recognition, is the ability to identify the stimulus as well as the ability to process subsets of input for recognition that are more digestible [15].

We want to investigate when given certain tasks what people choose to focus on.

Given the above conceptualizations, and in relation to RQ2 presented earlier on, we propose the following hypotheses:

H2: The number of peripheral tasks during a video conference session is inversely related to the visual attention fixation on the primary task video.
H3a: Visual attention fixation during the primary task video correlates with subjective learning performance.
H3b: Visual attention fixation during the primary task video correlates with objective learning performance (Fig. 1).

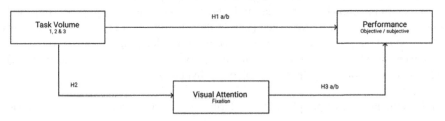

Fig. 1. Research model

3   Method

3.1   Data Collection

This study was approved by the ethics review board of the authors' institutions (#2021–4230). In this research, we conducted a within-subject design experiment separated into two phases of data collection. The first phase was conducted in April 2021, lasted 2 weeks, and data was collected remotely from participants based in Montreal, Canada, using Lookback (a user research online platform that allows the recording of participants' facial expressions, screen, and audio). The first phase's focus was to test the experimental design. The second phase of data collection was carried out in person at the authors' university laboratory, with adjustments having been made to the experimental design due to the inclusion of eye-tracking as a method to measure divided attention (a dimension not measured in Phase 1). Phase two was conducted in three waves during the summer and fall of 2021. The experiment typically involved participants multitasking by performing three desktop computer-based tasks. In phase one, participants were asked to multitask in two ways, either by having their single-screen split with dedicated screen area for each stimulus or by using multiple screens by switching between browser tabs, each containing one stimulus. In phase two, participants were only able to multitask in the split-screen condition, because the addition of eye-tracking as a method did not allow for accurate tracking of visual attention fixations in the tab-switching condition.

3.2 Participants

A total of 54 individuals between the ages of 19 and 45 (mean = 25) participated in this study. During the first phase, participants (n = 21) were recruited from our university research panel. The authors' laboratory research panel was created and aimed at using a proprietary device named Cobalt Bluebox to enable remote physiological data collection [22]. Participants of the first phase were compensated in the form of gift cards of CA\$25 for their participation in a 2-h-long study. During the second phase, participants (n = 33) were compensated with CA\$30. Eligibility requirements included participants being 18 years old or older with advanced reading and listening skills in French. All participants provided their informed consent. At any moment during the experiment, participants were allowed to quit or stop if necessary. Data from the two phases were combined since there are no statistical differences between the participants in each group.

3.3 Experiment

Experimental Design & Tasks. We used a within-subject experimental design to assess how increasing the number of peripheral tasks while in an e-learning video conference session affects their attention and performance in retaining information. In the baseline condition, only the primary task, i.e. the e-learning video conference session, was displayed. The second condition included the display of the primary task along with one peripheral task, i.e., a chat session. The third condition displayed the tasks of the second condition plus a second peripheral task, i.e., a sudoku logic-based, combinatorial number-placement game (see Fig. 2). Table 1 shows the tasks performed in each experimental condition. In conditions 2 and 3, the screen was split into 2 or 3 areas of interest (AoIs) respectively; these AoIs were held constant among all participants.

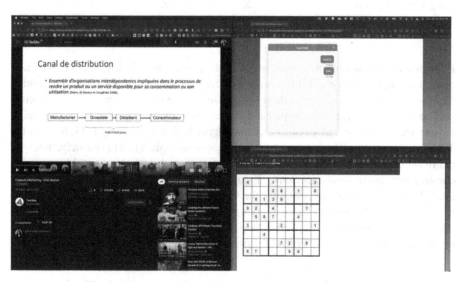

Fig. 2. Fixed setup displaying all 3 tasks in the third condition

Describing the tasks in more detail, for the video task, three different pre-recorded video conference sessions were used in each condition. Each 20-to-24-min-long video presented a different eMarketing topic and consisted of two segments: a lecture and a Q&A.

In the conditions where participants engaged in the chat task was present, Social Intent's Slack Live Chat browser widget [23] was utilized to facilitate communication. Participants were prompted general questions pertaining to their origins, interests in television shows and restaurants. These questions were pre-tested and grouped into six sets of questions with similar response lengths. Participants would be prompted three times with a different set of questions within conditions 2 and 3 (i.e., the two experimental groups). They would also be prompted with these questions at the same time intervals (two minutes, eight minutes and 10 min from the start of the video) to ensure a comparable and similar experience.

The sudoku task, present only in condition 3, was set to a medium level of difficulty. To sudoku puzzle game requires each participant to "fill in all the boxes in a 9 × 9 grid, so that each column, row, and 3 × 3 box have the numbers 1 through 9 without repetitions" [2]. The sudoku represented a task that required more concentration and time so as to imitate how people may be working on other work-related or otherwise cognitively-demanding tasks during a video conference session.

Table 1. Experimental stimuli present in each condition

	Video	Chat	Sudoku
Condition 1 (primary-task only)	X		
Condition 2 (2 tasks)	X	X	
Condition 3 (3 tasks)	X	X	X

Experimental Protocol. An email was sent to participants 24 h in advance of their session to validate their eligibility, review and complete the consent form, and to remind them of the time and location of their test session. Once the participant was welcomed (online in phase 1; in-person in phase 2), a research assistant guided them in placing sensors on their chest and wrist to measure physiological data using BIOPAC and the Tobii Pro eye-tracker. The research assistant went on to explain that the participant would multitask engaging in three tasks, and that between each task there would be a short questionnaire about their experience. Figure 2 Before each task, the research assistant used Windows shortcuts to configure the screen (e.g. Windows key + left arrow key) in order to have a consistent screen configuration across conditions. The order of the conditions was randomized across participants. Post-task questionnaires were answered immediately after each task. Figure 3 illustrates the experimental procedure.

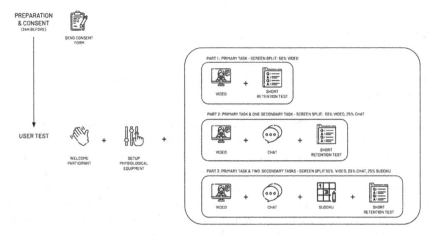

Fig. 3. Experimental procedure

Adjustments From Phase One (i.e. the Pilot Phase). In phase one of the study, data collection was completed remotely through Lookback (a user research online platform that allows the recording of participants' facial expressions, screen and audio) and as for the physiological data, it was collected using a proprietary device named Cobalt Bluebox [22]. Adjustments were made from the pilot protocol in phase two to account for in-person collection, adding the use of Tobii Pro Lab [24], an eye-tracker technology, and the use of BIOPAC [25] to collect physiological data. A pre-test questionnaire was completed 24-h before the test session. Another adjustment from phase one was that while in the pilot study one group multitasked by switching between tabs and the other had their screen split, in phase two the tab switching scenario was removed because the eye-tracker could not accurately track what the participants were looking at. Hence, eye-tracker data from the pilot study was not included in the data analysis of this study. Lastly, the split-screen configuration was made larger in phase two because participants had difficulty with the third task, i.e. during the pilot it had proved to be too small and many participants were scrolling and trying to change the configuration to make it more visible.

Measures. Investigating multitasking in a video conference or e-learning class setting, the measures of interest were attention and performance. To enable this measurement, a multi-method approach was used; specifically, a mixture of self-reported questionnaires (explicit measures) capturing user experience ex post, and physiological measurements (implicit measures) that capture real time experiences before, during, and after a task.

Attention. To capture implicit visual attention, we used Tobii Pro, a global leader in eye-tracking research solutions [23]. Areas of interest (AoIs) were created for each task in each condition. From the AoIs. we were able to extract the total fixation duration of each task, and the proportion of fixation duration of a task during a condition.

Learning Performance. Subjective learning performance was measured after each task, using an adapted five-point Likert scale [26]. Objective learning performance was measured as the number of correct answers divided by the total number of questions for each task [2]. Since the scoring for subjective and objective performance was different, to be able to compare them, the score of subjective performance was adjusted by a factor thus standardizing the two measures of performance.

Materials. In this study, all questionnaires were administered through qualtrics.com, an online survey platform.

Post Task Questionnaire. The post-task questionnaire consisted of two parts -the retention test and the self-assessment portion - and was administered after each condition. To build the retention tests with similar difficulty for each conference video, a bank of questions was created for participants to validate and measure the level of difficulty of each question. The questions were separated into either explicit or seen information, or implicit, heard or inferred information. Some questions were excluded if the percentage of participants who answered correctly was less than 70%. A total of ten questions, five explicit and five implicit questions were chosen for each video based on their level of explicitness and accuracy/correctness. Explicitness as mentioned above is defined by the way the information is presented, seen or not seen and correctness is defined by how many participants have correctly answered the question to determine the level of difficulty. The retention test's purpose was to measure how much information the participant had retained from the video. All questions were randomized and participants were also asked to rate their level of confidence with their answers to each question.

The second portion of the post task questionnaire is the self-assessment. Participants rated their own performance on their retention test and their ability to multitask using a Likert scale from strongly disagree to agree.

4   Analysis and Results

4.1   Impact on Performance

The mean scores for subjective and objective performance are shown in Table 2.

Table 2. Descriptive Statistics (subjective and objective learning performance)

	Task volume			p-value		
	1	2	3	1 vs. 2	1 vs. 3	2 vs. 3
Subjective performance	3.69	3.45	2.12	0.21	0.00	0.00
Objective performance	7.51	6.94	7.09	0.12	0.22	0.66

Linear regression was used to test whether the volume of peripheral tasks affects subjective learning performance. Results indicate a significant negative effect was observed ($F(2,32) = 32.61$, $p < 0.0001$), with said task volume explaining 32.50% of the variance in subjective learning performance (R-square $= .3250$). Hence, results show hypothesis 1a is supported. Pairwise comparisons between the conditions were subsequently performed to investigate this effect further. As can be seen from the results in Table 2, when participants performed only the primary task versus the primary task along with a peripheral task, there was no significant difference in the level of subjective learning performance (p = .2154). However, a significantly lower level of subjective learning performance was observed when participants performed the primary task along with two peripheral tasks compared to performing either (a) the primary task only (p < 0.0001), or (b) the primary task and one peripheral task (p < 0.0001).

Similarly, a linear regression was used to test whether the volume of peripheral tasks affects objective learning performance. Results indicate a non-significant effect (F(2,32) = 1.35, p = .2724) and a very low explained variance (R-square = .0253). Hence, results show hypothesis 1b is not supported.

4.2   The Mediating Effect of Visual Attention

We used linear regression to test whether the number of peripheral tasks during a video conference session is inversely related to the visual attention fixation on the primary task video. Results indicate there is a significant negative effect (F(8,32) = 266.43, p < 0.0001) with a high explanatory power (R-square = .8540). Hence, results show hypothesis 2 is supported. Pairwise comparisons between the conditions were subsequently performed to investigate further. Shown in Table 3, a significantly lower fixation duration on the primary task was observed across all conditions.

Table 3. Descriptive statistics of the percentage of time spent on the stimuli and the pairwise comparisons

Ratio TotTaskFixDur/Tottaskdur			Stimuli					
			1	2	3	1 vs 2	1 vs 3	2 vs 3
			Chat	Sudoku	Video			
			Means	Means	Means	p-value[1]	p-value[1]	p-value[1]
			n=99	n=99	n=99			
Task	1	n=99	0.0100	0.0227	0.7737	0.1637	0.0000	0.0000
	2	n=99	0.1580	0.0588	0.5880	0.0000	0.0000	0.0000
	3	n=99	0.1059	0.5021	0.1153	0.0000	0.0000	0.0000
	1 vs 2	p-value[1]	0.0000	0.2916	0.0000			
	1 vs 3	p-value[1]	0.0000	0.0000	0.0000			
	2 vs 3	p-value[1]	0.0005	0.0000	0.0000			

Again, linear regression was used to test the correlation between visual attention fixation during the primary task video with subjective learning performance. We found that the relationship was not significant (Coef = .1752, SE = 0.0936, p = .0703). Hence hypothesis H3a is partially supported. The third hypothesis also posited that visual attention correlates with objective performance (H3b). Using linear regression we observe that the correlation between them is not significant (Coef. = .0794, SE = 0.0939 p = .4040). Hence hypothesis 3b is not supported. Table 4 provides a summary of the hypothesis testing results conducted for this study.

Table 4. Hypothesis testing results

Hypothesis	From	To	Test result	P value	Status
H1a	Task volume	Subjective performance	$F(2,32) = 32.61$	0.000***	Supported
H1b	Task volume	Objective performance	$F(2,32) = 1.35$	0.2724	Not supported
H2	Task volume	Visual attention	$F(8,32) = 266.43$	0.000***	Supported
H3a	Visual attention	Subjective performance	Regression Coef. = .1752, SE = 0.0936	0.0703	Partially supported
H3b	Visual attention	Objective performance	Regression Coef. = .0794, SE = 0.0939	0.4040	Not supported

Note: * significant at 0.05 level; ** significant at 0.01 level; *** significant at 0.001 level

5   Discussion

5.1   Findings

This study examines the effect of an incremental number of peripheral tasks (or task volume) on learning subjective and objective performance while engaged in an e-learning video conference session. It also looks to explain the extent to which where individuals' attention is directed during multitasking mediates the relationship between task volume and learning performance.

Results confirmed the inverse relationship that exists between the number of peripheral tasks and subjective performance. More precisely, this effect was observed when two peripheral tasks in addition to the primary e-learning task demanded the attention of the user. However, an unexpected and interesting finding was that no significant difference in the actual, objective performance was observed as a function of task volume, since a significant effect on subjective learning performance was observed. The incongruency between subjective and objective learning performance in relation to task volume suggests that organizations need not worry when workers engage in a secondary task during video conference sessions. However, they should look deeper into the number and types of tasks workers engage in during such remote work sessions, as performance could indeed be negatively affected with a higher task volume or more cognitively demanding task types.

In terms of visual attention, our analysis of the results showed a drastic drop in visual attention towards the primary video task. Our results show that participants were looking at the video 77.37% of the time in the baseline condition. The addition of one peripheral task decreased visual attention on the primary task to 58.8% of the time. When two peripheral tasks were present, attention to the primary task was even lower at 11.53% of the time. Still, participants were retaining the information auditorily, as objective performance was not significantly negatively affected. While the relationship between visual attention fixation and objective performance was not significant, partial support was obtained for the positive effect of visual attention on subjective learning performance.

5.2 Limitations

There were several limitations from this study. This being a lab experiment, the setting differs from the participants' actual setup and experience when multitasking during a videoconference session in terms of equipment, the number of devices used, and the types of tasks engaged in. However, we simulated an environment for this study by pre-recording a video conference session containing content from actual online course sessions. We chose not to include multiple devices when multitasking since the eye-tracker, Tobii pro Lab [23] can only be set up on one device. Moreover, the testing environment varied between phases one and two.

6   Conclusion

To conclude we explored the effects of the number of peripheral tasks on subjective and objective performance as well as the mediating effects of visual attention on this relationship. We found that the number of peripheral tasks, or more generally task volume, influences people's subjective performance but not objective performance. Visual attention was found to be influenced by the number of tasks, but partial support was observed for the effect of attention on subjective learning performance and support was not observed for the former's effect on objective learning performance.

References

1. Cao, H., et al.: Large scale analysis of multitasking behavior during remote meetings. In: Proceedings of the 2021 CHI Conference on Human Factors in Computing Systems, pp. 1–13 (2021)
2. Adler, R.F., Benbunan-Fich, R.: Juggling on a high wire: multitasking effects on performance. Int. J. Hum Comput Stud. **70**(2), 156–168 (2012)
3. Czerwinski, M., Horvitz, E., Wilhite, S.: A diary study of task switching and interruptions. In: Proceedings of the SIGCHI Conference on Human Factors in Computing Systems, pp. 175–182 (2004)
4. Mokhtari, K., Delello, J., Reichard, C.: Connected yet distracted: multitasking among college students. J. College Read. Learn. **45**(2), 164–180 (2015). https://doi.org/10.1080/10790195.2015.1021880
5. Xu, S., Wang, Z.: Media multitasking. In: The International Encyclopedia of Media Effects, pp. 1–10 (2017)
6. Craik, F.I.M.: Selective changes in encoding as a function of reduced processing capacity. In: Klix, R., Hoffman, J., van der Meer, E. (eds.) Coding and Knowledge Representation: Processes and Structures in Human Memory. Elsevier, Amsterdam (1982)
7. Craik, F.I.M.: On the transfer of information from temporary to permanent memory. Philos. Trans. R. Soc. Lond. B **302**, 341–359 (1983)
8. Jett, Q.R., George, J.M.: Work interrupted: a closer look at the role of interruptions in organizational life. Acad. Manag. Rev. **28**(3), 494–507 (2003)

9. Iqbal, S.T., Grudin, J., Horvitz, E.: Peripheral computing during presentations: perspectives on costs and preferences. In: Proceedings of the SIGCHI Conference on Human Factors in Computing Systems, pp. 891–894 (2011)
10. Jeong, S.H., Hwang, Y.: Media multitasking effects on cognitive vs. attitudinal outcomes: a meta-analysis. Hum. Commun. Res. **42**(4), 599–618 (2016)
11. Pashler, H.: Dual task interference in simple tasks: data and theory. Psychol. Bull. **116**(2), 220–244 (1994)
12. Tombu, M., Jolicœur, P.: A central capacity sharing model of dual-task performance. J. Exp. Psychol. Hum. Percept. Perform. **29**(1), 3 (2003)
13. Jenkins, J.L., Anderson, B.B., Vance, A., Kirwan, C.B., Eargle, D.: More harm than good? how messages that interrupt can make us vulnerable. Inf. Syst. Res. **27**(4), 880–896 (2016)
14. Sana, F., Weston, T., Cepeda, N.J.: Laptop multitasking hinders classroom learning for both users and nearby peers. Comput. Educ. **62**, 24–31 (2013)
15. Evans, K.K., et al.: Visual attention. Wiley Interdisc. Rev. Cogn. Sci. **2**(5), 503–514 (2011). https://doi.org/10.1002/wcs.127
16. Posner, M.I., Snyder, C.R., Davidson, B.J.: Attention and the detection of signals. J. Exp. Psychol. Gen. **109**(2), 160 (1980)
17. Broadbent, D.E.: Perception and communication. Elsevier (2013)
18. Treisman, A.M., Gelade, G.: A feature-integration theory of attention. Cogn. Psychol. **12**(1), 97–136 (1980)
19. Wolfe, J.M., Cave, K.R., Franzel, S.L.: Guided search: an alternative to the feature integration model for visual search. J. Exp. Psychol. Hum. Percept. Perform. **15**(3), 419 (1989)
20. Desimone, R., Duncan, J.: Neural mechanisms of selective visual attention. Annu. Rev. Neurosci. **18**(1), 193–222 (1995)
21. Murphy, S. (ed.): The Oxford Handbook of Sport and Performance Psychology. Oxford University Press, Oxford (2012)
22. Courtemanche, S., Fredette, L.: COBALT - bluebox: système de synchronisation et d'acquisition sans-fil de données utilisateur multimodales. Declaration of invention No. AXE-0045, HEC Montréal, Montréal, Canada (2022)
23. Live Chat [Slack Chat widget] (2014). https://www.socialintents.com/
24. Tobii Pro [Software and Hardware] (2001). https://www.tobiipro.com/product-listing/tobii-pro-lab/
25. BIOPAC Sytems [Software & Hardware] (2001). https://www.biopac.com/corporate/about-biopac/
26. Wang, Z., et al.: Behavioral performance and visual attention in communication multitasking: a comparison between instant messaging and online voice chat. Comput. Hum. Behav. **28**(3), 968–975 (2012)

Factors Influencing Student Engagement in Online Synchronous Teaching Sessions: Student Perceptions of Using Microphones, Video, Screen-Share, and Chat

Mark Dixon[1]([✉]) and Katherine Syred[2]

[1] School of Engineering, Computing and Mathematics, University of Plymouth, Drake Circus, Plymouth PL4 8AA, UK
mark.dixon@plymouth.ac.uk
[2] Pathology Department, Derriford Hospital, Plymouth PL6 8DH, UK

Abstract. Worldwide, over the past two years the pandemic has had a significant impact on methods used in teaching. Sessions have moved away from face-to-face delivery toward activities exclusively being conducted online. Difficulties have been reported, such as a reluctance amongst students to engage online (with some describing a 'painful silence'). Students seem particularly uncomfortable engaging via screen-sharing, video-camera, and microphone facilities, but more post messages using chat. Several studies have employed student perception questionnaires to improve understanding of online teaching, but have not explicitly compared engagement facilities. This paper presents survey questionnaire results of undergraduate students perceptions of different engagement facilities during online synchronous teaching sessions, and the factors influencing engagement to improve effectiveness. More students reported a preference for face-to-face teaching sessions. However, this was divisive. There was also variation amongst students in prevalence and preference for microphone, screen-share, and video use. However, students were almost unanimous in being comfortable posting chat messages. Face-to-face sessions distinguish between speaking as part of the audience and standing on-stage as presenter. The engagement experience online is pushed toward being the presenter (which many students find difficult). There were contrasting student views, in areas such as distraction and recording sessions. An 'online privacy-visibility paradox' has been identified, where individuals require both visibility and privacy. The variation in student views and behaviour presents a challenge to deliver teaching sessions that meet the (often conflicting) diversity of needs to support inclusivity (in a manner that is sustainable for teaching staff and financially viable for institutions).

Keywords: Student engagement · Videoconference software · Online teaching · Privacy

P. Zaphiris and A. Ioannou (Eds.): HCII 2022, LNCS 13328, pp. 209–227, 2022.
https://doi.org/10.1007/978-3-031-05657-4_15

1 Introduction

1.1 Impact of COVID-19 Pandemic on Teaching

Over the past two years the pandemic has had a significant impact on the delivery methods used in teaching at all levels, including higher education. Worldwide, this has invariably led to a move away from face-to-face teaching sessions with a far greater proportion of (in many cases all) teaching activities being conducted online in both a synchronous and asynchronous manner. This has often been enforced by government restrictions relating to people meeting in person.

With synchronous teaching sessions, where staff and students need to meet at the same time videoconferencing systems (such as Zoom, and MS Teams) have been used as substitutes for class room based work (such as lectures, lessons, and tutorials). It is important to note that this technology is being utilised within an application domain that it was not explicitly designed for (teaching as opposed to conducting business meetings). Clearly there is considerable overlap but there are also some significant differences in terms of the nature of interactions between participants. In general, this approach has been successful in allowing teaching to continue throughout the pandemic. However, a number of difficulties have been reported in the literature.

Several authors reported a reluctance amongst students to engage online (Nickerson and Shea 2020; Singhal 2020), with some describing a 'painful silence' occurring within Zoom sessions (Lee et al. 2020). Students seem particularly uncomfortable sharing screens, sharing video, or speaking using their microphone, but more are inclined to post messages using chat (Singhal 2020), instant messaging and forum facilities. The Slack business communication platform was mentioned as providing additional chat functionality compared to that embedded within Zoom (Nickerson and Shea 2020).

Several papers (Williams 2021; Hu *et al.* 2022) have described 'Zoom Fatigue' where the loss of synchrony in online meetings causes an increase in cognitive load, requiring greater concentration, which results in a range of problems (such as stress and difficulty switching off). Joia and Lorenzo (2021) included reports from students describing an increased demand on concentration which resulted in fatigue (although the phase zoom-fatigue was not used).

Kay and Pasarica (2019) showed that using low effort (single click) facilities, such as reactions (raised hand and thumbs up) could have a positive impact on students engagement (Kay and Pasarica 2019).

Security concerns around the use of video conferencing technology have been reported (Mahr et al. 2021). In particular, 'Zoom bombing' has been recorded, where uninvited participants join and typically engage in disruptive, abusive and / or offensive behaviour, that often results in the session being abandoned. These concerns may impact upon student engagement.

There have been many studies that have employed student perception questionnaires (such as Oka and Suardita 2018; Heo *et al.* 2021; Stevanovic *et al.* 2021; Vishwanathan *et al.* 2021) to improve understanding of online teaching. However, they have not explicitly compared the use of different engagement facilities (microphone, screen-share, video-camera and chat) within video conferencing software.

There has been some interest in the role of student to student interactions in enhancing engagement (Gay 2020; Kay and Pasarica 2019) and the ease with which this can be encourage depending on which technology is used (Nickerson and Shea 2020). In particular, the more extensive chat facilities within Slack were found to support small group interactions more effectively than Zoom (Nickerson and Shea 2020).

1.2 Previous Work

Last year, Dixon and Syred (2021) reported observations of the limitations of current videoconferencing technology being used to deliver online teaching sessions and suggested some enhancements that may improve student engagement. It is important to identify how widespread these perceptions are and to understand the underlying contributing factors.

1.3 Understanding Student Engagement in Online Teaching Sessions

The present paper presents the results of a survey questionnaire of undergraduate students perceptions of their engagement during online synchronous teaching sessions using videoconferencing software. This includes the prevalence of active participation by students (by using chat, microphone, video, and screen sharing) during these sessions, the factors influencing their decision to engage or not, and what can be done to encourage participation and improve effectiveness.

2 Method

A mixture of qualitative and quantitative data were collected via a JISC online survey questionnaire from undergraduate students across two disciplines and four years (Foundation and Second year Computing, and third and fourth year Medicine). Generally, the participants were recruited via emails, which included a hyperlink to the survey. The survey was not linked explicitly to the students' teaching sessions, except for the third year medical cohort (where a link to the survey was included with an online quiz activity). Thematic analysis was conducted on the free-text responses (themes were emergent rather than pre-determined).

Table 1. Survey questionnaire questions.

	Text
1	I agree to participate
2	During an online session (such as Zoom or MS Teams), how often have you
2.1	spoken using your microphone
2.2	shared your screen with others

(continued)

Table 1. (*continued*)

	Text
2.3	shared your video with others
2.4	posted messages into chat
3	During an online session (such as Zoom or MS Teams), how many people would you be comfortable
3.1	hearing you speak via a microphone
3.2	sharing your screen with
3.3	seeing you via video camera
3.4	seeing message(s) posted by you
4	What influences your use (or not) of a microphone to speak to others in online sessions?
5	What influences you in sharing your screen (or not) with others in online sessions?
6	What influences you sharing (or not) your video camera to others in online sessions?
7	What influences your use (or not) of posting into chat in online sessions?
8	Is your behaviour during online sessions (such as Zoom or MS Teams) different to face-to-face sessions? If so, how?
9	Is there anything that the lecturer / tutor could do or has done to encourage or hinder your use of these online facilities (microphone, screen-share, video, chat)?
10	Is there any aspect of the technology (Zoom / MS Teams) that has encouraged or hindered your use of these online facilities (microphone, screen-share, video, chat)?
11	Is there anything that could be changed with the technology (Zoom and/or MS Teams) to encourage your use of these online facilities (microphone, screen-share, video, chat)?
12	Do you prefer online or face-to-face teaching sessions?
13	Please explain why you prefer this?

Table 1 shows the thirteen questions used in the survey. Question one related to participant consent and subsequent questions were only available if the user chose to participate (by selecting 'yes' to this question). Question two used categories, and aimed to elicit information regarding students' previous use of engagement facilities (microphone, screen-share, video camera, and chat). Question three also used categories, and aimed to elicit information regarding students' comfort levels with different engagement facilities (microphone, screen-share, video camera, and chat). Questions four to seven were free-text and looked at factors influencing student engagement. Questions eight to eleven were also free-text and looked at behaviour (both student and lecturer) and technology in the engagement process. Question twelve collected students' preferences for online or face-to-face teaching sessions, and question thirteen aimed to understand the reasons behind their choice.

3   Results

A total of twenty three students responded to the survey. No data was recorded if someone declined, so it was not possible to determine how many decided not to participate.

3.1   Prevalence of Modes of Engagement

This section describes the results from questions regarding the prevalence of different modes of engagement (microphone, screen-share, video, and chat) amongst students.

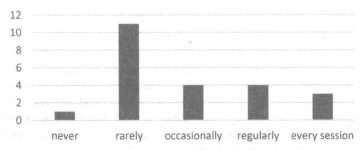

Fig. 1. Bar Graph showing how often students had used their microphone during online teaching sessions (Question 2.1).

Figure 1 shows a graph of responses indicating how often students had used their microphone during online teaching sessions. The graph is skewed toward the less frequent end of the scale. The most prevalent response was rarely, with a single student saying never and similar spread of responses on the other categories.

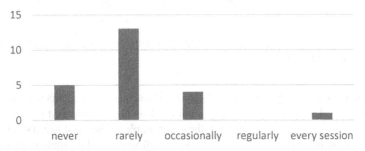

Fig. 2. Bar Graph showing how often students had shared their screen during online teaching sessions (Question 2.2).

Figure 2 shows a graph of responses indicating how often students had shared their screen during online teaching sessions. This graph is also skewed toward the less frequent end of the scale. The most prevalent response was rarely, with a five students saying never, four students saying occasionally, and one student saying every session (which seems

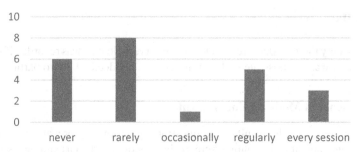

Fig. 3. Bar Graph showing how often students had shared their video during online teaching sessions (Question 2.3).

unlikely in every online lecture, but more likely during a small number of tutorial type online sessions). No students indicated that they shared screen regularly.

Figure 3 shows a graph of responses indicating how often students had shared their video camera during online teaching sessions. The graph is bimodal with two distinct grouping at either end of the response range. Six students said they had never shared video and eight rarely. In contrast, three students indicated that they had shared video in every session and five regularly. Only one student gave the response occasionally. This question seems to divide the students more than any other.

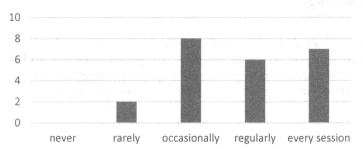

Fig. 4. Bar Graph showing how often students had posted messages into chat during online teaching sessions (Question 2.4).

Figure 4 shows a graph of responses indicating how often students had posted messaged into chat during online teaching sessions. This graph is skewed toward the more frequent end of the scale (in contrast to the other graphs). The most prevalent responses were occasionally, regularly, and every session (all with similar numbers of students - eight, six, and seven respectively). Two students said they rarely posted to chat and no students indicated they never used chat.

3.2 Comfort with Modes of Engagement

This section describes the results from questions regarding student comfort with different modes of engagement (microphone, screen-share, video, and chat) amongst students for different group (audience) sizes.

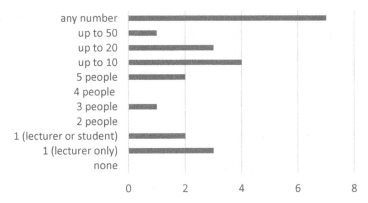

Fig. 5. Bar Graph showing how many people students would be comfortable speaking to using their microphone during online teaching sessions (Question 3.1).

Figure 5 shows a graph of how many people students would be comfortable speaking to using their microphone during online teaching sessions. It is multimodal, with peaks at 'any number', 'up to 10' and '1 (lecturer only)'. The responses fall into three groups. Seven students indicted that they would be comfortable using a microphone with any number of people. Nine students indicated they would be comfortable with between five and twenty people. Five students indicated they would only be comfortable with a single person (three of them would only be comfortable with the lecturer).

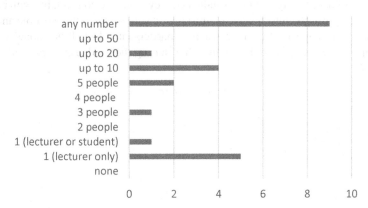

Fig. 6. Bar Graph showing how many people students would be comfortable sharing their screen with during online teaching sessions (Question 3.2).

Figure 6 shows a graph of how many people students would be comfortable sharing their screen with during online teaching sessions. It is multimodal, with peaks at 'any number', 'up to 10' and '1 (lecturer only)'. The responses fall into three groups. Nine students indicted that they would be comfortable sharing their screen with any number of people. Seven students indicated they would be comfortable with between five and twenty people. Six students indicated they would only be comfortable with a single person (five of them would only be comfortable with the lecturer).

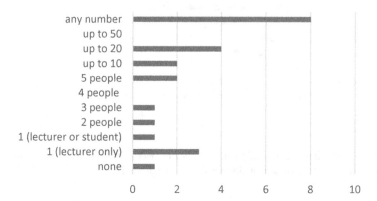

Fig. 7. Bar Graph showing how many people students would be comfortable sharing their video camera with during online teaching sessions (Question 3.3).

Figure 7 shows a graph of how many people students would be comfortable sharing their video camera with during online teaching sessions. It is multimodal, with peaks at 'any number', 'up to 20' and '1 (lecturer only)'. The responses fall into three groups. Eight students indicted that they would be comfortable sharing their video camera with any number of people. Eight students indicated they would be comfortable with between five and twenty people. Seven students' responses were between three people and none. This is the only engagement mode where a participant selected the 'none' category indicating that they would not be comfortable sharing their video camera at all.

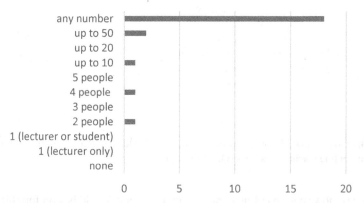

Fig. 8. Bar Graph showing how many people students would be comfortable seeing their messages posted in chat during online teaching sessions (Question 3.4).

Figure 8 shows a graph of how many people students would be comfortable seeing their messages posted in chat during online teaching sessions. In contrast to the other engagement modes, it is unimodal and heavily skewed toward the 'any number' category (eighteen students reporting), with two students selecting the 'up to 50' category. The remaining three participant responses are spread across categories from ten to two people, forming a low plateau.

3.3 Factors Influencing Student Engagement

This section describes the results from questions regarding factors influencing use of different modes of engagement (microphone, screen-share, video, and chat) amongst students.

Table 2 shows the emergent themes regarding what influences student use (or not) of a microphone to speak to others in online sessions. Six students commented that smaller group sizes encourage this type of engagement, one of whom also mentioned familiarity with group members having the same influence. Five students mentioned being influenced by the behaviour of other students (not wanting to be the first to speak), with one describing being wary of accidentally interrupting others who were speaking. Two students mentioned their subject knowledge influencing engagement. Individual students mentioned factors that discourage engagement, such as recording of sessions, lecturer tone or criticism of student responses (especially incorrect ones), bandwidth problems and discomfort with 'public speaking'.

Table 2. Emergent themes regarding what influences student use (or not) of a microphone to speak to others in online sessions (Question 4).

Participant count	Theme description
6	Group size
5	Other students
3	Lecturer questions
2	Breakout rooms
2	Technology mishaps
2	Lecturer support
2	Lecturer criticism/tone
2	Subject knowledge
1	Interrupt
1	Familiarity
1	Public speaking
1	Recording
1	Communication barrier
1	Bandwidth problems
1	Others need help

Table 3 shows the emergent themes regarding what influences students sharing their screen (or not) with others in online sessions. Four students mentioned group size (smaller groups encourage engagement). Four students indicated that they would only do this when required. Four students indicated that they would only do this when there was a clear purpose or that it was more effective. Three students indicated that screen-sharing was something they associated with presenting or leading the session (one of which mentioned 'stage fright' as an inhibitor). One student indicated that their limited familiarity with the videoconferencing technology inhibited their engagement.

Table 3. Emergent themes regarding what influences students sharing their screen (or not) with others in online sessions (Question 5).

Participant count	Theme description
4	Group size
4	Required
4	Purpose/effectiveness
3	Presenting/leading/stage fright
1	Technology unfamiliar

Table 4 shows the emergent themes regarding what influences students sharing (or not) their video camera to others in online sessions. Six students indicated that they would only do this if required to do so. A further three students indicated that they would 'just rather not' do this, was 'just uncomfortable in front of a camera', and mentioned 'anxiety about appearance and background'. Four (other) students indicated that smaller group size made sharing their video camera more likely. Two students indicated that familiarity with group members also made this more likely. Two students said that video was distracting during sessions. One student being influenced by other students not responding to requests to share video. Another student indicated that they would share video to make it easier for others to hear what they were saying.

Table 4. Emergent themes regarding what influences students sharing (or not) their video camera to others in online sessions (Question 6).

Participant count	Theme description
6	Required
4	Group size
3	Rather not/anxiety
2	Bandwidth
2	Familiarity

(*continued*)

Table 4. (*continued*)

Participant count	Theme description
2	Distracting
1	Others not responding
1	Hearing

Table 5 shows the emergent themes regarding what influences students posting (or not) into chat in online sessions. Two students indicated that chat allowed them to engage without interrupting the speaker and another student commented that chat allowed them time 'to think what I mean' when composing the post. There were contrasting views, as one student indicated that chat allowed them 'to get my point across when I don't feel comfortable using the mic', while another said that they could not 'usually type fast enough to answer using the chat' so 'would preferentially unmute and speak'.

Table 5. Emergent themes regarding what influences students posting (or not) into chat in online sessions (Question 7).

Participant count	Theme description
2	Not interrupting speaker
1	Time to compose
1	Set activities
1	Uncomfortable with mic
1	Easiest
1	Follow others
1	Typing speed

3.4 Behaviour and Technology

This section describes the results from questions regarding student behaviour, lecturer behaviour and technology.

Table 6 shows the emergent themes regarding differences in student behaviour during online compared to face-to-face sessions. Eight out of twenty three students indicated that there was no difference in their behaviour. The other participants provided a variety of comments, suggesting limitations of both face-to-face and online delivery. Five students indicated they were less engaged in online sessions. However, one student indicated they were more engaged during online sessions. Two students described concern regarding online interruption inhibiting their engagement (that it is 'harder to tell when others will speak online'). One student mentioned face-to-face distractions and two students mentioned online distractions. Another student mentioned greater freedom to move around in online sessions (such as going 'to the bathroom whenever you want') and that this would not disrupt the session.

Table 6. Emergent themes regarding differences in student behaviour during online compared to face-to-face sessions (Question 8).

Participant count	Theme description
8	No
5	Online less engaged
2	Online interruption
2	Online distraction/less focused
1	Face-to-face distraction
1	Online more audible
1	Online hiding
1	Online non-attendees
1	Online talking to yourself
1	Bandwidth
1	Online more engaged
1	Group influence
1	Online more relaxed
1	Online greater freedom
1	Face-to-face disruption

Table 7 shows the emergent themes regarding lecturer/tutor behaviour that encourages or hinders student use of microphone, screen-share, video, and chat (Question 9). Eleven out of twenty three students (just under half) could think of nothing the lecturer could do to influence student use of engagement technologies. However, the other twelve students provided twelve comments, which included not recording online sessions, using interactive tasks (such as quizzes or polls), using breakout rooms, and avoiding being 'very critical towards wrong answers' given by students. One response regarding not recording sessions mentioned 'screen shots of people were shared on social media'. It seems likely that this caused distress, but is not clear whether it was done by the lecturer or other students.

Table 7. Emergent themes regarding lecturer/tutor behaviour that encourages or hinders student use of microphone, screen-share, video, and chat (Question 9).

Participant count	Theme description
11	No
2	Online not record
2	Online quiz/poll
2	Breakout room
1	Lecturer criticism
1	Lecturer non-response
1	Online training
1	Group size
1	More face-to-face
1	Online com barrier
1	Online privacy breech
1	Online interactive
1	Don't force engagement

Table 8 shows emergent themes regarding aspects of the technology that encourages or hinders use of microphone, screen-share, video, and chat. Four students mentioned bandwidth being insufficient to support the use of the engagement mechanisms (especially when multiple facilities are used at the same time by multiple students). One student mentioned a related issue of the equipment limitations (of their laptop) struggling to support the engagement mechanisms.

Table 8. Emergent themes regarding aspects of the technology that encourages or hinders use of microphone, screen-share, video, and chat (Question 10).

Participant count	Theme description
8	No
4	Bandwidth
1	Online tech clarity (privacy)
1	Online accounts
1	Equipment limitations
1	Allow exercises in lecture
1	Online public speaking

(continued)

Table 8. (*continued*)

Participant count	Theme description
1	Video very uncomfortable
1	Online rewatch
1	Zoom easier than Teams

Table 9 shows the emergent themes regarding changes to the technology that would encourage student use of microphone, screen-share, video, chat. Two students commented that ensuring the lecture's microphone was good enough quality to clearly pick up their audio would help. One student suggested providing facilities that would allow lecturers to monitor the chat more effectively (presumably students posts were not responded to at times). Another explicitly requested the ability to 'privately voice chat with the lecturer' and also asked for the ability to 'toggle being able to see yourself in the Zoom participant panel when your camera is on'. It was not clear if this was to just not see yourself or if it was a request that only the lecture could see your video. Individual students also requested small breakout rooms and an 'introductory session' to ensure students are familiar with videoconferencing technology to prevent time being lost.

Table 9. Emergent themes regarding changes to the technology that would encourage student use of microphone, screen-share, video, chat (Question 11).

Participant count	Theme description
12	No
2	Lecturer mic
1	Lecturer monitor chat
1	Smaller breakout rooms
1	Disable camera
1	Private mic with lecturer
1	Online intro session

3.5 Preference Between Face-To-Face and Online

This section describes the results from questions regarding preference for face-to-face and online sessions amongst students.

Figure 9 shows student preference for online or face-to-face. There seems to be a general preference for face-to-face sessions (eleven students), although this is not unanimous with five students preferring online sessions. It is interesting the in both groups there are more students in the strong category. This question seems to be quite divisive amongst students. There was only one student who said they had no preference. There were six

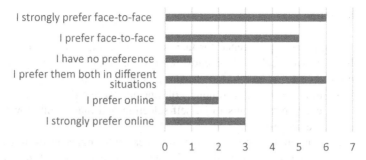

Fig. 9. Bar graph showing student preference for online versus face-to-face teaching sessions (Question 12).

students who indicated a shifting preference depending on circumstances. However, two students who selected 'I prefer them both in different situations' commented that they 'prefer face-to-face' but gave specific criteria for online being necessary (convenience and travel).

Table 10 shows emergent themes regarding students explanations of their preference for either online or face-to-face teaching sessions. Eleven students commented that face-to-face sessions were easier. Seven students indicated that it was easier to focus in face-to-face sessions (fewer distractions). Two students indicated that face to face sessions allowed them to approach the lecturer privately at the end of the session (and that online sessions tended to end immediately and not provide this opportunity). Three students mentioned reduction in travel as a benefit to online sessions. Three students also indicated that online sessions allowed them to use their own machine to take notes and undertake work (one specifically mentioned not owing a laptop). One student stated that face-to-face sessions were an 'unnecessary risk … in the middle of a pandemic'.

Table 10. Emergent themes regarding students explanations for their preference of either online or face-to-face teaching sessions (Question 13).

Participant count	Theme description
11	Face to Face interaction easier
7	Face to Face easier to focus, fewer distractions
3	Travel
3	Use own machine - take notes, work
2	Prefer face to face
2	Rewatch recording
2	Privacy/after lecture
1	Pandemic risk

4 Conclusions

More students reported a preference for face-to-face teaching sessions. However, the topic was divisive, with peaks at both ends of the scale (suggesting strongly opposing views). The preference for face-to-face teaching is an interesting outcome given that the survey was administered asynchronously on-line and recruited via email (one might think this could cause participants to be self-selecting and bias results toward those students with online preference).

There is variation amongst students; some find it easier to engage face-to-face, others find it easier to engage online, and others have similar engagement with both (but still report slightly different experiences). Some students are still engaged online, even though they are not visible (they like that lack of visibility, it feels more private and this makes them more relaxed which allows them to engage better).

4.1 Prevalence and Preference of Engagement Mode

There was variation amongst students in prevalence and preference for microphone, screen-share, and video use. These modes of engagement divided the students - there were peaks at either end of the spectrum. Some students used them frequently and were very comfortable with them and other students tended not to use them and were uncomfortable with them.

However, students were almost unanimous in being far more comfortable engaging in on-line sessions by sharing chat messages that the three forms of engagement mentioned above.

4.2 Factors Influencing Student Engagement During Online Sessions

In face-to-face sessions there is a distinction between speaking when seated as part of the audience and standing at the front of the room as the presenter. The engagement experience online is pushed toward being the presenter at the front of the room (which many students find far less comfortable). There seems to be an association amongst some students between the role of presenter and engagement via microphone, screen-share, and video. This may be reenforced by the absence (for these engagement modes) of facilities to privately communicate with just the lecturer (leading to feelings of public speaking and stage-fright for some students).

Previous work has provided evidence that students are most comfortable and most frequently use chat compared to other mechanisms (Singhal 2020). The current study confirms this, but also offers an indication of the underlying reasons for this behaviour. The other modes of engagement (microphone, video, screen-share) have an increased perception of potentially interrupting the speaker. The nature of chat allows students to:

- take time to compose their message,
- engage without interrupting the speaker, and
- engage privately with the lecturer

The first two are due to the asynchronous nature of chat, while the third is a factor of the functionality provided by some of the technology.

There were several contrasting views from students, such as:

- distraction: some students commented that distraction occurred in the home environment during online sessions and other students described distraction during face-to-face sessions (this seemed to influence their preference, in a mutually exclusive manner)
- recording sessions: previous work includes comments from students regarding the benefits of being able to review a recording at a later time. The present study includes similar comments. However, it also contains comments from other students explicitly requesting that sessions are not recorded, and the recordings inhibit their engagement (which does not seem to have been elicited by previous studies). One comment indicated that the sharing of screen-shots of people on social media contributed to this. Although most systems have editing facilities, this can create an impractical time burden for staff.

The key here seems to be that it is the lecturer who students want to hear, but recordings will pick up students too. Students may be more comfortable with anonymous interactions (such as via quiz/polling systems) but this prevents staff from knowing who is engaging (or being able to identify those who are not and may need help).

Ironically the least contentious medium (chat) is the only one that (in Zoom) offers the facility to privately communicate with the lecturer alone. However, the availability of this facility may influence the high level of comfort and frequency with its use. All other mechanisms (microphone, screen-share, and video camera) broadcast to everyone. MS Teams offers no private communication. Students indicated that Zoom was preferred to MS Teams, but did not say why. This lack of one-to-one private chat facility within MS Teams may be a contributing factor, or students may just be more familiar with Zoom.

Small group size was a commonly described factor to encourage student engagement. However, the disruptive nature of breakout rooms can make it difficult for staff to rapidly group and regroup students during a session (both in terms of the time it takes to create and move between rooms, and the disorienting user-interface changes that occur).

There seems to be an 'online privacy-visibility paradox', where individuals need to be both visible and yet have their privacy respected. In face-to-face sessions this is easier to achieve, sessions were very rarely recorded (for privacy reasons) but everyone could see who was present and how engaged they were. In online sessions, using cameras and microphones to engage makes people more visible but puts people in the position of being the presenter more than they would in face-to-face sessions and raises privacy issues that were far less present during face-to-face sessions. Alternatively, not using these aspects of the technology allows people to 'hide', which can lead to a reduction in engagement. Both approaches can cause disengagement, with significant variation amongst students.

The results of this study suggest student behaviour can be very different online and face-to-face (i.e. different students find it easier to engage in the different situations).

4.3 Recommendations for Delivery of Online Sessions

The variation in student views and behaviour presents a challenge to deliver teaching sessions in a way that meets the (often conflicting) diversity of needs to support inclusivity (in a way that is sustainable for teaching staff and financially viable for institutions).

There were comments requesting better microphone equipment to improve the lecture's audio, but there were no similar comments regarding screen-sharing or video camera. This suggests that students place high value on being able to hear the lecturer and that this sometimes falls short.

The lecturer should have as much control as possible to record what they need and avoid recording students. It may be useful to be strategic and clear regarding when sessions are recorded. Generally, students are more interested in recordings of the lecturer's delivery of content (and less interested academically in recordings of other students unless those students are presenting). Student engagement may be inhibited if they are being recorded, so consider if this has pedagogic value (prior to the pandemic, blanket recording of all participants in teaching sessions would have been be been very unusual in face-to-face teaching, and would have raised ethical and privacy concerns).

The facility to only share video, screen, microphone with a single person (mainly the lecturer/host) was requested as a means to encourage student engagement.

It is very challenging for staff to be delivering, dealing with face-to-face questions, ensuring screen is projected in room, ensuring screen-share is working, ensuring mic is working (on mute when privacy needed, speaking to students, and not talking on mute when presenting) and monitoring/responding to chat. A possible solution is to schedule face-to-face and online sessions separately rather than attempting to run hybrid sessions.

4.4 Further Work

In the present study, the number of questions in the survey were intentionally limited to encourage participation (and as the relatively low numbers of responses may have identify individuals). However, it would be beneficial to consider:

- staff perceptions
- the students' discipline and year group (so that comparisons may be made)
- disability and mental health (such as social anxiety or dyslexia) to determine if there is a relationship (there are suggestions that the issues surrounding online learning may be more intense for those with disabilities, for example Williams 2021 mentions autism)
- the quality of student engagement and whether this is visible in a synchronous online session or occurs asynchronously outside scheduled teaching sessions.
- the comparison of online versus face-to-face student engagement (is it the same students who are engaging online and face-to-face)

References

Dixon, M., Syred, K.: Teaching lung pathology during a pandemic: can further developments of an online quiz primer improve the engagement of students in a completely on-line delivery? In: Zaphiris, P., Ioannou, A. (eds.) HCII 2021. LNCS, vol. 12784, pp. 409–426. Springer, Cham (2021). https://doi.org/10.1007/978-3-030-77889-7_29

Gay, G.H.E.: From discussion forums to emeetings: integrating high touch strategies to increase student engagement, academic performance, and retention in large online courses. Online Learn. J. **24**(1), 92–117 (2020)

Heo, H., Bonk, C., Doo, M.Y.: Enhancing learning engagement during COVID-19 pandemic: self-efficacy in time management, technology use, and online learning environments. J. Comput. Assist. Learn. **37**, 1–13 (2021)

Hu, Y., Ow Yong, J.Q.Y., Chng, M.L., Li, Z., Goh, Y.S.: Exploring undergraduate nursing students' experiences towards home-based learning as pedagogy during the COVID-19 pandemic: a descriptive qualitative exploration. BMC Nurs. **21**(13), 1–9 (2022)

Joia, L., Lorenzo, M.: Zoom in, zoom out: the impact of the COVID-19 pandemic in the classroom. Sustainability **13**(5), 2531 (2021)

Kay, D., Pasarica, M.: Using technology to increase student (and faculty satisfaction with) engagement in medical education. Adv. Physiol. Educ. **43**(3), 408–413 (2019)

Lee, A.Y., Moskowitz-Sweet, G., Pelavin, E., Rivera, O., Hancock, J.T.: "Bringing you into the zoom": the power of authentic engagement in a time of crisis in the USA. J. Child. Media **15**, 91–95 (2020)

Mahr, A., Cichon, M., Mateo, S., Grajeda, C., Baggili, I.: Zooming into the pandemic! a forensic analysis of the zoom application. For. Sci. Int. Dig. Invest. **36**, 1–12 (2021)

Nickerson, L.A., Shea, K.M.: First-semester organic chemistry during COVID-19: prioritizing group work, flexibility, and student engagement. J. Chem. Educ. **97**(9), 3201–3205 (2020)

Oka, H., Suardita, K.: Japanese dental students' perceptions of videoconferencing lectures in the global classroom. MedEdPublish **7**(9), 9 (2018)

Singhal, M.K.: Facilitating virtual medicinal chemistry active learning assignments using advanced zoom features during COVID-19 campus closure. J. Chem. Educ. **97**(9), 2711–2714 (2020)

Stevanovic, A., Bozic, R., Radovic, S.: Higher education students' experiences and opinion about distance learning during the Covid-19 pandemic. J. Comput. Assist. Learn. **37**, 1682–1693 (2021)

Vishwanathan, K., Patel, G., Patel, D.: Impact and perception about distant online medical education (tele-education) on the educational environment during the COVID-19 pandemic: experiences of medical undergraduate students from India. J. Family Med. Prim. Care **10**(6), 2216–2224 (2021)

Williams, N.: Working through COVID-19: 'Zoom' gloom and 'Zoom' fatigue. Occup. Med. **71**(3), 164 (2021)

An Instrument for Self-assessment of Data Literacy at the Micro, Meso, and Macro Educational Levels

Belén Donate[1]([✉]) [iD], Francisco José García-Peñalvo[1] [iD], Daniel Amo[2] [iD],
Eduard de Torres[2] [iD], and Javier Herrero-Martín[3] [iD]

[1] University of Salamanca, 37008 Salamanca, Spain
`belendonate@usal.es`
[2] La Salle, Universitat Ramon Llull, 08022 Barcelona, Spain
[3] Centro Superior de Estudios Universitarios La Salle, 28023 Madrid, Spain

Abstract. In only two years, COVID-19 has forced the transformation of the educational system with emergency and radical changes concerning the digitalisation and virtualisation of classrooms. A new hybrid teaching-learning context is opening in which learning analytics becomes relevant as teaching support to adapt instruction to the different learning rhythms of connected learners. As well as for students to make decisions in their self-regulated learning. However, for its proper implementation at the micro, meso and macro educational levels, it is necessary to detect and fill those gaps through training to have a sufficient level of data literacy of the roles involved. However, the educational inquiry doesn't provide any data literacy self-assessment tools. This paper aims to provide an instrument for self-assessment of data literacy at micro, meso and macro levels in the educational context. The methodology of the work has been designed considering two phases. The first is based on the development and validation of the questionnaire through a documentary methodology with a qualitative approach. The second is based on its implementation, through a descriptive methodology with a quantitative approach. Aiming to precisely determine the wording according to the population of interest, the validity of the banks of items constructed and their content, have been carried out employing the expert consultation method.

Keywords: K-12 education · Data literacy · Learning analytics

1 Introduction

COVID-19 has generated a significant impact on society in recent years, particularly the pandemic situation that has pushed educational institutions to react by enhancing the digitisation of teaching [1–3]. The introduction of these new practices firmly supported by digital tools [4, 5], could constitute a bridge towards the development of learning analytics for educational improvement [6]. In this respect, learning analytics is based on "the measurement, collection, analysis and presentation of data about learners and their contexts to understand and optimise learning and the environments in which it

P. Zaphiris and A. Ioannou (Eds.): HCII 2022, LNCS 13328, pp. 228–237, 2022.
https://doi.org/10.1007/978-3-031-05657-4_16

occurs" [7]. Thus, they are recognised as a reference area in the field of Learning Technologies, because they facilitate decision-making in education through technical and methodological approaches to data management [8].

Similarly, they are limitations in data management at certain educational levels that have to be examined to make accessible this scientific field. One factor of particular relevance is the implications and risks derived from privacy, confidentiality and security policies for using data of underage students in the K-12 stages [9]. However, it is possible to establish the necessary conditions to create a private and secure environment for using student data in online contexts to study and analyse this information [10]. In the same way, working with data local is possible considering the possibilities of local technologies as mediators of teaching-learning processes [11]. In any case, to recognise and address these privacy problems, educational needs, improvements in teaching-learning processes and certain levels of data literacy, must be achieved.

1.1 Data Literacy Competencies

The concept of "Data literacy" has been defined by multiple authors. They coincide in that it is "the extraction, management and processing of data with an ethical and critical approach" (Raffaghelli, 2018). According to [13] literature review of 8 frameworks for data literacy, it can be identified the following elements or competencies: awareness, access, engagement, management, communication, ethical use and preservation.

- Awareness is competence-based on the understanding of data and its role in society.
- Access is the identification, location, and appropriate use of data streams.
- Engagement is an element encompassing data-driven decision making. It refers to the assessment, analysis, administration, and interpretation of data.
- Management encompasses data planning and management, including administration and analysis, security protocols for data storage, data exchange and data-driven documentation.
- Communication is competency-based in the process of synth, creating displays, and presenting data effectively.
- Ethical use is an element based on an understanding of the issues involved in the use of data.
- Preservation is referred to the long-term practices of storing, using, and reusing data.

Authors addressing educational data literacy seek to assess data management for practice, information and learning analytics [12]. In the literature review conducted by [13], the following categories of teaching competencies for data literacy have been taken as reference:

- Data awareness and understanding.
- Access to data.
- Engagement in interpretation and decision making.
- Management and planning.
- Communication and ethical use.
- Preservation or storage.

In turn, Juliana E. Raffaghelli (2018) y Mandinach & Jimerson (2016) set out the knowledge or activities that define them. However, the transferability of data literacy skills to different professional sectors (business, social media, research laboratories, education) entails several risks in the educational K-12 environment. In this line, according to Raffaghelli (2018), most works and questionnaires on educational data literacy focus on the teaching perspective, with the most important contributions coming from Higher Education [15, 16]. On the other hand, Buckingham (2012) highlights in this idea the potential for learning analytics to have a positive impact on teaching. He points out that it would be achieved through sound pedagogical design, their systematic application, and the transmission of the necessary data handling skills. He further argues that learning analytics considers different analytical ranges that converge with each other, distinguished at the following levels:

- Micro-level: refers to the processes of monitoring and interpreting learner data at individual and group levels. These data can be managed by both teachers and students themselves, generating a double benefit: the assessment of at-risk students and the proportion of an appropriate intervention; an insight into their learning habits, and recommendations for improvement for self-management of learning. Such data could be obtained through serious games, automatic tagging, educational data mining, computer-supported collaborative learning, recommender systems, intelligent tutoring systems/adaptive hypermedia, information visualisation, computational linguistics and argumentation, and social network analysis.
- Meso-level: operates at an institutional level. To the extent that educational institutions share similar processes with sectors that already benefit from educational data management. In this way, it supports decision-making, with a better understanding of the impact of different variables in a shared way. In turn, it improves management decision-making and the allocation of organisational resources.
- Macro-level: enables a type of inter-institutional analytics. So it means improved access to standardised assessment data. Whether at the state level or across students' lifetimes.

These three levels define different data literacy competencies or skills. Therefore, is established a taxonomy based on the roles of learner, teacher and and high school management staff.

1.2 Proposal

This paper will address one of the barriers that can most significantly condition the use of learning analytics at these levels: data literacy in K-12 schools. In this line, as stated by [18], the emergence of new digitalised educational practices has revealed a lack of digital skills and data literacy among K-12 teachers. In response to this, the present work focuses on the elaboration of a self-assessment instrument, to determine the current status or level of data literacy for the development of K-12 learning analytics in Spain [19]. The general and specific objectives are defined as follows:

To design an instrument to measure the level of data literacy of the management team, coordinators, teachers, and students in the K-12 stages.

- To establish the first approximation of the validation of the self-assessment instrument in data literacy.
- To evaluate limitations and detect improvements in the items of the questionnaire.
  The document has been organised into four sections. Sect. 1 presents the introduction of the problem and the objectives of the work. Then, in Sect. 2, the methodology of the instrument design and the initial validation process are presented. Subsequently, Sect. 3 shows the results obtained in the questionnaire validation. The paper ends with Sect. 4, which discusses the results and draws conclusions.

2   Method

A documentary methodology with a qualitative approach to preparing this self-assessment instrument has been used.

For this purpose, several works on this subject that could constitute a framework have been selected. The steps followed for the development of the work are described in more detail below:

2.1   Documentary Analysis and Selection of Frameworks

Aiming to establish a set of frameworks, a type of documentary research technique was carried out: a content analysis. This research technique allows the evaluation of the discourse nature, the internal structure of the information or its form of organisation [20]. Hence, this type of analysis allows for the contextualisation of the data and its validity. Bearing in mind the incipient nature of learning analytics at K-12 educational levels [21], an attempt has been made to establish a search for reference frameworks that may fit with their characteristics in data literacy. To this end, we have used as a criterion that the competencies of each framework have sufficient conceptual breadth to adjust the different educational segments. Likewise, it has ensured that the complexity of the knowledge and self-assessment tasks match the education levels at a basic level of data handling.

Hence, considering these criteria, a pre-selection of two frameworks was performed [12, 22].

As a fundamental approach, the work of Raffaghelli (2018) has been analysed. According to the literature review of [14] in [12], to manage data, teachers must identify problems, use data, transform data into useful information and evaluate the results.

The following table shows how the competencies developed by these authors are developed in knowledge or tasks which are represented in Table 1 below:

Table 1. Competencies-Knowledge/Tasks [14] in [12].

Competencies	Knowledge/Tasks
Identify Problems	• Use data to identify problems in educational practice within groups, levels of education or high school • Use data to address an educational problem, reporting on solutions created at an institutional level
Use data	• Identify institutional data sources and their purposes
Transform data into information	• Make decisions data-based for the school's pedagogical projects and activities
Lowest Level Heading	• Understand how to visualise, represent, and share data from school projects and pedagogical actions • Consider ethical aspects of all data-driven processes
Evaluate outcomes	• Determine the steps of monitoring, diagnosing, and adjusting teaching, with understanding of the contexts surrounding decisions • Support learner data literacy and pedagogical data literacy by discussing the data sets adopted throughout a learning process/activity

Based on the above framework, it should be considered that data management involves a set of people performing different tasks: teachers, coordinators, managers, and students. Thus, the approach of Buckingham Shum (2012) has followed to cover the different levels surrounding each educational segment which are represented in Table 2 below:

Table 2. Data Literacy Levels [17].

Level	Educational Agent
Micro	It corresponds to teaching practice and students as active agents in their learning, using data to solve educational problems
Meso	It refers to the coordinators of pedagogical activities and projects of the educational institution
Macro	This level involves high school management and is associated with inter-institutional actions

2.2 Instrument Design

The design of the self-assessment instrument has aimed at the collection of personal perceptions of teachers, students, coordinators, and managers about their abilities in data literacy processes. Therefore, the items haven't been meant to collect correct or incorrect answers about competencies in this area, but rather aspects related to self-perception of effectiveness. In this way, a Likert-type scale to express the degree to which the person who completes it considers that "he/she feels capable of developing knowledge or tasks in data management" was developed. For this purpose, a scale from 1 to 6 has been established, where 1: "I do not feel able", 2: "With help, I can accomplish this task", 3: "Without help, I can accomplish this task in a basic way", 4: "Without help, I can completely accomplish this task in its entirety", 5: "I have enough theoretical-practical knowledge to help others in this task", and 6: "I have enough theoretical-practical knowledge to help and teach others in this task".

The scale design process consists of two phases, which were decisive for the items development.

In the first phase, a division of the contents into four scales has been established. Consequently, each scale according to the activities developed by each level (micro, meso and macro) has been elaborated. [17]. Secondly, the competencies and the knowledge/task, proposed by [12, 14], were used to make adaptations adjusted to the activities carried out by educational agents: students, teachers, coordinators and high school management staff. The following table shows some examples of statements or items following the micro-level scales and their relationship with the competencies presented by the authors:

Table 3. Items and competencies in micro-level data literacy.

Competencies	Levels	Items
Identify Problems	Micro-level teachers	I use data from digitised learning environments (e.g., virtual classroom learning activities, applications or other tools) to identify learning problems of the students and groups I teach
	Micro-level students	I use data from virtual classroom activities, applications, or other digital tools to understand the improvement of my learning
Use data	Micro level-teachers	I use different data sources to conclude my teaching practice and student learning
Transform data into information		I can test assumptions about the students' learning process or my teaching practice through data representation
Evaluate outcomes	Micro level-teachers	I can generate actionable information on student performance and needs through data management
	Micro level-students	I visualise and monitor my learning data in digital environments

Regarding the instrument meso-level, aimed at coordinators, items were included based on the knowledge and activities of the frameworks, with adaptations to the type of activity they carry out. In this way, the items included aspects connected to institutional management such as the development, monitoring and programming of the school's pedagogical projects or activities. Concerning the macro level, items based solely on the competencies of identifying problems and evaluating results have been established. The main reason for this was the inter-institutional nature of this level, which does not so much examine data management processes as the exchange of results obtained through them. The same is true for the micro-level questionnaires, represented in Table 3, addressed to students. In this case, the items have been established based on the two competencies above because the rest of them may be of a complexity that a K-12 learner would not be able to address.

2.3 Instrument Validation

According to [23], questionnaires require indicators of the degree of precision they measure. So, following this author, guaranteeing their validity and reliability is a fundamental aspect. Also, the content of the item bank constructed requires attention in the validation [24]. Thus, two external validations and one documentary validation had developed.

On the one hand, the expert consult had developed by sending the questionnaire to professionals. This process aims to judge more precisely the wording and approach of the items for the population of interest. On the other hand, the questionnaire had sent to students for their assessment. In addition, it had added an exhaustive bibliographical review of literally sources.

3 Results

The validation by twenty teaching experts leaves the following comments and average response times:

- It takes an average of 6 min to answer the questionnaire.
- The items seem well structured, elaborated, and well thought out.

Validation by ten students leaves the following comments and average response times:

- It takes an average of nine minutes to answer the questionnaire.
- Explanations are requested on the meaning of several terms such as "K-12 stages in education" or "Data Literacy" used in the questionnaire presentation.
- They indicated that the items were easy to understand, "I understood the questionnaire and would not add anything else". Except for the item "I visualise and monitor data on my learning in digital environments", where they point out that it could be drafted in a way that is easier to understand.

The most relevant limitations identified by the teaching experts, in the wording of the items, recommended that to assess the perception of ability, the conjugated verb should be replaced by its infinitive: "I use data" instead of "I use". In this way, they emphasised that it is necessary to point out in the items that the aim is to measure the perception of "competence" rather than its application. Along these lines, some experts point out that "the results are subjective to the participant and not objectively validated in quantitative terms". Therefore, they suggested that instead of writing the item "I use different sources of data to conclude my teaching practice and student learning", the action verb "use" or "I consider the data" should be replaced by "I am or would be able to". Similarly, they recommend that instead of including "Data Literacy in Education Questionnaire Validation" in the title, "Assessment of self-perceived competence in data literacy and data management" should be used.

On the other hand, they recommend including definitions and examples of concepts that are difficult to understand, such as Data Literacy, K-12, data literacy and data management tools. At the same time, they ask for examples of data to contextualise certain statements, for example, "platform accesses, total time, deliveries, notes or interactions".

Finally, they highlight the need to redefine some items as there are no differences in their content. These are: "I use evaluation, content transmission or visualisation tools that allow me to work with raw data to extract quick and elaborated results" and "I use tools that allow me to process raw data in statistical tools for the extraction of results (e.g., cleaning, merging and creating visualisations of the data)".

4   Discussion and Conclusions

According to the results, the following improvement questionnaire elements have been detected:

- The need to redefine items to make their wording clearer and more suitable for K-12 practice.
- Improvements are needed in the wording to make it easier to understand what is to be measured: "personal perception of competence in data handling".
- Definitions and clarifications of concepts that may be new to this population should be included in the wording.
- Practical examples of data management relevant to the K-12 teacher's context are requested. That is to say, data management software, or the specification of the type of data to be collected: access to the platform, total time, deliveries, notes or interactions.

These results suggest that the population will require simplification of the knowledge or activities of the items. At the same time, students seem to be unfamiliar with data management concepts. All of this shows the need to reformulate the instrument to improve the comprehension of the items.

Finally, we cannot ignore the fact that the frameworks encompass a broader population than the K-12 stages.

For this reason, it is relevant to point out the relevance of this type of validation to identify several needs, for instance, by readapting the vocabulary and the background of the items.

Therefore, this work fosters to continuation to collect comments and assessments that reflect the data literacy of educational agents at these stages. That will improve the validity and reliability of the instrument.

Acknowledgments. The research that has given rise to these results has been carried out through funds from Secretariat of Universities and Research of the Generalitat de Catalunya, and Ramon Llull Univ. Ref. Project: 2021-URL-Proj-057.

References

1. García-Peñalvo, F.J., Rector, R.R.-O., Rodríguez-Conde, M.J., Rodríguez-García, N.: The institutional decisions to support remote learning and teaching during the COVID-19 pandemic. In: 2020 X International Conference on Virtual Campus (JICV), pp. 1–5 (2020). https://doi.org/10.1109/JICV51605.2020.9375683
2. Gil-Fernández, R., León-Gómez, A., Calderón, D.: Influence of COVID on the educational use of social media by students of teaching degrees. Educ. Knowl. Soc. **22**, E23623 (2021)
3. Knopik, T., Oszwa, U.: E-cooperative problem solving as a strategy for learning mathematics during the COVID-19 pandemic. Educ. Knowl. Soc. EKS. **22**, e25176–e25176 (2021)
4. García-Peñalvo, F.J., Corell, A.: La COVID-19: ¿enzima de la transformación digital de la docencia o reflejo de una crisis metodológica y competencial en la educación superior? Campus Virtuales. **9**, 83–98 (2020)
5. García-Peñalvo, F.J., Corell, A., Abella-García, V., Grande-de-Prado, M.: Recommendations for mandatory online assessment in higher education during the COVID-19 Pandemic. In: Burgos, D., Tlili, A., and Tabacco, A. (eds.) Radical Solutions for Education in a Crisis Context: COVID-19 as an Opportunity for Global Learning, pp. 85–98. Springer, Singapore (2021) https://doi.org/10.1007/978-981-15-7869-4_6
6. Amo, D., Santiago, R.: Learning Analytics: la narración del aprendizaje a través de los datos. Editorial UOC (2017)
7. About SoLAR: https://www.solaresearch.org/about/, Accessed 13 Jan 2022
8. García-Peñalvo, F.J.: Learning analytics as a breakthrough in educational improvement. In: Radical solutions and learning analytics, pp. 1–15. Springer (2020)
9. Amo, D., Alier, M., García-Peñalvo, F., Fonseca, D., Casañ, M.J.: Privacidad, seguridad y legalidad en soluciones educativas basadas en Blockchain: Una Revisión Sistemática de la Literatura. RIED Rev. Iberoam. Educ. Distancia. **23**, 213–236 (2020). https://doi.org/10.5944/ried.23.2.26388
10. Amo, D., Navarro, J., Casañ, M.J., García-Peñalvo, F.J., Alier, M., Fonseca, D.: Evaluación de la importancia de la ética, privacidad y seguridad en los estudios de Learning Analytics. In: en el Marco de las Conferencias LAK, (2019). https://doi.org/10.26754/CINAIC.2019.0073
11. Amo, D., Gómez, P., Hernández-Ibáñez, L., Fonseca, D.: Educational warehouse: modular, private and secure cloudable architecture system for educational data storage. Analysis Access. Appl. Sci. **11**, 806 (2021)
12. Raffaghelli, J.E.: Educators' Data Literacy. MEDIA Educ. STUDI Ric. BUONE Prat. pp. 91–109 (2018). https://doi.org/10.4399/97888255210238
13. Maybee, C., Zilinski, L.: Data informed learning: A next phase data literacy framework for higher education (2015)
14. Mandinach, E.B., Jimerson, J.B.: Teachers learning how to use data: a synthesis of the issues and what is known. Teach. Teach. Educ. **60**, 452–457 (2016)

15. Calvani, A., Fini, A., Ranieri, M., Picci, P.: Are young generations in secondary school digitally competent? a study on Italian teenagers. Comput. Educ. **58**, 797–807 (2012)
16. Slavin, R.E.: Evidence-based education policies: transforming educational practice and research. Educ. Res. **31**, 15–21 (2002)
17. Buckingham Shum, S.: Learning Analytics. https://www.solaresearch.org/core/unesco-policy-brief-learning-analytics/ (2012)
18. Domínguez Figaredo, D., Reich, J., Ruipérez-Valiente, J.A.: Analítica del aprendizaje y educación basada en datos: un campo en expansión. RIED Rev. Iberoam. Educ. Distancia. **23**, 33 (2020). https://doi.org/10.5944/ried.23.2.27105
19. Donate, B., García-Peñalvo, F.J., Amo, D.: Learning Analytics in K-12 Spanish education: a systematic mapping study. In: 2021 XI International Conference on Virtual Campus (JICV), pp. 1–4 (2021) https://doi.org/10.1109/JICV53222.2021.9600315
20. Martín, S.N.: El "análisis de contenido" como técnica de investigación documental: aplicación a unos textos de prensa educativa, y su interpretación mediante "análisis de correspondencias múltiples." Rev. Investig. Educ. RIE. **10**, 179–200 (1992)
21. Donate, B., García-Peñalvo, F.J., Amo, D.: Learning Analytics in K-12 Spanish education: a systematic mapping study. In: 2021 XI International Conference on Virtual Campus (JICV), pp. 1–4. IEEE (2021). https://doi.org/10.1109/JICV53222.2021.9600315
22. Raffaghelli, J.E.: Developing a framework for educators' data literacy in the European context: proposal, implications and debate. In: International Conference on Education and New Learning Technologies EDULEARN, pp. 10520–10530 (2019)
23. Muñiz Fernández, J.: Las teorías de los tests: teoría clásica y teoría de respuesta a los ítems. Papeles Psicólogo Rev. Col. Of. Psicólogos. (2010)
24. Sireci, S.G.: The construct of content validity. Soc. Indic. Res. **45**, 83–117 (1998)

Designing Dashboards to Support Teachers in Online Learning Tools

Sidra Iftikhar[✉] [iD], Carles Garcia-López[✉] [iD], David García-Solórzano[✉] [iD], Enric Mor[✉] [iD], and Ana-Elena Guerrero-Roldán[✉] [iD]

Universitat Oberta de Catalunya, Barcelona, Spain
{Siftikhari,Carlesgl,Dgarciaso,Emor,aguerreror}@uoc.edu

Abstract. Online learning contexts make it difficult for the teachers to be aware of the progress of their classrooms. As the absence of in-person interaction in online learning inhibits students' perceptions about their learning to be conveyed to the teacher. Considering the context of online programming education, similar problems arise. Designing data rich interfaces for teachers that provide them with desired information about the classroom and learners will facilitate the teachers to monitor the progress of learners. In this work we present the design of teachers' dashboards for an online learning programming laboratory tool. This tool encourages students to acquire programming skills by practicing concepts and has been incorporated in two online programming courses of two different bachelor's degree programs. Even though the teachers could view each learner's solved activities, it was still difficult for them to have a clear view of how each learner is progressing in their practice and what is the learning status of the entire classroom. The identification of this issue is a consequence of the user-centered design (UCD) approach that has been carried out to design the dashboards, actively involving the course teachers. The involvement of teachers made it possible to identify user scenarios that were helpful in definition of the key performance indicators (KPIs) and views for the different dashboards. The designed teachers' dashboards for the online learning laboratory are an effective tool for the teachers to make timely decisions related to the classroom that could affect the students' learning, performance, and engagement.

Keywords: User-centered design · Online learning · Learning tools · Dashboards · Teachers' dashboards · Learning to code

1 Introduction

The acquisition of programming skills, like any other skill acquisition, is effectively done by virtue of practice [1, 2]. However, in online settings, challenges are posed, such as the communication gap between students and lecturers that exists throughout the teaching-learning process [3]. Many online courses promote asynchronous communication in which there is limited or no face-to-face interaction between the learners and teachers. As a result, students have the control of their own learning process, whereas the teacher is no longer a transmitter of knowledge, but a facilitator who constantly guides each student

P. Zaphiris and A. Ioannou (Eds.): HCII 2022, LNCS 13328, pp. 238–252, 2022.
https://doi.org/10.1007/978-3-031-05657-4_17

through their learning process and arranges meaningful learner-centered experiences [4]. Given this shift of the roles, lecturers and teachers need appropriate ways to monitor the learners in terms of their learning process, performance and engagement that will enable them to provide learners with just-in-time feedback and assistance. In this regard, the learner data that is stored in the learning management systems (LMS) can be used. However, the amount of data is so huge that teachers need some support to manage it in an effective way and make it useful. To overcome such a problem, the use of visual learning analytics (VLA) is a good solution. VLA is defined "as the use of computational tools and methods for understanding educational phenomena through interactive visualization techniques" [5]. Such techniques generate visual representations that reveal facts and trends that allow users to infer unknown information by combining the visual inputs with their knowledge of data.

One of the most relevant and useful VLA tools is the dashboard. Dashboards are instruments intended to improve decision-making by amplifying or directing cognition and capitalizing on human perceptual capabilities [6]. Such tools for an online learning programming environment may help to draw the teachers' attention to the problems learners are facing with practice of programming activities, for instance the students find activities difficult. As a result, teachers may provide relevant feedback and make timely pedagogical decisions. Therefore, in this work we propose the design of a set of teachers' dashboards (TD) for an online programming learning laboratory tool called CodeLab. This tool is based on the learning-by-doing approach and provides students with the opportunity to learn to program by the virtue of practice, as learning to code is achieved by continuous practice. A set of detailed learning itineraries containing learning activities based on coding concepts is presented to the learners for practicing. In CodeLab, where there are no face-to-face experiences between teachers and learners, through this study we identified that the teachers need to know about the learning, practice, progress, and perceptions of the entire classroom and of each learner. For the whole classroom, often a quick overview is sufficient to be aware of the progress, which is hard to attain in an online learning programming laboratory.

The online laboratory tool, CodeLab has been designed and developed through a user-centered design (UCD) approach involving the course teachers at all stages [7]. The involvement of teachers in the UCD process first helped us identify the main user scenarios in this case; that are the "overview of the course" and "overview of each student". After the definition and creation of user scenarios the relevant key performance indicators (KPIs) and views have been identified that can provide teachers with information on learners' practice and performance. Due to the relevance of practice in the learning process of programming, and that the tool encourages the learners to practice learning the programming concepts, data related to practice of learning activities was considered a main KPI. The scope of this work includes the presentation of the design process of the first scenario, "overview of the course" in detail. Since the teachers have been involved throughout the design and development process, constant feedback from the teachers helped us deliver the dashboards that proved to be useful for teachers in terms of addressing their teaching goals. The rest of the article is structured as follows: Sect. 2 discusses the related work, Sect. 3 presents the methodology, Sect. 4 discusses the design process for teachers' dashboards and finally Sect. 5 provides discussion and conclusion.

2 Related Work

Several research works suggest the use of student tracking systems to gather data from LMS, transform them into a form convenient for processing and generate graphical representations that can be explored by instructors. Such tools consist of a set of visualizations that represent different aspects of the teaching-learning process. Two of the pioneering students tracking systems are CourseVis [8] and its successor, GISMO (Graphical Interactive Student MOnitoring tool) [9], which allow teachers to examine social, cognitive, and behavioral aspects of their learners. Likewise, Zhang et al. [10] designed a plug-in for Moodle called Moodog which, besides displaying student tracking data, also sends automatic reminders to learners. In spite of the benefits of student tracking systems, they also had some drawbacks. The most relevant one was that switching among various views in order to see all the data could be a time-consuming and tedious task for instructors. As a result, dashboards have been suggested in recent years.

Dashboards are defined by Schwendimann et al. [11] as "a single display that aggregates different key performance indicators (KPIs) about learners, learning processes, and/or learning contexts into one or multiple visualizations". Over the past decade, several learning analytics dashboards have been created and introduced in the literature that provide various kinds of information about learners, for example, about academics and performance. This is the case of the Zeitgeist dashboard [12], which provides simple metrics as a result of analyzing user interactions with resources stored in a LMS called MAZE, e.g., the number of downloaded items. Similarly, Podgorelec and Kuhar [13] created two dashboards, one for lecturers and one for teaching assistants. The KPIs were collected in a survey sent to 183 users. It was noticed that, although both users shared most of the needs, there was some information that was more relevant for lecturers than for teaching assistants and vice versa. Both dashboards used different types of visualizations, such as box and whiskers diagrams for having an overview of the grades from practical work, line diagrams showing both attendances and submitted assignments, a table with sparklines and bullet diagrams, etc. Another early dashboard was the Student Activity Meter (SAM) [14], which focused on higher-level indicators in order to display time spent on learning activities and document use statistics. To do this, SAM used basic graphical representations such as bar charts, an animated tag cloud and parallel coordinates. Likewise, Charleer et al. created LARAe (Learning Analytics Reflection & Awareness environment) [15], a dashboard which delivered visualizations that helped get insights about how learners interact with content and with other classmates, teams, and external users. The novelty of this dashboard is that it uses badges to abstract essential milestones of the course, such as achieving course goals, writing a specific number of posts, receiving comments, etc.

Dashboards have also used in face-to-face scenarios in order to have key indicators in real time so that the teacher can adapt their instruction according to the needs of the classroom for example, MTDashboard [16] provided teachers with real-time key indicators while students worked in small groups in a collaborative face-to-face activity in an enriched multi-tabletop classroom. This dashboard thus displayed radar charts for displaying the number of touches on the tabletop per student and the equality among group member touches.

In recent years, dashboards have added data that go beyond the learning process itself but necessary for teachers. For example, EMODA [17] presents students' emotions from four data sources: audio, video, self-report, and interaction traces. Likewise, the current focus is also put on other educational stakeholders, such as study advisers (SA). This is the case of LISSA (Learning dashboard for Insights and Support during Study Advice) [18], a dashboard that was designed to facilitate communication between SAs and students by visualizing commonly available grade data. Other dashboards for academy advisers are Student Explorer [19] and LADA (Learning Analytics Dashboard for Advisers) [20]. Moreover, contemporary learning dashboards [21] do not only show feedback based on outcomes, but they also give information about how students can improve themselves by looking for inefficient processes (e.g., showing common learning patterns and their correlation to assignment results).

Several studies also focus on the design process of the dashboards itself. In this context, Abel discusses the design of a teacher's dashboard for an iPad application for middle school mathematics teachers [22]. A combination of design approaches including participatory design, conceptual design and activity theory have been used for the dashboards to identify relevant data and wireframes were created and validated by the teachers. Likewise, Molenaar et al. [23] designed of teachers' dashboards to facilitate primary school mathematics teachers by following Verberts' learning analytics process [24]. The dashboard displays students' performance by marking the completed, reattempted and incorrectly performed learning activities. A color-coded scheme has been used to highlight the students' progress. Ahn et al. [25], in turn, use a human centered design (HCD) approach to design a dashboard for middle school mathematics teachers. In a similar scenario, Aleven et al. [26] discuss the user centered design of the teachers' dashboard for an intelligent tutoring system for school level students. Usage scenarios related to how teachers can reflect on students' practice have been created additionally and the prototypes have also been validated by teachers. In a similar scenario, Holstein et al. [27] present a user centered design approach for the teachers' dashboard, Luna, that is also based on intelligent tutoring.

To the best of our knowledge, few studies present the design process of dashboards for tools related to learning to program. Regarding this, Basawapatna [28] proposed the design for teachers' dashboard for a game-based application that has been incorporated to the computer programming students of K-12 level. Similarly Santos et al. built StepUp [29], a PI system in the form of a dashboard that empowered second year engineering students to reflect on their own activity (e.g. the time spent with different tools, such as Eclipse IDE) and that of their peers in a course in which the learners developed software in Java. Likewise, Fu et al. [30] conducted a study that aims to propose dashboards for teachers that are teaching C programming language to novice learners. The dashboards report the students' progress by providing an insight of the type of errors the students make when learning to program. For remote labs, Joan and Uttal [31] present a teachers' dashboard with the aim of providing students' progress data in terms of submission statistics of lab journals. Additionally, the students who require support from the teachers are highlighted so that teachers can provide them with help. However, a detailed design approach has not been discussed in this study.

In online settings dashboards play a vital role for teachers to facilitate and enhance their teaching process, by presenting them all the required information. Designing dashboards through a design process that involves the users, in this case teachers, helps to identify clear design goals related to the teaching process. The teachers can express their needs and facilitate the identification and definition of the user scenarios that comprise of the relevant data necessary for them to carry out their online teaching. In case of this work, where we propose the dashboards for CodeLab tool, the teachers' dashboards aim to address a major issue faced by the teachers that is being aware of the progress of the online programming classroom. Unlike other studies that involve the teachers in the design process, our work has involved teachers at all stages, from the design to the development stage and ensured that the teachers were in close collaboration with the design and development team concerning all the decisions taken during this process.

3 Methodology

Universitat Oberta de Catalunya (UOC) is a fully online university which aims to provide online learners with quality personalized higher education. Addressing this aim of UOC, an online programming learning laboratory tool called CodeLab has been designed and developed to support students throughout the learning process while they are enrolled in programming courses [7]. This tool enables students to learn to program through practice, fostering autonomy. In addition, the tool allows communication between peers and the teacher through synchronous conversational communication channels. The tool has been incorporated in two online programming courses in two different degree programs: Bachelors of Digital and Design Creation, and Bachelors of Multimedia. The medium of education of both degree programs are Catalan and Spanish language and this aspect has also been considered for the design of the tool. The total number of students in both the courses were 229. Particularly, CodeLab is used in courses to learn to code in not STEM studies. This means that in some cases, learning to program becomes a challenging task for learners. For this purpose, CodeLab was designed to provide students with a setting where they can learn to program through practice and, at the same time, be able to monitor and organize their own learning progress.

3.1 Design Goals

Tools and environments to learn programming have been in existence for a long time, many of which are face-to-face. These face-to-face environments make it somewhat more accessible for the teachers to monitor the learner's progress, as they share the same physical space where they can interact and are well aware that the learners are engaged. This common situation in a face-to-face setting becomes a challenge in online settings, where communication and interactions between teachers and students are mediated by an online learning platform. Despite this complexity, some teachers were already carrying out monitoring tasks through systems that they had defined themselves. In some cases, for example, teachers used spreadsheets to take notes on some of the data they had on students. Although at that point of the project CodeLab offered other relevant functionalities, a new challenge was identified to facilitate this monitoring activity for teachers.

In this regard, a challenge is presented that takes the form of a design goal that was divided into a twofold objective: enable teachers to monitor the overall progress of (1) the class as a whole and of (2) the individual students.

3.2 Design Process

Given the complexity of the design challenge, the process was addressed through a user-centered design (UCD) approach, following the principles and phases of the ISO 9241-210 human-centered design process [32]. The iterative and participatory nature of a user-centered design process can be particularly enriching in the design of digital learning contents and tools [33]. Although, as described in [7], the users of the learning tool are students and teachers, for the design presented in this work, we focused on teachers, who were actively involved in each of the design phases, rather than only participating in evaluation phases at the end of each iteration of the process. Specifically, a total of 12 teachers were involved in design workshops. Of this, 8 teachers during the test and pilot of dashboards in real settings; and 4 teachers were fully involved in the design and development meetings as well as in the workshops carried out during the design process. Furthermore, it is worth highlighting that the teachers participated actively in the design and evaluation of prototypes during workshops and design meetings.

Design scenarios describe the tasks that a specific user wants to perform in a specific context to sketch out technological solutions [34, 35]. Thus, during the first phase of the design process, two main scenarios were identified (Table 1) with teachers according to the design goal described above. These scenarios were the starting point for the design of the solution presented in this work.

Table 1. Scenarios of use

Scenario	Details
1. Overview of the course	Teachers should be able to proactively see the overall progress of the classroom at a glance
2. Overview of a specific student	Teachers should be able to proactively and reactively monitor a student's overall progress at a glance

Key Performance Indicators (KPI) can measure and monitor the progress of the educational goals to improve the students' performance [36], allowing teachers to identify strategies for effective teaching and learning [37]. Therefore, for each of these scenarios, together with the teachers we defined a list of KPI that teachers considered relevant in order to monitor the progress of students' learning. The gathering of these indicators proposed by teachers and those identified in the literature resulted in a long list of indicators. With the two scenarios described above in mind, and during the working sessions with the teachers, it was identified that providing the teachers with the list of KPIs was not sufficiently illustrative to get an overview of the monitoring of the class, since they do not convey what teachers need. In this sense, as pointed out in [38], a dashboard is a way to offer the user different interfaces to make the interaction between the user and the KPIs easier. Thus, the need to design different dashboards that could meet the scenarios and allow teachers to monitor the overall progress of both the class and an individual student was defined. Although two scenarios were initially defined (Table 1), this iteration of the design process focused on the design of a solution for Scenario 1: Overview of the course.

4   Dashboards' Designs

Designing a dashboard is a difficult task, as it involves understanding the teacher's needs to identify and visually represent the KPIs to convey the information that address the user needs. KPIs summarize key information about how students use the learning tool, but they do not convey a clear understanding to the teacher. That is why an important aspect, and one that generated the most discussion, was to identify the best graphical representation for each KPI. In this regard, one of the first aspects that were discussed with the teachers was the definition of the visual representations of the KPIs listed above (Table 2).

Table 2. KPI in course dashboard

KPI	Visual representation
Activities	**Pie chart** with the completed challenges or activities in relation to the total of the course
Annotations	**Pie chart** with the number of activities or challenges that contains personal annotations
Access	**Bullet graphs** displaying the number of times the student has accessed the course, the challenge or the activity in comparison to their peers
Time spent	**Bullet graphs** displaying the time the student has spent in the course, the challenge or the activity in comparison to their peers
Messages	**Bullet graphs** displaying the messages the student has published in the course or the challenge in comparison to their peers
Perceptions	Graphics with numbers with the average value of the perceptions of the activities of the course
Status	When did the learner last connected to the tool

Nevertheless, it is not only about how the user views the selected KPI, but also how the user interacts with the platform that presents the information. That is, how the user uses the system. In this regard, use cases are a convenient approach to defining how the user interacts with a system [39] to address the design of an interface [40].

Due to the participation of diverse teachers, it was challenging to design use cases that met the needs of all of them. Although all teachers initially had similar profiles, the reality was that there were significant differences in needs and in the ways, they monitor students' performance. In order to define these use cases by considering the teachers' goals, two elements were taken into account:

The case had to describe how teachers monitor students according to the scenarios described in Sect. 3.1.

These designs had to reflect in one form or another the structure of the courses themselves.

Regarding this second element, and as detailed in CodeLab [7] contents are structured as follows: (1) course, (2) challenges and (3) activities. First, for each course, CodeLab provides learners with a set of challenges designed by teachers. Each challenge aims to ensure that students acquire the knowledge and practice the skills related to a programming concept. To this end, each challenge provides a specific itinerary of programming activities. All activities are classified according to two criteria: difficulty and type of activity. Furthermore, in order to give students more autonomy in their learning process, the activities are open for practice since the beginning of the course.

These three levels of structure were taken as dimensions of information to allow teachers to access the information about their classrooms.

4.1 Navigation

As mentioned above, the design not only focused on the different interfaces, but also on the navigation between these screens. In terms of information architecture, two key aspects were defined that have a major influence on the navigational system (Fig. 1):

1. The teacher should first find an entry page (Home) that allows access to the rest of the information and, at the same time, shows a summary of some key information.
2. The teacher should find all the information easily from the homepage.

A major reason for these design decisions was the analogy with a face-to-face laboratory, where the teacher can have an overview of the whole classroom from the same spot, without having to move from one place to another.

Fig. 1. Structure of the information provided in the dashboards.

4.2 Home Page

During the design workshops carried out with teachers, they all expressed their satisfaction in having an entry page (Fig. 2) that allows them to have such an overview at the click of a button from that page. As previously mentioned, this entry page not only provides links to further information, but also presents a summary of some of the relevant information. On the one hand, the teacher can see the overall progress in each of the challenges of the course through progress bars. These indicate which challenges are completed, in progress or not started (a in Fig. 2). On the other hand, they can also see an overview of the notifications on the communication channels, including the number of messages and mentions received. This information is also segmented by challenge (b in Fig. 2). Finally, in the lower section of the page, the teacher is provided with drop-down sections for each challenge of the course, where the list of activities can be seen (c in

Fig. 2). Regarding the list of activities, the teacher can also observe the average progress bar for each of the activities and the average of the students' perceptions about the level of difficulty, time taken and level of satisfaction. These perceptions have been gathered for different learning activities in CodeLab and on the homepage the average has been summarized.

4.3 Course Dashboard

As explained above, the broadest dimension in CodeLab is the course dimension. Course dashboard provides the most overall information of the course. The interface adopts the same structure as the entry page but with different information. First, the teacher can find the general data of the course in the first layout of the screen (a in Fig. 3). This part contains information about the communication in the course and information about the average of the students' perception ratings. In the second layout of the interface, the general progress of each of the challenges that configure the course is displayed (b in Fig. 3), but in more detail compared to the home page. A major distinction from the home page is the third layout (c in Fig. 3). Here the list of the students of the course can be seen with some information about each of them according to the course dimension. Table 2 shows how the information is displayed for each student.

Fig. 2. CodeLab home page (teacher view).

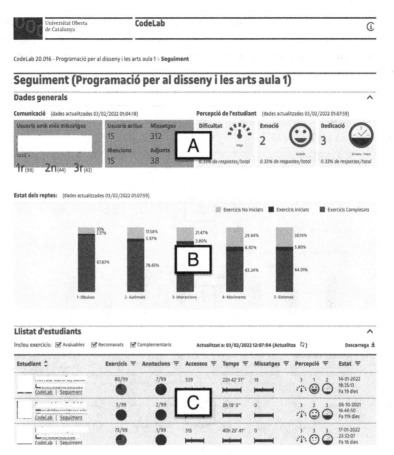

Fig. 3. Dashboard of a course in CodeLab.

4.4 Challenge Dashboard

In terms of the challenge dimension, we designed a dashboard to be able to visualize the key information of each challenge of the course. The interface layout of the dashboard containing the information about a challenge is like the one that provides information about the course. Interface wise, it is also similar to the homepage. The difference is concerned with the level of detail this dashboard provides. In Fig. 4-part a, as can be seen the average of perception ratings and student activity on the CodeLab communication channel, per challenge is averaged. Similarly, later in part b, the progress of each activity in the challenge can be seen.

4.5 Activity Dashboard

The most fine-grained information is displayed at the activity level dashboard. Information corresponding to each learning activity for the classroom is presented. As presented in Fig. 5, for the activity "hello world", the average learner perceptions and the average number of messages on the communication channel about the activity are displayed. Later the list of students is also presented that provides information about the completion status of the activity, number of times it was accessed, learner perception and the time spent on the activity.

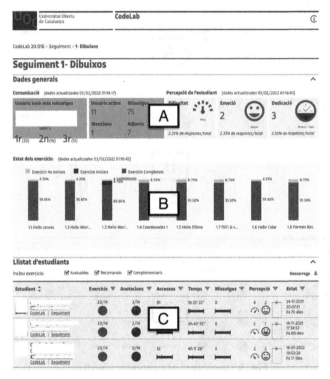

Fig. 4. Dashboard of a challenge in CodeLab.

5 Discussion and Conclusions

The design and development of the teachers' dashboards for CodeLab has been user centric at all the stages. Implying that the teachers were not just involved to identify the need for the teachers' dashboards, but they were also present and actively involved in all the design and development meetings and workshops that aimed to discuss the user scenarios, use cases for views and relevant KPIs. Each design decision for the inclusion or exclusion of information, number of dashboards required addressing the scenarios were discussed, designed and validated in detail with the teachers. Even at the development stage, the teachers were involved in the discussion of the final version of the dashboards with the developers. As mentioned, the CodeLab learning tool has already been used in the previous 2 semesters before the designing and development of the teachers' dashboards. The teachers' previous usage experience also provided an advantage. Initially, when the laboratory tool was designed and developed, the teachers were only involved in certain phases, whereas this time for the teachers' dashboards they provided continuous feedback to the designers and presented complete participation.

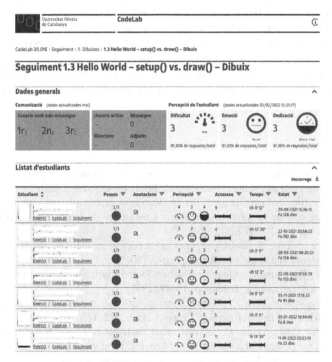

Fig. 5. Dashboard of an activity in CodeLab.

Design workshops were useful not only to define scenarios, use cases and dashboards but also to evaluate the design solutions. The 8 teachers that used the new dashboards in a course with students were satisfied with the fact that they could clearly have the overview of the classroom, at all the levels: course, challenge, and activity. The three new dashboards had provided them the opportunity to monitor the progress of the classroom, but they could also identify the issues faced by the students collectively, know about the student engagement and they also addressed collective issues in the communication channel. In this regard, and more specifically, in the beginning of the semester teachers were able to identify that the classroom was practicing less than expected. This allowed teachers to early detect learners at risk and provide feedback to motivate practice.

Although the major design goals were achieved, the new teachers reported that it was hard for them to navigate through the system especially when using it for the first time. For instance, teachers had difficulty in seeing information about an activity for the classroom from the home page. This leads to a conclusion that more emphasis should be put on the navigation aspects of the tool in design meetings and make it easy to use. The teachers also expressed that they believed there was room for improvement in the analysis of a few KPIs. For example, it was pointed out that the KPI "time spent on activities" has not been calculated accurately, since it overlaps the time of writing the code and time of being accessing the activity page. Similarly, the student status KPI on the dashboards could be refined, in terms of the number of activities preformed rather than considering the last connection time.

As future work, different objectives are defined to be undertaken. First, scenario 2 identified in this work, would be addressed to allow teachers to have an overview of each learner's performance. Secondly, the identified areas for improvement need to be addressed, such as the navigation through the tool and the refining of some visual representations. Finally, it is also important to start a design process that leads to the development of dashboards for students, which could foster their autonomy and self-awareness of the learning process.

References

1. Stigberg, H., Stigberg, S.: Teaching programming and mathematics in practice: a case study from a Swedish primary school. Policy Futur. Educ. **18**, 483–496 (2020)
2. Peng, W.: Practice and experience in the application of problem-based learning in computer programming course. In: 2010 International Conference on Educational and Information Technology, pp. V1–170. IEEE (2010)
3. Paulsen, M.F., Nipper, S., Holmberg, C.: Online education: learning management systems: Global e-learning in a scandinavian perspective. (2003)
4. Salomon, G.: The changing role of the teacher: From information transmitter to orchestrator of learning. Eff. responsible Teach. pp. 35–49 (1992)
5. Vieira, C., Parsons, P., Byrd, V.: Visual learning analytics of educational data: a systematic literature review and research agenda. Comput. Educ. **122**, 119–135 (2018)
6. Yigitbasioglu, O.M., Velcu, O.: A review of dashboards in performance management: implications for design and research. Int. J. Account. Inf. Syst. **13**, 41–59 (2012)
7. Garcia-Lopez, C., Mor, E., Tesconi, S.: CodeLab: an online laboratory for learning to code. In: Zaphiris, P., Ioannou, A. (eds.) HCII 2021. LNCS, vol. 12784, pp. 437–455. Springer, Cham (2021). https://doi.org/10.1007/978-3-030-77889-7_31
8. Mazza, R., Dimitrova, V.: Visualising student tracking data to support instructors in web-based distance education. In: Proceedings of the 13th International World Wide Web Conference on Alternate Track Papers & Posters, pp. 154–161 (2004)
9. Mazza, R., Milani, C.: Gismo: a graphical interactive student monitoring tool for course management systems. In: International Conference on Technology Enhanced Learning, Milan, pp. 1–8 (2004)
10. Zhang, H., Almeroth, K., Knight, A., Bulger, M., Mayer, R.: Moodog: tracking students' online learning activities. In: EdMedia+ Innovate Learning. pp. 4415–4422. Association for the Advancement of Computing in Education (AACE) (2007)
11. Schwendimann, B.A., et al.: Perceiving learning at a glance: a systematic literature review of learning dashboard research. IEEE Trans. Learn. Technol. **10**, 30–41 (2016)
12. Schmitz, H.-C., Scheffel, M., Friedrich, M., Jahn, M., Niemann, K., Wolpers, M.: CAMera for PLE. In: Cress, U., Dimitrova, V., Specht, M. (eds.) EC-TEL 2009. LNCS, vol. 5794, pp. 507–520. Springer, Heidelberg (2009). https://doi.org/10.1007/978-3-642-04636-0_47
13. Podgorelec, V., Kuhar, S.: Taking advantage of education data: advanced data analysis and reporting in virtual learning environments. Elektron. ir Elektrotechnika. **114**, 111–116 (2011)
14. Govaerts, S., Verbert, K., Duval, E., Pardo, A.: The student activity meter for awareness and self-reflection. In: CHI'12 Extended Abstracts on Human Factors in Computing Systems, pp. 869–884 (2012)

15. Charleer, S., Santos, J.L., Klerkx, J., Duval, E.: Improving teacher awareness through activity, badge and content visualizations. In: International Conference on Web-Based Learning, pp. 143–152. Springer (2014)
16. Martinez-Maldonado, R., Kay, J., Yacef, K., Edbauer, M.-T., Dimitriadis, Y.: MTClassroom and MTDashboard: supporting analysis of teacher attention in an orchestrated multi-tabletop classroom. (2013)
17. Ez-Zaouia, M., Lavoué, E.: EMODA: A tutor oriented multimodal and contextual emotional dashboard. In: Proceedings of the seventh international learning analytics & knowledge conference, pp. 429–438 (2017)
18. Charleer, S., Moere, A.V., Klerkx, J., Verbert, K., De Laet, T.: Learning analytics dashboards to support adviser-student dialogue. IEEE Trans. Learn. Technol. 11(3), 389–399 (2017)
19. Lonn, S., Aguilar, S.J., Teasley, S.D.: Investigating student motivation in the context of a learning analytics intervention during a summer bridge program. Comput. Human Behav. **47**, 90–97 (2015)
20. Gutiérrez, F., Seipp, K., Ochoa, X., Chiluiza, K., De Laet, T., Verbert, K.: LADA: A learning analytics dashboard for academic advising. Comput. Human Behav. **107**, 105826 (2020)
21. Dourado, R.A., Rodrigues, R.L., Ferreira, N., Mello, R.F., Gomes, A.S., Verbert, K.: A teacher-facing learning analytics dashboard for process-oriented feedback in online learning. In: LAK21: 11th International Learning Analytics and Knowledge Conference, pp. 482–489 (2021)
22. Abel, T.D., Evans, M.A.: Cross-disciplinary participatory & contextual design research: creating a teacher dashboard application. Interact. Des. Archit. **19**, 63–76 (2014)
23. Molenaar, I., Knoop-Van Campen, C.A.N.: How Teachers Make Dashboard Information Actionable. IEEE Trans. Learn. Technol. 12(3), 347-355 (2019). https://doi.org/10.1109/TLT. 2018.2851585
24. Verbert, K., Ochoa, X., De Croon, R., Dourado, R.A., De Laet, T.: Learning analytics dashboards: the past, the present and the future. In: Proceedings of the Tenth International Conference on Learning Analytics & Knowledge, pp. 35–40 (2020)
25. Ahn, J., Campos, F., Hays, M., Digiacomo, D.: Designing in context: reaching beyond usability in learning analytics dashboard design. J. Learning Analytics 6(2), 70–85 (2019). https://doi. org/10.18608/jla.2019.62.5
26. Aleven, V., Xhakaj, F., Holstein, K., McLaren, B.M.: Developing a teacher dashboard for use with intelligent tutoring systems. CEUR Workshop Proc. **1738**, 15–23 (2016)
27. Holstein, K., Xhakaj, F., Aleven, V., McLaren, B.M.: Luna: a dashboard for teachers using intelligent tutoring systems. Education **60**, 159–171 (2010)
28. Basawapatna, A., Repenning, A., Koh, K.H.: Closing the cyberlearning loop: enabling teachers to formatively assess student programming projects. In: SIGCSE 2015 - Proceedings. 46th ACM Technical Symposium Computer Science Education, pp. 12–17 (2015). DOI https:// doi.org/10.1145/2676723.2677269
29. Santos, J.L., Govaerts, S., Verbert, K., Duval, E.: Goal-oriented visualizations of activity tracking: a case study with engineering students. In: Proceedings of the 2nd International Conference on Learning Analytics and Knowledge, pp. 143–152 (2012)
30. Fu, X., Shimada, A., Ogata, H., Taniguchi, Y., Suehiro, D.: Real-time learning analytics for c programming language courses. In: Proceedings of the Seventh International Learning Analytics & Knowledge Conference, pp. 280–288 (2017)
31. Jona, K., Uttal, D.: Don't forget the teacher: new tools to support broader adoption of remote labs. In: 2013 10th International Conference on Remote Engineering and Virtual Instrumentation (REV), pp. 1–2. IEEE (2013)
32. ISO, B., STANDARD, B.: Ergonomics of human-system interaction. (2010)
33. Garcia-Lopez, C., Mor, E., Tesconi, S.: Human-centered design as an approach to create open educational resources. Sustainability. **12**, 7397 (2020)

34. Nardi, B.A.: The use of scenarios in design. ACM SIGCHI Bull. **24**, 13–14 (1992)
35. Bodker, S.: Scenarios in user-centred design-setting the stage for reflection and action. In: Proceedings of the 32nd Annual Hawaii International Conference on Systems Sciences. 1999. HICSS-32. Abstracts and CD-ROM of Full Papers, p. 11 (1999). DOI https://doi.org/10.1109/HICSS.1999.772892
36. Mohammed Badawy, A., El-Aziz, A., Hefny, H.: Exploring and measuring the key performance indicators in higher education institutions. Int. J. Intell. Comput. Inf. Sci. **18**(1), 37–47 (2018). https://doi.org/10.21608/ijicis.2018.15914
37. Bijan, M.: An innovative model for constructing a teaching-learning performance indicator. Int. J. Innov. Learn. **7**, 151–170 (2010)
38. Yoo, Y., Lee, H., Jo, I.-H., Park, Y.: Educational dashboards for smart learning: review of case studies. Emerg. Issues Smart Learn. 145-155 (2015)
39. Cockburn, A.: Structuring use cases with goals. J. object-oriented Program **10**, 56–62 (1997)
40. Constantine, L.L., Lockwood, L.: Structure and style in use cases for user interface design. Object Model. User Interface Des. **1**, 245–280 (2001)

An Analysis on Social Media Use for Learning Under the COVID-19 Condition in Japan

Toshikazu Iitaka(✉)

Kumamoto Gakuen University, Oe 2-5-1, Chuo-Ku, Kumamoto, Japan
iitaka2@yahoo.co.jp

Abstract. An analysis of the use of social media among Japanese students under the COVID-19 condition is presented in this study. Online research on the use of the Internet among Japanese was conducted in 2020. We collected data from 560 persons and compared the result of this research with those of similar research in 2018. We investigate the influence of COVID-19 on social media use for learning. We use analysis of variance to estimate changes among Japanese students under the COVID-19 situation. Furthermore, we analyze these changes through the Pearson correlation coefficient. These analyses allow the creation of meaningful research questions for future studies.

Keywords: Social media · COVID-19 · e-learning

1 Introduction

We will show the analysis on the use of social media for learning among Japanese students under the COVID-19 condition herein. A study [1] conducted comparable research. The analysis of literature [1] was based on research data from 2018. COVID-19 has altered the landscape of online learning. Many people have been compelled to work or study online because of COVID-19. Therefore, some remote working and learning questions are added to the questions presented in literature [1]. The results of the online research conducted in 2018 are then compared with those of a study conducted in 2020. We obtained some remarkable results that could be helpful in creating new research questions, which will facilitate the investigation on the use of social media for learning after COVID-19.

First, the significance and background of this research are presented in this study. Then, the research questions are described and the statistical analysis is presented. Finally, the limitation of this research and new research questions for future studies are described.

2 Significance and Background of This Research

This section reviews previous studies. This review will show that the current research is important. The major background of this study lies in social media use for learning. The current study is mainly is based on literature [1].

P. Zaphiris and A. Ioannou (Eds.): HCII 2022, LNCS 13328, pp. 253–264, 2022.
https://doi.org/10.1007/978-3-031-05657-4_18

First, we present the results of previous studies on the use of social media for learning. Literature [2] already reported the potential of social media for learning and teaching. Literature [2] mainly focused on the use of social media data for investigating effective teaching and learning, thus leading to the examination of the recommendation engine for learning. Therefore, literature [2] considers social media as a source of big data. Existing research indicated the advantage of social media in enabling users to connect with friends [3]. Another research revealed that social media provides a baseline for various learning materials [4]. These studies did not consider the direct use of social media for learning. However, some studies examined direct learning approaches using social media. For example, Ozawa pioneered the use of Twitter during lectures [5]. Ozawa indicated that interactive lectures can be realized by comments of attendants through Twitter. The presentation of Iitaka, which focused on digital note-taking, implied that collaboration of digital note-taking and note-taking via social media is relevant [6]. Literature [6] indicated that many Japanese students (approximately 40%) use social media for note-taking. This phenomenon can be maximized for effective collaboration (Fig. 1).

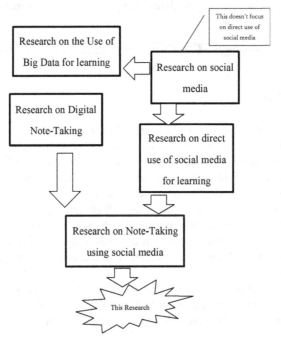

Fig. 1. Previous studies

Iitaka conducted online research based on the previous studies [1, 7]. Literature [1, 7] revealed that numerous Japanese students utilize social media, particularly Twitter, for note-taking (40% of students have used Twitter for digital note-taking). The distinction between students and nonstudents was statistically significant.

Considerable changes are prevalent because of COVID-19, and many people are forced to work or study online. Therefore, this study will examine the influence of these changes on learning using social media.

3   Research and Analysis

3.1   Research Feature

This section will present the features of this study, which is online research. The research was conducted in August 2020 to examine the influence of COVID-19.

The research was held by the same research company that conducted the previous research in 2018. The research design and distribution of samples are almost the same as those in 2018. Literature [1] analyzes the result of the online research. This study compares the result of the study conducted in 2018 with that obtained from the study conducted in 2020.

Table 1. Research feature.

Type of Survey		Online research
Period		2020.8.11–2020.8.20
Number of Samples		560
Gender		%
Female		50
Male		50
Age	%	Number of Samples
-19	25.2	141
20–29	31.8	178
30–39	10.4	58
40–49	10.2	57
50–59	10	56
60–69	7.1	40

Table 1 shows that the composition of samples is similar to the findings of Iitaka [1]. The research of literature [1] aimed to examine the use of social media for learning. We need additional samples that include frequent learners. Therefore, half of the samples are students who must learn more frequently than others.

Furthermore, we must define the independent variables before checking the research questions, thus allowing the examination of the use of social media for learning. Literature [1] studied only note-taking. However, we still investigated the general use of social media for learning.

The questions in Table 2 are four-scale questions. We created two variables based on the answers to the questions in Table 2. The first variable is "use of Facebook for

Table 2. Uses of social media for learning

Q1 Use Facebook to obtain information for learning
Q2 Use Facebook to ask someone what the users want to know
Q3 Use Facebook to connect with people who have the same learning objective
Q4 Use Facebook to record user learning
Q5 Use Facebook for note-taking (text data) (Literature [1] examined this aspect.)
Q6 Use Facebook for recording the photo of notebooks
Q7 Use Facebook for recording the photo of teaching materials with comments
Q8 Upload videos of practices on Facebook
Q9 Use Facebook for reading notes (including notes written by others)
Q10 Use Facebook for referring to photos of notebooks (including notes written by others)
Q11 Use Facebook for watching videos of explanation or performance for learning
Q12 Use Twitter to obtain information for learning
Q13 Use Twitter to ask someone what the users want to know
Q14 Use Twitter to connect with people who have the same learning objective
Q15 Use Twitter to record user learning
Q16 Use Twitter for note-taking (text data) (Literature [1] examined this aspect.)
Q17 Use Twitter for recording the photo of notebooks
Q18 Use Twitter for recording the photo of teaching materials with comments
Q19 Upload videos of practices on Twitter
Q20 Use Twitter for reading notes (including notes written by others)
Q21 Use Twitter for referring to photos of notebooks (including notes written by others)
Q22 Use Twitter for watching videos of explanation or performance for learning

learning," which comprises the answers from Q1–Q11. The second variable is "use of Twitter for learning," which comprises answers from Q12–Q22.

We must check the general changes in net use under the COVID-19 condition. Therefore, we examine the frequencies of the following online activities before and after the COVID-19 pandemic.

The questions in Table 3 are four-scale questions. We created two variables, namely "net use before COVID-19" and "net use during COVID-19," based on the questions in Table 3.

Table 4 shows that the distributions of variables are only slightly different from the normal distribution, except for "Note-taking using Facebook." Therefore, we will not use the variable "Note-taking using Facebook" for the analysis, which requires normal distribution.

Table 3. Questions regarding frequencies of net use.

Text	Abbreviation
Share(d) materials online and work(ed) or learn(ed) at home using these materials.	Share material
Watch(ed) movie of lectures online.	Watch movie
Learn(ed) or work(ed) at home receiving email or message of applications.	Mail or apps
Learn(ed) or work(ed) at home using a Web conferencing system.	Web conference

Table 4. Variables for the analysis of this study

	Mean	Std. Deviation	Skewness	Kurtosis	Reliability
Remote Learning or Working before COVID-19	7.00	3.71	0.99	−0.24	0.92
Remote Learning or Working during COVID-19	8.38	4.32	0.41	−1.26	0.93
Use of Facebook for Learning	15.54	7.86	1.65	1.69	0.98
Use of Twitter for Learning	16.47	8.04	1.44	1.10	0.96
Note-taking using Facebook(Q5)	1.42	0.79	1.83	2.32	–
Note-taking using Twitter(Q16)	1.47	0.82	1.61	1.46	–

3.2 Research Questions

This section introduces the research questions examined by the current study. This study focused on the research questions regarding the change under the COVID-19 situation.

We created the following research questions.

RQ1 Does the use of social media for learning among Japanese students change?

RQ2 Are the frequencies of remote working or learning related to the use of social media for learning?

3.3 Statistical Analysis

This section presents the statistical analysis based on the aforementioned research questions.

First, we examine RQ1. As previously stated, social media is currently used by a growing number of students for educational purposes. Iitaka indicated that an increased number of students tend to use social media for educational purposes [1]. We can assess the reproducibility of the outcome using crosstab analysis and t-test to compare pupils and others. We first present the crosstab analysis on note-taking.

Table 5. Crosstab analysis on note-taking

	Use Facebook for note-taking (text data)			
	Never	Seldom	Sometimes	Often
Not student	226	28	18	8
	80.7%	10.0%	6.4%	2.9%
Student	190	45	35	10
	67.9%	16.1%	12.5%	3.6%
Total	416	73	53	18
	74.3%	13.0%	9.5%	3.2%
	Use Twitter for note-taking (text data)			
	Never	Seldom	Sometimes	Often
Not student	225	35	14	6
	80.4%	12.5%	5.0%	2.1%
Student	175	42	51	12
	62.5%	15.0%	18.2%	4.3%
Total	400	77	65	18
	71.4%	13.8%	11.6%	3.2%

Table 5 shows that an increased number of students use social media for note taking. Then, we can demonstrate statistically significant differences in the use of social media for learning between students and others (Twitter: $t(545.54) = 5.84$, $p < 0.01$, Facebook: $t(551.35) = 3.19$, $p < 0.01$). Therefore, the result is reproducible considering this aspect.

Table 6. Frequencies of social media use for learning

		Mean	STD Deviation
Use of Twitter for Learning (2018)	Student	20.25	8.66
	Not student	14.24	6.89
	Total	17.25	8.38
Use of Facebook for Learning (2018)	Student	18.5	8.68
	Not student	14.19	6.8
	Total	16.34	8.08

(continued)

Table 6. (*continued*)

		Mean	STD Deviation
Use of Twitter for Learning (2020)	Student	18.4	8.38
	Not student	14.54	7.2
	Total	16.47	8.04
Use of Facebook for Learning (2020)	Student	16.59	8.22
	Not student	14.49	7.36
	Total	15.54	7.86

However, the usage frequencies of social media for learning among students have decreased as shown in Table 6. Therefore, we use a two-way analysis of variance to examine the interaction. The interplay between research date and sample attribution can then be discovered. We uncover statistically significant interactions considering the use of Twitter and Facebook for learning (Facebook, $F (1,1116) = 5.65$, $p < 0.05$; Twitter, $F (1, 1116) = 5.29$, $p < 0.05$) (Fig. 2).

The aforementioned figures reveal that the students in 2018 tend to use Twitter and Facebook for learning more often than those in 2020 (Facebook, $F (1, 1116) = 8.47$, p < 0.01; Twitter, $F (1, 1116) = 7.87$, $p < 0.01$). We can find a similar tendency in the use of other social media.

This phenomenon is associated with the increasing use of the network because of remote work or remote learning. Therefore, RQ2 must be examined (Table 7).

The use of social media for learning correlates with frequencies of remote working and learning before the COVID-19 pandemic (that is, the research in 2018). The usage of social media for learning in 2020 is still associated with remote working and learning. However, the correlation coefficient has decreased. Then, we establish a new variable by subtracting the frequency of remote working and learning before COVID-19 pandemic from that in 2020. We can evaluate if the samples began to work or study online regularly owing to the influence of COVID-19. Then, we can find a negative correlation between the use of social media for learning and this new variable of students (Facebook, $r = -0.272$, $p < 0.001$; Twitter, $r = -0.247$, $p < 0.001$).

Then, we examine the influence of remote learning or working on social media use for learning by multiple regression analysis. The independent variables are components of "remote learning or working before COVID-19" and "remote learning or working during COVID-19."

Figure 3 shows a difference between Facebook and Twitter. "Watch Movie during COVID-19" only affects the use of Twitter for learning. However, a similar tendency is observed. The same analysis is performed only on the data of students (Fig. 4).

We can find differences considering the use of Twitter. The analysis shows the negative effect of "mail or apps before COVID-19" and "share material during COVID-19."

This section presents the statistical analysis on the use of social media for learning among Japanese students. The first research question focuses on the change in the use of

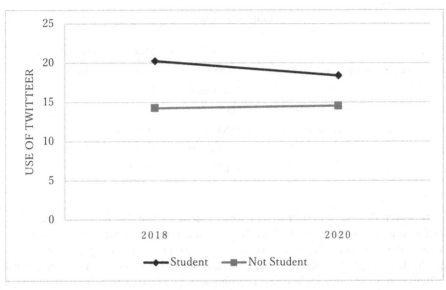

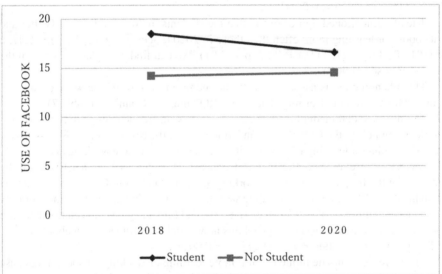

Fig. 2. Interaction on the use of social media for learning

Table 7. Relationship between the use of social media for learning and remote working or learning.

		Use of Twitter for Learning (2020)	Use of Facebook for Learning (2020)
(a) Remote Learning or Working before COVID-19	Not Student	0.687***	0.656***
	Student	0.494***	0.475***
(b) Remote Learning or Working during COVID-19	Not Student	0.575***	0.536***
	Student	0.212**	0.166**
(b)-(a) Newly started	Not Student	− 0.107	− 0.124*
	Student	− 0.247***	− 0.272***

The number is Pearson's correlation coefficient, ** $p < 0.01$, *** $p < 0.001$.

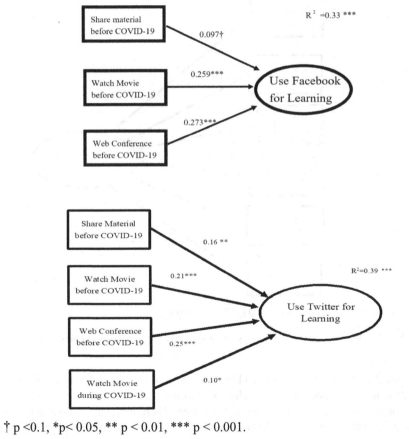

† $p < 0.1$, * $p < 0.05$, ** $p < 0.01$, *** $p < 0.001$.

Fig. 3. Multiple regression analysis on social media use for learning.

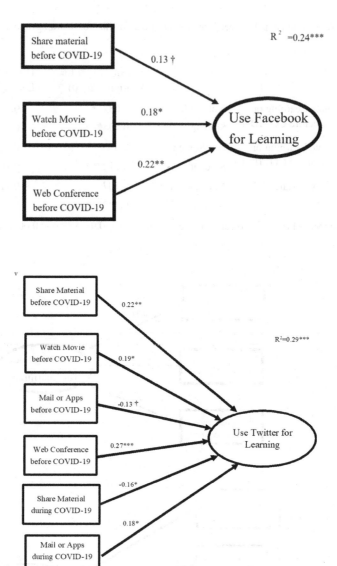

† p <0.1, *p< 0.05, ** p < 0.01, *** p < 0.001.

Fig. 4. Multiple regression analysis on social media use for learning among students.

social media for learning. Literature [1] utilized only the frequencies of note-taking using social media as dependent variables. However, we use comprehensive variables i. e. social media usage for learning, in the current research. Therefore, we can comprehensively estimate the influence of the COVID-19 condition. The analysis presented in this section shows that the result of the research conducted in 2018 is reproducible. An increased number of students in Japan tend to use social media for learning. However, the difference between students and others in the research conducted in 2020 is smaller than that conducted in 2018. This section described a hint to investigate the background of this phenomenon. The investigation of the second research question provides this particular hint. The frequencies of remote working and learning are related positively to the usage of social media for learning, and the positive relations are consistent. However, the relations are weakening.

4 Discussion of Result and Limitation

This section discusses the result of the analysis, thus helping us create new research questions. The limitation of this study is described below.

The analysis revealed that fewer students tend to use social media for learning in 2020 compared with those in 2018. We examine the correlation between the frequencies of remote learning and the usage of social media for learning and found that the correlation of students in 2018 is stronger than that in 2020. Thus, we consider the following hypotheses. The institutions to which students belong to may help identify official remote learning technologies and instruct them on their use. Many students can then use such applications in place of social media.

Therefore, we will conduct new research based on the aforementioned hypotheses. However, the online research in this study has some limitations. Thus, we will attempt to resolve such problems in the new research. The design of this research paper is unsuitable for online research according to the "Japanese Society for Information and Media Studies" and "The Society of Socioinformatics." However, conducting offline research is difficult owing to financial constraints. Therefore, we will first obtain convincing and meaningful results through online research. Then, we can build effective research questions, which will provide substantial investment to facilitate offline research.

The current study and literature [1, 6, 7] implied that the analysis of the use of social media for learning is crucial to the investigation on the use of big data for learning. Therefore, further research on the use of social media for learning will subsequently contribute to the study on the use of big data. Thus, demanding financial aid for such research will be valid.

Acknowledgement. This work was supported by JSPS KAKENHI Grant Number JP15K12175 and 20K03196.

References

1. Iitaka, T.: An analysis on digital note-taking using social media in Japan. In: Stephanidis, C., Antona, M. (eds.) HCII 2020. CCIS, vol. 1226, pp. 177–184. Springer, Cham (2020). https://doi.org/10.1007/978-3-030-50732-9_24
2. Iitaka, T.: Integration of online learning groups and research communities by Xoops. IEICE Tech. Rep. **109**(387), 1–6 (2010)
3. Paton, C., Bamidis, P., Eysenbach, G., Hansen, M., Cabrer, M.: Experience in the use of social media in medical and health education. Yearb. Med. Informa. **20**(01), 21-29 (2011). https://doi.org/10.1055/s-0038-1638732

4. Davis, C.H., Deil-Amen, R., Rios-Aguilar, C., Gonzlez Canch, M.S.: Social media, higher education, and community colleges: a research synthesis and implications for the study of two-year institutions. Community Coll. J. Res. Pract. **39**(5), 409-422 (2015) https://doi.org/10.1080/10668926.2013.828665

5. Ozawa, S.: Twitter wo katsuyoushita souhoukouzyugyouno dounyuuto tenbou, In: The 30th Conference of Japan University Association for Computer Education, (2018), Tokyo

6. Iitaka, T.: An analysis of the note-taking function of the audience response system. In: Zaphiris, P., Ioannou, A. (eds.) LCT 2017. LNCS, vol. 10295, pp. 364–374. Springer, Cham (2017). https://doi.org/10.1007/978-3-319-58509-3_29

7. Iitaka, T.: A survey on use of social networking service for digital note taking. IEICE Tech. Rep. **117**(469), 223–228 (2018)

Computer-Mediated Communication for Collaborative Learning in Distance Education Environments

Chrysoula Lazou(✉) ⓘ and Avgoustos Tsinakos

AETMA Lab, Department of Informatics, International Hellenic University, Agios Loukas, Kavala, Greece
{chrlazo,tsinakos}@cs.ihu.gr

Abstract. This paper discusses the benefits and potential challenges associated with the use of some form of Computer-Mediated Communication (CMC) in a specific learning situation. More specifically, it focuses on the importance of asynchronous and synchronous tools leveraged as to facilitate the completion of a collaborative project in tertiary education. The paper consists of three parts. The first part reviews literature with regards to CMC benefits and challenges while group of learners are working on a project. The second part develops arguments on how any problems might be addressed leveraging facilities and group dynamics in a collaborative project completion for the requirements of an online course as well as the effective management of the CMC activity. The third part elaborates on a process implemented as to assess the success of the use of CMC tools and if the intended learning outcomes have been met. The paper concludes that CMC, if appropriately leveraged, facilitates networked learning and allows for high level creativity and innovation in an ever accelerating digitally connected world.

Keywords: CSCL · Group work · Benefits · Challenges · Networked learning · Problem resolution

1 Introduction

Computer-mediated communication (CMC) is defined as any human communication that occurs through the use of two or more electronic devices [1]. It is "one of the methods for online communication, whether one-to-one, one-to-many, or many-to-many" interaction [2], providing learners with the means for accessing databases and sending and receiving documents diminishing time and spatial barriers world-wide. Its use implies some values and assumptions about learning, collaboration, communication, and community, with [3] attributing to it the role of an agent for socialization and communication. Computer-mediated communication can be broken down into two forms, namely, into synchronous and asynchronous. Synchronous computer-mediated communication refers to communication which occurs in real time though not necessarily same location, with all parties engaged in the communication simultaneously. On the contrary, asynchronous computer-mediated communication refers to communication which takes

P. Zaphiris and A. Ioannou (Eds.): HCII 2022, LNCS 13328, pp. 265–274, 2022.
https://doi.org/10.1007/978-3-031-05657-4_19

place when the parties engaged are not communicating in unison, which involves the possibility that the sender does not receive an immediate response from the receiver.

In light of the above, with regards to its role in education, [3] stress that CMC provides an active environment for social learning, fostering networks among learners, teachers, peers, and other members of the world community, diminishing transactional distance, as discussed by [4], and, thus, promoting learning in a mode that "has an even greater potential in education than does the stand-alone, knowledge-server type of computer" (p. 1). [5] defines computer-mediated communication approaches as distance education systems that are leveraged to achieve the aim of teaching a dispersed student body [1] further discusses that the properties that separate CMC from other media also include transience, its multimodal nature, and its relative lack of governing codes of conduct.

Collaborative or group learning is premised upon a learner-centered model that treats the learner as an active participant who construes knowledge from a wide range of experiences, information sources, and interaction with others [6, 7]. Some agreement on common goals and the pooling of individual competencies for the benefit of the group as a whole is necessary for successful collaboration. On this premise, as [8] posit, the focus in CMC is on reducing participant isolation and dependence upon the instructor, enhancing empowerment through independence and positive interdependence of the participants, and on the experience by learners of "mastery and community". To this end, the learning model is constructivist and as [9] contends, "[i]n using emerging computer-based technology as a resource, learners are encouraged to explore their own interests and to become active educational workers, with opportunities to solve some authentic problems" (p. 1). Inquiry-based and problem-solving learning is further facilitated by CMC as they foster learning communities with "a general sense of connection, belonging, and comfort … among members of a group who share purpose or commitment to a common goal" [10] (p. 2).

2   Review of Related Literature

Literature on pedagogical methods generally agrees on the value of collaborative learning outcomes, such as high order critical thinking skills discussed by [11]. In the context of distance education, where students are often expected to be studying independently, online group work can yield favorable results. The emergence of CMC has brought about a new perspective in learning, especially as to foster learning communities that might be geographically dispersed, thus, heterogeneous in demographics, cultural and socio-economical context. Nevertheless, these communities bear basic common attributes that make them homogeneous in a deeper sense, namely, their attitudes and interests [3] describe CMC as ideally producing "'online communities' meeting in 'virtual space'" (p. 28). Community, as [2] pose, implies that "the participants, at a minimum, share a sense of purpose and a commitment to achieving commonly valued goals". With regards to collaborative work, they contend that though sharing common experiences and other background elements may sometimes assist in developing social cohesion, it is diversity and heterogeneity that can create a "more cosmopolitan interpersonal and learning environment", allowing for creativity and innovation to flourish [12] further supports that CMC enables 'liberative discourse' to take place which increases motivation and fosters more active participation in an online course than the one observed in face-to-face (f2f) education, as it "encourages personal viewpoints and diversity of opinion rather than... offering authoritative solutions to the problems posed in [a] course..." (p. 208).

As [13] posit, virtual community members tend to have more homogeneous attitudes, allowing for exchange of support, information, and a sense of belonging, despite earlier fears about possible dehumanizing effects. They observe that virtual communities combine the characteristics of online virtual classrooms and computer-supported workgroups that provide emotional support and sociability, and information and instrumental aid related to shared tasks. More specifically, the authors summarize studies of how CMC affects community interaction and survey examples of different kinds of communities communicating online with a focus on asynchronous learning networks (ALN). They find that computer-supported cooperative work relationships generally focus on accomplishing tasks through coordinating activities and providing information and restricting relationships in content. Nevertheless, as they enthusiastically continue to support, in virtual communities these exchanges are often accompanied by emotional support and sociability, and a sense of belonging despite the exchange of information and services. Thus, virtual communities promote emotional intelligence in a world that, as they describe, turns into "The People of the Web" where loyalties to local communities are likely to weaken, whereas "geographically dispersed communities of interest" will strengthen, becoming part of the continuing social transformation toward global connectivity.

CMC is often based on some assumptions and convictions that according to [14] could be summarized into:

- Useful knowledge can be gained through dialogue with others. ("This knowledge takes various forms and allows the surfacing of tacit, personal and experiential understandings.").
- Electronic conferencing is unique: social and textual cues that regulate and influence group behavior are missing; authority and control structures shift rapidly; the usual discriminators of the race, age, and gender "are almost hidden."
- Users' appreciation of CMC generally does not appear to depend on previous computer literacy or experience.
- "Learning through computer mediation is an experiential, self-determined and largely self- motivated process. It cannot be legislated for in advance nor totally controlled at the time" (p. 90-91).

Nevertheless, [13] list some examples of constraints when virtual communities have to accomplish a common task including: the limited bandwidth of CMC that can reduce "social presence and cues"; its good implementation for exchange of information, opinions, and suggestions but less suited for communicating agreement or disagreement, resolving conflict or negotiating; there is no "turn-taking", so participants can key in entries whenever they like; there is more equality in participation than in f2f interaction. They contend that while asynchronicity makes interaction more convenient, it raises new coordination problems, such as information overload. Accordingly, [15] decries the fast pace of many online communications, and the high degree of stimulation provided by Internet-based interaction. The author expresses the fear that our over-stimulation by and over-indulgence in Internet-based information ("information obesity") will create a form of attention deficit disorder (ADD), making its victims unable "to concentrate on any one thing for more than a few moments ... their minds wander[ing], and frequently find[ing] themselves involved in several things at once." (p. 36). He maintains that technology can produce ADD in people who otherwise do not manifest its symptoms.

Additional limitations to effectiveness in CMC collaborative learning may include learner low competence [16] draw attention to the learner CMC competence as an important factor to the motivation to generate, use, and distribute information. They contend that learners who are more knowledgeable and skilled at using intermediary communication media are more likely to facilitate the collaborative process and play a significant role in the successful diffusion of information. Low CMC competence may inhibit purposeful and meaningful delivery of opinion and exchange of contribution in the process, "thus resulting in learning burnout and frustration and further affecting the collaborative learning effectiveness" (p. 1). The researchers identified that key elements to explore CMC learner competence are the "communication behavior" and "communication objectives". The communication behavior can be analyzed by two subsets, namely, (a) the total number of posts written and responded in the discussion board and (b) the total number of instant messages received from peers, while the communication objective by the total number of sending the shared type instant messages for communication and (b) the total number of replying to the shared type instant messages for communication.

Nevertheless, literature suggests that certain factors can ameliorate and address considerations [17] posits that in order to ameliorate barriers and problems it is critical that the instructor be effective; there is a need for careful planning, detailed preparations, and the mastery of the basic teaching competencies in light of using instructional technology. He continues to stress that the use of technology is secondary to well-designed learning goals and objectives and this relates to the "purposefulness of the designers and developers in provoking certain intelligent responses to the learning materials, context, and environment" (p. 1). The role of the educator is also stressed by [18], noting that "[t]echnology itself does not improve teaching and learning, though it can and does, at least in the hands of skilled distance educators, facilitate the process" (p. 43).

As aforementioned, computer-supported collaborative learning emerged as a strategy rich with research implications for the growing philosophies of constructivism and social cognitivism [19]. Especially in the case of asynchronous CMC, high order critical thinking can be achieved, reaching higher levels of Bloom's Taxonomy [20], in a creative, innovative learning environment. As literature supports, the reach of the Internet opens up and drives collaborations between people geographically separated. As work expands globally, so do differences in the culture, language, background, and work practices of those who are collaborating. Working across these divides is a challenge when developing their joint work practices, as they are first discovering differences and then learning and adopting ways of working with these differences [21–23]. Nevertheless, it is this diversity that fosters plurality of ideas and democratization of knowledge, as it broadens the scope of each joint work, allows for multiple perspectives to be discussed, and aims to meaningful transfer of knowledge according to context. Conferencing software and communication can ameliorate the feeling of disconnection and alienation that a learner might feel, reducing the transactional distance, boosting learner's confidence and providing extra motivation and engagement. A Community of Inquiry (CoI) is established under a social-constructivist approach, addressing the new knowledge requirements of the 21st century [24].

CMC can promote a very different type of learning experience. Most courses in distance education programs involve the collaborative work of small group of learners that have to accomplish a specific task, despite some anticipated barriers, namely, possible lack of coordination and equal contributions, delay in response, information overload, not sharing what needed and when needed, frustration and agitation. Nevertheless, [25] discusses that during this process, group members acquire skills, attitudes, and construction of knowledge. It is of primary importance that they develop collaborative skills summarized in: the ability to reduce negative emotions; manage stress; be assertive and express difficult emotions when necessary; stay proactive, not reactive; bounce back from adversity; and express intimate emotions in close, personal relationships. Synchronous CMC in CSCL can play a role, as voice and some body language and visual cues can ameliorate possible problems, facilitate and enhance bonds of trust among peers, and allow for a fruitful collaboration to flourish. It has been found that using synchronous communication tools in online group activities offers real-time collaboration, immediate response and feedback, many low-cost and free solutions, useful for one-to-one communication, and allows limited body language and tone of voice [26].

Nevertheless, it is the asynchronous tools that allow for flexibility, care in responding, deep learning and opportunity for reflection [27]. The researchers observed that during synchronous sessions there was a spontaneity in responses, less time to think and reflect on others' responses, chatting with each other, while not all participants could share their opinion due to time restrictions [3] provide examples of possible uses and outcomes of CMC in CSCL which can be summarized in brainstorming while conducting group projects, meaningful collaboration continuing classroom discussions, peer learning, examining diverse opinions, and comparing opinions widely. High order critical thinking is boosted as there is more emphasis on clear expression of views, critiquing, and collegiality and higher motivation to complete assignments. Asynchronous CMC offers 24-h access to material and new information, the opportunity for annotations and meaningful discourse, based on inquiry-based learning though not dependent on spontaneous, non well-researched responses. Intensity and quality of interaction is superior, especially for graduate learners; also, performance is greater as it allows for more commitment to assigned readings and preparation [13] found that the majority of students felt motivated to be diligent to their collaborative assignments because other students would be reading them, and thus they tended to work harder.

3   Assessing the Outcomes of CSCL

CSCL can foster meaningful learning in an online learning environment. Nevertheless, when assessing if the intended outcomes have been met, it is essential that we take into account certain variables. More specifically, [13] posit that virtual communities may vary as relationships cannot be neatly divided into discreet off-line and online sets. Online contact may be interspersed with f2f, telephone, and written contact. If this is the situation, the medium does itself play a minor role in the overall functioning of the community, including conferencing, groupware, email systems in many corporations, and interactive web pages by organizations. If the situation is that of a social network that is formed and sustained online, asynchronous CMC represents the most appropriate medium for groups that might involve examples such as thousands of a car brand enthusiast messaging on how to maintain or modify their cars, multi-user domains with participants highly involving social worlds, temporary project teams that dissolve when the project is over, or courses and degree programs through the Virtual Classroom as the one at the New Jersey Institute of Technology (NJIT).

Additionally, as [28] mentions, "[e]xperiences in virtual environments are like snowflakes—no two are alike" (p. 62). When setting goals and objectives, the instructor does not only focus on the final product of the groupwork but on other elements and benefits online groupwork may yield, namely, the change in skills, attitudes, and knowledge that group learning involves. With regards to the efficiency of group dynamics as to resolve conflict and achieve the intended learning outcomes, [29] conducted a survey on asynchronous group decision making. A field experiment was conducted with the intent to analyze the process and contents of group discussions that precede decision. More specifically, groups were assigned to solve a case study, as one of the assignments in a course, either orally or through an asynchronous computer-mediated communication system. The main goal of the experiment was to fill the gap found in literature related to analyzing in depth the process whereby the groups arrived at their decisions or produced their outcomes. Through content analyses, this study examined three key process variables to compare asynchronous with face-to-face group interaction, namely: (a) discussion breadth, (b) transfer efficiency, and (c) coordination approach. To this end, the following research questions based on group decision making were posed:

a) How is a face-to-face discussion different from an asynchronous text-based exchange of ideas?
b) What is the effect of these differences on the decision-making process and outcome?

In order to address these research questions, the content of discussions and final reports of groups supported by an asynchronous computer-mediated communication system were analyzed and compared to face-to-face groups that worked without computer support. With reference to content analyses of group sessions and reports, interesting insights into the nature of group coordination were reported. In sum, face-to-face and asynchronous groups adopted different coordination approaches. All face-to-face groups followed a combination of concurrent and sequential mode to discuss the case and develop the report, while asynchronous groups followed parallel and pooled approaches. Findings showed that asynchronous groups had broader discussions and submitted more complete reports than their face-to-face counterparts. More specifically, the breadth of asynchronous discussions was higher than the number of ideas mentioned face-to-face. This finding was mainly attributed to the very nature of asynchronous interaction, which allows one to reflect and come up with new ideas, and discuss more issues than in face-to-face meetings.

The discussion of a wider variety of issues had a positive impact on the completeness of the final report due to "the ability to pool more information along with the ease of compiling individual contributions from the written transcripts [which] led to longer reports for online groups" (p. 465). It was also noted that asynchronous groups adopted more loosely coupled interaction approaches, where they could work in parallel in different sections of the report or just pool their responses to produce the final write-up, which led to longer reports than their face-to-face counterparts. Nevertheless, the authors noted that in asynchronous groups, most of the time was consumed in the solution of the disagreements (discrepancy reduction) or discussion of new issues that came up. Additionally, not all groups decided on the same way of sharing the work as three groups appointed a representative to compile the individual contributions and develop a group report (pooled coordination), while two groups decided to assign each participant a different part of the final report (parallel coordination).

It was noted that face-to-face groups covered the questions in the worksheet in a sequential way, with each students making short contributions based on the individual position statements, on their consultation of books, and notes "on the spot". In order to prepare the final report, every manual group appointed a member in charge of taking notes during the discussion and submitting the group report at the end of the session. Sometimes, the rest of the group had to wait until the note-taker could write down the important aspects of the discussion. In a few cases, the note-taker added extra ideas to the final report, which explains why some issues not mentioned in the discussion appeared in a few group solutions. The implications of the findings are manifold and could be summarized as:

− Asynchronous groups experience clear process gains and their discussions are broader than exchanges in unsupported face-to-face meetings.
− Asynchronous groups are able to submit more complete reports, which are more thorough and longer than the ones submitted by manual groups, as a result of rich discussions.
− The difference in electronic communication support does not seem to affect the efficiency with which groups transfer information from the discussion to the reports.
− In terms of coordination style, groups adopt different approaches depending on the requirements of the task and possibilities of the communication medium.

4 Discussion

In light of all the aforementioned, it is clear that CSCL has brought about revolutionary changes in the contemporary pedagogy and practice in distance education and the benefits are multifaceted. Its social-constructivist dimension leveraging group dynamics fosters activities that provide several important benefits in online teaching and learning environment that could be summarized in the following as [30] clearly state:

− Help participants discuss concepts that promote deeper understanding of the material.
− Engage participants in the learning process and increase participation.
− Allow participants to tackle more complex problems.
− Give each participant experience in handling interpersonal processional relations, which is critical in "real-world" settings.

– Provide or improve practice evaluation skills as working professionals.
– Help create a sense of learning community, which is important for online students.
– Allow group members to assess other members of the team as well as self-evaluation.
– Assist participants to develop skills in independent judgments and encourage sense of involvement and responsibility on the part of students.
– Provide data that might be used in assigning individuals grades for team assignments.
– Improve learning and produce higher quality results.
– Reduce instructors' workload involved in assessing and grading.

Nevertheless, the specific learning situation proved that no theory and its application is without limitations. In order for this socio-constructivist approach to work, CSCL groups operate on three hierarchical levels, namely, coordination, cooperation, and co-construction. More specifically, as [31] suggest, coordination produces harmony and interaction flow, cooperation denotes recognition of group as well as personal goals, and co-construction recognizes that participants are building shared goals together, over time (p. 164–165). They schematically present their model of the collaborative educational process combining alternating group and individual activities, as follows:

- Individual: basic references and readings; individual problem views
- Group: view-building
- Individual: search for and of material
- Group: multiple ideas generated
- Individual: elaboration of ideas
- Group: integration, comments, and suggestions (p. 165).

Additionally, the assessment of groupwork effectiveness in CSCL shows that it cannot be overgeneralized, as each group bears its unique characteristics and it is each group dynamics and the effective management and instructor's mastery of careful planning and basic teaching competencies in light of using instructional technology that can ameliorate barriers and enhance benefits [32] contend that the best prescription for any problems that might arise is not to study traditional, offline communications paths as to "abstract the key properties of successful communications and replicate them electronically". They posit that "CMCS's are a new medium with their own advantages, disadvantages, social dynamics, problems, and opportunities" (p. 680). Abrami and Bures [33] argue that CSCL is capable of producing both enabling and disabling effects. Among the potential enabling effects are:

– Allowance for reflective rather than impulsive or spontaneous comments.
– Potentially increased (because asynchronous) communication.
– A permanent transcript of the discussion.
– More opportunity for shy participants.
– Greater ease in identifying the sources of contributions.

5   Conclusion

CSCL offers the workspace of the individual and the group, supports mutual transfer of data, information, and knowledge in the workspaces. It may include various information media, shared screen image and shared operations. Today's digitally connected world allows for unlimited opportunities for the individual to connect and interact with others that though sparsely populated may share common interests and build meaningful knowledge, broaden horizons, and achieve sustainability in a variety of fields. In the field of education and collaborative learning both synchronous and asynchronous tools bear affordances and limitations to be considered. In order to maximize their effective use, barriers are to be examined and surpassed under the discreet supervision of the instructor and the development of collaboration skills that are of lifelong value on the personal and professional level. Our digital era calls for skills and attitudes that promote collaboration, worldwide ties, and emotional intelligence in the workplace of our networked world and CSCL has a distinguished place as to achieve this.

References

1. McQuail, D.: Mcquail's Mass Communication Theory, 5th edn. SAGE Publications, London (2005)
2. Fahy, J.P., MacGregor, M.: Teaching and Learner Support Technologies in Distance Education – MDDE 621—Study Guide. Athabasca University, Canada (2017)
3. Lauzon, A., Moore, G.: A 4th generation distance education system: Integrating computer-assisted learning and computer conferencing. In: Moore, M.G. (Ed.), Distance Education for Corporate and Military Training. (Readings in Distance Education, 3). Penn State University, American Centre for the Study of Distance Education, pp. 26-37 (1992)
4. Moore, M.G.: Theory of transactional distance. In: Keegan, D. (ed.) Theoretical Principles of Distance Education. Routledge, New York (1993)
5. Rumble, G.: 'Open learning', 'distance learning', and the misuse of language. Open Learn. J. Open, Distance e-learning 4(2), 28–36 (1989)
6. Harasim, L.: Online education: an environment for collaboration and intellectual amplification. In: Harasim, L. (ed.) Online Education. Perspectives on a New Environment, Praeger, New York (1990)
7. Laurillard, D.: Rethinking University Teaching: A Framework for the Effective Use of Educational Technology. Routledge, London (1993)
8. Davie, L., Wells, R.: Empowering the learner through computer-mediated communicat ion. In: Moore, M.G. (Ed.), Distance education for corporate and military training. (Readi ngs in Distance Education, No. 3). The Pennsylvania State University, Ameri can Centre for the Study of Distance Education, pp. 104-112 (1992)
9. Berge, Z.: Computer-mediated communication and the online classroom in distance learn ing. Computer-Mediated Commun. Mag. 2(4), 6 (1995)
10. Conrad, D.: Building and maintaining community in cohort-based online learning. J. Dist. Educ. 20(1), 1–20 (2005)
11. O'Donnell, M.: Blogging as pedagogic practice: Artifact and ecology. Asia Pacific Media Educator 1(17), 5–19 (2006)
12. Rumble, G.: Interactivity, independence and cost. In: Paper presented at the Interaction and Independence Conference, Cambridge, England (1989)
13. Hiltz, S.R., Wellman, B.: Asynchronous learning networks as a virtual classroom. Com munications of the ACM 40(9), 44–49 (1997)
14. Nixon, T., Salmon, G.: Computer-mediated learning and its potential. In: Mills, R., Tait, A. (Eds.), Supporting the learner in open and distance learning, pp. 88–100. Pitman Publishing, London (1996)

15. Shenk, D.: Data Smog. HarperCollins Publishers, Inc, New York (1997)
16. Chih-Ming, C., Ying-You, L.: Developing a computer-mediated communication com petence forecasting model based on learning behavior features. Comput. Educ. Artificial Intell. **1**, 100004 (2020)
17. Berge, Z.: Facilitating computer conferencing: Recommendations from the field. Educa tional Technology, pp. 22-30 (1995b)
18. Beaudoin, M.: Reflections on research, faculty and leadership in distance education. Bibliotheks-und Informationssystem der Universitat Oldenburg, Ol denburg (2005)
19. Resta, P., Laferrière, T.: Technology in support of collaborative learning. Educ. Psychol. Rev. **19**, 65–83 (2007). https://doi.org/10.1007/s10648-007-9042-7
20. Bloom, B.S.: Taxonomy of Educational Objectives, Handbook I: The Cognitive Domain. David McKay Co Inc., New York (1956)
21. Haythornthwaite, C.: Communicating knowledge: articulating divides in distributed knowl-edge practice. In: Paper Presented at the Annual Meeting of the International Communication Association. Caroline, New Orleans, LA (2004)
22. Haythornthwaite, C.: Introduction: computer-mediated collaborative practices. J. Comput.-Med. Commun. **10**(4), 00–00 (2005). https://doi.org/10.1111/j.1083-6101.2005.tb00274.x
23. Haythornthwaite, C., Lunsford, K.J., Kazmer, M.M., Robins, J., Nazarova, M.: The generative dance in pursuit of generative knowledge. In: Proceedings of the 36th Hawaii In- ternational Conference on System Sciences. IEEE Computer Society, Los Alamitos, CA (2003)
24. Vaughan, N.D., Cleveland-Innes, M., Garrison, D.R.: Teaching in blended learning envi-ronments: Creating and sustaining communities of inquiry. Athabasca University Press (2013). https://www.aupress.ca/app/uploads/120229_99Z_Vaughan_et_al_2013-Teaching_in_Blended_Learning_Environments.pdf
25. Preston, N.: How to Increase Your Emotional Intelligence - 6 Essentials [Blog post]. https://www.psychologytoday.com/us/blog/communication-success/201410/how-inc rease-your-emotional-intelligence-6-essentials (2014, October 5). Accessed 1 Feb 2022
26. Wang, S.K.: The Effects of a Synchronous Communication Tool (Yahoo Messenger) on Online, Learners' Sense of Community and their Multimedia Authoring Skills, New York Institute of Technology, New York, Journal of Interactive Online Learning, www.ncolr.org/jiol, Volume 7, Number 1, Spring 2008, ISSN: 1541–4914 (2008)
27. Khalil, H., Ebner, M.: Using electronic communication tools in online group activi ties to develop collaborative learning skills. Universal J. Educ. Res. **5**(4), 529–536 (2017)
28. DiPetta, T.: Community on-line: new professional environments for higher education. New Dir. Teach. Learn. **76**, 53–66 (1998)
29. Benbunan-Fich, R., Hiltz, S.R., Turoff, M.: A comparative content-analysis of face- to- face vs. asynchronous group decision making. Decision Support Syst. **34**, 457–469 (2003)
30. Kadriye, O., Lewis, D.: Evaluating of Online Group Activities Intra- Group Member Peer Evaluation, In: 22nd Annual Conference on Distance Teaching and Learning, (2006) www.uwex.edu/disted/conference/Resource_library/.../06_4136.pdf
31. Santoro, F.M., Borges, M.R.S., Santos, N.: Evaluation of collaborative learning pro- cesses. Adv. Technol. Learn. **1**(3), 164–173 (2004)
32. Hiltz, S.R., Turoff, M.: Structuring computer-mediated communication to avoid infor mation overload. Commun. ACM **28**(7), 680–689 (1985)
33. Abrami, P., Bures, E.: Computer-supported collaborative learning and distance educa- tion. American J. Distance Educ. **10**(2), 37–42 (1996)

A User Profile Based Method for Usability Assessment of Distance Learning Systems

Heber Miranda Floriano[1]([⊠]), Rodrigo Bonacin[1,2], and Ferrucio de Franco Rosa[1,2]

[1] University of Campo Limpo Paulista (UNIFACCAMP), Campo Limpo Paulista/SP, São Paulo, Brazil
`hebermiranda@gmail.com`, `{rodrigo.bonacin,`
`ferrucio.rosa}@faccamp.br`
[2] Renato Archer Information Technology Center, Campinas/SP, Brazil

Abstract. Usability is a key factor to well-succeeded software development. Usability assessment is crucial in the web systems development process, especially for those aimed at distance education. With the massive use of e-learning and Learning Management Systems in the educational field, it is necessary to research and propose innovative methods and techniques for evaluating the usability of these systems. This article describes the proposal and application of a new method focused on the accessibility evaluation of e-learning systems, based on the users' profile associated with a broad set of criteria and metrics. By applying the method, the assessment results are synthesized in an indicator that represents the system's usability level. A case study with Moodle platform was conducted, and the results point to the feasibility, limitations, and future evolution of the method.

Keywords: E-learning · LMS · Assessment · Usability · Method · Distance learning

1 Introduction

Nowadays, e-learning systems have been increasingly used in a worldwide way. With the massive use of information and communication technologies, large-scale teaching methods (such as those using distance learning systems) present several problems [1]. Usability is a key issue related to problems of distance learning systems; however, it is dependent on each user profile, e.g., a usability issue reported by a novice student may not be a relevant problem for an experienced system administrator.

Usability is often being neglected in the design of Learning Management Systems (LMS) [2]. Thus, it is imperative to develop usability assessment methods that allow us to identify indicators and possibilities for improvement in distance learning systems.

We propose a method for evaluating the usability of e-learning systems, which takes into consideration the users' profile and a broad set of criteria and metrics synthesized in indicators. This method aims to support test analysts and developers to improve the accessibility of their systems. The method also aims to provide indicators for LMS administrators during the choice and configuration of their e-learning institutional systems. A case study with Moodle platform was carried out to illustrate the application of the method in a practical scenario, as well as to point out challenges and future research needs.

The remaining of this article is structured as follows: Sect. 2 presents the literature review and related work on usability assessment; Sect. 3 details the method and its application process; Sect. 4 presents a case study with Moodle; Sect. 5 presents the conclusions and the next steps in this research.

2 Literature Review and Related Work

First, it is necessary to identify the state of the art of usability assessment methods aimed at computer-based educational systems. We analyzed 35 articles in our Systematic Literature Review (SLR) [3] on usability assessment of e-learning systems (e.g., LMS), which also included m-learning and accessibility issues. The approach used in our SLR was based on the guidelines proposed by Kitchenham in [4] and the review process used by De Mendonça et al. [5], allowing the verification and analysis of current problems related to usability assessment.

Our SLR revealed that most educational institutions have unsatisfactory usability levels in their e-learning systems, as well as they do not prioritize addressing this need. We also observed that when an e-learning system is developed to meet high usability levels, the users' experience and satisfaction are increased. Therefore, the assessment of accessibility becomes a key tool to support learning. A synthetic description of the related works is presented in the following.

Several usability assessment methods for web-based systems were proposed, however, they mostly focus on assessing the usability of any/generic web applications, and concern time, financial and technological constraints [6]. Thus, Anandhan et al. [6] propose an approach that uses various methods, which resulted in the proposal of the CARE methodology (Cheap, Accurate, Reliable, Efficient testing), to reduce costs and increase the efficiency of usability tests of web systems.

Munir et al. [7] propose the use of the Nielsen Attributes of Usability (NAU) evaluation model. In their study, a Web portal was developed for the technology campus of a university. During the development of the portal, usability tests were carried out using a questionnaire based on the NAU model. These usability tests aimed to assess the principles of learning, efficiency, memorization, errors, and satisfaction. The objective of their study was to develop a web portal that would solve perception problems, such as being unattractive, monotonous, or confusing to the user.

Goh et al. [8] assessed the customer's perceived trust in an e-commerce website. The authors used four evaluation methods (Feedback Capture After Task, Retrospective Think Aloud, Retrospective Think Aloud with Eye Movement and observation) to carry out usability tests to identify the usability-related issues during the execution of tasks on e-commerce websites.

Virgos et al. [9] propose accessibility and usability guidelines as well as recommendations for Web systems to be accessible to users with Down syndrome.

Sivaji et al. [10] propose the Hybrid Usability Methodology (HUM), which is a result of the combination of the Laboratory Based Usability Test (LBUT) and the Exploratory

Heuristic Evaluation (EHE) approaches. The authors argue that "traditional" usability testing techniques are not sufficient due to the increasing complexity of websites. According to the authors, EHE is prone to false-positive results and LBUT can be expensive. LBUT has lower coverage than EHE. The main objective was to present a feasible approach and to provide stakeholders with a decision-making framework for usability testing strategies, which considers real-world constraints.

Table 1 presents a summary of the related works and a comparison with the proposed method. Our work differs from other works in the following aspects: i) Regard-ing CARE [6], our method proposes specific criteria for evaluating e-learning systems. Furthermore, CARE focuses on decreasing the costs involved in the testing activity; ii) Concerning [7], our method uses principles additional to those proposed by Nielsen, such as accessibility, complexity, audibility, and reuse of data entry; iii) Concerning [8], our method proposes criteria, weighting, and analyzes of specific usability aspects for e-learning. Furthermore, our method does not use a multi-method approach, thus reducing the complexity of the usability assessment process; iv) Concerning [9], our method is not focused on people with Down syndrome, it focuses on a wider audience covering students, teachers, and coordinators of educational institutions, including people with disabilities in general; v) Concerning [10], HUM focuses on reducing costs and increasing coverage, while our method aims to provide a usability indicator based on criteria and flexibility, with the possibility of weighting the calculations.

Table 1. Summary of related works domains and contributions

Reference	Application Domain					Contribution			
	A	B	C	D	E	1	2	3	4
Anandhan et al. [6]				X			X		
Munir et al. [7]	X						X		
Goh et al. [8]					X		X		
Virgós et al. [9]			X	X				X	
Sivaji et al. [10]				X			X		
This study	X	X	X			X	X		X

Application Domain: (A) E-learning; (B) M-learning; (C) Accessibility; (D) Web Systems in general; (E) E-Commerce.
Contribution: (1) Process; (2) Method; (3) Conceptualization; (4) Software Prototype.

3   The Proposed Method

We present the Method for Usability Assessment of Educational Systems (MUAES). Figure 1 presents an overview of the MUAES, which considers the user's profile and the characteristics of the platform under evaluation. Using this information as input, the method is applied to assess the degree of usability of the e-learning system.

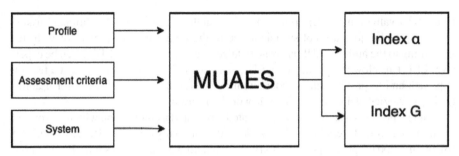

Fig. 1. Overview of MUAES.

To start the usability assessment, MUAES receives as input parameters the User Profiles (coordinator, teacher, student, evaluator), the e-learning system to be evaluated (e.g., LMS), and the assessment criteria (e.g., complexity, accessibility). The principles presented by Munir et al. [7] were considered in MUAES, including the ability to learn, efficiency, memorization, and errors.

The following Assessment Criteria (*ac*) and their respective Assessment Functions (*af*) are considered when processing the method:

Complexity. This criterion concerns the following aspects (or factors): a) number of system functions; b) number of pages; c) average number of clicks to perform basic tasks.

Accessibility. This criterion concerns the following aspects (or factors): a) availability of virtual assistant (e.g., Alexa) [11]; b) need to insert audiovisual content into the systems [12]; c) availability of subtitles for hearing impaired users [13]; d) need for a sign language interpreter [14]; e) availability of screen zoom for the visually impaired users; f) larger click areas on buttons (and other control fields) for motor-impaired users; g) plain text to facilitate the reading of people with dyslexia (and screen readers for visually impaired users).

Intuitiveness. This criterion concerns the following aspects (or factors): a) intuitive arrangement of screens with related functions; b) menus with easy access; c) conceptual model that resembles the mental model; d) minimization of memory load; since human short-term memory is limited, simple views are required, the frequency of window movement should be reduced, and codes, mnemonics, and action sequences minimized [15].

Efficiency. This criterion concerns whether the system meets the users' needs or not. As an example, by using data analysis techniques it is possible to verify if the users' needs are met [16].

Error Tolerance. This criterion concerns whether the system can hide errors to the point that they become imperceptible to users [17] and to have mechanisms that can avoid possible errors that users may make.

Auditability. This criterion concerns the system's ability to verify data integrity and to track significant updates to the data [18].

Reuse of Data Entry. This criterion concerns whether the system has an interface that optimizes user time, for instance, reusing data from tasks that have already been executed [19].

A set of formulas was developed to systematize the usability analysis. A value is assigned for each user profile, which is considered in a global index we named User Profile Index $(I\alpha)$; *i.e.*, $I\alpha$ is a composition of the Coordinator $(I\alpha_c)$, Teacher $(I\alpha_t)$, and Student $(I\alpha_s)$ indices.

Before the use of the formulas, the responsible for conducting the evaluation needs to define a maximum value of the usability evaluation $(Vmax)$ and to define the weight of each evaluation criterion (W), according to each user profile. Table 2 shows examples of weights assigned for the *ac* according to each user profile. The W values are defined according to the form of use and the needs of each user.

Table 2. Examples of assigning weights to assessment criteria according to user profile

ac	Student	Teacher	Coordenador
	(W_s)	(W_t)	(W_c)
1. Complexity	0.5	0.5	0.5
2. Accessibility	1	0.5	0.5
3. Intuitiveness	1	1	1
4. Efficiency	0.5	1	1
5. Error Tolerance	1	0.5	0.5
6. Auditability	0.5	1	1
7. Reuse of Data Entry	0.5	0.5	0.5
Vmax	5	5	5

In the example of Table 2, Accessibility, Intuitiveness, and Reuse of Data Entry received greater weights for the student profile. In this example, we have students with deficiency (Accessibility), with greater difficulty and barriers to interact with the system (Intuitiveness), and with a higher possibility of making mistakes (Error Tolerance). Intuitiveness, Efficiency, and Auditability received higher weights for the teacher and coordinator profiles, due to the task that they do in the system. Furthermore, it was considered that these profiles received training on how to use the system, as well as they have access to advanced technical support, unlike students.

MUAES is flexible since it allows changes in weights according to the needs of the institution and situation (e.g., during the development of an LMS or tool), in which the usability assessment is applied. Once defined the initial parameters (*Vmax* and W) are defined, it is possible to obtain the maximum value of the evaluation of each criterion

(∂). To do so, as shown in Eq. 1, we divide *Vmax* by the number of criteria (*Nac*) and multiply by *W*:

$$\partial = W_i * \left(\frac{\textbf{Vmax}}{\textbf{Nac}} \right)$$ (1)

Considering the example in Table 2, we have: i) For the Student profile: ∂_2 (Accessibility) = $1 * (5/7) = 0.714$; ii) For Teacher profile: $\partial_2 = 0.5 * (5/7) = 0.357$; iii) For the Coordinator profile: $\partial_2 = 0.5 * (5/7) = 0.357$. *I$\alpha$* is defined using the ∂ value, however, it is important to note that each criterion (*ac*) has its attributes (*af*) and the maximum value of the attributes will always be equal to *Vmax*. The next step is to calculate the value obtained by each criterion. For this, we must sum the value obtained in the evaluation of each of its attributes (*Vaf*). With these values, we can define *Iα* by multiplying ∂ by the result of dividing the criterion value by the multiplication between *Vmax* and *Naf*, as shown in Eq. 2.

$$I\alpha = \partial . \sum_{x=1}^{ac} \frac{\sum_{x=1}^{N_{af}} Vaf_x}{Vmax * N_{af}}$$ (2)

For example, considering the values presented in Table 2, where the student profile is evaluated, we have: i) Complexity: $ac = 0.5 * (14/(5 * 3)) = 0.47$; ii) Accessibility: $ac = 1 * (17/(5 * 7)) = 0.49$; iii) Intuitiveness: $ac = 1 * (15/(5 * 4)) = 0.75$; iv) Efficiency: $ac = 0.5 * (5/(5 * 1)) = 0.50$; v) Error tolerance: $ac = 1 * (5/(5 * 1)) = 1.00$; vi) *Auditability*: $ac = 0.5 * 4/(5 * 1)) = 0.40$; vii) Data entry reuse: $ac = 0.5 * (1/(5 * 1)) = 0.30$.

At the end of the calculation of the values of the criteria, we must take them to obtain the value of the Student profile index, as follows: $I\alpha_s = 0.47 + 0.49 + 0.75 + 0.50 + 1 + 0.40 + 0.30 = 3.90$. Once the value of *I$\alpha$* has been calculated, the value of the General Index (*Ig*) can be obtained by dividing the value of the sum *Iα* of all profiles by the number of profiles, as shown in Eq. 3. Finally, for our illustrative example, where $I\alpha_t = 4.54$ and $I\alpha_c = 4.51$, we have: $Ig = 3.90 + 4.54 + 4.51 = 4.32$.

$$I_g = \frac{1}{N_{I_\alpha}} \sum_{i=1}^{N_{I_\alpha}} I\alpha_i$$ (3)

3.1 Application Process of MUAES

This section presents the MUAES application process, which specifies the steps needed to apply this method in practice. The process is intended to be used by test analysts, developers, or system administrators of educational institutions interested in evaluating e-learning systems and tools. Figure 2 presents an overview of the proposed application process.

As shown in Fig. 2, to conduct the MUEAS method to carry out the usability assessment, the steps described in the next paragraphs must be followed.

Step 1. Platform Definition: Define the platform (application, system, tool, or system module) to be evaluated, such as: Moodle, Canvas, Sakai, among others, including their modules or plug-ins.

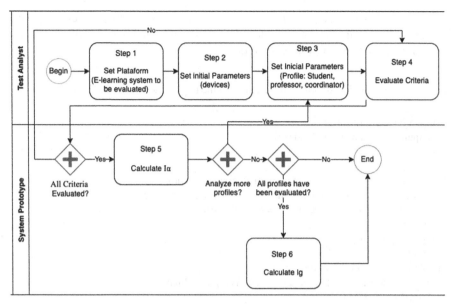

Fig. 2. Overview of the application process.

Step 2. Definition of Initial Parameters (devices): It must be informed on which type of device the evaluation will be carried out. For example: mobile, desktop, among others.

Step 3. Definition of Initial Parameters (profile): The profile that will be evaluated must be defined, namely: 0 for Student, 1 for Teacher, and 2 for Coordinator.

Step 4. Criteria Evaluation: With the initial parameters defined, we must open the system and log in according to the profile to be evaluated. Then, the evaluation begins, according to the *af* of each *ac*. We highlight for each *af* we will have the answer options from 0 to 5 and that each one of these options represents a percentage that the e-learning system meets, namely: Option 0, does not meet in any aspect; Option 1, meets 20% of requirements; Option 2, meets 40% of requirements; Option 3, meets 60% of requirements; Option 4, meets 80% of requirements; Option 5, meets 100% of requirements.

With all input information necessary for the method, in steps 5 and 6, the output information (indicators) is calculated.

Step 5. Calculate Profile Index (*Iα*): Once the *af* assessments are completed, Eqs. 1 and 2 must be applied to obtain the profile score.

Step 6. Calculate General Index (*Ig*): With all profiles evaluated, and calculated the *Iα* of each profile, we use Eq. 3 to obtain the general index. We emphasize that it is possible to obtain the index of each profile individually, though to obtain the *Ig* it is mandatory to evaluate all profiles.

3.2 Software Prototype that Implements the Application Process

A software prototype was developed to implement the proposed application process, aimed at calculating the indicators for all profiles (Student, Teacher, and Coordinator) and the general index. The algorithm (pseudocode) for generating the indexes is presented in Table 3. To obtain the general index (Ig), the resulting indexes ($I\alpha$) of the Student, Teacher, and Coordinator profiles are required.

Table 3. Algorithm for calculating the profile and general indexes

---

1. Input: integer α (profile)
2. Output: profile and general indexes
3.
4. Begin
5. Int Vmax $\leftarrow$ 5 (initialize the maximum assessment value)
6. Int Nac $\leftarrow$ Count(ac) (initialize the number of assessment criteria)
7. $\alpha \leftarrow$ [0 = Student, 1 = Teacher, 2 = Coordinator]
8. Read α
9. $W[\alpha] \leftarrow [ac_n, W_{ac}]$
10. While x $\geq$ 1 and x $\leq$ Nac do
11. While j $\geq$ 1 and j $\leq$ Naf do
12. Vaf = (read values of assessment functions (af), $\leq$ Vmax);
13. SumVaf = SumVaf + Vaf
14. End while (end assessment functions)
15. $\partial = W_{\alpha}[ac_i]$ * (Vmax / Nac)
16. $I\alpha_x = (\partial$ * SumVaf) / (Vmax * Naf)
17. SumIα = SumIαx + Iαx
18. End while (end assessment criteria)
19. Print Iα_x
20. IG = SumIα / Nα
21. Print Ig
22. End

---

4   Case Study

This section presents a case study, in order to describe the application steps of the method and evaluate the feasibility and limitations of the MUEAS. The application process (cf. section 3.1) was carried out and the results obtained in each step are presented in tables. A Brazilian university (UNISEP – *União das Instituições de Serviços, Ensino e Pesquisa*, in Portuguese language) was chosen to carry out the case study. UNISEP, a 50 years old institution, is focused on undergraduate courses, with approximately 7.000 students enrolled in its distance learning system. We applied the method to verify if the LMS used by students, teachers, and university coordinators meets the minimum usability requirements as well as what is the achieved score.

In Step 1, it was defined that the Moodle should be evaluated, as the institution has been widely using it during approximately 13 years.

In Step 2, the initial parameters (devices) were defined. The computer used was a desktop with all operational audio and video devices; the browser was Google Chrome, and the operating system was Windows 10.

Table 4. Assigning grades to attributes (*af*) and calculating criteria (*ac*) with Student profile.

ac	af	af Score	ac calculated
Student Profile			
Complexity	Number of system functions	5	0.47
	Number of system pages	5	
	Average number of clicks to perform basic tasks	4	
Accessibility	Virtual Assistant	0	0.49
	Audio Visual	0	
	Subtitles	2	
	Sign Language	0	
	Screen Zoom	5	
	Larger click areas	5	
	Simple text	5	
Intuitiveness	Grouping screens with related functions	5	0.75
	Menus with easy access	5	
	Conceptual model resembles the mental model	3	
	Memory load minimization	2	
Efficiency	Needs are met	5	0.50
Error Tolerance	Error tolerance	5	1.00
Auditability	Data integrity	4	0.40
Reuse of data entry	Time optimization by reuse of previously included information	3	0.30

In Step 3, the initial parameters (profiles) were defined. All profiles were evaluated in the following sequence: student, teacher, and, finally, the coordinator.

In Step 4, to evaluate the criteria, the test analyst logged in according to the parameters defined in steps 2 and 3 and started the calculation of the *af* according to the feedback from the Moodle. The same process was performed for all profiles, as detailed in Tables 4, 5, and 6.

In steps 5 and 6, *Iα* and *Ig* were calculated. With the weights defined and the evaluation questionnaire completed, Eq. 2 was applied by the developed software prototype (*cf.* 3.2). The results of *ac*, *Iα* of each profile, and the percentage of compliance with the usability requirements are presented in Tables 7 (Student), 8 (Professor), and 9 (Coordinator).

Table 5. Assigning grades to attributes (*af*) and calculating criteria (*ac*) with Teacher profile.

ac	af	af Score	ac calculated
Teacher Profile			
Complexity	Number of system functions	5	0.50
	Number of system pages	5	
	Average number of clicks to perform basic tasks	5	
Accessibility	Virtual Assistant	0	0.24
	Audio Visual	0	
	Subtitles	2	
	Sign Language	0	
	Screen Zoom	5	
	Larger click areas	5	
	Simple text	5	
Intuitiveness	Grouping screens with related functions	5	0.90
	Menus with easy access	5	
	Conceptual model resembles the mental model	4	
	Memory load minimization	4	
Efficiency	Needs are met	5	1.00
Error Tolerance	Error tolerance	4	0.40
Auditability	Data integrity	5	1.00
Reuse of data entry	Time optimization by reuse of previously included information	5	0.50

Table 6. Assigning grades to attributes (*af*) and calculating criteria (*ac*) with Coordinator profile.

ac	af	af Score	ac calculated
Coordinator Profile			
Complexity	Number of system functions	4	0.47
	Number of system pages	5	
	Average number of clicks to perform basic tasks	5	
Accessibility	Virtual Assistant	0	0.24
	Audio Visual	0	

(*continued*)

Table 6. (*continued*)

ac	af		*af* Score	*ac* calculated
Coordinator Profile				
	Subtitles		2	
	Sign Language		0	
	Screen Zoom		5	
	Larger click areas		5	
	Simple text		5	
Intuitiveness	Grouping screens with related functions		5	1.00
	Menus with easy access		5	
	Conceptual model resembles the mental model		5	
	Memory load minimization		5	
Efficiency	Needs are met		4	0.80
Error Tolerance	Error tolerance		5	0.50
Auditability	Data integrity		5	1.00
Reuse of data entry	Time optimization by reuse of previously included information		5	0.50

Table 7. Results of *ac* calculated, *Iα* of the Student profile, and Percentage of usability requirements met

ac	Student	
	ac calculated	Percentage
Complexity	0.47	94%
Accessibility	0.49	49%
Intuitiveness	0.75	75%
Efficiency	0.5	100%
Error Tolerance	1	100%
Auditability	0.4	80%
Reuse of Data Entry	0.3	60%
	Iα$_S$	*3.90*

Table 8. Results of *ac* calculated, *Iα* of the Teacher profile, and Percentage of usability requirements met

ac	Teacher	
	ac calculated	Percentage
Complexity	0.5	100%
Accessibility	0.24	48%
Intuitiveness	0.9	90%
Efficiency	1	100%
Error Tolerance	0.4	80%
Auditability	1	100%
Reuse of Data Entry	0.5	100%
	Iα$_t$	*4.54*

Table 9. Results of *ac* calculated, *Iα* of the Coordinator profile, and Percentage of usability requirements met

ac	Coordinator	
	ac calculated	Percentage
Complexity	0.47	94%
Accessibility	0.24	48%
Intuitiveness	1	100%
Efficiency	0.8	80%
Error Tolerance	0.5	100%
Auditability	1	100%
Reuse of Data Entry	0.5	100%
	Iα$_c$	*4.51*

After all the profiles were evaluated, the value of the general index (Ig) of the usability assessment carried out on the Moodle platform for the educational institution UNISEP was 4.32. To obtain the *Ig*, Eq. 3 was applied by the developed software prototype (*cf.* 3.2). By considering that we have: i) for the Student profile: $I\alpha_s = 3.91$, ii) for the Teacher profile: $I\alpha_t = 4.54$, iii) for the Coordinator profile: $I\alpha_c = 4.51$; *Ig* is *Ig = (3.91 + 4.54 + 4.51) / 3*, resulting in *Ig = 4.32*.

5   Discussion on the Results

By applying the method in a usability assessment, we were able to identify the strengths and weaknesses of the e-learning system in a clearly way.

Regarding the Student profile, we can verify that its usability score was *3.9*, reaching 78%. However, it is also important to analyze each criterion individually. We verified, by the Accessibility criterion, that the system needs to be improved. In this context, we suggest using plug-ins to deal with this issue. Another aspect to be improved is the reuse of data entry, something that a developer could solve with some ease.

The Teacher and Coordinator profiles obtained similar scores (*4.54* and *4.51* respectively), reaching *90%*. Analyzing the criteria individually, the Accessibility criterion had the worst performance, followed by the Efficiency criterion.

The Moodle system used by the educational institution met the evaluator's expectations, achieving *86%* of the total grade. The proposed method makes it possible to make a careful comparison between LMSs to identify points of improvement and complementary aspects in the systems.

During this study, it was crucial to define which criteria would indicate the level of usability of the e-learning system under evaluation. Furthermore, after defining the criteria, it was challenging to develop the equations that systematize the proposed usability evaluation process.

6 Conclusion

The proposed method is innovative since it produces three usability indicators according to each user profile and a general usability indicator is synthetized. The main contributions are: (i) a conceptual method for evaluating the usability of e-learning systems; (ii) an implementation process to assist developers in the application of MUAES; (iii) a set of usability criteria for evaluating LMS (desktop and mobile), considering users with special needs.

The case study made it possible to verify that MUAES can support the identification of usability problems of e-learning systems in a systematic way. MUAES can also be used during the development process of LMS, providing requirements and evaluation criteria.

As future work, in addition to applying MUAES to other LMS, we intend to address the limitation of receiving information and performing analyzes after the completion of the calculations. A system able to obtain the input data and make the calculations of the profile and general indexes will be developed to this end. It will provide us a comparative analysis with other evaluations. We also planned to build a graphical interface for the developed prototype.

References

1. Kataoka, Y., Thamrin, A.H., Murai, J., Kataoka, K.: Effective Use of Learning Management System for Large-Scale Japanese Language Education, In: Proceedings of the 10th International Conference on Education Technology and Computers, pp. 49–56 (2018) https://doi.org/10.1145/3290511.3290564
2. Mtebe, J.S., Kissaka, M.M.: Heuristics for evaluating usability of learning management systems in Africa. In: 2015 IST-Africa Conference, pp. 1–13, (2015) https://doi.org/10.1109/ISTAFRICA.2015.7190521.

3. Floriano, H.M., Jino, M., de F. Rosa, F.: A Study on Usability Assessment of Educational Systems (Submitted) (2022)
4. Kitchenham, B.: Procedures for performing systematic reviews. Keele, UK, Keele Univ., 33(TR/SE-0401), 28 (2004) doi: 10.1.1.122.3308
5. de Mendonça, R.R., de Franco Rosa, F., Bonacin, R.: UM ESTUDO SOBRE ANÁLISE, REPRESENTAÇÃO E DETECÇÃO DE INTENÇÕES DE CRIMINOSOS EM POSTAGENS EM MÍDIA SOCIAL. 27 (2019) WWW/INTERNET
6. Anandhan, A., Dhandapani, S., Reza, H., Namasivayam, K.: Web Usability Testing — CARE Methodology. In: Third International Conference on Information Technology: New Generations (ITNG'06), pp. 495–500, (2006) https://doi.org/10.1109/ITNG.2006.141
7. Munir, S., Rahmatullah, A., Saptono, H., Wirani, Y.:Usability evaluation using NAU method on web design technique for web portal development in STT Nurul Fikri. In: 2019 Fourth International Conference on Informatics and Computing (ICIC), pp. 1-6, (2019) https://doi.org/10.1109/ICIC47613.2019.8985913.
8. Goh, K.N., Chen, Y.Y., Lai, F.W., Daud, S.C., Sivaji, A., Soo, S.T.: A comparison of usability testing methods for an e-commerce website: a case study on a Malaysia online gift shop. In: 2013 10th International Conference on Information Technology: New Generations, pp. 143–150, (2013) https://doi.org/10.1109/ITNG.2013.129
9. Alonso-Virgós, L., Baena, L.R., Crespo, R.G.: Web accessibility and usability evaluation methodology for people with Down syndrome. In: 2020 15th Iberian Conference on Information Systems and Technologies (CISTI), pp. 1–7, (2020) https://doi.org/10.23919/CISTI4 9556.2020.9140858
10. Sivaji, A., Abdullah, M.R., Downe, A.G., Ahmad, W.F.W.: Hybrid usability methodology: integrating heuristic evaluation with laboratory testing across the software development lifecycle. In: 2013 10th International Conference on Information Technology: New Generations, pp. 375–383, (2013) https://doi.org/10.1109/ITNG.2013.60
11. Melton, M., Fenwick, J.: Alexa skill voice interface for the moodle learning management system. J. Comput. Sci. Coll. 35(4), 26–35 (2019)
12. Siqueira Bine, L.M., Fondazzi Martimiano, L.A.: Digital inclusion through the insertion of acessibility in the netanimations online repository. In: IEEE Latin America Transactions, vol. 16, no. 1, pp. 240–247, (2018) https://doi.org/10.1109/TLA.2018.8291479
13. Hersh, M.:Accessibility and usability of virtual learning environments. In: 2008 Eighth IEEE International Conference on Advanced Learning Technologies. pp. 991-992, (2008) https://doi.org/10.1109/ICALT.2008.155.
14. Antunes, D.R., Guimarães, C., García, L.S., Oliveira, L.E.S., Fernandes, S.:A framework to support development of sign language human-computer interaction: building tools for effective information access and inclusion of the deaf. In: 2011 FIFTH INTERNATIONAL CONFERENCE ON RESEARCH CHALLENGES IN INFORMATION SCIENCE, pp. 1-12, (2011) https://doi.org/10.1109/RCIS.2011.6006832.
15. Shneiderman, B.: Designing the User Interface: Strategies for Effective Human-Computer Interaction. Pearson Education – India (2010)
16. Gharibpoor, M., Sargazi, S., Aref, M.: Efficiency evaluation of e-learning compared to traditional education in human resource development (case study: small and medium enterprises in Shiraz). In: 7th International Conference on e-Commerce in Developing Countries:with focus on e-Security, pp. 1–8, (2013) https://doi.org/10.1109/ECDC.2013.6556736
17. Ongsiriporn, O., Senivongse, T.: UML profile for fault tolerance patterns for service-based systems. In: The 2013 10th International Joint Conference on Computer Science and Software Engineering (JCSSE), pp. 240–245, (2013) https://doi.org/10.1109/JCSSE.2013.6567352
18. Bajerski, C.D., et al. Qualidade de Software -Usabilidade. Revista Bate Byte, n 38, abr. (1994)
19. Pressman, R.S.: Software Engineering: A Practioner's Approach, 3rd edn. McGraw-Hill, New York (1992)

How Prepared Was the World for Emergency Distance Learning in K-12 Education? A Literature Review

José Reyes-Rojas[1][(✉)] and Jaime Sánchez[2]

[1] Pontifical Catholic University of Chile, Santiago, Chile
jgreyes2@uc.cl
[2] University of Chile, Santiago, Chile
jsanchez@dcc.uhile.cl

Abstract. The present study answers the question of how prepared the world was in school distance education. The situation of primary and secondary education is deepened around experiences in distance education focused on students, in the period that includes the decade between 2010 and 2019. Designs and modalities of distance education, types of interaction, recurring themes, and impact of reported experiences were analyzed. The results reveal a low preparation in distance school education, compared to the high demand for online education that has arisen since the COVID-19 pandemic. The blended learning design appears as the most used modality, while the type of asynchronous interaction was the most frequent before the pandemic. In addition, differences are recognized in the impacts reported in the analyzed literature, which allows establishing a type of impact that includes distance education as its independent variable, and another that considers it as a more contextual element while studying the relationships between other variables.

Keywords: Distance education · K-12 · Blended learning · Online education · COVID-19 · Synchronous and asynchronous education

1 Introduction

The 2020s began radically changing the routines of people practically all over the world. Through distance education, millions of children and young people have had to adapt to new learning environments in which digital connectivity and learning from home appear as the main attributes of educational practices deployed in health emergency contexts. This adaptation has been transversal for both education workers and students of all educational levels, who have found in the remote modality a way to sustain the teaching-learning processes necessary to complete their work goals or their respective training processes.

Various authors have considered the advances in trends related to distance education through literature reviews, such as the study of e-learning, blended learning, flipped classroom, MOOC (Kebritchi et al. 2017; Lee 2017), the computational thinking as content of online education (Kirwan et al. 2018, p. 6), inclusive virtual education (Fermín-González 2019, p. 162), learning communities, instructional design and characteristics of learners in contexts distance education (Zawacki-Richter et al. 2009), among others.

All these studies have as a common element the approach of the respective tendencies in the context of higher education. However, for school education (K-12), the study of experiences in distance education prior to the pandemic is less abundant, highlighting exceptionally reviews that can address specific emerging technologies (Queiroz et al. 2018). For Barbour and Reeves (2009, p. 413), the need to increase research on the factors that affect performance in the context of virtual and distance education for the school population (K-12), is a pending challenge that arises when verify that most of the research in the area focuses on adult learners, a perspective that is negatively complemented by the lack of studies on information and communication technologies in developing countries (Kozma and Vota 2014, p.892). On the other hand, for Arnesen et al. (2019, p. 20), while the field of online education grows, studies on school education (K-12) remain narrow, even though it shows signs of growth when studying scientific production between 1994 and 2014.

The less investigative attention in distance education at the school level is contradictory with the amount of child and youth world population that currently suffers from the problem of not having had sufficient experiences or material conditions, to face to some extent the teaching-learning scenario during a pandemic. Moreover, knowing studies that analyze or report experiences in distance education focused on learners throughout the planet, emerges as a necessity so that educational systems around the world can consider significant antecedents around the policies and decisions made in education in the past, while projecting potential capacities for educational management into the future.

In this way, the question about how prepared the school was throughout the world to face emergency distance education from previous experiences focused on learners, is proposed as a route that allows investigating distance education practices at the school level. during the past decade.

The purpose of this study is to characterize and analyze the experiences in distance modality in school education carried out before the pandemic caused by COVID-19 based on the main topics, designs and types of interaction reported, and the impact of the experiences on learning, so that it can serve as input for the evaluation of policies, actions and projects related to distance education at the global level.

On the other hand, it is sought that the scientific and school community can access new antecedents on which educational practices arising from the emergency are sustained, compare distance education scenarios in normal contexts in contrast to the health emergency that has arisen since 2020, analyze hybridization possibilities in methodological designs, and potentially make decisions regarding ways to design, implement, evaluate and promote distance education modalities considering experiences given in non-urgent environments, with different forms of technology use.

Finally, the results of the review seek to help researchers in the evaluation of the relevance of the knowledge developed so far on distance education in primary and secondary education, in a search to promote reflections on the relevance of the knowledge raised in problematic situations, such as those caused by the forced change from face-to-face to digital distance education.

In the following sections the methodology will be developed, where criteria and search procedures are described. Then the results grouped in the descriptive and analytical characteristics of the sample study will be presented. Finally, the findings will be discussed, and limitations and projections of the research field will be exposed.

2 Methodology

2.1 Search

To answer the research question posed, a literature review of scientific articles hosted in the main collection of the Web of Science (WOS) academic database was carried out, covering a personalized time interval, between the years 2010 and 2019. The search was made up of two values separated by the Boolean term "AND", and within each one, different concepts separated by the Boolean "OR". Thus, the first value contained different keywords related to distance education, while the second referred to the educational segments of interest, also expressed in their keywords, in this way: *("distance education" OR "long-distance education" OR "long distance training" OR "distance teaching" OR "distance learning" OR "distance training" OR "online distance education" OR "remote education" OR "remote teaching" OR tele-education OR "distance e-learning" OR "mobile distance learning" OR "blended learning") AND (K-12 OR "primary education" OR "secondary education" OR "elementary school" OR "high school").*

2.2 Inclusion Criteria

– English language: Being a search open to everyone, the English language was used as the common basis for scientific reports.
– Primary and secondary education (K-12): Educational experiences carried out in primary and secondary education, including the final phases of secondary education, were considered as vocational experiences with the condition that they continue to be part of secondary school and not university exclusively.
– Considered the period between the years 2010 and 2019: To better define the borders of the decade, 10 years were considered to count from 2010 for the search for articles, even though they report educational experiences prior to 2010. To avoid confusion or add more filters to the review, only the year of publication will be considered.
– Student-centered experiences: It is a central part of the study to restrict the search to articles that account for the knowledge created from active experiences that have students as protagonists, regardless of whether these actors can relate to others both in the collection and in the analysis of the data of each article.
– Empirical articles: Finally, only scientific articles were considered as baseline criteria that ensure the search for experiences evaluated around their means and their results.

2.3 Exclusion Criteria

– Experiences centered on teachers: Articles focused on teachers will be left out of the study, fundamentally due to the student-centered perspective that this study intends.

– Education for adults: By focusing the study on childhood and youth, although there may be experiences of adults at primary or secondary educational levels, they will be excluded from the sample.
– Preschool education: This educational level was not addressed by the present study due to the complexity of technological insertion in preschool and the differences in coverage worldwide.
– Homeschooling or non-formal education: When discussing the forced change from face-to-face and mass education to distance education, other types of education such as home education or forms of non-formal education are left out.
– Technological applications that do not necessarily cover distance education: There is a large literature that, using concepts typical of the search, does not necessarily address aspects of distance education. Therefore, a distinction was made between articles that described digital uses in school, with those that were situated in an educational design that involved distance education in some of its parts.
– Secondary data: Articles such as reviews or evaluations based on secondary data were excluded, considering the intention of investigating specific educational experiences in primary or secondary education and focused on students.

The search initially yielded 542 results, which, when filtered by language (English) and type of document (articles and reviews), resulted in 261. Although the reviews were not part of the inclusion criteria, they were considered given the possibility to find papers related to the objectives of this study.

Summaries of all document results were read. After the identification of articles that coincided with the inclusion criteria, a superficial reading of the article was carried out, paying attention to the methodological section and the research procedures, with the aim of applying exclusion criteria. The process resulted in a selection of 29 documents, which after being read in depth, were reduced to 23 that are part of the final sample.

3 Findings

3.1 Main Topics

Although the documents analyzed expose different approaches, contexts of realization and educational topics, it is possible to identify three large thematic categories that bring together this diversity of efforts to promote teaching-learning spaces mediated by distance technology in the school, that is, characteristics of student-users, trends and innovation in distance education, and the role of teachers.

These categories allow us to approach the sample from an identification of the way in which they characterize the students-users-participants, throughout different educational experiences, they account for trends and emerging technological innovations located in the field of education and, finally, they highlight the role of teachers as fundamental actors to understand the effectiveness of the educational exercise in remote conditions.

Characteristics of Student-Users. This category groups articles that address aspects of students, such as motivation (Pardanjac et al. 2010), attitude towards learning (Chao et al. 2015; Kim et al. 2012; Kirby and Sharpe 2010), predispositions (de la Varre et al.

2014; Malinovski et al. 2014), preferences (Randler et al. 2014), and tensions towards distance learning (Tochon 2015).

The papers vary both in the disciplines they address and in their methodological approaches. Thus, while Kirby and Sharpe (2010) seek to characterize the factors of students that affect the possibility of taking a distance course through logistic regression, the work of Tochon (2015) presents a critical autobiography from which he proposes conceptual crossings with theories of power. There are also studies such as those by Randler et al. (2014) who set out to find the relationship between the chronotypical preferences of students and the development of their attitudes towards online distance education.

The documents, in general, highlight the positive attitude of the students towards the innovations and new technologies used in the reported interventions, which could be a precedent that allows contrasting the impact of remote experiences when they are controlled and sporadic, as in the past decade, in contrast to contexts of health emergency where massive and distance digital education has been an obligation, as in the current decade.

Trends and Innovation in Distance Education. The category brings together documents that show innovative uses of technology applied to distance learning, such as interactive videoconferencing (Anastasiades et al. 2010; Thompson and Nutta 2015; Xiong et al. 2017), the use of automatic scaffolding in web browsing (Huertas et al. 2015, 2018), the innovative use of flipped classrooms and blended learning (Burdina et al. 2019; Gariou-Papalexiou et al. 2017), and the application of distance learning for disciplines related to creation and art (Edward et al. 2018; Garcia-Garcia et al. 2017).

The documents, although diverse in their thematic approach, share creative and advanced proposals in the panorama of the past decade regarding digital distance learning. Thus, the work of Xiong et al. (2017) proposes a classroom format where teachers and students converge online, and face-to-face teachers and students synchronously, in a controlled context but increasing the possibilities of interaction in mixed teaching. On the other hand, we find articles that address issues related to creation, although in different disciplines, as is the case of Edward et al. (2018) who propose a mixed learning model for teaching oriental music, unlike the project developed by García-García et al. (2017), which promotes group and online plastic creation to develop knowledge and interest in engineering. In short, the category brings together advanced experiences that can serve as a background or tool in the new contexts of massive use of distance education.

Role of Teachers. The articles gathered in this category are those that propose, from the student-centered research experience, a substantive importance in the role of teachers in distance learning (Burdina et al. 2019; Kim et al. 2012), as well as we can also find articles that distinguish different formats of pedagogical accompaniment, both face-to-face and remote (Borup et al. 2019; Thompson & Nutta 2015; Xiong et al. 2017).

In the documents that are part of this category, the work of Borup et al. (2019) where important distinctions are made from the students' reports about the support of online teachers in contrast to face-to-face tutors or facilitators. On the other hand, investigations such as that of Xiong et al. (2017) highlights the importance of being able to count on excellent teachers remotely despite the material difficulties in balancing access to education.

In general, the documents that address the issue of the role of teachers agree on the importance they have in accompanying remote scenarios. The influence of their timely responses, the fact that they are actively perceived in the students' process, as well as their ability to involve different resources in their innovative design of educational sequences, have a significant impact on both the results and the results. in attitudes toward learning.

On the other hand, the review documents also propose different ways of carrying out the pedagogical work, distinguishing different types of accompaniments, such as online teachers, online tutors, and face-to-face teachers, which can interact synchronously or asynchronously with the students, always having a substantive importance when posing learning challenges.

3.2   Types of Interaction in Distance Education

The sample showed that, despite the diversity of educational contexts and initiatives identified, distance education designs were limited. Blended learning was the most used educational design (8), followed by interactive videoconference (4), virtual school (2) and flipped classroom (2). However, there were multiple studies that did not specify the type of design used, even when they do specify the type of interaction in distance education, namely, synchronous, asynchronous, or mixed interaction.

For Watts (2016), the different levels of synchrony in distance education are possible to approach as types of interaction, thus existing a synchronous and an asynchronous interaction. The present study will consider such a conceptual use to group the different experiences in school distance education, with the incorporation of a type of mixed interaction in which synchronous and asynchronous interactions converge simultaneously. In this way, the sample was analyzed according to types of interaction since it is a characteristic reported in all the studies (Table 1), unlike the type of educational design whose description is non-existent in almost a third of the data corpus.

Regarding mixed face-to-face designs, such as blended learning and the flipped classroom, that part of the design that involves distance learning outside the school space synchronous-face-to-face with respect to the teacher has been considered as asynchronous interaction. On the contrary, those experiences that in their design considered both synchronous and asynchronous non-face-to-face interactions were considered as mixed modalities of distance education.

By separating the documents by asynchronous, synchronous, and mixed interaction, it is the former that concentrates most of the reported educational experiences. In addition, blended learning is the most used design of mixed presence. On the other hand, both the mixed and the synchronous designs concentrate the same number of appearances in the sample, where the interactive videoconference is the most frequent educational design between both types of interaction. Initiatives such as the flipped classroom like blended learning are also emerging with respect to mixed presence, and virtual schools, with greater online mass and with possibilities of synchronous and asynchronous interaction.

Regarding interactive videoconferences, it should be noted that these are applied in different ways in their respective contexts. Thus, we can find videoconferences in which

Table 1. List of documents grouped according to type of interaction, impact, sample, and methodologies

Type of interaction	Reference	Design	Sample	Methodology
Asynchronous	Pardanjac et al. (2010)	Not reported	w/n	Quantitative
	Kirby and Sharpe (2010)	Not reported	324	Quantitative
	Ümit Yapici and Akbayin, (2012)	Blended learning	107	Quantitative
	Kalamković. et al. (2013)	Not reported	99	Quantitative
	De la Varre et al. (2014)	Not reported	w/n	Quantitative
	Randler et al. (2014)	Not reported	769	Quantitative
	Huertas et al. (2015)	Blended learning	75	Quantitative
	Tochon (2015)	Not reported	1	Qualitative
	Chao et al. (2015)	Flipped classroom	91	Quantitative
	Sulisworo et al. (2016)	Blended learning	62	Quantitative
	García-García et al. (2017)	Blended learning	25	Qualitative
	Lin et al. (2017)	Blended learning	54	Quantitative
	Gariou-Papalexiou et al. (2017)	Flipped classroom	17	Qualitative
	Huertas-Bustos et al. (2018)	Blended learning	75	Quantitative
	Nishanti et al. (2018)	Blended learning	360	Mixed methods
	Dey and Bandyopadhyay (2018)	Blended learning	228	Qualitative
	Borup et al. (2019)	Virtual school	70	Qualitative
Synchronous	Anastasiades et al. (2010)	Virtual school	459	Quantitative
	Thompson and Nutta (2015)	Interactive videoconference	158	Quantitative
	Xiong, Ge et al. (2017)	Not reported	430	Quantitative

(continued)

Table 1. (*continued*)

Type of interaction	Reference	Design	Sample	Methodology
Mixed	Kim et al. (2012)	Interactive videoconference	46	Qualitative
	Malinovski et al. (2014)	Interactive videoconference	4	Qualitative
	Burdina et al. (2019)	Interactive videoconference	152	Qualitative

there is a regular face-to-face class of teachers and students, but without incorporating a second educator who is connected in real time to support the learning of a second language (Thomson and Nutta 2015). A videoconference format with interaction between two courses where the end of the process is reinforced with a face-to-face milestone (Anastasiades et al. 2010), and a design of multimedia classrooms with online teachers, face-to-face teachers, face-to-face students, and online students, in cooperation and coordination in real time (Xiong et al. 2017).

3.3 Types of Impact

To address the impact reported in the sample, it is important to note the diversity of methodologies and variables of interest evaluated in the different studies. While some studies report changes in the learning of subjects or in attitudes towards learning (Anastasiades et al. 2010; Lin et al. 2017; Ümit Yapici and Akbayin, 2012), there are studies that explore other types of relationships between variables that, although they occur in a distance education context, are not able to explain a possible impact of this modality on specific aspects of learning (De la Varre et al. 2014; Huertas-Bustos et al. 2018; Borup et al. 2019).

Thus, the analysis of the sample led to a distinction of the impact according to the approach of the distance education modalities as a factor of change in the academic performance or attitudes towards student learning. We will call direct impact that which describes a relationship between the distance education experience and academic performance or attitude towards learning. On the other hand, we will call indirect impact that whose results do not refer directly to the improvement in academic performance or in the attitude towards learning from an experience in distance education and, instead, consider the exploration of other variables in where distance education is more of a context than an object of study.

Direct Impact. Most of the documents that report this type of impact do so in a positive way with respect to learning and attitudes towards learning. In other words, it is mostly considered that having a distance education experience improves performance in multiple disciplines and increases qualities such as the motivation of learners in distance education scenarios. There are also documents that report an impact on both academic performance and attitude towards learning simultaneously (Chao et al. 2015; Lin et al. 2017; Sulisworo et al. 2016).

Regarding the direct impact on academic performance, it is possible to sustain that all the documents that report this type of impact do so in a positive way. To the extent that distance learning experiences are implemented, school performance improves. In this way, we can find an increase in academic performance in the subjects of biology (Ümit Yapici and Akbayin 2012), mathematics (Lin et al. 2017), musical arts (Edward et al. 2018) and science (Kalamković. et al. 2013). There are also other impact studies on school performance that, although they specify the factors and conditions that would improve such academic performance, do not pay attention to the subjects or contents where the improvement is visible (Burdina et al. 2019; Chao et al. 2015; Dey and Bandyopadhyay, 2018; Sulisworo et al. 2016; Xiong et al. 2017). This is possibly explained by the emphasis placed by the authors on highlighting the characteristics of distance educational design, instead of detailing aspects of learning a disciplinary content.

The direct impact on attitudes towards learning brings together documents that report improvements in aspects such as the perception of internet use (Ümit Yapici and Akbayin 2012), positive attitudes towards the language and the Hispanic Latino community (Thompson and Nutta 2015), development and strengthening of autonomy (Gariou-Papalexiou et al. 2017), and a general attitude of positive predisposition towards possible new experiences in distance education (Pardanjac et al. 2010). On the other hand, there are also studies that stress the relationships between well-being and permanent connection via mobile devices, since they focus on subjectivity and living conditions arising from the in-depth account of a single case (Tochon 2015).

However, not all findings are obtained with equal rigor. One of the documents reports improvements in all subjects and especially in science, after having used the resources available for the co-management of the learning process from home (Kalamković et al. 2013). Even when the article is a contribution to the approach of the use of LMS (Learning management systems) as a complement to traditional courses, the analysis of the main variable (the use of educational resources that can be accessed from Moodle) is not conclusive, unknown if there are other variables that could explain the increase in academic performance between one semester and another. Similar is the case of a study on the importance of motivation in distance education, which states that most of the participants saw an increase not only in the attitude towards virtual environments of distance education, but also in the attributes of this modality (Pardanjac et al. 2010). However, the means to reach the conclusions can be questioned, especially in aspects such as effectiveness and the supposed reduction in learning times, problems that the authors consider resolved only with the data of the responses of students when asked about the use of time, but without conducting any empirical study to confirm it. At the same time, a programming language is proposed, but there are no tests that allow validating the results. In fact, the exact number of participants is not specified, both in the two schools and in the university under study.

These examples that are part of the sample, propose a measured and critical approach that contrasts with the optimism of the impact around the implementation of distance learning courses. A supposed increase in academic performance must be contrasted with the low number of experiences that report this type of direct impact, even more so when there are disciplines not covered by the sample. On the other hand, the improvement in attitudes must also be approached with care not to fall into excessive optimism regarding the qualities that distance education experiences provide to the school population, considering the low number of impact reports identified in the sample, and the possible methodological disparities present through the documents studied.

In short, the distance education modality deployed in school education during the decade prior to the pandemic reported having the ability to improve both academic performance and attitudes towards learning and towards new experiences possible in a similar modality. However, such a positive impact must be contrasted with the methodological weaknesses and the absence of sample evidence that allows such findings to be contrasted.

Indirect Impact. In this section we find studies that, in a heterogeneous way, seek to relate new variables in comparison with those studies included in the direct impact, always in a context of distance school education. There are studies that propose models to predict which factors affect the completion of distance courses (Kirby and Sharpe 2010) and which factors have to do with the motivations that lead a student to enroll in one of these courses (Kim et al. 2012). While the first study proposes that it is the variable of self-efficacy in reading skills that mostly increases the chances of taking and completing a distance course, the second study identifies the positive predisposition to teamwork as the main predictive factor when it comes to explain the motivations that make students take an online course. It is also possible to identify factors such as excessive academic load, technological accessibility problems or parental dissatisfaction with the distance education process of their children as possible causes of dropout from online courses in rural educational contexts (de La Varre et al. 2010). Unlike the direct impact, in this type of impact it is possible to identify contrasts on the same topic addressed from distance education, as occurs with the factors that affect taking an online course. This allows an analysis to be carried out that, despite the limited number of related investigations present in the sample, can be contrasted with educational realities different from those of origin for the case of each study.

In short, the analysis of the indirect impact allows the study of distance school education to be opened to topics other than academic performance and learning attitudes, by incorporating new variables that account for the importance of inequalities of origin or previous material conditions. to the educational experiences studied in a possible performance in distance modality. This allows qualifying the individual characteristics of learners highlighted in the direct impact studies with more structural factors, such as gender, socioeconomic level, parental education, among others.

4 Discussion

Among the multiple topics that emerge from the study, the attitudes of students and the active role of teachers or tutors appear as essential aspects when evaluating the success or failure of an educational experience in distance mode. Students prefer a communicative tutor who is attentive to their concerns, rather than a kind of technical advisor who gives instructions on how to use the platform (Borup et al. 2019; Xiong et al. 2017). However, the finding regarding the importance of online teachers or tutors does not necessarily represent a specific feature of distance education in school education, but rather aligns with a long tradition of studies in the field of online education. distance (Berge and Mrozowski 2001, p. 7; Moore and Diehl 2018, p. 155; Schlosser et al. 1994, p. 2). Furthermore, there are studies that contradict the findings regarding the importance of teachers in distance education, stating that variables such as online feedback or computer-mediated communication are not significant when measuring the effectiveness of distance courses. in different types of learners (Arnesen et al. 2019, p. 36). The findings on the importance of online tutors and teachers are part of a tradition in the scientific literature on distance education, in which it is considered that, just as teachers must be well prepared to carry out their face-to-face activities, In the same way, they must be prepared to carry out distance educational processes (Keagan 1996; Keegan 1980; Moore and Diehl 2018; Schlosser et al. 1994). In the context of a drastic change in modality from the COVID-19 pandemic, lines of future work are proposed that include the acquisition of new skills by school education teachers, as well as knowing the process of change by the which old skills had to be updated or replaced by new knowledge management skills, management of online resources, and communication skills in digital environments by teachers.

Before the pandemic, mixed or hybrid modalities of synchronous and asynchronous interaction had already been experimented with. Interactive videoconferences on some occasions even considered the possibility of having both face-to-face teachers and students, as well as remote teachers and students connected and communicating in a synchronous interaction (Xiong et al. 2017). This design has been explored by other studies as a possibility to cover access needs in rural education contexts (Buccelli et al. 2013; de Melo et al. 2011), highlighting the opportunity to incorporate teachers of excellence overcoming the geographical distances, or the possibility of interacting with peers from another educational establishment during the same class session (Xiong et al. 2017). In this way, educational innovations can be projected in both directions, namely, both in the inclusion of new teaching actors, from other schools or higher education, as well as groups of students not only from geographically distant establishments, but also culturally distant, due to socioeconomic, linguistic, ethnic barriers, etc.

Within the type of asynchronous interaction, the Blended Learning design was the most used. Even though the study sample is limited compared to the amount of the world's school-age population that could have had distance education experiences throughout the world, the results are not far from other studies that suggest the greater effectiveness of this type of designs that integrate presence and distance, in contrast to purely face-to-face or purely distance methods (Means et al. 2013, p. 35). In other words, blended learning for both school education and other educational levels not only contributes with a greater number of pre-pandemic experiences in school education, but also appears as a more effective design in the acquisition of new knowledge, and at the same time, it is projected towards hybrid modality scenarios with a view to post-pandemic education.

5 Conclusions

Distance education has been a modality that is currently impossible to separate from technological advances in the digital age. Before the COVID-19 pandemic, some schools around the world had the opportunity to experience distance education modalities, both in synchronous and asynchronous interaction types, although scientific reports communicated in the past decade show an underuse of these educational designs, which in turn limits the generalizability of the findings around such experiences. In this way, the question about how prepared the planet was to face a drastic change from face-to-face modalities to others at a distance in a school education scenario, it is difficult to answer without considering the low number of reports found, which contrasts with the massive and even obligatory emergency remote education that weighs on primary and secondary education in much of the globe.

Despite this restriction, the findings of this study allow us to affirm that the distance educational experiences deployed before the pandemic, for the most part, aroused the interest of the students, increased the academic performance of the learners, and improved their attitudes. towards distance learning. Furthermore, the world school reality was objectively more prepared for educational designs in distance mode with asynchronous interactions than synchronous interactions, which is mainly sustained by the greater presence of this type of interaction in the decade prior to the pandemic. This data can be analyzed in depth in future research, in consideration of the speed and effectiveness with which the different educational systems of the world reacted to the need to support the educational exercise with the aim of continuing to ensure the right and access to education of children and adolescents, through access and coverage with different types of interaction during the school period affected by the international health crisis.

Going back to the question about how prepared the school was throughout the world to face emergency distance education in school education, and taking into account the intention of this study to characterize and analyze the experiences in distance modality in education school carried out before the COVID-19 pandemic, it is possible to conclude that the world was not sufficiently prepared for a change in educational modality of the magnitude with which the health emergency demanded of the educational systems of the planet. Instead, the few experiences reported were mostly asynchronous experiences and mixed face-to-face design, while they did not necessarily report conclusive findings regarding the impact of the distance education modality or the type of interaction as such. However, the content analysis allows generating a story between emerging trends and certain possibilities of innovation and study on modalities that have currently attracted the attention of multiple educational systems in the world, such as the development of a hybrid education from of experiences, for example, such as interactive videoconferencing. On the other hand, in this scenario of radical change, teachers continue to play a fundamental role, although sometimes different from that of the classic face-to-face teacher. Online tutors appear, who synchronously or asynchronously attend to both the technical and educational needs of the students, while the apprentices prefer a teacher or tutor taking care their concerns, who answers their questions in a timely manner and who shows interest in the learning process of their students.

The different experiences analyzed, added to the distance education initiatives forged in the emergency context, can collaborate in the creation of a projective scenario of post-pandemic hybrid education, where the activities and modalities of the traditional teaching exercise concur, with the new ones. capacities developed by educational communities around the world, to build a more inclusive education and that puts technological development at the service of education.

Acknowledgements. This work was funded by CONICYT's Basal Funds for Centers of Excellence, Project FB0003.

References

Anastasiades, P., et al.: Interactive videoconferencing for collaborative learning at a distance in the school of 21st century: A case study in elementary schools in Greece. Comput. Educ. **54**(2), 321–339 (2010)

Arnesen, K., Hveem, J., Short, C., West, R., Barbour, M.: K-12 online learning journal articles: Trends from two decades of scholarship. Distance Educ. **40**(1), 32–53 (2019)

Barbour, M., Reeves, T.: The reality of virtual schools: A review of the literature. Comput. Educ. **52**(2), 402–416 (2009)

Berge, Z., Mrozowski, S.: Review of research in distance education, 1990 to 1999. Int. J. Phytorem. **21**(1), 5–19 (2001)

Borup, J., Chambers, C., Stimson, R.: K-12 student perceptions of online teacher and on-site facilitator support in supplemental online courses. Online Learn. J. **23**(4), 253–280 (2019)

Buccelli, D., Espuny, H., Cavaleiro, J., Neto, P., Lopes, R., Romano, S.: Education mediated by technology: Strategy to spread high school learning in Piauí state, Brazil. IFIP Adv. Inf. Commun. Technol. **415**, 334–341 (2013)

Burdina, G., Krapotkina, I., Nasyrova, L.: Distance learning in elementary school classrooms: An emerging framework for contemporary practice. Int. J. Instr. **12**(1), 1–16 (2019)

Chao, C., Chen, Y., Chuang, K.: Exploring students' learning attitude and achievement in flipped learning supported computer aided design curriculum: A study in high school engineering education. Comput. Appl. Eng. Educ. **23**(4), 514–526 (2015)

de la Varre, C., Irvin, M., Jordan, A., Hannum, W., Farmer, T.: Reasons for student dropout in an online course in a rural K–12 setting. Distance Educ. **35**(3), 324–344 (2014)

de La Varre, C., Keane, J., Irvin, M.: Enhancing online distance education in small rural US schools: A hybrid, learner-centred model. ALT-J. Res. Learn. Technol. **18**(3), 193–205 (2010)

de Melo, J., Ferraz, L., da Silva, M.: Communication Processes at the "Distance Learning in the Amazon Forest Project." In McLuhan Galaxy Conference Understanding Media Today, pp. 266–277. UOC Editorial, Barcelona (2011)

Dey, P., Bandyopadhyay, S.: Blended learning to improve quality of primary education among underprivileged school children in India. Educ. Inf. Technol. **24**(3), 1995–2016 (2018). https://doi.org/10.1007/s10639-018-9832-1

UNICEF DATA. https://data.unicef.org/topic/education/covid-19/. Accessed Jan 26, 2022

Edward, C.N., Asirvatham, D., Johar, M.G.M.: Effect of blended learning and learners' characteristics on students' competence: An empirical evidence in learning oriental music. Educ. Inf. Technol. **23**(6), 2587–2606 (2018). https://doi.org/10.1007/s10639-018-9732-4

Fermín-González, M.: Research on virtual education, inclusion, and diversity: A systematic review of scientific publications (2007–2017). Int. Rev. Res. Open Dist. Learn. **20**(5), 146–167 (2019)

Garcia-Garcia, C., Ramos, V., Serrano, J.: Sculpture development as an informal activity for learning engineering abilities in K-12 students. Int. J. Eng. Educ. **33**(1), 332–345 (2017)

Gariou-Papalexiou, A., Papadakis, S., Manousou, E., Georgiadu, I.: Implementing a flipped classroom: A case study of biology teaching in a Greek high school. Turkish Online J. Dist. Educ. **18**(3), 47–65 (2017)

Huertas, A., López, O., Sanabria, L.: Effect of a metacognitive scaffolding on information web search. Electr. J. E-Learning **16**(2), 91–106 (2018)

Huertas, A., Vesga, G., Vergara, A., Romero, M.: Effect of a computational scaffolding in the development of secondary students' metacognitive skills. Int. J. Technol. Enhanced Learn. **7**(2), 143–159 (2015)

Kalamković, S., Halaši, T., Kalamković, M.: Distance learning applied in primary school teaching. Croatian J. Educ. **15**(3), 251–269 (2013)

Keagan, D.: Foundations of Distance Education, 3rd edn. Routledge, London (1996)

Kebritchi, M., Lipschuetz, A., Santiague, L.: Issues and challenges for teaching successful online courses in higher education. J. Educ. Technol. Syst. **46**(1), 4–29 (2017)

Keegan, D.: On defining distance education. Distance Educ. **1**(1), 13–36 (1980)

Kim, P., Kim, F., Karimi, A.: Public online charter school students: choices, perceptions, and traits. Am. Educ. Res. J. **49**(3), 521–545 (2012)

Kirby, D., Sharpe, D.: High school students in the new learning environment: A profile of distance e-learners. Turkish Online J. Educ. Technol. **9**(1), 83–88 (2010)

Kozma, R., Vota, W.: ICT in developing countries: Policies, implementation, and impact. In Handbook of Research on Educational Communications and Technology. 4th ed., pp. 885–894 (2014). Springer New York

Lee, K.: Rethinking the accessibility of online higher education: A historical review. Internet High. Educ. **33**, 15–23 (2017)

Lin, Y., Tseng, C., Chiang, P.: The effect of blended learning in mathematics course. Eurasia J. Math. Sci. Technol. Educ. **13**(3), 741–770 (2017)

Malinovski, T., Vasilleva, M., Vasileva Stojanovska, T., Trajkovik, V.: Considering high school students' experience in asynchronous and synchronous distance learning environments: QoE prediction model. Int. Rev. Res. Open Dist. Learn. **15**(4), 91–112 (2014)

Means, B., Toyama, Y., Murphy, R., Baki, M.: The effectiveness of online and blended learning: A meta-analysis of the empirical literature. Teach. Coll. Rec. **115**(3), 1–47 (2013)

Moore, M., Diehl, W.: Handbook of Distance Education, 4th edn. Routledge, New York (2018)

Pardanjac, M., Radosav, D., Jokic, S.: Motivation of users - How important and what is its impact on distance learning. Techn. Technol. Educ. Manage. **5**(1), 181–188 (2010)

Queiroz, A., Nascimento, A., Tori, R., da Silva Leme, M.: Using HMD-based immersive virtual environments in primary/K-12 education. In: International Conference on Immersive Learning, pp 160–173. Springer International Publishing, Missoula (2018)

Randler, C., Horzum, M., Vollmer, C.: The influence of personality and chronotype on distance learning willingness and anxiety among vocational high school students in Turkey. Int. Rev. Res. Open Dist. Learn. **15**(6), 93–110 (2014)

Schlosser, C., Anderson, M.: Distance Education: A review of the literature, 1st edn. AECT Publication Sales, Washington (1994)

Sulisworo, D., Agustin, S., Sudarmiyati, E.: Cooperative-blended learning using Moodle as an open source learning platform. Int. J. Technol. Enhanced Learn. **8**(2), 187–198 (2016)

Thompson, G., Nutta, J.: Trying to reach more children: Videoconferencing in the Spanish foreign language elementary school classroom. Hispania **98**(1), 94–109 (2015)

Tochon, F.: Mobile experiences of an adolescent learning Spanish online in a twenty-first century high school. Int. J. Pedagogies Learn. **10**(2), 91–106 (2015)

Ümit Yapici, I., Akbayin, H.: The effect of blended learning model on high school students' biology achievement and on their attitudes towards the internet. Turkish Online J. Educ. Technol. **11**(2), 228–237 (2012)

Watts, L.: Synchronous and asynchronous communication in distance learning: A review of the literature. Q. Rev. Dist. Learn. **17**(940), 23–32 (2016)

Xiong, C., Ge, J., Wang, Q., Wang, X.: Design and evaluation of a real-time video conferencing environment for support teaching: an attempt to promote equality of K-12 education in China. Interact. Learn. Environ. **25**(5), 596–609 (2017)

Zawacki-Richter, O., Bäcker, E., Vogt, S.: Review of distance education research (2000 to 2008): Analysis of research areas, methods, and authorship patterns. Int. Rev. Res. Open Dist. Learn. **10**(6), 21–50 (2009)

Estimation of Online Lecture Quality Using Fundamental Frequency Characteristics ExTracted from Student Utterances

Tomoyuki Takata[✉] and Yumi Wakita

Osaka Institute of Technology, Osaka, Japan
e1918047@oit.ac.jp, yumi.wakita@oit.ac.com

Abstract. The number of online lectures has increased against the backdrop of the COVID-19 pandemic. With the increase in online lectures, more methods of evaluating their quality and improving lecture styles are being developed. We proposed a method of estimating online lecture quality using the SD-F0 values of students' response utterances. First, we confirmed the effectiveness of the SD-F0 values of students' response utterances in estimating students' understanding of lectures. Through identification experiments using an online lecture video database, the precision rate of "Understanding" was found to be 80.6%. This suggests that when the SD-F0 value was high, with a high probability, the student understood the lecture content. Next, we analyzed the relationship between the SD-F0 values of the students' utterances and lecture quality. We confirmed that during the first thirty minutes of a lecture, when the SD-F0 value was high, the lecture was considered high-quality. If the SD-F0 values of the 10% or 20% utterances in a lecture exceeded a boundary set by the SVM (the boundary between high- and low-quality lectures), the lecture could be regarded as high-quality. The identification rate was greater than 80%.

Keywords: Online lectures quality · Conversation analysis Understanding level · Standard deviation of Fundamental frequency

1 Introduction

The number of online lectures has increased against the backdrop of the COVID-19 pandemic. Online lectures have several merits, such as offering an efficient study arrangement and learning at one's own pace, and even after the pandemic ends, teachers may continue their online teaching styles. With the increase in online lectures, more methods of evaluating their quality and improving lecture styles are being developed.

In general, online lectures are evaluated using student questionnaires and comprehension tests. Recently, to accelerate this evaluation, several simple questionnaire counting methods have been proposed [1]. However, evaluation using questionnaires is strongly influenced by individuality; hence, lecture evaluation quality is occasionally distorted. Consequently, several evaluation methods that automatically assess online lecture quality have been proposed [2, 3], such as those based on student facial expressions using

© The Author(s), under exclusive license to Springer Nature Switzerland AG 2022
P. Zaphiris and A. Ioannou (Eds.): HCII 2022, LNCS 13328, pp. 304–312, 2022.
https://doi.org/10.1007/978-3-031-05657-4_22

machine learning. However, these methods have several problems; for example, assessment performance depends on factors such as the individuality of the facial expression and filming environment.

We previously proposed a method of estimating the degree of decline in the understanding levels using the standard deviation of the fundamental frequency (SD-F0) of each utterance in their daily conversations [4]. In our previous paper, we indicated that the SD-F0s of their response utterances to a partner's speech are effective in estimating an elderly person's understanding of that speech.

In this paper, we propose a method of estimating online lecture quality using the SD-F0 values of student response utterances. First, we discuss the effectiveness of the SD-F0 values in estimating students' understanding of lectures.

2   Acoustic Analysis of Conversations Between Teachers and Students in Online Lectures

2.1   Online Lecture Video Database

In this study, online English lectures for high school students were analyzed. Both the students and teachers participated in the lectures from their respective homes using online video communication services, such as Zoom. The ratio of students to teachers in each lecture was 1:1. The content of each session consisted of the lecture by the teacher, the student's questions, and the teacher's answers. There were no exercises or examinations conducted by the students.

The lecture videos were recorded, including facial images and conversations between the teachers and students. We analyzed the fundamental frequency (F0) and speech power level (SPL) of each utterance extracted from their conversations during the online lectures and confirmed the probability of estimating the quality of the online lecture from time variation characteristic differences, such as the standard deviation of the F0s and SPL. Table 1 shows the specifications of the online lecture video data used for acoustic analysis.

Table 1. Online lecture video for acoustic analysis

Lecture No	Lecture Length	Student
9	67 min	Female
11	104 min	Male
12	83 min	Male
16	72 min	Male
18	82 min	Female
20	100 min	Male
22	86 min	Male
24	62 min	Male

2.2 F0 Extraction

Figure 1 shows the pitch extraction method used in this experiment. The frequency characteristics after the FFT process were used for pitch extraction. To achieve noise-robust extraction, the liftering results were processed via FFT again, and F0s were extracted from the frequency characteristics after excluding the liftered spectrum. The F0 values were extracted from multiple candidates, and the Viterbi algorithm was used to select the F0 frequency that was most naturally connected to the previous frames, thus achieving noise-robust F0 extraction. The F0 extraction conditions are listed in Table 2.

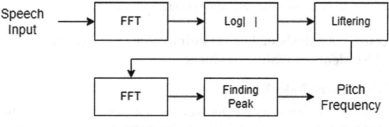

Fig. 1. F0 extraction process

Table 2. The acoustic analysis conditions

Sampling Frequency	16 kHz
Window length	0.1 ms
Frame shift length	0.025 ms
FFT analysis order	4096
Cepstrum analysis order	4096

3 Estimation of Students' Understanding Levels

3.1 Relationship Between the student's Understanding Level and the Standard Deviation of the student's Response Utterances

Using free speech among elderly people, we previously confirmed that the SD-F0 and the standard deviation of the SPLs (SD-SPL) of each response utterance to the other person's speech are effective parameters in estimating how much of the other person's speech is understood in a conversation [4]. Therefore, we focused on the students' response utterances in the online lecture videos and extracted only those utterances in which the student was responding to the teacher's statements. We calculated the SD-F0 and SD-SPL values of each utterance and examined the relationship between these values and the students' understanding of the lectures.

We asked four people to watch lecture videos including these response utterances and then categorize the understanding level of the students into two groups: "Understanding" and "Not Understanding." Table 3. shows the number of lectures, students, and utterances categorized into each group.

Table 3. Number of lectures, students, and response utterances for F0s and SPLs SD analysis

Number of lectures	8
Number of students	4
Number of response utterances Understanding: Not Understanding:	 54 51

Figure 2 shows the relationship between the SD-F0s and SD-SPLs of students' response utterances. The red squares indicate the utterances categorized as "Understanding," and the blue dots indicate the utterances categorized as "Not Understanding." In this figure, the area plotted by the "Not Understanding" values (blue dots) is smaller than that plotted by the "Understanding" values (red squares). Additionally, almost all of the "Not Understanding" values are below the dashed line; however, the area of "Understanding" goes beyond the dashed line. These results indicate that these areas cannot be easily distinguished; however, it is possible to identify the area plotted only by the "Understanding" utterances. This suggests that the SD-F0s and SD-SPLs are only useful for extracting normal speech utterances.

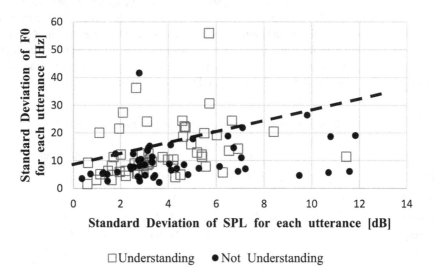

□ Understanding   ● Not Understanding

Fig. 2. Relationship between the SD-SPL and SD-F0 of students' response utterances.

3.2 Identification of Understanding Level Using SD-F0 and SD-SPL Values

Using a support vector machine (SVM) and the SD-F0 and SD-SPL values, we confirmed the performance of this method in identifying the difference between the "Understanding" and "Not Understanding" utterances. The experimental conditions for the SVM are listed in Table 4. Three identification experiments were conducted using different utterance datasets, and Table 5 indicates the number of utterances used for training and evaluation in each experiment. The utterances used for training were different from those used for testing.

Table 4. SVM conditions for identification

Type	C-SVC
Kernel	RBF
Cost	1000

Table 5. Number of utterances for identification

	Dataset 1	Dataset 2	Dataset 3
Number of utterances for training	49	59	42
Number of utterances for testing	10	18	24

The identification results are listed in Table 6. The average recall and precision rates were 30.3% and 80.6%, respectively. These results indicate that when the SD-F0 was low, it was difficult to estimate the understanding level. However, when the SD-F0 value was high, with high probability, the student's understanding of the lecture was high. Nevertheless, the identification rate was dependent on the dataset, which means that identification performance depends on the students and lectures.

Table 6. The identification of students' understanding levels

Dataset	Recall	Precision	f-measure	Accuracy
Dataset 1	0.6	0.75	0.67	0.7
Dataset 2	0.14	1	0.25	0.67
Dataset 3	0.17	0.67	0.27	0.54
Average	0.303	0.806	0.394	0.636

4 Estimation of Online Lecture Quality Using the SD-F0s of Student Utterances

4.1 Relationship Between Online Lecture Quality and SD-F0 Values

Online lecture videos have already been evaluated by educational experts and identified as either high- or low-quality lectures. However, from the results in Sect. 3, we found that SD-F0 tended to be higher when students understood the content of the lecture. In this section, we present how SD-F0 differs between high- and low-quality lectures.

Using the lecture videos indicated in Table 7, we analyzed students' response utterances. These included 104 utterances extracted from 6 high-quality lectures and 70 utterances extracted from 5 low-quality lectures. Figure 3 shows the results of this analysis and indicates how the SD-F0s of the students' response utterances changed from the beginning to the end of the lecture.

The results show that during the first thirty minutes, the SD-F0s values of utterances in the high-quality lectures tended to be larger than those in the low-quality lectures. However, in the final part of lectures, the SD-F0 values were low, even for the high-quality lectures, and differences between the SD-F0 values of the high- and low-quality lectures were not recognized.

Figure 4 shows the results for the teachers' utterances. all teachers are males. In this case, there was no difference between the SD-F0 values of the high- and low-quality lectures.

Table 7. Online lecture videos for identification experiments

Lecture No	Lecture Length	Student
5	95 min	Male
9	67 min	Female
11	104 min	Male
12	83 min	Male
18	82 min	Female
19	59 min	Female
20	100 min	Male
21	105 min	Male
22	86 min	Male
24	62 min	Male
25	22 min	Male

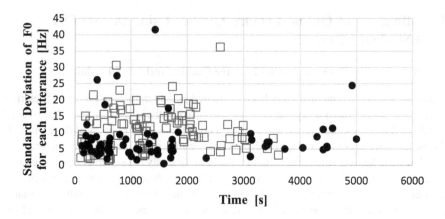

Fig. 3. The SD-F0 values for students' utterances

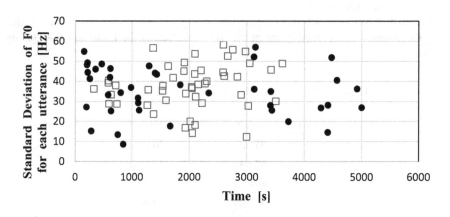

Fig. 4. The SD-F0 values for teachers' utterances

4.2 Relationship Between Online Lecture Quality and SD-F0 Values

According to the results in Sect. 4.1, if the utterance rate, in which the SD-F0 value is greater than the boundary value, is higher than a threshold rate, the lecture can be considered a high-quality lecture. Conversely, if the utterance rate, in which the SD-F0 value is greater than the boundary value, is lower than the threshold rate, the lecture is regarded as low-quality.

To confirm that SD-F0 values are effective in estimating lecture quality, a boundary between the SD-F0 values of high-quality lectures and those of low-quality lectures was set using the SVM method. Additionally, we calculated the utterance rates that exceeded the threshold rate. Figure 5 shows the relationship between the threshold and accuracy rates of lecture quality estimation. The figure indicates that the most suitable threshold rate was 10% or 20% because the accuracy rate for both high- and low-quality lectures could be estimated with high accuracy as over 80%.

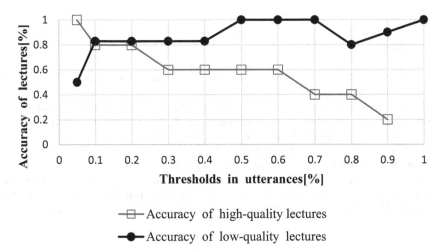

Fig. 5. The estimation performance of online lecture quality

5 Conclusion

With the increase in online lectures, more methods of evaluating their quality and improving lecture styles are being developed. We proposed a method of estimating online lecture quality using the SD-F0 values of students' response utterances.

First, we confirmed the effectiveness of the SD-F0 values of students' response utterances in estimating students' understanding of lectures. Through identification experiments using an online lecture video database, the precision rate of "Understanding" was found to be 80.6%. This suggests that when the SD-F0 value was high, with a high probability, the student understood the lecture content.

Next, we analyzed the relationship between the SD-F0 values of the students' utterances and lecture quality. We confirmed that during the first thirty minutes of a lecture, when the SD-F0 value was high, the lecture was considered high-quality. If the SD-F0 values of the 10% or 20% utterances in a lecture exceeded a boundary set by the SVM (the boundary between high- and low-quality lectures), the lecture could be regarded as high-quality. The identification rate was greater than 80%.

However, the relationship between the SD-F0 values of students' utterances and the quality of online lectures depended on the students; therefore, in future studies, it will be necessary to consider the students' utterance characteristics when setting the boundary between high- and low-quality lectures.

Acknowledgment. I would like to express my gratitude to Mr. Shozo Kamiya, Mr. Kotaro Ando, and Mr. Yasuhiro Nose of IBY, Inc., for providing the online lecture video database and useful advice for this study. This work was also supported by JSPS KAKENHI (grant number 19K04934).

References

1. Ramachandran, R. et al.: Development of a new questionnaire to study students' perception toward online classes. J. Med. **16**(4), 143–145 (2020)
2. Chollet, M., et al.: Exploring feedback strategies to improve public speaking: An interactive virtual audience framework. In Proceedings of the ACM 2015 International Joint Conference on Pervasive and Ubiquitous Computing, pp.1143–1154 (2015)
3. Liu, Y., et al.: Using context information for dialog act classification in DNN framework. In Proceedings of the CEMNLP 2017, pp. 2170–2178 (2017)
4. Kana, N., Wakita, Y., Nakatoh, Y.: Estimating age-dependent degradation using nonverbal feature analysis of daily conversation. In: Duffy, V.G. (ed.) HCII 2019. LNCS, vol. 11582, pp. 222–231. Springer, Cham (2019). https://doi.org/10.1007/978-3-030-22219-2_17

Diversity in Learning

Design and Neuroergonomics in Identification of Elements Restorers of ADHD Care in Educational Environments: A Systematic Literature Review (SLR) Based on the PRISMA Method

Layane Araújo[1]([✉]), Sheila Albuquerque[1], and Marcelo M. Soares[2]

[1] Design, Federal University of Pernambuco, Recife, Brazil
layane.araujo@ufpe.br
[2] Southern University of Science and Technology –
SUSTech and Federal University of Pernambuco, Recife, Brazil

Abstract. This study aimed to contextualize ADHD, establishing its connection with Neuroscience, Ergonomics, Design, Restorative Environments Theory and Educational Spaces. Therefore, a Systematic Literature Review (RSL) was carried out, based on the Preferred Reporting Items for Systematic Reviews and Meta-Analyses (PRISMA) method. The aim was to seek studies that addressed the learning process/attention of adults with ADHD, teaching strategies, and design interventions in classrooms based on the presented objectives. The searches took place on the Journal Portal of the Higher Education Improvement Coordination (CAPES). The filters used were papers published in the last ten years (2011–2021), peer-reviewed in English only. The research founds a total of 77,654 papers. The first 100 were analyzed in order of relevance, totaling 1,257 papers analyzed, and thus, excluding repeated ones, 52 papers were selected by evaluating the titles and abstracts. After a dynamic reading, 13 papers remained, divided into three groups: A, B, and C. Therefore, the papers were found to relate only to the areas proposed by the study of neuroscience, educational environment, learning, and attention focused on ADHD. No research was found that addresses all the points sought together, especially the field of Ergonomics and Theory of Restorative Environments, thus proving the need for research that addresses these contexts since there are possibilities for further studies on these themes.

Keywords: TDAH · Design · Neuroergonomics · PRISMA

1 Introduction

Attention Deficit Hyperactivity Disorder (ADHD) is a neurobehavioral disorder in childhood and often accompanies the individual throughout his life. According to the Brazilian Attention Deficit Association (ABDA), ADHD affects 3% to 5% of children in regions of the world. About 2/3 of them with ADHD continue with the disorder's symptoms

© The Author(s), under exclusive license to Springer Nature Switzerland AG 2022
P. Zaphiris and A. Ioannou (Eds.): HCII 2022, LNCS 13328, pp. 315–334, 2022.
https://doi.org/10.1007/978-3-031-05657-4_23

in adulthood. Studies show that 4.4% of adults across the globe have ADHD with full symptoms (ABDA, 2016).

One of the main complications associated with ADHD is problems with concentration and consequently with learning (Arruda et al. 2015, p.5). This fact highlights the need for specialists to turn their attention to this public in educational environments based on the person's right to go to school, participate, interact and develop.

Thus, the present study aimed to contextualize ADHD, establishing its connection with Neuroscience, Ergonomics, Design, Theory of Restorative Environments and Educational Spaces. To this end, a Systematic Literature Review (SLR) was carried out, based on the Preferred Reporting Items for Systematic Reviews and Meta-Analyses (PRISMA) method (Salameh et al. 2020). The aim was to search for studies that addressed the learning process/attention of adults with ADHD, teaching strategies, and design interventions in classrooms.

2   Design, ADHD, Neuroergonomics and Restorative Environments

To better understand the concepts of Design, Ergonomics, ADHD, Neuroscience, and the Theory of Restorative Environments, this topic is divided into two parts. The first part aims to establish a relationship between Design, Ergonomics, and teaching environments. The second part, further on, seeks to highlight the link between ADHD, Neuroscience, and the Theory of Restorative Environments.

2.1   Design, Ergonomics and Educational Environment

Design is a Latin word, designare, which means to develop and conceive (Bürdek 2010). The designer creates artifacts, environments, and services. According to the author mentioned above, Design comes from the industrial process and serial production of the 19th century, seen as a discipline based on the creative process, planning, and organization of products, systems, and services.

Therefore, Design comprises a multidisciplinary field encompassing social, anthropological, psychological, marketing, and ergonomic aspects. Since Ergonomics is one of its areas of study, it is understood as a necessary process to combine Design and Ergonomics in social and educational interventions practices. According to Iida (2016), ergonomic requirements make it possible to maximize comfort, satisfaction, and user safety.

In this way, ergonomics is an area that aims to transform and adapt not only the work but the space to the different needs of the human being, taking into account its limitations and characteristics.

Therefore, the combination of Design and Ergonomics can benefit projects related to the educational environment. According to Soares (2021, p. 47), Ergonomics can contribute to the generation of design concepts, providing designers with an understanding of users' physical and cognitive needs to generate solutions compatible with the function to be performed.

Furthermore, the National Guidelines for Special Education in Basic Education, presented by the Brazilian Ministry of Education (MEC) (2001), states that it is not the student who shapes or adapts to the school. Still, the school is aware of its function and is available to the student, becoming an inclusive space (Brasil, 2001).

Because of these statements, Adaskina (2016) argues that the teaching environment must be effective to contribute to the successful adaptation of individuals with ADHD to the schooling process. Besides, Harrison et al. (2019) claim that Design interventions in the educational environment can improve the quality of teaching and learn for this audience.

A deeper understanding of ADHD, the concept of Neuroscience, and the Theory of Restorative Environments will be addressed in the following topic.

2.2 ADHD, Neuroergonomics and Restorative Environment Theory

Arruda et al. (2015) define ADHD as a neurobiological disorder, usually genetic and hereditary, characterized by a dysfunction in the prefrontal cortex, part of the brain responsible for decision-making, action planning, and emotion control that influences cognitive abilities and behavior of the individual from childhood.

The ADHD spectrum brings together cases with different variations of the neurological disorder. According to the Diagnostic and Statistical Manual of Mental Disorders: DSM-5 (2014), there are three distinct types of ADHD: the combined one, which occurs when the individual has hyperactivity, impulsivity, and attention deficit; predominantly inattentive, characterized when the person shows only a lack of attention; and the principally hyperactive/impulsive, which can manifest as extreme restlessness, rash actions that occur at the moment without premeditation, and/or making important decisions without considering the long-term consequences.

The NeuroSaber Institute (2016) states that all care offered to individuals with ADHD may minimize its complications, such as behavior, mood, and cognition. However, according to Kuhnen and Puff (2014), people with ADHD often have a low-performance index in academic activities.

In addition, several multidisciplinary areas are interested in studying human thought and behavior, such as Environmental Psychology, Cognitive Psychology, and Neuroscience. According to Paiva (2018), the last two, added to Ergonomics, result in Neuroergonomics.

According to Parasuraman and Rizzo (2007), Neuroergonomics converges concepts from the disciplines of Neuroscience and Ergonomics and aims to study neural structures and human behavior in carrying out activities, emphasizing the context of cognition and behavior of individuals in environments.

According to Bins Ely (2003) and Paiva (2018), the influence of the built environment on the individual's behavior is related both to the requirements of the task performed in the environment and the characteristics and needs of the user. Activities carried out in physical spaces are mediated by human cognition and perception, in the sense of optimizing the physical, psychological and emotional needs required by users for these environments.

Therefore, when combined with Neuroergonomics, Design can be understood as a factor that constitutes a device that aims at physical and psycho-emotional well-being, capable of expanding human capabilities and potential.

Given this, the environment can provide a restorative space that helps in the behavior, conduct, and performance of its user. Thus, the concept of restorative environment, originally from Environmental Psychology, is used to describe the process of feelings aroused by the environment, which can positively influence the health and well-being of the individual (Altman and Wohlwill, 1983); Kaplan and Kaplan, 1982; Korpela 1989).

In their studies, Kaplan and Kaplan (1982) investigate how properties of environments, natural or built, can restore fatigue and attention to their users. For the authors, environments said to be restorative are those that allow the renewal of directed attention and, consequently, the reduction of mental fatigue; that is, the space must provide a means by which this attention arrives at a state of equilibrium.

In the opinion of Ulrich (1991), the environment is understood as restorative when there is the absence of stressful demands and the awakening of the user's interest, pleasure, or calm. Therefore, restoration would be the process of recovery or renewal of psychological, physiological, and social resources of individuals, compromised by the demands posed by contemporary environments.

Thus, Oliveira et al. (2019) emphasize that a welcoming/restorative educational space should promote students' health and constitutes a significant public health issue, with personal, environmental, social, and institutional impact.

Therefore, in order to study and identify other works in the literature that addressed the issue in question, bibliographic searches were carried out in the databases of the Periodicals portal of the Coordination of Superior Level Staff Improvement (CAPES), Brazil. The methodological procedure adopted for data collection was the Systematic Literature Review (SLR). The search method will be described in the next topic.

3 Method

The Systematic Literature Review (SLR) was developed based on the PRISMA method. The study comprised a qualitative and analytical SLR. It deeply evaluated the information collected, aiming to seek studies that addressed the learning/attention process of adults with ADHD, teaching strategies, and design interventions in classrooms based on the objective presented above.

Based on the Ministry of Health of Brazil (2012), the PRISMA method emerged from a review and update of the QUOROM (Quality Of Reporting Of Metaanalyses). Its guideline is to help authors improve the quality of SLR and Meta-Analysis data reporting. It is carried out through a checklist pre-defined by the researcher that allows reaching the study's objective. Figure 1, below, describes the method steps..

The first step consisted of data collection that took place on the CAPES Journal Portal, selected due to the numerous inclusion of journals in the search: Scopus (Elsevier), SciELO (CrossRef), MEDLINE, PubMed (NLM), among others. The filters used were papers published in the last ten years (2011–2021), peer-reviewed in English only.

In addition, the following keywords were used as descriptors: "Neuroscience, Ergonomics, Human Factors, Neuroergonomics, Educational Environments, Learning Process, Learning, Teaching, Classroom, Design, Interior Design, and Restorative Environments, combined with the terms ADHD and Attention Deficit Hyperactivity Disorder", and in some cases also with the terms "NOT Drug", "NOT Treatment" and "NOT Medicine".

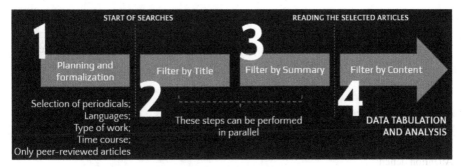

Fig. 1. PRISMA method steps. Source: Authors (2021)

The Inclusion and Exclusion criteria of the analyzed works were:

- Inclusion – papers that addressed the issue of adults with ADHD in the teaching environment; research focusing on the learning of adults with ADHD; studies that addressed teaching strategies and design interventions in classrooms for adults with ADHD from the perspective of neuroergonomics and/or the Theory of Restorative Environments;
- Exclusion – surveys that sample children and/or adolescents with ADHD; works that only address clinical pathologies and/or use drugs in analysis and treatment; studies that address other conditions in addition to and/or combined with ADHD, such as Autism Spectrum Disorder (ASD).

For the second and third stage, in the advanced search, the categories "Any – Any" were chosen, bringing together all the other categories offered by the platform: search by Title, Author, and Subject. The Boolean operators selected for the searches were 'and' and 'not' since the use of the Boolean 'or' did not generate results directed to the study. Thus, 18 combinations of the keywords were performed, which can be verified in Table 1.

Table 1. Data collection results

Combinations	Results of combinations	Selected by title and abstract	Selected by content
Neuroscience AND Attention deficit hyperactivity disorder; ADHD	17.703	9	3
Neuroscience AND Attention deficit hyperactivity disorder; ADHD; NOT Drug	8.924	5	1

(continued)

Table 1. (*continued*)

Combinations	Results of combinations	Selected by title and abstract	Selected by content
Neuroscience AND Attention deficit hyperactivity disorder; ADHD; NOT Medicine	2.866	2	0
Neuroscience AND Attention deficit hyperactivity disorder; ADHD; NOT Treatment	5.169	1	0
Human Factors AND Attention deficit hyperactivity disorder; ADHD	155	0	0
Ergonomics AND Attention deficit hyperactivity disorder; ADHD	172	4	3
Neuroergonomics AND Attention deficit hyperactivity disorder; ADHD	16	0	0
Neuroergonomics AND Attention deficit hyperactivity disorder; ADHD; NOT Drug	13	0	0
Neuroergonomics AND Attention deficit hyperactivity disorder; ADHD; NOT Medicine	4	0	0
Neuroergonomics AND Attention deficit hyperactivity disorder; ADHD; NOT Treatment	7	0	0
Educational environments AND Attention deficit hyperactivity disorder; ADHD	229	5	1

(*continued*)

Table 1. (*continued*)

Combinations	Results of combinations	Selected by title and abstract	Selected by content
Learning Process AND Attention deficit hyperactivity disorder; ADHD	725	3	1
Learning AND Attention deficit hyperactivity disorder; ADHD	16.466	11	3
Teaching AND Attention deficit hyperactivity disorder; ADHD	3.538	7	0
Classroom AND Attention deficit hyperactivity disorder; ADHD	4.401	4	0
Restorative Environment AND Attention deficit hyperactivity disorder; ADHD	17	0	0
Design AND Attention deficit hyperactivity disorder; ADHD	17.249	1	1
Interior Design AND Attention deficit hyperactivity disorder; ADHD	0	0	0
-	**77.654**	**52**	**13**

In this way, a total of 77,654 papers were found, and the filter by title and abstract were carried out in parallel since, often, only analyzing the title of the work, it is not possible to infer the content addressed by it.

To this end, the first 100 most relevant papers from each group of combinations of the keywords presented in Table 1 were evaluated, totaling 1,257 titles and abstracts analyzed. After this analysis and selection of the works, the exclusion of repeated papers was carried out, still at this stage, obtaining a total number of 52 papers to be evaluated, in order to verify if the content of the works in question were by the inclusion and exclusion criteria described above. Finally, after dynamic reading of the texts, 13 papers remained.

In order to illustrate the review up to this stage, a graphic was developed, presented in Fig. 2 below.

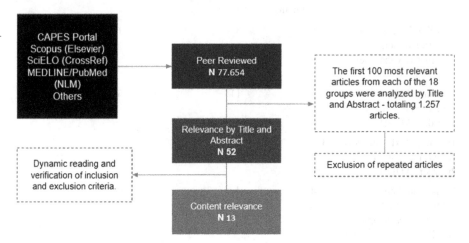

Fig. 2. Application of SLR. 2021 Source: Authors ()

In the fourth and final stage, a complete reading of the 13 selected works was carried out in order to explore the material analytically. From the PRISMA method, the information of the papers was systematized in an Excel spreadsheet with the following categories: title of the work, author(s), reference, country of origin of the work, the object of study, objectives, methods, and tools used, main results, conclusion, and classification of the relevance of the works, which were divided into three groups: A, B, and C, which will be better explained in the following topic.

4   Results and Discussion

This topic presents the works belonging to each group: A, B, and C.

4.1   Group A

The A group brings together studies that address interventions and Restorative Environments in ADHD, focusing on Neuroscience, Ergonomics, Theory of Educational Environments, Design and Educational Environments. However, the works found, in general, were designed especially for ADHD to Neuroscience, designed for studies of neurological functions, namely: Arabaci and Parris (2018), Gabay et al. (2018), Kim et al. (2014a, 2014b), Woltering et al. (2012), Gu et al. (2018), Rubia (2018), Thoma et al. (2014) and Keune et al. (2014).

The first research analysis, developed by Arabaci and Parris (2018) in Bournemouth, England, sought to examine the positive relationship between types of mind-wandering and ADHD at clinical and subclinical levels. However, the DSM-V is said to attribute mind-wandering only to inattention, and it is thought that only inattention results from impaired executive function linked to mind-wandering. Therefore, this work did not consider the relationship between mind-wandering and the main symptoms of ADHD: inattention, hyperactivity, and impulsivity.

Thus, the study had a sample of 80 undiagnosed adults. And for their method, the standard and easy versions of the Sustained Attention Response Task (SART) were used, measuring both the mind in its spontaneous function and the deliberate wandering.

As a result, the authors found that spontaneous mind-wandering was related to self-reported inattention, traits when the task was more cognitively challenging (standard SART). However, the hyperactive and impulsive traits were related to spontaneous mind wandering regardless of task difficulty.

Thus, the authors concluded that inattentive traits are not exclusively related to mind-wandering, and adults with hyperactivity/impulsive characteristics were more likely to experience mind-wandering, suggesting that mind-wandering may not be a helpful diagnostic criterion for inattention.

This second study, from Israeli, Gabay, Shahpari-Khateb, and Mendelsohn (2018), examines feedback-based probabilistic learning during conditions. The study involves procedural and declarative learning systems to varying degrees in adults with and without ADHD.

Based on some emerging studies, ADHD, in addition to being mainly associated with deficits in brain executive function, can also compromise the individual's procedural learning. Therefore, the authors show that feedback-based procedural learning is selectively impaired in ADHD, and these results coincide with the dopaminergic changes associated with this condition.

The method of this study includes 26 participants with ADHD and 28 without ADHD selected for the control group, totaling 54 participants. All participants are students from the University of Haifa, Israel. They performed a probabilistic learning task in which they were required to learn to associate between cues and outcomes. The outcomes were presented either immediately or with short/long delays. The test took place in an attenuated sound chamber. Participants were seated in front of a computer monitor throughout the experiment, in which stimuli were presented to record response time and accuracy, controlled by an E-PRIME computer program.

It was observed that the performance in probabilistic learning in participants with ADHD was comparable to control participants, without ADHD, under conditions of delay in the feedback/response time. However, during the learning and testing phase, these individuals' performance declined when feedback was immediate. In addition, ADHD symptom severity was negatively correlated with the ability to learn from direct feedback.

The authors concluded that probabilistic feedback-based learning could be improved in ADHD, provided that under certain conditions, such as shifting the load from the midbrain/striatal systems to declarative memory mechanisms. Thus, behavioral performance in people with ADHD can be remedied.

The third and fourth studies of this group belong to authors Kim et al. (2014a, 2014b), in these studies of Canadian and American origin, the authors addressed retinal perception and color differentiation by people with ADHD.

In the third study, the objective was to test the dopaminergic hypothesis of the retina. It postulates that the deficient perception of the blue color in ADHD, resulting from the hypofunction of the Central Nervous System and retinal dopamine, to which the blue cones are extremely sensitive. In addition, supposed sex differences in red color perception were explored.

For this purpose, 30 young adults diagnosed with ADHD and 30 healthy young adults matched by age and sex were tested. In addition, both groups performed a psychophysical task to measure blue and red color saturation and contrast discrimination ability and measures to assess visual function, such as the Visual Activity Questionnaire (VAQ) and the Farnsworth-Munsell 100 test (FMT).

As a result, women with ADHD were less accurate in discriminating blue and red color saturation compared to control subjects but did not differ in contrast sensitivity. Female participants in the control group were better at discriminating red saturation than males, but no sex difference was present in the ADHD group.

Thus, it is concluded that the lower discrimination of red and blue color saturation in the female ADHD group may be partially attributable to a hypodopaminergic state in the retina. It occurs since the perception of colors (blue-yellow and red-green) is based on the entry of S-cones (short-wavelength cone system) at the beginning of the visual pathway.

In the fourth study by the same authors, the objective was to investigate the impact of exogenous covert attention on chromatic colors (blue and red) and chromatic visual perception in adults with and without ADHD.

Therefore, this study also used a sample of 30 adults diagnosed with ADHD and 30 healthy adults, separated by age and sex. They look like a psychophysical task designed to measure the effects of perceived color perception (blue, red) and contrast sensitivity.

As a result, the effects of covert exogenous attention on saturation, contrast, and sensitivity levels perceived in blue and red coloration were similar in both groups, with no differences between men and women. Specifically, covert exogenous attention improved blue saturation perception and contrast sensitivity but did not affect red saturation perception.

Thus, it was concluded that exogenous covert attention is intact in adults with ADHD and does not explain the observed deficiencies in the perception of chromatic saturation (blue and red).

The fifth paper in this study was carried out in the United Kingdom by Woltering et al. (2012). The research object analyzed the typical development of adults with ADHD due to high levels of slow oscillatory activity (theta) and reduced fast oscillatory activity (alpha and beta) through electroencephalography in the resting state.

Eighteen participants with ADHD and 17 healthy controls were assessed using 129-channel electroencephalography (EEG). Furthermore, the Adult Self-Report Scale (ASRS v1.1) was also applied in the study to assess the symptoms of adults with ADHD. In addition, the Woodcock Reading Fluency subscale, Johnson-III Achievement Tests, Wechsler Adult Digit Span subtest, the Intelligence Scale (WAIS-IV) were used to assess auditory-verbal working memory and MATLAB 7.5 for exporting EEG data.

The main results showed that people with ADHD had lower power in the fast oscillations for all electrodes. Furthermore, the main effect of eye condition was found in the alpha band for all electrodes; as expected, closed eyes showed increased alpha compared to open eyes. Compared to the ADHD participants, the healthy control group showed a stronger decrease in alpha power when they had their eyes closed.

Therefore, the ADHD group showed a lower variability in the fast oscillatory band (alpha and beta) and the occipital electrodes for alpha. In addition, for the eyes closed condition, the ADHD group showed greater relative power in theta oscillation compared to the control group.

In summary, the authors noted the decrease in alpha power for the ADHD group, which is related to the slow-wave oscillations shown in relative power calculations. However, the study also highlighted that the analyzed adults with ADHD increased oscillatory power at fast frequencies.

Therefore, it is concluded that adults with ADHD presented a distinct neural pattern during the resting state, suggesting that the oscillatory power - alpha is a valuable index to reflect differences in neural communication of these individuals in early adulthood.

The sixth RSL study, prepared by Gu et al. (2018) in the United States, had the investigation of college adults with ADHD (non-medicated) as its object of study. They were matched with 27 healthy gender peers (41% female) at the University of Toronto between the years 2011 to 2013 to evaluate the neural and behavioral indices, considering the aspects of working memory.

The study adopted the following methods: the Adult Self-Report Scale (ASRS v1) and the Cognitive Failures Questionnaire. In addition, the Cambridge Neuropsychological Testing Automated Battery (CANTAB) was applied, as well as the Wechsler Vocabulary and Matrix Reasoning subscales. In addition, E-prime 1.2 was used for time stimulus control and collecting performance measures.

EEG was applied with a 128-channel sensor network in conjunction with the EGI Netstation software (Electrical Geodesic Inc). Then the data was transferred to Matlab 9.1. And for the analysis of variance, the ANOVA tool was applied.

The main results showed that the ADHD group demonstrated more symptomatology and cognitive problems compared to their peers. Furthermore, this group did not differ from its peers in terms of visual-spatial accuracy.

Furthermore, the authors showed that participants with ADHD did not differ from their peers on most behavioral indices of working memory and performance. However, the data showed more significant neural compromise in the brains of individuals with ADHD. For this reason, these individuals were found to be dedicating a similar amount of neural resources to the high and low load conditions.

In summary, it is concluded that the study contributed to research related to working memory in subjects with ADHD from the perspective of a neural system. In addition, it was found that the brains of individuals with ADHD process the maintenance of information differently from their healthy peers.

The seventh work evaluated by this group refers to studies carried out in the United Kingdom by the author Rubia (2018), in which the study object was: Meta-analyses referring to Electrophysiological Neurofeedback (NF-EEG); Transcranial Direct Current Stimulation (tDCS); Transcranial Magnetic Stimulation (rTMS) and Functional Magnetic Resonance Imaging (fMRI). Thus, the evaluations' objective consisted of the investigation of research applied to cognitive neuroscience for people with ADHD, focusing on Functional Magnetic Resonance Imaging (fMRI) and other neuromodulation techniques.

For this, the author highlighted in her analyses tools applied in neuromodulation such as Working Memory Tasks (WM), Visual-Spatial Task, Executive Functions (EF) Tasks, and Stop and Go/no-go Tasks.

There is evidence that deficits in the basal ganglia may be seen more in children with ADHD, while cortical dysfunctions are more persistent or more substantial in adults with ADHD. Furthermore, the reviews carried out by the author highlighted those specific abnormalities of ADHD may be more context-dependent on the conditions presented during cognitive control than in Executive Functions (EF).

In summary, one of the author's main positive findings on all Neurofeedback (NF) modalities, including EEG-NF, NIRS-NF, and fMRI-NF, is the evidence for the effects of delayed consolidation in the long term. Furthermore, they show to be more evident during follow-up than post-NF assessments.

The author concluded that people with ADHD have dissociated deficits in the cognitive domain in several areas of the brain. Furthermore, the author also concludes that brain stimulation associated with suitable cognitive training tasks is more likely to contribute to increased brain plasticity in ADHD than individual brain stimulation.

The penultimate paper evaluated in this group was prepared in Germany by Thomas et al. (2014). The study proposed to analyze 14 adults with ADHD of the combined subtype and 14 healthy participants of the control. They performed an observational and active probabilistic reward-based learning task. At the same time, an electroencephalogram (EEG) recorded the participants' brain activities. However, the study's main objective was to evaluate changes in the electrophysiological correlates of monetary reward processing in adult patients with ADHD.

The main methods applied in the study were: the Wender-Reimherr-Interview and the Multiple Choice Vocabulary Test. In addition, all participants engaged in an observational and active feedback learning task, both being adaptations of the probabilistic selection task.

The Presentation software controlled the stimulus time and the recording of the subject's responses, and each learning phase consisted of 20 trials for each pair of stimuli, totaling 60 trials. In addition, the EEG was recorded using the Brain Vision Recorder software.

Patients had reduced learning performance during the no-feedback test phases and increased FRN amplitudes in response to positive and negative feedback. For the no-feedback trials only, patients scored lower than controls.

In the end, it is concluded that for the first time, an improvement in FRN was demonstrated in association with reduced learning performance during active and observational reward learning in adults with ADHD. For this reason, it may be speculated that the reward prediction is often affected. Furthermore, the authors also concluded that there were no significant correlations between learning performance, FRN amplitudes, and clinical symptoms.

The last work evaluated by Group A refers to the research developed by Keune et al. (2014) in Germany, whose object of study was the evaluation of the relationship between

ADHD symptoms (men and women - adults, between 18 and 65 years old), depression and alpha asymmetry.

The study investigated ADHD because of the relationship between motivational dysfunction and behavioral symptoms by analyzing frontal brain asymmetry in the alpha band using the 24-channel electroencephalogram (EEG).

In analyzing the inferred methods, was identified to obtain the specific diagnoses of ADHD were applied the scales of Rösler et al. (2008). However, the EEG data were obtained through two assessments, with two weeks between them.

In summary, 52 data sets were considered in the final statistical analysis.

The main results showed that the ANOVA technique revealed that the regression of alpha activity in ADHD symptoms varied by Region and Hemisphere. Furthermore, simple comparisons for each region highlighted the right hemisphere's strongest anterior relative alpha activity in females compared to males in the lateral and mid-frontal areas. Women also scored higher on the self-reported depression measure.

Thus, the authors concluded that the symptoms of ADHD, similar to motivational dysfunction, involve a pattern of frontal brain asymmetry and information about the temporal properties of alpha asymmetry in ADHD and the supposed gender differences and the relationship with depression are scarce.

In summary, new gender-specific findings and a mediating role of ADHD symptoms were obtained with an atypical relationship between alpha asymmetry and depressive symptoms.

It can be seen that even the papers in group A, considered to be of greater relevance, individually, showed only studies in the field of Neuroscience, especially clinical studies. Therefore, the analyzed works did not address research related to Ergonomics, Theory of Restorative Environments, Design and Educational Environments focusing on ADHD.

The studies found were well distributed geographically, and almost all of them had adults with ADHD as their target audience. The exception is Arabaci and Parris (2018). Although they approached undiagnosed adults, they sought to assess the positive relationship between the types of mind-wandering and ADHD at clinical, subclinical levels through the SART rating scale.

The other studies had the research sample distributed as follows: five studies carried out their experiments with a control group of healthy individuals and people with ADHD (Woltering et al., 2012; Kim et al., 2014a, 2014b; Thoma et al., 2014; Gabay, Shahpari-Khateb and Mendelsohn, 2018; Rubia, 2018 and Gu et al., 2018); and only one paper defined its sample exclusively for the audience with ADHD (Keune et al., 2014).

However, regarding the Neuroscience tools, it was identified that four studies used the EEG to record the participants' brain activities, namely: Thoma et al. (2014); Keune et al. (2014); Rubia (2018), and Woltering et al. (2012).

To this end, two studies used the ANOVA tool for data analysis of variance (Keune et al., 2014 and Gu et al., 2018); Two papers used the E-Prime tool to assess participants' probabilistic learning based on feedback, controlling the stimulus and time of the experiment (Gabay et al., 2018 and Gu et al., 2018). Only two studies used the MATLAB software to execute EEG data (Gu et al., 2018 and Woltering et al., 2012).

Other tools were also used to ensure more significant support for the studies, such as questionnaires, scales, and tests shown above, highlighting: Adult Self-Report Scale (ASRS), used by Gu et al. (2018) and Woltering et al. (2012).

In summary, the results found in this group were different. Keune et al. (2014) and Woltering et al. (2012) showed dysfunctions in the alpha-band neural patterns of people with ADHD. On the other hand, Gabay et al. (2018) and Thoma et al. (2014) found, respectively, in their studies, that probabilistic learning based on feedback can be improved and that the learning performance of individuals with ADHD can present a reduction in active and observational reward stimuli.

In turn, Kim et al. (2014a, 2014b) portrayed the individual's attention with ADHD focused on the perception of chromatic saturation. Arabaci and Parris (2018) evaluated the traits of inattention associated with mind-wandering. On the other hand, Rubia (2018) and Gu et al. (2018) evidenced in their research the importance of neuromodulation as a fundamental tool for cognitive training and brain stimulation of working memory in individuals with ADHD.

Next, group B will be presented.

4.2 Group B

The studies in group B, on the other hand, focused on interventions aimed at psychotherapeutic relationships in adults with ADHD due to the high number of studies identified in this area.

Three studies were identified, Hirsch et al. (2018, 2019) and Allyson Camp et al. (2021), who highlighted research emphasizing changes in emotional experiences to understand and develop innovative therapeutic intervention strategies for people with ADHD.

In the first study of this group of German origin, Hirsch et al. (2018) developed a model that distinguishes positive and negative affect, problems with self-concept, and emotion regulation skills as distinct factors. Furthermore, the study points out the correlation with the symptom domains of inattention, hyperactivity, and impulsivity in adults, as clinical observations suggest that adults have more diverse deficits than children with ADHD.

Two hundred thirteen adults recently diagnosed with ADHD participated in this study (62.9% male, mean age 33.5 years). Symptoms were self-reported on the Adult ADHD Rating Scales: Conners; Positive and Negative Affect Scale; Regulation of Emotions and Skills Questionnaire.

Therefore, the model developed adequately considered the relevant clinical and therapeutic characteristics of adult ADHD. Thus, he suggested therapeutic interventions aimed at the successful and flexible use of adaptive emotion and emotion regulation skills for the public with ADHD.

The second paper evaluated in this group refers to the findings by Hirsch et al. (2019), from Germany, whose object of study was directed to the assessment of Emotional Regulation Deficit (ERD) in adults with ADHD.

The study objectives explore a person-centered approach with ADHD based on cluster analysis for subtypes of patients in the relative presence or absence of Emotional

Regulation Deficits (ERD) to obtain vital information to individualize the treatment decisions.

The sample consisted of 385 adult individuals (233 men (60.5%) with a mean age of 32.4 years and 152 women (39.5%) with a mean age of 32.5 years) newly diagnosed with ADHD, in which they did not use medications. In addition, clinical interviews based on the DSM-IV were conducted; Conners Adult ADHD Rating Scales (CAARS-L); the questionnaire for diagnostic ratings; and the application of the Amsterdam Short Term Memory Test (ASTM) and the Beck Depression Inventory.

Two clusters analyzed the experiment, and an infrared camera used the Quantified Behavior test. Cluster 1 composed 181 (47%) and cluster 2 of 204 (53%) patients. The subjects in cluster 2 had a higher symptom burden on the CAARS, less positive affect, greater negative affect, greater difficulties in emotion regulation, and greater symptom burden in all personality disorders included in the applied questionnaire.

Both cluster 1 and cluster 2 report significantly less emotion regulation skills than two independent samples of healthy controls. The effect sizes for cluster 1 show that, compared to healthy samples, deficits in ER are small to medium. For cluster 2, the same comparison revealed large deficits.

Thus, the authors concluded that most ADHD studies do not routinely assess emotion dysregulation, so it may be possible that these symptoms have been misinterpreted as anxiety and/or depressive symptoms, particularly in women with ADHD. The latter has a higher rate of emotion dysregulation.

The third paper analyzed in this group, carried out in the United States, referred to studies by Allyson Camp et al. (2021). It sought to evaluate devices aimed at neurostimulation, as a therapeutic intervention for ADHD, due to the neurological condition and its effects reflected in the behavior, learning, and social aspects of individuals with ADHD.

Some techniques aimed at the diagnosis of ADHD highlighted by the authors are: Quantified Behavioral Test (QB); Computerized QB Test Plus (Qb +); Vanderbilt Child Health Quality Assessment Scale (NICHQ); Swanson, Nolan and Pelham-IV Questionnaire (SNAP-IV); Adult ADHD Self-Report Scale (ASRS); Gordon Diagnostic System (GDS) and the Executive Function Behavior Assessment Inventory (BRIEF).

However, on neuromodulation issues, the authors highlighted the following devices: electroencephalography (EEG); Neurofeedback; invasive methods, such as: stimulating and non-invasive microelectrodes, such as transcranial magnetic stimulation (rTMS) or Transcranial Electrical Stimulation (tES); Transcranial direct current stimulation (tDCS); Transcranial Alternating Current Stimulation (tACS); Trigeminal Nerve Stimulation (TNS) and Cognitive Behavioral Therapy (CBT).

In addition, according to the authors, several companies are looking to develop portable neurostimulation devices for in-clinic and at-home therapy. For example, NeuroSigma was the first company to receive Food and Drug Administration (FDA) clearance to use its neurostimulation device for ADHD, called The Monarch®. The device's function is to generate pulses to stimulate the trigeminal nerve.

Finally, the authors concluded that innovation in treating people with ADHD through therapeutic neuromodulation interventions is fundamental for the management and understanding of these individuals' symptoms. In addition, it emphasizes the importance of studies in identifying genetic factors and environmental factors that influence the etiology and progression of ADHD.

Based on the papers discussed in group B, we observed that the geographic distribution was also different. Furthermore, all the works aim at individuals with ADHD (Hirsch et al. (2018, 2019; Allyson Camp et al., 2021); however, only the works by Hirsch et al. (2018, 2019) carried out their studies with healthy samples.

Thus, even considering less relevant studies and not addressing the main themes sought in SLR, this group brought together studies that addressed research related to the analysis of stimuli, behaviors, and emotional assessments of people with ADHD. The studies aim to understand the relationship of these aspects with therapeutic intervention strategies.

In clinical studies by Hirsch et al. (2018, 2019), the authors point out that the Conners Adult ADHD Rating Scales (CAARS-L) is applied to assess the participants' symptoms.

Furthermore, the experiments performed by the authors mentioned above were identified as complementary. Hirsch et al. (2018) addressed the development of a model that differentiates positive and negative affect. Problems with self-concept and emotion regulation skills as distinct factors correlated with inattention, hyperactivity, and impulsivity in adults with ADHD were also observed. In addition, the investigations by Hirsch et al. (2019) consisted of the comparative analysis between the participants, where it was seen that the Emotional Regulation Deficit (ERD) of people with ADHD varies between small and medium-sized.

Thus, the last paper of the group, by authors Allyson Camp et al. (2021), showed in their analysis the importance of neurostimulation, based on studies that addressed innovative devices and tests/scales fundamental to the therapeutic treatment and evaluation of the symptoms of people with ADHD.

The following subsection presents the C group.

4.3 Group C

Group C aimed to leverage research essentially of a qualitative nature, addressing experiences of educators and students with ADHD in the teaching environment. However, only one study was identified: Lasky et al. (2016), who addressed reports of individuals with ADHD concerning their daily activities, including occupational and educational contexts.

This US study aimed to employ a developmental psychopathology perspective to explore the impact of young adult ADHD occupation in post-secondary educational settings.

Therefore, the authors aimed to answer the following questions:

- Does context change play a role in declining ADHD symptoms in adulthood?
- Do the new contexts in which young adults find themselves alter their experiences of ADHD?
- Are there specific professional or educational contexts in which young adults report functioning better than others?

The authors conducted semi-structured interviews based on the Ecocultural Family Interview (EFI) model by Weisner et al., 1997, 2014) to examine these questions. The interviews were carried out on four US websites in 2010–11 with 125 young adults, 39 of whom were selected and 86 randomly selected from a sample of 579 subjects in a US qualitative complementary multimodal treatment of ADHD study (MTA - Multimodal Treatment Study of ADHD). The sample evaluates the relation to their work environment and post-secondary education.

As a result, 55% of subjects (65 individuals) described their symptoms as context-dependent. In some contexts, participants reported feeling better able to concentrate; in others, symptoms appeared more strongly. Modal descriptions included stressful and challenging tasks, new tasks, physically demanding or practical, and/or intrinsically interesting.

Therefore, the authors concluded that ADHD is experienced as an interaction between subjects and their environments consistent with a developmental psychopathology.

These findings demonstrate that the role of context needs to be taken into account in our understanding of ADHD as a psychiatric disorder, mainly when it manifests in young adulthood. Thus, this single study evaluated in this group highlighted the importance of assessing the relationship between people's experience with ADHD and the characteristics of the context in which it is inserted.

5 Conclusion

Based on the Systematic Literature Review, an enormous geographic diversity of studies involving adults with ADHD was found: Germany (4); United States (3); United Kingdom (3), Canada in partnership with the United States (2) and Israel (1). In addition, the systematization and distribution of papers into three groups allowed a better understanding of the studies found.

As a result of the SLR, the works relate only to the areas proposed by the study of neuroscience, educational environment, learning, and attention focused on ADHD. No research was found that addresses all the points sought together, especially the field of Ergonomics and Theory of Restorative Environments, thus proving the need for research that addresses these contexts since there are possibilities for further studies on these themes.

The group's interventions were generally considered positive and effective for understanding the behavior, learning, emotional regulation deficit, among other topics addressed, of adults with ADHD. The works verify the importance of understanding the experiences of adults with ADHD. Therefore, it is possible to propose Design and Neuroergonomics interventions more adequate to the needs of this public.

Corroborating with Soares (2021) on the importance of Design centered on user needs, as well as the reflections of Parasuraman and Rizzo (2007) on Neuroergonomics, it can be considered that the tools presented can contribute to the investigation of Restorative Elements (Kaplan and Kaplan, 1982). Furthermore, the application of the tools is observed when it comes to educational contexts, as identified in the analysis by Lasky et al. (2016). Examples of the contribution of Design in Restorative Elements are the studies of Allyson Camp et al. (2021), Thoma et al. (2014), and Rubia (2018).

For the next steps of this study, it is planned to expand the bibliographic search for Dissertations and Theses, aiming to complement the content of this Systematic Literature Review.

It is intended to carry out a new bibliographic search to carry out a deep study focused on Neuroscience and Psychology tools applied to ADHD, such as the EEG and the ASRS-18 scale. In addition, the study will support the Ph.D. thesis, which aims to study the application of Design and Neuroergonomics in the identification of restorative elements of attention for adults with ADHD in educational environments.

The authors wish to thank the Foundation for the Support of Science and Technology of the State of Pernambuco (FACEPE), Brazil, for the financial support to the research.

References

Adaskina, A.A.: Adaptation strategies of children with ADHD to the educational process [Elektronnyi resurs]. Sovremennaia zarubezhnaia psikhologiia. J. Modern Foreign Psychol. **5**(3), 35–40 (2016). https://doi.org/10.17759/jmfp.2016050303

Altman, I., Wohlwill, J.F. (eds.): Behavior and the natural environment. Plenum, New York and London, vol. 6 (1983)

American Psychiatric Association – APA: Manual diagnóstico e estatístico de transtornos mentais: DSM-5. Artmed, Porto Alegre (2014)

Arabaci, G., Parris, B.A.: Probe-caught spontaneous and deliberate mind wandering in relation to self-reported inattentive, hyperactive and impulsive traits in adults. Sci. Rep. (2018)

Arruda, M.A., Querido, C.N., Bigal, M.E., Polanczyk, G.V.: ADHD and mental health status in Brazilian school-age children. J. Attention Disorders **19**(I), 11–17 (2015)

Bins Ely, V.H.M.: Ergonomia + Arquitetura: buscando um melhor desempenho do ambiente físico. In: Anais do 3° Congresso Internacional de Ergonomia e Usabilidade de Interfaces Humano-Tecnologia: Produtos, Programas, Informação, Ambiente Construído. Rio de Janeiro: LEUI/PUC-Rio (2003)

Brasil. Ministério da Educação. Diretrizes nacionais para a educação especial na educação básica/Secretaria de Educação Especial – MEC; SEESP, 79 p. (2001)

Brasil, Ministério da Saúde, Secretaria de Ciência, Tecnologia e Insumos Estratégicos. Departamento de Ciência e Tecnologia. S Me. (2012)

Bürdek, B.E.: História, Teoria e Prática do Design de Produtos. Tradução Freddy Van Camp. Edgard Blücher, São Paulo (2010)

Camp, A., Pastrano, A., Gomez, V., Stephenson, K., Delatte, W., Perez, B.; Syas, H., Guiseppi-Elie, A.: Understanding ADHD: Toward an Innovative Therapeutic Intervention. Bioengineering (2021)

Características de Jovens e Crianças com TDAH. Neurosaber, 2016. Disponível em: Acesso em: 19 de set. de (2020)

Chao G.; Zhong-Xu, L., Tannock, R., Woltering, S.: Neural processing of working memory in adults with ADHD in a visuospatial change detection task with distractors. PeerJ (2018)

Gabay, Y., Shahbari-Khateb, E., Mendelsohn, A.: Feedback timing modulates probabilistic learning in adults with ADHD. Sci. Rep. (2018)

Gu, et al.: Neural processing of working memory in adults with ADHD in a visuospatial change detection task with distractors. PeerJ **6**, e5601 (2018). https://doi.org/10.7717/peerj.5601

Harrison, J.R., Soares, D.A., Rudzinski, S., Johnson, R.: Attention deficit hyperactivity disorders and classroom-based interventions: Evidence-based status, effectiveness, and moderators of effects in single-case design research. Rev. Educ. Res. **89**(4), 569–611 (2019). https://doi.org/10.3102/0034654319857038

Hirsch, O., Chavanon, M.L., Riechmann, E., Christiansen, H.: Emotional dysregulation is a primary symptom in adult Attention Deficit/Hyperactivity Disorder (ADHD). J. Affective Disorders (2018)

Hirsch, O., Chavanon, M.L., Christiansen, H.: Emotional dysregulation subgroups in patients with adult Attention-Defcit/Hyperactivity Disorder (ADHD): a cluster analytic approach. Sci. Rep. (2019)

Iida, Itiro; Guimarães, Lia Buarque de Macedo. Ergonomia: Projeto e Produção. 3 ed. Blucher, São Paulo (2016)

IEA (International Ergonomics Association). What is ergonomics. Disponível em: . Acesso em março de (2021)

Kaplan, S., Kaplan, R.: Cognition and Environment: Functioning in an Uncertain World. Praeger, New York, NY (1982)

Katya, R.: Cognitive neuroscience of attention deficit hyperactivity disorder (ADHD) and its clinical translation. Front. Hum. Neurosci. (2018)

Keune, P. M., Wiedemann, E., Schneidt, A., Schönenberg, M.: Frontal brain asymmetry in adult attention-deficit/hyperactivity disorder (ADHD): Extending the motivational dysfunction hypothesis. Clin. Neurophysiol. (2014)

Kim, S., et al.: Colour vision in ADHD: Part 1 - Testing the retinal dopaminergic hypothesis. Behav. Brain Func. (2014a)

Kim, S., et al.: Color vision in ADHD: Part 2 - Does Attention influence Color Perception? Behav. Brain Func. (2014b)

Korpela, K. M. Place-identity as a product of environmental self-regulation. J. Environ. Psychol. 9(3), 241–256 (1989)

Kuhnen, A., Puff, S.: Psicologia ambiental: a percepção de ambientes/espaços restauradores nas escolas e em educandos com TDAH. Revista Uniasselvi Pós. (2014)

Lasky, A.K., et al.: ADHD in context: Young adults' reports of the impact of occupational environment on the manifestation of ADHD. Soc. Sci. Med. (2016)

O que é TDAH. Associação Brasileira do Déficit de Atenção (2020). Disponível em: https://tdah. org.br/sobre-tdah/o-que-e-tdah/. Acesso em: 20 de set. de 2020

Oliveira, R.A., Almeida, T.F., Suzart, N.S.: Psicologia Ambiental E A Subjetivação Do Espaço Acadêmico: Um Relato De Experiência. In: Seminário Nacional e Seminário Internacional Políticas Públicas, Gestão e Práxis Educacional, vol. 7, no 7. (2019)

Paiva, M.M.B.: Percepção de Salas Residenciais por Idosos – uso das técnicas de Seleção Visual, Realidade Virtual e Eletroencefalografia. Tese (Doutorado em Design) – Centro de Artes, Cultura e Comunicação, Departamento de pós-graduação em Design, Universidade Federal de Pernambuco. Recife, p. 300. (2018)

Parasuraman, R., Rizzo, M.: Introduction to neuroergonomics. In: Parasuraman, R., Rizzo, M. (eds.) Neuroergonomics: The Brain at Work, pp. 3–11. Oxford University Press Inc, New York (2007)

Rösler, M., Retz-Junginger, P., Retz, W., Stieglitz, R.D.: Homburger ADHS-Skalen für Erwachsene (Homburger ADHDScales for Adults). Hogrefe, Göttingen, Germany (2008)

Rubia, K.: Cognitive Neuroscience of Attention Deficit Hyperactivity Disorder (ADHD) and Its Clinical Translation. Front. Hum. Neurosci. 12, 100 (2018). https://doi.org/10.3389/fnhum. 2018.00100

Salameh, J., Bossuyt, P.M., Mcgrath, T.A., Thombs, B. D., Hyde, C.J., Macaskill, P.: Preferred reporting items for systematic review and meta-analysis of diagnostic test accuracy studies (PRISMA-DTA): Explanation, elaboration, and checklist BMJ, 370, m2632 (2020). https:// doi.org/10.1136/bmj.n.2632

Soares, M.M.: Metodologia de ergodesign para o design de produtos : uma abordagem centrada no humano, 294 p. Blucher, São Paulo (2021)

Thoma, P., Edel, M., Suchan, B., Bellebaum, C.: Probabilistic reward learning in adults with Attention Deficit Hyperactivity Disorder—An electrophysiological study. Psychiatry Research (2014)

Ulrich R.S., Simons R.F., Losito B.D., Fiorito E., Miles M.A., Zelson M.: Stress recovery during exposure to natural and urban environments. J. Environ. Psychol. 11(3), 201–230 (1991)

Woltering, S., Jung, J., Zhongxu, L., Tannock, R.: Resting state EEG oscillatory power differences in ADHD college students and their peers.al. Behav. Brain Func. (2012)

Characterization of Spaces and Didactic Units for the Improvement of Diversity Gaps

David Fonseca[1]([⊠]) [iD], Monica Sanchez-Sepulveda[1] [iD], Elena Jurado[1] [iD], Alicia García-Holgado[2] [iD], Roger Olivella[1] [iD], Francisco José García-Peñalvo[2] [iD], Daniel Amo[1] [iD], Giuseppe Maffeo[3], Ömer Yiğit[4], Christian Hofmann[6], Kirsten Quass[5], Gülay Sevinç[7], and Yasin Keskin[4]

[1] GRETEL – Group of Research on Technology Enhanced Learning, La Salle Ramon Llull University, Barcelona, Spain
{david.fonseca,monica.sanchez,elena.jurado,roger.olivella, daniel.amo}@salle.url.edu
[2] GRIAL Research Group, Research Institute for Educational Sciences, University of Salamanca, Salamanca, Spain
{aliciagh,fgarcia}@usal.es
[3] FIDAE – Federazione Istituti Di Attività Educative, Rome, Italy
g.maffeo@fidae.it
[4] BURSA – Bursa Il Milli Egitim Mudurlugu, Bursa, Turkey
[5] CLEMENS – Clemens-Brentano-Europaschule, Lollar, Germany
kirsten.quass@cbes-lollar.eu
[6] STUDIENSEMINAR – Studienseminar GHRF, Giessen, Germany
christian.hofmann@kultus.hessen.de
[7] SADETTIN – Sadettin Türkün Ortaokulu, Bursa, Turkey

Abstract. Currently, most educational centers have specific spaces where, depending on the technology available in them, specific practices are carried out. Some examples of these spaces are the computer labs, electronics, biology, chemistry, or maker spaces. The CreaSTEAM project aims to create STEAM spaces in schools, so that they are multidisciplinary and transversal spaces where elements and technologies of all kinds coexist, and above all, rather than being focused on technology, they are focused on the development of STEAM skills and vocations, especially to reduce gaps in diversity. This article focuses on the design of an instrument that allows the conceptualization of STEAM practices in these new educational environments, contemplating and relating both educational methodologies, technologies, and diversity gaps to be solved or studied.

Keywords: STEAM education · STEAM-Labs · Diversity gap · Erasmus + project · Education · Learning

P. Zaphiris and A. Ioannou (Eds.): HCII 2022, LNCS 13328, pp. 335–346, 2022.
https://doi.org/10.1007/978-3-031-05657-4_24

1 Introduction

Many schools are experiencing rapid growth in the number of students of color, culturally and linguistically diverse students, and students from low-income families [1]. It
seems like our communities and our classrooms are more diverse than ever before, more
multicultural in their race and ethnic compositions than previous generations.

As demographics continue to shift, so does the opportunity to offer all students,
equitable opportunities and pathways to succeed. However, in some different sectors,
there is a lack of diversity, especially gender inequality and social background, especially
latent in the context of the fields of Science, Technology, Engineering (and the recently
added concept of Arts), and Mathematics (STEAM), from primary school to university
level and, therefore, labor market [2].

When we talk about diversity, we are worried about attracting representative people from all sectors of society, different cultures, disabilities, ethnic groups, gender or
sexual orientation. Part of the base for a prosperous society lies in providing accessible
advancement opportunities for its citizens. The low diversity in STEAM studies has been
identified as one of the main problems that needs to be solved in order to reduce the
diversity gap that exists in these sectors. Low diversity in STEM studies, but growing,
has been identified as one of the main problems that needs to be resolved in order to
reduce the diversity gap that exists in these sectors [3–9].

Schools recognize the value that curriculum and environmental changes can have in
positively impacting student advancement. The project CreaSTEAM addresses this, not
only from the gender gap perspective, but also with a broad approach covering diversity
and social inclusion as a way to create inclusive spaces in which to promote STEAM
[10].

The project aims to provide an actualized map of the resources focused on reducing the diversity gap using STEAM approaches and select from these resources better
solutions to create a framework to implement STEAM-Labs into secondary schools.
The approach is focused on creating good practices in these spaces to promote diversity in STEAM, where diversity also covers gender equity and social inclusion for the
promotion of STEAM vocations [2].

The CreaSTEAM project included in its methodology a previous and very important
step: teacher training [11]. The design of ubiquitous training materials and methods must
allow not only training in technical aspects, perhaps the most worked, but also conceptual
aspects, such as, for example, in CreaSTEAM, aspects of inclusion, diversity, gaps, and
fit with the socio-cultural reality that surrounds each educational center [12], which is
very diverse and can be rapidly changing [13–19]. From this point of view [20], the
adaptation of training to the teacher's profile, needs, interests or resources of the center
is a priority [21–24].

Considering the described process, and starting from the teacher training that will
allow contextualizing, creating/designing, implementing, changing and/or improving
the spaces of their school to subsequently carry out STEAM projects and practices, the
next conceptual step to be carried out is the characterization of such practices, exercises
or projects. The present work is focused on showing the creation of an instrument that
allows collecting in a systemic way the good practices designed in each center with the

objective that they can be parameterized, scalable and reproducible by other courses, as well as in other centers.

In Sect. 2 we will present the context of the study, followed by the section three where the Unit Plan instrument is presented. Finally, in section four we present the main conclusions of the development.

2 Context

In order to define a didactic unit that is scalable, reproducible and sufficiently detailed to be a working guide, an initial aspect to be taken into account is the teacher training [25, 26].

In the first part of the project, and parallel to the design of the Unit Plan, a series of training sessions were designed and implemented for school teachers. Any educational innovation or change needs the achievement of a preliminary and crucial step: teacher training [11].

Without prior training, a teacher's motivation to implement a change in their classes, regardless of whether it will lead to an improvement in the acquisition of student competencies, may be met with a reaction against the change, not only on a personal level but also at an institutional level, because the necessary resources are not properly calibrated [27]. To summarize, how a method is implemented in detail has a significant impact on achievement.

Adapting training to the teacher's profile, requirements, interests, or center resources is a priority from this perspective [21–24]. We followed a work plan in CreaSTEAM that centered on the user, the teacher. Working groups were identified by pro-files and centers based on an introduction online knowledge session to make a first approach to the needs connected to the implementation of STEAM-Lab in their center. From then, progress was established in the demands and interests in a second session, allowing the creation of six training sessions in the form of pills [28], related to: How to address diversity topics in class, 3D printing, using CAD models and augmented reality, educational robotics with Micro:bit, photo composition techniques for social media, and usability studies addressed to measure the efficiency of STEAM practices.

These pills were generated using a flipped classroom model, in which a series of videos and step-by-step instructions were created and made available to instructors prior to a presentation and question-and-answer session [29]. Given the difficulties of performing the training in situ [30] (because of the Covid-19 pandemic) [31, 32], the goal of this format was to deliver the key data regarding learning methods, technology, and diversity data to develop projects and practices in the STEAM-Labs [33, 34].

At this stage, in the project's present phase, instructors can design a Unit Plan for their activity, together with the materials they deem required, and begin implementation in the STEAM-Lab.

3   The Unit Plan Instrument

At this point, teachers are already in a position to define a Unit Plan of their activity with the resources they consider necessary and start the implementation in the STEAM-Lab. We have designed and created the Unit Plan (see Fig. 1).

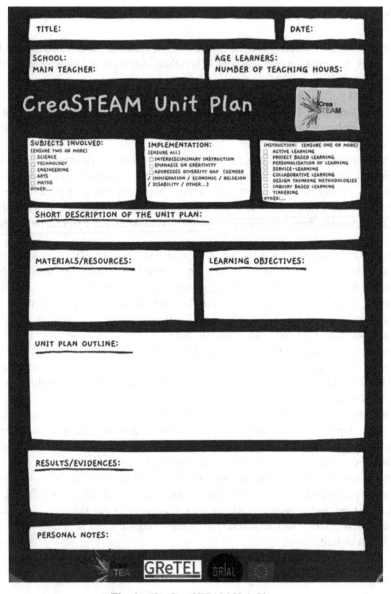

Fig. 1. The CreaSTEAM Unit Plan.

Section 1 of the form begins with basic data that characterize the activity, such as name, date, school, and main teacher. Within this heading, the last two pieces of information requested are very important as they help contextualize the activity: age of the students and number of teaching hours designed for the activity. This data helps to understand the needs that may exist depending on the experience and training of the students, as well as the time distribution in which the activity has been designed. For example, it is not the same an activity of four continuous hours in a space on a given day, as an activity with periodic access of one hour every week for four weeks. The level of depth of the activity, preparation of materials, experimentation, or simple arrangement of the elements to be used modifies the learning process and development of the exercise, and should and can be adjusted according to the educational level or school (taking into account the teaching plan) [35–37].

The second section of the form focuses on selecting the subjects involved in each exercise or project, what type of implementation will be carried out, and the training method.

In the aspect related to the subjects, the five areas that the STEAM acronym integrates are contextualized: science, technology, engineering, arts and mathematics, but since the objective is to improve these competencies and they can be applied in other subjects, the option is left open for other areas of knowledge to be indicated [38–40]. For example, and concretely, the first approaches have already been identified that seek to involve subjects such as languages or language in STEAM practices, to improve the integration of immigrant students. In other words, in cases such as the one described above, a STEAM project seeks to improve the competencies of subjects external to this conceptualization and thus reduce a specific diversity that affects a class or school.

In this same section, teachers should also contextualize the type of implementation they will carry out, differentiating whether, for example, they will seek a multidisciplinary instruction (indicating which disciplines they want to relate), a development focused on enhancing creativity, and/or in a complementary way what type of diversity gap they want to study, improve, or transmit to their students [41–46]. This second question of the section [47]is clearly related to the third [48]: the methodology to be implemented [9, 49–53]. It has been demonstrated that the application of active methodologies in the classroom not only improves student motivation, but also their concentration, satisfaction and, in a directly proportional way, their academic results [54–62].

Identifying the methodology is very interesting insofar as the same practice can be carried out from different methodological perspectives, being able in a next phase to evaluate and identify which type of methodology can be better adjusted according to the described objectives of each practice, the student's educational level and even the geographical area.

The profile of students has changed significantly throughout history, but with the digital revolution that we are living, it is clear that it is necessary to modify the teaching structures so that the student feels comfortable, motivated and adapted to new environments that mix both physical and digital elements, and where the teacher becomes a mentor, a guide who can resolve specific doubts and guide the student in the learning process, and information management. Involving the student as a central part of his and his classmates' training is essential nowadays, and in this sense, contextualizing each exercise from the instructional point of view is fundamental for the characterization of good practices.

In resume, this second section of the Unit Plan tool concretely contextualizes each exercise, allowing to subsequently evaluate to what extent the designed approach can be improved and scaled in future iterations.

The third and last section of the Unit Plan form is purely descriptive. In it, the teacher should provide all the details related to the following points of the educational activity [35, 44, 63]:

- Description of the Unit Plan: The detail of procedures and generic objectives to be achieved with the designed lesson should be included.
- Learning Objectives: Whether there are one or more subjects involved, this section is about defining in detail the learning objectives, both cross-cutting and specific, that are intended to be addressed.
- Materials to be used: Fundamental point of the unit plan, where all the materials, systems and technologies to be used and their intended use must be specified. A correct description will allow substitution and/or replication with analogous or similar systems in case another plant or activity cannot use them.
- Outline of development of the Unit Plan: Detail of the designed implementation process. As we have previously mentioned, it is not the same to design the use of a space for four hours at a time, as it is to design it for one hour periodically. Likewise, what is to be achieved with each session, or what is the same, the work objectives and their relationship with the learning objectives per work session and/or use of the space, are aspects to be indicated at this point.
- Outcomes and/or evidence: In this section the teacher has to describe what deliverables or final products are intended to be achieved with the lesson, and what evaluation methods, rubrics or systems will be used to evaluate the achievement of the learning objectives as well as the usage objectives and other cross-cutting objectives, such as whether or not the student's motivation for STEAM domains has increased, his or her satisfaction with the lesson, etc.
- Other notes or information of interest provided: Finally, there is a section for the teacher to comment on any other aspect that he/she considers relevant for the characterization and explanation of the lesson, always with the objective that it can be replicated and scalable in his/her center or any other, and even changing the educational level.

In the first iteration of Units Plans completed (13), the subjects involved have mainly focused on aspects of science, technology and mathematics, but there are also heterogeneous approaches such as physics, geography and politics (Fig. 2). In terms of the diversity gap on which the lessons focus, gender stands out, followed by economic factors and disabilities (Fig. 3).

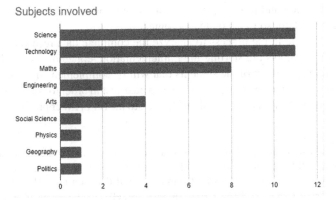

Fig. 2. Unit Plan results related to the subjects involved.

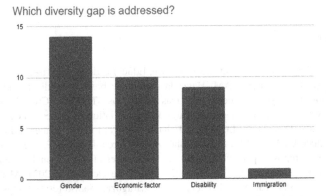

Fig. 3. Unit Plan results related to the diversity gap studied.

From a curricular perspective, multidisciplinary instruction was selected by 95% of the Unit Plans collected. In addition, about 50% also selected to improve creativity and reduce specific gaps identified in the schools. Forty percent cited all three aspects together in their objectives.

The most selected instructional method was project-based learning (about 80%), followed by collaborative and design thinking-based methodologies, with a combination of about 40%. The most cited materials are based on 3D printing of prototypes to be integrated into Arduino sets, as well as programming in Scratch and systems based on augmented/virtual reality using tablets and cardboards.

4   Conclusions

The Unit Plan is already being implemented in schools, after they have conceptualized, redesigned and/or implemented STEAM-Labs. In some cases, we can find new spaces created, in others a regrouping service, and in others reassigning new nomenclatures to design, collaboration and implementation spaces, but now based on competencies and methodologies and not so much on technologies.

Currently we are in the process to analyze the complete data received in the Units Plans, and some schools are starting the implementation, collecting data related to the motivation and expectation of the students that will be complemented at the final stage, after the project/exercise implementation, with a post-test in order to collect the usability, satisfaction and motivation of the students related to the STEAM approaches and spaces used.

Acknowledgments. With the support of the Erasmus+ Programme of the European Union in its Key Action 2 "Cooperation and Innovation for Good Practices. Strategic Partnerships for school education". Project CreaSTEAM (Co-thinking and Creation for STEAM diversity-gap reduction) (Reference number 2020–1-ES01-KA201–082601). The content of this publication does not reflect the official opinion of the European Union. Responsibility for the information and views expressed in the publication lies entirely with the authors.

References

1. Howard, G.R.: As diversity grows, so must we. Educ. Leadersh. **64**, 16–22 (2007)
2. Fonseca, D.,et al.: CreaSTEAM. Hacia la mejora de brechas en diversidad mediante la recopilación de proyectos, buenas prácticas y espacios STEAM - [CreaSTEAM. Towards the improvement of diversity gaps through the compilation of projects, best practices and STEAM spaces]. In: Maria Luisa Sein-Echaluce, Ángel Fidalgo Blanco, F.J.G.-P. (ed.) In: Sein-Echaluce Lacleta, M.L., Fidalgo-Blanco, Á., García-Peñalvo, F.J. (eds.) Innovaciones docentes en tiempos de pandemia. Actas del VI Congreso In-ternacional sobre Aprendizaje, Innovación y Coope-ración, CINAIC 2021 (20–22 de Octubre de 2021, Madrid. pp. 38–43. Servicio de Publicaciones. Universidad de Zaragoza, Madrid (2021). https://doi.org/10.26754/cinaic.2021.0007
3. Tsui, L.: Effective strategies to increase diversity in STEM fields: A review of the research literature. J. Negro Educ. **76**, 555–581 (2007)
4. Unesco: Be part of the change! STEM and Gender Advancement (SAGA): improved measurement of gender equality in science, technology, engineering and mathematics (2016). https://unesdoc.unesco.org/in/documentViewer.xhtml?v=2.1.196&id=p::usmarcdef_0000244375&file=/in/rest/annotationSVC/DownloadWatermarkedAttachment/attach_import_9f397934-5f24-49cd-abd4-1b2871916831%3F_%3D244375eng.pdf&locale=en&multi=true&ark=/ark:/48223/p.
5. García-Peñalvo, F.J., Bello, A., Dominguez, A., Romero Chacón, R.M.: Gender balance actions, policies and strategies for STEM: Results from a world café conversation. Educ. Knowl. Soc. **20**, (2019). https://doi.org/10.14201/eks2019_20_a31
6. García-Holgado, A., Camacho Díaz, A., García-Peñalvo, F.J.: La brecha de género en el sector STEM en América Latina: una propuesta europea. V Congr. Int. sobre Aprendizaje, Innovación y Compet. 704–709 (2019). https://doi.org/10.26754/cinaic.2019.0143
7. García-Holgado, A., Díaz, A.C., García-Pěalvo, F.J.: Engaging women into STEM in Latin America: W-STEM project. In: Conde-González, M.Á., Rodríguez-Sedano, F.J., Fernández-Llamas, C., García-Peñalvo, F.J. (eds.) PervasiveHealth: Pervasive Computing Technologies for Healthcare. pp. 232–239. ACM, New York (2019). https://doi.org/10.1145/3362789.3362902

8. Garcia-Holgado, A., et al.: Gender equality in STEM programs: A proposal to analyse the situation of a university about the gender gap. In: IEEE Global Engineering Education Conference, EDUCON, pp. 1824–1830 (2020). https://doi.org/10.1109/EDUCON45650.2020.9125326

9. Conde, M., Rodríguez-Sedano, F.J., Fernández-Llamas, C., Gonçalves, J., Lima, J., García-Peñalvo, F.J.: Fostering STEAM through challenge-based learning, robotics, and physical devices: A systematic mapping literature review. Comput. Appl. Eng. Educ. **29**, 46–65 (2021). https://doi.org/10.1002/cae.22354

10. Amo, D., et al.: CreaSTEAM. Towards the improvement of diversity gaps through the compilation of projects, best practices and STEAM-Lab spaces. In: ACM International Conference Proceeding Series, pp. 92–97. Association for Computing Machinery, New York (2021). https://doi.org/10.1145/3486011.3486426

11. Schneider, M., Preckel, F.: Variables associated with achievement in higher education: A systematic review of meta-analyses. Psychol. Bull. **143**, 565–600 (2017). https://doi.org/10.1037/bul0000098

12. Mariscal, G., Jiménez, E., Vivas-Urias, M.D., Redondo-Duarte, S., Moreno-Pérez, S.: Virtual reality simulation-based learning. Educ. Knowl. Soc. **21** (2020). https://doi.org/10.14201/eks.20809

13. Gabster, B.P., van Daalen, K., Dhatt, R., Barry, M.: Challenges for the female academic during the COVID-19 pandemic (2020). https://doi.org/10.1016/S0140-6736(20)31412-4

14. Kumi-Yeboah, A., Kim, Y., Sallar, A.M., Kiramba, L.K.: Exploring the use of digital technologies from the perspective of diverse learners in online learning environments. Online Learn. J. **24**, 42–63 (2020). https://doi.org/10.24059/olj.v24i4.2323

15. Sivapunniam, N.: Virtual realities: A blended learning approach to bridge the gap between diverse ESL learners. Lang. Cult. Ceating Foster. Glob. Communities, 283–290 (2005)

16. Delamarre, A., Shernoff, E., Buche, C., Frazier, S., Gabbard, J., Lisetti, C.: The interactive virtual training for teachers (IVT-T) to practice classroom behavior management. Int. J. Hum. Comput. Stud. **152** (2021). https://doi.org/10.1016/j.ijhcs.2021.102646

17. Sveinbjörnsdóttir, B., Jóhannsson, S.H., Oddsdóttir, J., Sigurðardóttir, T.Þ, Valdimarsson, G.I., Vilhjálmsson, H.H.: Virtual discrete trial training for teacher trainees. J. Multimodal User Inter. **13**(1), 31–40 (2019). https://doi.org/10.1007/s12193-018-0288-9

18. Guerrero, M.V.L., Jiménez, T.L.: Using virtual platform for giving feedback in teachers' training. Pensam. Educ. **56** (2019). https://doi.org/10.7764/PEL.56.2.2019.5

19. Stavroulia, K.E., Christofi, M., Baka, E., Michael-Grigoriou, D., Magnenat-Thalmann, N., Lanitis, A.: Assessing the emotional impact of virtual reality-based teacher training. Int. J. Inf. Learn. Technol. **36**, 192–217 (2019). https://doi.org/10.1108/IJILT-11-2018-0127

20. Gil-Fernández, R., León-Gómez, A., Calderón-Garrido, D.: Influence of covid on the educational use of social media by students of teaching degrees. Educ. Knowl. Soc. **22** (2021). https://doi.org/10.14201/eks.23623

21. Hepp K, P., Prats Fernández, M.À., Holgado García, J.: Int. J. Educ. Technol. High. Educ. **12**(2), 30–43 (2015). https://doi.org/10.7238/rusc.v12i2.2458

22. Ally, M.: Competency profile of the digital and online teacher in future education. Int. Rev. Res. Open Distance Learn. **20**, 302–318 (2019). https://doi.org/10.19173/irrodl.v20i2.4206

23. Guasch, T., Alvarez, I., Espasa, A.: University teacher competencies in a virtual teaching/learning environment: Analysis of a teacher training experience. Teach. Teach. Educ. **26**, 199–206 (2010). https://doi.org/10.1016/j.tate.2009.02.018

24. Galikhanov, M.F., Khasanova, G.F.: Faculty training for online teaching: Roles, Competences, Contents. Vyss. Obraz. v Ross. **28**, 51–62 (2019). https://doi.org/10.31992/0869-3617-2019-28-2-51-62

25. Bautista, M.A., Cipagauta, M.E.: Didactic trends and perceived teachers' training needs in higher education: A case study. Int. J. Cogn. Res. Sci. Eng. Educ. **7**, 71–85 (2019). https://doi.org/10.5937/IJCRSEE1903071B

26. Artacho, E.G., Martínez, T.S., Ortega Martín, J.L., Marín Marín, J.A., García, G.G.: Teacher training in lifelong learning-the importance of digital competence in the encouragement of teaching innovation. Sustain. **12** (2020). https://doi.org/10.3390/su12072852

27. Gorozidis, G., Papaioannou, A.G.: Teachers' motivation to participate in training and to implement innovations. Teach. Teach. Educ. **39**, 1–11 (2014). https://doi.org/10.1016/j.tate.2013.12.001

28. Boice, K.L., Jackson, J.R., Alemdar, M., Rao, A.E., Grossman, S., Usselman, M.: Supporting teachers on their STEAM journey: A collaborative STEAM teacher training program. Educ. Sci. **11**, 1–20 (2021). https://doi.org/10.3390/educsci11030105

29. Campanyà, C., Fonseca, D., Amo, D., Martí, N., Peña, E.: Mixed analysis of the flipped classroom in the concrete and steel structures subject in the context of covid-19 crisis outbreak. A pilot study. Sustain. **13** (2021). https://doi.org/10.3390/su13115826

30. García-Peñalvo, F.J., Corell, A., Abella-García, V., Grande, M.: Online assessment in higher education in the time of COVID-19. Educ. Knowl. Soc. **21** (2020). https://doi.org/10.14201/eks.23013

31. García-Peñalvo, F.J., Corell, A.: The CoVId-19: The enzyme of the digital transformation of teaching or the reflection of a methodological and competence crisis in higher education? Campus Virtuales. **9**, 83–98 (2020)

32. Knopik, T., Oszwa, U.: E-Cooperative problem solving as a strategy for learning mathematics during the COVID-19 pandemic. Educ. Knowl. Soc. **22**, e25176–e25176 (2021). https://doi.org/10.14201/eks.25176

33. García-Peñalvo, F.J., Fidalgo-Blanco, Á., Sein-Echaluce, M.L., Conde, M.Á.: Cooperative micro flip teaching. In: Zaphiris, P., Ioannou, A. (eds.) LCT 2016. LNCS, vol. 9753, pp. 14–24. Springer, Cham (2016). https://doi.org/10.1007/978-3-319-39483-1_2

34. Sein-Echaluce, M.L., Fidalgo-Blanco, Á., Balbín, A.M., García-Peñalvo, F.J.: Flipped classroom insights after nine-year experience applying the method. In: in Alier, M., Fonseca, D. (ed.) ACM International Conference Proceeding Series, pp. 266–270. ACM, New York, Barcelona, October 27–29, 2021 (2021). https://doi.org/10.1145/3486011.3486458

35. Dell'Erba, M.: Preparing students for learning, work and life through STEAM education. Policy Brief, Educ. Comm. States, Arts Educ. Partnersh. 1–12 (2019)

36. McCusker, J.R., Burch, A.S., Andrade, J.M.: Work study play! In: ASEE Annual Conference and Exposition, Conference Proceedings (2020).https://doi.org/10.1007/978-3-030-359 22-5_2

37. Ruiz, E.: Analyzing gender disparities in STEAM: A case study from bioinformatics workshops in the University of Granada. Enseñanza y Aprendiz. Ing. Comput. (2020). https://doi.org/10.30827/digibug.53241

38. Taylor, P.C., Taylor, E.: Transformative STEAM education for sustainable development. In: Empowering Science and Mathematics for Global Competitiveness, pp. 125–131 (2020). https://doi.org/10.1201/9780429461903-19

39. Quigley, C.F., Herro, D.: "Finding the joy in the unknown": Implementation of STEAM teaching practices in middle school science and math classrooms. J. Sci. Educ. Technol. **25**(3), 410–426 (2016). https://doi.org/10.1007/s10956-016-9602-z

40. Conner, L.D.C., Tzou, C., Tsurusaki, B.K., Guthrie, M., Pompea, S., Teal-Sullivan, P.: Designing STEAM for broad participation in science. Creat. Educ. **08**, 2222–2231 (2017). https://doi.org/10.4236/ce.2017.814152

41. Liao, C.: Creating a STEAM map: A content analysis of visual art practices in STEAM education. In: Khine, M.S., Areepattamannil, S. (eds.) STEAM Education, pp. 37–55. Springer, Cham (2019). https://doi.org/10.1007/978-3-030-04003-1_3

42. Allina, B.: The development of STEAM educational policy to promote student creativity and social empowerment. Arts Educ. Policy Rev. **119**, 77–87 (2018). https://doi.org/10.1080/106 32913.2017.1296392

43. Quigley, C.F., Herro, D., King, E., Plank, H.: STEAM designed and enacted: Understanding the process of design and implementation of STEAM curriculum in an elementary school. J. Sci. Educ. Technol. **29**(4), 499–518 (2020). https://doi.org/10.1007/s10956-020-09832-w

44. MacDonald, A., Hunter, J., Wise, K., Fraser, S.: STEM and STEAM and the spaces between: An overview of education agendas pertaining to 'Disciplinarity' across three Australian States. J. Res. STEM Educ. **5**, 75–92 (2019). https://doi.org/10.51355/jstem.2019.64

45. Ramey, K.E.: FUSE Studios: Bringing Interest-driven, Integrated-STEAM Learning into Schools via Makerspaces. http://ezphost.dur.ac.uk/login?url=https://www.proquest.com/doc view/1964250413?accountid=14533%0Ahttp://palimpsest.dur.ac.uk/openurl/?genre=disser tations+%26+theses&issn=&title=FUSE+Studios%3A+Bringing+Interest-driven%2C+Int egrated-STEAM+Learning+into+Sch, (2017)

46. Stevens, R., et al..: Exploring the adoption, spread, and sustainability of an informal steam learning innovation in schools. In: Proceedings of International Conference of the Learning Sciences, ICLS, pp. 1203–1210 (2018)

47. García-Peñalvo, F.J., Alarcón, H., Dominguez, A.: Active learning experiences in engineering education (2019)

48. Alonso De Castro, M.G., García-Peñalvo, F.J.: Overview of European educational projects on eLearning and related methodologies: Data from Erasmus+ Project Results Platform. In: ACM International Conference Proceeding Series, pp. 291–298. IGI Global (2020). https:// doi.org/10.1145/3434780.3436550

49. Vicente, F.R., Llinares, A.Z., Sánchez, N.M.: "Sustainable City": A steam project using robotics to bring the city of the future to primary education students. Sustain. **12**, 1–21 (2020). https://doi.org/10.3390/su12229696

50. Boytchev, P., Boytcheva, S.: Gamified evaluation in STEAM for higher education: A case study. Inf. **11** (2020). https://doi.org/10.3390/info11060316

51. Bertrand, M.G., Namukasa, I.K.: STEAM education: Student learning and transferable skills. J. Res. Innov. Teach. Learn. **13**, 43–56 (2020). https://doi.org/10.1108/jrit-01-2020-0003

52. Bassachs, M., Cañabate, D., Nogué, L., Serra, T., Bubnys, R., Colomer, J.: Fostering critical reflection in primary education through STEAM approaches. Educ. Sci. **10**, 1–14 (2020). https://doi.org/10.3390/educsci10120384

53. Vicente, F.R., Zapatera Llinares, A., Montes Sánchez, N.: Curriculum analysis and design, implementation, and validation of a STEAM project through educational robotics in primary education. Comput. Appl. Eng. Educ. **29**, 160–174 (2021). https://doi.org/10.1002/cae.22373

54. Fonseca, D., Redondo, E., Villagrasa, S.: Mixed-methods research: a new approach to evaluating the motivation and satisfaction of university students using advanced visual technologies. Univ. Access Inf. Soc. **14**(3), 311–332 (2014). https://doi.org/10.1007/s10209-014-0361-4

55. Fonseca, D., Canaleta, X., Climent, A.: Evaluación de la usabilidad y la satisfacción del estudiante de formación profesional en función de su motivación inicial: Curso de comercio electrónico mediante metodologia SCC Curso de comercio electrónico mediante metodologia SCC. In: Iberian Conference on Information Systems and Technologies, CISTI (2017). https:// doi.org/10.23919/CISTI.2017.7975915

56. Fonseca, D., García-Peñalvo, F.J.: Interactive and collaborative technological ecosystems for improving academic motivation and engagement. Univ. Access Inf. Soc. **18**(3), 423–430 (2019). https://doi.org/10.1007/s10209-019-00669-8

57. Petchamé, J., Iriondo, I., Riu, D., Masi, T., Almajano, A., Fonseca, D.: Project based learning or the rethinking of an engineering subject: Measuring motivation. In: García-Peñalvo, F.J. (ed.) ACM International Conference Proceeding Series, pp. 267–272 (2020). https://doi.org/ 10.1145/3434780.3436542

58. Fonseca, D., Villagrasa, S., Valls, F., Redondo, E., Climent, A., Vicent, L.: Motivation assessment in engineering students using hybrid technologies for 3D visualization. In: 2014 International Symposium on Computers in Education, SIIE 2014, pp. 111–116 (2014). https://doi.org/10.1109/SIIE.2014.7017714
59. Sanchez-Sepulveda, M. V., et al.: Evaluation of an interactive educational system in urban knowledge acquisition and representation based on students' profiles. Expert Syst. **37** (2020). https://doi.org/10.1111/exsy.12570
60. Fonseca, D., Valls, F., Redondo, E., Villagrasa, S.: Informal interactions in 3D education: Citizenship participation and assessment of virtual urban proposals. Comput. Human Behav. **55**, 504–518 (2016). https://doi.org/10.1016/j.chb.2015.05.032
61. Fonseca, D., et al.: Mixed assessment of virtual serious games applied in architectural and urban design education. Sensors **21** (2021). https://doi.org/10.3390/s21093102
62. Sanchez-Sepulveda, M., Fonseca, D., Franquesa, J., Redondo, E.: Virtual interactive innovations applied for digital urban transformations. Mixed approach. Futur. Gener. Comput. Syst. **91**, 371–381 (2019). https://doi.org/10.1016/j.future.2018.08.016
63. Khine, M.S.: STEAM education theory and practice. In: STEAM Education, p. 192 (2019)

Using Technology to Support Speaking in the Heterogeneous Young Learners' EFL Classroom

Andreas Kullick[✉]

University of Education Schwäbisch Gmünd, 73525 Schwäbisch Gmünd, Germany
andreas.kullick@ph-gmuend.de

Abstract. In this study, I investigate the potential of technology-enhanced tasks to support oral communication in the heterogeneous young learners' English as a foreign language (EFL) classroom. It has been established that technology holds potential for the development of learners' oral communication skills in foreign language learning. However, most studies have mainly focused on adolescent or adult learners so far. Here I present a classroom-based research project carried out with 3rd graders in a German primary school. Together with two other projects, it is part of a qualitative study for a PhD dissertation that examines possibilities to employ technology-enhanced tasks to support primary school pupils in speaking English. Interviews with in-service and pre-service teachers were conducted to shed light on how they see the potential of technology-enhanced tasks to promote oral communication in a heterogeneous EFL primary classroom. First preliminary findings are presented in this paper.

Keywords: Young learners · EFL · Speaking · Heterogeneity · Tasks · Technology · Primary school · Classroom-based Apps

1 Introduction

Research has shown many benefits of using technology in the foreign language classroom. For example, technology can facilitate learner-centered and communication-oriented approaches (e.g. Blume and Würffel 2018) or offer opportunities for differentiation, individualisation, and personalisation (e.g. Cutrim Schmid 2017). Moreover, it can promote learners' interaction, encourage them to give feedback, help improve their pronunciation, and enable extended production, intercultural awareness, and strategy-development (Edelenbos 2006). Additionally, technology helps teachers to control the scope and the difficulty of the tasks.

However, the possibilities that the fusion of technology and task in the classroom holds for foreign language learning have scarcely been investigated. Furthermore, studies conducted on this topic mostly took place at secondary level or with adult learners (e.g. Van den Branden 2006; Stockwell 2010). Although some researchers have pointed to the benefits that technology-mediated learning environments can offer even to a heterogeneous group of young learners (e.g. Pinter 2015, Müller-Hartmann and Schocker-v.

Ditfurth 2011; Whyte and Cutrim Schmid 2014, González-Lloret 2016) the number of studies that consider technology-enhanced language learning tasks is still very limited (Pellerin 2014; Gonzáles-Lloret 2017). Hence, the need for multilevel research on technology-enhanced tasks, to which Chapelle (2001) already drew attention more than 20 years ago, has been neglected so far (Gonzáles-Lloret 2017).

This paper contributes to the little research in this field. It presents a small-scale project conducted in an English as a foreign language (EFL) primary school classroom in the German federal state of Baden-Württemberg. The objective of the project was to promote young learners' oral communication using technology-enhanced tasks. The project is part of the research for a PhD dissertation exploring teachers' perspectives on the use of new technologies to promote oral communication in task-supported language learning in the heterogeneous EFL primary classroom. As the dissertation is still work in progress, the initial findings presented here should be regarded as preliminary. By presenting the project step by step, we begin with the research background.

2 Background

The dissertation seeks to answer the following overarching research question: What are in-service and pre-service EFL primary school teachers' perspectives on promoting oral communication through the use of technology-enhanced tasks in heterogeneous English as a foreign language (EFL) primary classrooms. More specifically:

a) Do the teachers think that technology-enhanced tasks have the potential to support oral communicative EFL learning in the heterogeneous primary classroom?
b) If so, what aspects of the use of technology in the EFL classroom do they consider have a relevant impact on the development of learners' oral communicative competence?

Therefore, my classroom-based research is concerned with four different areas: heterogeneity, communicative competence, task-supported language learning, and technology. For a clearer understanding of my research, I would like to briefly give an account of the four areas in the following sections (Fig. 1).

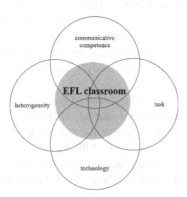

Fig. 1. Interconnected areas in the EFL classroom affected by the research approach.

2.1 Heterogeneity in the Young Learners' EFL Classroom

German primary school classes are considered very heterogeneous. The term *heterogeneity* refers to social categories as well as to the different performance levels of students (Budde 2013; Trautmann and Wischer 2020; Walgenbach 2017). In addition to differences such as gender, age, socio-economic background, learning speed, and motivation (Giesler, Schuett and Wolter 2016), learners in the English as a foreign language (EFL) classroom differ above all in their levels of performance. Their proficiency relating to a range of abilities and speaking skills (Goh and Burns 2012) varies considerably. Müller-Hartmann and Schocker-von Ditfurth point out that heterogeneity is even "*the* constituent feature of primary classrooms" (2011: 12, emphasis in original).

This poses two main challenges for all teachers. They need to design lessons that meet the diverse needs of their learners and they need to create learning opportunities so that learners can appreciate and benefit from heterogeneity (Chilla and Vogt 2017; Eisenmann 2019). In a nutshell, the question is how best to support both weaker and stronger pupils (Budde 2012). However, as Chilla and Vogt (2017) point out, foreign language didactics still seem to be reluctant to discover the subject area of heterogeneity. Since my research is on oral performance heterogeneity, we will next take a look at communicative competence in the primary classroom.

2.2 Communicative Competence in the Young Learners' EFL Classroom

According to the syllabus for English as a foreign language in primary schools in Baden-Württemberg, *communicative competence* is the main goal of EFL learning and refers to the ability of pupils to successfully communicate in the target language (Ministerium für Kultus, Jugend und Sport 2020). The focus is on developing listening and speaking skills, rather than on reading and writing. Young learners should be able to acquire intelligible pronunciation, use clear intonation for communicative purposes, make themselves understood with the help of phrases and short sentences (monologic speaking), and participate increasingly actively in conversations (dialogic speaking). To achieve this, different chunks and structures are used in English lessons. For example, a set of vocabulary on topics such as *me and my family, school, animals,* or *free time* is provided for learners to use in structures such as 'My name is...', 'My favourite subject is...', 'On the farm, there are...', or 'Do you like...?' (ibid.: 17ff.). In addition to that, EFL learning at primary level follows a thematic and not a grammatical progression (Kuty 2018a). Since young learners "will not have even developed sufficient grammatical resources to produce utterances that are morphologically or syntactically accurate" (Goh and Burns 2012:16), the focus of communication in primary school English lessons is on meaning. The principle of fluency before accuracy is thus at the centre of the lessons.

Research has shown that one approach for the development of communicative competence is *task-supported language learning* (Ellis 2009). For this reason, our attention will next turn to TSLL.

2.3 Task-Supported Language Learning in the Young Learners' EFL Classroom

The concept of *task-supported language learning* (TSLL) has first been introduced by Ellis (2009). He uses the term to describe English learning that works with tasks, is based on "a structural syllabus and typically involves 'PPP' (presentation-practice-production)" (ibid.: 224). The difference to *task-based language teaching* (TBLT), which was developed in the 1980s, is that TBLT consists of a syllabus of "unfocused tasks" (ibid.) that have to be completed, thus specifying the content. In Baden-Württemberg, EFL teachers usually use coursebooks, worksheets, or other teaching aids for their classes. To them, tasks serve not as the basis of their lessons but as an add-on. Therefore, TSLL rather than TBLT is implemented in primary schools in Baden-Württemberg (Müller-Hartmann and Schocker-von Ditfurth 2011).

Different researchers have offered various definitions of *task* and *task design* (e.g. Long 1985; Willis 1996; Ellis 2003; Samuda and Bygate 2008). One definition that stands out from all others comes from Van den Branden (2006: 4): "A task is an activity in which a person engages in order to attain an objective, and which necessitates the use of language." What is distinct about his definition is that he puts the learners at the centre and takes their perspective into account. This is important because we know that pupils engage in tasks that give them the opportunity to communicate their own meanings, content, or feelings (Müller-Hartmann and Schocker 2016). In other words, it is important that learners can take agency of their actions. Following Dewey's (Dewey 1997/1938) idea of *learning by doing*, González-Lloret (2017: 2) also points to this aspect when she explains that "we learn a language by doing something with it rather than knowing about it."

For the implementation of TSLL in EFL primary classrooms in Baden-Württemberg, Müller-Hartmann and Schocker-von Ditfurth (2011) propose a four-step *framework for sequencing tasks* that we can use as a guide. In their framework, the authors consider the coursebook as "the basic tool in TSLL contexts" (ibid.: 91) and suggest that as a first step teachers use the coursebook as a resource, analyse it and pre-select tasks. However, the teachers who participated in my research did not consider the coursebook as the basic tool of their English lessons. Two of the teachers did not even use a specific coursebook at all. Rather, various textbooks were part of a pool of resources that also included worksheets, copy templates, online printable materials, and activity books. From this pool, the teachers compiled materials that they adapted for their English lessons. Therefore, the *framework for sequencing tasks* needed to be adapted to this situation, resulting in the following four steps:

1. Planning lessons: analysing resources and pre-selecting tasks.
2. Pre-task: negotiating task choice, activating, and pre-teaching language.
3. Task cycle: doing the task, preparing, and presenting results.
4. Post-task: giving feedback, reflecting, and evaluating.

However, since the teachers in my research did not just use tasks, but technology-enhanced tasks, we will next take a look at the topic of technology in the classroom.

2.4 Technology in the Young Learners' EFL Classroom

When talking about *technology*, we do not necessarily have to refer to a specific device. Etymologically, the term *technology* derives from Greek *tekhnē* (art, skill) and *logos* (reason). Hence, technology is "the practical and purposeful application of knowledge" (Huang, Spector and Yang 2019: 7). In common usage, however, *technology* refers to "physical things as in smartphones, tablet computers, interactive whiteboards, and so on" (ibid.). Educational technology in the classroom then is the sound and effective use of digital tools "to support or facilitate learning, performance, and instruction" (ibid.: 8). Technology-enhanced lessons offer new learning opportunities and benefits even to a heterogeneous group of young learners (e.g. Pinter 2015; Kuty 2018b). Various studies show that technology in EFL learning can create not only options for differentiation, individualisation, and personalisation (e.g. Bates 2019) but also promote oracy and interaction (Edelenbos, Johnstone and Kubanek 2006: 149f.). In particular, the possibility to support young learners in developing their oral language competencies and communication skills is one benefit of using technology in the classroom that several other authors also point out (e.g. Pellerin 2014; Legutke 2015). Moreover, technology can easily be adapted to the learning environment and provide immediate feedback to learners. It can help increase pupils' control over task management and thereby even remove social barriers that might otherwise put communicative pressure on learners (Kaliampos 2019). So next, let us bring tasks and technology into the primary school classroom.

2.5 Task and Technology in the Young Learners' EFL Classroom

The combination of tasks and technology in foreign language education holds enormous possibilities. According to González-Lloret (2017), tasks are ideal for fully exploiting the potential of technologies for foreign language learning. However, the requirement set out by Graumann (2002) for teaching in heterogeneous classes also applies to the use of technology-enhanced tasks: The lesson design has to cater for the individual needs of the pupils. With a focus on performance heterogeneity this includes, for example, individualised instruction, a variety of media, open forms of teaching and learning, and adequate scaffolding (Eisenmann 2019).

To implement technology-enhanced tasks that take into account primary school children's various needs, we can draw on Chapelle's "criteria for CALL task appropriateness" (2001:55). These criteria include technology-enhanced task language learning potential, learner fit, focus on meaning, authenticity, positive impact on learners, and practicality, i.e. the suitability of the chosen technology to support the language learning activity. For task evaluation, Chapelle suggests analysing three "objects of evaluation" (ibid.: 53): software, teacher-planned activities, and learners' performance. In the context of the research presented here, one more object needs to be added to Chapelle's objects of evaluation, namely the *implications for technology-enhanced task design*. In the following, I am presenting my methodology.

3   Methodology

Whereas we can evaluate the objects software and teacher-planned activities by the use of judgmental methods, i.e. investigate "software and task in terms of criteria drawn from research on SLA" (Chapelle 2001:54), we need empirical methods to examine learners' performance and the implications for the design of technology-enhanced tasks. The reason for this is that with empirical methods we can consider the same criteria, but we use the "data gathered to reveal the details of CALL use and learning outcomes" (ibid.).

To collect empirical data, I conducted my classroom-based research at three cooperating primary schools. From each school, one EFL teacher participated in the research. Each of the three in-service teachers was assisted by a pre-service teacher (students of EFL teaching at the University of Education Schwäbisch Gmünd). The tandems were responsible for developing, creating, and implementing one small-scale project using technology-enhanced tasks to support pupils in speaking English at each school. Thus, the research design promoted collaboration between pre- and in-service teachers (Cutrim Schmid and Hegelheimer 2014). However, before creating the tasks for the projects, I first visited the teachers and observed their EFL lessons. This gave me a first impression of their classes. Also, the children had the chance to get used to me. After all, I would be coming more often. Then, I held a workshop for all participants, which was tailored to their needs regarding the project and in which they could bring in their own questions and concerns. The topics covered in the workshop included task design, how to use an iPad or a laptop, how to use a Smartboard, and how to work with different apps and software. After the workshop, the first interview was conducted with the in-service teachers. For the interviews, a semi-structured interview guide was developed. Subsequently, the three projects, which were integrated into the EFL curriculum of the respective school, were carried out in the scope of three to six lessons each. The lessons were video-recorded and made available to the participants so that they could watch the lessons again, if they wanted to. Finally, the second semi-structured interview was taken, this time also with the pre-service teachers (Fig. 2).

Classroom observation		
Participant workshop (in-service- & pre-service teachers)		
Interview 1 (in-service teachers)	3x1 classroom project	Interview 2 (in-service- & pre-service teachers)

Fig. 2. Data collection instruments.

Next, I will briefly introduce the instruments that I used to analyse the collected data.

4   Data Analysis Instruments

In the research design two tools are used for data analysis. The first tool is reflexive Thematic Analysis (TA) as suggested by Braun and Clarke (2006). TA is a qualitative method for identifying patterns of shared meaning, so-called *themes*, organised around a core concept across datasets. TA "emphasizes meaning as contextual or situated, reality or real*ities* as multiple, and researcher subjectivity as not just valid but a *resource*" (Braun et al. 2019: 848, italics in original). Braun and Clarke (2022: 34ff.) introduce a six-phase process of applying TA: familiarising with the dataset, coding, generating initial themes, developing and reviewing themes, refining and defining themes, and writing up. The initial coding of the data was inductive to generate themes informed by the content of the data. Later, focused coding with a deductive orientation followed. The coding took into account both semantic and latent meanings. Then, according to Corbin and Strauss's (2015) principle of *axial coding* (i.e. coding for context), the codes were divided into conditions, actions-interactions, and consequences. To support this process, the researcher used a second data analysis tool.

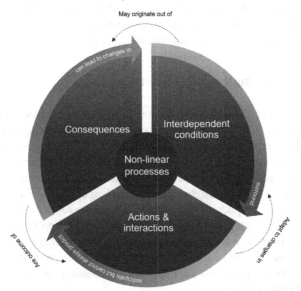

Fig. 3. Coding paradigm (based on Corbin and Strauss 2015).

This second tool is an adaptation of the coding *paradigm* as suggested by Corbin and Strauss (ibid.). The paradigm is a tool that assists researchers in axial coding or coding around categories. These categories are also called "themes" (ibid.: 35). In my research, the themes arise from the preceding TA. The paradigm has got three main features: conditions, actions-interactions, and consequences. Since "the paradigm is only a tool and not a set of directives" (ibid.: 229), it allows us to ask questions and find linkages in the data in order to work out concepts whilst keeping action-interaction in the centre. It also enables us to show processes and not just to give static descriptions of situations. However, if we want to understand and explain processes, we have to put them into context. Context is a broad term and includes, amongst others, the circumstances or conditions that make up a situation, the meanings people give to these, the actions and interactions people undertake to achieve a goal, and the consequences that result from these actions (ibid.: 226). Like links in a chain, one action often leads to another that in turn is followed by another, and so on, which is why the consequences of an action-interaction cannot always be predicted. Therefore, "the relationships between conditions, subsequent interaction, and consequences rarely follow a linear path" (ibid.: 233). Rather, they follow non-linear processes. As conditions can change, action-interaction may also need to change in order to achieve the desired outcome. And since consequences are the result of actions, they often become part of the conditions that lead to the next actions and interactions.[1]

---

[1] The connections between conditions, action-interaction, and consequences in non-linear processes are illustrated in Fig. 3.

In axial coding, i.e. in coding for context, we locate and link "action–interaction within a framework of subconcepts that give it meaning and enable it to explain what interactions are occurring, and why and what consequences real or anticipated are happening because of action–interaction" (ibid.: 227). Thus, with the help of the coding paradigm we can not only explain the actions-interactions in EFL lessons, but also place them in their respective context in order to understand why they were carried out (conditions), and what results they had (consequences).

5 Example of a Small-Scale Classroom Project

To give the reader a better impression of how the small-scale classroom projects were implemented, I would like to briefly present one of them as an example. The project was carried out with 3rd graders at a primary school in a rural area. It was integrated into the first English lessons after a long phase of school lockdowns and home schooling, during which no English lessons had been held. 13 girls and 10 boys attended this class and it was their first year in learning English as a foreign language. The English teacher, who was also the class teacher, decided to create a task on the topic *Present your favourite toy*. For the task, she wanted to work with iPads and use the App *ChatterPix Kids*, both of which she had been introduced to in the workshop. The teacher scheduled six lessons in total for the project. Four lessons for the introduction, the pre-task and the core task and two lessons for the presentation of results and reflection (post-task). The core task had two educational objectives:

1. The pupils are able to understand, pronounce and apply the vocabulary increasingly confidently.
2. The pupils are able to use the vocabulary and sentences in their own video production.

For the project, the pupils had been asked to bring their favourite toys with them to school. With the help of *Sally, the Kangaroo*, a hand puppet that the children know from a textbook, the teacher introduced the topic and reactivated the vocabulary. For this, she had brought real toys that she now presented to the children. Then she asked the pupils if they had any suggestions on how to make the toys talk so that they could introduce themselves and Sally would not have to do it anymore. The children quickly had the idea of making a video about it. To give the pupils an idea of where the project could be going and what a possible task outcome could look like, the teacher then showed two example videos in which *Sally, the Kangaroo* introduced herself. The first video showed a basic introduction and the second an extended one for pupils who worked better, faster, or needed a greater challenge. Both videos had been recorded using the "ChatterPix Kids" app by the researcher before the start of the project (Fig. 4).

However, before the pupils were allowed to make their first recording, they had to fill in a worksheet or create an individual text to introduce the toy of their choice. This gave them a template to which they could later refer when recording. The children were also provided with a word bank which, together with the example videos and the worksheet, served as scaffolding and language support. More language support was provided by dictionaries, pictionaries, and the teacher and classmates who were available for assistance. For pupils who had finished their recording, the teacher had prepared

Fig. 4. *Sally, the Kangaroo* in an example video of the "ChatterPix Kids" app.

another task where they had to work in pairs to create a dialogue between two toys. Again, the pupils were provided with an example video that the researcher had recorded. At the end of the core task, the teacher asked all pupils to save their individual results so that they could present them to their classmates and reflect on them in the next two English lessons (post-task phase) (Fig. 5).

Name: _____   Date: _____

MY TOY

1: Hello, my name is _____ (name of your toy).
I belong to _____ (your name).
I am a _____ (colour) _____ (what toy).
Have a nice day, goodbye.

OR

2: Hello, I am a _____ (what toy)
and I belong to _____ (your name).
I am _____ (colour).
Have a nice day, goodbye!

4: Hello, I am a _racing car_____ (what toy) and my name is
_____Jimmy_____ .
I belong to _____Andreas_____ (your name).
I am not a _____bike_____ (doll/horse/teddy
bear/...).
I am _____red and yellow_____ (colour).
I like _____driving fast_____ , _____winning races_____ and
_____good streets_____ . I don't like _____snow_____ and
_____rain_____ . See you later, bye bye!

Finished?

Fig. 5. Examples of worksheets for language support.

After their presentations in class, the researcher asked the pupils for one or two sentences as feedback on the project. Their comments were positive throughout. For instance, the children said that they thought the app was really cool and that working with it was great fun, that it was very exciting, that it was funny that the animals could open their mouths, and that it was great that everyone presented something.[2] After the six lesson-project, a second interview with the teacher, in which she reflected on the implementation of the technology-enhanced task in her EFL lessons, was conducted. In

---

[2] In the following lessons without the researcher, the children of course reflected on the project with their teacher and received detailed feedback.

the following section I will present a summary of first preliminary findings from this interview.

6   First Preliminary Findings

As pointed out earlier, in my research I investigate primary school EFL teachers' perspectives on promoting speaking through the use of technology-enhanced tasks in their heterogeneous classrooms. For this reason, all preliminary findings presented in the following represent only the view of the English teacher who implemented the project introduced above. Does she think that the technology-enhanced task she created has the potential to support oral communicative EFL learning in her class? And if so, what aspects of the use of technology in her EFL lessons does she consider to have a relevant impact on the development of her learners' speaking competence?

At the present stage of my research, I am focusing on analysing interview data using the coding paradigm. Thus, I would like to outline some preliminary findings that have emerged from this. At this point, I concentrate on the theme *oral performance*. One condition is to develop learners' communicative competence and support them in speaking English. Therefore, the action-interaction taken implements technology-enhanced tasks. In the interview after the project, the English teacher gave information about the consequences she had observed and which she found had resulted from the use of technology and task concerning the oral performance of the young learners. For example, the teacher (T5) thought that the task "completely worked. I mean, using the iPad and this app they all were motivated [..] at all costs they all wanted to speak into it and introduce their soft toy and make it talk. I think they all felt addressed" (interview 2_T5).[3] Regarding the objective of the task (children create a video and speak English) the teacher stated that "[e]veryone reached the goal of the task. Yes, they all have, according to their proficiency level. Some with three sentences and [...] all the others have done it very elaborately with the longer version or with an individual version. [...] They all reached the goal, on different levels though" (interview 2_T5). As a final example, here is the teacher's perception of the performance of the weaker learners in her class: "The two weakest children of the group, who always refrain from speaking, [...] bent over it (the iPad, t.a.) and tried to speak as quietly as possible so that the others do not hear it, but they all spoke" (interview 2_T5).

Regarding the theme *oral performance*, a preliminary summary of the results from this teacher's perspective shows that the technology-enhanced task helped to promote speaking in her heterogeneous EFL primary classroom. According to the teacher, all pupils felt addressed by the task. This suggests that technology-enhanced tasks have the potential to already meet the needs of young learners. Moreover, the teacher stated that the technology-enhanced task encouraged the use of the target language by all pupils. Furthermore, she noted that the children not only spoke English but they also spoke a lot. She observed the use of the target language even in weak learners, who usually always refrain from speaking English. A reason for this might be found in the safe space that technology gives to learners allowing them to speak without fear of being

---

[3] The interviews were conducted in German. The teacher's answers and comments have been translated into English by the author.

judged by someone else. What may also contribute to this is that the children receive immediate feedback and have the opportunity to revise and re-record their result, again in a protected setting. They can perform the task as many times as they like until they are happy with their outcome. Eisenmann (2019) suggests making conscious efforts to engage quieter or weaker learners in EFL lessons so that they feel more valued and involved. The more protected learning environment that the teacher created through the technology-enhanced task might have been a contribution to this. Another observation made by the teacher was that all pupils reached the goal of the task, i.e. they all produced a video. Finally, the teacher noted that the technology-enhanced task also entailed a higher degree of differentiation and individualisation. Therefore, from this teacher's point of view, technology-enhanced tasks are suitable for dealing with the high level of performance heterogeneity in her EFL lessons. Although the learners were not involved in real-world-interaction with people outside the classroom, the language they were using can be transferred to such authentic interactions. This is also indicated by the dialogues that some children in the project produced with a partner (Fig. 6).

Condition	Developing communicative competence						
Action-interaction	Using technology-enhanced tasks						
Consequences	All pupils are addressed	All pupils use target language	Pupils speak a lot	Weak and shy pupils also speak English	Pupils can perform task more often & repeat recordings	All pupils reach goal and produce task outcome	Task entails higher degree of differentiation & individualisation

Fig. 6. Overview: First preliminary findings representing T5's perspectives on using technology-enhanced tasks to support speaking in EFL learning with a heterogeneous group of young learners (theme: oral performance).

7   Final Words and Future Work

In this paper, I have presented the first preliminary findings of my research on teacher's perspectives on the potential of technology-enhanced tasks in promoting speaking in heterogeneous EFL primary classrooms. In the next phase of my research, I will further analyse the interviews, reduce the data to a few themes, and try to find connections between them. Then, with the help of the coding paradigm, I will code for context around these themes in order to find out what linkages between conditions, actions-interactions, and consequences the pre-service and in-service teachers consider as beneficial or detrimental when it comes to promoting oral communication with technology-enhanced tasks. This will also show what potential the teachers see in technology-enhanced tasks in this respect, if any. First preliminary findings at this stage suggest that it is not merely the technology but mainly specific features of technology-enhanced tasks that will make a difference regarding pupils' learning. Furthermore, we wish to understand two more things: What criteria for the design of technology-enhanced tasks that cater for the needs of a heterogeneous group of young learners are relevant for the teachers? What support do they consider helpful to be able to design such tasks? The support could, for example, be in terms of equipment, teacher training, handling of the technology, or sustainability.

References

Bates, A.W.: Teaching in a Digital Age –, 2nd edn. Tony Bates Associates Ltd., Vancouver, B.C. (2019)

Blume, C., Würffel, N.: Using technologies for foreign language learning in inclusive settings. Fremdsprachen Lehren und Lernen (FLuL) **47**(2), 8–27 (2018)

Braun, V., Clarke, V.: Using thematic analysis in psychology. Qual. Res. Psychol. **3**(2), 77–101 (2006)

Braun, V., Clarke, V.: Thematic analysis. A practical guide. Sage, London (2022)

Braun, V., Clarke, V., Hayfield, N., Terry, G.: Thematic analysis. In: Liamputtong, P. (ed) Handbook of Research Methods in Health Social Sciences, pp. 843–860. Springer, Singapore (2019)

Budde, J.: Problematisierende Perspektiven auf Heterogenität als ambivalentes Thema der Schul- und Unterrichtsforschung. Zeitschrift für Pädagogik **58**(4), 522–540 (2012)

Budde, J.: Unscharfe Einsätze – (Re-)Produktion von Heterogenität im schulischen Feld. In: Budde, J. (ed.) Unscharfe Einsätze: (Re-)Produktion von Heterogenität im schulischen Feld, pp. 7–26. Springer Fachmedien, Wiesbaden (2013)

Chapelle, C.: Computer Applications in Second Language Acquisition: Foundations for Teaching, Testing, and Research. Cambridge University Press, Cambridge (2001)

Chilla, S., Vogt, K.: Englischunterricht mit heterogenen Lerngruppen: Eine interdisziplinäre Perspektive. In: Chilla, S., Vogt, K. (eds.) Heterogenität und Diversität im Englischunterricht. Fachdidaktische Perspektiven, pp. 55–81. 1st, new edn. Peter Lang, Frankfurt a.M (2017)

Corbin, J. M., Strauss, A. L.: Basics of qualitative research. Techniques and procedures for developing grounded theory. 4th edn. Sage, London (2015)

Cutrim Schmid, E., Hegelheimer, V.: Collaborative research projects in the technology-enhanced language classroom: Pre-service and in-service teachers exchange knowledge about technology. ReCALL **26**(3), 315–332 (2014)

Cutrim Schmid, E.: Teacher Education in Computer-Assisted Language Learning. A Sociocultural and Linguistic Perspective. Bloomsbury, London/New York (2017)

Dewey, J.: Experience and Education. Simon & Schuster, New York (1938; 1997)

Edelenbos, P., Johnstone, R., Kubanek, A.: The main pedagogical principles underlying the teaching of languages to very young learners. Languages for the children of Europe. Published Research, Good Practice & Main Principles. Final Report of the EAC 89/04, Lot 1 study. European Commission, Brussels (2006)

Eisenmann, M.: Teaching English: Differentiation and Individualisation. Schöningh/UTB, Paderborn/Stuttgart (2019)

Ellis, R.: Task-based language teaching: Sorting out the misunderstandings. Int. J. Appl. Linguist. **19**(3), 221–246 (2009)

Ellis, R.: Task-based language learning and teaching. Oxford: Oxford Univ. Press (2003)

Giesler, T., Schuett, L., Wolter, F. J.: Wie können Lernziele und Rahmenbedingungen im differenzierenden Englischunterricht (besser) aufeinander abgestimmt werden? In: Doff, S. (ed.) Heterogenität im Fremdsprachenunterricht. Impulse – Rahmenbedingungen – Kernfragen – Perspektiven, pp. 61–76. Narr Francke Attempto Verlag, Tübingen (2016)

Goh, C.C.M., Burns, A.: Teaching Speaking. Cambridge University Press, A Holistic Approach. Cambridge (2012)

González-Lloret, M.: A Practical Guide to Integrating Technology into Task-Based Language Teaching. Georgetown University Press, Washington, D.C (2016)

González-Lloret, M.: Technology and task-based language teaching. In: Thorne, S.L., May, S. (eds.) Language, Education and Technology Encyclopedia of Language and Education ELE, pp. 193–205. Springer, Cham (2017). https://doi.org/10.1007/978-3-319-02237-6_16

Graumann, O.: Gemeinsamer Unterricht in heterogenen Gruppen: Von lernbehindert bis hochbegabt, Bad Heilbrunn/Obb.: Klinkhardt (2002)

Huang, R., Spector, J. M., Yang, J.: Educational Technology. A Primer for the 21st Century. Springer, Singapore (2019)

Kaliampos, J.: Scaffolding learner agency in technology-enhanced language learning environments. In: Blume, C., Gerlach, D., Benitt, N., Eßer, S., Roters, B., Springob, J., Schmidt, T. (eds.) Perspektiven inklusiven Englischunterrichts: Gemeinsam lehren und lernen, n.p. (2019). https://inklusiver-englischunterricht.de/2019/08/scaffolding-learner-agency-in-techno logy-enhanced-language-learning-environments. Accessed 02 July 2022

Kuty, M.: Der Englischunterricht in der Primarstufe. In: Haß, F. (ed.) Fachdidaktik Englisch. Tradition - Innovation – Praxis, pp. 32–41. 2nd, revised edn. Ernst Klett Verlag, Stuttgart (2018a)

Kuty, M.: Arbeitsmittel und Unterrichtsmedien. In: Haß, F. (ed.) Fachdidaktik Englisch. Tradition - Innovation – Praxis, pp. 280–305. 2nd, revised edn. Ernst Klett Verlag, Stuttgart (2018b)

Legutke, M., Müller-Hartmann, A., Schocker-v. Ditfurth, M.: Teaching English in the Primary School. 2nd edn. Klett-Lerntraining, Stuttgart (2015)

Long, M.H.: A role for instruction in second language acquisition: Task-based language training. In: Hyltenstam, K., Pienemann, M. (eds.) Modelling and Assessing Second Language Acquisition, pp. 77–99. Multilingual Matters, Clevedon, Avon (1985)

Ministerium für Kultus, Jugend und Sport Baden-Württemberg (ed.): Bildungsplan der Grundschule – Englisch (ab Klasse 3/4). Neckar-Verlag GmbH, Villingen-Schwenningen (2020)

Müller-Hartmann, A., Schocker-von Ditfurth, M.: Task-Supported Language Learning. Schöningh, Paderborn, München, Wien, Zürich (2011)

Müller-Hartmann, A., Schocker, M.: Aufgabenorientierung. In: Burwitz-Melzer, E., Mehlhorn, G., Riemer, C., Bausch, K.-R., Krumm, H.-J. (eds.) Handbuch Fremdsprachenunterricht, pp. 325–330. 6th, revised edn. Francke, Tübingen (2016)

Pellerin, M.: Language tasks using touch screen and mobile technologies: reconceptualizing task-based CALL for young language learners. Can. J. Learn. Technol. **40**(1), 1–23 (2014)

Pinter, A.: Task-based learning with children. In: Bland, J (ed.) Teaching English to young learners. Critical Issues in Language Teaching with 3–12 Year Olds, pp. 113–128. Bloomsbury Academic, London/New York (2015)

Samuda, V., Bygate, M.: Tasks in Second Language Learning. Palgrave Macmillan, Basingstoke, England (2008)

Stockwell, G.: Using mobile phones for vocabulary activities: Examining the effect of the platform. Lang. Learn. Technol. **14**(2), 95–110 (2010)

Trautmann, M., Wischer, B.: Theoriebildung im Diskursfeld Heterogenität. In: Harant, M., Thomas, P., Küchler, U. (eds.) Theorien! Horizonte für die Lehrerinnnen- und Lehrerbildung, pp. 219–229. Tübingen University Press, Tübingen (2020)

Van den Branden, K.: Task-Based Language Education. Cambridge University Press, From theory to practice. Cambridge (2006)

Walgenbach, K.: Heterogenität – Intersektionalität – Diversity in der Erziehungswissenschaft. 2nd edn. Opladen and Toronto: Barbara Budrich (2017)

Whyte, S., Cutrim Schmid, E.: A task-based approach to video communication with the IWB: a French-German primary EFL class exchange. In: Cutrim Schmid, E., Whyte, S. (eds.) Teaching Languages with Technology. Communicative Approaches to Interactive Whiteboard Use, pp. 50–85. Bloomsbury, London and New York (2014)

Willis, J.: A Framework for Task-Based Learning. Longman, Harlow (1996)

Flexible Ontology-Driven Educational Apps and Social Media for Learners with a Disability

Julius T. Nganji[1]([✉]) [iD], Mike Brayshaw[2], and Neil Gordon[2] [iD]

[1] University of Toronto, Toronto, ON M5G 1V7, Canada
j.nganji@utoronto.ca
[2] University of Hull, Hull HU6 7RX, UK

Abstract. This paper explores how to build ontology-driven learning systems from a flexible disability-aware mentality and augment them into a learning blend that embraces social media. The approach emphasizes the use of user centered flexible software in a blended approach to learning. The paper starts with a discussion of how learners learn, including their recent fascination with Apps and social media. The need to provide disability-aware personalization of the educational Apps that are developed is discussed. The emphasis is on designing learning systems for learners with disabilities rather than providing for them as an afterthought. The paper introduces social media as a way of facilitating and supporting e-learning. It notes the recent changes that have taken place in the use of social media. Taking e-learning as a case study the paper demonstrates how various models of e-learning, emphasizing flexible learning, can be enhanced linking back the whole while of integrating into disability-aware information systems. Some practical approaches to modeling the learner with ontologies are provided. Finally, caution is noted on how we have to use social media. We detail some of the potential problems and pitfalls that may be a contemporary consequence of using this media, then offer some suggestions and work rounds.

Keywords: Human computer interfaces design · Virtual communities · Social computing · Social networks

1 Introduction

With the explosion and increased diffusion of information technology devices comes a massive increase in the number of information systems that are being developed to respond to the ever-increasing demands of users. With the advent of social media, the facilities and networking potential of these users is greatly enhanced. However, designers and developers of information systems by default, tend to design for users without disabilities (Nganji 2019, 2021). This has enormous consequences for people with disabilities, especially when they are not able to access the systems that have been designed. Thus, the need for a careful consideration and inclusion of their needs.

This paper therefore aims to propose an ontology-driven and disability-aware approach that ensures the needs of all learners, including those with disabilities are captured

© The Author(s), under exclusive license to Springer Nature Switzerland AG 2022
P. Zaphiris and A. Ioannou (Eds.): HCII 2022, LNCS 13328, pp. 361–375, 2022.
https://doi.org/10.1007/978-3-031-05657-4_26

throughout the development cycle. Practical approaches such as the use of personas to capture the needs of the learner are discussed.

This paper addresses the integration of social media into learning systems. Within the scope of e-learning we show how we can provide increased flexibility for communication and delivery of our material. The information system design and e-learning elements will be of interest to both Psychologists and Computer Scientists, whilst the social computing elements embraces other disciplines as well.

The paper starts with a discussion of learning styles, and in particular the learning styles of people with disabilities. All individuals exhibit preferred learning styles, and this literature will be discussed. In relation to individual learners with disabilities, the preferred style may well be influenced by their actual needs. Any AI methodology that works with the user thus must take this into consideration. Support and increasing motivation are a further key consideration when designing learning technology.

In an analogous manner to the use of Games and Gaming in learning, this paper will discuss how we can include peoples' fascination with Apps and social media as motivational provisions within technology enhanced learning. We see and hear daily how people are glued to their social media apps. Social media also provides a means of supporting collaboration, both peer-to-peer and student-teacher collaborations. In the recent age of lockdowns, social media has been a vital communication tool and is already a big part of many users' technologies landscapes. For people with disabilities these lockdowns have meant social media has taken on a leading role in communication and interaction. We here explore how this might be developed within the learning context.

Following on from this we discuss the need to provide disability-aware personalization of the educational Apps that are developed. The emphasis is on designing learning systems for learners with disabilities rather than providing for them as an afterthought. The paper introduces social media as a way of facilitating and supporting e-learning. Taking e-learning as a case study the paper demonstrates how various models of e-learning, emphasizing flexible learning, can be enhanced linking back the whole while to integrating disability-aware information systems. We introduce inclusive learning personas as a method for effective user profiling including collaboration preferences and histories. Such personas can then be used as an effective way of designing the learning environment which puts the users as the central core, both in the design of learning environment and the design and use of social media. Then using these ontologies to model the learner and social media consideration, appropriate and personalized educational Apps can be designed and implemented. Some practical approaches using this methodology to model the learner with ontologies are provided.

Finally, when we are dealing with social media, we must note some words of caution. We detail some of the potential problems and pitfalls that may be a consequence of using this contemporary media and go on to offer some suggestions and work arounds that enable such problems to be faced and managed.

2 Background

2.1 Learning Styles and Learners with Disability

Human beings are different, even among identical twins, there exist distinguishing traits. In the same way, people have different preferences. In the field of education, learners have different preferences for accessing learning content which could be visual, auditory, or kinesthetic. This preference for learning is what is known as learning styles. There are various learning style models including Kolb Learning Styles Theory (Kolb 1985) which is based on experiential learning and describes the experiences of the learner. This model consists of four core elements: concrete experience, observation and reflection, the formation of abstract concepts and testing in new situations. In this model, concrete experience and abstract conceptualization are grasping experiences while reflective observation and active experimentation are transforming experiences.

Honey and Mumford's Index of Learning Styles (Honey and Mumford 1992) on the other hand describes four types of learners: activists who learn by doing and enjoy new experiences, reflectors who learn by observing and reflecting on what happened, theorists who are logical in approach and want to understand the theory behind actions and pragmatists who are very practical in approach.

A model which is of interest to this study, and which relates to learners with disabilities' preferences for learning materials due to their disability type is the VARK model (Fleming 2001). This model describes four types of learners: visual learners who are those with preference for seeing and hence, find visual aids very useful in their studies. If a learning environment is designed to incorporate video, such as incorporating video-driven social media, these learners will greatly benefit from it and might interact more with the learning environment. Auditory learners are those who learn best by listening, hence have a high preference for audio-based learning materials and benefit from participating in group discussions. Thus, for this group of learners, the presence of social media applications (Apps) within a learning environment will be very useful. Reading/writing preference learners prefer to take notes while a lecture is being delivered and thereafter spend time reading them to synthesize and assimilate the material. Finally, kinesthetic learners learn well by doing, thus involvement in activities such as experiments, practical demonstrations and interaction with the world are very helpful. Also, for this group of learners, collaboration in a social media enriched learning environment could be of great interest.

Learners with disability might find themselves preferring a specific format for learning materials perhaps not because it is influenced by their learning styles, but because of their disability. A learner with dyslexia, depending on its severity may either prefer text-based learning materials or audio materials. Thus, some would use text to speech assistive technologies such as Kurzweil 3000 (which helps with reading and writing) to convert text-based learning materials into audio which will be more beneficial to them. On the other hand, although the disability might influence their choice of the format of learning materials, some students with disabilities might prefer some formats because it is their learning style. Thus, in this case, the interplay between learning style and disability is beneficial to the learner and when the learning materials are presented to them in the format of their preference, will facilitate their learning. The question now is how we can be effective in designing a learning environment considering this vast array of choices and needs.

With this great diversity of learning preferences, it is still possible to develop educational Apps for all learners but then still design to meet specific individual learner needs, including those with special needs arising from disability. To accomplish this, personalization is the answer. A vast amount of research in e-learning have used learning styles for personalization. For instance, Chookaew et al. (2014) presented a personalized e-learning environment which facilitated programming for learners through a personalization of their learning styles, learning achievement and learning problems. During such personalization and to produce effective and efficient educational Apps that are tailored to the needs of the learner, the learner's knowledge level also needs to be considered (Dwivedi and Bharadwaj 2013).

2.2 Exploiting Learners' Fascination with Social Media and Apps

The internet is now a communication location of war, conflict, and crime (e.g., Karatzogianni 2006, 2015). It is also where we interact often sharing our most private and intimate details. Starting with the dawn of email, bulletin boards, and newsgroups, we now have popular Apps like Facebook and Twitter whose very nature are to promote social interaction and communication.

When we look to propose the design of educational Apps and to incorporate social media into contemporary learning environments, it is important to consider why this is important. There are countless Apps available for people to download to their devices and use for various purposes. These Apps are mostly accessed nowadays via mobile devices and people are increasingly also using these devices to access social media. Understanding the need to stay connected, developers have developed social media Apps for users to remain connected with one another even when travelling. Whether this newfound intimacy and bonding is real, and an adequate substitution for face-to-face interaction is an evolving question (Turkle 2011). This is revisited later when considering the current context of the work reported here.

Undivided attention when studying could be very helpful for a learner, thus as is commonly noticed in communal places nowadays, peoples' fascination with their devices or social media has led to them addictively interacting with their devices in such a way that they may even not notice or perhaps acknowledge others around them (Aagaard 2016). Although spending a considerable amount of time on mobile devices could lead to musculoskeletal pains (Xie et al. 2017), such interest in engaging with content could be exploited to build educational Apps and social media to respond to learners' needs (Nganji 2018). Educational Apps could be designed for learners to download and interact with in such a way that could help them improve their knowledge on a course and to collaborate with other learners, hence improving performance.

The importance of designing disability-aware educational Apps and incorporate social media for collaboration within learning environments cannot be overemphasized. Educators tend to include learning activities that may require collaboration between peers. Although this may be done asynchronously (for instance via email), this means does not exploit the available trend and tendency for people to communicate synchronously. Nowadays, with the existence of Apps such as WhatsApp which is a very affordable (for those connected to the Internet) means of synchronous communication allowing for group collaboration (Pacholek et al. 2021), learners are used to and aware of the numerous powerful means of facilitating learning. Even without the direction of educators, learners are forming groups and collaborating to bring about increased knowledge and to also form better relationships with peers. Contemporary learning environments need to respond to the learning needs of learners considering existing trends and technology. This vast choice of Apps and learning resources allows for flexibility in learning.

2.3 Social Media in Times of Lockdown

The role of social media in learning and collaboration has rapidly evolved due to the contemporary (i.e., often lockdown related) situation we have endured. Social Media has often been the only way of talking to people, socializing, and in this context a pathway to learning (e.g., Khan et al. 2021).

What many futurologists have claimed that they saw as possible ways of working in the future and the embrace of working online (and from home) has been brought forward by many years. So how things might have evolved more slowly over a time has been brought into sharp contemporary reality. It is an open question how this rapid change has affected the affordances of this technology and its use in long term relationships compared with a few years ago (c.f. Turkle 2011). Therefore, the context in which we might have envisaged using this technology, as well as the way we all as users, has changed because of contemporary events.

These changes have involved an increased use of Computer Mediated Communication and the necessity of working and sharing with others. So existing social tools and social media platforms have been pressed into use to provide vital support and enabling platforms for this rapidly adopted new working infrastructure. It is thus most timely to consider how me might use and exploit this new and changing social media use (and our shifting affordances to it), taken together with our existing use of AI, and apply it to learners with disability.

2.4 Ontology-Driven Personalized E-Learning

As earlier discussed, current learning environments do not incorporate the necessary Apps that could be used by students, not to talk of providing personalized content that could be vital for improving the learner's knowledge and hence increased performance. The ability for learners to study electronically is leading to changing roles for the educator (Shaikh and Khoja 2014) who is no longer the main actor. This shift from traditional systems of learning becomes even more radical when personalization is used to present content to learners (Childress and Benson 2014; Hsieh et al. 2013). With personalized provision of educational content for learners, it is easier to find information. To accomplish personalization, it is important to know more about the learner through some of their characteristics and behavior. For instance, if we understand the studying habits and trends via their past activities, we could tailor search results to meet their needs more precisely and thus provide relevant and specific content (Zhuhadar et al. 2008) to meet their learning needs.

The presence of social media allows for collaboration between learners and this collaboration could also be a means of personalized content provision for the needs of the learner. Although this will encourage students to be involved and active in the learning process, they will often need guidance from experts. Generally, the learner 's profile which contains information about the learner is used to provide them with specific learning materials (Tzouveli et al. 2008). Personalization based on user profiling (Biletskiy et al. 2009; Kritikou et al. 2008; Tzouveli et al. 2008) can also be used to predict the preferences of the learner to personalize or adapt the learning environment to meet their needs. Thus, educational Apps could be designed and through the learner's profile could be used to push specific content to the learner.

Learning styles which were discussed above could also be used to personalize learning (Klasnja-Milicevic et al. 2011; Pukkhem and Vatanawood 2011). By knowing the learning styles of the learner, it is possible to recommend appropriate learning materials (Halbert et al. 2011).

The semantic web provides a means for humans to communicate with machines and to understand each other and has been used to provide personalized recommendations (Nasraoui and Zhuhadar 2010). Bergman (2007) asserts that ontologies can provide a more effective basis for information extraction. Web ontologies can be used to model learning content that can be used for the educational Apps and to also represent the learner through their profile. Ontology-based web personalization has been successfully achieved in news recommendation (Cantador et al. 2008) and could thus be employed to push specific announcements to learners in their learning space. Also, ontologies have been used to recommend learning materials (Liu et al. 2010).

3   A Case Study in E-Learning

3.1   New Approaches to Education

Social computing marks a new interface between people and learning technology. This new interface changes how schools and universities can work. Physically, co-location is no longer a pre-requisite. In this paper modes of delivery, assessment, management, analytics, and pedagogical blending are re-visited for students with disabilities. We wish to reimage how universities can evolve from traditional models, change in terms of working, and blend into the world of learning and social computing that can scale for those who traditional attendance is an issue. New channels of learning offer novel mixtures of delivery media and pedagogy allowing for a blended approach to be exploited. Learning can be either highly personal or very shared. Delivery can be via a traditional location but using social computing software. Such blending of tracks leads to new didactics and management of these voyages and the extended analytics that they now afford. Such analytics can be a major influence on content, design, and management (Okoye et al. 2020). The lack of physical constraints in the interaction also allows a fundamental review of what we do and how. As a delivery device, social computing plays a new evolutionary role. It changes our presence with and affordances to educational material.

We are by our very nature a social animal and there is no surprise that when we attend school, college, or university a big part of that experience is social. Ties and bonds may last for a long time. That there is a relationship between social interaction and learning is long established (Vygotsky 1934; Bruner 1961, 1966; Wood, et al. 1976). It is thus timely to look at how this can be revisited in the world of social computing and how a blended, multi-pedagogic approach might benefit learners. The advent of social media and social networking allows us to look at this anew.

Allen (2007) introduced the idea of blended learning, that providing different approaches side by side that blend, results in a better learning experience. Given that we can now develop this to include different social media in this blend and different delivery modes e.g., via Webinars, MOOCS (Massive Open Online Courses) and virtual and augmented reality, then we are able to think about what we can now deliver, and how and when to deliver. We are now in the position to choose how to do this, considering the needs of learners with disability, in the context of disability-aware software – that this social media can not only carry content but also the social aspects of university life is a double bonus.

Flexible learning (Higher Education Academy 2013; Gordon 2014; Ceretta et al. 2002) alongside blending has been highlighted as an important educational goal. The notion of flexibility has been an important notion running centrally throughout this paper. For our target audience again, we can look at what and how to deliver our educational material. As we have noted before, sometimes the disability itself may dictate the media choice. In both blended and flexible approaches, the actual paradigm of instruction employed may also change. So too might the type of interaction that you have. Fordham and Goddard (2013) present two case studies using Facebook, to show some activities can be better supported using specific Facebook tools. For instance, Facebook Timeline was shown to help teach a curriculum, support homework, revision, debates, peer mentoring and tutoring, allow sharing of ideas, and other media resources. Bruff (2011) talks about using specific Twitter resources, Conference Backchannel. Dunn (2014) discusses 100 ways to use Twitter in education, differentiating them by degree of difficulty.

In the context of the current paper, we can look at how we might exploit social media in our e-learning context to work as an adjunct to our disability-aware design mentality. Rather than re-invent the wheel we can look to use social media as an add-on to our existing software. They typically have APIs (Application Programming Interfaces) which allow both tight or loose coupling with the e-learning system.

In terms of e-learning provision, social media can support content provision, and interaction both peer-to-peer and group interactions. Wiki and Blogs – offer tools that can support cooperation and joint discussion and problem solving. They may enable social networking and this in turn can provide vital encouragement, support, and lead to the construction of a learning community (e.g., Holton 2013). Studying by yourself and at a distance can be a very lonely experience (e.g., Willems 2007) and being able to share that experience via social media stands a chance of mitigating against this. This social media interaction could be very helpful for some students with disabilities who might not be able to interact with others in a physical classroom due to anxiety or other disability. Other groupware tools can also help e-learners e.g., WebPA (Gordon 2010) allows students to submit a judgment of team members' relative contributions, which in turn generates a weighting to allocate an individual mark (allowing for individual marks from group task).

In terms of e-learning style of provision we can see social media being used alongside existing approaches. This can be done in a standard classroom style of delivery or existing e-learning modes of delivery. This can be expanded to other, nontraditional based delivery modes for example:

M-Learning – Mobile Based Learning. Learning on the move anywhere you are. The flexibility to choose where to study. LMS/VLE/MOOCs don't care where you are. The use of social media extends our learning environments. It means that the constraint of co-location with a university campus no longer figures in our choice of course.

G-Learning – Game Based Learning. It has been noted that we tend to play (Homo Ludens) – Huizinga (1955). Given that this is an activity that we undertake for pleasure it is a natural extension to try and use this in an education context. To maximize motivation if somebody enjoys this activity and willingly engages in it – then making this a location for learning is a natural extension. West (Brown and Burton 1978), Wunpus (Carr and Goldsterin (1977), Stansfield et al. 1976), and Shopping on Mars (Hennessy et al. 1989) are early examples of the use of gaming as a way of teaching. The user engages on a game that at the same time is teaching them some new skill.

P-Learning – Pervasive Based Learning. Increasingly we live in a world surrounded by computers but do not notice them. We live in a world of smart phones, Linux TVs, and the Internet of Things. Ubicom (Brush 2014) means that we can interact with virtual universities where and when we choose. Given the development of Ubicom delivery devices, the co-location of student and university campus is loosened even further. The constraint now is more one of bandwidth and appropriate receiving device like a Pad or console.

S-Learning – Social Learning. Learning using social media and social exchanges with others. Many now also use social media outlets as their source of news and information.

4   A Practical and Inclusive Approach to Educational Apps Design

Having examined learning styles, the fascination that learners have in engaging with Apps and social media, how learning can be personalized to meet their needs and how this can be used in education, it is important to consider some practical approaches to accomplishing these through a change in mindset, thus adopting a disability-aware mind set.

With the drive to use technology for delivering learning services online, a lot of the technological developments around these areas by default have often focused on meeting the needs of people without disabilities, thus leaving people with disabilities to seek appropriate assistive technologies to interact with such systems.

A lot of the difficulties people with disabilities face when interacting with most information systems are related to the lack of consideration of the needs of people with disabilities during the development cycle. In designing technological solutions, designers and developers need to understand that disability could affect different functions related to the senses and how this happens. Such designers need to develop a new mind set when it comes to designing systems that will be used by everyone. The difficulties and failures of existing information systems towards people with disabilities have necessitated the search for a better approach for designing and developing information systems. Thus, this article aims to propose a disability-aware approach to developing educational Apps and incorporating social media in learning systems to respond to the needs of learners with disabilities.

In developing products to meet the needs of people with disabilities, it is important to ensure that adequate analysis of their needs is carried out and that these needs are incorporated into the design. By developing this disability-aware mentality to learning systems design, the result is a flexible, accessible, and usable learning environment with all the Apps to facilitate learning and collaboration.

In the following sections, two practical considerations for developing such inclusive learning environment which leads to personalized content provision will be presented.

4.1 Designing Inclusive Learner Personas for Effective User Profiling

A persona is a representation of an ideal type user when designing the educational Apps and social media to respond to the needs of specific users. In the persona, the learner's characteristics are included. These are information that could be contained in the user's profile in the learning system.

When the needs of the learner are adequately captured in the persona and used to design the educational Apps and learning environment, it ensures that their needs are met, and that the system is also usable. An example persona is that of a learner with anxiety who prefers collaborating with others online rather than in a physical location.

The persona in Fig. 1 for instance is that for John Smith, a master's student studying information systems. John is in his final year of a two-year master's degree and due to his disability, he requires some accommodation, that of a mentor or a support worker to accompany him to classes. Although John appreciates the support, he sometimes feels he could be more independent if more of the physical group meetings with his peers to complete their coursework could be better delivered online where he can contribute more effectively and efficiently.

This information in John's persona could be considered when designing the learning environment to meet his needs. John is just one example, but when designing educational Apps and incorporating social media into learning systems, it is important to consider several differing needs and thus design to meet the needs of the learner. This persona could be captured through research sessions involving interactions with John.

John Smith: M.Sc. Information Systems Student

Institution: University of Ottawa

Background: B.Sc. in Library and Information Systems, University of Hull

Computer Skills: Expert, uses social media daily

Key Goals

John is a mature student who has severe anxiety and is an expert computer user who often spends much time interacting with his mobile device. Due to anxiety, he requires a personal support worker to accompany him to lectures. With the support worker always present for all study groups, John is not too comfortable and prefers group meetings where he can collaborate with his peers virtually. For this, he does not require the help of his support worker.

Daily Tasks

John attends classes twice a week at the university and spends another day accessing the online learning environment where he completes and submits his assignments. As John is in his final year of the master's program, he also has a lot of group work.

John finds that the learning environment used for his courses does not meet his need to be able to synchronously collaborate with his peers on assignments. He wants the learning environment to incorporate educational Apps including social media that will facilitate group communication and collaboration.

Fig. 1. The persona of John Smith, a student with severe anxiety

4.2   Using Ontologies to Model the Learner and Educational Apps

We earlier discussed how personalization could be achieved to meet the needs of learners and discussed the use of ontologies to provide personalization. The advantage of ontologies we said, was the ability for machines and humans to communicate well and understand each other.

Also, we pointed out that ontologies could be used to represent the user as well as represent various components of the learning environment. Figure 2 presents an example of how John Smith's profile which contains vital information about him that could be used to provide him personalized educational Apps and could be modeled using an ontology presented using the Friend of a Friend (FOAF) vocabulary.

John's profile contains information such as his first name, family or last name, his gender, the username for logging into the learning environment or App, his email address, the type, and severity of his disability. The ontology also stores information about his learning goals and his preferred medium of achieving this goal. In his case, John wants to be able to collaborate with his peers to submit their assignment on time, but he also prefers to be able to do this collaboration online so that he can fully participate free from the anxiety and sometimes the feelings of intimidation that is associated with him being present with others in the same physical room. Also, he wants to be more independent in his study and to avoid episodes of panic attacks.

```
:rdf: type        foaf:Person
:personDetails       "firstname, family_name, gender, username, password, mbox";
:person_concept hasfirstName: "John";
:person_concept hasfamily_name: "Smith";
:person_concept hasGender: "Male";
:person_concept hasuserName: "jsmith";
:person_concept hasmbox: "jsmith10@uOttawa.ca";
:person_concept hasDisability: "Anxiety";
:person_concept hasDisabilityDegree: "severe";


:rdf: type          foaf:LearningGoals
:learningGoals      "Collaborative learning with peers";


:rdf: type          foaf:LearningResource
:studyMedium        "classroom, social media, virtual environment";
: studyMedium _ prefersMedium: "social media";
: studyMedium _ prefersMedium: "virtual environment";
```

Fig. 2. Sample ontology-based profile data set for John Smith

4.3   Emerging Problems and Issues with Social Media

Before we conclude however we need to also consider some potentially harmful aspects of social media as not all you read is true on media sites. Once to get published was hard, you either had to go through scientific reviewers and/or editors to publish. Indeed, you often had to establish your technical background to be considered as a suitable source of copy. This leads into the whole issue of Fake News and its sad associate Fake Science. What we are told is true and a scientific fact is now a part of the problem. You only must look at the many stories that circulated during the recent health crisis to see an example of this (Hoa and Basu 2020).

Traditionally there are professional standards and checks and balances established. A teacher has a well-defined role, and it is often policed by professional organizations or government Agencies[1] where a teacher's legal right to teach may be removed. Teachers go through training for that professional vocation. In many locations the curriculum is already specified and the ability for the individual deliverer to go off message or into their own realm is limited. Again, this is limited when there are set learning outcomes and national exams at the end that limit educational deliverers going off-piste.

Not everyone out there is nice. This might involve inappropriate behavior in the teacher-learner relationship. The internet also contains some darker more sinister agents who engage in trolling, harassment, social games, career building at the sake of others, or sexual motivated behaviors. For this reason, we must think about how best to deploy social media within our context. The obvious solution is to do so in a controlled environment where content is reviewed and checked, interactions monitored, and standards and understood terms of references for use policed are enforced. Such facilities are already in many places like MOOCs or other social extensions to existing VLEs within established learning institutions. It is now common practice of broadcasters and others who wish to extend their media provision into social media to do so in a moderated form (e.g., BBC Have Your Say (HYS)). So, whilst we must be aware of the potential pitfalls and

---

[1] E.g., https://www.gov.uk/government/organisations/teaching-regulation-agency.

dangers that we are faced with here there are already very well-established measures to protect and support learners.

This does not mean that social media interaction has exclusively to stay within the confines of an in-house MOOC for example. The use of other popular social media platforms may increase the motivational hook to learning and collaborating on a particular course. This might involve having their own dedicated use of 3rd party social media platforms, for example lecturers/professors or universities having their own YouTube channel(s). However, if third parties are used it will be necessary to be clear where trusted sources come from and what are the clear rules of interaction. This is something educators need to be aware of and many are doing anyway. Since whether they are formally part of a course or not, modern users will use them anyway, so necessitates consideration.

5   Conclusion

In this paper it has been argued that learning environments should be designed for all users and how being minded of users with disability from the outset can better inform the design of educational Apps that allow for social and collaborative learning. We have argued for the importance of flexibility, so that users are able to personalize their learning experience. For students with disabilities, we have argued for a disability-aware approach for all users. We have also discussed delivery modes and techniques to achieve delivery. Above more conventional techniques, we have discussed the role of the semantic web with ontologies for personalization and have argued about the role social media should take alongside more standard learning methods.

This is not to say that all is necessarily good in the world of social networking. The teacher/tutor's role is a very important one and there always runs the risks that this relationship might become inappropriate given the nature of interacting using social media.

All learning environments and social computing leave an increased user footprint in their wake. Our very use of online learning and social media means that we are contributing, knowingly or not, to Big Data. This in turn leads to the possible deployment of deep learning analytics (e.g., Schmidhuber 2015; Bengio, et al. 2015) where we use machine learning to look for undiscovered knowledge in patterns of engagement and interaction within our e-learning experiences. This can be in terms of classification of Big Data or in terms of pattern analysis and discovery. Linking such data mining of e-learning data and social media learning would present a possible future development.

References

Aagaard, J.: Mobile devices, interaction, and distraction: a qualitative exploration of absent presence. AI Soc. **31**(2), 223–231 (2016). https://doi.org/10.1007/s00146-015-0638-z

Allen, B.: Blended Learning Tools for Teaching and Training. Facet Publishing, London (2007). ISBN: 978-1-85604-614-5

Bergman, M.: An intrepid guide to ontologies (2007). http://www.mkbergman.com/374/an-intrepid-guide-to-ontologies/

Bengio, Y., LeCun, Y., Hinton, G.: Deep learning, Nature **521**(28th May) 436–44 (2015)

Biletskiy, Y., Baghi, H., Keleberda, I., Fleming, M.: An adjustable personalization of search and delivery of learning objects to learners. Expert Syst. Appl. **36**(5), 9113–9120 (2009). https://doi.org/10.1016/j.eswa.2008.12.038

Brown, J.S., Burton, R.R.: Diagnostic models for procedural bugs in basic mathematical skills. Cogn. Sci. **2**, 155–192 (1978)

Bruff, D.: Encouraging a Conference Backchannel on Twitter, The Chronicle of Higher Education (2011). http://chronicle.com/blogs/profhacker/encouraging-a-conference-backchannel-on-twitter/30612. Accessed 13 May 2018

Bruner, J.S.: The act of discovery. Harv. Educ. Rev. **31**, 21–32 (1961)

Bruner, J.S.: Toward a Theory of Instruction. Belkapp Press, Cambridge, Mass (1966)

Brush, A.J.: The UbiComp Community (2014). http://www.sigchi.org/communities/ubicomp. Accessed 12 Mar 2014

Cantador, I., Ballogin, A., Castells, P.: Ontology-based personalised and context-aware recommendations of news items. Paper presented at the Proceedings of the 2008 IEEE/WIC/ACM International Conference on Web Intelligence and Intelligent Agent Technology (2008)

Carr, B.P., Goldstein, I.P.: Overlays: a theory of modelling for computer aided instruction, AI Memo 406, AI Laboratory, Massachusetts Institute of Technology (1977)

Ceretta, C., Warne, B., Stirling, D., Bain, S.: Blended learning educational system and method, US Patent 6,370,355 (2002)

Childress, S., Benson, S.: Personalized learning for every student every day. Phi Delta Kappan **95**(8), 33–38 (2014)

Chookaew, S., Panjaburee, P., Wanichsan, D., Laosinchai, P.: A personalized e-learning environment to promote students' conceptual learning on basic computer programming. In: Proceedings of the 5th World Conference on Educational Sciences, vol. 116, pp. 815–819 (2014). https://doi.org/10.1016/j.sbspro.2014.01.303

Dunn, J.: 100 Ways to Use Twitter in Education, By Degree of Difficulty, Edudemic: Connecting Education and Technology. http://www.edudemic.com/100-ways-to-use-twitter-in-education-by-degree-of-difficulty/. Accessed 16 Mar 2014

Dwivedi, P., Bharadwaj, K.K.: Effective trust-aware e-learning recommender system based on learning styles and knowledge levels. Educ. Technol. Soc. **16**(4), 201–216 (2013)

Fleming, N.: VARK: a guide to learning styles (2001). http://www.vark-learn.com/english/index.asp

Fordham, I., Goddard, T.: Facebook guide for Educators, The Education Foundation (2013). http://www.ednfoundation.org/wp-content/uploads/Facebookguideforeducators.pdf. Accessed 18 Mar 2014

Gordon, N.A.: Group working and peer assessment—using WebPA to encourage student engagement and participation. Innov. Teach Learn. Inf. Comput. Sci. **9**(1), 20–31 (2010)

Gordon, N.A.: Flexible Pedagogies: Technology-enhanced Learning. The Higher Education Academy, York (2014)

Hennessy, S., O'Shea, T., Evertsz, R., Floyd, A.: An intelligent tutoring systems approach to teaching primary mathematics. Educ. Stud. Math. **20**(3), 273–292 (1989). ISSN 0013-1954

Halbert, C., Kriebel, R., Cuzzolino, R., Coughlin, P., Fresa-Dillon, K.: Self-assessed learning style correlates to use of supplemental learning materials in an online course management system. Med. Teach. **33**(4), 331–333 (2011). https://doi.org/10.3109/0142159x.2011.542209

Hoa, K., Basu, T.: The Coronavirus is the first true social Media Infodemic, MIT Technology Review, 12th February 2020. https://www.technologyreview.com/2020/02/12/844851/the-coronavirus-is-the-first-true-social-media-infodemic/. Accessed 6 Feb 2022

Higher Education Academy: Flexible Learning (2013). http://www.heacademy.ac.uk/flexible-learning. Accessed 25 July 2013

Holton, D.: 80+ Educational Google+ Communities, EdTechDev (2013). http://edtechdev.wordpr ess.com/2013/11/15/80-educational-google-communities/. Accessed 12 May 2018

Honey, P., Mumford, A.: The Manual of Learning Styles (3rd ed.). Maidenhead, Peter Honey (1992)

Hsieh, T.C., Lee, M.C., Su, C.Y.: Designing and implementing a personalized remedial learning system for enhancing the programming learning. Educ. Technol. Soc. **16**(4), 32–46 (2013)

Huizinga, Johan, Homo ludens; a study of the play-element in culture. Boston: Beacon Press. ISBN 978–0–8070–4681–4. 1955

Karatzogianni, A.: The Politics of Cyberconflict. Routledge, London and New York (2006)

Karatzogianni, A.: Firebrand Waves of Digital Activism 1994–2014: The Rise and Spread of Hacktivism and Cyberconflict. Palgrave MacMillan, Basingstoke (2015)

Khan, M.N., Ashraf, M.A., Seinen, D., Khan, U.K., Laar, R.A.: Social media for knowledge acquisition and dissemination: the impact of the COVID-19 pandemic on collaborative learning driven social media adoption. Front. Psychol. 31th May 2021. https://doi.org/10.3389/fpsyg. 2021.648253. Accessed 6 Feb 2022

Klasnja-Milicevic, A., Vesin, B., Ivanovic, M., Budimac, Z.: E-Learning personalization based on hybrid recommendation strategy and learning style identification. Comput. Educ. **56**(3), 885–899 (2011). https://doi.org/10.1016/j.compedu.2010.11.001

Kolb, D.: Learning Style Inventory. McBer and Company, Boston, MA (1985)

Kritikou, Y., Demestichas, P., Adamopoulou, E., Demestichas, K., Theologou, M., Paradia, M.: User profile modeling in the context of web-based learning management systems. J. Netw. Comput. Appl. **31**(4), 603–627 (2008). https://doi.org/10.1016/j.jnca.2007.11.006

Liu, F., Li, X.Y., Gao, G.H.: Ontology-based personalized recommendation technology research of learning resources. Paper presented at the Proceedings of the ETP/IITA Conference on System Science and Simulation in Engineering (SSSE 2010), Hong Kong (2010)

Nasraoui, O., Zhuhadar, L.: Improving recall and precision of a personalized semantic search engine for e-learning. In: Fourth International Conference on Digital Society: Icds 2010, Proceedings, pp. 216–221 (2010). https://doi.org/10.1109/icds.2010.63

Nganji, J.T.: Towards learner-constructed e-learning environments for effective personal learning experiences. Behav. Inf. Technol. **37**(7), 647–657 (2018). https://doi.org/10.1080/0144929X. 2018.1470673

Nganji, J.T.: A Disability-Aware Mentality to Information Systems Design and Development. In: Mehdi Khosrow-Pour, D.B.A. (ed.) Advanced Methodologies and Technologies in Artificial Intelligence, Computer Simulation, and Human-Computer Interaction, pp. 267–278. IGI Global (2019). https://doi.org/10.4018/978-1-5225-7368-5.ch021

Nganji, J.T.: Towards disability-aware social media-enriched virtual learning environments. In: Mehdi Khosrow-Pour, D.B.A. (ed.), Handbook of Research on Modern Educational Technolo-gies, Applications, and Management, pp. 922–936. IGI Global (2021). https://doi.org/10.4018/ 978-1-7998-3476-2.ch057

Okoye, K., Nganji, J.T., Hosseini, S.: Learning analytics for educational innovation: a systematic mapping study of early indicators and success factors, Int. J. Comput. Inf. Syst. Ind. Manag. Appl. **12**, 138–154 (2020)

Pacholek, K., et al.: A Whatsapp community forum for improving critical thinking and practice skills of mental health providers in a conflict zone. Interact. Learn. Environ. (2021).https://doi. org/10.1080/10494820.2021.1890622

Pukkhem, N., Vatanawood, W.: Personalised learning object based on multi-agent model and learners' learning styles. Maejo Int. J. Sci. Technol. **5**(3), 292–311 (2011)

Schmidhuber, J.: Deep learning in neural networks: an overview. Neural Netw. **61**, 85–117 (2015)

Shaikh, Z.A., Khoja, S.A.: Personal learning environments and university teacher roles explored using Delphi. Australas. J. Educ. Technol. **30**(2), 202–226 (2014)

Stansfield, J.L., Carr, B.P., Goldstein, I.P.: WUMPUS Advisor 1: a first implementation of a program that tutors logical and probabilistic reasoning skills, AI Memo 381, AI Laboratory, Massachusetts Institute of Technology (1976)

Turkle, S.: Alone Together: Why We Expect More from Technology and Less from Each Other. Basic Books, New York (2011). ISBN 1541697596

Tzouveli, P., Mylonas, P., Kollias, S.: An intelligent e-learning system based on learner profiling and learning resources adaptation. Comput. Educ. **51**(1), 224–238 (2008). https://doi.org/10. 1016/j.compedu.2007.05.005

Vygotsky, L.S.: Though and Language. In: Kozulin, A. (ed.) MIT Press, Cambridge (1934)

WebPA: An Online Peer Assessment System (2008). http://webpaproject.lboro.ac.uk. Accessed 13 Mar 2013

Willems, J.: The loneliness of the distance education student. In: Scevak, J., Cantwell, R. (eds.) Stepping Stones: A Guide for Mature-aged Students at University, pp. 83–92. ACER Press (2007). ISBN: 9780864314147. http://search.informit.com.au/documentSummary;dn=361659 693144693;res=IELHSS

Wood, D.J., Bruner, J.S., Ross, G.: The role of tutoring in problem solving. J. Child Psychiatry Psychol. **17**(2), 89–100 (1976)

Xie, Y.F., Szeto, G., Dai, J.: Prevalence and risk factors associated with musculoskeletal complaints among users of mobile handheld devices: a systematic review. Appl. Ergon. **59**, 132–142 (2017). https://doi.org/10.1016/j.apergo.2016.08.020

Zhuhadar, L., Nasraoui, O., Society, I.C.: Semantic information retrieval for personalized e-learning. Paper presented at the 20th IEEE International Conference on Tools with Artificial Intelligence, Dayton, OH, 03–05 November 2008

Research on Phonetic Indexing Interface in *Xinhua Dictionary Based on* Differences of English and Chinese Letters

Zimei Zhao[1], Xumin Wu[1], and Xun Liang[2]([⊠])

[1] Wuhan University of Technology, Wuhan 430070, Hubei, China
[2] Beijing Technology and Business University, Beijing 100048, China
kasino_zzm@163.com

Abstract. *Xinhua Dictionary* is an indispensable reference book in Chinese primary school teaching. However, through observation, it is found that due to the different pronunciations of English and Chinese letters, elementary school students who are beginners in language use the order of English capital letters as the phonetic index order. When using a Chinese character dictionary, phonetic confusion is easy to occur, which affects the retrieval efficiency. Based on the above questions, this paper combines the literature of linguistics and psychology to conduct an in-depth analysis around people, products and usage scenarios. A comparative study of letters and pronunciations that are easily confused between Chinese and English was conducted to explore the regularity of phonetic confusion. Experiment design was carried out on the preliminary summary of confusing phonetic sounds, to evaluate the prevalence of phonetic confusion problems, and to obtain pronunciations with higher confusion frequency. Integrate design elements and propose reasonable design solutions. At the same time, the redesign and usability test of the dictionary sequence retrieval interface are carried out. It is hoped that the research will shed light on the design improvement of user search interfaces in dictionaries and other reference books.

Keywords: English and Chinese phonetics · Syllable indexing · Dictionary retrieval · Human-computer interaction

1 Different Homonyms Between Chinese and English Letters Can Easily Cause Phonetic Confusion

In the early stage of the research, through direct observation, we observed 20 primary school students using the phonological indexing method to retrieve the example word '看' [kàn]. Through the 'User Journey Map' tool, the basic retrieval process of primary school students using the phonological indexing method can be summarized as 7 steps, as shown in Fig. 1.

P. Zaphiris and A. Ioannou (Eds.): HCII 2022, LNCS 13328, pp. 376–388, 2022.
https://doi.org/10.1007/978-3-031-05657-4_27

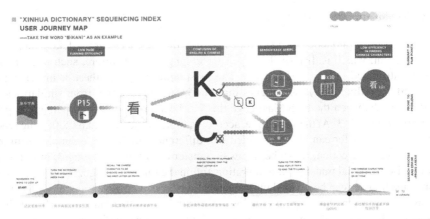

Fig. 1. User journey map of phonetic indexing in *Xinhua Dictionary* ——Taking the word '看' as an example.

Under the condition that the page turning efficiency is basically the same, the primary school students with slower indexing speed tend to lag behind in the third and fourth steps. This situation is mostly caused by 'recalling the first letter and judging the first letter of Pinyin' in the third step. There were mistakes in the link. The specific performance is that when they judge the pronunciation of '看', primary school students tend to confuse the Chinese pinyin letter 'k' with the letter 'C' which has /k/ pronunciation in English. Until they look for the syllable 'can' If the corresponding word is not found, the first letter of the pinyin is re-judged, and the initial letter 'K' in the pinyin is returned. To sum up, the English and Chinese phonetic confusion problem can easily lead to misjudgment of the first letter of the pinyin by primary school students, prolong the retrieval time, and affect the retrieval efficiency. Thus, it is preliminarily confirmed that the English and Chinese phonetic confusion will occur in the process of dictionary retrieval for primary school students.

2 Research on the Design of Retrieval Interface Based on Human-Computer Interaction Theory

Language is the only carrier of thinking, and 'speech or spoken language' is the acoustic image of language [1]. When conducting design research on the English and Chinese phonetic confusion in the phonological index and trying to improve it, it is bound to face the theoretical integration of linguistics, psychology, education and other disciplines. Human-computer interaction, as a comprehensive marginal discipline, can be combined with the theoretical knowledge and technical means of other basic disciplines, while combining the principles of visual communication design and interaction design to explore, so as to reveal the three elements of human, machine and environment. The law of the relationship between them [2]. Therefore, the researched literature information and pedagogical expert opinions are integrated, and the confusion problem is explored and summarized from the three aspects of users, products and usage scenarios.

2.1 Exploration from the User's Perspective

The problem of phonetic confusion occurs when the user sees capital letters and their arrangement, which is disturbed by the second language. Therefore, such phenomena can be attributed to language transfer. The most authoritative of these is the view put forward by Odlin (1989), who argues that 'the influence resulting from similarities or differences between the target language that has been previously (and perhaps imperfectly) acquired.' [3] At the same time, according to Javis and Pavlenko (2008), the types of language transfer can also be divided into different latitudes, for example, from the perspective of direction, it can be one-way transfer of different languages, or two-way or multi-directional transfer. Or a migration within the same language. From the results, language transfer can be divided into negative transfer and positive transfer. [4] Positive transfer is what one language promotes the learning of another language. This enables users to easily spell out the 'b', 'p' and other letters in Chinese Pinyin that have similar pronunciation habits to English letters. While negative transfer, named mother tongue interference, is mainly caused by the misinterpretation because of differences between their mother tongue and the second language [5]. The phonetic index interface of *Xinhua Dictionary* is not only sorted in uppercase English alphabetical order, but also uses uppercase letters Forms represent syllables. For elementary school students who lack subjective critical thinking and pay attention to imitation and perception [6] at the initial stage of English learning, it is easy to cause interference, resulting in phonetic confusion and affecting second language learning. However, the current research on negative language transfer is mostly concentrated in the fields of linguistics and education, and the research objects of Chinese phonetic transfer mainly focus on high school students and college students. The influence of English pronunciation [7], Li si-si (2015), based on the perceptual magnet effect, studies and analyzes the phenomenon of negative transfer in English pronunciation learning, and analyzes the causes of negative transfer [8]. However, most of them stay at the theoretical level, and there is a lack of quantitative data and design application research on the specific problem of speech confusion.

2.2 Exploration from a Product Perspective

Where there is a reference book, there must be an index. An index is a tool, and an index of a reference book is a tool of a tool. Lin Yushan (1989) once emphasized in his paper that the arrangement of index content is particularly important for dictionaries [9]. Regarding the setting of the phonetic index catalogue of the *Xinhua Dictionary*, Li Gongyi (1989) mentioned that although the phonetic indexing method rearranges the 417-syllable Chinese characters in the order of 23 English alphabets, the retrieval level is more concentrated. However, due to the 'unordered' characteristics of Chinese characters, it is difficult to retrieve Chinese characters, resulting in short distances for regular retrieval, wide retrieval area, and large number of characters to be searched, which affects retrieval efficiency [10]. At the same time, the reason for the practice of arranging the Chinese Pinyin search order in English alphabetical order is only briefly explained in the early journals as considering that the English alphabetical order is 'the easiest and most accurate arrangement in the world to find' [11]. It can be seen that at the beginning of the design of the phonological indexing method of *Xinhua Dictionary*, it did not take into account its own language characteristics and user needs. At the same time, it is not designed with the characteristics of user cognition.

2.3 Exploration from the Perspective of Usage Scenarios

Combining with the flow chart of human brain information processing proposed by Atkison & Shiffrin (1968), it can be found that when users use a dictionary to look up Chinese characters, they need to input the information of the Chinese characters they are looking up from the environment, and then enter the short-term memory after processing in the perceptual stage. [12] In order to prevent the loss of too much useful information from sensory memory, the brain will use the internal knowledge structure, such as general knowledge experience, cultural background, way of thinking and other subject factors to analyze and accept external stimuli [13] (Dember & Warm, 1979). However, the current usage situation is that when using the dictionary, the user needs to recall the phonetics of the searched Chinese characters and determine the initials. Then, recall the English alphabetical order and look for the first letter. Finally, associate Chinese phonetic sounds and judge syllables. In this case, the storage and processing of Chinese characters in short-term memory becomes very important.

3 Universal Assessment of English and Chinese Phonetic Confusion

Based on the above literature survey and expert consultation results, it further confirms the existence of English and Chinese phonetic confusion and its impact on indexing efficiency. The Dictionary phonetic indexing method has been in use since the 1950s, and there is no experimental data that can be cited to prove such a problem. Therefore, with the help of experimental research method, a quantitative study on the confusion of Chinese and English sounds in primary school students when retrieving dictionaries is carried out, and its universality is evaluated by the experimental results.

3.1 Experimental Procedure Design

Combined with the comparative research method, the phoneme comparison is carried out. To evaluate the universality of the pronunciation confusion of English and Chinese letters and summarize the easily confused letters and pronunciation, the pronunciation of English letters and Chinese pinyin letters, and the pronunciation of English letters in words are compared respectively, as shown in Table 1.

Table 1. Phonetic comparison of letters (Blue: Different phonemes. Yellow: Some phonemes are the same. Light Grey: Same Phoneme. dark grey: Not the first letter of Pinyin.)

Letters	Pinyin letters' pronunciation	English letters' pronunciation	The pronunciation of English letters in words			
Aa	/a/	/ei/	/ei/	/ai/	/ae/	/c/
Bb	/p/	/bi:/	/b/			
Cc	/tsʰ/	/si:/	/s/	/k/	/tʃ/	
Dd	/t/	/di:/	/d/			
Ee	/ɤ/	/i:/	/i:/	/ie/		
Ff	/f/	/ef/	/f/			
Gg	/k/	/dʒi:/	/dʒ/	/g/		
Hh	/x/	/eitʃ/	/h/			
Ii	/l/	/ai/	/i/			
Jj	/tɕ/	/dʒei/	/dʒ/			
Kk	/kʰ/	/kei/	/k/			
Ll	/l/	/el/	/l/			
Mm	/m/	/em/	/m/			
Nn	/n/	/en/	/n/	/n/		
Oo	/o/	/əu/	/əu/	/c/	/ʌ/	/u: /
Pp	/pʰ/	/pi:/	/p/			
Qq	/tɕʰ/	/kju:/	/k/			
Rr	/z/	/a:(r)/	/r/			
Ss	/s/	/es/	/s/	/tʃ/	/z/	
Tt	/tʰ/	/ti:/	/t/	/tʃ/	/θ/	
Uu	/u/	/ju:/				
Vv	/y/	/vi:/				
Ww	/w/	/ˈdʌblju:/	/o/			
Xx	/ɕ/	/eks/	/z/	/ks/	/gz/	
Yy	/i/或/y/	/wai/	/i/	/ai/		
Zz	/ts/	/zed/	/z/			

▮ Different phonemes　▮ Some phonemes are the same　▮ Same phoneme　▮ Not the first letter of Pinyin

Subsequently, through the circular chart, the pronunciation of the 23 pinyin initials in the dictionary phonetic index table was disassembled in Chinese and English. In the inner circle, in the form of a string diagram, summarize the confusion relationship between the first letters of the pinyin, and mark the single and complex vowels, initials and overall recognized syllables with similar pronunciations in different colors (the gray part is not easy to confuse the pronunciation). In the outermost circle, the number of rings indicates the easily confused frequency between the first letters of each pinyin, as shown in Fig. 2. And summarize the extracted information, see Table 2.

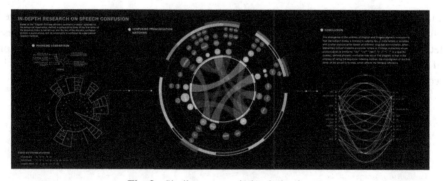

Fig. 2. Similar pronunciation induction

Table 2. A summary of confusing letters and sounds

Initials			Confused syllables	pronunciation	Confusing words
Aa	Ee		ei	/ei/	cake
Aa	Oo		ao	/ɔ/	our
Ee	Nn		en	/en/	—
Ee	Rr		er	/ɛ:/	bird
Cc	Ss		shi	/ʃ/	ocen
Cc	Ss		si	/s/	cenima
Cc	Kk		ka-,ke-,ko-,ku-	/k/	can
Qq	Kk		ku-	/k/	question
Ww	Oo		wu	/u:/	could
Zz	Gg	Jj	zhi	/dʒ/	suggest, jump
Zz	Xx		zi	/z/	xeric

It can be seen that the problem of English and Chinese speech confusion is due to the user's misjudgment of two or more letters or syllables with similar pronunciation based on different language environments. Not all letters will have phonological confusion, nor is it that English and Chinese letters with the same phoneme will not have phonological confusion (such as K). The emergence of English and Chinese phonetic confusion is partial, connected, and conditional. Therefore, the design of the experiment must be based on specific users and meet the usage scenarios of different language environments to evaluate the universality of the English and Chinese pronunciation confusion. The experimental process is shown in Fig. 3.

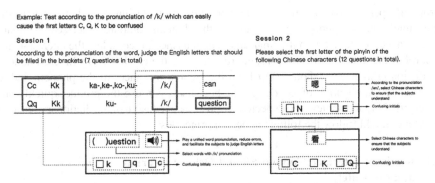

Fig. 3. Experimental procedure

3.2 Participants

The experiment was carried out in the No. 2 Experimental Primary School in Fangshan District, Beijing in May 2021. A total of 44 s-grade students who were receiving primary school Chinese teaching and who had mastered the phonological indexing method of *Xinhua Dictionary* participated in the experiment as subjects. The subjects included 21 boys and 26 girls, ranging in age from 7 to 9 years old. Before the experiment, each subject read the range of Chinese characters that may appear in the experiment (to ensure that they are familiar with the pronunciation) and was informed of the experimental procedure and points of attention.

3.3 Analysis of Results

After the experiment was carried out according to the above process, the experimental data were sorted out, and the experimental results were obtained as shown in Fig. 4.

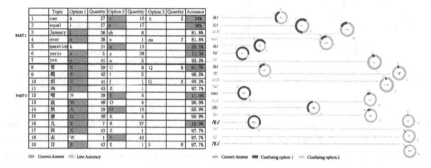

Fig. 4. Experimental results

4 Application Principles of Dictionary Search Interface Redesign

From the perspective of human-computer interaction design, the dictionary is the 'machine', and the phonetic index table is the 'human-computer interface'. Humans (users) need to interact with the 'man-machine interface' to complete the operation and control of the 'machine'. Therefore, in order to solve the English and Chinese phonetic confusion problem, we should start from the 'search interface' of the phonetic index. Through the application of the design method, users can use the product quickly and efficiently [14] and achieve the expected purpose. The redesign of the dictionary retrieval interface should follow the following design principles.

4.1 Retrieval Interface Content Should Deliver Information Quickly and Accurately

'Reading' is the process of obtaining information from visual materials [15]. The design of the retrieval interface is the process of visualizing information and making it easy to communicate. As a Chinese learning reference book, the content in the phonetic sequence retrieval interface of *Xinhua Dictionary* is mainly composed of Chinese pinyin letters, syllables, corresponding words and page numbers. Therefore, Pinyin letters can be redesigned with reference to the sorting characteristics and expression forms of Chinese Pinyin while satisfying the legibility and identification, focusing on the visual and sorting order to guide the user's indexing method, so that users can reduce the number of English letters. sequence association, so as to better integrate into the Chinese context. At the same time, in the selection of words corresponding to syllables, it is necessary to combine the cognitive range of primary school students. For confusing letters or syllables, visual codes such as size, color, and shape can be used to distinguish them, so as to enhance the recognition of the retrieval interface and alleviate the negative transfer of language.

4.2 The Principle of Proximity and Similarity

There are a total of 417 syllable combinations in Chinese Pinyin, and the current method of classifying and combining syllables with English initials is prone to confusion of English and Chinese pronunciation, and there are also problems such as serial indexing and low page turning efficiency. The principle of proximity and approximation are essentially the organizing principles for simplifying and integrating perceptual objects, that is, when people simplify cognitive objects, they tend to combine similar and close elements for cognition as a whole [16]. Therefore, in the design of the retrieval interface, it is possible to explore and try new alphabetical rules and arrangement sequences. While combining the psychological cognition and behavioral characteristics of users, it is necessary to have a logical and clear information structure and an easy-to-master retrieval process. Thereby, the syllable retrieval method is more effectively integrated, and the retrieval efficiency is improved.

4.3 The Principle of Consistency

Consistency has a direct impact on the user's mental ease of memory and load. Also, it is the source of the efficiency of product control [17]. In the process of designing, it is necessary to refine a theme or framework, and design through visual features and auxiliary elements to ensure that the structure, interface, style, operation of the *Xinhua Dictionary* retrieval interface is consistent with the user's mental model, so as to realize the retrieval process. systemic and complete. At the same time, in terms of style, redesign should be carried out around the psychological characteristics of primary school students, such as their strong curiosity, fondness for many colors, and memory characteristics based on mechanical memory and specific image memory [18]. On the premise of ensuring a clear and consistent search interface style and layout Next, pursue a certain artistic beauty. It can even further meet the higher-level needs of users, that is, emotional interaction, aesthetic taste, cultural belonging and added value needs.

5 Prototype Design and Usability Evaluation of Dictionary Search Interface

5.1 Retrieval Interface Content Should Deliver Information Quickly and Accurately

The dictionary was redesigned and prototyped by incorporating design elements. The improvement process is mainly divided into the following steps:

Alleviate Negative Language Transfer. By replacing English letters with Chinese pinyin letters and replacing the English arrangement order with pinyin order, the impact of negative English transfer of primary school students in the process of querying dictionaries is alleviated.

Improve Fault Tolerance. By refining the combination of Chinese pinyin letters (as shown in Fig. 5), the original five-page catalog was reduced to one page. At the same time, the order of the pages is rearranged, and the directory on the eleventh page that was originally located is placed on the cover of the dictionary, as shown in Fig. 6.

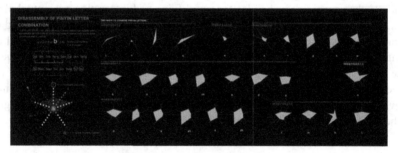

Fig. 5. Disassembly of pinyin letters' combination

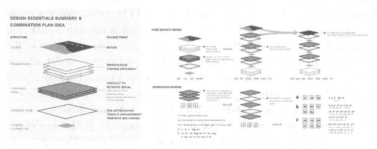

Fig. 6. Arrangement scheme design

While improving the indexing efficiency, it also reduces the time needed to turn to other pages due to speech confusion and improves the fault tolerance rate of negative language transfer. At the same time, in order to further verify the reading order with high retrieval efficiency, a variety of layout types of cover designs, such as left-to-right, top-to-bottom, and serpentine order, are carried out. Prepare for the next experimental session. Based on the above design process, a prototype of the dictionary is obtained, as shown in Fig. 7, and is ready for preliminary usability testing.

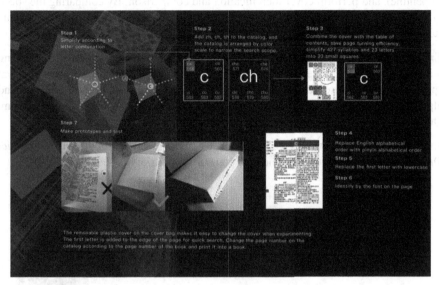

Fig. 7. Dictionary prototyping process diagram

5.2 Participants

The experiment was carried out in the No. 2 Experimental Primary School in Shijingshan District, Beijing in September 2021, and a total of 32 primary school students participated in the experiment. The subjects included 15 boys and 17 girls, ranging in age from 8 to 9 years old. Before the experiment, a dictionary retrieval test was performed on each participant, and the range of Chinese characters that may appear in the experiment was read (to ensure that they were familiar with the pronunciation of Chinese characters), and they were informed of the experimental process and points of attention.

5.3 Test Process Design and Result Analysis

On the basis of the dictionary prototype, in order to further explore the design key points of retrieval efficiency and the processing of pinyin letter coding types, three groups of experimental procedures were designed, and data was collected and analyzed. Before the start of the experiment, first select a sentence and let the participants spell it to test whether they can use the *Xinhua Dictionary* phonetic index method to search, after passing the test. Lead the participants to briefly sort out vowels, consonants, and overall recognition of syllables, and briefly familiarize themselves with the newly designed dictionary interface and usage process. After finishing the pre-experiment preparations, three groups of comparative experiments were carried out.

Experiment 1: Cover recognition comparison. Take out the three new retrieval interfaces arranged in different reading orders (from left to right, from top to bottom, and serpentine), and perform cover identification and comparison. By comparing the speed of indexing the same sentence, select the fastest retrieval interface A. By letting the subjects choose independently, the most popular dictionary cover B was counted.

Experiment 2: directory sorting comparison. Then, according to the order of unifying the reading order of the retrieval interface to A (the interface with the fastest retrieval speed), compare the retrieval speed of the two covers sorted by English alphabet and alphabetical order of Chinese Pinyin, and select the fastest average speed among them. Quick interface C.

Experiment 3: Indexing speed comparison. Compare B and C with the original *Xinhua Dictionary*, count the retrieval time, and compare the retrieval speed.

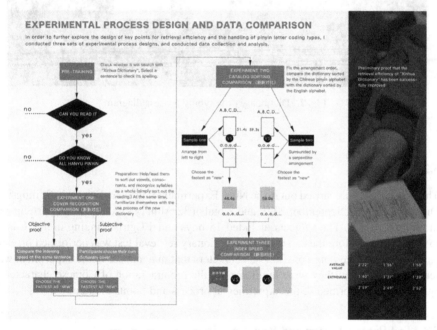

Fig. 8. Experimental process and data results

The above experimental process and the corresponding experimental results, as shown in Fig. 8, the user's favorite cover is the cover arranged in a serpentine structure, and the fastest retrieval speed is the interface with the reading order from left to right sorted by Chinese Pinyin, and the average retrieval time of this interface is shorter than that of *Xinhua Dictionary*, which preliminarily confirms the effectiveness of the design content.

6 Epilogue

English and Chinese phonetic confusion is a common but often overlooked problem in the phonological indexing method of *Xinhua Dictionary*, which affects the retrieval efficiency of primary school students for a long time. Scientific research methods lack in-depth research on the personality, age, and behavior of primary school students aged 6–12, and their application methods are also out of the essence of primary education [19]. Therefore, the viewpoints and experimental process proposed in this paper are not only the discovery and proof of potential pain points, but also a bold attempt to analyze and solve problems by combining multidisciplinary theoretical knowledge and using design tools. There is still room for improvement and improvement in its theoretical methods and experimental ideas. It is hoped that through analysis and research, it will play a positive role in the language learning process of primary school students and will have a certain role in improving the retrieval methods of dictionaries and other reference books for users. Inspirational meaning.

References

1. Liu Hao, F.: Language Transfer: Cross-linguistic Influence in Language Learning, 1st edn. China Textile Press, Beijing (2018)
2. Ding Yulan, F.: Ergonomics, 5th edn. Beijing Institute of Technology Press, Beijing (2017)
3. Terence Odlin, F.: Language Transfer: Cross-linguistic Influence in Language Learning, 1st edn. Cambridge University Press, Cambridge, UK (1989)
4. Scott Jarvis, F., Aneta Pavlenko, S.: Crosslinguistic Influence in Language and Cognition, 1st edn. Routledge, New York (1989)
5. Faerch, F., Kasper, S.: Perspectives on language transfer. Appl. Linguist. **8**(2), 111–136 (1987)
6. Meng Qingfeng, F.: On the negative transfer of Chinese pronunciation to oral English communication. Lang. Constr. **27**, 21–22 (2016)
7. Li Sisi, F.: Research on English phonetic acquisition based on the negative transfer of mother tongue. J. Changchun Inst. Educ. (03), 88–89+151 (2015)
8. Chai Yanzhen, F.: Research on the negative transfer phenomenon of high school students English phonetics acquisition from the perspective of the new curriculum. Ideol. Front **S1**, 273–276 (2013)
9. Li Gongyi, F.: The retrieval method of one pole to the end–introduction to the retrieval method of Chinese character information dictionary. Dict. Res. **05**, 99–103 (1989)
10. Lin Yushan, F.: On the index of reference books. Dict. Res. **04**, 85–90 (1989)
11. Wang Aiqin, F.: Question and answer on sound sequence searching method. Ningxia Educ. **08**, 26–36 (1985)
12. Wang Jun, F.: A Study on Foreigners' Acquisition of Chinese Characters, 1st edn. Peking University Press, Beijing (2020)
13. Dember, F., Warm, S.: Psychology of Perception, 1st edn. Holt, Rinehart & Winston, New York (1979)
14. Ruan Baoxiang, F.: Industrial Design Ergonomics, 3rd edn. Machinery Industry Press, Beijing (2017)
15. Ni Jincheng, F.: Cognitive Process and Validity of Interactive Reading Mode, 1st edn. Shanghai International Studies University Press, Shanghai (2013)
16. Liu Jin, F., Li Yue, S.: Breaking the Cocoon into a Butterfly–The Growth Road of User Experience Designers, 1st edn. People Post Press, Beijing (2014)

17. Chen Zhao-ni, F.: The application of cognitive psychology in UI interface. Packag. Eng. **38**(16), 30–33 (2017)
18. Guo Wei, F.: On the psychological characteristics of primary school students and effective classroom teaching. Curric. Educ. Res. (34), 154 (2018)
19. Liu He, F.: Problems and causes in the development of educational psychology in primary schools in my country. Asia Pac. Educ. **26**, 155–156 (2015)

Technology in Education: Practices and Experiences

Successful Erasmus+ Projects: Some Case Studies

María Goretti Alonso de Castro[1](✉) and Francisco José García-Peñalvo[2]

[1] Grupo de Investigación GRIAL, Doctorado Formación en la Sociedad del Conocimiento, Grupo de Investigación GRIAL, Universidad de Salamanca, Salamanca, Spain
malonsca@gmail.com
[2] Grupo de Investigación GRIAL, Departamento de Informática y Automática, Instituto Universitario de Ciencias de la Educación, Universidad de Salamanca, Salamanca, Spain
fgarcia@usal.es
https://ror.org/02f40zc51

Abstract. The analysis of successful projects provides valuable information for finding inspiration and learn from good practices to implement them in future projects. In the case of Erasmus+, there is a very rich project database with catalogued projects that allows access to them what is very useful to analyse the published data of good practice or success stories projects. In the research that is being carried out, reason for this article, a group of good practices or success story projects related to eLearning have been selected, they have been analysed based on the information found on the Erasmus+ Projects Results Platform, their coordinators have been surveyed to gather more information from the projects and interviews are being carried out with those coordinators whose projects have been, and continue to be, useful beyond the funding period even in the pandemic crisis. This article presents the methodology for the interviews and the first results obtained in four of them as an example. The main results for the success and sustainability have been the importance of analysing the needs of students and/or teachers in innovative themes, the integration of the project outcomes into the teaching-learning processes and a good relationship with the project partners. All that using ICT as a tool to better implement the project activities with an easy access from any place, at any time and with any type of device.

Keywords: Education · Technology · European projects · Interactive learning environments · Electronic learning

1 Introduction

The world is becoming increasingly technological with a greater use of Information and Communication Technologies (ICT) in the daily life of any person. Bank transactions, public administration management and shopping are becoming more digital and sometimes require the use of specific apps. This gives rise to the need to empower people with the necessary skills to participate effectively in a growingly digital world. However, as the OECD Trends Shaping Education 2022 [1] report points out *rapid technological*

P. Zaphiris and A. Ioannou (Eds.): HCII 2022, LNCS 13328, pp. 391–405, 2022.
https://doi.org/10.1007/978-3-031-05657-4_28

change is not always helping the most pressing social needs and, despite the increase in network connectivity, some feel alone and voiceless. Education is often the way to address the social challenges that arise, preparing people to be able to respond to them.

For this reason, in recent decades the use of digital technologies has been introduced to improve teaching-learning processes to improve education and find a way to deal with a challenging, complex, and constantly changing world. Additionally, COVID-19 pandemic broke out in 2020 causing our educational centres, teachers, students, and families to urgently adapt to distance learning methodologies using ICT. This crisis has shown the great need we have for advance in technological competence, especially in the field of education [2, 3].

Some examples of the interest in finding ways to improve educational processes are the multiple publications on ICT and eLearning. In the case of Higher Education there are several analyses regarding the digital transformation of teaching in the face of a methodological and skills crisis due to the COVID-19 pandemic [4–10].

To shed light on how to improve teaching, Grande-De-Prado et al. [11] has developed a guide of recommendations to provide tools to teachers and universities in the evaluation process motivated by the needs produced in the pandemic. In this way, it seeks to help many teachers who share this problem at this exceptional time throughout the planet. Mixed or distance classes have also been promoted in those places where it has not yet been possible to increase face-to-face classes.

The use of social networks for educational purposes, both before and after the lockdown, is a field that has also aroused great interest to analyse differences according to gender and the type of teaching at the university (face-to-face or online) [12].

In the field of Ibero-American educational institutions, analyses have also been carried out on the main difficulties encountered [13]. This analysis has led to the compilation of strategies used in the teaching and learning processes. An evaluation model was also designed together with the emergency situations in which they should be implemented, as well as possible special contingency plans.

Educational solutions have also been explored in collaborative environments, such as the case of the research on solving mathematical problems through cooperation with computer tools during the COVID-19 pandemic, which showed great motivation and learning results [14].

Learning through mobile learning in Higher Education has increased considerably and this has generated the need to evaluate good practices. For this reason, a system of quality indicators has been designed; it is composed with 25 indicators, grouped into 5 variables, aimed at university contexts that use the mobile learning methodology [15].

International and national institutions are aware of the need in achieving improvements in learning using ICT, including eLearning. In this area, an aspect detected in the International Computer and Information Literacy Study (ICILS) stands out, which indicates that although ICT are used by many teachers, the use for which they are intended is for solving simple tasks, not taking advantage of their potential for more complex tasks [16, 17].

To achieve improvements in educational institutions the European Union finances and promotes the development of European educational projects (https://bit.ly/3ABlri0). Through the Erasmus+ Program (https://bit.ly/3KNPLdV), as well as previous programs, numerous educational projects have been carried out in which new methodologies are analysed and explored to achieve the desired improvement in education.

All these facts are the motivation for the research presented in this article. Its purpose is to collect relevant information on the projects that are being developed in this field and extract indicators that make some of them to be considered good practice and success story. The objective is to extract useful lessons for future projects that can inspire educational centres that are starting or need ideas on how to develop projects with real impact and whose results can be sustainable and useful over time.

Next, different aspects of the research are presented, first, the state of the art related to the objectives pursued, followed by the methodology used to carry out the analysis of the projects, as well as the main results obtained so far. The article ends with the most outstanding conclusions.

2 Literature Review

It is necessary to set the scope of the research to adequately carry out the analysis of projects, for this reason it was decided to focus the study on the use of ICT in eLearning, since it is one of the areas in which the efficient use of these technologies for success is key in improving learning. Moreover, it is increasingly necessary to take advantage of the full potential of eLearning since its use has increased due to the pandemic.

Inclusive Virtual Education raises great interest to leave no one behind, recognizing the diversity of participants found in online courses and emphasizing the need to design and provide accessible educational platforms and resources [18].

The need to improve teacher training to adequately address distance education when face-to-face teaching is not possible, this has been highlighted in the recent situation due to COVID-19 [19, 20].

This type of teaching also helps all those who cannot continue their training in person, it allows lifelong learning in a flexible and optimal way, which is why it is a methodology in growing demand. In fact, some studies have been carried out on different methodologies that could enable flexible learning, such as:

- Mobile learning in Spain [21] evidenced the merely instrumental use, still scarce –although apparently growing.
- Mixed learning in Peru [22] shows the need to optimize the use of this methodology to achieve a more autonomous training, for a progressive insertion in the professional world.
- Joint programs and degrees [23] increase the mobility of students and teachers who often spend periods of study in the different participating institutions and provide opportunities for cooperation and peer learning between institutions.
- Smartphone use and its impact on attention [24], despite many unresolved questions about the effects of smartphone use on different domains of attention, smartphone use could have beneficial effects in certain processes.

- Interactive learning environments [25] can provide a more flexible learning approach that strengthens students' self-regulation of their learning process by providing services, tools, etc.

As regards to eLearning, the GRIAL group has numerous publications that analyse the current state and advances of eLearning, as well as the future trends of this teaching-learning methodology [26–28].

UNESCO has also analysed the effectiveness of eLearning [29] concluding that teaching through eLearning can make a great difference in learning. However, it pointed out that achieving an improvement in the learning results depends on the type of eLearning and the use made of it.

ICILS showed that schools and classrooms vary in the way teachers use ICT for instruction. Although eLearning is widely perceived as a means of achieving transformative effects in classrooms, its implementation has been relatively limited. Likewise, the effectiveness of ICT to promote learning seems to depend on educational practices and the ability to integrate digital technologies into teaching processes effectively [16, 17].

CEDEFOP [30] found the need of lifelong learning for the labour market with a combination of electronic resources and face-to-face interaction between students and teachers. The purpose is to make it possible to adapt the training to the context of the users and the time they have available.

UNESCO also promotes lifelong learning, including eLearning as one of the means to achieve it [31].

In addition, OECD, due to the recent COVID-19 pandemic, has published different reports with information related to the equipment in the centres and digital training of teachers and students, as well as school resources with data collected in the studies: Program for the Evaluation International Student Study (PISA) (https://bit.ly/3r0UOzv) and the Teaching and Learning International Survey (TALIS) (https://bit.ly/3KOU9tc), among others.

One of the main results of this work has been country notes explaining the main findings for OECD countries [32]. These country notes reflect how prepared were the educational systems based on the data collected through the studies in the field of ICT in education and allow reviewing the aspects that require the implementation of improvements in this field.

The European Union (EU) encourages the implementation of ICT-based projects in the European Educational Project Programs. In the case of Erasmus+, ICTs are one of the priorities and topics considered for project funding.

In the Erasmus Project Results Platform (E+ PRP) (https://bit.ly/3H6qJUT), which contains all the projects funded by the Erasmus+ Program and its predecessor programs in education, youth, and sport since 2007, we find more than 20,000 projects related to eLearning or ICT. These projects are classified; hence it allows the selection of those that are labelled as good practices or success stories.

In summary, all these analyses, and publications support the need to continue improving educational projects that involve ICT, including the eLearning projects that are the object of this research [33–40].

3   Methodology

The research presented in this article is based on a mixed methodology that combines quantitative and qualitative analysis [41], taking advantage of the combination of the strengths of each one to answer the research questions [42]. The guide for systematic reviews of research projects [43, 44] has been used as a reference to achieve that goal.

This methodology provides a way to analyse the projects, obtaining an overview of current trends and locating gaps and opportunities that help to define new advances in the field of research. In addition, this method allows comparing finalized projects and having an idea of the evolution of technological ecosystems [45] in the area of study.

The research process consists of four stages: study definition, selection definition, project selection and analysis. Presently, the research is on the analysis phase, in which we will try to quantitatively evaluate the first results obtained in relation to the common factors that have influenced the success of different Erasmus+ educational projects with eLearning or ICT, as well as the way in which the implementation, the results and the sustainability of these projects can help define guidelines to achieve good quality in future projects.

The analysis stage has been structured in three phases: firstly, the projects have been reviewed on the E+ PRP gathering the main data regarding their field of work, the results achieved, involved institutions, etc.; secondly, a questionnaire has been implemented and sent to the projects coordinators in order to collect important information related to their possible success and ICT used, and finally an interview phase is being carried out at the moment of writing this article, only with those projects with results sustainable along the time and with teachers or students involved.

The next two sections explore the questionnaire and the interview phases.

3.1   Questionnaire

The design of the survey has been based on diverse questionnaire design theories from different papers with the definition of different types of open or closed questions, the methodology, the way of writing the questions in clear language, grouped, and ordered, the recommended number of questions [46].

The survey is divided into six sections: Identification, Global aspects of the project, Students and ICT, Teachers and ICT, other aspects related to other areas in terms of the use and sustainability of the results obtained from the projects, among other things, and finally the main conclusions. It contained 21 questions, 19 with dichotomous options and 2 open-ended, and the average time to fill in it was 20 min.

It has been reviewed several questionnaires as a source of inspiration, such as the case the questionnaires of the ICILS Study [16, 17], the PISA Global Crisis Questionnaire Module of the OECD [47] and TALIS (https://bit.ly/3KOU9tc), in addition to the Erasmus+ Program Guide which specifies key aspects of impact indicators and the dissemination of Erasmus+ projects (https://bit.ly/3KNPLdV). All of them already tested and validated.

3.2 Interview

In all qualitative investigation, the interview as a technique is always linked to a research problem and this requires a specific strategy when thinking about its use. Therefore, it implies planning and designing it considering fundamental aspects of the investigation and the type of enquiry selected to collect the information. Depending on the objectives projected in the study, we will be guided towards the choice of the most appropriate type of interview for the collection of the necessary information in such a way as to guarantee the viability of the technique and the research work [41, 48].

The semi-structured interview modality is one in which the interviewees can be exposed to the same script, although with freedom in the axes that guide their answers, without forcing the order of the questions [41, 48].

For the research presented here, this modality has been chosen to collect information of interest from the interviewees in a friendly and open way, giving them the possibility of expressing themselves about the aspects that were of interest in relation to the success of the project. The three areas of interest were: first, to know to what extent and in what way teachers and students were involved; second, the usefulness of the results achieved in the project and its materials beyond its completion and, third, how these were useful in the pandemic.

With that goals the interview script was design (Table 1). The preparation of the interview script has been based on knowing specific aspects related to the areas already covered with the questionnaire but focused on the three areas indicated. And the implemented methodology is as follows:

1. First, questions related to the proposed topics have been considered, in addition to assessing the validity of the previous questionnaire.
2. Second, it has been analysed its link with the sections of the questionnaire (Table 2).
3. Third, the validity has been verified with the two initial interviewees.
4. Fourth, the interviews have been organized:

   a. An email was sent to all the coordinators of the selected projects that met the three proposed requirements.
   b. Those interested in collaborating have confirmed and it is established with them the day and date for the interview through Google Meet.
   c. Prior to the day of the interview, all the project information available on the E+ PRP and in the questionnaire is reviewed and included in the script file as background information.
   d. The interview is conducted in a friendly manner on the proposed day, transcribing the information related to the issues of interest.
   e. At the end of the interview, all the annotations are cleansed and sent to the interviewees so that they can review and correct what they consider necessary.

Once all the interviews are finished, a detailed analysis of all of them will be carried out using categorization to obtain quantitative data of the most significant qualitative aspects.

Table 1. Interview script.

Planned questions
1. One of the factors that can contribute to the success of educational projects is that they meet the real needs of the group of students or teachers for whom it is proposed, in the case of your project, what specific needs did you intend to solve in relation to the students and/or teachers?
2. Did you manage to solve your proposed needs? What improvements did you achieve in learning or teaching methods?
3. How were the students and teachers involved in the activities? Are they still participating today? How do they do it?
4. Was it focused on specific subjects or subjects or was it cross-cutting?
5. Are the results used in current teaching practice? Are they integrated into the educational project of the centre or institution?
6. Have the products developed in the project been transferred to other centres or institutions? Are they used by more groups than those who participated in the project during the funding period?
7. How have you managed to reach more groups? What dissemination activities have you done and continue to do?
8. Do you keep updating the materials you developed with the project?
9. What use was and is being made of ICT for the project? What have been the most outstanding ICT tools and methodologies and those that have had the most impact on improving learning?
10. Are the resources useful for online teaching or for eLearning? To what extent and how are they used?
11. In the previous questionnaire, you indicated that the resources had been useful to solve the problems that arose during the pandemic. How did you use the resources generated in the project during the confinement?
12. Have you carried out other subsequent projects based on what you achieved with this project?
13. What improvements would you propose in what has been developed so far with the project during and after the financing period?
Finally, it is very relevant to us to know your assessment in relation to the questionnaire you completed:
• Did you find it adequate in terms of the type of questions for the objectives that were posed?
• Did you find the questions pertinent to gather information on the purposes of the project, its main activities, use of ICT, dissemination, impact, and sustainability?
• Were the length and number of questions adequate? Was it easy for you to answer them?
• Was the time for completion as expected or did it take longer than expected?
• Was the interface used intuitive or did it cause you any problems?
• What aspects of the questionnaire would you improve?

Table 2. Mapping between the sections of the questionnaire and the interview questions.

Questionnaire section [38]	Interview questions
2. Global aspects of the project	1, 2, 3, 5, 10
3. Students and ICT	4, 9
4. Teachers and ICT	4, 9
5. Use and sustainability of the results obtained from the projects, among other things	6, 7, 8, 11, 12
6. Conclusions (open-ended questions)	5, 13

4 Results

The steps followed so far include the mapping of the projects based on specific criteria already defined [40, 41] and described below:

- They must be linked to the term eLearning/e-Learning (almost 10,000 projects).
- Only projects labelled as good practices or success stories (nearly 1,200 projects) are chosen.
- The key actions KA1 and KA2 are those in which schools are most involved.
- The interest is focused on those projects in which educational centres participate because they are an important element to analyse the improvement in the learning process. Therefore, those projects that did not involve educational centres were excluded.

The number of projects that met the first three requirements was 1,144 projects, of which 256 did not have any educational centre involved.

Once the projects meeting those criteria were filtered, contact information was collected using the data available on the E+ PRP (https://bit.ly/3H6qJUT) or on the websites of the coordinators and/or partners. There were 39 projects for which it was not possible to find a contact email nor a phone number. Therefore, the total number of institutions contacted was 849. The questionnaire was sent to all these contacts, from which responses were obtained for 187 projects, giving a response rate of 22%. Several analyses have been carried out with those results presented on different papers [34–39].

Once the questionnaire phase was finished an interview phase has started with those projects that indicated in the survey that the results of them proved useful during the pandemic and had the participation of both students and teachers in its exploitation and implementation, in addition to use and generate valuable digital resources for the community and they are still useful today. Only 58 projects meet those three requirements. The coordinators of these projects have been contacted to arrange an interview and presently 22 coordinators have confirmed to participate in the interview, of which, at the time of writing this article, 10 interviews have been carried out.

4.1 Main Results from the Questionnaire

The most outstanding results obtained through the questionnaire have been:

- Regarding the administration of the survey, the contact data of the project coordinators collected from the platform and its websites were used. At the same time, summaries of projects, as well as their results, were collected to obtain as much information as possible. The response rate of the survey has been 22%, which is adequate to obtain data of interest on projects.
- The most indicated success factors in relation to the projects are: attending to the real and concrete needs of the students and teachers of the educational sector of the project, coordination and collaboration of all the partners of the project before, during and after the project, sustainability of the project over time, since it continues to be used and updated, participation and involvement of teachers and students from the educational sector of the project.
- In the case of students and the use of ICT in projects, it should be noted that the most represented sector is School Education. ICT tools used by students focus on basic skills related to office management and presentations, as well as collaboration platforms. Regarding ICT devices, both laptops and desktops are the most used.
- In relation to teachers and their use of ICT, the results are very similar to those of students, School Education is also the most prominent sector, followed by Vocational Education and Training, Higher Education and Adult Education. ICT tools used by teachers are also related to office automation, presentations, and collaboration platforms. In addition, video and photo editing, the use of network resources and the digital learning environment. As regards as ICT devices, both laptops and desktops are the most used, and depending on the educational field, tablets and smartphones are also very common.
- In general, for more than 50% of the projects surveyed, it can be said that the results have been positive with sufficient funds to be able to carry them out and with the capacity to continue using them after the end of the funding period. In addition, they have also been useful on COVID-19. Small variations are observed between educational fields, although not very pronounced. The sector that differs most is Adult Education, a fact that is normal because it is a different target audience and includes continuous training processes.

4.2 Main Results from the Interview

In relation to the interview phase, it is still in progress, however, with the current progress, some aspects can be glimpsed that deserve to be considered. To begin with, it is worth pointing out the characteristics of the 4 projects that have been interviewed:

- Type of projects:

  - 1 KA1 project from Vocational Education and Training (VET) field (KA102).
  - 3 KA2 projects (strategic partnerships): 1 from School Education field (KA209), 1 from the Youth field (KA205), 1 from the Vocational Education and Training field (KA202).

- 2 of them of 2017, 1 of 2016, and 1 of 2014.

– Main facts identified in the projects:

- 2014 - KA202:

  - The objective was to build a solid knowledge base and source of information on the state-of-the-art intrapreneurial training and competences for successful implementation. It was implemented the Intrapreneurial Training Programme during the project.
  - The project was very innovative and therefore still valid, it has had projection until now. A great advance has been seen working on intrapreneurship within companies, employees can contribute a lot to improve their processes and opportunities.
  - The approach is aimed at promoting the continuous training of the personnel of technology companies with material for online or face-to-face training available.
  - Each institution adapts it to its needs and integrates it into its training platforms. During the lockdown for COVID-19, support continued with audio-conferences and videoconferences with the complete Microsoft Office package, Google Drive to collaborate and share project documents and Skype.

- 2016 - KA205:

  - It was designed to meet the need of a small town with little offer for young people in holidays seasons outside the school period. It was intended for a very closed area and far from big cities, where the diversity of cultural offer was scarce, and a solution was needed. The teachers assisted in the planning and design of the activities.
  - It guarantees its sustainability through the creation of a network with local institutions, NGOs, companies, communities, schools, sports clubs, City Halls with the resources of the project.
  - They have also created 4 free clubs for art and culture, another for science and technology, sports and outdoor activities, citizenship and entrepreneurship that are still working.
  - They used technology and robotics for students of some countries and a Moodle platform was made for the training of the monitors and during the period to carry out an assessment of the children's competencies after the technology-based activities to see the results obtained.

- 2017 – KA102:

  - Nursing assistant student mobilities were proposed with the clear objective of improving the labour insertion of students and 100% has been achieved. Teachers carried out mobilities to make contacts with health institutions and for job shadowing in the VET School partners.

- The teachers managed to learn how other VET Schools managed the training in work centres in three different countries, which is very useful for them, they tried to broaden horizons for the students in their apprenticeship period.
- They have a stable relationship with the partners, hence the activities and mobilities between schools go on project after project.
- They got a great improvement at the level of languages and ICT learning. They used specific software of nursing assistant profession and also collaborative working tools. For distance learning and online coordination at specific times they use Google Meet, Blackbloard, WhatsApp, and the website and social networks for dissemination.

- 2017 - KA219:

  - It was intended for improving the cultural and foreign language competencies of the students within the centres involved, as well as the use of ICT in the classroom.
  - All teaching staff and students participated actively, bilingualism have been established because of the project and the project materials were applied with the subjects indicated above and are still used today.
  - Due to the success of the relationships between the partners, they have managed to improve the relations between schools and continue to carry out joint activities.
  - For distance learning they mainly used eTwinning for exchanging ideas/resources/videos and dissemination, as well as Microsoft Teams, Zoom and Skype.

In short, some common aspects of the projects analysed are that they met the needs of their students and/or teachers and are associated with innovative topics that have a real incidence and use in the institutions involved, furthermore, they can be extended or transferred to stakeholders or peers. The learning outcomes and materials developed are used until now, adapted and integrated into the teaching processes, even sometimes in the curricula or students' jobs afterwards. In addition, they have coordinated very well with the partners keeping their relationship and implementing successive projects and, even in some cases, they have created networks. Regarding the use of ICT, all the projects used them as a complement to facilitate teaching and communication processes not as the main goal.

5 Conclusions

The research work presented in this article has as its main goal to provide effective indicators for teachers to design their projects, involving electronic learning, in a more effective way.

To provide a valuable guide for teachers, the educational projects collected on the Erasmus+ Projects Results Platform are being analysed. This allows an analysis of the type of projects, results, and topics and sees those classified as good practice or success stories. This database is the primary tool for collecting information together with the collaboration of the main participants of those projects that have been successful.

The analysis methodology used is that provided by the guidelines for a systematic review of research projects.

Currently, the research is in the phase of analysis and collection of additional information. The first stage was to analyse and gather information provided on the E+ PRP with Erasmus+ educational projects classified as good practice and related to ICT and/or eLearning of the key actions 1 and 2 of Erasmus+ with educational centres involved. The second stage has been the design of an online survey that was sent to all eligible project coordinators. It was finally completed by 187 and with them a preliminary analysis of the data provided through the survey has been carried out.

Afterwards, the next stage consists in conducting interviews with those institutions selected for having projects in which teachers and/or students have been involved, the results continue to be useful and have also been so due to the pandemic. The interview phase will be from December 2021 to May 2022. A script was prepared, the institutions have been contacted, and the interviews are being carried out presently. When this phase is over and after the analysis of the results, a focus group will be held to jointly analyse all the results collected and how they can help and serve as an example. educational centres in improving teaching-learning processes.

As main results so far, it is interesting to highlight the importance of analysing the needs of students and/or teachers in innovative topics that have a real incidence and use in the institutions involved. Adapt and integrate the project, its results and/or outcomes into the teaching-learning processes (the curricula, the educational project, etc.). Additionally, it is desirable to have a good and stable relationship with most of the partners.

In summary, the analysis of all the data collected in the different phases will allow teachers and teacher trainers to be guided to know the key factors for a good design of educational projects, as well as an optimal use of ICT resources and a real impact on the teaching-learning process.

Acknowledgments. This research work has been carried out within the Doctoral Program in Education in the field of the Knowledge Society of the University of Salamanca (http://knowledge society.usal.es) [49, 50] with the tutoring and supervision of Francisco José García-Peñalvo, as well as the support available from the University of Salamanca and specifically from the GRIAL group [51].

References

1. OECD: Trends Shaping Education 2022. OECD Publishing, Paris (2022)
2. Daniel, S.J.: Education and the COVID-19 pandemic. Prospects **49**(1–2), 91–96 (2020). https://doi.org/10.1007/s11125-020-09464-3
3. García-Peñalvo, F.J., Corell, A.: The COVID-19: the enzyme of the digital transformation of teaching or the reflection of a methodological and competence crisis in higher education? Campus Virtuales **9**, 83–98 (2020)
4. Cabero-Almenara, J., Llorente-Cejudo, C.: Covid-19: radical transformation of digitization in university institutions. Campus Virtuales **9**, 25–34 (2020)
5. Dietrich, N., et al.: Attempts, successes, and failures of distance learning in the time of COVID-19. J. Chem. Educ. **97**, 2448–2457 (2020)

6. Fatani, T.H.: Student satisfaction with videoconferencing teaching quality during the COVID-19 pandemic. BMC Med. Educ. **20**, 1–8 (2020)
7. García-Peñalvo, F.J.: Avoiding the dark side of digital transformation in teaching: an institutional reference framework for elearning in higher education. Sustainability **13**, 2023 (2021)
8. García-Peñalvo, F.J.: Digital transformation in the universities: implications of the COVID-19 pandemic. Educ. Knowl. Soc. **22**, 1 (2021)
9. Gatti, T., et al.: Practices at Coimbra Group Universities in response to the COVID-19: a collective reflection on the present and future of higher education in Europe. Coimbra Group (2020)
10. García-Peñalvo, F.J., Corell, A., Abella-García, V., Grande-de-Prado, M.: online assessment in higher education in the time of COVID-19. Educ. Knowl. Soc. **21** (2020)
11. Grande-de-Prado, M., García-Peñalvo, F.J., Corell, A., Abella-García, V.: Higher education assessment during COVID-19 pandemic. Campus Virtuales **10**, 49–58 (2021)
12. Gil-Fernández, R., León-Gómez, A., Calderón-Garrido, D.: Influence of COVID on the educational use of social media by students of teaching degrees. Educ. Knowl. Soc. **22** (2021)
13. Fardoun, H., González-González, C.S., Collazos, C.A., Yousef, M.: exploratory study in iberoamerica on the teaching-learning process and assessment proposal in the pandemic times. Educ. Knowl. Soc. **21** (2020)
14. Knopik, T., Oszwa, U.: E-cooperative problem solving as a strategy for learning mathematics during the COVID-19 pandemic. Educ. Knowl. Soc. **22**, e25176 (2021)
15. Aznar Díaz, I., Cáceres Reche, M.P., Romero Rodríguez, J.M.: Quality indicators to evaluate good teaching practices of mobile learning in Higher Education. Educ. Knowl. Society **19**, 53–68 (2018)
16. Fraillon, J., Ainley, J., Schulz, W., Friedman, T., Gebhardt, E.: Preparing for life in a digital age. In: The IEA International Computer and Information Literacy Study International Report. Springer, Cham (2014). https://doi.org/10.1007/978-3-319-14222-7
17. Fraillon, J., Ainley, J., Schulz, W., Friedman, T., Duckworth, D.: Preparing for life in a digital age. In: IEA International Computer and Information Literacy Study 2018 International Report. Springer, Cham (2020)
18. Crisol-Moya, E., Herrera-Nieves, L., Montes-Soldado, R.: Virtual education for all: systematic review. Educ. Knowl. Soc. **21** (2020)
19. García-Peñalvo, F.J., Corell, A., Abella-García, V., Grande-de-Prado, M.: Recommendations for mandatory online assessment in higher education during the COVID-19 pandemic. In: Burgos, D., Tlili, A., Tabacco, A. (eds.) Radical Solutions for Education in a Crisis Context. COVID-19 as an Opportunity for Global Learning, pp. 85–98. Springer Nature, Singapore (2021). https://doi.org/10.1007/978-981-15-7869-4_6
20. García-Peñalvo, F.J., Corell, A., Rivero-Ortega, R., Rodríguez-Conde, M.J., Rodríguez-García, N.: Impact of the COVID-19 on higher education: an experience-based approach. In: García-Peñalvo, F.J. (ed.) Information Technology Trends for a Global and Interdisciplinary Research Community, pp. 1–18. IGI Global, Hershey (2021)
21. Fuentes, J.L., Albertos, J., Torrano, F.: Towards the mobile-learning in the school: analysis of critical factors on the use of tablets in spanish schools. Educ. Knowl. Soc. **20**, 1–17 (2019)
22. Turpo-Gebera, O., Hurtado-Mazeyra, A.: Scientific productivity on blended learning in peru: approaches to its evolution from university theses. Educ. Knowl. Soc. **20** (2019)
23. Delgado, L.: Joint programmes and degrees in the european higher education area. Educ. Knowl. Soc. **20** (2019)
24. Liebherr, M., Schubert, P., Antons, S., Montag, C., Brand, M.: Smartphones and attention, curse or blessing? - a review on the effects of smartphone usage on attention, inhibition, and working memory. Comput. Human Behav. Rep. **1**, 100005 (2020)

25. Conde-González, M.Á., García-Peñalvo, F.J., Rodríguez-Conde, M.J., Alier, M., García-Holgado, A.: Perceived openness of Learning Management Systems by students and teachers in education and technology courses. Comput. Hum. Behav. **31**, 517–526 (2014)
26. García-Peñalvo, F.J., Seoane-Pardo, A.M.: An updated review of the concept of eLearning: tenth anniversary. Educ. Knowl. Soc. **16**, 119–144 (2015)
27. García-Peñalvo, F.J.: Learning analytics as a breakthrough in educational improvement. In: Burgos, D. (ed.) Radical Solutions and Learning Analytics: Personalised Learning and Teaching Through Big Data, pp. 1–15. Springer, Singapore (2020). https://doi.org/10.1007/978-981-15-4526-9_1
28. García-Peñalvo, F.J.: Reference model for virtual education at face-to-face universities. Campus Virtuales **9**, 41–56 (2020)
29. Chatelier, G., Voicu, L.: E-Learning within the framework of unesco. In: Proceedings of the Fourteenth International Conference on eLearning for Knowledge-Based Society, 18 March 2018. Assumption University, Thailan, (2018)
30. CEDEFOP: Más que nuevos empleos: la innovación digital como apoyo a la trayectoria profesional. European Commission (2019)
31. Elfert, M.: UNESCO's Utopia of Lifelong Learning: An Intellectual History. Routledge, London, UK (2018)
32. OCDE: School education during COVID-19: Were teachers and students ready? Country notes (2020)
33. Alonso de Castro, M.G., García-Peñalvo, F.J.: Methodological guide for the successful use of digital technologies in education. Improvement of learning through European educational projects. In: García-Peñalvo, F.J. (ed.) Proceedings TEEM 2020, Eighth International Conference on Technological Ecosystems for Enhancing Multiculturality, Salamanca, Spain, 21–23 October 2020. ACM, New York (2020)
34. Alonso de Castro, M.G., García-Peñalvo, F.J.: Overview of european educational projects on elearning and related methodologies: data from erasmus+ project results platform. In: García-Peñalvo, F.J. (ed.) Proceedings TEEM 2020. Eighth International Conference on Technological Ecosystems for Enhancing Multiculturality, Salamanca, Spain, 21–23 October 2020. ACM, New York (2020)
35. Alonso de Castro, M.G., García-Peñalvo, F.J.: Erasmus+ educational projects on eLearning and related methodologies: data from erasmus+ project results platform. In: García-Peñalvo, F.J. (ed.) Information Technology Trends for a Global and Interdisciplinary Research Community, pp. 111–133. IGI Global, Hershey (2021)
36. Alonso de Castro, M.G., García-Peñalvo, F.J.: Most used ICT methodologies for student learning in Erasmus+ projects related to eLearning. In: Balderas, A., Mendes, A.J., Dodero, J.M. (eds.) Proceedings of the 2021 International Symposium on Computers in Education (SIIE), Málaga, Spain, 23–24 September 2021. IEEE, USA (2021)
37. Alonso de Castro, M.G., García-Peñalvo, F.J.: ICT methodologies for teacher professional development in Erasmus+ projects related to eLearning. In: García-Holgado, A., García-Peñalvo, F.J., González-González, C.S., Infante-Moro, A., Infante-Moro, J.C. (eds.) Proceedings XI JICV 2021, XI International Conference on Virtual Campus, Salamanca, Spain, 30 September–1 October 2021. IEEE, USA (2021)
38. Alonso de Castro, M.G., García-Peñalvo, F.J.: Outstanding methodologies in Erasmus+ projects related to eLearning. In: Alier, M., Fonseca, D. (eds.) Proceedings TEEM 2021. Ninth International Conference on Technological Ecosystems for Enhancing Multiculturality, Barcelona, Spain, 27–29 October 2021, pp. 657–661. ACM, New York (2021)

39. Alonso de Castro, M.G., García-Peñalvo, F.J.: ICT tools highlighted and their usefulness during the pandemic: Erasmus+ projects related to eLearning. In: Alier, M., Fonseca, D. (eds.) Proceedings TEEM 2021. Ninth International Conference on Technological Ecosystems for Enhancing Multiculturality, Barcelona, Spain, 27–29 October 2021, pp. 219–224. ACM, New York (2021)
40. Alonso de Castro, M.G., García-Peñalvo, F.J.: Successful educational methodologies: Erasmus+ projects related to e-learning or ICT. Campus Virtuales **11** (2022)
41. Creswell, J.W.: Research Design: Qualitative, Quantitative, and Mixed Methods Approaches. SAGE, Thousand Oaks (2013)
42. Creswell, J.W., Klassen, A.C., Plano Clark, V.L., Smith, K.C.: Best practices for mixed methods research in the health sciences. Office of Behavioral and Social Sciences Research. National Institutes of Health, EEUU (2011)
43. García-Holgado, A., Marcos-Pablos, S., Therón, R., García-Peñalvo, F.J.: Technological ecosystems in the health sector: a mapping study of European research projects. J. Med. Syst. **43**, 1–11 (2019)
44. García-Holgado, A., Marcos-Pablos, S., García-Peñalvo, F.J.: Guidelines for performing systematic research projects reviews. Int. J. Interact. Multimedia Artif. Intell. **6**, 136–144 (2020)
45. García-Holgado, A., García-Peñalvo, F.J.: Validation of the learning ecosystem metamodel using transformation rules. Futur. Gener. Comput. Syst. **91**, 300–310 (2019)
46. García Alcaraz, F., Alfaro Espín, A., Hernández Martínez, A., Molina Alarcón, M.: Diseño de Cuestionarios para la recogida de información: metodología y limitaciones. Revista Clínica de Medicina de Familia **1**, 232–236 (2006)
47. Bertling, J., Rojas, N., Alegre, J., Faherty, K.: A tool to capture learning experiences during Covid-19: the PISA Global Crises Questionnaire Module. OECD Education Working Papers (2020)
48. Schettini, P., Cortazzo, I. (eds.): Técnicas y estrategias en la investigación cualitativa. Editorial de la Universidad Nacional de La Plata (EDULP), Argentina (2016)
49. García-Peñalvo, F.J.: Education in the Knowledge Society, an interdisciplinary PhD Programme. Educ. Knowl. Soc. **15**, 4–9 (2014)
50. García-Peñalvo, F.J., Rodríguez-Conde, M.J., Verdugo-Castro, S., García-Holgado, A.: Portal del Programa de Doctorado Formación en la Sociedad del Conocimiento. Reconocida con el I Premio de Buena Práctica en Calidad en la modalidad de Gestión. In: Durán Ayago, A., Franco Pardo, N., Frade Martínez, C. (eds.) Buenas Prácticas en Calidad de la Universidad de Salamanca: Recopilación de las I Jornadas. REPOSITORIO DE BUENAS PRÁCTICAS, (Recibidas desde marzo a septiembre de 2019, pp. 39–40. Ediciones Universidad de Salamanca, Salamanca (2019)
51. García-Peñalvo, F.J., Rodríguez-Conde, M.J., Therón, R., García-Holgado, A., Martínez-Abad, F., Benito-Santos, A.: Grupo GRIAL. IE Comunicaciones Revista Iberoamericana de Informática Educativa, 33–48 (2019)

User Experience of Universal School-Based e-Mental Health Solutions

Exploring the Expectations and Desires of Adolescent Users

Erfan Badawi[✉], Constantinos K. Coursaris, Sylvain Sénécal,
and Pierre-Majorique Léger

HEC Montréal, Montréal, Canada
{erfan.badawi,constantinos.coursaris,sylvain.senecal,pml}@hec.ca

Abstract. Due to lack of in-person social interactions and stressful conditions resulting from schools' closures, major lockdowns, and other restrictions imposed for preventing the further spread of COVID-19, there has been a great concern regarding adolescents' mental well-being and their access to mental health resources. Now, e-mental health resources that schools can develop and offer to all their students could play a much more important role: as a valuable, accessible, and affordable means for educating and empowering adolescents to maintain a balanced mental and emotional well-being. In this paper, we aim to explore the expectations and desires of adolescent students from the user experience of universally delivered school-based e-mental health solutions. Through conducting qualitative exploratory interviews with adolescent students and performing contextual analysis, we have identified the core needs, expectations and desires that were shared between high school students pertaining to e-mental health resources. By reporting our findings via diagrams and tables, we offer HCI/UX designers and developers a means to help them create a better strategy for their universal e-mental health solutions and put a more focused effort into addressing the core needs, expectations, and desires of adolescent students from said solutions: first, by providing them the solutions' must-haves (the identified user expectations from the UX of e-mental health solutions), and then, by targeting to include the solutions' nice-to-haves (the identified factors that can make the experience of e-mental health solutions more desirable for the students).

Keywords: School-based mental health interventions · E-Mental health · Computer-based learning · Human-computer interaction · User experience · User needs

1 Introduction and Background

1.1 Current State of Adolescent Students' Mental Health

Recent grey literature surrounding North American adolescents' mental health reveal that psychological distress, anxiety and depression symptoms have been rapidly rising

© The Author(s), under exclusive license to Springer Nature Switzerland AG 2022
P. Zaphiris and A. Ioannou (Eds.): HCII 2022, LNCS 13328, pp. 406–419, 2022.
https://doi.org/10.1007/978-3-031-05657-4_29

among the youth, especially since the start of the COVID-19. Compared to other age-groups, Canadian adolescents have experienced the greatest decline in their mental well-being due to the restrictions imposed for preventing the further spread of COVID-19 [1]. The results of Statistics Canada's 2021 crowdsourced data on the topic of children and youth's health show 57% of adolescents aged 15–17 had self-reported to be in 'worse' or 'much worse' mental health condition compared to their condition before COVID-19 era's drastic measures, i.e., several months with complete lockdown, schools' closures, and strict physical distancing measures across Canada [2]. Similarly, in the US, studies found adolescents' stress, anxiety, and depression symptoms have been rising. In October 2020, American Psychological Association (APA) declared a national mental health crisis after publishing the results of its study which was conducted through surveying the US residents of different age groups during the pandemic: in APA's report, from 1,026 adolescent students aged 13–17 who responded to the survey, 43% stated their life stresses had increased since the start of the pandemic [3].

1.2 The Schools' Role in Addressing Adolescents' Mental Health Needs

Due to adolescents' alarming mental health conditions and lack of access to mental health resources and education, the high school setting could become the optimal resource center for educating the students and for providing them the appropriate tools and resources for their mental health, and specifically, by doing so through accessible and non-discriminatory universal mental health programs. Compared to targeted programs which focus on risk status of the students for mental illness prevention and/or treatment, the universal programs either deliver general mental health education and resources throughout the school or provide grade-specific programs – tailored to the specific needs of the students' age and grade – as part of the formal curriculum or as an after-school activity [4].

When designing a universal mental health intervention program, schools can choose to use information and communications technology to their benefit by developing an e-mental health[1] solution either as an extension to their program or as the primary method of the program's delivery. Through e-mental health solutions, which could be comprised of web-based, mobile and/or other kinds of digital and online applications and interfaces, schools can deliver inexpensive, flexible, timely, and readily available access to mental health resources for their students which would have been otherwise not possible for them [6].

1.3 Research Objectives

As we saw a great need – especially due to concerns raised since the start of COVID-19 pandemic – for better understanding adolescent students' subjective experiences with universal school-based e-mental health resources, and since we found it to be a gap

---

[1] As outlined by Mental Health Commission of Canada, e-mental health is an umbrella term for mental health services and resources delivered or enhanced through the use of information and communications technologies, including internet and computerized resources and apps, peer support platforms through social media or other technologies [5].

in the qualitative academic literature, we attempted to identify the factors that could positively impact the overall user experience of these resources for their adolescent end-users. More specifically, we sought to learn the subjective opinions, experiences, and preferences of adolescent users regarding both e-mental health and traditional mental health programs in order to better understand what kind of experience they expect to have with school-based e-mental health programs and how these programs can become more desirable for them.

In this paper, we aim to uncover some of the main expectations and desires of adolescent users from universal e-mental health solutions' user experience, and also to specify how schools can target the users' expectations and desires when developing/redesigning an e- mental health solution or when developing/redesigning the activities and features offered inside it. Our goal is to present human-computer interaction (HCI) and user experience (UX) designers and developers a means to help their universal school-based e-mental health solutions meet the needs, expectations and desires of its intended users, and as a result, increase the likelihood that these solutions could provide a more satisfactory experience for their users.

Through our exploratory study, we hope to extend the body of knowledge in the context of the needs specific to adolescents' mental health, also contribute to the practice by informing the user experience of e-mental health solutions. At a broader level, our methodological approach may be used in other situational contexts thereby contributing to advancing the body of knowledge pertaining to HCI and UX studies concerning adolescents' well-being.

2 Key Concepts

In this section, we will briefly present the definitions of key HCI/UX-related concepts used in this paper, also when applicable, the extent to which the definition would apply to the context of our research.

2.1 User Experience

Adapted from the definition provided by International Organization for Standardization (ISO), we define the user experience (UX) of a specific universal school-based e-mental health solution for an individual user as the user's perceptions, opinions, beliefs, also emotional, behavioral, and other psychological and physiological responses resulting from interacting with and anticipating using the solution [7]. Since our exploratory study's scope does not include any stakeholders other than the intended end-users of universal e-mental health solutions, i.e., adolescent students, we will only focus and comment on the experiences that these solutions provide for them.

2.2 Expectations from the User Experience

In accordance with our definition of *user experience*, expectations from the user experience for an adolescent student is defined as the individual's anticipations and/or predictions – based on past experiences, knowledge, and intuitive feelings – from the experience of using and continuing the use of a specific solution. Therefore, in this paper, the interchangeable terms "expectations from the UX" and "user expectations", which could also be translated as what users consider to be a "solution's must-haves", would encompass any anticipated or predicted emotional, behavioral, physical, mental, belief-related, and achievement-related outcome for the end-user.

2.3 User Desires from the User Experience

In accordance with our definitions of *user experience* and *user expectations* related to universal school-based e-mental health solutions, we define an individual user's desires from the user experience of a solution to encompass not only the user expectations, i.e., the *solution's must-haves*, but also additional factors that would make the experience more desirable for the user, i.e., the "solution's nice-to-haves".

2.4 Core User Needs

To uncover and identify the user expectations and desires from the UX of e-mental health resources, especially the ones that were not explicitly expressed by the participants, we deemed it necessary to use a classification model that could explain what underlying factors were driving the users' experiences with e-mental health resources. For this purpose, we adapted the *Four Fundamental Human Needs*[2] model to classify our findings. This model which proved to have close similarities with the direction and objective of our study, can help explain the behaviors of digital consumers and support digital disruptors in creating better product strategies [8].

  We will illustrate how we adapted this model to classify our participants' core needs – the main factors driving and defining their experiences with e-mental health resources – later and in our results section (see Table 1).

3 Methodology

3.1 Research Questions

To reach our research objectives and explore the areas that would require special attention from HCI/UX developers in order to increase the likelihood that the experience of their universal school-based e-mental health solutions could meet the expectations and desires of its adolescent users, we adopted a qualitative methodology. The specific research questions on which we focused in our exploratory qualitative study were the following:

1. What are the main factors that drive the adolescent students' experiences with universal school-based e-mental health solutions?
2. What do adolescent high school students expect from the user experience of universal school-based e-mental health programs?

---

[2] In this model, *Comfort, Connection, Uniqueness,* and *Variety* are described as the four fundamental needs of digital users [8].

3. What factors could make universal school-based e-mental health solutions more desirable for adolescent students?

After agreeing on our study's scope and research questions, we developed the study protocol and the semi-structured interview questions with which we could better explore the experiences and opinions of adolescent students with mental health resources – both non-digital and e-mental health solutions – and their motivations and goals from using them. To this end, we determined the interviews' preliminary and follow-up questions in a way that could help us focus on: a) finding the answers to 'when', 'why', and 'how' each adolescent's experiences with mental health resources started and continued; b) uncovering each adolescent's positive and negative experiences with these resources and their consequent impacts; and, c) discovering each adolescent's subjective opinions about the resources' shortcomings and the improvements that these resources would require in order to meet the user expectations and desires, and to help in achieving the individual's mental health goals.

Following the submission of our complete study protocol to HEC Montréal's Research Ethics Board (REB) and receiving the certificate of approbation for our research from the board, we started the recruitment and data collection processes from mid-May 2021.

3.2 Data Collection

In our data collection period, we conducted individual semi-structured interviews through a video conferencing platform with 8 different adolescent participants, each lasting 40 ± 10 min, depending on how the conversation unfolded. To participate in our interviews, the requirement for the students was to be fitted into at least one of the two following categories:

1. High school students who have participated in and have a good recollection of their experiences with traditional/non-digital mental health-related activities that were not pursued for mental illness treatment or rehabilitation purposes ($n = 6$).

Adolescents of the first participant group had experiences in one or more preventive or promotive mental health-related activities such as meditation, yoga, and deep-breathing exercises. Out of these 6 participants, half of them were students at public schools while the other half were studying at private schools:

- The public-school students were all from the same high school that offered an optional traditional (non-digital) mental health course: the course had a mental health instructor who was present during the class times and apart from educating the students about the psychophysiology of stress, anxiety, calmness and other relevant topics, the instructor would teach them different exercises and techniques for stress management and increasing awareness; the instructor would also engage in moderating and assisting in the group exercises (deep breathing, meditation, yoga, etc.) and facilitating the discussion periods in which the students exchanged their experiences, shared their struggles and success stories regarding improving and/or maintaining their mental well-being.

- The other students who had not been offered a similar class by their private high schools were adolescents who were interested in pursuing yoga or meditation for the benefits that those would give them. These students had all started their journeys with mental health exercises either with a non-professional guide, such as one of their parents, or through attending a professional instructor's sessions with one of their close family members.

All the participants from this participant group were residents of the Quebec province except one that was from Ontario province, and the majority of interviews (4 out of 6) were conducted in French.

2. High school students who have had experiences in using e-mental health resources and have a good recollection of these experiences (n = 6).

Adolescents of the second participant group had experiences using resources related to meditation, yoga, mental focus, sleep aid, anxiety and/or stress control/relief. Out of these 6 adolescents, half were students at public schools while the other half were studying at private schools. The majority of these students were residing in the Quebec province (4 out of 6) while the rest were from Ontario; however, 3 interviews for this participant group were conducted in English and the other 3 in French.

Overall, out of a total of 8 participants, 4 adolescents (2 students from public high schools and 2 students from private high schools) met both interview categories' requirements and responded to our interviews' semi-structured and follow-up questions pertaining to both participant groups.

3.3 Qualitative Analysis of the Interviews

Data Analysis Process for Individual Interviews. After the completion of each interview in either of the two participant groups, we immediately started our qualitative analysis by first developing the transcript of each interview through listening to each recorded interview. As we were also interested in uncovering each participant's underlying needs and those expectations and desires that were not explicitly expressed during the interviews, we performed additional steps: we started listening to the audio recording for each interview again, but this time to extract the contextual cues, information, and insights from the interview and to fill the gaps between what was expressed and what was concealed or remained undiscovered by each participant. The findings from the second listening were directly added into each interview transcript as a side note. This method was used since due to privacy concerns and following REB's recommendations, we decided not to capture the video outputs, but only to record the audio outputs of our interviews with our adolescent participants – and only after receiving their written consent before the interviews, and the verbal confirmation at the beginning of our interviews with each participant – and therefore, it was important for us to listen more closely and to pay more attention to changes in tones, pauses and other vocal expressions and cues that could provide additional insights and contexts to each student's answers.

To maximize efficiency and accuracy, we set out to complete all the above steps within a maximum of 48 h from the starting time of each interview; this way, we could ensure our memories from each participant and the discussions that took place during each interview could still remain fresh, and therefore, we could have a more accurate and quicker way to extract, organize, and further analyze our findings in the consequent steps.

Process for Analyzing the Interviews Within a Participant Group. After finishing data collection in each participant group and completing the analysis for all individual interviews of that group, we analyzed each annotated transcript individually to extract each participant's opinions, motivations, goals, positive and negative experiences pertaining to mental health interventions and resources. The output from this round of analysis was in the format of short phrases, each in the language that was chosen for the interview by its participant. We then grouped all the short-phrase findings of each participant group together with the following method: **A)** For those phrases that had similarities with each other: **1)** If they were from the same participant, only one of the phrases that was more representative was kept and the others were discarded; **2)** If they were not from the same participant and if there was a phrase that represented all the other similar phrases, we kept that phrase and discarded the others while taking note of the number of similarities to the phrase that was kept; and, **3)** If they were not from the same participant and there was no phrase that represented all the other similar phrases, we generated a more representative phrase and added all those similar phrases as bullet points under it; **B)** For phrases that had no similarities with each other: they were kept as is for this round of analysis.

Process for Combining the Findings of Both Participant Groups. After the data collection period and data analysis process for both participant groups completed, we color-coded the short-form and bullet-pointed phrases that belonged to either participant group. Then, we combined our findings together with the following method: **A)** For those phrases that had similarities with each other: **1)** If there was a phrase that represented all the other similar phrases, we kept that one and discarded the others while changing the color-code to a new one to represent the phrase belongs to both participant groups; we also took note if there were numbers (representing similar ideas that were previously discarded) associated with either the phrase that was kept or the one(s) that were discarded; and, **2)** If there was no phrase that represented all the other similar phrases, we generated a more representative phrase and added all those similar phrases as bullet points under it while changing its color-code to the one representing both participant groups and taking note of the numbers associated with any phrases before combining it with others; **B)** For phrases that had no similarities with each other: they were kept as is for this round of analysis.

Process for Analyzing the Combined Findings. After combining our findings from both participant groups, we first set out to classify all the remaining phrases via the following groups that are based on our study's group-specific objectives:

- Essential benefits of e-mental health solutions and resources for the users
- Critical disadvantages/shortcomings of e-mental health solutions and resources for the users

- Desired areas of improvement for e-mental health solutions and resources
- Factors motivating the users in pursuing the betterment of their mental health
- Shared goals of the users pursuing/completing mental health-related activities

Then, as we aimed to use an inductive approach to generate themes among our findings, we took a closer look in order to find patterns among the phrases. However, since not all the phrases had the same structure (as they were mostly derived directly from the interview transcripts), it was first required that we transform all the phrases into ones that would have a common structure: because our goal was to focus on the users and understand their core needs, expectations and desires from e-mental health solutions, we decided to transform the phrases that were about e-mental health resources' benefits, shortcomings and desired improvements – which were derived either directly from the results for the second participant group or were discovered via comparison of results in both participant groups – into phrases that would consider the point-of-view of the users who would have felt that benefit, the lack, or the need.

The following example presents an instance where we transformed the structure of a phrase related to shortcomings of e-mental health solutions into a phrase that represented the unmet need for adolescent users.

Example. The phrase "Not communicating the expected outcome or learning objective from specific activity" was derived from both participant groups, hinting that both traditional mental health and e-mental health programs and resources have had a similar shortcoming for their adolescent participants. Therefore, this finding suggests that the developers of school-based mental health solutions should follow the point-of-view of the users and plan for providing their students sets of clear expectations about the outcomes, learning objectives, and the effort required for reaching them. Therefore, we transformed the original phrase into the phrase "Being able to set clear expectations for a mental-health related activity", which was what the users felt lacking when using the e-mental health solutions.

Next, after ensuring all the structures of phrases were similar and from the point-of-view of the users, we intended to identify the main themes that were shared between them: the main factors – core needs – that drove our participants' experiences with mental health solutions and resources. The themes that emerged from our attempt to reorganize our findings based on the core needs that were shared between our adolescent participants were consistent with *four fundamental human needs* model: the fundamental needs for connection, comfort, variety, and uniqueness [8]. We therefore named our core needs' categories after these fundamental needs, and to classify our findings, we adapted that model to our specific context (see Table 1).

After reorganizing our findings to generate the main themes (i.e., core user needs), we then sought to discover the most important phrases related to each core user need (which would constitute the user expectations and desires). To this end, we identified the phrases that either had the most recurrence or had the most weight:

- For identifying the most recurrent phrases, we performed the following steps:

    a. We first identified in which participant group(s) the phrase was shared: if it was shared in <u>both groups</u>, therefore, it was deemed <u>one time more recurrent</u> than the others who had the same occurrence.
    b. Then, we checked whether or not the phrase was one that <u>was generated to represent a combination of similar phrases</u>: if in fact it was, the number of bullet-point form phrases that were listed below it was deemed to be the total number of the phrase's occurrence; therefore, the total number of recurrences would be <u>one less than the total number of bullet-point form phrases</u>.
    c. Consequently, we verified if we <u>had noted the number of a phrase recurrence</u> next to it; this practice was done after each time we had combined similar phrases or had discarded less-representative similar phrases during different rounds of our analysis: if there was a number next to a phrase, it would indicate <u>how many more times the phrase was recurrent.</u>
    d. Lastly, by calculating the number of additional occurrences identified in the steps above for each of the phrases, we determined which ones were more recurrent than the others, and therefore represented those expectations and desires that were shared between the users more than the others.

- For identifying phrases with the most weight, we revisited our interview notes where we had noted the benefits, shortcomings, positive and negative experiences related to mental health interventions and resources that were deemed more urgent and sensitive to focus on. The urgency and sensitivity of such topics were recognized either by the participants themselves, when during the interviews they had explicitly or implicitly put more emphasis on the matter, or the gravity of positive or negative effects of the discussed topic throughout the interviews were acknowledged by the research team. After establishing which topics should have more weight, we identified the phrases that were related to them.

By only keeping the phrases that had the most recurrence and/or more weight and by discarding the others, we were able to identify the most essential needs, motivations, and goals that either the adolescents expect or desire to address via their experiences with e-mental health solutions.

4 Results and Discussion of Practical Implications

In this section, we will gradually present the results of our study via diagrams and tables. For the purpose of clarity, we will use color-coded tables and figures to demonstrate how our findings from each stage would contribute to other stages.

4.1 Core User Needs from e-Mental Health Solutions

As the starting point in our classification, and to answer our first research question, we identified the core user needs that drive the adolescent students' experiences with e-mental health solutions These needs were derived from the main themes among the needs, motivations, and goals that were shared between all the participants in our study, and as explained before, were named after four fundamental human needs model: Comfort, Connection, Variety, and Uniqueness [8]. In Table 1 we present the definition for each core user need and what each could represent for HCI/UX designers and developers; we will later clarify how each HCI/UX concept could be used to inform the design of e-mental health solutions.

Table 1. Core user needs driving the user experience of e-mental health solutions, adapted from Forrester Research's four fundamental human needs model [8].

Core User Needs	Comfort	Connection	Variety	Uniqueness
Definition	The need to remove ambiguity, complexity, and sources of stress associated with the experience	The need to belong with others and to feel welcomed and supported in the course of the experience	The need to feel excited about possibilities and to anticipate new experiences and diversions from monotony in the course of the experience	The need to feel special, capable, and optimistic about opportunities for improvement in the course of the experience
HCI/UX Connection	Knowledge Psychological Safety Usefulness Ease-of-Use	Ease-of-Use Usefulness	Engagement Personalization Customization Usefulness	Self-Efficacy Knowledge Personalization Usefulness

4.2 Users' Expectations from School-Based e-Mental Health Solutions' UX

Next, to answer our second research question, we identified the needs, motivations, and goals that adolescent users expected to address through their experiences with e-mental health solutions. In Fig. 1, we present these user expectations from the user experience of high schools' universal e-mental health programs.

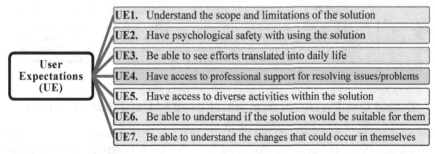

Fig. 1. User expectation from the UX of school-based e-mental health solutions. *Note:* Here, each user expectation's color scheme corresponds to that of core needs depicted in Table 1. (Color figure online)

The description of each expectation (**UE1–7**), their connections to the core user needs (the main driving factors of user experience of e-mental health solutions for students), and their practical implications in HCI/UX are presented in more details in Table 2.

Table 2. Descriptions of identified user expectations from the UX of e-mental health solutions. *Note:* Here, the color scheme corresponds to the color schemes presented in Fig. 1 and Table 1.

Related Core Need	UE#	Description
Comfort	1	This expectation that is a critical shortcoming of mental health resources, is concerned with removing unneeded ambiguities and providing clear communications about the scope and limitations of a solution to help the users make an informed decision.
	2	A critical shortcoming in and an essential motivating factor for using e-mental health solutions, this expectation is about the need to use a solution without additional concerns such as chances of failure or criticism, and it could be addressed by removing unneeded sources of such stresses and ensuring psychological safety of the users.
	3	This expectation is concerned with a critical shortcoming in and an essential motivating factor for pursuing any type of mental health-related activities: the users require to be able to anchor the activities and learnings from the mental health resources into their daily life, otherwise they might not find it to add value or be useful for them.
Connection	4	This expectation represents a valuable factor for the users who would need to be able to remove complexities, as they arise during or throughout their experience with an e-mental health solution, by receiving professional support. For the designers, ensuring there would be no major usability issues or complexities leading to this need for the user is vital, but providing an easy access to support is also a crucial consideration.
Variety	5	An essential motivating factor for the users and a critical shortcoming of e-mental health solutions, this expectation is about maximizing the engagement via personalization for those groups of users who would welcome more possibilities and access to more contents and activities within the solution.
Uniqueness	6	A critical shortcoming in and an essential motivating factor for using e-mental health solutions, this expectation is concerned with providing information and guidelines to allow users to have a clear understanding about their capabilities and opportunities for improvement, the benefits associated with the solution and/or its activities, also the efforts and time required for their optimal effects.
	7	An essential motivation for the users, this expectation is concerned with educating and providing adequate resources that will help user identify, anticipate, and track the changes in their mental and emotional wellbeing (improvements or deterioration).

4.3 Desired User Experience from School-Based e-Mental Health Solutions

Consequently, in order to answer our third and final research question, we identified the needs, motivations, and goals of adolescent users that could contribute towards making a more desirable user experience for universal school-based e-mental health solutions. These contributing factors, outlined in Fig. 2, would be in fact additional desires of adolescent students from the UX of e-mental health solutions. This means that in order to provide the desired user experience to adolescent users, first, the focus of HCI/UX designers and developers should be on providing the user expectations (**UE1–7**), and then, on addressing the additional desirable factors (**AD1–6**); this way, when developing a new e-mental health solution or redesigning an existing one for high schools, developers and designers can focus on maximizing the likelihood that the UX of their solution could be desirable for their intended users.

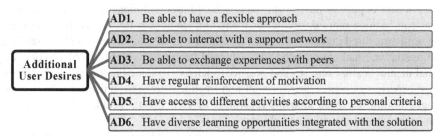

Fig. 2. Additional desires of users from the UX of school-based e-mental health solutions. *Note:* Here, the color scheme for each additional desire corresponds to that of core users' needs depicted in Table 1. (Color figure online)

And lastly, the description of each additional desire from the UX of school-based e-mental health solutions (**AD1–6**), its connection to the core user needs and its practical implication in HCI/UX are presented in Table 3.

Table 3. Descriptions of additional user desires from the UX of e-mental health solutions. *Note:* Here, the color scheme corresponds to the color schemes presented in Fig. 2 and Table 1.

Related Core Need	AD#	Description
Comfort	1	If this desire is met, users will be able to remove excess complexity and stress that could follow if the solution is not easy to use and/or cannot be adapted to the users' schedules and preferences. Users desire to be allowed to follow the e-mental health resources at their own pace, within their comfort zone, or on their own (unaided).
Connection	2	If this desire is met, users will see more value in the solution as they would feel reassured to have access to a support system, which should consist of individuals who would understand the context and situation and would not be judgmental or critical of other users but instead could help alleviate stresses and complexities for them.
	3	If this desire is met, users will have feelings of belonging within a community and connected to those who are also in a journey with them, both of which will add to the subjective value of the solution and help motivate the users to use it more.
Variety	4	If this desire is addressed through engagement drivers, users will exhibit internal feelings of excitement and will attempt to push themselves for getting more involved with e-mental health activities for the benefits or outcomes they could provide them.
	5	If this desire is met through customization capabilities that solution would provide to the users, they will be empowered to choose from activities they feel could be more valuable and suitable for them and/or to change and adapt program or activities' criteria (type of activity, level of complexity, etc.) based on their preference and/or need of the day.
Uniqueness	6	If this desire is met through delivering personalized educational contents and resources for the users who would welcome it, they will feel more knowledgeable and motivated than before in using the solution as they would associate more value to it.

5   Conclusion and Future Work

The presented article offers insights from an exploratory study that was conducted in order to better understand the factors that contribute to the overall user experience of universally delivered school-based e-mental health solutions from the point-of-view of adolescent users; more specifically, we sought to learn what kind of experience these users would expect to have from these school-based solutions and how these solutions can become more desirable for them. Our findings were derived from conducting semi-structured qualitative interviews with a total of 8 adolescent students residing in Canada who had experiences with e-mental health resources (n = 6) and/or traditional mental health exercises and practices such as yoga, meditation, etc. (n = 6), and these experiences were either through non-treatment-focused, universal school-based programs (offered to all students regardless of their mental health risks) or through non-school-based activities and classes.

As our goal was to present our study's findings together with the practical implications that they would have for HCI/UX designers and developers in the most accessible way, we attempted to organize and present our findings via interrelated visualizations (tables and diagrams): **a)** first, we presented the 4 core user needs (the motivating factors which we identified to be the drivers of the users' experiences with mental health resources) in Table 1 and outlined the HCI/UX concepts which we deemed were correlated to them; **b)** we then presented the 7 essential needs, goals and motivations that users expect to address through their experiences with e-mental health solutions in Fig. 1 and further discussed their practical implications inside Table 2; and lastly, **c)** we outlined 6 additional factors that could make the user experience of e-mental health solutions more desirable for their intended end-users in Fig. 2 and subsequently expanded on their practical implications inside Table 3. We recommend the developers and designers of school-based e-mental health solutions to first focus on providing what the end-users consider as the *solutions' must-haves* (by addressing the seven user expectations) and then, to focus on offering the *solutions' nice-to-haves* (by focusing on additional desires of users from the UX of e-mental health solutions).

We hope our results could be used as a means for HCI/UX designers and developers to help them put a more focused effort and create a better product/service strategy when developing or redesigning school-based e-mental health solutions and resources. However, we also acknowledge that due to the exploratory nature of our study, and since we focused on better understanding the goals, needs, and motivations of the intended end-users of school-based e-mental health solutions through qualitative analysis, we can neither at this point provide any concrete evidence about the feasibility of integrating our recommendations into a solution, nor attest to their consequent usability once they are embedded in a school-based program; these concerns were beyond the scope of this research and could be further explored and tested in practice and/or via usability testing.

References

1. Statistics Canada: Impacts on Mental Health (2020). https://www150.statcan.gc.ca/pub/11-631-x/2020004/pdf/s3-eng.pdf. Accessed 10 Feb 2022

2. Statistics Canada: Canadian Health Survey on Children and Youth (2020). https://www150.sta tcan.gc.ca/n1/daily-quotidien/200723/dq200723a-eng.htm. Accessed 10 Feb 2022
3. American Psychological Association: Stress in America™ 2020: A National Mental Health Crisis (2020)
4. Fisak, B.J., Richard, D., Mann, A.: The prevention of child and adolescent anxiety: a meta-analytic review. Prev. Sci. **12**(3), 255–268 (2011)
5. Neil, A.L., Christensen, H.: Efficacy and effectiveness of school-based prevention and early intervention programs for anxiety. Clin. Psychol. Rev. **29**(3), 208–215 (2009)
6. Tedder, M., Shi, L., Si, M., Franco, R., Chen, L.: eMindfulness therapy—a study on efficacy of blood pressure and stress control using mindful meditation and eating apps among people with high blood pressure. Medicines **2**, 298–309 (2015)
7. International Organization for Standardization: Ergonomics of human-system interaction–Part 210: Human-centred design for interactive systems (2019). https://www.iso.org/obp/ui/#!iso: std:77520:en. Accessed 10 Feb 2022
8. McQuivey, J.: Digital consumers want to fulfill their needs. In: Digital Disruption: Unleashing the next wave of innovation. Forrester Research, Inc., pp. 54–68 (2013)

Multisubject PBL: Implementing, Maintaining and Evolving Through 15 Years

Patricia Compañ-Rosique[iD], Carlos J. Villagrá-Arnedo[iD],
Rafael Molina-Carmona[(✉)][iD], Francisco J. Gallego-Durán[iD],
Rosana Satorre-Cuerda[iD], and Faraón Llorens-Largo[iD]

Grupo de investigación Smart Learning, University of Alicante, Alicante, Spain
{patricia.company,villagra,rmolina,fjgallego,
rosana.satorre,faraon.llorens}@ua.es
https://web.ua.es/en/smart-learning/

Abstract. Project Based Learning (PBL) is an active learning methodology with many advantages, but also with some natural challenges to be tackled. Planification, coordination, flexibility and adaptability amonst others are required qualities that will pose challenges for teachers and students implementing PBL. This work presents a particular implementation of PBL at the University of Alicante and its evolution through fifteen years, ending being applied to a complete one-year course in the Multimedia Engineering Degree.

To present this evolution, an analogy with the development cycle of a computer game is established, as the projects students develop are computer games. Same as a computer game evolves as a product through several planned versions, presented implementation has changed and developed its own "versions" until achieving its current consolidated status, that could confidently be called "the final product". This latest implementation is currently working nominally in practice, and is stable, flexible, escalable and transferable.

Present work shows the value of the continuous improvement spiral a way to accumulate improvements and arriving to better implementations, also contributing the results of the experience with PBL through fifteen years, summarizing challenges and solutions adopted.

Keywords: Project based learning · Active learning · Deming cycle

1 Introduction

Higher education must prepare students for being the best possible professionals. The last academic year is of great relevance, specifically for engineers. A great way to foster their preparation and motivation is making them work like in a professional environment. For instance, in the Computer Games industry they will work in projects, structured in development stages, with tight timing schedules and organized into teams and roles. Therefore, they need to familiarize

P. Zaphiris and A. Ioannou (Eds.): HCII 2022, LNCS 13328, pp. 420–432, 2022.
https://doi.org/10.1007/978-3-031-05657-4_30

with planification, deadlines, roles and intra e inter-team communication (i.e. performing presentations). All this work should be carefully oriented towards delivering the best possible final product on time.

To acomplish this task, the University of Alicante applies Project Based Learning methodology (PBL) to the fourth year of the Multimedia Engineering Degree (MED), particulary in its branch on Development of Digital Entertainment (DDE). Several authors define PBL in different ways ([2,17]), but there is common agreement on actively involving students as main characteristic. It mainly fosters teamwork, active self-planification, autonomous learning, development of oral and written skills, self-regulation, critical thinking, simulation of real situations and interdisciplinarity. There is a growing interest in achieving learning. PBL is considered a good practice due to its characteristics. In [5] authors review methodological advances in European projects on learning technologies. For instance, in [13] authors perform a literature review focused on different implementations of PBL in higher education, while in [21] authors focus on applications of PBL to computer engineering. There are also experiences of implementation in primary education [25].

Our experience with PBL starts fifteen years ago in the Computer Engineering Degree (CED). We started implementing PBL in four separated subjects in CED and learnt how to properly apply and adapt it. This experience helped selecting PBL as choice methodology for MED and its DDE branch. Presently, the DDE branch has nine years of experience with the PBL methodology, and a tenth year running. During these years, its PBL implementation has evolved to better accomodate student and teacher's needs. The present work describes this evolution splitted in stages. The first stage shows the original ideas, design and conceptualization of the methodology, during MED creation. Next stages explain progressive consolidation of PBL after its implementation, and most relevant details changed to improve the quality of students' learning process. It also shows how PBL has resisted CoViD emergency challenges, adapting to remote situation with minimum changes, showing its sostenibility, fault tolerance and transferability.

The organization of this work into stages mimics the planification students follow during one year of PBL developing their products (computer games). This planification comes from real-world projects' schedules. Therefore, this work makes an analogy to real-world professional game development and the PBL implementation it explains.

Summarizing, the planification to get from a game idea to a final product is divided in four stages, milestones and deliverables as follows: first, elaboration of a game concept and initial design; second, a minimum viable product, also called mechanics alpha version; third, closed stable beta version, with all required technologies integrated; and fourth, polished final product and deployment/publication.

The four development stages can be mapped to four evolution stages of the implementation of the PBL methodology, as shown in Table 1.

Table 1. Analogy between game developing milestones and PBL implementation stages

Milestone	Stage
0: idea/concept	0: Original PBL implementation
1: Minimum viable product (alpha)	1: First PBL DDE 1-complete-year impl.
2: Stable version (beta)	2: Consolidated PBL DDE impl.
3: Final product	3: Ready to transfer/deploy PBL DDE impl.

2   Context

The PBL methodology described in this work is currently implanted in the DDE branch of the MED at the University of Alicante. The MED was created as an intermediate degree between traditional engineering and computer engineering. The main aim is to produce IT professionals with skills to develop and direct Multimedia projects in the sectors of Digital Entertainment, Computer Games and Content Management on Information Networks [23].

Since MED inception, PBL was thought as choice methodology to convey quality formation for students, with four reasons in mind:

- MED was a freshly-created degree. That let us design a studies plan based on desired competencies and learning objectives, without the influence of already established degrees.
- Estimated number of students for fourth year, varying from fourty to seventy, is adequate for PBL. It lets building diverse student teams of a managable size, having eight to twelve teams from four to six students.
- Developing projects is key in the formation of engineers, and that is the main focus of PBL. Therefore, PBL is optimal to train students for their real world future professional attributions.
- There was previous successful experience implementing PBL. It had already been implemented in four subjects in the Computer Engineering Degree, and the projects the students developed there were also computer games.

The first academic year of MED was 2010/11. Students from the first promotion arrived to fourth year in 2013/14. So, 2013/14 was the first academic year implementing PBL in MED. The fourth year of MED is divided into two branches or specializations: Development of Digital Entertainment (DDE) and Content Management (CE). Fourth year students have two mandatory subjects and select another five optional ones. Each branch has its own five optional subjects. However, students can select their five optional at their own will among the available ten. They only have one restriction: to get their degree with branch mention, they need to get at least four subjects from the desired branch. Consequently, most common selections are the complete pack of five subjects, or four subjects and a free fifth from the other branch.

Table 2 shows the seven subjects (two mandatory and five optional) that make up the DDE branch, along with a description of their aims. Each one of them is wighted six European Credit Transfer System (ECTS) credits [9].

Table 2. Subjects composing the Developmeng of Digital Entertainment branch

Subject	Type	Aims
Multimedia Projects	Mandatory	- Plan, manage and control the development of the project - Know and apply IT legal and ethic aspects
Advanced Graphics Techniques	Mandatory	- Know and apply the required methods, algorithms and data structures for an efficient graphical representation - Develop the graphics engine of a computer game
Video Games I	Optional	- Deepen in the knowledge and abilities to design and develop computer games - Develop playing mechanics, artificial intelligence and network engine of a computer game
Digital Post-Production	Optional	- Know what digital post-production is and most useful tools - Develop team logo, a poster, a trailer and the credits of a computer game
Sound Design Techniques	Optional	- Know and apply the concepts and techniques required for sound design - Develop and implement the sound engine of a computer game, along with music, sounds and effects
Video Games II	Optional	- Know the most common physics and graphics engines for 3D computer games - Develop or integrate a physics engine into a computer game - Introduce in the engine specific game development techniques
Virtual Reality	Optional	- Learn the basic principles of Virtual Reality and its applications - Develop sketches, models, textures, animations, environments and other elements of a computer game - Use motion capture to create characters' animations of a computer game

3   PBL Evolution

In order to implement a novel methodology like PBL, is important to adopt a continuous improvement strategy to constantly supervise the teaching-learning process. Starting simple and grow based on experience is advisable, instead of trying to design a perfect implementation before starting. Presented implementation has followed the Deming cycle for continuous improvement [8], adapted to the docent process. Deming stablishes four key steps: Planning, Doing, Verifying and Acting. Planning corresponds to the docent team proposal. Doing maps to the lessons and activities imparted by teachers and their interaction with students. Verifying involves obtaining results and data from the learning process and analysing it. Finally, Acting results in using data and analysis to create an updated docent team proposal aimed at improving results next year. Figure 1 summarizes this process visually.

Fig. 1. Continuous improvement strategy

Deming cycle from Fig. 1 has been followed every one of the previous fifteen years, redesigning and improving the presented implementation of PBL methodology in the DDE context. To summarize this evolution four milestones have been highlighted, creating a paralellism with the four milestones the students meet to produce their final products. Following subsections present these four milestones.

3.1   Stage 0: Original PBL Implementation

This first milestone includes first PBL experiences conducted in the CED at the University of Alicante. This experiences are experimental implementations of PBL, and part of the learning process to master the methodology. Initially, there was a group of four teachers involved that started by learning about PBL in seminars and papers from M. Valero [24]. After this learning period, the group designed a basic PBL methodology and individually applied to four subjects in the CED:

- Computer Games and Virtual Reality
- Advanced Graphics and Animation
- Computer Assisted Manufacturing Models
- Reasoning

The four subjects were completely optional for students: they could pick one, two, three, the four or none of them, depending entirely on their own interests. None of the four subjects was required for them to complete their degrees.

The details of this first implementation are described in [22]. Although PBL was applied individually in each subject, a common project was defined for the four subjects as a whole: a computer game. This project included the learning goals of all the four subjects: all subjects contributed to the project, and also received from it, making the experience interdisciplinar. So, students formed groups and had to develop a single project (their computer game) that should include the requirements from the subjects they had opted in.

As PBL had great demands on students' intercommunication, a web-based groupware based on redmine [14] called *ABP-Forja* (PBL-forge) was created and deployed. The creation, setup, advantages, disadvantages and strategies used is discussed in detail in [15], with all the necessary steps to transfer it to other disciplines.

In fact, PBL was implemented not only on the CED, but also in a completely different discipline: law. An adapted version of the methodology was designed for Informatics for Lawyers [10], an optional subject from the degree in law. The project was adapted to become the development of a journal issue of computer engineering for lawyers. Students worked in groups learning about interesting computer-based technologies like databases, remote control, terminal usage, basic programming, web server administration and also advanced spreadsheet usage. Their aim was to learn about the tecnologies and then write articles for their own journal explaining the tecnologies learnt and how to learn them.

This experience had all the componentes of PBL: a project as main focus, student autonomy in learning, the teacher in the guidance role, competencies as main learning object instead of contents, learning by doing and a formative assessment. Results showed that the methodology worked successfully even on non-technologically oriented fields like law. Moreover, it showed that, under propper motivational conditions, law students became interested in more advanced technological contents than the traditional offimatic contents.

3.2   Stage 1: First PBL DDE One-complete-year Implementation

The experiences at this point can be considered as the minimum viable product. They happened at the start of 2013/14, first implementation of PBL in the DDE branch of MED. In this implementation, PBL was applied to all the subjects in the fourth year at the same time, not individually, but together. The complexity of this implementation revealed a lot of improvement points that were addressed in subsequent milestones.

The most important focus at this stage was to implement the new design as a whole year, instead of individual subjects, train and convince the new teachers not involved in previous experiences, and show that it was viable and scalable. Additionally, it was important to solve potential administrative issues derived from rigidity of administrative procedures. The most difficult part was to make the advantages of the methodology overcome the additional cost to be assumed in teacher dedication, specially at this initial implementation point.

The way projects are managed is described in [30], highlighting the organizing role of the Multimedia Projects subject. The main tool for managing project continued to be a custom version of the redmine software, which this time was called *Cloud*. The central supportive role of Multimedia Projects is expanded in [26], explaining the way in which the subject helps in teams management and projects follow up. This support helped students progress towards having a final product at the end of the year. This time, the final product will have much greater dimensions: groups of four to six students, up to seven subjects per students contributing to the project, and a complete year developing. This made final products a great contribution to students' professional portfolios.

One of the main innovations in this milestone was the initial budget for students' projects. Each team had to design their game concept, and initial plan, and a budget at the start of the year. The bugdet document would represented a contract proposal between the student team and the teachers: it stated the technical characteristics that the game will include as a list of deliverables, the hours that each deliverable will take and the marks they will receive for completing it. The total amount of budgeted hours had to match the corresponding hours the students were expected to perform acording to the amount of ECTS credits they had enrolled in. As each subject was measured as six ECTS credits, that means a student was expected to work for 150 h. Therefore, seven subjects add up to 1050 working hours. A team with five members would then have a total budget of 5750 h to work in their project. Similarly, each subject was assessed with marks from 0 to 10 points. A student with seven subjects would add up to 70 points, therefore a team with five members would have a total budget of 350 points.

Another important obstacle to overcome was administrative assessment. The subjects were equally distributed in both semesters and their administrative time-span is limited to one semester. This implies that first-semester subjects had to fill in their achievement records before the start of the second semester. However, the projects are conceived to have an unlimited one-year time-span, and it would have been unnatural to split the projects in half. Therefore, students were required to accept having a temporary unfilled record in their first-semester subject, that is filled at the end of the year when they submit their projects for final assessment. This temporary status was also negotiated with administrative representatives, having all parties involved in the methodology.

Moreover, there was an important decision to state about final assessment. Some implementations of PBL treat the project as a whole, meaning that students either pass or fail completely. In this case, this would have implied either passing or failing seven subjects in block, for four to six students at the same time. That would have represented a high risk that students probably would have preferred not to face. Moreover, it could have been criticized for being unfair, not without proper reasons, because some students could have performed enough merits to pass some subjects while still requiring more effort on others. This was predicted as a common case, hence the decision was not to treat pass or failure as a whole. Instead, the decision was to assess each subject with respect to the budget, concrete deliverables submitted and a variable percentage of marks that each subject reserved. This reserved percentage of marks varies between zero to thirty percent of the total marks of each subject, and teachers can assign it to students based on individual works for that subject, apart from the main project. Therefore, each subject emits a final assessment mark for each team of students, with the total ammount of points they have earned via deliverables and reserved works. Then, teams of students have the opportunity to decide on how to distribute the total ammount of points between their members, which has not necessarily to be an equal distribution. This distribution takes the form of a proposal from each team that the teacher has to approve. With these mechanisms, subjects retain their own personality through the reserved works, while contributing to the project, and the project contributes to the subjects by not being assessed as a whole, but depending on concrete deliverables submitted by students.

3.3 Stage 2: Consolidated PBL DDE Implementation

At this point in time, the PBL implementation at the University of Alicante had evolved up to an stable point. Most of the problems founds in previous years had been addressed with different adaptations and there was no need of more changes. The PBL implementation was consistently using same procedures every academic year, all teachers were used to the procedures and everything worked nominally.

From this point onwards, proposed changes became improvement experiments on the verge of the implementation, generally not affecting the core established procedures.

One relevant question addressed in [32] is how to provide students with the necessary information. At the start of the year, students ellaborate an initial report describing the game project, the tools and technologies required and a planification. Initial implementation of PBL provided guidelines, and the task proved to be extremely difficult for students, as they had no previous experience. Guidelines were then changed into templates. This change standarized the format of student proposals and made more simple for them their initial creation acts. It also lost a bit of creativity and unguided exploratory work, but the overall effect is perceived as quite positive either from students or from teachers point of view.

Another improvement introduced was the creation of the team supervisor figure. Each team was assigned a teacher as their supervisor, becoming their personal guidance person along the whole project. Altough all teachers collaborated in guiding students, supervisors helped by having more direct and continuous contact with the team and its members, better understanding their personal problems and necessities and doing a more detailed follow up of the progress of the project. The relevance of this figure is highlighted in [1] as a success driver for PBL methodology.

The choice tool for project management also changed from the traditional custom redmine into github [27]. Github [11] provided same basic tool for working (version control through git) along with other standard tools, but had two main advantages: it was becoming an industry standard, and liberated teachers from the burden of maintaining a custom server.

Previous evolution and obtained staibility in the application of PBL lead to many interesting debates like the one in [7], including representatives from heterogeneus experiences from different universities. The report in [7] summarizes many details from described improvements and other interesting questions that arised during that meeting.

Many of the improvements and changes that lead to the stability point reached came from analyzing student opinions and contributions. Those were known by conducting yearly surveys as long as inviting student representatives to teacher meetings after every project milestone. The work in [28] summarizes the content of these surveys and meetings, and the relevant results and information extracted that guided evolution of the PBL implementation.

Socioemotional competences of students was also considered as object of study. Works [20] and [19] describe many difficulties students had to properly work in teams. High level of socioemotional competences lead to students becoming efficient professionals with management and leadership abilities [3,4]. Additionally, people with high levels of emotional intelligence are more successful professionally [6].

At the end of this PBL implementation milestone, a complete and exhaustive guide on how to apply PBL was published [31]. This guide summarizes all lessons learnt and key aspects on implementing PBL to a whole academic year, incorporating all the subjects of the year in a single project.

3.4   Stage 3: Ready to Transfer/Deploy PBL DDE Implementation

At this final milestone, the PBL implementation as a product was completed, sustainable, escalable and transferable. To foster knowledge transfer, additionally to all previously cited works, specific courses were conducted [12].

In this sense, [29] highlights the way in which student presentations of their products were organized and conducted over the year. Student presentations generated a feedback loop of value to the whole implementation. Presentations were streamed over the Internet and industry professionals were invited to give comments and feedback to students. This generated a link between students, industry and general public that enhanced the whole system, provided prestige and promoted knowledge transfer.

Additionally, [18] discusses another tool developed, in the form of a flow diagram, called Action Plan. This tool helped in project creation and starting up, yielding an almost automatic planification for the PBL year, based on Deming methodology.

During the second semester of the academic year 2019/20, CoViD-19 pandemic burst. Universities were forced to change to online from one week to the next. As described in [16], the PBL implementation then proved to be resilient to such changing conditions, as an additional unexpected benefit. Even becoming suddenly confined at home, students could continue working on their projects without interruption, and teachers were able to suppervise and guide students remotely from the first day of change. Almost two years after that, careful analyses have been conducted to determine the major factors contributing to this success:

- Intercommunication is an inherent part of PBL, being continuous, frequent and rich in all successful student teams. Students are already used to work remotely and communicate via instant messaging, video conference and social networks. Losing the classroom has an impact in socializing, but is not determinant to maintain communication and teamwork.
- PBL makes students autonomous by definition, which helps them easily continue working remotely. Students are more proactive and less worried about their assessment, because PBL helps them focus on a project, a goal, through continuous tracking and teacher supervision and guidance.
- Technological tools are mature and students are used to them because they are part of their day to day job.

3.5   Continuous Improvement Spiral

The very same concept of continuous improvement implies an iterative application, which easily becomes an spiral. Figure 2 shows the spiral followed along these fifteen years.

The PBL implementation started its initial experiences focalizing student autonomy and teachers as guidance. At stage 1, the coordination role was considered important and assigned to one subject, and the assessment procedure was designed to be flexible through the budget. Then, the stable version of the methodology at stage 2 included better, more structured information for teams to start up and manage their projects. Moreover, it added a team supervisor and consolidated the measurement instruments for self-assessment. Finally, the last stage presented a final product, mature, transferable and escalable, with the focus on its deployment and on expanding students horizons beyond classes through streamed presentations and relations with industry professionals.

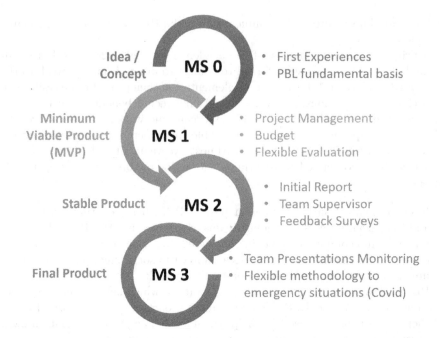

Fig. 2. Continuous improvement spiral

4   Conclusions

This work has overviewed and summarized the evolution of a PBL implementation at the University of Alicante along fifteen academic years. It started being applied individually to four optional subjects of the Computer Engineering Degree. Since then, it started an spiral improvement evolution that has driven it to a final implementation in the Multimedia Engineering Degree involving a single one-year project as main work for all the seven subjects included in that academic year.

The initial implementation has evolved by means of analysing results obtained from the experience, surveys and direct participation of students in teacher meetings. Many aspects of the methodology have been improved: central coordination, flexible evaluation, teacher supervision and guidance, continuous feedback and follow ups, guidelines and templates, milestones, presentations, streaming and industry involvement.

The final version of the implementation has been shown as mature, CoViD resilient, escalable, transferable and ready to be deployed. This final implementation summarizes all the experience gained during fifteen years of continuous improvement and is now working nominal year after year.

Although latest implementation has been deemed as mature, it does not mean it has stopped evolving. There always be aspects to improve and circumnstances that will require adaptation. This is, in fact, another important value presented in this work: a continuous improvement spiral applied year after year is certain to accumulate improvements over the years and lead to mature implementations. In this case, measurement instruments are simple (yearly surveys and direct student participation) yet effective. However, that is probably a next improvement step: finding better instruments to measure and redefine aims with respect to metrics in better ways.

References

1. Andrade, T.: Project based learning activities in engineering education. In: 2012 15th International Conference on Interactive Collaborative Learning (ICL), pp. 1–6. IEEE (2012)
2. Blumenfeld, P.C., Soloway, E., Marx, R.W., Krajcik, J.S., Guzdial, M., Palinc-sar, A.: Motivating project-based learning: sustaining the doing, supporting the learning. Educ. Psychologist **26**(3–4), 369–398 (1991)
3. Boyatzis, R.E.: Competencies in the 21st century. J. Manage. Dev. (2008)
4. Brotheridge, C.M., Lee, R.T.: The emotions of managing: an introduction to the special issue. J. Managerial Psychol. (2008)
5. Alonso de Castro, M., García-Peñalvo, F.: Metodologías educativas de éxito: proyectos erasmus+ relacionados con e-learning o tic successful educational methodologies: erasmus+ projects related to e-learning or ICT. Campus Virtuales **11**, 95–114 (2022). https://doi.org/10.54988/cv.2022.1.1022
6. Cooper, R.K.: Applying emotional intelligence in the workplace. Train. Dev. **51**(12), 31–39 (1997)
7. Reverte, C., Usandizaga Lombana, I., Molina-Carmona, R.: Aprendizaje Basado en Proyectos entre asignaturas: tres experiencias, muchas preguntas y algunas respuestas. In: XXV Jornadas de Enseñanza Universitaria de la Informática, pp. 79–86. Murcia (2019)
8. Deming, W.: Out of the Crisis. MIT Press, Massachusetts Institute of Technology, Center for Advanced Engineering Study (2000), https://books.google.es/books?id=LA15eDlOPgoC
9. European Commission: (2022), https://education.ec.europa.eu/es/sistema-europeo-de-transferencia-y-acumulacion-de-creditos-ects
10. Gallego-Durán, F.J., Llorens Largo, F.: 'Aprendizaje Basado en Proyectos? ¡Pero si mi carrera no es técnica! In: XIII Jornadas sobre la Enseñanza Universitaria de la Informática, pp. 231–238. Teruel (2007)
11. GitHub Inc: Github (2022), https://github.com/
12. IES Torrellano: Eurobotique. erasmus+ (2016-1-es01-ka201-024990) (2016), https://web.ua.es/es/i3a/eurobotique.html
13. Kokotsaki, D., Menzies, V., Wiggins, A.: Project-based learning: a review of the literature. Improving Schools **19**(3), 267–277 (2016)
14. Lang, Jean-Philippe: Redmine (2014), https://www.redmine.org/
15. Llorens Largo, F., Molina-Carmona, R., Gallego-Durán, F.J., Villagrá-Arnedo, C.J., Aznar Gregori, F., et al.: Abpgame: un videojuego como proyecto de aprendizaje coordinado para varias asignaturas (2013)
16. Llorens-Largo, F., Villagrá-Arnedo, C., Gallego-Durán, F., Molina-Carmona, R.: Covid-proof: cómo el aprendizaje basado en proyectos ha soportado el confinamiento. Campus Virtuales **10**(1), 73–88 (2021)

17. Markham, T., Larmer, J., Ravitz, J.: Project Based Learning Handbook: A Guide to Standards-Focused Project Based Learning for Middle and High School Teachers. Buck Inst for Education, 2a edn. (2003)
18. Molina-Carmona, R., Villagrá-Arnedo, C.J., Gallego-Durán, F.J., Llorens Largo, F.: Convencido del aprendizaje basado en proyectos, ¿por dónde empiezo? In: XXVI Jornadas de Enseñanza Universitaria de la Informática, pp. 117–124. Valencia (2020)
19. Pertegal-Felices, M.L., Molina-Carmona, R., Jimeno-Morenilla, A., Villagrá-Arnedo, C.: Difficulties associated with teamwork in a project-based learning experience. In: Education and New Developments 2017, pp. 652–655. Lisboa (2017)
20. Pertegal-Felices, M.L., Molina-Carmona, R., Marcos-Jorquera, D., Villagrá-Arnedo, C.J., et al.: Evaluación de las competencias socioemocionales en entornos de aprendizaje colaborativo de alumnos de ingeniería multimedia (2017)
21. Pucher, R., Lehner, M.: Project based learning in computer science-a review of more than 500 projects. Procedia Soc. Behav. Sci. **29**, 1561–1566 (2011)
22. Reverte, J., Gallego, A.J., Molina-Carmona, R., Satorre Cuerda, R.: El aprendizaje basado en proyectos como modelo docente. Experiencia interdisciplinar y herramientas groupware. In: XIII Jornadas de Enseñanza Universitaria de la Informática. Teruel (2007)
23. Universidad de Alicante: Degree in multimedia engineering verified memory (2020), https://utc.ua.es/es/documentos/sgic/sgic-eps/grados/memoria-verificada/c205-memoria-verificada.pdf
24. Valero García, M., García Zubia, J.: Cómo empezar fácil con pbl. In: XVII Jornadas sobre la Enseñanza Universitaria de la Informática, pp. 109–116. Sevilla, July 2011, http://hdl.handle.net/2099/11951
25. Valle-Ramón, D., García-Valcárcel, A., Basilotta Gómez-Pablos, V.: Aprendizaje basado en proyectos por medio de la plataforma youtube para la enseñanza de matemáticas en educación primaria. Educ. Knowl. Soc. (EKS) **21**, 9 (2020). https://doi.org/10.14201/eks.23523
26. Villagrá, C., et al.: ABPgame+ o cómo hacer del último curso de ingeniería una primera experiencia profesional. In: El reconocimiento docente: innovar e investigar con criterios de calidad, pp. 1384–1399. Universidad de Alicante (2014)
27. Villagrá-Arnedo, C.J., et al.: Uso de la herramienta github en la gestión y monitorización de proyectos abp en cuarto curso del grado en ingeniería multimedia (2017)
28. Villagrá-Arnedo, C.J., et al.: Desarrollo de una metodología abp para el itinerario creación y entretenimiento digital del cuarto curso del grado en ingeniería multimedia (4002) (2018)
29. Villagrá-Arnedo, C.J., et al.: Las presentaciones de los proyectos en la metodología abp del itinerario de creación y entretenimiento digital de cuarto curso del grado en ingeniería multimedia (4606) (2020)
30. Villagrá-Arnedo, C.J., Gallego-Durán, F.J., Molina-Carmona, R., Llorens Largo, F.: ABPgame+: siete asignaturas, un proyecto. In: XX Jornadas sobre la Enseñanza Universitaria de la Informática, pp. 285–292. Oviedo (2014)
31. Villagrá-Arnedo, C.J., Molina-Carmona, R., Llorens Largo, F., Gallego-Durán, F.J., et al.: Aprendizaje basado en proyectos grandes: experiencia y lecciones aprendidas (2020)
32. Villagrá-Arnedo, C.J., Gallego-Durán, F.J., Llorens Largo, F., Molina-Carmona, R.: Movimientos pendulares al situar al estudiante en el centro del proceso de aprendizaje. In: XXII Jornadas de Enseñanza Universitaria de la Informática, pp. 285–291. Almería (2016)

Teaching Learning Interactions in Secondary School: Towards a New Narrative Learning Context

Javier Herrero-Martín[1]([⊠]) [iD], Xavier Canaleta[2] [iD], Javier del Valle[3],
and Ricardo Torres[2] [iD]

[1] Centro Superior de Estudios Universitarios La Salle, Universidad Autónoma de Madrid,
Madrid, Spain
j.herrero@lasallecampus.es
[2] La Salle, Ramon Llull University, Barcelona, Spain
{xavier.canaleta,ricardo.torres}@salle.url.edu
[3] Colegio La Salle Palencia, Equipo Distrital NCA-ARLEP, Madrid, Spain
javivalle@sallep.net

Abstract. This paper describes the impact of the creation and deployment of a new interaction and learning ecosystem (NCA/NLC) and how it contributes to educational success in secondary education, based on the overall improvement and quality assurance of the learning process. The associated technological infrastructure allows for a consistent and coherent approach, by providing a framework that integrates and facilitates several elements: the integrated connection between the methodological and didactic developments of the rest of the educational stages (vertical connection), the integration of content and learning processes, creating an ecosystem with its own meaning; the assurance of the legislative, normative and curricular quality of the teaching and learning process; and the ecological and comprehensive connection with the events and conditions of the current world.

Keywords: Learning systems · Methodologies · Narrative processes

1 Introduction

Secondary education is a key part of what is usually perceived as the typical school development. In a traditional view, which has often been challenged (Resino et al. 2019), students must face, sequentially, specific assessment periods through which their skills and abilities, mainly intellectual ones, are assessed, in order to achieve specific learning outcomes (Ohlsen 2007). In traditional education, technological integration has been progressively incorporated at the same time that specific needs for updating content or forms of learning were emerging. In this way, technological advances have been presented as progressive-added possibilities for innovation from a perspective of improving the pre-existing way of teaching (Hillmayr et al. 2020).

P. Zaphiris and A. Ioannou (Eds.): HCII 2022, LNCS 13328, pp. 433–444, 2022.
https://doi.org/10.1007/978-3-031-05657-4_31

Far from this consideration, new educational trends raise a fundamental issue, that of a necessary balance between intellectual development, meaningful learning and emotional quality of education (Vílchez 2002), taking into account two elements: the instrumental character of the learning activity, which brings into play the operative practice of mental processes applied to contextualized everyday life experiences and events (Lo and Hew 2020); and the mediating role and leadership of teachers in the context of the educational activity (Leithwood et al. 2020).

Rethinking education entails a general reconsideration of how teachers, as learning mediators, and students, as major players, use technology support and digital resources, both conceptually and operationally (Adell et al. 2019; Ekberg and Gao, 2018). Consequently, the way in which the technological layer acts upon the pedagogical layer must also change (Bretscher 2021), adapting in a way that fits this new perception of learning contexts.

It is clear that this kind of initiatives propose a clear paradigm shift in secondary education (Harris and Bruin 2017), seeing that the current educational (pedagogical and methodological) models lack the necessary conditions to provide instructional designs according to new insights derived from how we analyze today those learning needs (Top et al. 2021). Furthermore, considering this changing perspective in the way of understanding how human beings learn, from a multidisciplinary perspective (Kuo et al. 2019), this present scenario has promoted the emergence of new ways of teaching, displacing the traditional concept of teaching by the more current concept of interaction.

Along with the change in the pedagogical framework we are also facing, as a consequence, a fundamental need: the provision of an adequate learning environment for designing of digital ecosystems adapted to this new condition. In fact, accepting the challenge of methodological change means rethinking a new general educational model in which technological and digital framework could offer a clear response to the demands of the new operative scenario. Moreover, the post-covid era is bringing out a paradigm shift in the way learning contexts are viewed. While the needs for digitization and interaction between humans and technology are still valid, due to the pandemic of intrinsic needs, the current educational reality has provided a broader and more diverse way of understanding access, both to knowledge and to shared resources. This general framework shows an ideal field for the design of new learning ecosystems that foster different ways of achieving individual and collective competencies.

In this context, interactive learning systems are created as polyhedral, multisensory environments, where people can find a space both for assimilation and construction of new knowledge and also for its use in mutual-context collaborations. Thus, the different elements that make up a learning ecosystem interact between them, while mutually influencing each other, in such a way that the system itself learns from its own model of mutual influence and interaction.

1.1 Human-Computer Interaction in the XXI Century Context

The evolution of technology nowadays is mostly driven by a number of social requirements derived from how people use and interact with technology and each other; this translates into the educational world, where educational solutions based on technology are also based on how learners interact with each other, with facilitators, and with pedagogical and methodological content. In this context, the usability of technological resources and facilities is an indicator of how humans connect the digital (virtual, technological) with the physical (biological and neurocognitive) representation of the world they live in. Furthermore, if we bring this idea closer to the pedagogical field, it would be necessary to bound the scope of the innovation, as well as its effect on people, in terms of creative learning potential, proper use, reliability, comprehensiveness and even ethical boundaries (Churchill et al. 2013), It could be stated that digital ecosystems offer the appropriate counterpart to biological ecosystems (Briscoe et al. 2011), conserving some properties derived from those, that make them useful for building robust environments, with scalable architectures, capable of solving complex problems of a dynamic, self-organizing and self-managing nature, whose automation potential generates greater value in terms of productive efficiency (Levin 1998).

Accordingly, HCI designs in education need to face the critical issue of the recognition of formal representation structures that gather, in an integrative way, each of the existing pieces of information (Rinaldi and Russo 2020) so people may appreciate the whole project as unique and indivisible.

It is important to note the relevance of teachers as facilitators in the technology mediated process of multidisciplinary learning practices; although the vast majority of learners are likely already familiar with technologies, the contextual and digital ecosystem will need to be able to generate smart learning mechanisms, adapted to interindividual student conditions (Stephanidis et al. 2019). To sum up, there are two relevant factors, when considering an interaction system: first, those features and conditions defined by the technological environment; second, the fundamental consideration regarding the human factor as a central point in the design and implementation of learning systems (Chen and Wang 2019).

A current, up-to-date vision of education should consider these two aspects when designing learning contexts. The advances and developments of technology enhanced learning (TEL) systems, shows a growing interest in the importance of data analytics and its connection with the educational world, an interaction that gave way to the emergence of the learning analytics concept. The convergence between learning design and learning analytics provides an adequate framework for a) making implicit knowledge and learning explicit, and b) the significance of practical and instrumental learning processes (Mangaroska and Giannakos 2011) .

1.2 Current Research Context

The research project described in this paper is contextualized within the framework of evaluation and methodological deployment known as Nuevo Contexto de Aprendizaje (New Learning Context, NLC, known as NCA for its initials in Spanish and Catalan); it is a nation-wide educational experience, developed and led by the La Salle Institution, based on a theoretical model that impacts 76 educational centers, with a country-wide scope (Spain and Portugal), at secondary education level (12–16 years). The start of the deployment process takes place during the 2021–22 academic year and will be implemented gradually over the following three years, until that education level has been fully covered.

The main research question focuses on how the creation and deployment of a new interaction and learning ecosystem (NCA/NLC) contributes to educational success in secondary education, in terms of indicators of change, improvement and quality assurance.

As a main research question, we wonder how the creation and deployment of a new interaction and learning ecosystem (NCA/NLC) contributes to educational success, in secondary education, in terms of indicators of change, improvement and quality assurance.

2 Method

2.1 Research Design

The research is contextualized within the general framework of the NCA/NLC evaluation design (Herrero-Martín et al. 2020) A mixed, parallel and convergent design is proposed (Creswell 2014), combining, on the quantitative side, an analysis based on learning outcomes (ANOVA, MR) and, on the qualitative side, an incidental non-probabilistic design, with complete saturation (Hennink and Kaiser 2022), based on the generation of discussion groups formed by students and teachers.

2.2 Participants and Sampling

In terms of quantitative variables, the sample is made up of a total of 1,436 students of the first year of Secondary Education (Spanish curriculum), enrolled in schools in 15 autonomous communities. The educational centers are all part of the La Salle-Arlep network (Spain and Portugal). A stratified cluster sampling (Sedgwick 2013) was selected for the qualitative phase of the research. For both dimensions, three levels were defined: education sector (region); province, and educational center.

2.3 Development of the Model. Integration Between the Current Educational Legislation and the NCA Framework

The structural design of NCA at the secondary education level (ESO) is referenced in a double sense, formulated in terms of needs: the integration of the autonomous educational legislation and the NCA framework, and the adaptation to learning preferences, formal and non-formal, by means of a digital context.

The initial development process synchronizes, based on the curricular evaluation criteria, the different legislative frameworks for each region of the state (in Spain, Autonomous Communities). Then, the system connects the curricular base with the methodological and didactic (narrative learning, and other NCA didactic environments) and, finally, with the pedagogical principles of the model.

2.4 Technological Layer and Digital Ecosystem Features

For the development of the integrated virtual learning system, a specific technological proposal has been developed, based on

a) Sallenet ©. A platform developed in-house, based on open source LMS Moodle.
b) A Varnish server that acts as an HTTP accelerator, in order to take concurrency into account. This is a reverse HTTP proxy cache.
c) Apache 2.4.18 server technology on Ubuntu 16.04 LTS and PHP 7.0.33 and MariaDB 10.2.23 database
d) Backup System, with a daily backup. These daily copies are stored for 4 months; and after that only one monthly copy is stored indefinitely.

The learning ecosystem is based on the technological development, through a limited set of dynamic properties:

1. Ecological context. Non-formal learning is established as a priority through transmedia access.
2. Autonomy and personalization of learning. Diversity of formats and asynchronous availability. This allows adapting the inter-individual conditions of the learner based on the smart personalization of the properties of the system, and at the same time increasing the degrees of freedom in accessing content and activities.
3. Usefulness and usability of the curricular content and the learning evaluation process.
4. Data analytics. To make it easier for the evaluation process (continuous, comprehensive and complex) to be carried out with the greatest possible rigor, NLC/NCA proposes a digital tool that helps us automate the data collection and reporting processes. An essential condition of the ecosystem is the optimal use of informative data (use, participation, learning, evaluation and feedback).
5. Comprehensive learning environment. Many of the learning outcomes are automated and viewable in real time by students, teachers, and families. From a psycho pedagogical point of view, the ecosystem must enable the recognition of barriers to learning. In this sense, both the meta-analysis of data and the direct reflection of the educator allow for the ultimate understanding of the progress of the students.
6. Coherence with the methodological design. It is essential to guarantee the coherence and alignment of the development process, from the didactic innovation layer to the evaluation process.

2.5 Methodological Design

Narrative Learning Concept in NLC/NCA. The pedagogical object of the narrative consists of confronting each scenario with the personal history of the learner so that, together with the learning itself, an adequate human evolution and development takes place.

Recent research considers the relevance of multidisciplinary narrative use as a mediator of learning (Niemi and Kiilakoski 2020). In this way, didactic narratives and the consideration of storytelling help to understand the world in which we live and to know how to value it from the perspective of culture and history (Lee et al. 2011).

For methodological purposes, and starting from the educational legislation at national level, we then connected the national and local curricula with the NCA methodological design through different narrative proposals, which will connect knowledge both horizontally (interdisciplinary) and temporally. This $360°$ reality is epistemologically based on the idea of knowledge connected to the world and the events that occur in it, beyond the isolated concept of the subject as an individual and unique object of learning. Narratives understand people and societies, not subjects.

Besides curriculum projection, the proposed design uses the layers model depicted by Pratten (2011) for the development of transmedia narratives:

a) Narrative layer (describes the story in terms of plot and character or events development). We approach a learning object from an interdisciplinary perspective, where each area contributes its specificity for the understanding and elaboration of a final product. The plot that unifies the process unfolds in the welcoming and closure learning areas through events or characters that keep the common thread of the story.
b) Presentation layer (describes the platform, channels and means used to deliver the previous layers). We use a proposal that is well-known to young people, ecological, in transmedia format as detailed below.
c) Interactive layer (describes the mechanics, events and logic that provide the experience). It is based on activities that simultaneously serve as learning and evaluation.
d) Layer of experience (describes the moments created and the emotional journey of the audience). Attributed to experiences of metacognition and learning/service, as well as celebration and public display of learning.

2.6 Operational Database

The methodological design operates technologically from the operational integration of different databases that are then related to each other. Its basic properties are detailed below.

a) Legislative: uses the different levels and adaptations of curriculum specification, linking stage objectives with competencies, area objectives, content blocks, evaluation criteria and evaluable learning standards. In this way, each evaluation criterion is referenced to the different levels of specification mentioned above.
b) Didactics: each evaluation criterion categorized in the different areas is referenced, related to the didactic areas described in the model, as well as to the pedagogical principles and their transversal connections with the different content areas.
c) Curricular contents. Differentiated by areas of knowledge and educational levels. Also diversified, using text, graphics and audiovisual formats.

d) Educational activities.

   1. Moodle tasks: forums, work documents, deliverable files (text, image, audio…)
   2. Moodle Quiz and Adaptive quiz
   3. H5p type interactive activities.

2.7 Digital Didactic Sequence

The learning proposal is shown in a single didactic sequence, using a digital format. It proposes differentiated access and content for teachers and students with a visual support that is attractive and familiar, similar to what students find on the Internet, and works as the center of interest for learning processes (autonomy, protagonism and personalization). Figure 1 represents the internal algorithm designed to connect the development of integrated content and the interactive learning interface, based on an adaptive and customizable process.

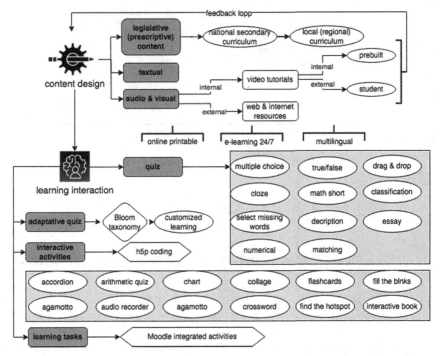

Fig. 1. Content-learning design in new learning context. Main features description of general model in secondary level education.

2.8 Evaluation Proposal

The NLC/NCA design has a specific evaluation tool. Starting from the predefined and weighted set of interrelated evaluation criteria, the levels of activity, didactic field,

		1ª Evaluación	2ª Evaluación		3ª Evaluación
Calificaciones	Área				
CV Convalidado	Biologia y Geologia	7	10	Notable	8
RE Refuerzo Educativo	Educacion fisica	RE 5	7	Bien	6
	Matematicas	6	8	Suficiente	5
	Religion	4	8	Bien	6
	Geografia e Historia	4	9	Notable	7
	Educacion Plastica, Visual y Audiovisual	3	6	Sobresaliente	9
	Tecnologia	6	9	Suficiente	5
	Primera Lengua Extranjera: Ingles	5	8	Notable	7
	Segunda Lengua Extranjera: Frances	4	7	Notable	8
	Lengua castellana y literatura	CV	CV		CV
	Cultura Clasica (2 ESO)	1	2	Insuficiente	3

Tutor/a

Periodo 1 A ESO / 3ª Evaluación

Curso académico 2021-2022

La Salle Institución Madrid / nca

Comentarios

Biologia y Geologia: Estas trabajando muy bien! (3)

Educacion fisica: Educacion fisica - Lorem Ipsum is simply dummy text of the printing and typesetting industry. Lorem Ipsum has been the industry's standard dummy text ever since the 1500s, when an unknown printer took a galley of type and scrambled it to make a type specimen book. It has survived not only five centuries, but also the leap into electronic typesetting, remaining essentially unchanged. It was popularised (3)

Tecnologia: Tienes que concentrarte un poco mas en clase (3)

Cultura Clasica (2 ESO): Tienes que esforzarte un poco mᵃs para superar esta materia pendiente

Incidencias

Falta	2	Falta justificada	1
Retraso	0	Retraso justificado	0

Competencias

01	02	03	04
Competencia artv≠stica	Competencia social y cv≠vica	Competencia tecnolv≥gica	Competencia cientv≠fica

05	06	07
Competencia matemv"tica	Competencia en comunicaciv≥n lingvTv≠stica y literaria	Competencia motriz

Una persona competente es capaz de responder a demandas complejas y llevar a cabo tareas diversas de forma adecuada. La competencia supone una combinación de habilidades prácticas, conocimientos, motivación, valores éticos, actitudes, emociones, y otros componentes sociales y de comportamiento que se movilizan conjuntamente para lograr una acción eficaz.

✂ -

Justificante de calificación

Periodo	1 A ESO / Tercera evaluacin	Firma padre / madre / Tutor
Alumno	Lucia Abad Calleja	

Fig. 2. School Report. Output featuring of human-computer interactive ecosystem in NLC/NCA

area and subject, learning competencies, stage objectives and pedagogical principles are connected, for each of the levels corresponding to the educational stage.

In this way, the technological design of the evaluation system allows the automatic connection of the direct assessment of the teacher on an activity, with the rest of the levels and curricular dimensions.

The development of the tool allows multiple adaptive uses, applicable to different contexts. In this way, the output reports can be multiple and customizable, allowing for diversity awareness of the student body. In addition, it is possible to use the data to assess learning from different perspectives, both quantitatively and qualitatively (Fig. 2).

It is also possible to retrieve qualification data to assess competency-type learning. As each evaluation or qualification task is linked to one or several skills, the algorithm allows the establishment of filters by learning skills. In this way, the teacher will be able to have a clear vision of how the student is progressing in one competence or another, collecting information from different tasks, in different areas and connecting, in turn, the interpretation between different teachers.

Likewise, the design incorporates analysis filters for the characteristics and conditions of the student's personal development, in parallel to the formal learning process (data referring to each didactic field), allowing to generate both analytical and graphical outputs of the state in real time.

3 Results

Preliminary results point to a learning context enriched by the numerous interconnected variables, compared to the pre-existing model (linear, based on physical support, textbook and activities, and teaching with specific technological supports). The main characteristics found in the first phase of deployment may be summarized as a) greater motivation towards learning; b) significant increase in peer interaction, and development of interpersonal skills and human development; c) greater commitment to learning processes and d) greater control over the assessment system.

In addition to the improvement of individual learning conditions, the system created guarantees legislative, regulatory and curricular compliance for each learning process and activity, guaranteeing its supervision in real time, which allows total assurance of educational quality. and its supervision at all times.

4 Discussion and Conclusions

In the current scientific literature there is evidence of how the use of narrative processes as a means to encourage learning produces positive effects in different disciplines (Prins et al. 2017; Engel et al. 2018). In this same approach, there are different contrasted experiences that support the relevance of narrative development in the development of knowledge strategies and high-level cognitive competence (Mangione et al. 2011).

Ongoing research supports the principle of improving learning conditions by establishing an integrated interaction framework that allows the connection of content, processes and adaptable forms of inter-individual participation and self-regulation. The development of interactive learning ecosystems based on narrative development proposals makes it possible to approach, in a special way, between the formal learning context and its projection on the new technological-industrial and socio-cultural dynamics of the surrounding environment (Sánchez-Mesa et al. 2016). The development proposed in this research, within the framework of the NLC/NCA, allows, in this sense: a) the integrated connection between the methodological and didactic developments of the rest of the educational stages (vertical connection); b) the integration of content and learning processes, creating an ecosystem with its own meaning; c) the assurance of the legislative, normative and curricular quality of the teaching and learning process; and d) the ecological and comprehensive connection with the events and conditions of the current world.

This way, a consistent and coherent approach is ensured and facilitated by the proposed development, in the form of an integrated framework.

References

Author, F.: Article title. Journal **2**(5), 99–110 (2016)

Author, F., Author, S.: Title of a proceedings paper. In: Editor, F., Editor, S. (eds.) CONFERENCE 2016, LNCS, vol. 9999, pp. 1–13. Springer, Heidelberg (2016)

Author, F., Author, S., Author, T.: Book title, 2nd edn. Publisher, Location (1999)

Author, F.: Contribution title. In: 9th International Proceedings on Proceedings, pp. 1–2. Publisher, Location (2010)

LNCS Homepage. http://www.springer.com/lncs. Accessed 21 Nov 2016

Adell, J.S., Llopis, M.A.N., Esteve, M.F.M., Valdeolivas, N.M.G.: El debate sobre el pensamiento computacional en educación. RIED. Revista Iberoamericana de Educación a Distancia **22**(1), 171–186 (2019). http://dx.doi.org/10.5944/ried.22.1.22303

Bretscher, N.: Challenging assumptions about relationships between mathematics pedagogy and ICT integration: surveying teachers in English secondary schools. Res. Math. Educ. **23**(2), 142–158 (2021). https://doi.org/10.1080/14794802.2020.1830156

Briscoe, G., Sadedin, S., De Wilde, P.: Digital ecosystems: ecosystem-oriented architectures. Nat. Comput. **10**(3), 1143 (2011). https://doi.org/10.1007/s11047-011-9254-0

Chen, S.Y., Wang, J.H.: Human factors and personalized digital learning: an editorial. Int. J. Hum.-Comput. Interact. **35**(4–5), 297–298 (2019). https://doi.org/10.1080/10447318.2018.154 2891

Churchill, E.F., Bowser, A., Preece, J.: Teaching and learning human-computer interaction: past, present, and future. Interactions **20**(2), 44–53 (2013). https://doi.org/10.1145/2427076.2427086

Creswell, J.W.: Research Design: Qualitative, Quantitative, and Mixed Methods Approaches, 4th edn. SAGE Publications, Thousand Oaks (2014)

Ekberg, S., Gao, S.: Understanding challenges of using ICT in secondary schools in Sweden from teachers' perspective. Int. J. Inf. Learn. Technol. **35**(1), 43–55 (2018). https://doi.org/10.1108/IJILT-01-2017-0007

Engel, A., Lucido, K., Cook, K.: Rethinking narrative: leveraging storytelling for science learning. Child. Educ. **94**(6), 4–12 (2018). https://doi.org/10.1080/00094056.2018.1540189

Harris, A., de Bruin, L.R.: Secondary school creativity, teacher practice and STEAM education: an international study. J. Educ. Change **19**(2), 153–179 (2017). https://doi.org/10.1007/s10833-017-9311-2

Hennink, M., Kaiser, B.N.: Sample sizes for saturation in qualitative research: a systematic review of empirical tests. Soc. Sci. Med. **292**, 114523 (2022). https://doi.org/10.1016/j.socscimed.2021.114523

Herrero-Martín, J., Canaleta, X., Fonseca, D., Rodríguez-Merino, C., Kinnear, L., Amo, D.: Designing a multi-scale and multi-dimensional assessment for a new national educational context. In: Eighth International Conference on Technological Ecosystems for Enhancing Multiculturality, pp. 791–796 (2020). https://doi.org/10.1145/3434780.3436567

Hillmayr, D., Ziernwald, L., Reinhold, F., Hofer, S.I., Reiss, K.M.: The potential of digital tools to enhance mathematics and science learning in secondary schools: a context-specific meta-analysis. Comput. Educ. **153**, 103897 (2020). https://doi.org/10.1016/j.compedu.2020.103897

Kuo, H.-C., Tseng, Y.C., Yang, Y.T.C.: Promoting college student's learning motivation and creativity through a STEM interdisciplinary PBL human-computer interaction system design and development course. Think. Skills Creat. **31**, 1 (2019). https://doi.org/10.1016/j.tsc.2018.09.001

Lee, S.Y., Mott, B.W., Lester, J.C.: Modeling narrative-centered tutorial decision making in guided discovery learning. In: Biswas, G., Bull, S., Kay, J., Mitrovic, A. (eds.) AIED 2011. LNCS (LNAI), vol. 6738, pp. 163–170. Springer, Heidelberg (2011). https://doi.org/10.1007/978-3-642-21869-9_23

Leithwood, K., Harris, A., Hopkins, D.: Seven strong claims about successful school leadership revisited. Sch. Leadersh. Manage. **40**(1), 5–22 (2020). https://doi.org/10.1080/13632434.2019.1596077

Levin, S.: Ecosystems and the biosphere as complex adaptive systems. Ecosystems **1**, 431–436 (1998). https://doi.org/10.1007/s100219900037

Lo, C.K., Hew, K.F.: A comparison of flipped learning with gamification, traditional learning, and online independent study: the effects on students' mathematics achievement and cognitive engagement. Interact. Learn. Environ. **28**(4), 464–481 (2020). https://doi.org/10.1080/10494820.2018.1541910

Mangaroska, K., Giannakos, M.: Learning analytics for learning design: a systematic literature review of analytics-driven design to enhance learning. IEEE Trans. Learn. Technol. **12**(4), 516–534 (2011). https://doi.org/10.1109/TLT.2018.2868673

Niemi, R., Kiilakoski, T.: I Learned to cooperate with my friends and there were no quarrels: pupils' experiences of participation in a multidisciplinary learning module. Scand. J. Educ. Res. **64**(7), 984–998 (2020). https://doi.org/10.1080/00313831.2019.1639817

Mangione, G.R., Orciuoli, Pierri, F.A., Ritrovato, P., Rosciano, M.: A new model for storytelling complex learning objects. In: Third International Conference on Intelligent Networking and Collaborative Systems, pp. 836–841 (2011). https://doi.org/10.1109/INCoS.2011.27

Ohlsen, M.T.: Classroom assessment practices of secondary school members of NCTM. Am. Second. Educ. **36**(1), 4–14 (2007). https://www.jstor.org/stable/41406094

Pratten, R.: Getting started with transmedia storytelling. CreateSpace (2011)

Prins, R., Avraamidou, L., Goedhart, M.: Tell me a Story: the use of narrative as a learning tool for natural selection. Educ. Media Int. **54**(1), 20–33 (2017). https://doi.org/10.1080/09523987.2017.1324361

Resino, D.A., Amores, I.A.C., Muñoz, I.A.: La repetición de curso a debate: Un estudio empírico a partir de PISA 2015. Educación XX1 **22**(2) (2019). https://doi.org/10.5944/educxx1.22479. Article 2

Rinaldi, A.M., Russo, C.: Sharing knowledge in digital ecosystems using semantic multimedia big data. In: Hameurlain, A., et al. (eds.) Transactions on Large-Scale Data- and Knowledge-Centered Systems XLV. LNCS, vol. 12390, pp. 109–131. Springer, Heidelberg (2020). https://doi.org/10.1007/978-3-662-62308-4_5

Sánchez-Mesa, D., Aarseth, E., Pratten, R., Scolari, C.A.: Transmedia (Storytelling?): a polyphonic critical review. Artnodes: revista de arte, ciencia y tecnología **18**, 8–19 (2016). https://doi.org/10.7238/a.v0i18.3064

Sedgwick, P.: Stratified cluster sampling. BMJ **347**, 7016 (2013). https://doi.org/10.1136/bmj.f7016

Stephanidis, C., et al.: Seven HCI grand challenges. Int. J. Hum.–Comput. Interact. **35**(14), 1229–1269 (2019). https://doi.org/10.1080/10447318.2019.1619259

Top, E., Baser, D., Akkus, R., Akayoglu, S., Gurer, M.D.: Secondary school teachers' preferences in the process of individual technology mentoring. Comput. Educ. **160**, 104030 (2021). https://doi.org/10.1016/j.compedu.2020.104030

Vílchez, P.S.: Evolución de los conceptos sobre inteligencia. Planteamientos actuales de la inteligencia emocional para la orientación educativa. Educación XX1, 5 (2002). https://doi.org/10.5944/educxx1.5.1.385

Are Learning Theories Being Used to Support the Implementation of Learning Technologies Within Higher Education? A Systematic Review

Pedro Isaias[1](✉), Paula Miranda[2], and Sara Pifano[3]

[1] Institute for Teaching and Learning Innovation (ITaLI) and UQ Business School, The University of Queensland, Australia, Level 2, Colin Clark Building (#39), St Lucia, QLD 4072, Australia
`pedro.isaias@uq.edu.au`
[2] Setubal School of Technology, Polytechnic Institute of Setubal, Setúbal, Portugal
`paula.miranda@estsetubal.ips.pt`
[3] ISRLab – Information Society Research Laboratory, Lisbon, Portugal
`sarap@isrlab.org`

Abstract. A main concern associated with the implementation of learning technologies pertains to its lack of support from learning theories. In light of this concern, this paper aims to identify which theories of learning, if any, are used by educators to support the employment of learning technologies in higher education. A thematic analysis was performed in the context of a systematic review of 285 papers on the subject of learning technologies, for the period of 2007–2017, within the context of higher education. The results demonstrate that learning theories are not being used to support the incorporation of technologies in higher education. These findings bring to light the absence of a theoretical justification for technology implementation.

Keywords: Learning technologies · Learning theories · Higher education · Systematic review

1 Introduction

Societal transformations have impacted the choice of both learning theories and learning technology [27]. In the context of a connected and predominantly digital world, it is unfitting to resort to learning theories that are exclusively founded upon principles deriving from traditional teaching settings in the classroom. The continuous change affecting education and the growing variety of learning settings demand a reassessment of the theories that are employed to scaffold the design of both learning tasks and technologies [4]. Learning theories argue that the selection of instructional approaches depends on the learning goals that are to be established [25].

Selwyn [40] argues that there is a global perception that technology is both an integral part and an inevitable feature of current forms of education, which has led a significant part of research to focus exclusively on the technical and procedural aspects

© The Author(s), under exclusive license to Springer Nature Switzerland AG 2022
P. Zaphiris and A. Ioannou (Eds.): HCII 2022, LNCS 13328, pp. 445–460, 2022.
https://doi.org/10.1007/978-3-031-05657-4_32

of technology implementation, namely on how to deploy it more fruitfully. This paper argues that these technical and procedural aspects are central to the debate about the practical use of learning technologies and that they provide valuable insight for future implementation. Nonetheless, examining procedural and technical aspects is insufficient and it is essential to explore the theoretical foundations that validate the use of learning technologies.

With regards to theory, Oliver [33] highlights the lack of theories of technology to justify how it can be conducive to learning. This indicates, according to the author, a significant deficiency of research in this area, as the absence of theoretical justification prevents the establishment of a decisive connection between the deployment of technology and learning. Rather than focusing on the theory of technology, as determinant as it is, this paper emphasises instead the importance of theories for learning. It follows Pentoney, Halpern, Butler [36] who advocate that the swiftness of technological progress demands, namely, that emerging technologies be informed by current knowledge about how individuals learn. Despite its importance, previous research [21, 24] has highlighted a lack of connection between learning theory and learning technology design and use.

In light of these arguments and given the research gap that exists on the connection between technology and theory, this study aims to address the following research question, in the context of higher education:

- Which theories of learning, if any, are used by educators to support the implementation of learning technologies?

To address this research question, three core objectives will be pursued: a) to analyse the publication patterns of the selected papers; b) to determine which learning technologies are most often cited by the papers; and c) to analyse the references to learning theories. This paper begins by exploring the role that learning theories have in the integration of technology in education. The methods section follows with a presentation of the systematic review and the processes associated with it. The paper concludes with the analysis and discussion of the results.

2 Learning Theories and the Integration of Technology

The integration of technology in education poses the challenge of identifying the ways in which technology impacts the students' cognitive process [39]. As it's been argued, "it is not surprising that as the scope of changes in learning enabled by technologies increases, so does our need to expand the repertoire of theories and research approaches." [4]. Moreover, one of the most fundamental aspects to examine is how learning theories are being transformed by the adoption of technology in education and which of these theories are being used to validate the deployment of technology in educational settings [26]. Referring to Web 2.0 tools in particular, Bates [3] highlights the importance of resorting to a clearly defined educational theory to inform teachers' selection and deployment of technology in learning environments. Also, according to Yuen, Yaoyuneyong, Yuen [50] "using a Web 2.0 technology or tool in the classroom without considering pedagogical theory could be compared to using power tools to construct a house without first consulting an architect". As such, learning theories provide a much needed structure to the implementation of technology in educational contexts.

Mayes, De Freitas [30] equally claim that, within technology-enhanced learning, a sound pedagogical design requires the adoption of a learning theory. It is fundamental that there is guiding frame to assess if the learning and teaching practices that are implemented will actually result in the envisioned learning results. However, the connection between the design of learning scenarios where technology is employed and learning theories is intricate, as the compatibility between the theoretical underpinnings of learning and the design aspects pertaining to learning technologies isn't always achievable [25]. Hung [20] argue that rather than perceiving learning theories as conflicting, it is more beneficial to match the different pedagogical approaches that each of them defends to the most appropriate learning technologies to achieve specific learning objectives. Behaviourism, for example, can be more compatible with quizzes and a linear production of information, while constructivism can be more suitable to guide simulations and virtual worlds [41].

The potential that technology has to offer to education requires a stable basis of a strong understanding of learning to be accomplished [15]. According to Bell [4] educational stakeholders are attempting to incorporate technology in both formal and informal learning environments, searching for theoretical frames that can guide their initiatives. The author postulates that the selection of the most relevant learning theory is influenced by the intervention's goal and spectrum, the financial resources that are available and the teacher/researcher's own philosophical standpoint and experience. Moreover, different theories originate different "conceptions of information processing and knowledge acquisition that influence technology use. Given the central function of education to help learners acquire declarative, procedural and conditional knowledge, learning theories and technologies are fellow travellers." [27]. Thus, different learning theories have different conceptions about the effect of technology, how it should be deployed and what purpose it serves. The convergence between the progress of learning theories and the affordances that technology provide allow teachers in higher education to benefit from exceptional possibilities [19].

Nonetheless, research is sparse in connecting the use of learning technologies with definite learning models. The studies that mention learning theories, often do so superficially and with an excessive reliance on theories that are not necessarily pertinent to digital settings [11]. In the systematic review performed by Bartolomé, Castañeda, Adell [2] of literature between 1960 and 2015, the authors focused on the specific issue of personalisation in educational technology and posited that some types of learning technologies do not attempt to incorporate pedagogical foundations in the pursuit of personalisation. Furthermore, in another systematic review about the use of digital card games in the context of education, Kordaki, Gousiou [24] concluded that although most papers embraced basic elements of social and constructivist theories of learning, only a few explicitly stated the theory that they used. Similarly, in their systematic review in the context of nursing education, Kaakinen, Arwood [21] set out to examine how learning theories were being deployed in the design and learning assessment of simulations. The authors revealed that only a very limited segment of the studies that they examined used a theory of learning or development as a foundation for their use of simulations.

2.1 Learning Theories

From the panoply of existing learning theories, some are more relevant in the context of technology deployment. The main theories here considered, for the guidance of technology implementation in education, are behaviourism, cognitivism, connectivism and constructivism. Zingiswa, Mohapi [54] argue that behaviourism and constructivism are the leading theories at the foundation of many existing learning technologies. Besides behaviourism and constructivism Harasim [18] also highlights cognitivism as a theory for explaining and modelling learning technology application. Connectivism can equally be used in the context of technology deployment to promote both self-directed and collaborative learning [44].

Behaviourism. The core of behaviourism is the idea of a reaction following a specific stimulus. In this learning theory, learning is merely the acquirement of a novel behaviour. According to behaviourists there are two types of conditionings that can justify how people can be taught: classical conditioning and operant conditioning. Classical conditioning involves the strengthening of a natural impulse or another action that happens in response to a specific incentive. Operant conditioning, on the other hand, constitutes the most important kind of behaviourist learning. It can be defined as a reinforcement of a behaviour through a reward [37]. In the context of learning technologies, behaviourism represents a pertinent and feasible theory to provide the basis and the direction of the adoption of educational technology [9].

Cognitivism. Cognitivism is based on a cognitive orientation that focuses on facilitating the mental processing and on orienting the learner process and interaction. According to cognitivism, learning is more related with what the students know and the processes by which they have acquired it. The emphasis is placed on the attainment of knowledge and on the internal structures of the learners. Within this theory, the learners are regarded as being active contributors for the learning process. Also, cognitivism promotes the development of learning settings that enable and encourage learners to establish a link with content that they had previously learned, and that provide knowledge with meaning [17]. In terms of technology, cognitivism relates to tools that can model the mind and depict knowledge. Intelligent tutoring systems and artificial intelligence are examples of technologies that are based on representations of the human mind [18].

Connectivism. Connectivism regards learning as a process happening in uncertain settings with shifting elements that is not completely within the control of the learner. This learning theory is motivated by the assumption that new information is continuously being obtained and therefore the capacity to distinguish between information that is relevant and that which is irrelevant becomes crucial. It posits that it is fundamental to understand the effect that new information has on a context that was based on previous, outdated information. Hence, it is more important to know how to learn, than to possess knowledge that might become obsolete [42]. Connectivism also supports the control shift from the teacher to the students. Nonetheless, it is believed that by itself, connectivism, in a connected world and a dynamic context, is insufficient to guide technology enhanced learning as it lacks the comprehensiveness, as most single learning theories do, to account for all possible scenarios and purposes [4].

Constructivism. Constructivism regards learning as the product of a mental construction. This means that learning occurs at the moment where the new knowledge is created into and added to a person's existing structure of knowledge [37]. Constructivism shapes learning environments by promoting learning through activities, interaction and the development of authentic assessment techniques. Also, in terms of instructional strategies, it is suitable for discussions, inquiry teaching and discovery learning [39]. Furthermore, "socio-constructivist theories and technology-supported communities of learning and practice have become dominant, at least as a frame of reference within the community of educational technologists." [27]. Social constructivism advocates that learning is an active rather than passive process, that it has a social nature, where students learn meaningfully by engaging in social activities [1].

3 Methods

The systematic review followed the structure of the three core phases of the process, according to Bryman, Bell [8]: stipulating the research question and creating a strategy for the review process; performing the review; and reporting the results. Also, the PRISMA framework was consulted to assist the entirety of the project. More specifically, to assist the reporting of the systematic review, the PRISMA for abstracts checklist [5] and the PRISMA checklist [31] were used as a reference in the entirety of the process. Despite claims of researcher's bias and insufficient meticulousness, systematic reviews are valuable as evidence-based methods [8]. A central aspect of systematic reviews is transparency and it requires a clear description of the methods and procedures upon which the review is based [14]. In this sense, the next subsections intend to provide a clear depiction of the entirety of the process associated with this systematic review.

3.1 Inclusion Criteria

Google Scholar was used as the database for the search for papers. Google scholar was chosen because, as an academic database, it is at the moment, notwithstanding all its limitations, the system that offers the widest coverage of publications. It "offers viable avenues for searching and disseminating research that might otherwise remain in the depths of journal collection" Zientek, Werner, Campuzano, Nimon [52]. The initial search was guided by the expression "learning technologies higher education" within the 2007–2017 time period. With this expression, Google Scholar returned 186 000 results. To address the overwhelming amount of publications, the following inclusion criteria were established:

a) Pertains to the use of technology for learning (including both learning technologies in general or any learning technology in particular);
b) Describe either conceptual or empirical studies;

c) Refers to the higher education sector;
d) Published between 2007 and 2017;
e) Publications in English;
f) Research papers from conferences and journals or book chapters;
g) Full text available online;
h) Must contain the selected keywords in the title of the paper.

This last criterion was established to obtain a more manageable number of publications and since it could objectively be applied, it helped to reduce the impact of the researchers' biases. As was mentioned above, the overwhelming number of results that our initial search produced required a criterion that could narrow the results to a number that we could realistically analyse. The assessment of the quality of the studies is an essential part of conducting a systematic review, so it is important to include quality criteria [7]. Nonetheless, quality evaluation is very challenging, as not all studies report on the same components of research practice. Thus, criteria like journal ratings should be avoided, as they do not guarantee that all the essential elements of high quality research have been met [14]. Rather than adopting a strict list of quality criteria which would greatly reduce the number of publications that were selected, in this paper, to ensure a more complete understanding of the subject being studied, the quality assessment of the publications was done by following Pawson's (2006) argument of including publications based on their contribution to the understanding of the subject in question. As such, for the purpose of this systematic review, inclusion criteria a), b) and e) were also used as quality criteria to evaluate the studies, in addition to a mandatory compliance with the established structure of a research paper.

3.2 Search Keywords for Paper Selection

The selected keywords for the search were: higher education, learning technology/technologies, educational technology/technologies. To apply the search criteria, the advanced search option was used and the keywords were searched as "with all of the words" and "in the title of the article", from 2007 to 2017. The decision of not including any specific learning theory as a search keyword was made to collect papers that referred to any learning theory. Using specific theories or using the general expression "learning theories" would have limited the results. As one of the aims of the systematic review was to assess the importance that learning theories were given in the literature, the focus was on the collection of general studies about learning technology in higher education, rather than on literature that specifically addresses learning theories. Additionally, in previous systematic reviews the inclusion [21] or exclusion [24] of the expression "learning theories" resulted in similar findings pertaining to the theories of learning. Figure 1 illustrates the process of the paper selection.

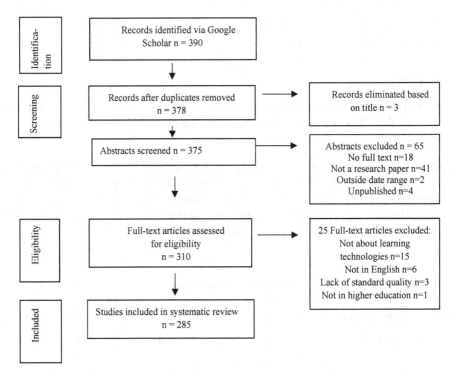

Fig. 1. Paper selection process. Adapted from Moher et al. [31]

3.3 Paper Analysis

The final 285 papers were examined using thematic analysis, a core method of qualitative research [6]. The trustworthiness of this type of analysis is greatly determined by precision, consistency and exhaustiveness in the data analysis [32]. In this research, the papers were screened individually and the most relevant references related to the research question were extracted into a universally applied form with several items that served as preliminary codes, which included:

- Category;
- Type of study;
- Type of technology used/discussed;
- Guiding learning theory.

The form was designed by three researchers and the papers were coded according to the data collected in each of the items of the form. The initial codes were based on a review of the literature and adjusted through the coding process, where new information emerged. The coding was performed by one coder with the revision of two other coders. In case of disagreement the initial coding was consulted as a guide. The codes pertaining to learning theories were further coded according to purpose and context of use. The content of this data extraction was then the subject of a qualitative content analysis in

Nvivo 10, as it is described in more detail in the analysis of the results section. The presentation of the results is textual, tabular and diagrammatic (word tree).

3.4 Results

The analysis of the 285 papers is divided into three sections: a presentation of publication patterns; a depiction of the most frequently mentioned technologies; and a scrutiny of learning theories.

Publication Patterns. With concern to the first objective of this research pertaining to publication patterns, as can be seen in Table 1, which displays the publication year, most papers were published between 2013 and 2017. This pattern demonstrates the existence of a growing research interest. Also, it suggests that the great majority of the papers that were analysed in the systematic review were based on recent research.

Table 1. Publication year

2007	2008	2009	2010	2011	2012	2013	2014	2015	2016	2017
8	12	16	26	23	25	33	43	36	32	31

In terms of the classification of the papers, there was a predominance of journal publications. In total, 32 are book chapters, 100 are published as conference papers and 151 are journal papers. Additionally, 1 working paper and 1 panel were equally considered. In terms of the type of research, the majority of the papers are empirical (180), while 101 are conceptual and 4 are applied.

Most Popular Learning Technologies. In addressing the second objective of this paper, related to the most popular learning technologies, it was important to establish which specific learning technologies were mentioned in the papers. With concern to the itemisation of the various learning technologies, this list follows the information provided by the selected papers. It was more consistent to use this method, as some papers clearly refer to the specific technologies that they were using and others were more evasive. There were references to a wide variety of technologies that can be used for learning purposes. The table below depicts the 10 most cited technologies in the papers that were analysed (Table 2).

Table 2. Most frequently mentioned learning technologies

Learning technologies	Number of papers
Web 2.0 technologies	60
Learning management systems	26
Mobile technologies	25

(continued)

Table 2. (*continued*)

Learning technologies	Number of papers
E-learning technologies	24
Information and communication technologies	18
Video	15
Web technologies	13
Virtual learning environments	7
Student response systems	6
Massive open online courses	6

The majority of the papers did specify a learning technology, but a significant portion (129) mentioned solely learning technologies in general, without referring to a particular example. From the analysis of the papers that did focus on particular technologies, the predominance of Web 2.0 technologies becomes evident. Learning Management Systems, Mobile technologies and e-learning technologies were equally popular among the selected publications. Furthermore, 49 papers mentioned technologies that were classified as other in the codification of the data, since they were mentioned only 1 to 3 times. These include cloud computing, assistive technologies, learning analytics, wearable technology, e-portfolios and emerging technologies. Over 60 papers mentioned more than one technology or technology class and 16 papers were grouped under a category entitled various technologies, for having mentioned over 5 technologies.

Theories of Learning in the Implementation of Learning Technologies. In response to the third objective, to analyse the references to learning theories, it is addressed here in connection to this paper's main research question and it revealed that an expressive majority of the papers, 228, did not mention any learning theory. The 57 papers that made reference to a learning theory chose mainly constructivism as the most adequate learning theory in the context of learning technology. The predominance of constructivism is followed by its social variance, social constructivism. Table 3 shows the specific number of papers and the learning theories that they mention. This list is based on the references of the papers and on the views of the authors from the selected papers. The analysis was based on their own definition of each learning theory.

Table 3. Learning theories referenced in the papers

Learning theory	Number of papers
Not mentioned	228
Constructivism	38
Social constructivism	17
Behaviourism	10

(*continued*)

Table 3. (*continued*)

Learning theory	Number of papers
Cognitivism	9
Connectivism	8
Only mentions their importance	6
Constructionism	3

In total, 38 papers mentioned constructivism. An additional 17 papers selected social constructivism, a branch of constructivism. Behaviourism (10), cognitivism (9) and connectivism (8) were also mentioned in a few papers, mainly referred together as a group of popular learning theories. A few publications (6) mentioned only the importance of learning theories. With regards to constructionism, only 3 papers mentioned its importance. Besides these learning theories, 12 others were mentioned in the papers, but solely once. These include, for example, 21st century skills, learning preference theories, cooperative freedom, collagogy grounded in learning theory and adult learning theory.

A further analysis into the context in which each of the learning theories was mentioned aimed to determine more explicitly the reasons behind these references. As there were only a few references relating to behaviourism, cognitivism and connectivism, these were analysed manually. These three learning theories were mentioned in two main contexts: they are cited collectively or individually to describe existing or dominant learning theories and they are mentioned as being suitable for the support of learning technologies, as can be seen in Table 4.

Table 4. References to behaviourism, cognitivism and connectivism

Context	Learning theory	Example of papers
Description of existing or dominant learning theories	Behaviourism	Papachristos, Arvanitis, Vassilakis, Kalogiannakis, Kikilias, Zafeiri [34]
	Cognitivism	Torres-Coronas, Monclús-Guitart, Rodríguez-Merayo, Vidal-Blasco, Simón-Olmos [45]
	Connectivism	Makina [29]
Suitability to support/frame learning technology	Behaviourism	Yun, Ming-Lei [51]
	Cognitivism	Kivunja [22]
	Connectivism	Kizito [23]

Social constructivism, in its turn, in the 17 papers where it was mentioned, is cited mainly in association with learning as a social activity. In this case, the thematic analysis was equally performed manually. In 12 papers, it was referenced in the context of learning as a process that occurs in collaboration with others. In the other 5 papers it was cited as a learning theory (2) and it was characterised as being compatible with social media (1), the new generation of learners (1) and a more flexible learning delivery (1). Also, it mentioned in some papers in direct connection to learning technologies: its role in assisting technology design and as a suitable theory to support the implementation of learning technologies, as is illustrated in Table 5.

Table 5. Context for social constructivism references

Context for social constructivism	Example of papers
Actual Support for learning technologies	Vahtivuori-Hänninen, Suomalainen, Karaharju-Suvanto [47]; Donaldson [16]
Suitability for technology support	Comrie [13]; Lyons [28]

Constructivism was the learning theory with the most references and as such a preliminary thematic analysis was performed in Nvivo 10. The text associated with constructivism was coded in Nvivo in a node that was then the object of word frequency query, using a 50-word range. The 5 more cited words were further analysed via individual text search queries: learning (60 references), students (14), active (13), process (13), technologies (13). Learning was connected with learning theory, learning environments and collaborative and active learning. Students were mentioned in relation to their control over learning, the focus on students rather than on teachers and students as the constructors of knowledge. Active, as portrayed in Fig. 2, was associated mainly with the student and with the learning process.

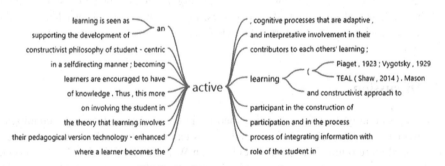

Fig. 2. Active text query word tree

The word tree above depicts how constructivism was referred to in the papers in relation to active students engaging in an active learning process, through actual participation and knowledge construction. The word process was used as learning process, active and interactive process and as a self-developing process. Finally, the term technologies was employed in connection with multimedia, networking, social media and education technologies.

To complement the analysis that was performed in Nvivo, each reference to constructivism in the papers was analysed and coded according to the context in which it was cited. The thematic coding of each reference resulted into five main contexts where constructivism was mentioned: as a learning theory for technology deployment, as a base for the design of technology enhanced learning, constructivist view on students' control over learning, constructivist perspective on students as constructors of knowledge, and constructivist view of learning as an active, collaborative process (Table 6).

Table 6. References to constructivism

Context	Examples of papers
Constructivism as a learning theory for technology deployment	Yu, Jo [49]; Zijdemans-Boudreau, Headley, Ashford [53]
Constructivism as a base for the design of technology enhanced learning	Trepule, Tereseviciene, Rutkiene [46]; Papachristos et al. [34]
Constructivist view on students' control over learning	Casanova, Moreira, Costa [10]; Stevens, Guo, Li [43]
Constructivist perspective on students as constructors of knowledge	Pusey, Meiselwitz [38]; Torres-Coronas et al. [45]
Constructivist view of learning as an active, collaborative process	Wood [48]; Cleveland-Innes, Garrison [12]

In association with technology, constructivism was mainly referred to as a learning theory suitable to support the deployment of technology and a foundation for the design of technology enhanced learning. It was equally highlighted by the authors due to three of the fundamental precepts that it advocates: the students' control over learning, the role of the learners as constructors of knowledge, and learning as an active, collaborative process.

4 Discussion

Prior to examining the role of learning theories in the context of learning technologies deployment, the analysis of the selected papers examined the technologies that were mentioned more often. The special incidence on Web 2.0 technologies, LMSs, mobile technologies and e-learning technologies, places an emphasis on particular technologies, which can assist teachers in the selection of technology with stronger pedagogical potential. Further research can explore the purpose for which they were deployed and examine more deeply their pedagogical value.

By understanding what originates learning it is possible to more effectively implement technology, as it becomes guided by theoretical precepts that allow educators to select the most appropriate technologies for attaining their envisioned learning goals. The importance given to learning theories in the literature review section [4, 19, 27] was not matched by the results of the analysis. The results revealed insufficient information to justify this lack of references to learning theories, which can be further explored in prospective research ventures. Regardless of motive, this absence of consideration of theory has significant consequences for the deployment of learning technologies. As Yuen et al. [50] argue, it fails to provide implementation with a theoretical foundation that is responsible for its solid structure. Where learning theories were mentioned, constructivism and social constructivism were the dominant paradigms in the context of technology adoption. They were mentioned in connection with their suitability for learning technology design and implementation. Also, their description in the selected papers highlights their value for practice as important allies to teachers who wish to deploy technology in the context of active and collaborative learning and of student-centred approaches to leaning.

While conducting this systematic review there are several limitations that had an impact on the results. Firstly, this study's results can solely be interpreted in light of the selected papers and cannot be generalised to the entirety of the existing literature. While the sample of papers that were selected does portray varied perspectives, methodologies, publication patterns and formats, it cannot be characterised as being representative. Secondly, any term connected with learning theories was excluded from the keywords used in the search of publications. This was done to assess if general literature (not specific of learning theories) mentioned their importance or impact in the implementation of learning technologies. The inclusion of such keywords would have possibly produced different outcomes, but it would have equally directed the search for papers in a targeted direction, which was not the intent of this study.

5   Conclusion

The growing importance of the deployment of technology in the context of educational settings demands a continuous scrutiny of its value. This paper contributes with a systematic review about the use of learning technologies in the context of higher education, with a focus on learning theories. The results revealed a prevalence of Web 2.0 technologies, LMSs and mobile technologies as the most cited instructional tools, which opens way to a further examination of their pedagogical worth and the reasons why they are being focused on by educational research. The findings also revealed the lack of importance attributed to the use of learning theories as guides for the implementation of technology, which seems to highlight a lack of theoretical foundation for learning technologies adoption. This can, in the future, have repercussions at the level of students' learning outcomes and the design of learning activities which are mediated by technologies. Finally, the review of the studies emphasised constructivism and social constructivism as the learning theories more often associated with the deployment of learning technologies.

Future systematic reviews can use different inclusion criteria, focusing solely on empirical research papers where technology has been applied to real learning environments to provide a knowledge base for technology implementation. Additionally, the use of learning theories as a foundation for the implementation of technology in education can be further explored by resorting to a more targeted search with criteria that exclusively address specific learning theories. Finally, future research avenues can complement the findings of this research with more direct methods of data collection questioning teachers and learning technologies designers as to their views on and use of learning theories.

References

1. Balakrishnan, V., Gan, C.L.: Students' learning styles and their effects on the use of social media technology for learning. Telematics Inform. **33**(3), 808–821 (2016). https://doi.org/10.1016/j.tele.2015.12.004
2. Bartolomé, A., Castañeda, L., Adell, J.: Personalisation in educational technology: the absence of underlying pedagogies. Int. J. Educ. Technol. High. Educ. **15**(1), 1–17 (2018). https://doi.org/10.1186/s41239-018-0095-0
3. Bates, T.: Understanding Web 2.0 and its implications for e-learning. In: Lee, M., McLoughlin, C. (eds.) Web 2.0-Based E-Learning: Applying Social Informatics for Tertiary Teaching, pp. 21–42. IGI Global, Hershey (2011)
4. Bell, F.: Connectivism: its place in theory-informed research and innovation in technology-enabled learning. Int. Rev. Res. Open Distrib. Learn. **12**(3), 98–118 (2011)
5. Beller, E.M., et al.: PRISMA for abstracts: reporting systematic reviews in journal and conference abstracts. PLoS Med. **10**(4), e1001419 (2013)
6. Braun, V., Clarke, V.: Using thematic analysis in psychology. Qual. Res. Psychol. **3**(2), 77–101 (2006)
7. Bryman, A.: Social Research Methods, 4th edn. Oxford University Press, New York (2012)
8. Bryman, A., Bell, E.: Business Research Methods. Oxford University Press, New York (2015)
9. Burton, J.K., Moore, D.M.M., Magliaro, S.G.: Behaviorism and instructional technology. In: Handbook of Research on Educational Communications and Technology, pp. 15–48. Routledge, New York (2013)
10. Casanova, D., Moreira, A., Costa, N.: Technology Enhanced Learning in Higher Education: results from the design of a quality evaluation framework. Procedia Soc. Behav. Sci. **29**, 893–902 (2011)
11. Castañeda, L., Selwyn, N.: More than tools? Making sense of the ongoing digitizations of higher education. Int. J. Educ. Technol. High. Educ. **15**(1), 1 (2018). https://doi.org/10.1186/s41239-018-0109-y
12. Cleveland-Innes, M., Garrison, D.R.: Higher education and postindustrial society: new ideas about teaching, learning, and technology. In: Moller, L., Huett, J. (eds.) The Next Generation of Distance Education, pp. 221–233. Springer, Boston (2012). https://doi.org/10.1007/978-1-4614-1785-9_15
13. Comrie, A.: Future models of higher education in Scotland: can collaborative, technology-enhanced learning offer solutions? Campus-Wide Inf. Syst. **28**(4), 250–257 (2011)
14. Denyer, D., Tranfield, D.: Producing a systematic review. In: The Sage Handbook of Organizational Research Methods, pp. 671–689. Sage Publications Ltd, Thousand Oaks (2009)
15. Derry, J.: Epistemology and conceptual resources for the development of learning technologies. J. Comput. Assist. Learn. **23**(6), 503–510 (2007)
16. Donaldson, L.: Integrating Web 2.0 learning technologies in higher education: the necessity, the barriers and the factors for success. All Ireland J. Teach. Learn. High. Educ. **6**(3), 2021–2042 (2014)
17. Ertmer, P.A., Newby, T.J.: Behaviorism, cognitivism, constructivism: comparing critical features from an instructional design perspective. Perform. Improv. Q. **26**(2), 43–71 (2013)
18. Harasim, L.: Learning Theory and Online Technologies. Routledge, New York (2012)

19. Herrington, A., Herrington, J.: Authentic mobile learning in higher education. In: Proceedings of the AARE 2007 International Educational Research Conference, Fremantle, Western Australia (2007)
20. Hung, D.: Theories of learning and computer-mediated instructional technologies. Educ. Media Int. **38**(4), 281–287 (2001)
21. Kaakinen, J., Arwood, E.: Systematic review of nursing simulation literature for use of learning theory. Int. J. Nurs. Educ. Scholarsh. **6**(1), 1–20 (2009)
22. Kivunja, C.: The use of social media technologies in collaborative learning in higher education. Int. J. Concept. Manage. Soc. Sci. **3**(4), 74–80 (2015)
23. Kizito, R.N.: Connectivism in learning activity design: implications for pedagogically-based technology adoption in African higher education contexts. Int. Rev. Res. Open Distrib. Learn. **17**(2), 19–39 (2016)
24. Kordaki, M., Gousiou, A.: Digital card games in education: a ten year systematic review. Comput. Educ. **109**, 122–161 (2017). https://doi.org/10.1016/j.compedu.2017.02.011
25. Kyza, E.A., Erduran, S., Tiberghien, A.: Technology-enhanced learning in science. In: Balacheff, N., Ludvigsen, S., Jong, Td., Lazonder, A., Barnes, S. (eds.) Technology-Enhanced Learning, pp. 121–134. Springer, Dordrecht (2009). https://doi.org/10.1007/978-1-4020-9827-7_8
26. Loveless, A., Williamson, B.: Learning Identities in a Digital Age. Routledge, Oxford (2012)
27. Lowyck, J.: Bridging learning theories and technology-enhanced environments: a critical appraisal of its history. In: Spector, J., Merrill, M., Elen, J., Bishop, M. (eds.) Handbook of Research on Educational Communications and Technology, pp 3–20. Springer, New York (2014). https://doi.org/10.1007/978-1-4614-3185-5_1
28. Lyons, J.: Learning with technology: theoretical foundations underpinning simulations in higher education. In: Brown, M., Hartnett, H., Stewart, T. (eds.) ASCILITE - Australian Society for Computers in Learning in Tertiary Education Annual Conference. ASCILITE, pp. 582–586 (2012)
29. Makina, A.: Challenging the boundaries of incorporating educational technologies in e-Teaching & Learning at higher education institutions. In: Mastorakis, N.E., Brooks, A.L., Rudas, I.J. (eds.) Proceedings of the 11th International Conference on Educational Technologies (EDUTE 2015). Advances in Computers and Technology for Education, pp. 111–118. WSEAS Press (2015)
30. Mayes, T., De Freitas, S.: Technology-enhanced learning: the role of theory. In: Beetham, H., Sharpe, R. (eds.) Rethinking Pedagogy for a Digital Age: Designing for 21st Century Learning, 2nd edn., pp. 17–30. Routledge, Oxon (2013)
31. Moher, D., Liberati, A., Tetzlaff, J., Altman, D.G., Group, P.: Preferred reporting items for systematic reviews and meta-analyses: the PRISMA statement. PLoS Med. **6**(7), e1000097 (2009)
32. Nowell, L.S., Norris, J.M., White, D.E., Moules, N.J.: Thematic analysis: striving to meet the trustworthiness criteria. Int. J. Qual. Methods **16**(1), 1609406917733847 (2017)
33. Oliver, M.: Learning technology: theorising the tools we study. Br. J. Edu. Technol. **44**(1), 31–43 (2012)
34. Papachristos, D., Arvanitis, K., Vassilakis, K., Kalogiannakis, M., Kikilias, P., Zafeiri, E.: An educational model for asynchronous E-learning. A case study in a higher technology education. Int. J. Adv. Corp. Learn. (iJAC) **3**(1), 32–36 (2010)
35. Pawson, R.: Evidence-Based Policy: A Realist Perspective. Sage Publications, London (2006)
36. Pentoney, C.S., Halpern, D.F., Butler, H.A.: The impact of learning technologies. In: Scott, R., Kosslyn, S. (eds.) Emerging Trends in the Social and Behavioral Sciences. Wiley, New York (2015)
37. Pritchard, A.: Ways of Learning: Learning Theories and Learning Styles in the Classroom, 2nd edn. Routledge, Oxon (2009)

38. Pusey, P., Meiselwitz, G.: Heuristics for implementation of wiki technology in higher educa-
    tion learning. In: Ozok, A.A., Zaphiris, P. (eds.) OCSC 2009. LNCS, vol. 5621, pp. 507–514.
    Springer, Heidelberg (2009). https://doi.org/10.1007/978-3-642-02774-1_55
39. Schunk, D.H.: Learning Theories: An Educational Perspective, 6th edn. Pearson Education
    Inc., Boston (2012)
40. Selwyn, N.: Distrusting Educational Technology: Critical Questions for Changing Times.
    Routledge, Oxon (2013)
41. Sieber, V., Andrew, D.: Learning technologies and learning theories. In: Ghaoui, C. (ed.)
    Usability Evaluation of Online Learning Programs, pp. 218–232. IGI Global, Hershey (2003)
42. Siemens, G.: Connectivism: a learning theory for the digital age. Int. J. Instruct. Technol.
    Distance Learn. **2**(1), 3–10 (2005)
43. Stevens, K., Guo, Z., Li, Y.: Understanding technology mediated learning in higher education:
    a repertory grid approach. In: Myers, M.D., Straub, D.W. (eds.) Proceedings of the Thirty
    Fifth International Conference on Information Systems. Association for Information Systems,
    Atlanta, GA (2014)
44. Thota, N.: Connectivism and the use of technology/media in collaborative teaching and
    learning. New Dir. Teach. Learn. **2015**(142), 81–96 (2015)
45. Torres-Coronas, T., Monclús-Guitart, R., Rodríguez-Merayo, A., Vidal-Blasco, M.A., Simón-
    Olmos, M.J.: Web 2.0 technologies: social software applied to higher education and adult
    learning. In: Adult Learning in the Digital Age: Perspectives on Online Technologies and
    Outcomes, pp. 208–218. IGI Global, Harshey (2010)
46. Trepule, E., Tereseviciene, M., Rutkiene, A.: Didactic approach of introducing technology
    enhanced learning (TEL) curriculum in higher education. Procedia Soc. Behav. Sci. **191**,
    848–852 (2015)
47. Vahtivuori-Hänninen, S., Suomalainen, K., Karaharju-Suvanto, T.: Pen-based learning tech-
    nologies in higher education: teaching and studying radiographic anatomy in mobile learn-
    ing environment. In: E-Learn: World Conference on E-Learning in Corporate, Government,
    Healthcare, and Higher Education, pp. 3265–3274. Association for the Advancement of
    Computing in Education (AACE) (2008)
48. Wood, S.L.: Technology for teaching and learning: moodle as a tool for higher education. Int.
    J. Teach. Learn. High. Educ. **22**(3), 299–307 (2010)
49. Yu, T., Jo, I.-H.: Educational technology approach toward learning analytics: relationship
    between student online behavior and learning performance in higher education. In: Pro-
    ceedings of the Fourth International Conference on Learning Analytics and Knowledge,
    pp. 269–270. ACM, New York (2014)
50. Yuen, S.C.-Y., Yaoyuneyong, G., Yuen, P.K.: Perceptions, interest, and use: teachers and web
    2.0 tools in education. Int. J. Technol. Teach. Learn. **7**(2), 109–123 (2011)
51. Yun, Z., Ming-Lei, M.: Applications of modern educational technologies in higher arts
    education. In: Zhang, W. (ed.) Advanced Technology in Teaching, pp. 487–494. Springer,
    Heidelberg (2012). https://doi.org/10.1007/978-3-642-29458-7_72
52. Zientek, L.R., Werner, J.M., Campuzano, M.V., Nimon, K.: The use of Google Scholar for
    research and research dissemination. New Horizons Adult Educ. Hum. Resour. Dev. **30**(1),
    39–46 (2018)
53. Zijdemans-Boudreau, A., Headley, S., Ashford, R.: Do Educators Need a Second Life? Explor-
    ing possibilities for technology-based distance learning in higher education. In: Proceedings
    of the Society for Information Technology & Teacher Education International Conference,
    pp. 1617–1622. Association for the Advancement of Computing in Education (AACE) (2009)
54. Zingiswa, J., Mohapi, S.: Educational theories, methodologies and technology integration in
    the classroom. In: Callaos, N., Horne, J., Sánchez, B., Savoie, M., Tremante, A. (eds.) Proceed-
    ings of the 8th International Multi-Conference on Complexity, Informatics and Cybernetics
    (IMCIC 2017), Orlando, USA, pp. 130–134 (2017)

TPS^2 Approach Applied to Requirements Engineering Curriculum Course

Fernando Moreira[1,2](✉) ⓘ, Maria João Ferreira[1] ⓘ, Natércia Durão[1] ⓘ,
Carla Santos Pereira[1] ⓘ, David Fonseca[3] ⓘ, César A. Collazos[4] ⓘ,
and Alex Sandro Gomes[5] ⓘ

[1] REMIT, Universidade Portucalense, Rua Dr. António Bernardino de Almeida, 541, 4200-072
Porto, Portugal
{fmoreira,mjoao,natercia,carlasantos}@upt.pt
[2] IEETA, Universidade de Aveiro, Aveiro, Portugal
[3] Architecture Department, La Salle, Universitat Ramon Llull, Barcelona, Spain
david.fonseca@salle.url.edu
[4] Universidad del Cauca, Street 5 # 4-70, Popayan, Colombia
ccollazo@unicauca.edu.co
[5] Centro de Informática, Universidade Federal de Pernambuco, Recife, Brazil
asg@cin.ufpe.br

Abstract. In the information systems area, besides the problem of involvement, students often have difficulties learning in course units such as Requirements Engineering, namely in identifying and writing requirements and specifying the new information system based on requirements identified. The reasons for these difficulties are well known and described in the literature, referring to critical thinking/problem-solving, creativity, communication, and collaboration, among others. Knowing the value of flexible and personalized learning, teachers are changing the way they teach, using different active learning methodologies, such as the flipped classroom and project-based learning. This paper describes an experiment carried out with students that aims to improve the learning experiences of students enrolled in the degree courses (Computer Science and Computer Engineering) at the curricular units Information Systems Development and Requirements Engineering. Specifically, the experiment carried out aimed to create a catalogue of requirements for a rental agency. In solving the case study, it was proposed to use a new approach, based on active methodologies, titled Think-Per-Share & Switching (TPS^2). At the end of the experiment, the students were invited to evaluate the approach. The results of the student's evaluation are promising, and we will apply the TPS^2 in the next academic year.

Keywords: Disruption · Learning ecosystems · Active learning techniques · Higher education

P. Zaphiris and A. Ioannou (Eds.): HCII 2022, LNCS 13328, pp. 461–477, 2022.
https://doi.org/10.1007/978-3-031-05657-4_33

1 Introduction

The mandatory change of teaching-learning processes (TLP), imposed by COVID-19 since March 2020 [1–3], leads to a shift in understanding regarding the teaching procedures that have become as or more important than the learning contents themselves. In addition to this "*new reality*", different perspectives depending on the actors' perspectives. For example, from the professors' view, "*the frustration caused by the lack of participation, disinterest and devaluation on the part of students about the classes and the strategies created to attract their attention*" is highlighted, and from students' view "*complain about the routine, boring classes and little dynamic*" [4]. The new educational conception of the school centered on learning, which is developed based on competencies, is justified by theories that try to explain how the individual learns, reinforcing what has been indicated in [5]. It is imperative to make the subject active in the production of knowledge. In this context, traditional teaching techniques became part of the investigation process, intending to identify deficiencies and propose new teaching-learning methodologies.

The trends of the 21st century indicate that the central characteristic of education is the shift from an individual focus to a social, political, and ideological focus [6]. Teaching takes place throughout life, constituting a permanent process. For example, in [7], four pillars of knowledge and continuing education are indicated, considered essential: i) learning to know; ii) learning to do; iii) learning to live together, and iv) learning to be. These pillars allow the updating of existing educational methodologies, as well as the introduction of differentiating academic proposals, which meet the necessary disruption that education as a whole, but particularly in higher education, to respond to the challenges listed in [8], namely, what are the competences of the future?

The teaching process establishes a differentiated relationship with the student, where a trajectory of knowledge construction and learning promotion is observed. It is a relationship "*that activates the learning process in terms of particular abilities to be acquired*" [9]. Teaching and learning are ontologically linked. Thus, "*the meaning of teaching depends on the meaning given to learning, and the meaning of learning depends on the activities generated by teaching*" [9].

Teachers become facilitators and motivators of students, so that they are more active in the learning process, thus demanding that students have, among others, critical thinking skills. Critical thinking is one of the skills indicated by the World Economic Forum as one of the main skills to face the challenges of the 21st century [8]. In addition to critical thinking, the skills "Critical thinking/problem-solving", "Creativity", "Communication", and "Collaboration" are also of high importance.

In this context and to respond to these challenges, in the last decades of the 20th century, Active Methodologies (AMs) emerged, which can be understood as a set of methods/techniques that seek to develop students' autonomy in the knowledge acquisition process. AM's are teaching strategies developed with a focus on students' effective participation in their educational process in a flexible and interconnected way. However, the use of AMs requires planning, organization, and control, so that the respective feedback accompanies every moment on the task(s) being performed. AMs present alternatives that can complement traditional teaching, i.e., with methods that make the student an active being, with a greater critical capacity, and always show the students' autonomy in their teaching and learning processes.

The options for developing active teaching-learning methodologies are multiple, including the problematization strategy, problem-based learning (PBL), team-based learning (TBL), of Think-per-Share, among others. Complementarily, other procedures allow the creation of active teaching-learning methodologies, such as: seminars, group work, socialization, round tables, plenary sessions, dialogued exhibitions, thematic debates, workshops, commented readings, portfolios, films presentation, musical interpretations, dramatizations, oral evaluation, among others [10].

Higher Education Institutions (HEI) policy regarding the improvement in TLP is to encourage the adoption of active methodologies because it is believed to, on the one hand, be adequate for success in the acquisition of competencies and, on the other hand, meet the characteristics of the students who are coming to HEIs [11–13].

Among the AMs proposed in the literature, collaborative learning through techniques such as Think Pair Share (TPS) [14] are shown to be an outstanding approach for developing critical thinking. However, the use of TPS alone is not enough to develop the four core competencies ("Critical thinking/problem-solving", "Creativity", "Communication" and "Collaboration") identified and which are the fundamental and critical basis for the skills to be developed by students in this new era. In this context, to develop the four competencies mentioned, extending the TPS for solving one task per group to several groups participating or building, to solving the same task/problem.

In this paper, a validated approach will be presented, in which an innovative learning approach developed to a curricular unit of two first-cycle courses were introduced. In addition to the motivational aspects, the proposed method took into consideration the fusion of several learning strategies for the development of new competencies, framed in the current and future moment, in which the digital transformation predominates. The new approach was named as Think-Per-Share & Switching (TPS^2), and it is a new approach based on Think-per-share methodology.

The TPS^2 approach can be considered as a combination of merge approximations to give rise to a new approximation. The essential principle development of the method is that the students acquire the necessary skills for the twenty-first century in an effective and efficient way. The proposed approach thus relies on different active methodologies and resources, including some digital teaching materials.

2 Literature Review

Requirements Engineering (RE), as defined in [15], is a branch, sub-area, of Software Engineering that studies the process of determining the requirements, and it has been traditionally looked upon as the "front-end" of the software life cycle. Its main goal is to produce specifications from informal ideas for the problem to be solved. A new area started in 1993 when the 1st International Symposium on RE was organized.

Requirements emerge in a highly collaborative and social process that involves stakeholders, project teams, management, and the product itself [16]. The goal of RE is to understand the client's needs and provide a solution with the support of methods, techniques, and tools. RE is an often-underutilized discipline in software development [17–20].

Despite the added value that "*a good requirement will cause system success, but sometimes the system will fail because of lack of controlling and monitoring on the system design*" [15], related TLP with RE is complex [21]. The current approach to teaching RE might have several limitations because an RE course requires skills development. Therefore, more practical methods should be employed to produce better results from the course.

The role-playing approach is one of the active methodologies. In [22], the authors have used this methodology using groups of undergraduate students and instructors (lecturer and graduate students). Instructors, besides lecturing, play the role of consultants. At the same time, each group of students plays the role of three types of companies: a startup, a requirements construction, and an auditing one.

In [23], the authors report the results of an exploratory pilot study conducted to assess the effectiveness of Case-Based Learning (CBL) methodology in facilitating the learning of several RE concepts. They have used only the CBL active methodology without any methodology improvement.

A novel pedagogical approach was presented in [24], for training student analysts in the art of elicitation interviews. This study was conducted in two parts: first, the authors performed an observational study of interviews performed by novices and were presented a classification of the most common mistakes made; second the mentioned list of errors made by students was used to monitor their progress through out three sets of interviews to discover the individual areas for improvement. They conducted an empirical study involving role-playing and authentic assessment in two semesters on two different cohorts of students.

García et al. [25] have presented a solution to provide undergraduate students with an interactive learning environment to help the introduction of ISO/IEC/IEEE 29148. The main game objective is to strengthen the comprehension and application of the main processes of the standard and some related requirements engineering techniques. Requengin was designed to simulate an academic library where players must apply the requirements engineering processes to change the traditional management system by a software system while they receive, at the same time, preliminary training in ISO/IEC/IEEE 29148 [25].

SaPeer and reverSeSaPeer presented in [26] are two pedagogical approaches. SaPeer uses role-playing, peer review and self-assessment to enable students to experience first-hand the difficulties related to the interviewing process, reflect on their mistakes, and improve their interview skills by practice and analysis. reverSeSaPeer builds on the first approach and includes a role reversal activity in which participants play the role of a customer interviewed by a competent interviewer.

Traditional methodologies and class projects alone have proven unsuitable for teaching the software process. To overcome this limitation, in [27], the authors have implemented a playful methodology for teaching and learning the construction of software requirements based on Pre-Conceptual Schemes is proposed.

de Souza Filho et al. [28] have conducted an exploratory study to investigate how Design Thinking (DT) benefits the development of a data-driven requirements elicitation tool. To do so, they applied the Double Diamond process, having in mind Brown's DT Cycles, supported by a set of DT techniques. The results indicate that DT techniques can be integrated into the development process, allowing a better understanding of the problem and supporting the development of user-centered solutions.

After reviewing the literature carried out previously, it is possible to verify that in none of the research works, the use of the active Think-per-share methodology was found as a possible solution. For this reason, this work will present an approach based on Think-per-share, introducing a concept that will allow students to develop a large part of the skills defined in [8].

3   Research Methodology

The main goal of this research is to propose and validate an approach, named TPS^2, to teaching two curricular units, "Requirements Engineering" and "Information Systems Development" of two first-cycle courses. The approach has the main goal to motivate students to acquire knowledge and develop hard and soft skills, based on previous experimentation which has shown how increasing the motivation of the student in the proposed tasks increases their knowledge, as well as their satisfaction with the tasks and the course design [29–38].

The value recognition of a research project's value and scientific validity is guaranteed by the scientific methodology on which the work is based. The research methodology must be carefully chosen because it is based on philosophical assumptions that guide and aim to achieve the research project's success. To achieve that success, we chose the Design Science Research (DSR) methodology [30] as a theoretical basis that supports the scientific validation of this study.

The use of the DSR allows the design and implements the proposed model, leading it in interaction with persons (students and teachers), technology and the organization (HEI), which needs to be managed if it is to consider a successful application of the model/approach [31].

Additionally, this research used the quantitative methodology, which can be generically defined as a method of social research that uses statistical techniques to collect and analyze data. This approach aims essentially to find relationships between variables to make descriptions using the statistical treatment of collected data and to draw conclusions [32]. The selection of the quantitative methodology is justified by the need to collect the opinions of the students, i.e., the study was descriptive in nature, and the data collection was carried out with the use of a questionnaire. The use of questionnaires requires special care, since it is not enough to collect the answers on the issues of interest, it is also important to perform a statistical analysis for the validation of the results. Aspects such as sample size, questionnaire formulation, data analysis, among others, were considered in the study.

The questionnaire adapted from [33] was submitted to the evaluation of four experts in the area and consists of 34 questions (Q1 a Q34) distributed by six topics, namely: Students' perspective on Lab (Q1 to Q5); Students' perspective on Learning and Skills Developed (Q6 to Q11); Students' perspective on Teamwork (Q12 to Q16); Students' perspective on Professor's Role (Q17 to Q22); Students' perspective on Student Assessment (Q23 to Q27); Students' perspective on TPS^2 as Teaching-Learning Methodology (Q28 to Q34).

The first topic consists of 5 questions which include for example, the importance of the laboratory in the future profession of the students and its suitability for the learning process. The second topic consists of 6 questions regarding the skills developed, for example, oral and written skills and project management skills. The third topic contains 5 questions about teamwork between students. The professor's role/relation to the students' learning process represents the fourth topic. Fifth topic, consisting of 5 questions, is related to the students' assessment of their work and the respective results obtained. Finally, the sixth topic with 7 questions, reflects the opinions of the students about TSP^2 as a teaching-learning methodology.

All questions were close-ended type and measure on a five-point Likert scale ranging from "Strongly Disagree" (1) "Disagree" (2), "Not sure" (3), "Agree" (4) and "Strongly Agree" (5). We collected 34 valid answers from 56 Computer Science and Computer Engineering students. Data collected were treated by using the IBM SPSS Statistics 27.0 software. The statistical analyses used in our study were Descriptive Analysis (frequency analysis, descriptive measures and graphical representations), reliability analysis (Cronbach's Alpha), correlation analysis and Exploratory factor analysis (EFA).

4 TPS^2 Approach

4.1 Rationale

During the academic year 2020/2021, in the context of pedagogical training on Active Learning promoted by the HEI, teachers were encouraged to create active approaches/methodologies that would contribute to the development of technical/hard and soft skills of their students. From this challenge emerged a new active learning approach, designated as Think-Per-Share & Switching (TPS^2), to provide an answer to the problems identified in previous academic years related to students' difficulty in acquiring soft skills (critical thinking/problem solving, creativity, communication, and collaboration), and hard skills (the creation of a requirements catalogue following the ISO/IEC/IEEE 29148 standard).

4.2 Approach

Based on the challenge and problems presented above, the main goal of the proposed approach is to improve the TLP in the Information Systems Development and Requirements Engineering curricular units. So, an extension to TPS is proposed to incorporate a component designed as "Switching" to reach the main goal. This component will allow students to share the work between groups, several times by enabling each group to participate in the mentioned list of errors made by students was used to monitor their progress through carrying out the work of all groups, to develop the skills mentioned above. With the new component, the new teaching-learning model will be known as Think-Per-Share & Switching (TPS^2), as shown in Fig. 1.

As shown in Fig. 1, the TPS^2 is composed by six phases: (1) Problem Definition/Initial Tasks; (2) Group composition and facilitator appointment; (3); Adapted Think per share, by group; (4) Switching, (5) Evolution of the results obtained; (6) Final document production.

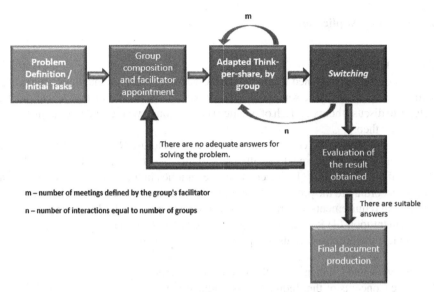

Fig. 1. Think Pair Share and Switching (TPS^2).

In the first phase (1), the problem is defined/presented, and the teacher carries out a description of the tasks that must be developed. Then, the working groups are defined in the second phase (2), and the facilitator appointment is carried out. With these two initial phases, the objective is to develop the "Communication" and "Collaboration" skills. This task is followed by phase (3), in which the different groups try to answer the problem, having a version per group per group; the groups get together and try to find a single solution based on the conclusions of each group. In phase (3), the moderator defines the number of sessions (m) that are necessary to carry out before moving on to phase (4). In phase (3), soft skills ("Critical thinking/problem-solving", "Creativity", "Communication" and "Collaboration") and hard skills ("the creation of a requirements catalogue following the ISO/IEC/IEEE 29148 standard"), are developed. The teacher coordinates all activities. When the number (m) of sessions ends, the groups exchange the works among themselves, and thus phase (4) is carried out, and phase (3) begins again. Phase (3) and (4) is repeated n times, with n representing the number of groups. After *n* exchanges (in each exchange, there were *m* interactions), phase (5) begins. In this phase, the teacher and each group evaluate whether the results have reached the objectives defined initially. If the results already follow the defined goals, then phase (6) starts, and the whole process ends. When the results do not follow the objectives defined initially, the process returns to phase (2). In this new interaction, it is possible, for example, to change the group's moderator or even to change elements of each group. As a result of this process, it is possible to develop the soft and hard skills mentioned above. To illustrate the application of the TPS^2 approach, in the following section, a practical case developed during the current academic year (2021–2022), On the 1st-semester classes of the previously defined curricular units, will be presented.

4.3 Practical Application

Course Overview

The RE course was designed following the ACM/AIS guidelines and the BT referential. It runs for 15 weeks (one semester) and consists of two hours of theoretical/practice lectures to discuss theory and 2 h of practice (lab sessions), where students put in practice the learned theory.

The main goal of the course is to induce students to use RE in their future work as a designer in the development of software systems. So, it is expected that a student, at the end of the course, can (1) Select and use techniques in the requirements engineering process according to the proposed problem; (2) Evaluate and use different techniques for prioritizing requirements according to the problem to be solved; (3) Use a requirements management tool; (4) Recognize technical developments in the area.

To meet the proposed goals, the programmatic contents are:

1. Overview and Challenges of Requirements Engineering;
2. Basic Concepts of the Requirements Engineering;
3. The Requirements Engineering Process;
4. Requirements Engineering – Process (Elicitation; Analysis, Negotiation and Prioritization; Modeling and Specification; Documentation; Validation);
5. Requirements Management – Use of a management requirements tool;
6. Future Directions and discussion.

The theoretical/practice lectures use the expositive method. However, it is still intended to have active participation of students through direct interpellation between teacher and students and vice versa. Students must solve case studies that approximate them to real-world situations in laboratory lectures.

Case study

At the beginning of the semester, it was proposed to students to develop their technical skills in the creation of a requirements catalogue following the ISO/IEC/IEEE 29148 standard through the TPS^2 methodology. The selected theme of the case study is believed to be easily understood by students who should enjoy its working method and the business environment.

The paragraph below presents a part of the text that served as a basis for the students' work proposal, using the TPS^2 approach, i.e., the creation of a requirements catalogue.

System Rental Agency - RentAgen

"The core business of the rental company "RentAgen" is the rental of real estate. The company has several branches.

The properties are classified by groups taking into consideration the typology and location. For example, group 1 includes one-bedroom flats in Porto - Downtown. The monthly rental value is attributed to the function of the group to which a given property belongs. In a given typology, there may be several properties.

About a specific property, you want to know several pieces of information, including address, year of construction, state of conservation, and equipment (e.g., air conditioning, WIFI, kitchen with appliances, ...). In addition, it is intended to know at which filial a property in a given group has been rented out. Customers can make reservations with a maximum duration of 8 days; the reservation is automatically cancelled at the end of this period. A customer can be an individual person or a legal entity."

At the end of the case study, a final version/solution of the requirements catalogue was shared. All students collaboratively participated in its construction, contributed to the final solution, and consequently agreed on that solution.

As mentioned, the final product of this case study was a catalogue of requirements, from which we extract and present three functional requirements as an example.

System Rental Agency – RentAgen
Requirements catalogue
....
RF02 - The system should allow a client to view the details of a property
RF03 - The system must allow an employee to query the filial in which a
              property was rented.
RF04 - The system should allow a customer to reserve a property for rental.
....

---

5   Results and Discussion

At the end of the semester and before the final assessments, the 56 students from the two curricular units in the degrees courses of CS and CE answered the questionnaire mentioned in Sect. 3. As a result, 34 valid responses were obtained. The results obtained and the discussion carried out in this section aim to study the proposed methodology (TSP^2) in developing students' soft and hard skills.

In order to verify whether the variability in the answers results from the opinions of each student, the internal consistency measured by Cronbach's alpha was calculated. Internal consistency is defined as the proportion of variability in responses that result from differences in respondents. This measure is one of the most used to verify the internal consistency of a set of items, varying between 0 and 1, and the higher the value of alpha, the greater the internal consistency. According to Pestana and Gageiro [43], values above 0.7 are week, for values between 0.7 and 0.8 internal consistency is considered reasonable and between 0.8 and 0.9 is considered good. With the exception of the questions of topic V all the values are good (see Table 1).

Table 1. Cronbach's alpha coefficients for the topics.

Topic	Cronbach's alpha	N° of items
1	0.857	5
2	0.870	6
3	0.819	5
3	0.869	6
5	0.642	5
6	0.881	7

A low Cronbach's Alpha coefficient may reflect the wrong coding of the items of the respective dimension because it assumes as presupposition that the various items are categorized in the same sense which does not happen for questions Q25 and Q26 that we chose at this point to remove them from the analysis. The new dimension V has only three items and the corresponding Cronbach's Alpha is 0.784, so the values obtained lead us to a comfortable position to proceed the study.

In order to assess student's global opinion about the questions that composes each topic we constructed 6 dimensions Dim_1 to Dim_6 (corresponding to the six topics), calculating the arithmetic mean of the variables (score) that integrate each dimension.

To identify if these dimensions were associated, we calculate Pearson correlation coefficient. The results show that exists strong positive correlation (all correlation significant at the 0.01 level except between Dim_3 and Dim_5 which is significant only at 0,05 level), that is, the students that most agree in one dimension also most agree in other dimension. In more detail, the high positive correlation between "TPS^2 as teaching-learning method" and "Learning and skills developed" ($r = 0.836$) and with "Lab" ($r = 0.853$). Also high correlation between "Lab" and "Learning skills developed". According to the students, the positive impact of TPS^2 and the Lab leads to the development of better oral, written and technical skills (decision skills, organization, problem solving, time management) as well as the development of a critical thinking and greater autonomy (Table 2).

It also makes sense to calculate descriptive measures (mean, median and coefficient of variation – C.V.) for each dimension (see Table 3). According to these results, the dimension that most stands out is dimension 3 (Teamwork), that is, the one in which students have a strong positive opinion about teamwork as an enhancer of the learning process as well as skills acquired at the level of interpersonal relationships essential for their professional training. However, it should be noted that given the values obtained, all other dimensions have a very positive evaluation by the students, and it is verified, given the low coefficients of variation, great homogeneity in these opinions.

Table 2. Pearson correlation between dimensions.

Correlations		Dim_1	Dim_2	Dim_3	Dim_4	Dim_5	Dim_6
Dim_1	Pearson correlation	1	**,831****	**,735****	**,598****	**,728****	**,853****
	Sig. (2-tailed)		,000	,000	,000	,000	,000
	N	34	34	34	33	34	34
Dim_2	Pearson correlation	,831**	1	**,657****	**,781****	**,616****	**,836****
	Sig. (2-tailed)	,000		,000	,000	,000	,000
	N	34	34	34	33	34	34
Dim_3	Pearson correlation	,735**	,657**	1	**,487****	**,429***	**,554****
	Sig. (2-tailed)	,000	,000		,004	,011	,001
	N	34	34	34	33	34	34
Dim_4	Pearson correlation	,598**	,781**	,487**	1	**,597****	**,768****
	Sig. (2-tailed)	,000	,000	,004		,000	,000
	N	33	33	33	33	33	33
Dim_5	Pearson correlation	,728**	,616**	,429*	,597**	1	**,812****
	Sig. (2-tailed)	,000	,000	,011	,000		,000
	N	34	34	34	33	34	34
Dim_6	Pearson correlation	,853**	,836**	,554**	,768**	,812**	1
	Sig. (2-tailed)	,000	,000	,001	,000	,000	
	N	34	34	34	33	34	34

**. Correlation is significant at the 0.01 level (2-tailed).
*. Correlation is significant at the 0.05 level (2-tailed).

Table 3. Descriptive measures for the dimensions.

	Dim_1	Dim_2	Dim_3	Dim_4	Dim_5
Mean	3,6353	3,8627	**4,2353**	3,9697	3,9020
Median	3,8000	4,0000	**4,4000**	4,1667	4,0000
Std. deviation	,85772	,77684	,70405	,74004	,84698
C.V	23,6%	20,1%	16,6%	18,6%	21,7%
Mean	3,6353	3,8627	**4,2353**	3,9697	3,9020

Given that dimension 3 stood out from the others, it was also decided to present in detail the questions that constitute this one. To do so, the bar plot below was constructed (see Fig. 2).

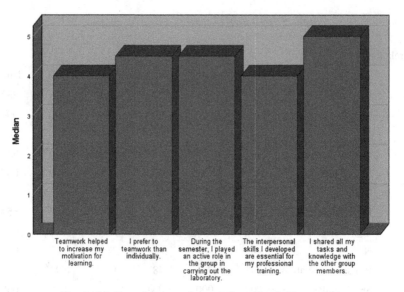

Fig. 2. Median of the questions of dimension 3 (Teamwork)

Figure 2 shows us that all the questions are critical with median at least 4, that is, at least the students agree. The question that presented the highest degree of agreement is the one that refers to the sharing of tasks and knowledge with other members of the group.

In view of this results, it is interesting to analyze the structural relationship between the dimensions. For this, it will be used the exploratory technique EFA with application of the principal components method followed by a Varimax rotation (is the rotation that produce a more interpretable solution) for extraction the factors.

According to the percentage of variance explained by the model (85.3%), two factors (components) were retained. To assess the validity of the EFA, the KMO criterion was used with the classification criteria defined in [44] having obtained KMO = 0.802 (in the interval [0.8, 0.9] it is considered good), which allows the EFA to be carried out as this exploratory analysis is suitable for the data matrix under study. Table 4 summarizes the factor weights for each dimension in each of the two factors.

The first factor (component) has high factor weights ($>0,7$) in dimensions 6 (TPS[2] as Teaching-learning methodology), 5 (Student assessment), 4 (Professor's rule) and 2 (Learning and skills developed) and explains 52,1% of the total variance. The second factor, with a high factorial weight (0.946) explains 33,2% of the total variance (overall the two factors explain 85,3% of the total variance). Note that dimension 1 (Lab) saturates the two factors, reflecting the fact that student's opinion regarding the laboratory can be explained simultaneously by both factors. The first factor can be designated as "Impact of TPS[2] and professor support on skills developed by students" and the second factor is designated by "Teamwork".

Table 4. Feature rotated component matrix.

	Component	
	1	2
Dim_1	,652	,671
Dim_2	**,702**	,597
Dim_3	,220	**,946**
Dim_4	**,788**	,311
Dim_5	**,875**	,183
Dim_6	**,881**	,395

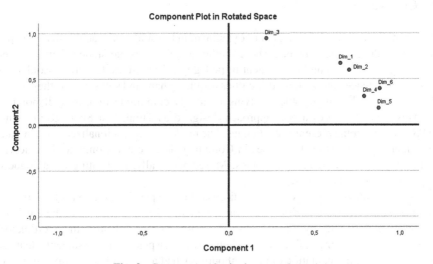

Fig. 3. Component plot in the rotated space

Table 4 and Fig. 3 together allow to obtain in detail the conclusions that follow.

In factor 1, taking into account the responses provided by students to the various questions addressed in these dimensions, it can be concluded that the teaching-learning methodology implemented had a great positive impact on students, facilitating their integration and socialization with their peers and professor, effectively contributing to the reduction of school failure. Factor 2 shows how important, in the students' opinion, teamwork is contributing for the increase of the motivation for learning and in the development of essential skills for their professional training.

6   Research Limitations and Future Directions

Despite its contributions, the research presented has limitations, and for that reason, there should be continuity in future work. One of the limitations is that the model was only tested once and was limited to one topic of the CU syllabus contents.

A second limitation is that the approach was only applied in one institution. For that reason, its use should be extended to more syllabuses, more courses and other institutions. Since a larger sample of higher education institutions would provide more robust results and allow comparisons between countries and the identification of cultural differences.

The workload for students and teachers is high, although at different times. For teachers, the workload is heavy in the materials preparation and monitoring phase of the method application, in which the teacher functions as coordinator. The students' workload is heaviest during catalogue creation and discussion with peers.

Finally, it was not addressed how teachers could use the proposed approach to align the different active learning techniques in course units within the first cycle of the course for optimal dissemination.

7   Conclusions

Active methodologies allow a greater dynamism in the students' teaching-learning process of programmatic contents. These methodologies promote students' involvement and bring satisfaction and enrichment to pedagogical practices. Generally, students in Computer Science courses have difficulties acquiring hard and soft skills, as they need to develop critical thinking/problem-solving, creativity, communication, and collaboration.

This paper proposes a new approach designed as Think Pair Share & Switching (TPS^2) to answer the presented challenges. The model was operationalized and evaluated by students of the 1st cycle courses in Computer Science and Computer Engineering in the requirements engineering topics. More specifically, in creating a catalogue of requirements based on a case.

Based on the results presented and discussed in the previous sections, it can be seen that the issues related to written and oral technical skills and success in the curricular unit were substantially by the students. The teacher's role, adapting the coordinator's profile instead of the transmitter of knowledge, was very positive in the students' learning progress. The implementation of the methodology had a tremendous positive impact on students, facilitating their integration and socialization with their peers and professor, effectively contributing to reducing school failure. Another conclusion is how important, in the students' opinion, teamwork contributes to the increase of the motivation for learning and the development of essential skills for their professional training [45–47].

In summary, this paper has addressed the reasons for developing a comprehensive approach to the teaching and learning process for a curriculum unit part of first cycle courses. The TPS2 approach was developed to address the complexity of the teaching and learning process in a real context where students are digital, and technologies are constantly evolving. The student's evaluation of the model encourages its reuse in other curricular units.

Funding. This work was supported by the FCT – Fundação para a Ciência e a Tecnologia, I.P. [Project UIDB/05105/2020].

References

1. World Economic Forum. COVID-19's impact on jobs and education: using data to cushion the blow. https://www.weforum.org/agenda/2021/12/this-is-how-to-use-data-to-manage-covid-19-s-impact-on-jobs-and-education/, Accessed 12 Dec 2021
2. Cano, S., Collazos, C.A., Flórez-Aristizabal, L., Moreira, F., Ramírez, M.: Experiencia del aprendizaje de la Educación Superior ante los cambios a nivel mundial a causa del CoVId-19. Campus Virtuales **9**, 51–59 (2020)
3. Grande-de-Prado, M., García-Peñalvo, F.J., Corell, A., Abella-García, V.: Evaluación en Educación Superior durante la pandemia de la COVID-19. Campus Virtuales **10**, 49–58 (2021)
4. Diesel, A., Baldez, A.L.S., Martins, S.N.: Active teaching methodologies principles: a theoretical approach. Revista Thema **14**(1), 268–288 (2017)
5. Brito, C.A.F., Campos, M.Z.: Making higher education learning process easier: the role of active learning strategies. RIAEE Revista Ibero-Americana de Estudos em Educação **14**(2), 371–387 (2019)
6. Gadotti, M.: Perspectivas atuais da educação. São Paulo Perspectivas **14**(2), 3–11 (2000). http://www.scielo.br/pdf/spp/v14n2/9782.pdf, Accessed 21 Nov 2021
7. Delors, J.: Educação: um tesouro a descobrir. Relatório para a Unesco da Comissão Internacional sobre Educação para o Século XXI. 4. ed. Cortez/Unesco, São Paulo/Brasília (DF) (2000)
8. World Economic Forum: These are the top 10 job skills of tomorrow – and how long it takes to learn them. https://www.weforum.org/agenda/2020/10/top-10-work-skills-of-tomorrow-how-long-it-takes-to-learn-them/, Accessed 12 Dec 2021
9. Saint-Onge, M.: O ensino na escola: o que é e como se faz. 2. ed. Loyola, São Paulo (2001)
10. Siqueira-Batista, R.: Os anéis da serpente: a aprendizagem baseada em problemas e as sociedades de controle. Ciênc Saúde. **14**(4), 1183–1192 (2009)
11. García-Peñalvo, F.J., Corell, A., Abella-García, V., Grande-de-Prado, M.: Online assessment in higher education in the time of COVID-19. Educ. Knowl. Soc. **21** (2020)
12. Knopik, T., Oszwa, U.: E-cooperative problem solving as a strategy for learning mathematics during the COVID-19 pandemic. Educ. Knowl. Soc. **22**, e25176 (2021)
13. García-Peñalvo, F.J., Corell, A., Abella-García, V., Grande-de-Prado, M.: Recommendations for mandatory online assessment in higher education during the COVID-19 pandemic. In: Burgos, D., Tlili, A., Tabacco, A. (eds.) Radical Solutions for Education in a Crisis Context. COVID-19 as an Opportunity for Global Learning, pp. 85–98. Springer Nature, Singapore (2021). https://doi.org/10.1007/978-981-15-7869-4_6
14. Pllana, D.: Think-pair-share: teaching strategy unravels uncertainty. In: UBT International Conference, vol. 197 (2020). https://knowledgecenter.ubt-uni.net/conference/2020/all_events/197, Accessed 14 Dec 2021
15. Zakaria, N.H., Haron, A., Sahibuddin, S., Harun, M.: Requirement engineering critical issues in public sector. Int. J. Inf. Electron. Eng. **1**(3), 200–209 (2011)
16. Haron, A., Sahibuddin, S.: the roles of an actor in requirement engineering process. In: Proceedings of the 3rd IEEE International Conference on Computer Science and Information Technology ICCSIT '10, Chengdu, China (2010)
17. Panian, Z.: User requirements engineering and management in software development. In: Proceedings of the European Computing Conference, pp. 609–620 (2009)
18. García-Holgado, A., Vázquez-Ingelmo, A., García-Peñalvo, F.J., Rodríguez-Conde, M.J.: Improvement of learning outcomes in software engineering: active methodologies supported through the virtual campus. IEEE Revista Iberoamericana de Tecnologías del Aprendizaje (IEEE RITA) **16**, 143–153 (2021)

19. García-Peñalvo, F.J., García-Holgado, A., Vázquez-Ingelmo, A., Sánchez-Prieto, J.C.: Planning, communication and active methodologies: online assessment of the software engineering subject during the COVID-19 crisis. RIED. Revista Iberoamericana de Educación a Distancia **24** (2021)

20. Vázquez-Ingelmo, A., García- Holgado, A., García-Peñalvo, F.J.: C4 model in a Software Engineering subject to ease the comprehension of UML and the software development process. In: 2020 IEEE Global Engineering Education Conference (EDUCON), Porto, Portugal, 27–30 April 2020, pp. 919–924. IEEE, USA (2020)

21. Memon, R.N., Ahmad, R., Salim, S.S.: Critical issues in requirements engineering education. In: Handbook of Research on Emerging Advancements and Technologies in Software Engineering, pp. 19–40. IGI Global, Hershey (2014)

22. Quintanilla P.R.L., Engiel, P., Pivatelli, J., Sampaio, J.C.: Facing the challenges of teaching requirements engineering. In: 2016 IEEE/ACM 38th International Conference on Software Engineering Companion (ICSE-C), ICSE-C, pp. 461–470 (2016)

23. Tiwari, S., Ameta, D., Singh, P., Sureka, A.: Teaching requirements engineering concepts using case-based learning. In: IEEE/ACM International Workshop on Software Engineering Education for Millennials, SEEM, pp. 8–15 (2018)

24. Bano, M., Zowghi, D., Ferrari, A., Spoletini, P., Donati, B.: Teaching requirements elicitation interviews: an empirical study of learning from mistakes. Req. Eng. **24**(3), 259–289 (2019). https://doi.org/10.1007/s00766-019-00313-0

25. García, I., Pacheco, C., León, A., Calvo-Manzano, J.: A serious game for teaching the fundamentals of ISO/IEC/IEEE 29148 systems and software engineering – lifecycle processes – requirements engineering at undergraduate level. Comp. Stand. Interf. **67**, 103377 (2020)

26. Ferrari, A., Spoletini, P., Bano, M., Zowghi, D.: SaPeerandReverseSaPeer: teaching requirements elicitation interviews with role-playing and role reversal. Req. Eng. **25**(4), 417–438 (2020)

27. José Hernández-Reinoza, H., Villota-Ibarra, C., Alberto Jiménez-Builes, J.: Metodología lúdica para la enseñanza de la ingeniería de requisitos basada en esquemas preconceptuales. Revista EIA **18**(35), 1–15 (2021)

28. de Souza Filho, J.C., Nakamura, W.T., Teixeira, L.M., da Silva, R.P., Gadelha, B.F., Conte, T.U.: Towards a data-driven requirements elicitation tool through the lens of design thinking (2021)

29. Fonseca, D., Martí, N., Redondo, E., Navarro, I., Sánchez, A.: Relationship between student profile, tool use, participation, and academic performance with the use of Augmented Reality technology for visualized architecture models. Comput. Human Behav. **31**, 434–445 (2014)

30. Fonseca, D., et al.: Mixed assessment of virtual serious games applied in the architectural and urban design of learning processes. Sensors **21**(9), 3102 (2021)

31. Arango-López, J., Gutiérrez F.L., Paderewski, P., Moreira, F., Fonseca, D: Using geolympus to create a pervasive game experience in the higher education context. Universal Access in the Information Society. In press (2021)

32. Fonseca, D., García-Peñalvo, F.J.: Interactive and collaborative technological ecosystems for improving academic motivation and engagement. Univ. Access Inf. Soc. **18**(3), 423–430 (2019). https://doi.org/10.1007/s10209-019-00669-8

33. Petchamé, J., Iriondo, I., Riu, D., Masi, T., Almajano, A., Fonseca, D.: Project based learning or the rethinking of an engineering subject: measuring motivation. In: Eighth International Conference on Technological Ecosystems for Enhancing Multiculturality (TEEM 2020), Salamanca, Spain, 21–23 October 2020, pp. 267–272. Association for Computing Machinery, New York (2020)

34. Santos, C., Durao, N., Fonseca, D., Ferreira, M.J., Moreira, F.: An educational approach for present and future of digital transformation in portuguese organizations. Appl. Sci. **10**(3), 757 (2020)
35. Fonseca, D., García-Peñalvo, F.J., Camba, J.D.: New methods and technologies for enhancing usability and accessibility of educational data. Univ. Access Inf. Soc. **20**, 421–427 (2021)
36. Moreira, F., Ferreira, M.J., Pereira, C.S., Gomes, A.S., Collazos, C., Escudero, D.F.: ECLEC-TIC as a learning ecosystem for higher education disruption. Univ. Access Inf. Soc. **18**(3), 615–631 (2019). https://doi.org/10.1007/s10209-019-00682-x
37. Moreira, F., Ferreira, M.J., Pereira, C.S., Fonseca, D., Collazos, C., Gomes, A.: Higher education teachers training (HET2) model: active learning in higher education environment. In: Rocha, Á., Adeli, H., Dzemyda, G., Moreira, F., Ramalho Correia, A.M. (eds.) Proceedings of WorldCIST 2021. Trends and Applications in Information Systems and Technologies. Advances in Intelligent Systems and Computing, Terceira Island, Azores, Portugal, 30 March–2 April 2021, vol, 1367, pp. 103–112 (2021)
38. Centeno, E., et al.: A comparative study of the application of lesson study in different university learning environments. In: Zaphiris, Panayiotis, Ioannou, Andri (eds.) HCII 2020. LNCS, vol. 12205, pp. 425–441. Springer, Cham (2020). https://doi.org/10.1007/978-3-030-50513-4_32
39. Bichler, M.: Design science in information systems research. Wirtschaftsinformatik **48**(2), 133–135 (2006). https://doi.org/10.1007/s11576-006-0028-8
40. Peffers, K., Rothenberger, M., Tuunanen, T., Vaezi, R.: Design science research evaluation. In: Peffers, K., Rothenberger, M., Kuechler, Bl. (eds.) DESRIST 2012. LNCS, vol. 7286, pp. 398–410. Springer, Heidelberg (2012). https://doi.org/10.1007/978-3-642-29863-9_29
41. Goertzen, M.J.: Introduction to quantitative research and data. Lib. Tech. Rep. **53**, 12–18 (2017)
42. Fernandes, S., Abelha, M., Fernandes, S.M., Albuquerque, A.S.: Implementation of PBL in a social education programme at the Portucalense University. In: Proceedings of the Conference: 9th International Symposium on Project Approaches in Engineering Education and 15th Active Learning in Engineering Education Workshop, pp 446–455 (2018)
43. Pestana, M., Gageiro, J.: Análise de dados para Ciências Sociais. A complementaridade do SPSS, Edições Sílabo, 6a Edição (2014)
44. Marôco, J.: Análise Estatística com o SPSS Statistics. 7ª edição. ReportNumber, Lda (2018)
45. Sein-Echaluce, M.L., Fidalgo-Blanco, A., García-Peñalvo, F.J., Fonseca, D.: Impact of transparency in the teamwork development. Appl. Sci. **11**(9), 3887 (2021)
46. Necchi, S., Peña, E., Fonseca, D., Arnal, M.: Improving teamwork competence applied in the building and construction engineering final degree project. Int. J. Eng. Educ. **36**(1), 328–340 (2021)
47. Aláez, M., Romero, S., Fonseca, D., Amo, D., Peña, E., Necchi, S.: Auto-assessment of teamwork and communication competences improvement applying active methodologies. Comparing results between students of first academic year in architecture, economics and engineering degrees. In: Zaphiris, P., Ioannou, A. (eds.) HCII 2021. LNCS, vol. 12784, pp. 193–209. Springer, Cham (2021). https://doi.org/10.1007/978-3-030-77889-7_13

Collaborative Learning Using Technological Tools - A Framework for the Future

Tord Talmo[1]([⊠]), Maria Sapountzi[2], George Dafoulas[3], and Alessia Valenti[4]

[1] Norwegian University of Science and Technology, Trondheim, Norway
tord.m.talmo@ntnu.no
[2] Radbound University Nijmegen/Active Citizens Partnership, Athens, Greece
[3] Middlesex University, London, Great Britain
g.dafoulas@mdx.ac.uk
[4] CESIE, Palermo, Italy
Alessia.valenti@cesie.org

Abstract. This paper focuses on educational technology designed for collaborative learning, or more correct these tools' abilities for enhancing collaboration in the learning environment. The paper reports on findings from the Erasmus+ -project Learning Through Innovative Collaboration Enhanced by Educational Technology (iLikeIT2). The main aim of the project is to develop a new response technology directed towards collaboration in the learning environment, but in order to do so it is necessary to investigate previous development within the area. The paper presents data from analysis of 48 different tools, and their abilities to be applied in collaborative environments. Secondly the paper reports on 7 different pilots done with different tools, and the qualitative data collected from questionnaires and reflectional conversations with 31 students and instructors after the pilots. The paper thus investigates a wide range of different functionalities that are useful for collaboration, coordination and communication when doing case work in a learning environment. The paper presents pros and cons with different tools, trying to answer the research question: "How can educational technology best enhance collaborative work, and which functionalities need to be present in order to make the tool work positively for the collaborative work?". Even if the paper is not able to conclude in a significant direction, 28 areas of interest for collaborative work with Educational Technology are identified. The paper points at possible improvements for both the tools themselves, but also for the methodology being applied when using the tools.

Keywords: Collaborative learning · Collaborative work · Education · Technology · Digital tools

1 Introduction

A mantra in modern teaching is collaboration and active learning in the student group. Drawing heavily on theories developed by Piaget and Vygotsky, constructivism has been a dominating principle on how knowledge is constructed. The idea is that students

P. Zaphiris and A. Ioannou (Eds.): HCII 2022, LNCS 13328, pp. 478–496, 2022.
https://doi.org/10.1007/978-3-031-05657-4_34

should participate actively in exactly constructing their knowledge more than simply acquire it passively: Thus constructivism does not believe that there are set principles for learning "which [...] are to be discovered and tested, but rather that learners create their own learning" [1, p. 230]. These theories have brought a change in the pedagogy in the 21st Century, that is further enhanced with the major impact of digital tools, skills and opportunities in the educational system arising and constantly being improved throughout the beginning of the century.

Digital skills are considered as vital 21st century skills. This has greatly impacted the educational sector, which is also needed. We know that there is an increasing worldwide demand for higher education. According to the European Commission this demand is expected to make an increase of the number of students from 100 million currently to 250+ million by 2025 [2]. Following the growth in students as well as the demand for more constructivist ideas of learning, it is obvious that Higher Education Institutions (HEI) needs to explore the opportunities provided by digital solutions. This is also vital for the wider society, and for the competencies sought by employers when studies are finished.

In the 21st century digitalization of the society is vital for achieving higher rates of satisfaction, efficiency and improved learning outcome. This is also considered by the European Commission. In their European Framework for Digitally Competent Educational Organizations, which is a key component in the Europe 2020 strategy, the emphasize on this type of competence is highly recommended. It is greatly encouraged that educational institutions consider their institutional strategies in order to coop with the new demands: "To consolidate progress and to ensure scale and sustainability, education institutions need to review their organizational strategies, in order to enhance their capacity for innovation and to exploit the full potential of digital technologies and content" [3]. As shown in a previous article by Talmo et al. this change has not yet been fully considered: "Still, the majority of job announcements do not mention the need for digital skills at all. One could, of course, discuss the necessity for what we have defined as old-fashioned skills, but at least these announcements relate to the strategies at some level." [4, p. 411]. In this study the need for digital competencies when being hired in HEI was investigated. It was anticipated that the priorities from the Commission, as underlined in "Digital strategy for the period 2015–2019": "The internet and digital technologies are transforming our world. Barriers online can deny people the full benefits that digital developments can offer" [5], should penetrate also the strategies on institutional level. EU shows the importance of reevaluating and increasing the knowledge of digital skills in all sectors, which makes it necessary also to research the learning effects and the availability and usage of digital tools and software in HEI.

As the last element of the background for this study it is necessary to mention the ability to work in groups. This is a part of the constructionist theory, enhancing the construction of meaning through collaboration with peers, and is also considered vital for the development of 21st Century skills: "The collaborative learning environment challenges learners to express and defend their positions, and generate their own ideas based on reflection" [6]. Combining digitalization of Education and society together with constructivist ideas of pedagogy, shows clearly that the development of new digital innovations can aid the success of collaboration in modern classrooms: "With the development of new ICTs innovative forms of collaboration are also emerging (Leadbeater, 2008, p. 10)" [7]. Accordingly, recent studies show that using response technology facilitates more classroom interaction and communication [8].

Thus this study aims at answering the research question: "How can Educational Technology best enhance collaborative work, and which functionalities needs to be present in order to make the tool work positively for the collaborative work?".

2 Background

The research reported in this article has its basis in three different phases. In the first phase forty-eight tools already available in the market was tested to see how well they facilitated for collaborative work. It was designed a template for summarizing and assessing the characteristics of the tools. Beside identifying information, the designed template aimed to assess each tool according to the following main criteria:

- *Functional + Usable - Ease of Use* (degree to which the tool can be used by the specified users to achieve the specified objectives): including assessment of learnability, efficiency, effectiveness and memorability of the tool;
- *Reliable - Data, Privacy & Security* (Is the solution set up to give you the data you need in a sustainable way and are you clear and comfortable with the privacy policies?): including identity and access management, data privacy and protection compliance and quality of support;
- *Pleasurable - User Experience* (how a person feels about using the tool): including Satisfaction and Social value;
- *Scalability* (Does the system has the potential to grow or be adapted to a differed need?).

In total seven researchers were involved in the testing of these tools, meaning that it was essential to create a solid and reliable template that was recognizable for all. To achieve this, there was agreement that the research should focus on three keywords/terms in all aspects; **1) Communication, 2) Collaboration** and **3) Coordination**; the three C's. Based on previous research towards what functions when designing a new collaborative software, the three C's seems as the most functional framework for development [9–11]. The research aimed at identifying tools that had a clear potential for to be used for collaborative work. Initially the aim was to look at in-class-usage, but due to the pandemic situation, the aim was modified to also include possibilities for enhancing collaborative work in online environments.

The tools were tested, analyzed and noted by the researchers, and discussed during weekly meetings in the whole period lasting from March 2021 till September 2021. Additionally, one technical expert assessed the solutions for the tools to ensure quality control. The results were displayed in a comparative table (Fig. 1) that gave an overview of different characteristics found in each tool.

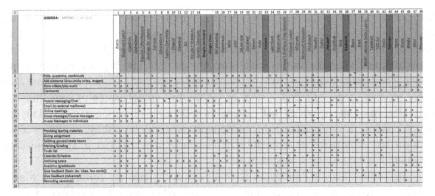

Fig. 1. Table of characteristics existing tools for collaborative work

Figure 1 shows all the criteria that the researchers used to assess the tools, categorized according to the three C's. The marks indicates if the tools possess the functionality in some way, or fulfills the functionality in any way at all. Based on the accessibility to functionality tools were picked to pilot the most valuable functionalities for collaborative work in phase three.

In phase two the aim was to identify the functionalities that needs to be inherit in the tools to enhance the collaboration aspect of a learning process. This was done through literature review, and ended up in eight different functionalities that suits the three C's in an educational tool:

1. Chat/video/recording/messaging system - (communication)
2. Shared whiteboard/screen - (collaboration)
3. Accumulation/internal voting/internal - (communication)
4. Content development - (coordination)
5. Teacher interaction - (coordination)
6. Presentations/sharing doc internally - (collaboration)
7. Group formation/role allocation - (coordination)
8. Assessment/feedback - (collaboration)

Comparing the table presented in Fig. 1 with the functionalities, eight different tools was picked for the piloting in phase three. These were ZOOM [12], MiroBoard [13], forms.app [14], GoogleDocs [15], iLike [16], Microsoft365 [17], Blackboard [18] and Kahoot [19]. The tools did not necessarily need to provide opportunities for all the three C's, but at least one of these. It was the functionalities that was important for this study, not the tools themselves. Thus the researchers when moving into phase three needed to focus on isolating the functionality to be used more than focusing on the tool itself. The third phase is described under "4 Methodology".

3 Theoretical Framework

It is crucial to point out what collaborative learning - work means in terms of education. Firstly, it refers to a teaching technique that teachers, educators, or trainers adopt during their classes. The term has been clearly and thoroughly explained by Goodfell, Smith & MacGregor in their research *What is Collaborative Learning* (1994). According to them, this educational term includes the intellectual merger attempt made by students together or students and teachers. In this case, students are split into a group of two or more people. Their main goal is to work together, cooperate, find a common solution, create a final product, come to a conclusion, or get the full apprehension of something they study. Regarding the activities that students in collaborative work are involved in, these vary according to the needs of the curriculum. Nevertheless, these activities always focus on the "exploration or application of the course material" [20, p. 1] and not solely implementing the teacher's presentations.

Collaborative learning and work have a point to replace the common teaching- or lecture-centered learning in classrooms or tertiary education [20]. Collaborative work enforces and reinforces the students' intercourse and diligent work alongside the traditional method of taking notes during the lecture. As Goodfell, Smith & MacGregor mention, educators who implement this learning technique during their classes tend to consider themselves as "expert designers of intellectual experiences for students- as coaches .... of a more emergent learning process." [20, p. 1].

With the breakthrough of Information and Communication Technologies (ICTs) and their constant usage in the educational sector by academics, today more than ever it is effortless for students to access learning anywhere and any time [21]. In this context, professors and students should be flexible and motivated to apply and participate in this learning process since the technological achievements change or are updated rapidly [21].

3.1 Collaborative Learning and Work in Technological Ecosystems

But what happens when the modern mobile applications and learning platforms, such as MOOCs, online systems, robots programming, the usage of augmented virtual reality, etc., take advantage of the learning and teaching process and become more and more widespread day by day? According to Fonseca and Garcia-Penalvo (2019), the recently updated teaching techniques "based on gamification and collaborative interaction with the context and the learning process" drive to the alternation of the teacher's role [21].

Research has shown that when academics make use of such alluring technologies that caption students' attention, they are capable of engaging students and increasing their motivation to participate in the lecture and advance their academic results [21].

3.2 Effectiveness of the Collaborative Work

Pombo et al. (2010) studied a university-based environment by examining the effectiveness of making use of solely one digital tool. The results had "practical implications for the design of the collaborative activities and innovative assessment in blended learning environments" [22, p. 217]. By utilizing only, a digital tool, inter-group collaboration was boosted amazingly.

The results were quite positive when the students-participants called to use asynchronous communication tools for peer assessment. This technique would allow them to be aware of each other's assignments and performance to become more collaborative in the digital environment. For instance, while students were working together their comments were elevated. Thus, this means the effectiveness of the collaboration process showed high interaction [22]. The same results can be found in a study by Nielsen et al (2014) in Norway. More than 200 h of video materials on students using a response tool, showed how interaction increased in class, and how strategic methodological approaches from the instructor enhanced the leaning outcome from the work: "Change of methodology, from classic to peer instruction, increases the argumentation time with 91%. Most of this time is used to present explanations, related to curricula." [23].

Through the study of Cesar and Santos (2006), the results were quite impressive and more than expected. The most crucial of them revealed that through collaborative peer work, the students acquired an interest in courses that they did not like to, accepted sharing roles, succeeded in collaboration, and started promoting other students' work. Furthermore, Cesar and Santos concluded that students working in inclusive learning environments could support working in various pulses without making them feel restrained. It was also reported the enhance "higher mental functions, like language and reasoning" by advancing "social and cognitive competencies" [24, p. 339]. To conclude, most of the students agreed that working collaboratively led them to feel included in the learning process.

3.3 Theoretical Framework Software Development

When developing an educational tool for collaborative one needs to focus on providing those functions that are deemed essential for supporting collaborative work in educational contexts. The main challenge is to determine how different technical features can be combined to support the various social aspects associated with collaborative learning. The work carried out in this research falls under the umbrella of (CSCW), which places "emphasis on collaborative work settings, where social interactions and analysis are paramount" [25]. This indicates that educational tools should provide the necessary platform to support Computer Supported Collaborative Learning (CSCL) which results in improving "student motivation and critical thinking" [26].

During the early years shaping CSCL Lehtinen et al. (1999) argued that "there are not too many well controlled experiments, which could answer the questions concerning the wider applicability of CSCL in normal classrooms and the added value of computers and networks in comparison to collaborative learning environments without technology" [27]. Since then there was a dramatic increase in CSCL solutions, which are usually classified as (i) virtual learning environments (e.g. repositories of educational content), (ii) collaborative platforms (e.g. whiteboards), and (iii) communication tools (e.g. video conferencing). An aim is to combine certain functions to support the communication, coordination and collaboration of learners online. This is illustrated in the following figure, representing a software development framework implemented in the ongoing EU co-funded project Learning Through Innovative Collaboration Enhanced by Educational Technology (iLikeIT2) [28]. The framework includes six categories of features that are commonly met in the CSCL solutions identified above. When designing the iLikeIT2 tool we focused on integrating a number of features that are essential for collaborative work in different learning scenarios. More specifically, the six elements of the iLikeIT2 framework are:

- *Delivery* – we believe it is necessary to enable instructors and learners to collaborate and communicate without interrupting the delivery of learning that may involve a teaching presentation, demonstration of an application, use of browser to show a website, display of visual content or video, as well as sharing of files.
- *Interaction* – we determined that the main exchanges between instructors and learners during a teaching session would be in the form of assessment, questioning and polling.
- *Learner support* – we anticipated that learner support during scheduled sessions is affected by the fact that emphasis is on covering certain content, therefore small interventions should be driven by the instructor's ability to access statistics about the progress of the entire class, the performance of certain groups and achievement of individual learners.
- *Communication* – we expected that instructors and learners would use either audio or chat functions to exchange information during a session.
- *Collaboration* – we determined that collaboration would require the formation of teams and allocation of roles.
- *Coordination* – we established that instructors would need to coordinate the learning activity by (i) reflecting whether certain tasks need improvements, (ii) appraising which topics are challenging for the learners, (iii) testing which questions are appropriate for the session, (iv) evaluating whether groups perform according to certain thresholds and (v) assessing individuals' knowledge and understanding.

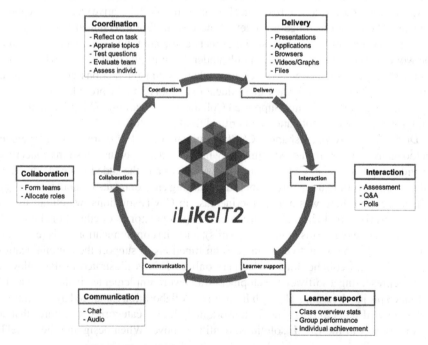

Fig. 2. The iLikeIT2 software development framework

Thus, the aim of this research is to address the activity needs of collaborative learning by addressing both analytic and design components as defined by for example Stahl et al. (2006). More specifically "analysis of meaning making is inductive and indifferent to reform goals", while design is "inherently prescriptive—any effort toward reform begins from the presumption that there are better and worse ways of doing things" [29]. The six elements of the iLikeIT2 software development framework enable users of the tool to engage in various learning activities during scheduled, synchronous sessions. Combined with pedagogical practices and theory, this background provides a framework for the research and results being presented in this article, and aids answering the research question: "How can educational technology best enhance collaborative work, and which functionalities need to be present in order to make the tool work positively for the collaborative work?".

4   Methodology

Phase three of the study included seven pilot tests in four different countries with participants from different sectors and levels of the educational system (see "5 Results"). Pilot testing help to identify the issues related to the use of a tool for collaborative work and to know how user-friendly and how easy a tool should be for an individual to navigate through its features. Pilot testing's primary purpose is to scope out user requirements and collect input to see how the functionality affects the collaborative aspects in a group.

The researchers needed to provide real-life scenarios for the groups. The participants to the pilot testing were selected from previous experience, actual studies and/or based on previous experience, motivation and expertise. It is important to secure input from as many areas as possible in order to obtain good qualitative data in a pilot-phase like this. The pilots were organized as seen in the bullet points below:

Organization of pilot testing:

a. Modus: Small focus groups of 5–10 participants
b. Participants' profile:

  i.   Instructors/Teaching staff: Lecturer and senior lecturers, Trainers, Learning support workers, Academic developers
  ii. Technicians
  iii. Students

c. Equipment: Case work plan. equipment to test the tools (laptop, tablet, smartphone) + tools to be tested
d. Time limit: Between two and three hours for the whole pilot including questionnaires and reflectional conversation)
e. Pilot settings:

  i.   Groups: Groups of 4 or five participants with one facilitator running the cases.
  ii. 1 facilitator observe the collaborative work
  iii. Additional technician to ensure that the tool functions if needed

    iv.   Actual teaching situations might include more students.

f. Requirements: For recording of pilot testing might partners need to comply with national and institutional law regarding privacy protection. Participants need to sign a statement of consent

g. Pilot workplan:

    i.   Preparation: Participants provided with all the necessary information regarding the project and the activity: aim of the pilot testing and what participants had to do during the testing period, accurate description of the chosen tool and case and intentions regarding the expected final results. Lastly, a time limit was provided for carrying out the chosen cases' single tasks or main activity to participants for the test.

    ii. Deployment: Ensured that all the participants have understood the project's goals and the activity basic working, proceed on working on the chosen case with the tool required to be tested.

To ensure the correct data being collected, and that the functionalities would be the focus point, the researchers made one subject specific case for each pilot. These cases were developed based on both the level of the participants, their previous knowledge, the subject the instructor was familiar with and to ensure that the participants needed to actually work together on the same task. Each case was planned to use an activity plan that included information about:

- Objective of the case
- Time required to deliver the case
- Methodology for delivering the case
- How to collect data about the use
- What to do with the data

Additionally, based on the same activity plan, the researchers included one generic case, about successful communication, that all pilots should run, no matter the participant's profile. This was to ensure that all participants were exposed to one similar task, so that the reflectional conversations would be more focused and obtain the same type of data afterwards. The generic case was modified a bit in each pilot due the tool being chosen for testing. When the participants were done with their testing, their inputs about what they feel about the activity and what changes they would like to see in the tool they worked with was collected through a questionnaire[1] and a reflectional conversation. The use of Reflectional conversations (focus groups) is a research method that is intended to collect data, through interactive and directed discussions. In this study the reflectional conversation took form of a 'reflection-on-action' [30]. This can take place in tranquility or designers can pause in the midst of the action to make a "stop-and-think". In either case, the reflection has no direct connection to the present action. Designers can pause to think back over what they have done, exploring the understanding that they have brought

---

[1] The results from the questionnaire are not included in this research.

to the handling of the task." [30, p. 2] The conversation was done after the tasks being done in the focus group, but still in the process of developing a new software based on the information provided in the conversations.

A focus group is a form of qualitative research where a group of people are asked about their perceptions, opinions, beliefs, and attitudes towards certain issues that the researcher wants to study. Using focus groups can be categorized as a form of qualitative research where a group of people are asked about their perceptions, opinions, beliefs, and attitudes towards certain issues that the researcher wants to study. This allows deeper insight, as well as providing the researcher with the opportunity of asking follow-up questions.

Although focus groups are similar to in-depth interviews, they have some fundamental differences. The researcher asks some questions in an interactive group setting where participants are free to talk with other group members. The researcher uses a discussion guide that has been prepared in advance of the focus group to guide the discussion. Generally, the discussion starts with overall impressions and gradually becomes more specific. By using this approach, it is possible to gain access to the experiences of many different individuals and, as individuals interact with one another, data is enriched, enabling views to be reformulated through exchange.

For this study the researchers developed guidelines for the reflectional conversation based on the main points shown in Fig. 2 (Fig. 3):

Main principles for reflectional conversations. iLikeIT2

	How ?	Why ?
Moderator/facilitator	Dual structure	One facilitator to lead the conversation, one instructor included in the conversation. The instructor will provide valuable insight to the case.
Structure	Semi-structured	The conversation has an aim, and it is necessary to not deviate too much from this. Participants should be urged to discuss freely.
Settings	Formal	Part of a lecture in some cases. Needs to be recorded and transcribed.
Communication	Flexible	Balancing act between flexibility, allowing a free-flowing conversation, and structure, ensuring that the conversation does not stray too far from research objectives. Flexibility will allow a larger number of responses from all participants.
Cooperation	Equality of contribution	Moderation between introvert/extrovert persons. Allowing instructor to participate without dominating.
Expressions/Limitations	Personalized	Subjective meanings are interesting in this study. Discussions are welcome and the facilitator should moderate for such.
Time frame	30 min.	It is foreseen that the participants might be tired if the conversation last longer than 30 minutes. Still, if interesting discussions and engagement, this is not a maximum.

Fig. 3. Main principles reflectional conversation

Based on these main principles in Fig. 2, the following guidelines were designed and distributed to all facilitators:

1. As participants arrive, the facilitator should welcome them and thank them for coming. Once everybody is present and seated, the facilitator should provide a brief introduction outlining the purpose of research. Next, each participant introduces themselves, giving name and a brief bit of background.
2. Upon completion of the piloting, facilitator ask participants to sit in a circle. The facilitator lays ground rules for conversation (one person to talk at a time, all views welcome, confidentiality) and stress that there is no hidden agenda, and that all views will be treated in confidence. The participants are asked to sign a statement of consent.
3. The facilitator introduces the opening topic/question, which should be fairly general, and capable of generating discussion. Attempts should be made to make everyone contribute. It may be necessary for the facilitator to intervene quite a bit by asking questions, and generally keeping the discussion going.
4. During the discussions, the facilitator needs to make sure that all points are covered and promote group discussion.
5. The facilitator will use a guide with a list of topics/questions to be covered. It is advisable however to have memorized this list in advance, as to read from questions will look forced and inhibit discussion.
6. The groups should discuss every topic.
7. Before ending the focus group, participants should be encouraged to state their final position on key topics and offer any additional comments relevant to the group's key purpose. It is very important to end the discussion on a positive note and also to thank people for coming.

Even if it is not advisable that the facilitator intervenes, participates or lay restraints on the discussion the facilitator needs to get the participants started and intervene if the discussion in moving towards a side-track or stops entirely. Some pre-made questions are made available for the facilitator in order to cover the most important parts of the research question:

1) Describe a normal setting for collaborative work in your learning environment?
2) What helps you to use collaborative tools effectively in your teaching?

   a. Perceived usefulness - Degree to which they believe that using a particular technology would enhance their job performance: Work more quickly? Improved job performance? Increased productivity? Effectiveness? Useful?
   b. Perceived ease-of-use - Degree to which they believe that using a particular system would be free from effort: Easy to learn? Clear and understandable? Easy to use? Controllable? Easy to remember?
   c. Attitude toward use – teacher's positive or negative feeling about using the tool
   d. Behavioral intention - The degree to which the teacher has formulated conscious plans to use the tool
   e. Social influence processes

3) Do you have any advice for those who would like to use collaborative tools in their courses?

4) Which functionalities are working according to the intention of the case?
5) What functionalities of the tools do you consider to be important and useful for collaborative work?
6) Identify the limitations of the tool according to the intention of the case?
7) What challenges do you see in using this tool for collaborative work?
8) What functionality do you miss? Is there any function that you wish you could use in your courses?

5   Results

In total seven pilots have been run in five different countries: Norway, Italy, Greece and Spain. A total number of 11 different cases has been used, where three of these were based on the same generic case about communication. A total number of 86 informants have been participating in the pilots. Five of the pilots have been done solemnly online, while two were done with physical presence.

A total number of 31 informants have been participating in the reflectional conversations:

Students, age 22–30: 11
Instructors: 20

In the student group, only students at NTNU, Norway had some previous experience with the tool being used in one of the pilots (Google Docs). In the instructor group seven instructors were used to the tool being used (iLike and Micosoft365). In one of the pilots there were difficulties when logging into the tool, which meant that the instructors changed to a familiar tool (Microsoft365). The low number of physical presences in the pilots is due to the pandemic situation (Covid19) throughout the world and restrictions put in place by institutions. In an Educational Technology-project/research this was not considered to have any effect on the results.

The results from the reflectional conversation were collected in a focus group grid, focusing on six main thematic areas:

1. Normal setting for collaborative work
2. Effective use of collaborative tools
3. Advices
4. Working functionalities
5. Limitations/Challenges
6. Needs /Wishes

During the interpretation of the conversations, the researchers identified sub-themes within each of the main categories. These sub-themes were identified through specific statements from the participants. Several of the sub-themes were identical, even if the tools in use being different, and the functionalities being tested were not the same. Thus, we claim that we have found a total of 28 areas that must be taken into consideration when designing and using educational tools to enhance collaborative learning in the learning environment. Table 1 shows an overview of the different areas identified, with a short explanation to each of them based on input from the reflectional conversations.

Table 1. Areas identified as essential for making collaboration better when using Ed.Tech.

CSCL categories	Areas of interest	Description
Delivery	Time efficency & control	The instructor's ability to monitor the work being done and the time saved when delegating tasks and groups
	Split screen	Possibility of sharing multiple content at the same time
	Visuals	Results need to be visualized in a clear and appealing fashion for the plenary/group
	Dynamics	The ability the tool provides for organization and creation of continuous work
	Misuse	The tools need to be used for the intention, not for everything else, i.e. laziness from the instructor, private chats, games or similar
	Cost & fees	Important that the tools deliver what you expect them to do, indifferently the cost and/or fees being paid
	Connection	All technical solutions need to be secure and available, like internet connection and AV-equipment, as well as an easy access/registration for all participants
Interaction	Recording	The ability to record the session, allowing both students and instructor to watch the session post activity
	Learning effect	The opportunity to increase motivation and provide immediate feedback on tasks
	Responsibility	The possibility to monitor and access the peers work, thus making responsibility for the tasks clearer
	Teacher view	The instructor is allowed easy monitoring and access to all aspects of the collaborative work, in real time and after ended task
	Statistics/results	Both displaying results immediately and saving statistics for later discussions

(*continued*)

Table 1. (*continued*)

CSCL categories	Areas of interest	Description
Learner support	**Initiation**	The ability of instantly getting into interaction and in-depth learning
	Preparation	Easy to understand for the students, and abilities of preparing for different scenarios
	Control system for the moderator	The ability of customization. Also important to monitor and moderate misuse
	Learning design	Clear guidelines and explanation of the task. Needs to be available in the tool somehow
Communication	**Sharing**	The ability of not being physically present to attend and contribute in a collaborative work
	Communication	The possibility of exchanging ideas and discuss during the task, written or orally
	Regularity	Both students and instructors need to be used to the tool and methodology
	Messaging system	The ability of answering specific messages and create new threads of communication
Collaboration	**Peer learning**	The idea of students helping and aiding each other
	Collaboration	The ability to communicate efficiently and interact with other members of the group, both for students and instructors
	Indicating uncertainty	The ability to show the group and/or instructor uncertainty with the answer or disagreement with the groups result
	Roles	The possibility of selecting a "leader", and to identify who is responsible for each task

(*continued*)

Table 1. (*continued*)

CSCL categories	Areas of interest	Description
Coordination	**Collaboration/Assignments**	The ability of creating both individual and collaborative tasks. Allowing the instructor to easily change between the two according to the learning design
	Coordination	The ability to delegate tasks, store materials and work simultaneously in the same task
	Grouping	Allowing flexibility when dividing in groups
	Teachers' preparation	Instructors needs to be prepared, both for the methodology, but also for the possibilities the tools allow for

The table is sorted according to the six categories found in the CSCL framework. The description of the areas are interpreted from a synopsis of different statements from both students and instructors during the conversations.

6 Discussion

As seen previously there are clear indications in literature that educational technology can improve the learning process for the students. Based on this study there are especially two things that are essential for making the process positive; 1) The tools chosen must be appropriate and contain the correct functionality, and 2) the instructors need to be prepared, strategic in their learning design and know the tools capabilities. In this study, the eight functionalities being researched clearly shows that there are several tools delivering functionality good enough for using in a learning environment, even if there seems always to be lacking something[2]: "In Zoom: there is no 'someone has raised their hand' emoticon, nor does it have a sound to alert me." or "what you showed us with the graphics etc., can absorb the attention of the students and the individual,". Most of the statements are agreed upon by other informants in the conversation, and also appear more commonly than others. It seems as if the instructors are often looking for functionality that resembles the physical group work: "The students may participate either through the chat or by raising their hand and you give them permission to enable the microphone." There are several of the areas identified for successful collaborative work in Table 1 that points towards this, like "Time efficiency and control", "Teacher view", "Misuse" and "Control system for the moderator". The instructors are still positive to the effects the tools are providing and implementing, which is also emphasized by the students.

---

[2] All quotes in this part are quoted directly from the transcripts. These are available by contacting the authors of this publication.

Mainly it seems as if the students like the opportunities of creating new dynamics, easy communication and coordination of the group work: "Dividing people in group, make them able to act simultaneously on the same task is a great asset for lessons."

Additionally, it is obvious that the instructor's role as a facilitator for learning is essential. Technology is nothing without methodology, and when applying educational technology in the learning environment, it is vital that the instructor know the tool and its possibilities: "If the teacher was two hours without looking at the chat. They were two hours without responding to anything." This is something the instructors in the study is well aware of: "... can immediately motivate the student, get into in-depth learning, meaning there is interaction, and since technology is constantly evolving, I think we are all called upon to keep up with all these modern media, because the learning environment is becoming more modern.". No matter the access to the new tools, instructors need to allocate their time between accessing new tools and focusing on learning design: "I discover potential and functionalities of tools but I do not have the time to try them". Thus, the areas identified in Table 1 connected to the instructor's part as a facilitator, like "Control system for the moderator", "Statistics" and "Teachers preparation", is something that needs to be supported in an efficient educational tool for collaborative work. Other areas, like "Indicating uncertainty", "Learning design", and "Preparation" are aspects that are perceived as important. In order to design a functional tool one needs to develop for flexibility when creating new questions or selecting from existing ones. This is as part of the interaction element of the tool. The visualization of results is critical. All results and statistics must be easily accessible and visually attractive to the participants. It is also essential that the tool emphasize the importance of the instructor being the facilitator of collaborative learning.

It is always interesting to look for areas where the agreement is higher than others. In this research it seems as three areas is especially interesting. Firstly, there are several informants, both instructors and students pointing at the importance of making sure the systems/tools are working. If the tools are inadequate for the work being designed, the session will not be very useful: "It happened I had to completely change what I had planned because the tool was not helpful." A useful tool needs to be secure, working and useful for the task.

Secondly there is a common agreement that the tools need to provide additional engagement and motivation in the student group: "A tool needs to be appealing also in terms of graphics". Even if the graphics might be more important for the younger targets, a nice graphic stimulates the feeling of fun and game. As important as the gamification of the tool, is the opportunity to make the work more efficient and dynamic: "When working in group, a shared document makes dividing tasks easier". This area is something that several emphasize and agree upon in the conversations.

Thirdly it seems to be common agreement about the ability to communicate with peers:

"I would like to say that the plan helps on 2 levels: individually for each person because it helps them to place their thoughts as a central idea and then to develop them, because it gives them easier goals, that is, starting from a central idea and slowly managing to break it down more to divide it into smaller branches, so that the final result becomes easier. Also, when you are a team, everyone can create their own branch and this way everyone in the team is more comfortable and they can have control over everyone's project."

This is not surprising, but there are informants providing information that even the most common tools do not have the necessary communication channels available for the work that needs to be done:

"Well, I am thinking about the discussions that appear while we sit and write for example. Now we have to call or use a different tool compared to when we wrote the definition about communication, then the communication part was constant, and we therefore came to a conclusion."

Even if there is much to discuss it is possible to conclude on the research question for this paper: "How can Educational Technology best enhance collaborative work, and which functionalities needs to be present in order to make the tool work positively for the collaborative work?". In the results part we have identified 28 areas of interest when assessing and identifying tools that may enhance the learning effect in a collaborative work. These areas clearly underline the two main factors identified in the literature: the tools inherit functionalities and the instructor's ability to use them in a meaningful way. It is possible to see some areas as more important than others, but still there is several informants pointing at all areas, and it seems to be agreement among the participants on these 28.

There are several limitations to the results obtained in the study. The results have been collected and interpreted by five different researchers only able to communicate and discuss online. This may affect the results. All transcripts are available via the authors and will be published at a later stage[3].

The fact that there were eight different tools with different functionalities available being included in the study provides a large amount of data but might also make the focus less sharp. The study aimed at looking at functionalities, and cases were run according to the latter. This reduces the focus on the tool itself.

It is difficult to claim that the results are significant due to the low number of participants. Still, almost five hours of reflectional conversations are analyzed. All recordings are available via the authors.

It is also a possible uncertainty in the 28 areas identified. Not all of them are mentioned as often as the others, and some of them are not agreed upon by all. The study was concerned about agreement, this was included in the focus grid designed before the pilots, and areas only mentioned by one participant and not agreed upon, has not been included.

This research is not sufficient to make clear conclusions. Still the recommendations are valid, and the 28 areas identified are significant when applying Educational Technology in modern learning environments. For the future there should be done studies on the learning effects on groups using different tools, to identify achieved academic performance and to figure out how the implementation of the tools changes the dynamics of the collaborative work. Even if there are 28 areas identified, these could be more

---

[3] All results and appendices will be published in the project Learning Through Innovative Collaboration Enhanced by Educational Technology (iLikeIT2) [30].

detailed, and research could have been done in order to figure out which areas are more important.

Acknowledgement. Parts of this has been co-funded funded with support from the European Commission through the project Learning Through Innovative Collaboration Enhanced by Educational Technology (iLikeIT2) (Nr. 2020-1-NO01-KA203-076434). This publication reflects the author's views only, and the Commission cannot be held responsible for any use which may be made of the information contained therein.

References

1. Schunk, D.H.: Learning Theories: An Educational Perspective, 6th edn. Pearson Education Inc., Boston, MA (2012)
2. European Commission: Report to the European Commission on New modes of learning and teaching in higher education (2014). ISBN 978–92–79–39789–9. https://doi.org/10.2766/81897
3. EU Science Hub: European Framework for Digitally Competent Educational Organisations (2019). https://ec.europa.eu/jrc/en/digcomporg
4. Talmo, T., et al.: Digital competences for language teachers: do employers seek the skills needed from language teachers today? In: Book: Learning and Collaboration Technologies. Designing, Developing and Deploying Learning Experiences (2020). https://doi.org/10.1007/978-3-030-50513-4_30
5. European commission: Priorities, Digital Single Market (2019). https://ec.europa.eu/commission/priorities/digital-single-market_en
6. Anderson, T., Dron, J.: Three generations of distance education pedagogy. The international review of research in open and distributed learning, vol. 12, no. 3 (2011). https://doi.org/10.19173/irrodl.v12i3.890
7. Scott, C.L.: The futures of learning 3: What kind of pedagogies for the 21st Century?" UNESCO series Education Research and Foresight. Working papers (2015). http://unesdoc.unesco.org/images/0024/002431/243126e.pdf
8. Einum, E.: Discursive lecturing: An agile and student-centred teaching approach with response technology. J. Educ. Change **20**(2), 249–281 (2019). https://doi.org/10.1007/s10833-019-09341-7
9. Stahl, G.: Group practices: a new way of viewing CSCL. Int. J. Comput.-Support. Collab. Learn. **12**(1), 113–126 (2017). https://doi.org/10.1007/s11412-017-9251-0
10. Lazareva, A.: International Conference on Interactive Collaborative Learning (ICL). (2015). https://doi.org/10.1109/ICL.2015.7318066
11. Ze, S., Ruihua, K., Xiongkai, S.: CSCW-based virtual team cooperation platform analysis and design. In: Conference proceedings Informatics in Control, Automation and Robotics (CAR), 2010 2nd International Asia, vol. 3 (2010). https://doi.org/10.1109/CAR.2010.5456698
12. https://zoom.us/
13. https://miro.com/
14. https://forms.app/
15. https://www.google.com/docs/about/
16. https://www.one2act.no/
17. https://www.microsoft.com/en-us
18. https://www.blackboard.com/about-us
19. https://kahoot.com/

20. Goodfell, A., Smith, B.L., MacGregor, J.: Collaborative Learning: A Sourcebook for Higher Education. Natl Center on Postsecondary (1994)
21. Fonseca, D., García-Peñalvo, F.J.: Interactive and collaborative technological ecosystems for improving academic motivation and engagement. Universal Access Inf. Soc. 18(3), 423–430 (2019). https://doi.org/10.1007/s10209-019-00669-8
22. Pombo, L., Loureiro, M.J., Moreira, A.: Assessing collaborative work in higher education blended learning context: strategies and students' perceptions. Educ. Media Int. 47(3), 217–229 (2010). https://doi.org/10.1080/09523987.2010.518814
23. Nielsen, K.L., et al.: How the initial thinking period affects student argumentation during peer instruction: students' experiences versus observations. Stud. High. Educ. (2014). https://doi.org/10.1080/03075079.2014.915300
24. César, M., Santos, N.: From exclusion to inclusion: Collaborative work contributions to more inclusive learning settings. Eur. J. Psychol. Educ. 21(3), 333–346 (2006). https://doi.org/10.1007/bf03173420
25. Pratt, W., Reddy, M.C., McDonald, D.W., Tarcazy-Hornoch, P., Gennari, J.H.: Incorporating ideas from computer-supported cooperative work. J. Biomed. Inform. 37(2), 128–137 (2004)
26. Knutas, A., Ikonen, J., Porras, J.: Computer-supported collaborative learning in software engineering education: a systematic mapping study. Int. J. Inf. Technol. Secur. 7(4) (2019)
27. Lehtinen, E., Hakkarainen, K., Lipponen, L., Veermans, M., Muukkonen, H.: Computer Supported Collaborative Learning: A Review (1999)
28. iLikeIT2 (2022). Homepage iLikeIT2. https://ilikeit2.eu/
29. Stahl, G., Koschmann, T., Suthers, D.: Computer-supported collaborative learning: An historical perspective. In: Sawyer, R.K. (ed.), Cambridge Handbook of the Learning Sciences, pp. 409–426. Cambridge University Press, Cambridge, UK (2006)
30. Reymen, I.M.M.J.: Research on design reflection: overview and directions. In: Folkeson, A., Gralèn, K., Norell, M., Sellgren, U. (eds.), Proceedings of the 14th International Conference on Engineering Design, pp. 33–35, Stockholm: KTH, Royal Institute of Technology (2003)

Teaching Programming Amid the Digital Churn: Guidelines and Curriculum for a Laboratory

Dante Tezza[✉] and Ben Abbott

St. Mary's University, San Antonio, TX 78228, USA
{dtezza,babbott1}@stmarytx.edu

Abstract. In the modern and digital society, the importance of software development is undeniable. Therefore, educating the next generation of software developers is crucial. However, learning how to program is challenging, and research on improving programming pedagogy is essential. Adding a laboratory component to programming courses can enhance the education. In this work, we first elicited requirements and guidelines for an introductory programming lab curriculum based on a literature review and feedback by instructors with years of experience. These included the use of (1) current and adequate tools, (2) collaborative learning environment, (3) formative assessment, (4) appropriate assignments for the target audience, (5) pedagogical innovations, and (6) to prepare students to be lifelong learners of the subject. Following, we present a curriculum for an introductory undergraduate programming lab based on the Raspberry Pi platform. It teaches students how to program following software development best practices and integrate software and hardware through a series of cyber-physical assignments, including developing a rover vehicle. We successfully piloted the curriculum with 30 students, and we present the highly positive feedback provided by them. Although the course was based on the C programming language, the underlying foundation on programming principles will allow students to apply the concepts in any language. Furthermore, this curriculum is not intended to be a one-size-fits-all approach to programming education. However, it can be a strong starting point for readers to tailor it to fit their audience, school needs, and student learning outcomes.

Keywords: Curriculum · Education · Engineering education · Programming · Software

1 Introduction

The churning digital transformation has become a directing factor in society's evolution. Some now consider it a software-driven society [16]. Therefore, it is natural that the demand for software developers and software development education continues to accelerate. Skills in algorithms and programming are essential intellectual tools and should be included in basic education [8]. However, software development is a continuously evolving field where new techniques, technologies, and programming languages often replace their predecessors. Although software education has incorporated these rapid-advancing topics, the core pedagogy has not experienced significant change [14].

Outcome-based programming metrics are typically focused on goals such as: to teach students programming competence, to understand the logic behind programming [15], to develop problem-solving abilities, and to be able to use a programming language to implement their solutions [11]. Correspondingly, this portion of their education should emphasize the foundations of mathematics, science, and engineering principles [10], enabling students to be lifelong learners. However, students' failure in programming disciplines suggests that traditional pedagogy is not suitable for many [11].Therefore, it is essential to actively research and adapt programming education to improve our pedagogy. Additionally, we must remember the importance of teachers' training [5]and develop appropriate curriculum.

Computer programming is challenging to learn [12,29]. For instance, it takes roughly ten years for a beginner to become an expert computer programmer [31]. Thus, based on society's fast pace, it is not surprising that many students give up before reaching the expert level. Programming education poses significant mental challenges to many novice students [8], and their struggles have been attributed to a lack of problem-solving abilities [11,20], poor pedagogical methods, and low self-efficacy [20]. Additionally, programming education can be challenging as it is unfamiliar for many undergraduate students who have never taken a software class before. Computer programming is a creative process hard to master by reading. Students can learn more effectively by writing programs [9]. Therefore, it is reasonable to include hands-on laboratory components in programming courses, and an accepted approach to enhance programming education is to increase practical lab hours [20].

In this study, we first elicited requirements and guidelines for an introductory programming lab curriculum based on a literature review and feedback by instructors with years of experience. These included the use of (1) current and adequate tools, (2) collaborative learning environment, (3) formative assessment, (4) appropriate assignments for the target audience, (5) pedagogical innovations, and (6) to prepare students to be lifelong learners of the subject. Following, we present a curriculum for an introductory undergraduate programming lab. The curriculum consists of 12 lab sessions based on the Raspberry Pi platform. It is designed to teach students how to apply programming principles, software development best practices and train them in essential development tools. For instance, students must submit their assignments using version control (git) and learn how to remote connect to their computers using VNC. Additionally, students learn hardware and software integration through a series of cyber-physical assignments. Throughout 12 lab sessions, students work with LEDs, buzzers, PWM signals, and brushless motors. During the last five lab sessions, students program a ground rover vehicle. The last assignment consists of an autonomous race in which students compete with their programmed rovers. Students show mastery of the subject they studied throughout the semester in this engaging and fun task.

This curriculum was piloted during the Fall 2021 semester with 30 students, and in this paper, we discuss the lessons learned and present the students' feedback. Students accepted the curriculum with highly positive feedback. Although, the curriculum presented in this paper was developed using the C programming language. The underlying foundation on programming principles will allow students to apply the concepts in any language. Furthermore, this curriculum is not intended to be a one-size-fits-all approach to programming education. However, it can be a strong starting point for readers to tailor it to fit their audience, school needs, and student learning outcomes.

2   Literature Review

Research suggests that computer programming is considered a difficult subject to learn [11]. It can be even more challenging in environments where academic and socioeconomic factors impact the learning experience, such as in developing countries [20]. Students' poor performance and high failure rate highlights the difficulties in learning programming [20]. A survey found that passing rates are on average only 67% [2], and such high failure rates have been a popular research topic [11]. Additionally, this issue has been known for decades. For instance, researchers in 1997 documented that "programming was considered the most challenging and least interesting subject by most first-year students in computing courses" [13]. Furthermore, programming pedagogy research spreads among various topics. For instance, an analysis of research papers published from 2005 to 2008 demonstrates that 40% of them explored ability, aptitude, and understanding of the subject; 35% explored difference teaching, learning, and assessment techniques; 9% discussed teaching, learning, and assessment tools; 6% are related to theories and models, and only 4% presented programming course curriculum's [23].

A primary reason why many students struggle when learning to program is their lack of the core abilities of generic problem solving [20]. To us, this explains why program design is the most challenging aspect of introductory programming [4]. For instance, many students start programming their solution before first analyzing and understanding the problem [20]. Consequently, if students can improve their problem-solving abilities, programming courses will be positively impacted [11]. Another challenging aspect of programming education is that students try to communicate with a computer as if they were communicating with another human being. For instance, they do not emphasize the importance of the order in which statements are executed [8]. Therefore, students must understand and follow the formal rules of the programming environment [8].

A classic debate for the first programming course concerns the choice of the appropriate language for students to implement their solutions. Many instructors and researchers advocate using commonly used languages such as C++ and

Java. Others support higher-level conceptual languages or the use of toolkits and even games, allowing students to focus on the logic required to implement the solution [4]. Additionally, the instructor must balance the lecture between providing support for low-level issues such as programming syntax and covering the highly complex conceptual areas required by efficient program design techniques [4]. Researchers also found a loss of intentionality in programming students, which happens when students "use and adapt other programs" [3]. This becomes a problem when students no longer try to understand the program and don't improve their problem-solving thought process. When faced with a new problem, their programming skills rely on (1) pattern matching and (2) random modifications based on automatic feedback provided by compilers and IDEs [3].

Students start to struggle early in the programming courses, leading to dropouts and harder-to-overcome challenges later in the semester [27]. Therefore, it is beneficial to identify students struggling earlier than later in the course. Researchers have explored data mining to analyze students' performance and identify struggling students early on [26]. Broader artificial intelligence algorithms have also been used to support programming education [6]. For example, Lisp-Tutor [1], C-Tutor [25], and Cimel ITS [19] are intelligent tutoring systems designed to support students.

Approaches such as employing drones in the classroom [28], puzzle-based techniques [21], and the use of games and gamification [18] have also been explored to enhance students' learning experience. For instance, [30] researched game elements in programming education and found that an essential factor shared between games and education is the use of feedback. Feedback is common in games, as it guides players towards the objective outcome, and it can also be used to influence students overall learning behavior [17]. Additionally, the use of automatic feedback is beneficial for both students and instructors. For instance, during an online Java course with an assessment tool that analyzes the code and supports predefined tests, researchers found that the automatic feedback decreased the instructor time required for manual assessment by a factor of four [9]. Furthermore, the instantaneous feedback was appreciated, and increased students' motivation [9]. Other game elements that can be used in programming education include assistance during tasks, challenges, dynamic difficulties, and a scoring system [17].

3   Programming Lab Guidelines and Requirements

Current and Adequate Tools - With the overwhelming quanity and variety of advanced tools supporting software development, it is essential to train students to use adequate tools. The course instructor should carefully decide what tools are appropriate to the students' skills and current industry requirements. However, the instructor must not select tools that are too advanced for their student's grade as they can be hard to use and hinder programming learning. Technological tools may not always enhance the learning experience [7], but if chosen adequately, they can be valuable assets to the classroom. For instance, using the

Arduino microcontroller can enhance learning attitude, problem-solving, academic interest, and flow of learning in computer programming education [24].

Software tools such as modern debuggers, integrated development environments (IDEs), and simulators can prepare students for the industry expectations. In addition, hardware devices such as microcontrollers (i.e., Raspberry Pi, Arduino, etc.), input/output devices (i.e., motors, LEDs, buzzers, etc.), and robots (i.e., rovers and drones) can increase students, interest, commitment, and engagement to the course. If possible, students should own or check the equipment out for the course duration. Keeping the equipment for the duration of the course can (1) increase the sense of ownership, (2) allow students to explore the tools, (3) work on extracurricular projects, and (4) enable students to configure and tailor the tools to their likening. Additionally, students are spending less time on campus and preferring to study off-campus in remote learning [4], and checking the equipment out, enables them to replicate the lab set up in their home environment.

Collaborative Learning Environment - Active learning techniques and collaborative learning, such as pair programming, can enhance students learning outcome success [32] and support programming education [22]. In addition, peer learning activities such as pair programming can be effective because although there are differences in the students' skill levels within a classroom, the knowledge gap between two students is generally smaller than the knowledge gap between a student and a professor [3]. Therefore, students helping each other can be an effective way to complement the instructor-led class.

The danger of peer learning activities such as pair programming is that some students might grow dependent on working with another and not develop the ability to solve problems independently. Therefore, a balance between team and independent work must be achieved. A possible approach is to alternate the methodology between each lab , one in which students can collaborate in pair programming and the following they have to work independently. This approach benefits from the advantages of collaborative learning and enhances students' ability to work in teams while still requiring students to work independently.

Formative Assessment - a lab environment can be very effective because it allows instructors to monitor and correct students' misunderstandings in real-time. As discussed in Sect. 2, early feedback and early detection of struggling students are beneficial. Therefore, formative assessment is appropriate for a lab environment. By providing early and constant feedback (versus solutions at the end of the class), instructors can guide students towards the solution while supporting critical thinking, discuss different approaches to the solution, and teach programming best practices. Additionally, receiving feedback as they work can enable students to clearly see their progress and build self-confidence to achieve high-quality solutions that they might not have been able to achieve independently without formative assessment.

Appropriate Task Selection - tasks should (1) lead to successful students' learning outcomes, (2) engage students in the class, and (3) prepare students for post-graduation careers. The tasks should directly support the learning outcomes established for the course. Most programming curricula require students to develop relatively small programs, but real-world software systems are usually much more extensive with thousands (or even millions) lines of code [14]. Additionally, many students see these short tasks as boring and not engaging. A different and effective approach is to provide students with a larger system where students have to either add new code or modify existing code. Using this approach will enable the instructor to develop stimulant activities and engage the students in the classroom. Alternatively, a more extensive project can also be broken into multiple lab sessions, allowing students to see their ability to work on larger and more complex projects.

Pedagogical Innovations - pedagogical innovations can effectively increase students' motivation, engagement, and commitment to the class, leading to successful learning outcomes. The instructors can adapt and vary innovations based on their students' knowledge level, learning styles, and institution culture. A lab environment allows the instructor to understand students' struggles deeper, enabling them to analyze and pick appropriate techniques for the situation. For instance, engaging material such as physical devices (rovers, drones, hardware components, etc.) are fun and can be used to engage students in the assignments. Another example is to use programming patterns provided in the pre-lab assignments as a foundation for students to build their solutions upon. Instructors can use this technique to guide students to high-quality solutions following industry best practices. For instance, the instructor can provide a starting code with task descriptions and missing functions and ask students to complete the code. As the semester evolves, the instructor can gradually provide fewer starting codes, shifting the complexity of the code to the student's responsibility.

Lifelong Learners - Software development is a continuously evolving field. For instance, new techniques, hardware components, programming languages, and software standards are often updated or replaced. Therefore, it would be prejudicial to the students to focus on temporary concepts. Instead, the instructor should focus on the discipline's stable and long-lasting concepts. Additionally, students should understand that software development is constantly evolving and learn to keep updated with modern concepts based on their fundamental knowledge of programming principles. Students' skills should allow them to quickly adapt to emerging technology waves [3], avoiding becoming obsolete in their careers [10].

4   Curriculum Implementation

This section presents a curriculum implementation following the guidelines discussed in Sect. 3. This curriculum was piloted with 30 students, and their feedback is also provided in this section. This curriculum was taught using the C Programming language. However, the underlying foundation on programming principles will allow students to apply the concepts in other languages. Lastly, this curriculum should be used as a starting point for readers to tailor it to fit their audience, school needs, and student learning outcomes.

4.1 Course Goals

At the end of this course, students are expected to be able:

1. To compile, link, debug and run C programs.
2. To use the basic C program structure; variables, constants, and operators.
3. To use the repetition constructs such as looping with for, while, and do-while statements.
4. To use the selection structures such as if, if/else, switch, conditional expression statement
5. To create program modules using functions (passing data to and returning values from functions)
6. To use arrays and pointers
7. To work with strings and string manipulating functions
8. To perform file, I/O operations
9. To develop structured, modular, and top-down design of software.

The Table 1 below links each lab session to the course goals presented above:

Table 1. Matrix linking lab sessions and course goals.

Week	Lab name	1	2	3	4	5	6	7	8	9
1	Introduction and setup	X	X							
2	Input and output	X	X							
3	LED control 1	X	X	X	X					
4	Motor control	X	X	X	X					
5	Light patterns	X	X	X	X	X				
6	LED control 2	X	X	X	X	X				
7	Morse encoder	X	X	X	X	X				
8	Rover control 1	X	X	X	X	X				X
9	Rover control 2	X	X	X	X	X	X			X
10	Rover control 3	X	X	X	X	X	X		X	X
11	Rover control 4	X	X	X	X	X	X	X		X
12	Rover competition	X	X	X	X	X	X	X	X	X

4.2 Equipment and Tools

The course utilized the Rasperry Pi platform. Each student checked out a Raspberry Pi 400 computer, shown in Fig. 1a for the duration of the course. Additionally, each student kit contained hardware components to complete the assignments, including a brushless motor, LEDs, resistors, a buzzer, a breadboard, a breakout board, and an assortment of wires. Lastly, students had access to ground rovers (shown in Fig. 1b), based on a Raspberry Pi 4 computer. This equipment was selected due to its (1) low cost, (2) wide availability, (3) flexibility that it provides to teach a wide variety of topics in a fun approach for the students.

(a)   (b)

Fig. 1. Lab equipment: (a) Raspberry Pi 400 computer, (b) ground rover

Appropriately using version control is a crucial skill for software developers. Therefore, it is natural to start using a version control tool during the lab assignments and final submission of their code. This pilot course was based on git versioning control software. Additionally, Github Classroom was used as the repository and class management software. Every assignment was posted in a template repository. Then, students cloned the repository, performed their work, and pushed their final repository to the remote origin, allowing the instructor to have access and grade the student work. Furthermore, students also used a VNC software to remotely connect to their Raspberry Pi.

4.3 Lab Sessions

Week 1 - Introduction and Setup - this session intends to introduce students to programming and set up their development environment. Students learn how to edit, compile, and execute code from the terminal and from an Integrated development environment. Additionally, students learn about the version control software and how to submit their assignments. This is achieved through exercises where the student must modify a code provided by the instructor, compile, execute, commit and push their work.

Week 2 - Input and Output - students learn the concept of standard input/output, how to read from the keyboard and print to the screen. In the first exercise, students print their name initials using asterisks. Following, students start to see the looping concepts by merging their first exercise with a looping code provided by the instructor to print their initials multiple times. Students are also introduced to timing functions, as they are asked to create a delay between each time the program prints their initials to the screen.

Week 3 - LED Control 1 - in this session, students work with the general-purpose input/output (GPIO) pins in the Raspberry Pi for the first time by controlling an LED. In the first exercise, students learn about pulse-width-modulation (PWM) and how to control the brightness of an LED by programming different PWM duty cycles to an output pin. Following, students strengthen their understanding of loops by creating a pattern where the LED brightness changes gradually from 0% to 100%.

Week 4 - Motor Control in this session, students reinforce the concepts learned during the previous week while learning how to use a debugger. Students use a GPIO pin to control a brushless motor to a speed entered by the user (0%to 100%). Following, students modify the code to create an acceleration pattern that will gradually speed the motor from 0% to the desired speed. This week, students must troubleshoot their development using a debugger.

Week 5 - Light Patterns - students are introduced to switch statements and how to use GPIO pins to read a push-button. They must control 4 LEDs to create light patterns. The code should have at least 4 different light patterns, and the user can change patterns by pressing the push button.

Week 6 - LED Control 2 - in this session, students integrate all the concepts learned in past lab assignments (selections, loops, PWM, GPIO, etc.) to control a LED with two pushbuttons. They are able to increase or decrease the LED brightness depending on which pushbutton is pressed. Students are asked to demonstrate their mastery of different types of loops and selection statements in this lab.

Week 7 - Morse Encoder - students create a Morse encoder. For each character input, the program controls a buzzer and an LED to generate the Morse output.

Week 8 - Rover Control 1 - this is the first of a series of sessions working with the rover. In this lab, students code the rover to move in different directions (forward, backward, turn left, turn right). Students learn how to test their code using LEDs (simulating the rover axis). Following they deploys their code to the rover and control it remotely using VNC.

Week 9 - Rover Control 2 - in this lab, students use arrays to store programmed paths for their rovers to execute autonomously. Their code must allow the (1) programming of new paths, (2) execution of programmed paths, and (3) deletion of programmed paths.

Week 10 - Rover Control 3 this week, students expand the autonomous racing capability developed in the previous week to store and load programmed paths from files. Following, students are required to implement two enhancements to their rover control, such as curve movements, smooth accelerations, and control trimming. Students are not required to implement the same tasks, and are encouraged to implement as much functionality as they would like to their rover. Students will use their code and implemented functionalities to compete against each other on on the last week.

Week 11 - Rover Control 4 students learn about strings and string manipulation to create a rover control interpreter. The code allows the user to control the rover with interpreted English commands such as "drive forward 30 cm" or "turn 90 °C".

Week 12 - Rover Competition in this last lab, students use the code they developed on the previous four labs to control their rover in a competition. Each student must control their rover through a racing course twice. During the first run, the student controls the rover manually (using keyboard, interpreter, etc.). During the second run, the rover must complete the course autonomously. Students are judged on the (1) time required to complete the track, (2) completed distance, (3) code implementation, and (4) style. For this fun activity, students are not limited to use tasks developed in their previous lab assignments. Instead, they are encouraged to implement additional functionalities that will enhance their odds in the competition. For instance, students can integrate their code with a joystick to provide better control during the manual race.

4.4 Student Feedback

The curriculum was piloted with 30 students, and this section discusses students' feedback at the end of the course. Overall, students appreciated the course and provided highly positive feedback. Some of the comments are summarized below, followed by a discussion on their feedback.

- Having hands-on experience with coding is vital to learning how to program, and I think this lab did a fantastic job of it.
- I loved the experiments that had hardware associated with them because there were tangible results from programming the hardware. My personal favorite was the programming of the car.
- The lab helped us apply the knowledge learned in the theoric class. For example, I started to understand loops once we used them in the laboratory.
- I have definitely learned much from this class. It has been educational fun and allows for some creativity as well. Using the Raspberry Pi Keyboard has definitely aided me in this class. It's simple and easy to get the hang of.

– The lab complemented my learning in the class by allowing me to practice the concepts taught in the course in a scenario where the implementation of the concepts would affect the performance and functionality of a program. I could integrate the knowledge learned in the class and my own manner of approaching problems. Resulting in a deeper understanding of the programming concepts and how I can use them to solve problems given to me.

Students' feedback suggests that the lab hours provided additional motivation to learn to program. One student wrote, "I never found myself not wanting to go to the lab. On the contrary, I always looked forward to it." or "lab tasks were enjoyable as a puzzle". They appreciated the use of hardware components in the classroom, and one student wrote, "interactive labs like this are so much fun and motivate you more since you to "play" in the assignments" and "it was amazing to see how a program be written to control hardware components, it makes you feel accomplished", and "I liked to see the output in the hardware instead of on the screen". Students also enjoyed working with hardware components as "it provided a physical and visual representation of what our code was meant to do." and some even associated with their career dreams. For instance, one student stated "I like the lab experiments with motors because I am interested in BCI in relations to advanced prosthetics". Students might also have been motivating as they found the lab easier to associate with real-life scenarios. They provided comments such as "it really helped me understand how programming was applied in real-life activities" and "it helped us apply the code to real-life situations". Such feedback reinforces the idea that hands-on activities in a lab environment are beneficial for programming pedagogy, especially to motivate students.

Additionally, when asked about the strengths of a lab course, many students highlighted the strength of formative assessment. A student summarized this strength as "one strength of the lab course was being able to practice the code while having professors available to help. Sometimes trying to learn on your own time, you get stuck and can't move on/feel very discouraged. Having the help to move you forward and help you learn was very good". Additionally, various students enjoyed the fact that the instructors did not provide direct answers, and instead, they were able to guide the students in finding their solutions. Another strength noted by students was the collaborative classroom environment, as students were allowed to help each other in specific assignments. One of them said, "the class is able to help each other out with the assignment, so we can collaborate using all our different strengths". Additionally, a student summarized the environment as "the open atmosphere of the room (I can talk across the table to my peers, instructors walking around), took the pressure off, let us enjoy the coding more, and allowed us to learn from each other".

5 Conclusion

Computer programming is a critical skill in our modern digital society. However, learning how to program is challenging, and programming courses usually present high failure rates. Therefore, it is important to develop tools and techniques to enhance our pedagogy. A laboratory component to programming classes is an effective way of improving students' learning. Labs should make use of (1) current and adequate tools, (2) collaborative learning environment, (3) formative assessment, (4) appropriate assignments for the target audience, (5) pedagogical innovations, and (6) prepare students to be lifelong learners of the subject. We designed an introduction programming lab course following the above guidelines. The curriculum consists of 12 classes with cyber-physical assignments based on the Raspberry Pi platform. We successfully piloted the curriculum with 30 freshman undergraduate students, and we found the curriculum to be easy to follow and effective in keeping students interested and engaged throughout the course.

Our work in this paper can serve as a starting point for instructors to tailor a programming lab course to their audience, school needs, and student learning outcomes. Our contribution is summarized as (1) a discussion on guidelines and considerations to teach programming in today's modern society, (2) a description of a 12-session introduction programming lab curriculum, and (3) a discussion on students' feedback provided at the end of the course.

References

1. Anderson, J.R., Reiser, B.J.: The lisp tutor. Byte **10**(4), 159–175 (1985)
2. Bennedsen, J., Caspersen, M.E.: Failure rates in introductory programming. AcM SIGcSE Bull. **39**(2), 32–36 (2007)
3. Boyer, N.R., Langevin, S., Gaspar, A.: Self direction & constructivism in programming education. In: Proceedings of the 9th ACM SIGITE Conference on Information Technology Education, pp. 89–94 (2008)
4. Butler, M., Morgan, M., et al.: Learning challenges faced by novice programming students studying high level and low feedback concepts. In: Proceedings Ascilite Singapore, pp. 99–107 (2007)
5. Condori, K.O.V.: Teaching formation to develop computational thinking. In: Global Implications of Emerging Technology Trends, pp. 59–72. IGI Global (2018)
6. Crow, T., Luxton-Reilly, A., Wuensche, B.: Intelligent tutoring systems for programming education: a systematic review. In: Proceedings of the 20th Australasian Computing Education Conference, pp. 53–62 (2018)
7. Dacko, S.G.: Narrowing skill development gaps in marketing and MBA programs: the role of innovative technologies for distance learning. J. Mark. Educ. **23**(3), 228–239 (2001)
8. Dagdilelis, V., Satratzemi, M., Evangelidis, G.: Introducing secondary education students to algorithms and programming. Educ. Inf. Technol. **9**(2), 159–173 (2004)
9. Fischer, G., von Gudenberg, J.W.: Improving the quality of programming education by online assessment. In: Proceedings of the 4th International Symposium on Principles and Practice of programming in Java, pp. 208–211 (2006)
10. Ghezzi, C., Mandrioli, D.: The challenges of software engineering education. In: Inverardi, P., Jazayeri, M. (eds.) ICSE 2005. LNCS, vol. 4309, pp. 115–127. Springer, Heidelberg (2006). https://doi.org/10.1007/11949374_8

11. Gomes, A., Mendes, A.J.: An environment to improve programming education. In: Proceedings of the 2007 International Conference on Computer Systems and Technologies, pp. 1–6 (2007)
12. Gomes, A., Mendes, A.J.: Learning to program-difficulties and solutions. In: International Conference on Engineering Education-ICEE, vol. 7 (2007)
13. Hagan, D., Sheard, J., Macdonald, I.: Monitoring and evaluating a redesigned first year programming course. In: Proceedings of the 2nd Conference on Integrating Technology into Computer Science Education, pp. 37–39 (1997)
14. Knight, J.C., Prey, J.C., Wulf, W.A.: A look back: undergraduate computer science education: a new curriculum philosophy and overview. In: Proceedings Frontiers in Education 1997 27th Annual Conference. Teaching and Learning in an Era of Change, vol. 2, pp. 722–727. IEEE (1997)
15. Lewis, C.M.: How programming environment shapes perception, learning and goals: logo vs. scratch. In: Proceedings of the 41st ACM Technical Symposium on Computer Science Education, pp. 346–350 (2010)
16. Manovich, L.: Software takes command, vol. 5. A&C Black (2013)
17. McGonigal, J.: Reality is Broken: Why Games Make us Better and How They can Change the World. Penguin, London (2011)
18. Melero, J., Hern, D., Blat, J., et al.: Towards the support of scaffolding in customizable puzzle-based learning games. In: 2011 International Conference on Computational Science and Its Applications, pp. 254–257. IEEE (2011)
19. Moritz, S.H., Wei, F., Parvez, S.M., Blank, G.D.: From objects-first to design-first with multimedia and intelligent tutoring. ACM SIGCSE Bull. 37(3), 99–103 (2005)
20. Oroma, J.O., Wanga, H., Ngumbuke, F.: Challenges of teaching and learning computer programming in developing countries: Lessons from tumaini university. In: Proceedings of INTED2012 Conference, Valencia, Spain, 5th–7th March 2012 (2012)
21. Oyelere, S., Agbo, F., Yunusa, A., Sanusi, I., Sunday, K.: Impact of puzzlebased learning in computer science education: the case of mobileedu. In: 18th IEEE International Conference on Advanced Learning Technology (ICALT), Maceio-AL, Brazil (2019)
22. Reuse-Durham, N.: Peer evaluation as an active learning technique. J. Instr. Psychol. 32(4), 1–9 (2005)
23. Sheard, J., Simon, S., Hamilton, M., Lönnberg, J.: Analysis of research into the teaching and learning of programming. In: Proceedings of the Fifth International Workshop on Computing Education Research Workshop, pp. 93–104 (2009)
24. Sohn, W.: Design and evaluation of computer programming education strategy using arduino. Adv. Sci. Technol. Lett. 66(1), 73–77 (2014)
25. Song, J., Hahn, S., Tak, K., Kim, J.: An intelligent tutoring system for introductory c language course. Comput. Educ. 28(2), 93–102 (1997)
26. Sunday, K., Ocheja, P., Hussain, S., Oyelere, S., Samson, B., Agbo, F.: Analyzing student performance in programming education using classification techniques. Int. J. Emerg. Technol. Learn. (iJET) 15(2), 127–144 (2020)
27. Teague, D., Corney, M., Ahadi, A., Lister, R.: Swapping as the 'hello world' of relational reasoning: Replications, reflections and extensions. In: Proceedings of the Fourteenth Australasian Computing Education Conference (ACE2012): Conferences in Research and Practice in Information Technology, vol. 123, pp. 87–94. Australian Computer Society (2012)

28. Tezza, D., Garcia, S., Andujar, M.: Let's learn! an initial guide on using drones to teach STEM for children. In: Zaphiris, P., Ioannou, A. (eds.) HCII 2020. LNCS, vol. 12206, pp. 530–543. Springer, Cham (2020). https://doi.org/10.1007/978-3-030-50506-6_36

29. Wiedenbeck, S., Labelle, D., Kain, V.N.: Factors affecting course outcomes in introductory programming. In: PPIG, p. 11. Citeseer (2004)

30. Willert, N.: A systematic literature review of gameful feedback in computer science education. Int. J. Inf. Educ. Technol. 11(10), 464–470 (2021)

31. Winslow, L.E.: Programming pedagogy-a psychological overview. ACM Sigcse Bull. 28(3), 17–22 (1996)

32. Xia, B.S.: An in-depth analysis of teaching themes and the quality of teaching in higher education: Evidence from the programming education environments. Int. J. Teach. Learn. Higher Educ. 29(2), 245–254 (2017)

A Hermeneutic Approach to Simplify Programming: Secondary Education Case Studies

Andrea Valente[1]([⊠]) [iD] and Emanuela Marchetti[2] [iD]

[1] The Maersk Mc-Kinney Moller Institute, SDU Game Development and Learning Technology, Odense, Denmark
anva@mmmi.sdu.dk
[2] Media, Department for the Study of Culture, University of Southern Denmark (SDU), Odense, Denmark
emanuela@sdu.dk

Abstract. A central concern in the field of CT deals with how to simplify programming, to make it accessible to individuals without a technical background. Although CT should not be only reduced to it, programming remains the main challenge in the design of CT pedagogical approaches and tools. In the past years we have developed an approach to simplify programming, centered on the creation of a theoretical framework that can describe the learning path of beginner programmers in terms of knowledge distance. Our framework combines the hermeneutic spiral with Notional Machines, NoMs for short, seen as a more operational counterpart to hermeneutics. To simplify the problem-solving aspect of programming for learners, our approach addresses computational problems that are specific to their studies, and leverages learners' preunderstanding of the digital media, that they have experienced as users. To concretize the connection between the hermeneutic spiral and NoMs, we designed a minimalistic Python multimedia library, called Medialib, aimed at enabling secondary education students to create visual media and games with simple code; the choice of multimedia as the main domain to introduce CT spawns directly from the hermeneutic spiral and learners' preunderstanding. This paper compares three case studies that we conducted in the past three years, at universities in Japan and Denmark, and in a Danish gymnasium. The main contribution of this paper is a theoretical understanding of how CT is being constructed as a school subject in Danish high schools and non-technical lines in university. Our studies show a convergence of CT towards design of multimedia in secondary education, especially regarding the high-fidelity prototyping phase.

Keywords: Computational thinking · Programming · Hermeneutics · Notional machines · Learning · Secondary education

1 Introduction

Computational Thinking (CT for short) has become a highly discussed educational field, where multiple understandings and experiments have been conducted on a global scale.

© The Author(s), under exclusive license to Springer Nature Switzerland AG 2022
P. Zaphiris and A. Ioannou (Eds.): HCII 2022, LNCS 13328, pp. 511–529, 2022.
https://doi.org/10.1007/978-3-031-05657-4_36

In general it has been agreed upon that CT also incorporates skills from design or social sciences, and should not be identified with programming [12]. However, how to teach novices to program is still a central challenge and programming is acknowledged as a precious skill, empowering young people as professionals and citizens in the contemporary information society. Our studies on CT are aimed at understanding how teachers in secondary education are tackling the challenge of teaching programming in non-technical curricula, where students are required to acquire CT-related skills and knowledge, but programming is not their main specialty. In a previous article [2], we have elaborated a theoretical framework which combines Hermeneutics and Notional Machines (or NoMs). This framework, that will be referred to as HeNoM in this paper, aims at articulating a pedagogical compass, to support teachers and schools to find effective strategies to simplify programming for their students. In this study we go one step further, investigating how teachers are concretely framing programming for their students in secondary education, based on the principles defined in our framework. In particular we focus on analyzing how teachers are paving the road to programming in the terms of the hermeneutic spiral, and in relation to how coding rules and structures are presented to the students (defined in terms of NoMs).

Our study builds on three case studies, to compare through our framework, how similarly and differently are non-technical students introduced to programming. The first two case studies involve university students from non-technical curricula in Japan and Denmark, and the third case involves Oerestad Gymnasium, a high school in Denmark.

In the next chapter we present our theoretical framework and a literature review, regarding CT from a pedagogical perspective. In Sects. 3 and 4 we detail our empirical case studies; Sect. 5 presents our analysis and discussions. Section 6 concludes the paper.

2 Theory and Related Work

In our studies, we are concerned in understanding how programming can be simplified to non-technical students in secondary education. Our focus is specifically on how non-technical students are being introduced to programming, within CT-framed courses. CT is defined as the cognitive processes that are involved in formulating problems, whose solution can be implemented through "information-processing agents" [34] such as digital hardware and software. The definition of CT is in itself a complex matter, as proved by the existence of various related concepts, such as "digital humanities", "Computational Literacy", "Computational Participation" and "Computational Empowerment" [34]. In order to address the conceptual complexity behind the notion of CT, we leverage a pedagogical theory, Hermeneutics (detailed in Sect. 2.1) that relates to knowledge acquisition, and a more technical framework that addresses the issue of guiding learners to create simple code, NoMs (in Sect. 2.2).

2.1 Hermeneutics

Hermeneutics is a philosophical theory on text interpretation [5, 14], which has been applied to understand how learning and sense making can be facilitated for novices. We find Hermeneutics as a promising theory to understand how to introduce novices to programming, as we approach programming as involving the understanding and the crafting of a text, the code, which novice programmers have to learn to compose following the specific syntax and semantic of artificial languages on a computer using a specialized editor [15]. The computer itself is a medium for composing and evaluating the semantic of this text.

The term Hermeneutics comes from ancient Greek "hermeneutikos", which means "meaning" and "to interpret". Hermeneutics is concerned with the nature of understanding of texts, which is defined as the outcome of a critical dialogue between the reader and the text [16, 18]. The readers approach the text from their individual perspective, leveraging already acquired knowledge [19].

In Hermeneutics, the understanding and interpretation of text takes place through a circle or spiral [16, 17]. The circle or spiral provides visual metaphors for the tentative process of meaning-making started by the learners. The spiral was suggested as a symbol for the increasing level of depth reached by the readers, as they move further in their understanding. While entering the spiral the readers leverage their pre-acquired knowledge, which provide concepts and means of comparison to the new concepts to be acquired in making sense of a new text [20]. A central aspect of the Hermeneutic spiral is about how the readers become able to recompose the whole and the parts of the new text ([20], pp. 24, [18]). Analyzing and writing code can be analyzed in the same way, as the programmers have to be able to use different syntactic units from the available programming languages, to create a whole code-text that could solve a specific problem.

Furthermore, we see interpretation as a key component in programming as in reading, since programming can be seen as a form of problem-solving, grounded on the scientific method and aimed at the creation of technological artefacts. Interpretation is crucial to problem-solving, as programmers have to be able to analyze and make sense of a problem, interpreting the problem in the terms provided by the structures of artificial programming languages and construct an algorithm which could solve it. Moreover, different programmers can interpret the same problem in various ways, hence crafting different solutions, depending on their individual mindset.

Gadamer argues that understanding implies a form of "anticipation" [16], in which as the readers dive deeper in the parts composing a text and attempt at recomposing these parts together, they are in fact envisioning and reflecting on meaning while they are constructing it. The Hermeneutic spiral culminates in the "fusion of horizons", which is defined as a harmonic combination between the learners' pre-understanding and the knowledge they are attempting to gain [16, 17]. The fusion of horizons is a metaphor for achieved understanding, in the terms of the learners' appropriation of new knowledge and meaning. Similarly in creating code, programmers are envisioning, how the combination of syntactic units of a programming language can lead to finding solutions to a given problem. We can argue that a fusion of horizons is achieved when the programmers succeed in making their code work on the computer and when their code properly addresses the problem to be solved.

In the Danish school, the pedagogical method called use-modify-create [15] has been widely adopted to introduce novices to programming, and it leverages on principles similar to the hermeneutic spiral. First of all it requires learners to start analyzing code provided by the teachers, the second step requires the learners to put the code to use, running it and reflecting on what it "does"; lastly the learners are required to edit existing code, and eventually create new code based on their understanding of the provided code. This third step can lead to personal changes and reinterpretations of the code, to cover slightly different cases of problem-solving. In this sense, programming employs a language and technology-specific form of understanding, in which the programmers have to approach the creation of a text-code, through their individual interpretation of the problem to be solved and of the possibilities offered by the available programming languages.

2.2 NoMs and the Simplification of Programming

In previous work [2] we have compared and analyzed the structure of beginners' books (such as [21, 22] and [23], with [24] being an outlier), of online courses [25] and [26], and the way popular libraries are presented (like Pygame Zero for instance [27]). Most of these materials are organized in a traditional, bottom-up fashion. The textbooks and online courses often do not cover a coherent narrative in which the learners are confronted with problems meaningful to them. Furthermore, concepts are typically introduced in a specific order mainly because of their importance in understanding concepts that will follow, i.e. an internal logic. Moreover, in our opinion beginners textbooks tend to focus too much on formal definitions and terminology, instead of helping the learners to build a solid, practical understanding of coding as a craft. McGugan [24] is an exception, and follows a spiral, iterative approach; functions for example are introduced only briefly in the first chapters, and then they are re-considered later in the book, after the Pygame library has been covered, finally providing a more complete and deep explanation of functions in Python. From our analysis we also found out that most materials adopt one or a few of a short list of strategies to simplify programming: removing theoretical explanations requiring further knowledge, providing block-coding tools to reduce the requirements on syntax memorization, providing practical exercises, and finally adopt creative coding often focusing on implementation of simple, interactive programs. Practical exercises are often framed to enable the creation of simple games in specially designed systems or programming environments, with the development of simple games seen mainly as a motivational resource, leveraging the learners' personal interests. However, most materials still follow a traditional bottom-up approach, to the extent that even books targeted at primary school learners tend to introduce graphics and multimedia in the second half of the text. Moreover, in our experience CT courses for non-technical students typically address learners from different faculties, providing generic knowledge, non-specifically related to their major. Considering these findings, the simplification of programming appears to be approached from a quantitative, reductionist perspective, cutting down and reducing the complexity of computational problems to be presented to learners. In our approach we are instead interested in a different meaning of complexity and simplification. Following current research [4, 28] and [3], we decided to adopt the idea of Notional Machines, or NOMs, and use them to reason about complexity (and simplicity) of programming and programming learning. NoMs were first introduced by DuBoulay in the 1980s [28], and are based on two main ideas:

1. that learners need a model to reason about computation,

2. but also that the model does not need to be complete or highly complex form the very beginning, and instead it would make more pedagogical sense to proceed with multiple models, in a spiral or incremental fashion

In [4] NOMs are presented as:

"[...] artifacts intentionally designed to serve the pedagogical purpose of representing and explaining the behavior of a computational system. A notional machine uses terminology and abstraction levels aimed at a particular audience to support their practices in a particular context. It is often a simplification and can be communicated in different formats."

Although we are inspired by [4], we prefer to look at NOMs more as a way to mentally and manually run code, to make sense of programs, than in relation to algorithm animation, as the authors of that paper do.

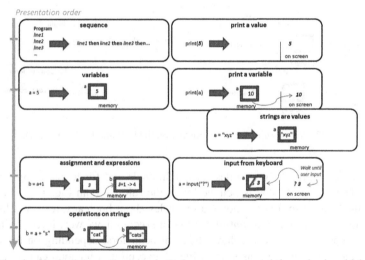

Fig. 1. Visual rules for interpreting simple Python programs, and the order in which they are introduced to the learners.

Our approach (that is detailed in [2]) proposes instead to take a few examples of programming tasks, solve them in the simplest, shortest and most readable way using 2 different programming environments (for example Python with Pygame, and Python with another library). Then using a similar method as the cognitive complexity, analyze and list all concepts, and their dependencies, needed to create a minimal NoM that beginners could use to manually execute the code in the different solutions. Once we have these two minimal NOMs, we compare them and conclude which one is simpler, i.e. which NOM is defined with fewer and least complex concepts. The idea that NoMs can be used to compare more than programs, but also entire programming languages is supported by papers like [29].

An example of NoM for the Python language can be seen in Fig. 1, where instead of using only natural language rules, as done in [117], we present a more visual representation of our NOM's rules. The rules in Fig. 1 only cover a minimal, imperative fragment of Python, with only numbers and strings as data types, no conditionals, loops or functions, and no support to handle images, sounds or even mouse inputs. Despite its limitations, the NoM in Fig. 1 offers a straightforward computation model for imperative programming, based on a before-after semantics that is inspired by operational semantics for imperative calculi (as discussed in the Plotkin's seminal book [6]). In Fig. 1 we specify the semantics of each operation, and we show for each box: the instruction, the state of the memory (when relevant) and what happens to the screen. The style attempts to bridge the need to be formal with the idea of keeping a minimal visual notation that learners can understand from their previous, non-technical experience. The strictly sequential and imperative nature of this fragment of Python helps in maintaining the rules simple enough. Following the original principle behind NoMs, we can then show the learners incrementally more complex NoMs, covering more and more of Python.

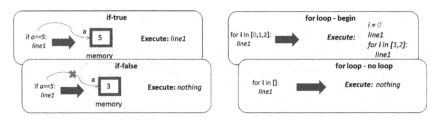

Fig. 2. Visual rules for conditionals (on the left) and for loop (right).

For example, Fig. 2 shows rules for conditionals and for loops, using our visual notation. The new NoM that is defined by all the rules in both Fig. 1 and Fig. 2; the learners might need to first be shown a few rules about booleans, tests and lists. And since the instructions in Fig. 2 control the flow of execution, we were forced to introduce a new concept: instructions can have different behaviors, depending on the contents of the memory. In particular as seen in Fig. 2, executing a for loop can result in two possible outcomes: executing the body of the loop with a specific value assigned to the loop variable, or exiting the loop.

The hermeneutic spiral presented in the previous section supports the idea of leveraging learners' preunderstanding, hence multimedia should be supported in our NoM. Our position is supported by current studies in the domain of CT targeting civil engineers and architects, where the creation of multimedia is proposed as a preferred domain to familiarize students to get to acquire CT-related competences [35].

However, even the new NoM is not enough to cover multimedia. To achieve that, yet keep the resulting NoM as simple as possible, we defined and implemented a minimalist multimedia library for Python, called Medialib [1]. The main inspiration for the Medialib design came from Processing[1], a language aimed at enabling designers to rapidly prototype visual and multimedia programs. Processing is not implemented

---

[1] Official page: https://processing.org/.

as a standalone programming language, but as a simplification of Java, an Embedded Domain Specifc Language (or EDSL for short, as discussed by Fowler in [8]) which offers a rather elegant programming style and is quite different and simpler than its host language. We see a strong connection between the idea of an EDSL and the concept of a NoM, therefore we decided to follow the same approach with the Medialib, which effectively extends the NoM in Figs. 1 and 2 with a few new operations that make it possible to work with images, audio and user input; the resulting new NoM still only uses a sequential execution model, blocking operations and primitive data-types. These few new commands are meant to appear to the beginner programmer as build-in instructions, and Medialib only uses primitive types and avoids complex parameters in the commands parameters, such as Python lists, tuples or objects. All operations in the Medialib are designed to look *atomic* to the programmer, so that the learner can be sure that her sequential model of execution is always respected. Adopting the Medialib, teachers of beginner programmers can avoid, or at least postpone, the discussion of object-oriented concepts, event-handling and function definitions, scope of variables, and instead start writing short, working and readable multimedia programs from the first lecture. The NoM induced by the imperative Python fragment and the Medialib can effectively be used as the start of a spiral of incrementally more complex NOMs.

In our research we see NOMs as the operational counterpart of Hermeneutics, regarding leading novices towards learning programming. The Medialib library represents a design exemplar of our approach [30], in the way it enables us to shorten the knowledge distance between non-technical students and the Python language, and more in general, programming.

3   Two Case Studies in University

The first two case studies regard the design and testing of our Medialib Python library, which we created as an exemplar of our HeNoM framework. Our multimedia library was developed through a loose participatory design method [31], as it addressed specifically the need of our colleague from Kyushu University (KU, in Fukuoka, Japan), Jingyun Wang, who had much experience in conducting a Python course for non-technical students, and asked us for help to cope with recurring issues (as detailed in [1]). She was in charge of a general introductory programming course at KU, targeted bachelor exchange students from different educations, mostly non-technical ones, to introduce them to programming and Python; that course became the basis for our first case study. Our second case study was a course held in Odense, Denmark, at the University of Southern Denmark (SDU) by the authors. The students at SDU were in the first year of their master, and their course was an introductory course in Data Science called Digital Methodologies, which included elements of CT and enabled us to introduce basic programming in Python with the Medialib, focusing on basic competences in Data Science.

Because of Covid-19 restrictions, both courses ran online through video conference, email, and local Content Management Systems for the distribution of course material and students' assignments. This caused additional issues to the quality of the courses and data gathering, hindering the teachers' ability to closely follow the students' technical and learning challenges. Both case studies were organized as inductive, qualitative, research through design investigations [30], and given the circumstances, we adopted a netnographic approach to our study [13, 32], collecting data through: video conference and note taking during online classes, analysis of the students' assignment during the class, questionnaires, and a series of final video interviews were conducted with a small focus group from the students at KU. The students of both courses were presented with the same questionnaire, with minor changes in relation to the course structure. The questionnaire included multiple choice questions, Likert scale and open-ended questions, in which the students had for instance to write about their major, list the software they use and how often. The collected data were analyzed through an interpretive thematic analysis of the students' responses, regarding their expectations with the course, what they found easy to understand or challenging in the use of the Medialib, the tasks we gave them, as well as new design requirements for the improvement of the library.

3.1 Introductory Programming Course in Fukuoka

This course was an introductory CT course at KU, with 15 90-min lectures, which ran in spring 2019. The course was mandatory and offered to exchange students enrolled in various non-technical educations, with the goal of providing basic programming skills in Python; the students perceived it as a way to gain technical skills that could improve their CV, and support their future studies. The students came from different educations, mostly related to biology and business, and only one student had taken programming courses before; all the students said that they did not feel confident in their mathematical knowledge, with 35% stating that they struggled with mathematics and preferred avoiding it.

Data was gathered through the teacher's observations of classes, note taking, questionnaires and a series of final interviews with a subgroup of the students. The questionnaire was proposed twice, during the course and at the end, to compare responses and to evaluate how the students' perception of the course and the Medialib tool changed over time. The final interviews were conducted with 16 students in a semi-structured form [4]. Starting from an initial set of five questions on their experience of the Medialib and of the course structure, the students were also asked to comment on specific answers they gave to the final questionnaire, in order to gain more details on their experience (details can be found in [1]).

The main challenge of this course was its generalist nature: programming is a very large field, involving a variety of problems and fields, each requiring a specific set of skills. For instance, programming to create a web page or to scrape data on-line represents two rather distant and different practices, requiring specific data structures, algorithms, and possibly different languages and NOMs. To face this challenge we started by restructuring the course, taking advantage of the "simple" NoM induced by the Medialib. Our choice of multimedia as the main domain for the course, for the tasks assigned to the students, and for our new library was dictated by our hermeneutic approach: it was an attempt at compensating for the lack of a common focus among the students, picking media as a familiar domain that could enable them to access the hermeneutic spiral, leveraging their preunderstanding of digital media as users [16, 18]. As a result the course materials focused around composition of and interaction with images and audio, through algorithmic thinking, leveraging student cultural and sensorial preunderstanding, to enable them to make sense of their code without having to recall or understand too many mathematical notions.

According to our findings the students were in fact able to connect elements of their code to specific features and behaviors, leading them to make sense of their code, and providing a sense of achievement. The students argued in the questionnaires and interviews that they started to spontaneously wonder "what could I do next?" with their code, conducting trial and error experiments. During interviews, the students were asked about the most interesting exercise in the course, and all of them agreed that it was the last one: implementing a game combining various materials gathered through the whole course. A girl from biology said that: *"[I liked] The game! It put all the lectures into perspective!"*, a boy and a girl from agriculture said that: *"[the game exercise] made everything more clear, [...] how the different parts of the language work together!"*. Moreover, three students said in their interviews that they felt "proud" when the code worked, especially when mistakes were made and they were able to correct them on their own. In this sense, these students pointed at the fact that being able to debug the code, enabled them to reach a degree of self-confidence during the course, which made them feel more motivated to attend and do the exercise.

3.2 Digital Methodologies Course in Odense

During the spring semester of 2021, the Medialib was deployed and tested with a class of 24 students, enrolled in their first year of the master programme in Media Studies at SDU in Denmark. The course ran for 12 three-hour lectures, one lecture per week, and it covered topics such as: research design, netnography, online interviews and surveys, content and thematic analysis, use of software to scrape data from the Internet, and visual representation of data through diagrams and infographics. The students also had to conduct an inquiry on a topic of their choice from the domain of Media Sociology, applying relevant methods and software tools presented in the course. Their inquiry would be discussed in a 20 pages report, structured as a research paper. Two central goals for this course are in fact preparing the students to tackle the methodological part of their master thesis project, and provide an opportunity to practice scientific writing.

This course had a narrower focus than the one discussed in the previous case study, i.e. Data Science. Moreover, the students had more homogeneous backgrounds, they were all Danish and humanists: 20 from the BA in Media Studies, 2 from the BA in multimedia design, and 2 from English Literature. The main challenge for us was actually to organize the course, since we could only use one third of the course (i.e. 4 lectures) for teaching basic programming in Python, introduce graphics programming, scraping, and cover the most common data formats for Data Science, such as JSON and CSV. Therefore, we proceeded to present: basic imperative programming in Python, simple data visualization techniques and user interaction with the Medialib, web-scraping through webAPI and basic data analysis. As in the KU course, on the last lecture of the programming module the students were given a recapitulating exercise, which they had to personalize and deliver together with their final report.

Similarly to the first case study, lockdown restrictions in Denmark forced us to conduct our course and data gathering online. We took notes during lectures and at the end of the course the students were sent the same questionnaire that we used at KU for the previous case study, to gain comparable data. A few alterations were added in the questionnaire, to better fit the course and the educational context, moreover, the Danish students filled the questionnaire only once (the KU students filled it twice), because the programming module at SDU was too short to mark significant differences in the students' experience of the Medialib.

The students' feedback registered during the course was generally positive on the Medialib and on the course. The students explained that the module was quite different from their typical courses, as they had to deal with coding and digital tools, instead of analyzing texts. A girl said that: *"It feels nice to have to make something work"* and that *"it feels good when it works!"*. The students approached the coding exercises constructively, as a trial-and-error practice, which led them to do more experiments when the code did not meet their expectations, even amid possible frustration. In conclusion, the course enabled the students to quickly engage with coding in a gradual way, as we leveraged Data Science as a topic to enable them to enter the hermeneutic spiral of programming.

4   Case Study in a Gymnasium

In the two studies presented in the previous section, we were in charge of the deployment of the library and we participated in conducting the teaching; this case is quite different as we investigate how the simplification of programming is approached by other teachers and in a Danish secondary education institution (the Oerestad Gymnasium in Copenhagen). In this case study we were able to adopt an ethnographic approach, thanks to reduced Covid-19 restrictions, following one semester of teaching at Oerestad gymnasium in the subject "Informatik" (defined in Danish by the ministry of education [11]), which is a course in Computational Thinking held by the Danish high schools. We have gathered qualitative data through:

- Interviews and discussion with the teacher about his strategy,
- Participant observations of teachers and students during lectures and real-world activities (such as visits to a local museum for a students' project),
- Analysis of newly published texts and materials,
- Analysis of the code produced by the students' groups for their project, with focus on the complexity of the code and the connection with the topics in the teaching materials.

4.1   The "Lodsmuseum" Project

At the beginning of the fall semester 2021 we approached Claus Witfelt, a teacher covering programming courses at the Oerestad Gymnasium. Claus was at the time in the process of publishing a digital book that he wrote about teaching CT (more precisely about "Informatik" [7]), aimed at other secondary school teachers; the book emerged from his experience and practices, and from the ways in which he organized his lectures and activities at the gymnasium. We were interested in comparing his ideas and approach to CT with our HeNoM framework, and in observing his class 3rd grade students, the highest class in Danish Gymnasiums. The class was composed of 26 students, between

18 to 20 years of age. Thanks to Claus' collaboration and availability, we could follow his students' work through the semester, documenting and analyzing their group work on a project with a local museum. Claus explained us that fall 2021 was the first semester in which he tried to have a project involving the "Danmarks Lodsmuseum" (which translates as "Pilot Museum of Denmark") in Dragor[2], which is administered by Amager Museum and focuses on local naval tradition.

The museum showcases the life of Danish maritime pilots, how they lived and worked, and the history of piloting in the seas between Denmark and Sweden. Modernization, such as advancements in GPS technologies, has rendered pilots obsolete and the entire complex was eventually converted into a museum. One building in particular that we visited with the class, has been restored to its original 1980s appearance in every detail, including the now retro-looking landline phones, newspapers and everyday products on the shelves of the kitchenette that pilots used when spending the night at the piloting station.

Claus told us that he first approached the director of the museum and they agreed to have the students produce documentation materials about the museum, in the form of web sites or mobile application prototypes.

4.2 Analysis of a Digital Book

In order to familiarize ourselves with the style of teaching and the materials used in the Oerestad Gymnasium, we analyzed the teacher's digital textbook [7]: Claus gave us preview access to the book in fall 2021, shortly before it was digitally published. The digital book, in line with the long Danish tradition of student-centered problem-based project work, presents itself as a website with navigation through chapters. There are 8 chapters and each has 4 to 9 modules, which represent possible lectures that a teacher can use to cover that chapter. A module defines an activity for the class and the teacher, and provides guidelines to support the teacher in assessing the results from the class for that module. For example Sect. 1 has 6 modules, and its title is *"Mini-project on the travel of my dreams"* (translated from the original Danish); the introduction of Sect. 1 explains that:

> *"[...] we [the students and the teacher] will work with travel and how they are presented online, and we will create a very simple app that can act as an online advertisement for a travel agency. [...] In this mini-project, we will work with different aspects of the subject, idea development, evaluation, design, development, IT security and much more."*

Criteria to be fulfilled are also described, to make it clearer for the students, but also to support other teachers in organizing their evaluation of Sect. 1; in particular the description mentions the following requirements for the mini-project:

- The user should be able to sign up for various destinations,
- It should be possible to see beautiful pictures and read about each destination,

---

[2] Official site: https://www.museumamager.dk/index.php?id=56.

- The user must also be able to book a trip,
- Each order should be placed in a shopping basket or possibly in a database,
- Students should be able to reflect on security and on how to create an innovative product.

These points and the previous quote are translations from Danish into English by the authors. After this introductory information, Sect. 1 proceeds to detail the activities to organize for each module in the chapter.

In our analysis we noticed that some chapters in the book tend to start from a design problem, focusing on iterative design, issues and practices; other chapters are more technical in nature and appear to begin with a presentation of theoretical contents, and only at a later stage engaging the learners in application of the theory. Our discussions with the author of the book confirmed that the book structure was in fact designed to balance both problem-solving and technical topics. Design focused chapters have the following progression:

- The first module defines a problem and/or theme
- The next module introduces some theories and/or methods
- Idea development and first iteration:

  – brainstorming
  – low-fi prototyping
  – design

- Implementation of a high-fidelity prototype, using AppLab from Code.org: second iteration
- Further development, agile methods, roles in team-work, pair programming, etc.
- Usability, testing methods, new version: third iteration
- Product documentation and final presentation, final testing. Support students' soft skills.

The technical focused chapters instead have a different progression: an intro to technical subject (e.g. arduino and robotics, or databases), a deeper dive in the subject, one or more tasks about the technical subject, and presentation of the solution of the tasks.

Also the overall structure of the book clearly follows a progression: it starts with design focused chapters, and later more technical chapters follow, to explore specific topics more in depth. The purpose seems to be to help students transition from users of IT systems to designers and developers; only later they are presented with more technical parts of IT and Computer Science. This approach in the new digital book [7] brings "Informatik" more in line with what we observed in university-level programming courses, and it conforms with our idea of the hermeneutic spiral. Interestingly, each chapter of the book can be seen as an introduction to a certain domain, and students will have to face a specific NoM (or progression of NoMs) in order to understand and apply the knowledge provided, as well as constructively engage in problem solving.

4.3   Interview with the Teacher

In this case study, the contact with the teacher was important to gain a deeper understanding of his approach in simplifying programming to his students. We collaborated in close contact with Claus observing his classes, visiting the museum with his students, and informally talking with him during our visits. Finally after the end of the course, we conducted a semi-structured interview online, with open questions. Our questions were about Claus' approach to simplify programming, what he considers to simplify programming, and what are his strategies to make coding easy for his students. Three main themes emerged from our interview with Claus:

- Motivating the students to code,
- Concretizing coding through development of media,
- Gradual progression of activities: from less to more technical.

At our questions regarding how he approaches the task of simplifying programming for his students, Claus started explaining that "it is important to motivate the students". He sees programming as a challenging skill to acquire, which demands for the students' motivation in order to practice enough. Interestingly Claus argues: "There I start from the social sciences: how can we change people's minds about something? And then go into programming." Moreover, Claus considers multimedia a good start to motivate students by asking them to "Make something interactive, interesting", and that "Quizzes are a very nice programming exercise". In fact, Sects. 2 and 3 from Claus' textbook focus on creating quizzes, which are seen as a medium that involves the creation of content, graphics, and relates to usability principles, needed to guide the users through the quiz.

Moreover, in order to elicit motivation, Claus argues that it is important to show the students that "coding can be important for people". Therefore, he decided to involve Lodsmuseum as a *client* for the students, who got the task of developing interactive media for the museum's website or exhibition: "This semester, it was the first time I tried involving a local museum. I discussed the possible projects with the museum, with the director. We ended up asking the students to produce documentation materials about the museum, like web sites." In this way, the students went through a User Centered Design cycle, starting with a user study, which involved a visit at the museum and informal chats with the director and other staff. Afterwards the students had to go through the typical phases of ideation, lo-fi and hi-fi prototyping [33], to end with a presentation at the museum, where the students could get feedback from the staff and the director. In the end, the students could not do the presentation as Covid-19 restrictions were tightened again, however, they managed to develop a series of simple prototypes in the given time. The project with the museum had a positive impact on the students, who felt that they were working on a meaningful problem. Interestingly, the project led to reflections also for Claus, who said during our interviews: "Now that I have more experience with this particular museum, I would do it differently next year: we could get more with programming games instead, still with the same goals".

The third theme identified during the interview deals with creating a gradual progression for the students, from less to more technical tasks. Claus is careful with selecting tools and language structures that are not too complex for the students: "We use code.org for apps and websites, it is a pretty good system!'". Claus explains that first graders are introduced to coding gradually, making web pages, and then progress to developing quizzes and "That is the first time they are actually coding. At that point they have to use blocks in code.org, which is both block-based and text-based, define variables, and use loops and conditionals". Through his experience teaching "Informatik", Claus developed his own strategies. He told us that for many years he followed "A fairly traditional approach to programming: start with variable declarations, conditionals, etc. But this does not work anymore. I cannot get students' attention in class". He says that he shifted from introducing programming structures on the blackboard to tutorial videos: "[in the video] I sit and speak and show how to code conditionals (for instance), and then let the students do it by themselves" and according to his experience the students prefer this method and engage with the code on their own. He added that with his third graders he experimented with traditional teaching with poor results: "when I did not have time to prepare video tutorials for a lecture, I started showing the class what to do [projecting from his computer], with the idea that they should follow me step by step [...]. A student stopped me and told me that this way was too stressful for her, and that I should give them a video tutorial instead. They are used to learn in that way".

Claus' approach can vary as his students' progress: "Sometimes I start from some theory, or drawing a flowchart, and then break down the problem into smaller pieces, then we go to coding. Other times I start by demonstrating what we will get at the end of the video, for example '*we are going to be making this game*', and to achieve that we will need this and that; breaking the problem down into smaller problems". A point-and-click game can in such cases provide a good starting point for Claus: "When you break down a point-and-click game you can discuss some of the theory behind games: what is a mechanic, what is an avatar, what is a world, etc. With a game like chess it would be much more complicated". Interestingly, we notice that in Claus' approach, no matter how technical are the tasks for the students, simple games and multimedia provide a preferred starting point to concretize coding and also to discuss the theory behind the topic. Moreover, Claus argues that "A point-and-click game has a story; in the case of the museum cooperation, the students could make the story about a ship pilot, in the appropriate historical context, and his daily activities [i.e. the focus of the museum exhibits]", so that these games can be easily adapted to different contexts and user groups.

In our previous research projects we also explored stand-ins for programming, proxies, activities that might be close to coding or programming, but simpler for beginners to approach. And we have shown that there exist activities in between editing parameters of an existing digital artifact and actual coding (see [9] and [10]). Therefore, we agree with Claus that creating a static webpage is less complex than actual programming, but can be used to transition beginners from user of digital technology to coders. Claus argued that regarding progression: "In my book we go from social problems with little code, then there are more technically centered chapters. The book follows the structure of the yearly course". In this sense, Claus' approach can be analyzed in the terms of our HeNoM framework, in which novices enter a hermeneutic spiral in coding, progressing from users to creators of digital artifacts. According to the structure of Claus' book, in the beginning the students can leverage their daily knowledge of social media as users, to start thinking as programmers: they keep both roles for the first chapter, and in further chapters are guided to take more and more a programmer role.

4.4 Analysis of Students' Deliveries

In our analysis, we also looked at students' delivery, to gain an understanding on how the students relate to Claus' approach in simplifying programming. The students worked in 6 groups of 2 (or alone, in a few cases), so that Claus received 6 reports at the end of the "Lodsmuseum" project. All deliveries are websites; in some cases the students have also published their website online using free services, external to the gymnasium. The deliveries vary in complexity and degree of completeness, from a few simple pages linked together via hyperlinks, to more finished websites, including "virtual tours" of parts of the museum exhibits, integrated JavaScript quizzes, and games. Online tools like replit[3] and code.org's Web Lab[4] have been used to create and possibly publish the deliveries. The game-like contents can be classified in 3 categories: quizzes, JavaScript canvas games, and point-and-click inspired games.

Three deliveries have quizzes, and the implementations range from a list of buttons or HTML radio-buttons per question, with immediate feedback with a JavaScript popup. Other quizzes were implemented with a submit button, and a function that actually counts the correct answers and provides differentiated answers to the player depending on the points collected.

The JavaScript canvas games appear to be mostly simple, generic games (such as side-scrollers where a box has to jump over obstacles). Instead the point-and-click mechanics were implemented in an interesting way: via images and HTML MAP tags, a classic HTML technique that allows defining multiple clickable links on a single image. When used creatively, MAP tags can give the impression of step-by-step navigation through a set of photos (in this case taken by the students during the visit). One of the student groups even went as far as to draw speech balloons on multiple copies of their photos, to give the impression of interactive information being displayed for the player of the game. Audio clips and videos were often embedded in the webpages, giving a feeling of mashup to the resulting site, and showing the ease with which the students could consider and compose various media styles and formats.

Two groups of students designed and implemented rather finished and usable websites, with advanced code (relative to the others) and relevant contents and a connected navigation graph across the pages.

5 Discussion

In accord with our framework, we found that the simplification of programming in high school is addressed along two dimensions: the contextualization in the real world of the programming tasks that the students have to solve, and the algorithmic complexity of the code that they produce. The algorithmic perspective can be defined in the terms of a series

---

[3] Official page: http://replit.com/.
[4] Official page: https://code.org/educate/weblab/.

of NoMs, as the teachers are acting to minimize and gradually increase the complexity of the NoM of reference for the students. For instance: gradual increase of complexity of the problems, creation of a stable tool chain, creation of good conditions for scaffolding so that the students can independently work on their code. On the other hand, we observed how the teacher at the Oerested gymnasium framed and offered scaffolding for the coding activity within a concrete design project, in this specific case in collaboration with the Lodsmuseum. This two-pronged approach addresses two main issues concretely: first, the gradual introduction to programming for problem-solving (in line with the hermeneutic spiral) supports the students who could find programming intimidating; secondly, the contextualization through a design process helps the students seeing how programming can be a resource within society, leveraging familiar media (webpages, interactive and social media) and the students' preunderstanding of those media. As a result, we find that programming in high school is being constructed as a creative designerly subject, where the writing of code is being contextualized as a design resource for the making of interactive content, together with graphic design and text writing. Design activities (such as the design cycle) also seem to contextualize programming-related activities like software design and debugging, although to a lesser extent. In this sense "Informatik" seems to be more rooted within the practice of high-fidelity prototyping in User Centered Design than in Computer Science, naturally incorporating also the soft skills involved in the CT manifesto [12].

Comparing the three case studies, we find that they all follow a spiral approach, where simpler concepts are followed by more complex ones, in an incremental progression. Moreover, multimedia appears as a central domain on which to base beginners' intuition, and not simply a way to motivate them, but more importantly because it leverages their preknowledge, in accord with the HeNoM framework. The materials and tasks given to the students in the Oerestad Gymnasium include the implementation of simple quizzes, simple 2D games, and game-like applications based on the point-and-click mechanic. Remarkably, the design of quizzes and point-and-click games were explored by the authors in previous papers (e.g. in [9] and [10]) while searching for a middle ground between editing digital contents and full blown programming. Quizzes and point-and-click games are also simple in terms of the NoMs that they would require by the learners.

Using our HeNoM framework as an analytical lens, and looking at how teaching materials combine or alternate between design thinking and technical topics (as in the chapters of Claus' digital book), we can see a trend in the way educational institutions are appropriating and attempt making sense of CT. This process shows a convergence towards an interpretation of CT as the high-fidelity prototyping phase of interaction design. Interestingly, Claus told us that he starts from the "social sciences", leveraging a User Centered Design process, and appears to introduce his students to programming via the typical stages of such a design process, from user study to ideation, to high-fidelity prototype and testing. An advantage of following the User Centered Design method is that it naturally gives time to the students to enter the hermeneutic spiral through a user study, building personal motivation and intuition for making their software. On the other hand, in university context, the specialization of students gains priority towards the framing of coding, living more room to trial-and-error practice with code and debugging as resources for sense making.

6   Conclusion

We propose a theoretical framework to address the simplification of programming that combines the hermeneutic spiral and notional machines. This novel approach allows regarding code as a particular form of text aimed at problem solving, and provides an interpretive perspective, respectful of the needs of non-technical university students, who need to approach programming and code from their own perspective.

The main contribution of this paper is a theoretical understanding of how CT is being constructed as a school subject in universities and Danish high schools, and insights on how CT teachers are tackling the difficult task of simplifying programming, to enable students to edit and write code.

An analysis of three case studies that we conducted in the past three years, suggests that secondary educational institutions are appropriating CT in specific ways. CT appears to be converging towards the high-fidelity prototyping phase of an interaction design process. Our plan is to continue to develop and test our theoretical approach and our Medialib library, to gain a deeper understanding on the matter of simplifying programming for non-technical students and to improve the Medialib tools for future employment in universities and high schools. Ongoing and future work includes observations of CT in primary schools, via a network of researchers in Denmark, England, and East Asia (in particular in Taiwan and Japan), to compare emerging strategies from the point of view of our framework.

Acknowledgements. Thanks to Claus Witfelt for his collaboration, availability and support.

References

1. Valente, A., Marchetti, E., Wang, J.: Design of an educational multimedia library to teach python to non-technical university students. In: Zaphiris, P., Ioannou, A. (eds.) Proceedings of the 9th International Congress on Advanced Applied Informatics (IIAI-AAI), pp. 169–175. IEEE, United States (2020)
2. Valente, A., Marchetti, E.: Simplifying programming for non-technical students: a hermeneutic approach. J. KI - Künstliche Intelligenz, 1–17 (2022). https://doi.org/10.1007/s13218-021-00748-0
3. Berry, M., Kölling, M.: Novis: a notional machine implementation for teaching introductory programming. In: International Conference on Learning and Teaching in Computing and Engineering, LaTICE 2016, Mumbai, India, IEEE Computer Society, pp 54–59 (2016)
4. Duran, R., Sorva, J., Leite, S.: Towards an analysis of program complexity from a cognitive perspective. In: Proceedings of the 2018 ACM Conference on International Computing Education Research, pp. 21–30. Association for Computing Machinery, New York, NY, USA, ICER'18 (2018)
5. Grondin, J.: Gadamer's Interest for Legal Hermeneutics. Law's Hermeneutics: Other Investigations. Routledge, Oxford, pp. 48–62 (2017). ISBN 9781138333567

6. Plotkin, G.D: A structural approach to operational semantics. Aarhus university (1981)
7. Witfelt, C.: Informatik for alle, https://informatikforalle.ibog.forlagetcolumbus.dk/. Accessed Feb 2022
8. Fowler, M.: Domain-Specific Languages, Addison-Wesley Professional (2010). https://doi.org/10.1007/978-3-642-03034-5
9. Marchetti, E., Andrea, V.: It takes three: re-contextualizing game-based learning among teachers, developers and learners. In: Proceedings of the European Conference on Games Based Learning (2016)
10. Valente, A., Marchetti, E.: The road towards friendly, classroom-centered interactive digital contents authoring. In: Chang, M., So, H-J., Wong, L-H., Shih, J-L., Yu, F-Y. (eds.) Proceedings of the 27th International Conference on Computers in Education: Taiwan: Asia-Pacific Society for Computers in Education, vol. 2, pp. 38–46. Asia-Pacific Society for Computers in Education (2019)
11. UVM: Informatik C, hhx, htx, stx, hf Vejledning. https://www.uvm.dk/gymnasiale-uddann elser/fag-og-laereplaner/laereplaner-2017/hhx-laereplaner-2017. Accessed 25 Feb 2022
12. Wing, J.: Computational thinking's influence on research and education for all. Italian J. Educ. Technol. 25(2), 7–14 (2017)
13. Drotner, K., Iversen, S.M.: Digitale metoder: At skabe, analysere og dele data. Samfundslitteratur (2017)
14. Balzer, W., Eleftheriadis, A., Kurzawe, D.: Digital humanities and hermeneutics. Philosoph. Inquiry 42(3/4), 103–119 (2018)
15. Kristensen, K., Marchetti, E., Valente, A.: The global challenge of designing e-learning tools for computational thinking: a comparison between east Asia and Scandinavia. In: e Lecture Notes in Computer Science (LNCS). Springer, Germany (2021). https://doi.org/10.1007/978-3-030-77889-7_33
16. Gadamer, H.G.: Truth and method (j. weinsheimer & d. g. marshall, trans.). New York: Continuum (1989)
17. Heidegger, M.: Being and time (j. macquarrie & e. robinson, trans.) (1962)
18. Tomkins, L., Eatough, V.: Hermeneutics: Interpretation, understanding and sense-making. SAGE handbook of qualitative business and management research methods, pp. 185–200 (2018)
19. Sotirou, P.: Articulating a hermeneutic pedagogy: the philosophy of interpretation. J. Adv. Compos. 365–380 (1993)
20. Schleiermacher, F.: Hermeneutics and Criticism and Other Writings. Cambridge University Press, Cambridge (1998)
21. Severance, C.R.: Online course - programming for everybody (getting started with python) https://www.coursera.org/learn/python?specialization=python. Accessed 25 Feb 2022
22. Sweigart, A.: Invent Your Own Computer Games with Python, 4th Edition - free online book. No Starch Press (2016). https://inventwithpython.com/invent4thed/. Accessed 25 Feb 2022
23. Vorderman, C.: Computer Coding Python Games for Kids. Dorling Kinderssley Limited, London (2018)
24. McGugan, W.: Beginning Game Development with Python and Pygame: From Novice to Professional (Beginning from Novice to Professional). Apress, USA (2007)
25. Malan, D.J.: Cs50 2019 - lecture 0 - Computational Thinking, Scratch (2019). https://www.youtube.com/watch?v=jjqgP9dpD1k. Accessed 25 Feb 2022
26. Severance, C.R., Blumenberg, S., Hauser, E.: Python for Everybody: Exploring Data in Python 3. CreateSpace Inde-pendent Publishing Platform, North Charleston, SC, USA (2016)
27. Pope, D.: Pygame zero - official webpage. https://pygame-zero.readthedocs.io/en/stable/int roduction.html. Accessed 25 Feb 2022
28. Duran, R.: Blog post "notional machines" (2019). https://compedonline.school.blog/2019/07/26/notional-machines. Accessed 25 Feb 2022

29. Seppälä, O., et al.: Notional machines for scratch and python. In: Dagstuhl Seminar 19281, pp. 18–19 (2019)
30. Zimmerman, J., Forlizzi, J.: Research through design in HCI. In: Ways of Knowing in HCI, pp. 167–189. Springer (2014). https://doi.org/10.1007/978-1-4939-0378-8_8
31. Björgvinsson, E., Ehn, P., Hillgren, P.A.: Participatory design and democratizing innovation. In: Proceedings of the 11th Biennial Participatory Design Conference, pp. 41–50 (2010)
32. Kozinets, R.V.: Netnography. The international encyclopedia of digital communication and society, pp. 1–8 (2015)
33. Sharp, H., Rogers, Y., Preece, J: Interaction Design: Beyond Human-Computer Interaction. Wiley, Hoboken (2019). ISBN: 978-1119547259
34. Dohn, N.B: Computational thinking – indplacering i et landskab af it-begreber. In: Dohn, N.B., Mitchell, R., Chongtay, R. (eds.) Computational Thinking. Teoretiske, Empiriske, og Didaktiske Perspektiver. Samfundslitteratur (2021). ISBN: 978-87-593-4044-8
35. Fonseca, D., Redondo, E. (eds.): Handbook of research on applied e-learning in engineering and architecture education. IGI Global (2016)

Author Index

Printed in the United States
by Baker & Taylor Publisher Services